DESKBOOK ENCYCLOPEDIA OF AMERICAN INSURANCE LAW

SEVENTH EDITION

"This publication is designed to provide accurate and authoritative information in regard to the subject matter covered. It is sold with the understanding that the publisher is not engaged in rendering legal, accounting or other professional service. If legal advice or other expert assistance is required, the service of a competent professional person should be sought." — *from a Declaration of Principles jointly adopted by a Committee of the American Bar Association and a Committee of Publishers and Associations.*

Published by
Data Research, Inc.
P.O. Box 490
Rosemount, Minnesota 55068

OTHER TITLES PUBLISHED BY DATA RESEARCH, INC.:

Deskbook Encyclopedia of American School Law
Students with Disabilities and Special Education
U.S. Supreme Court Education Cases
Deskbook Encyclopedia of Employment Law
Deskbook Encyclopedia of Public Employment Law
Private School Law in America

Copyright © 1993 by Data Research, Inc.

All rights reserved

Printed in the United States of America

ISBN 0-939675-35-8
ISSN 1068-543X

The Library of Congress has cataloged this book as follows:

Deskbook encyclopedia of American insurance law. — 7th ed.

p.   cm.
Includes index.
ISBN 0-939675-35-8
1. Insurance law—United States—Digests.
I. Data Research Inc. (Rosemount, Minn.)
KF1159.D47 1992   346.73'086—dc20
[347.30686]

PREFACE

The ***Deskbook Encyclopedia of American Insurance Law, Seventh Edition***, is a completely updated encyclopedic compilation based on state and federal appellate court decisions in the field of insurance. These decisions have been examined by the editorial staff of Data Research, Inc. for inclusion in the appropriate topic classifications. The topic classifications in this edition reflect the rapidly changing case law in the field of insurance, and the textual treatment is based on editorial examination of these court decisions. For the convenience of the reader, the full legal citation is supplied for each case. This edition offers a brief explanation of the American judicial system. The appendix includes a subject-matter table of insurance cases decided by the U.S. Supreme Court. Also included is a comprehensive appendix of law review articles on insurance law.

The intent of the ***Deskbook Encyclopedia*** is to provide insurance professionals and lawyers with access to important case law in the field of insurance.

EDITORIAL STAFF
DATA RESEARCH, INC.

INTRODUCTORY NOTE ON THE JUDICIAL SYSTEM

In order to allow the reader to determine the relative importance of a judicial decision, the cases included in the *Deskbook Encyclopedia of American Insurance Law, Seventh Edition*, identify the courts from which decisions have been rendered. For example, a case decided by a state supreme court generally will be of greater significance than a state circuit court case.

Almost all the reports in this volume are taken from appellate court decisions. Although most insurance law decisions occur at the trial court level, appellate court decisions have the effect of binding lower courts and administrators so that appellate court decisions have the effect of law within their court systems.

State and federal court systems generally function independently of each other. Each court system applies its own law according to statutes and the determinations of its highest court. However, judges at all levels often consider opinions from other court systems to settle issues which are new or arise under unique fact situations. Similarly, lawyers look at the opinions of many courts to locate authority which supports their clients' cases.

Once a lawsuit is filed in a particular court system, that system retains the matter until its conclusion. Unsuccessful parties at the trial court level generally have the right to appeal unfavorable determinations of law to appellate courts within the system. When federal law or constitutional issues are present, lawsuits may be appropriately filed in the federal court system. In those cases, the lawsuit is filed initially in the federal district court.

On rare occasions, the U.S. Supreme Court considers appeals from the highest courts of the states if a distinct federal question exists and at least four justices agree on the question's importance. The federal courts occasionally send cases to state courts for application of state law. These cases are infrequent and in general, the state and federal court systems should be considered separate from each other.

The most common system, used by nearly all states and also the federal judiciary, is as follows: a legal action is commenced in district court (sometimes called a trial court, county court, common pleas court or superior court) where a decision is initially reached. The case may then be appealed to the court of appeals (or appellate court), and in turn this decision may be appealed to the supreme court.

Several states, however, do not have a court of appeals; lower court decisions are appealed directly to the state's supreme court. Additionally, some states have labeled their courts in a nonstandard fashion.

In Maryland, the highest state court is called the Court of Appeals. In the state of New York, the trial court is called the Supreme Court. Decisions of this court may be appealed to the Supreme Court, Appellate Division. The highest court in New York is the Court of Appeals. Pennsylvania has perhaps the most complex court system. The lowest state court is the Court of Common Pleas. Depending on the circumstances of the case, appeals may be taken to either the Commonwealth Court or the Superior Court. In certain instances the Commonwealth Court functions as a trial court as well as an appellate court. The Superior Court, however, is strictly an intermediate appellate court. The highest court in Pennsylvania is the Supreme Court.

While supreme court decisions are generally regarded as the last word in legal matters, it is important to remember that trial and appeals court decisions also create important legal precedents. For the hierarchy of typical state and federal court systems, please see the diagram below.

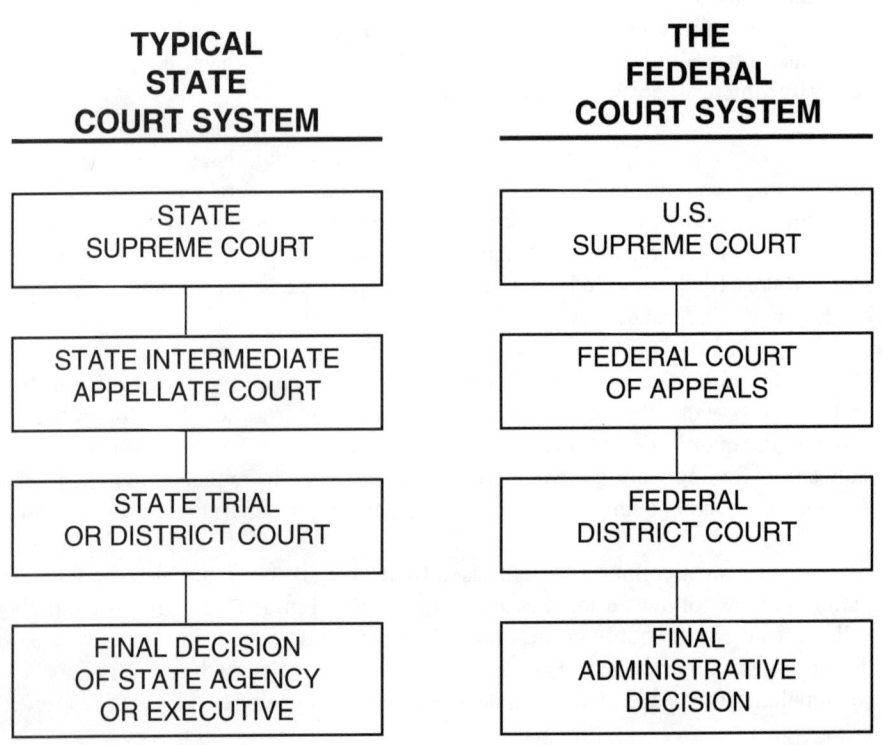

Federal courts of appeals hear appeals from the district courts which are located in their circuits. Below is a list of federal circuits and the states included in each circuit.

First Circuit	—	Puerto Rico, Maine, New Hampshire, Massachusetts, Rhode Island
Second Circuit	—	New York, Vermont, Connecticut
Third Circuit	—	Pennsylvania, New Jersey, Delaware, Virgin Islands
Fourth Circuit	—	West Virginia, Maryland, Virginia, North Carolina, South Carolina
Fifth Circuit	—	Texas, Louisiana, Mississippi
Sixth Circuit	—	Ohio, Kentucky, Tennessee, Michigan
Seventh Circuit	—	Wisconsin, Indiana, Illinois
Eighth Circuit	—	North Dakota, South Dakota, Nebraska, Arkansas, Missouri, Iowa, Minnesota
Ninth Circuit	—	Alaska, Washington, Oregon, California, Hawaii, Arizona, Nevada, Idaho, Montana, Northern Mariana Islands, Guam
Tenth Circuit	—	Wyoming, Utah, Colorado, Kansas, Oklahoma, New Mexico
Eleventh Circuit	—	Alabama, Georgia, Florida
District of Columbia Circuit	—	Hears cases from the U.S. District Court for the District of Columbia.
Federal Circuit	—	Sitting in Washington, D.C., the U.S. Court of Appeals, Federal Circuit hears patent and trade appeals and certain appeals on claims brought against the federal government and its agencies.

TABLE OF CONTENTS

PREFACE iii

INTRODUCTORY NOTE ON THE JUDICIAL SYSTEM v

TABLE OF CASES xvii

CHAPTER ONE
LIABILITY OF INSURERS

I. THE DUTY TO DEFEND AND INDEMNIFY 1
   A. Duty Found 1
   B. Duty Not Found 7
   C. Coverage of Insureds' Punitive Damages 12
      1. Coverage Found 12
      2. Coverage Not Found 14
   D. Other Actions Against Insurers 16

II. PUNITIVE DAMAGE AWARDS AGAINST INSURERS 19
   A. Punitive Damages Awarded 19
      1. Life, Health, Accident and Hospitalization Policies 19
      2. Liability, Workers' Compensation, Casualty and
         Automobile Policies 23
   B. Punitive Damages Denied 29

III. EXCESS INSURERS 36

IV. REINSURANCE 41

CHAPTER TWO
AGENTS, BROKERS AND EMPLOYMENT MATTERS

I. DUTY OF CARE 43
   A. Agent's Duty of Care—Generally 44
      1. Duty of Care Satisfied 44
      2. Duty of Care Not Satisfied 48
   B. Broker's Duty of Care—Generally 51
      1. General Rule 51
      2. Duty of Care Satisfied 52
      3. Duty of Care Not Satisfied 54
   C. Misrepresentation, Fraud and Deceptive Trade Practices 56
   D. Libel and Slander 59
   E. Releases 60
   F. Premiums 61

TABLE OF CONTENTS

- II. BINDERS 63
  - A. Insurers Effectively Bound 63
  - B. Insurers Not Bound 64

- III. LICENSING 65
  - A. Constitutionality of Agent Licensing Statutes 65
  - B. Revocation and Suspension of Licensing 66

- IV. AGENCY/BROKERAGE AGREEMENTS 68
  - A. Breach of Contract—Generally 68
  - B. "No Competition" Agreements 71
  - C. Bonus Renewal Commissions 73
  - D. Redlining 73

- V. EMPLOYMENT MATTERS 74
  - A. Race, Sex and Age Discrimination 74
  - B. Collective Bargaining 79
  - C. Adjusters 80
  - D. Employment Contracts 82

CHAPTER THREE
MOTOR VEHICLE INSURANCE

- I. SCOPE OF COVERAGE 86
  - A. Arising out of the Use or Maintenance of a Motor Vehicle 86
    1. "Motor Vehicle" Defined 86
    2. "Arising out of" Defined 88
       a. Coverage Allowed 88
       b. Coverage Denied 90
    3. Parked Vehicles 93
  - B. Accidents and Occurrences 95
  - C. Intentional Harm 97
  - D. Persons Eligible for Coverage 98
    1. Family Members and Household Residents 98
    2. Permissive Users 102
  - E. Vehicles Eligible for Coverage 105
    1. Replacement and Rental Vehicles 105
    2. School District Vehicles 107
    3. Dealers 108
    4. Motorcycles 110
    5. Other Vehicles 111
  - F. PIP Benefits 112
  - G. Misrepresentation 114

- II. DUTIES OF INSURERS 115

- III. DUTIES OF INSUREDS 119

- IV. STATE AND FEDERAL REGULATION 121

TABLE OF CONTENTS

      A. State Regulation 121
      B. No-Fault 125

V.   STACKING OF MULTIPLE POLICIES 126
      A. Stacking Allowed 127
      B. Stacking Precluded 129

VI. UNINSURED/UNDERINSURED MOTORIST BENEFITS 132
      A. Scope of Coverage 133
          1. Insurers' Obligations 133
          2. Accidents and Events Covered 134
          3. Hit-and-Run Accidents 137
          4. Physical Contact Rules 138
      B. Individuals Entitled to Coverage 140
          1. Coverage Allowed 140
          2. Coverage Denied 142
      C. Interception of Benefits by Creditors 145
      D. Insurers' Duty to Offer Coverage 145
          1. Duty not Satisfied 145
          2. Duty Satisfied 148
      E. Exclusions 149

VII. POLICY CANCELLATION 151
      A. Cancellation Notices 151
          1. Inadequate Notice 151
          2. Adequate Notice 153
      B. Nonpayment of Premiums 155
          1. Coverage Valid 155
          2. Coverage Void 155
      C. Transfer of Ownership 156
      D. Binders 157

VIII. SETOFF 159

IX. SEX-BASED RATE DIFFERENTIALS 161

X.   EXCLUSIONS 163
      A. Vehicles 163
      B. Persons 166
      C. Violations of Law 169

XI. STATUTE OF LIMITATIONS 170

CHAPTER FOUR
INSURANCE FRAUD BY CONSUMERS

I.   INSURANCE FRAUD FOUND 173

II.   INSURANCE FRAUD NOT FOUND 178

TABLE OF CONTENTS

CHAPTER FIVE
LIFE AND HEALTH INSURANCE

I. MISREPRESENTATION 186
   A. Application Misrepresentations Precluding Coverage 186
   B. Alleged Misrepresentations Not Precluding Coverage 191
   C. Incontestability Clauses 195

II. NONPAYMENT OF PREMIUM 197
   A. Policies Voided 197
   B. Policies Not Voided 199

III. GROUP LIFE AND HEALTH INSURANCE 201
   A. Scope of Coverage 201
      1. Types of Claims and Individuals Covered 202
      2. Regulation of Practice 210
      3. Injuries 211
      4. Policy Dates and Limitations Periods 211
   B. The "Actively at Work" Requirement 214

IV. DELIVERY OF POLICY 216

V. DOUBLE INDEMNITY AND ACCIDENTAL
   DEATH BENEFITS 219

VI. PAYMENT OF PROCEEDS 223
   A. Rival Claimants 223
   B. Change-of-Beneficiary Disputes 228
   C. Missing Persons 232

VII. EXCLUSIONS FROM COVERAGE 233
   A. Life Insurance 234
      1. Coverage Precluded 234
      2. Coverage Allowed 239
   B. Health and Medical Insurance 242
      1. Coverage Precluded 243
      2. Coverage Allowed 246
      3. Preexisting Conditions 250

VIII. SEX-BASED MORTALITY TABLES 253

CHAPTER SIX
HOMEOWNER'S INSURANCE

I. SCOPE OF COVERAGE 255

II. RESIDENCE AND DOMICILE MATTERS 267

TABLE OF CONTENTS

III. POLICY EXCLUSIONS 272
    A. Motor Vehicle Exclusions 272
    B. Intentional Acts Exclusions 275
    C. Business Pursuit Exclusions 284
    D. Earth Movement Exclusions 289

IV. MISREPRESENTATION 292

CHAPTER SEVEN
LIABILITY AND CASUALTY INSURANCE

I. SCOPE OF COVERAGE 296
    A. Liability and Casualty Insurance Distinguished 297
    B. Policy Terms 298
    C. "Accidents" and "Occurrences" 302
    D. Primary/Excess Insurance 306
    E. Cancellation 308
    F. Exclusions 310
    G. Joint and Several Liability 318

II. PREMIUMS 319
    A. Coverage Disputes 319
    B. Liability for Payment of Premiums 321

III. NOTICE/PROOF OF LOSS REQUIREMENTS 322

IV. BURGLARY AND THEFT INSURANCE 325
    A. Preconditions for Coverage 325
    B. "Visible Force and Violence" Requirements 327
    C. Exclusions 328

V. FIRE INSURANCE 330
    A. Arson Investigations 330
    B. Coverage Disputes Involving Arson 332
        1. Arson Allegations—Generally 332
        2. Joint Ownership 334
    C. Insureds' Misconduct 337
    D. Buildings Covered 340
    E. Insurers' Right to Repair or Rebuild 341
    F. Mortgagees vs. Mortgagors 343
    G. Technical Problems with Policies 345

VI. BUSINESS AND INDUSTRIAL INSURANCE 346
    A. Business Risks 346
    B. "All Risk" Policies 352
    C. "Occurrences" 354
    D. Exclusions 355
        1. Exclusions Generally 355

TABLE OF CONTENTS

        2. Polluter's Exclusions 360
    E. Products Liability 367

VII. AIRCRAFT INSURANCE 369
    A. Pilot Qualifications 369
        1. Coverage Awarded 369
        2. Coverage Denied 370
    B. Airworthiness Certification 372
    C. Conversions to Criminal Use 373
    D. Exclusions Generally 374

VIII. FEDERAL FLOOD INSURANCE 376

IX. MARINE INSURANCE 378
    A. Coverage Allowed 378
    B. Coverage Denied 381

X. "DRAM SHOP" LIABILITY 382

XI. TITLE INSURANCE 368

XII. STATE AND LOCAL GOVERNMENT LIABILITY 391

XIII. FARMOWNER'S INSURANCE 395
    A. Exclusions 395
    B. Theft Loss Coverage 399

XIV. FIDELITY BONDS 400

XV. CONSTRUCTION INSURANCE 403

CHAPTER EIGHT
PROFESSIONAL MALPRACTICE INSURANCE

I. COVERAGE FOR ACTIVITIES WITHIN THE SCOPE
    OF PROFESSIONAL SERVICES 409

II. POLICY COVERAGE DATES 415

III. FRAUD BY PROFESSIONALS 420

IV. SUITS BASED ON ERROR OR MISTAKE 422

V. LIABILITY OF A PROFESSIONAL'S EMPLOYER 423

VI. OTHER MALPRACTICE CASES 425
    A. Liability Limits and Subrogation Rights 425
    B. Bad-Faith Claims 428

TABLE OF CONTENTS

CHAPTER NINE
WORKERS' COMPENSATION

I. "ARISING OUT OF" AND "IN THE COURSE OF" EMPLOYMENT 432
   A. The Coming and Going Rule 432
   B. Personal Accidents in the Course of Employment 435
      1. Injuries Occurring While Engaged in Conduct Not Approved by Management 435
      2. Injuries Occurring Due to Intentional Acts of Third Parties .. 436
      3. Injuries Occurring While Engaged in Conduct Intended for Personal Comfort 436
      4. Injuries Occurring While Engaged in Company Activities Having a Dual Purpose of Business and Pleasure 438
   C. Accidents "in the Course of" but not "Arising out of" Employment 439
   D. Injuries Arising out of Accidents in Which the Employee-Employer Relationship was Disputed 440
   E. Chain of Causation: Chronic Conditions Initially Arising out of Work-Related Injuries 442
   F. Preexisting Conditions 444

II. MULTIPLE EMPLOYERS 446

III. THE EMPLOYEE'S EXCLUSIVE REMEDY 448
   A. Statutory Employment 448
   B. Tort Actions Based on Alleged Intentional Harm 450

IV. DISABILITY PAYMENTS UNDER WORKERS' COMPENSATION 451
   A. Temporary Total Disability 452
   B. Permanent Partial Disability 453
   C. Permanent Total Disability 454

V. DEATH BENEFITS 457

VI. SETOFF OF BENEFITS 459

VII. STATUTE OF LIMITATIONS 461

VIII. MISCELLANEOUS WORKERS' COMPENSATION CASES 463
   A. Employee Incarceration While Receiving Benefits 463
   B. Violation of Safety Laws by Employer 464
   C. Other Employer Misconduct 466

IX. THE LONGSHORE AND HARBOR WORKERS' COMPENSATION ACT (LHWCA) 467

TABLE OF CONTENTS

CHAPTER TEN
STATE AND FEDERAL LAW

I. FEDERAL REGULATION 471
   A. ERISA Cases 471
   B. Other Federal Cases 478

II. STATE LAW REQUIREMENTS 480
   A. State Regulatory Authority 480
   B. Arbitration 487
   C. Subrogation 489

APPENDIX A
   McCarran-Ferguson Insurance Regulation Act 495

APPENDIX B
   Subject Matter Table of Recent Law Review Articles 497

APPENDIX C
   Subject Matter Table of Insurance Cases Decided by the
   United States Supreme Court 517

APPENDIX D
   Glossary 521

INDEX 527

TABLE OF CASES

A

A. Copeland Enterprises v. Pickett & Meador, 322
AAA Pool Serv. & Supply v. Aetna Cas. & Sur. Co., 60
Abington Savings Bank v. Rock, 344
Abuhamra v. New York Mutual Underwriters, 345
Adams v. Blue Cross/Blue Shield of Maryland, Inc., 202
Adams v. Collins, 448
Aetna Cas. & Sur. Co. v. Duncan, 109
Aetna Cas. & Sur. Co. v. Gosdin, 331
Aetna Cas. & Sur. Co. v. Velasco, 50
Aetna Cas. and Sur. Co. v. Kenner, 161
Aetna Casualty & Surety Co. v. Cartigiano, 99
Aetna Casualty & Surety Co. v. Workers' Compensation Appeals Board, 433
Aetna Casualty Assurity Co. v. James J. Benes and Associates, 395
Aetna Life Ins. Co. v. Bunt, 230
Aetna Life Ins. Co. v. Lavoie, 36
Affiliated FM Ins. Co. v. Beatrice Foods Co., 16
Ahmad v. Loyal American Life Insurance Co., 74
Ainsworth v. Combined Ins. Co. of America, 20
AIU Ins. Co. v. FMC Corp., 361
AIU Ins. Co. v. Gillespie, 483
Al Zuni Trading Co., Inc. v. Penick, 224
Album Realty v. American Home Assurance Co., 403
Alcorn Bank & Trust Co. v. United States Fidelity & Guar. Co., 297
Alewine v. Horace Mann Ins. Co., 285
All American Ins. Co. v. Burns, 314
Allen v. Ind. Comm'n of Arizona, 462
Allen v. Simmons, 15
Allison v. Nationwide Mutual Ins. Co., 211
Allstate Ins. Co. v. Brooks, 276
Allstate Ins. Co. v. Calkins, 266
Allstate Ins. Co. v. Geiwitz, 273
Allstate Ins. Co. v. Hankinson, 102
Allstate Ins. Co. v. Hutcheson, 163
Allstate Ins. Co. v. Killakey, 139
Allstate Ins. Co. v. McCrae, 154
Allstate Ins. Co. v. Miller, 277
Allstate Ins. Co. v. Moraca, 259
Allstate Ins. Co. v. Pogorilich, 130
Allstate Ins. Co. v. Prudential Property & Cas. Ins. Co., 154
Allstate Ins. Co. v. Shockley, 268
Allstate Ins. Co. v. Tomaszewski, 257
Allstate Ins. Co. v. Zuk, 277
Alpha Therapeutic Corp. v. St. Paul Fire and Marine Ins. Co., 424

Alphin v. Marquesa Maritime, Inc., 468
Alvarino v. Allstate Ins. Co., 92
Amco Ins. Co. v. Haht, 277
American Casualty Co. v. Federal Deposit Insurance Corp., 318
American Continental Ins. Co. v. Estate of Gerkens, 371
American Continental Ins. Co. v. Marion Memorial Hospital, 416
American Eagle Ins. Co. v. Lemons, 370
American Economy Ins. Co. v. Canamore, 123
American Family Life Assur. Co. v. Bilyeu, 220
American Family Mut. Ins. Co. v. Nickerson, 288
American Family Mut. Ins. Co. v. Ward, 168
American Family Mutual Ins. Co. v. Johnson, 278
American Family Mutual Ins. Co. v. Pacchetti, 279
American General Life Ins. Co. v. First American Nat'l Bank, 199, 320
American Ins. Co. v. Ohio Bureau of Workers' Compensation, 490
American Modern Home Ins. Co. v. Rocha, 274
American Motorists Ins. Co. v. Republic Ins. Co., 409
American National Fire Ins. Co. v. Estate of Fournelle, 268
American Protection Ins. Co. v. McMahan, 5
American Reliance Ins. Co. v. Mitchell, 397
American Safety Razor Co. v. Hunter, 435
American Transit Ins. Co. v. Abdelghany, 138
Amos v. North Carolina Farm Bureau Mutual Ins. Co., 127
Anderson v. Minnesota Mut. Fire & Cas. Co., 58
Anderson v. St. Paul Fire & Marine Ins., 394
Andrews v. American Health & Life Ins., 193
Ann Arbor Trust Co. v. Canada Life Assur. Co., 236
Antonone v. Atlantic Mut. Fire Ins. Co., 342
APCIGF v. Helme, 428
Application of Aetna Life & Cas. and Schurr, 101
Arad v. Caduceus Self Ins. Fund, 421
Arkansas Blue Cross & Blue Shield v. Brown, 247
Arkansas Blue Cross & Blue Shield v. Fudge, 252
Arkansas Blue Cross & Blue Shield v. Long, 247
Arkansas Farm Bureau Ins. Fed. v. Ryman, 166
Arkwright-Boston Manufacturers Mut. Ins. Co. v. Aries Marine Corp., 307
Armstrong v. Pilot Life Ins. Co., 233
Arnold v. Metropolitan Life Ins. Co., 222
Arps v. Seelow, 99

TABLE OF CASES

Association Life Ins. Co. v. Jenkins, 250
Atlanta Cas. Co. v. Tucker, 125
Atlanta Casualty Co. v. Stephens, 103
Atlantic Container Service, Inc. v. Coleman, 467
Atlantic Mutual Ins. Co. v. Finker, 138
Atlantic Mutual Ins. Co. v. McFadden, 360
Attorneys' Title Ins. Fund, Inc. v. Rogers, 323
Aucompaugh v. General Electric, 435
Auto Club Ins. Ass'n v. New York Life Ins. Co., 493
Auto Owners Ins. Co. v. Rucker, 91
Auto-Owners (Mutual) Ins. Co. v. Stroud, 311
Auto-Owners Ins. Co. v. Selisker, 260
Auto-Owners Ins. v. Corduroy Rubber Co., 126
Automobile Club Ins. Co. v. Donovan, 152
Automobile Club Inter-Ins. Exchange v. State Farm Mutual Automobile Ins. Co., 124
Averbuch v. Home Ins. Co., 339
Avis Rent A Car System v. Liberty Mut. Ins. Co., 13
Awrey v. Progressive Cas. Ins. Co., 35

B

Baker v. Armstrong, 13
Baker v. Independent Fire Ins. Co., 266
Bank of the West v. Superior Court, 2, 18
Bankers Ins. Co. v. Pannunzio, 153
Barajas v. USA Petroleum Corp., 441
Barbara Corp. v. Maneely Ins. Agency, 321
Barber v. Wausau Underwriters Ins. Co., 174
Barciak v. United of Omaha Life Ins. Co., 187
Bardwell v. Kester, 159
Bare v. Associated Life Ins. Co., 207
Barker v. Goldberg, 235
Barney's Karts, Inc. v. Vance, 461
Baron v. Nationwide Mut. Ins. Co., 169
Bartholomew v. Foster, 162
Bartlett v. Amica Mutual Ins. Co., 150
Bartolina v. NN Investors Life Ins., 250
Barton-Barnes Inc. v. State, 122
Bass v. North Carolina Farm Bureau Mutual Ins. Co., 132
Bates v. Cole, 312
Bauer v. Kar Products, Inc., 301
Bay Automotive and U.S.F.& G. v. Allaire, 450
Bay Cities Paving & Grading, Inc. v. Lawyers' Mutual Ins. Co., 425
Bayly, Martin & Fay v. Pete's Satire, 56
Beaird v. Miller's Mut. Ins. Ass'n of Illinois, 80
Beaty v. Truck Insurance Exchange, 297
Beggs v. Pacific Mut. Life Ins. Co., 253
Behrensen v. Whitaker, 441
Belaire v. State Farm Mut. Automobile Ins. Co., 131
Belefonte Underwriters Ins. Co. v. Brown, 35
Bell v. Patrons Mutual Ins. Association, 155

Bennett v. State Farm Ins. Co., 117
Benson v. Bradford Mut. Fire Ins. Corp., 399
Bentley v. New York Life Ins. Co., 230
Berger v. Minnesota Mut. Life, 252
Bettigole v. American Employers Ins. Co., 356
Bettis v. Wayne County Mut. Ins. Ass'n, 397
Beveridge v. Hartford Acc. and Indem. Co., 234
Bill Brown Construction Co. v. Glen Falls Ins. Co., 56
Bischoff v. Old Southern Life Ins. Co., 58
Blake v. Union Mutual Stock Life Ins. Co. of America, 477
Bloebaum v. General American Life Ins. Co., 208
Blonsky v. Allstate Ins. Co., 53
Bluewater Ins. Ltd. v. Balzano, 41
Blumberg v. Guar. Ins. Co., 411
Boggs v. Whittaker, Lipp & Helea, Inc., 349
Bohannon v. Aetna Cas. & Sur. Co., 157
Bohannon v. Guardsmen Life Ins. Co., 201
Bolin v. Kitsap County, 433
Borg-Warner Corp. v. Ins. Co. of North America, 365
Borland v. Safeco Ins. Co. of America, 33
Borman's v. Michigan Property & Casualty Guaranty Ass'n, 479
Boryca v. Marvin Lumber & Cedar, 456
Boston Old Colony Ins. Co. v. Insurance Dep't., 485
Boston Old Colony v. Lumbermen's Mut. Cas., 61
Botway v. American Int'l Assur. Co. of New York, 192
Boudreaux v. Unionmutual Stock Life Ins. Co. of America, 245
Bowman v. Charter General Agency, Inc., 118
Boyd Motors, Inc. v. Employers Ins. of Wausau, 353
Boyd v. SAIF Corp., 434
Boyd v. United Farm Mutual Reinsurance Co., 351
Brack v. Allstate Ins. Co., 89
Brackin v. Metropolitan Life Ins.Co., 174
Brand v. Boatmen's Bank, 209
Brannen v. Golf Life Ins. Co., 209
Bratton v. St. Paul Surplus Lines Ins. Co., 341
Bremer v. Buerkle, 444
Briggs v. Nationwide Mutual Ins. Co., 261
Brill v. Indianapolis Life Ins. Co., 223
Brimhall v. Home Ins. Co., 436
Broderick v. Ins. Co. of North America, 130
Brooks, Tarlton, Gilbert, Douglas & Kressler v. United States Fire Ins. Co., 422
Brown v. American Intern. Life Assurance Co., 270
Brown v. Progressive Preferred Ins. Co., 155
Brown v. State Farm Fire & Casualty Co., 109

xviii

TABLE OF CASES

Brown v. United Services Automobile Ass'n, 138
Bryant v. Clark, 487
Buckeye Union Ins. Co. v. Carrell, 141
Buckner v. Motor Vehicle Accident Indem. Corp., 145
Buemi v. Mut. of Omaha Ins. Co., 174
Burke v. Hawkeye National Life Ins. Co., 69
Burkhart v. Harrod, 385
Burnsed v. Florida Farm Bureau Cas. Ins., 144
Burt Dickens & Co. v. Bodi, 72
Busby v. Simmons, 143
Busch Corp. v. State Farm Fire & Cas. Co., 324
Byrne v. Reardon, 48
Byrne v. State Farm Ins. Co., 91
Byrnes v. Donaldson's, Inc., 453

C

Cain v. Parent, 269
California Insurance Guarantee Ass'n v. Superior Court, 483
California Mut. Ins. Co. v. Robertson, 288
California State Auto. Assoc. Inter-Ins. Bur. v. Garamendi, 484
Calvert Ins. Co. v. Western Ins. Co., 9, 391
Calvert v. Farmers Ins. Co. of Arizona, 110
Campbell Soup Co. v. Liberty Mut., 9
Canadian Ins. Co. v. Ehrlich, 168
Cannon v. State Farm Ins. Co., 111
Cantrell v. Nationwide Mutual Fire Ins. Co., 340
Carfagno v. Aetna Casualty and Surety Co., 487
Caribbean Ins. Servs. v. American Bankers Life Assur. Co. of Florida, 70
Carlino v. Lumbermens Mutual Cas. Co., 128
Carroll v. Jackson National Life Insurance Co., 192
Central Dakota Radiologists v. Continental Casualty Co., 412
Century Companies of America v. Krahling, 222
Cerullo v. Allstate Ins. Co., 91
Chacon v. American Family Mut. Ins. Co., 279
Chase v. William Penn Life Ins. Co., 193
Chen v. Metropolitan Ins. and Annuity Co., 240
Chester v. State Farm Ins. Co., 23
Chifici v. Riverside Life Ins. Co., 193
Childs v. American Com. Liability Ins., 95
Christensen v. Sabad, 229
Chrysler Credit Corp. v. Noles, 491
Chubb/Pacific Indemnity Group v. Ins. Co. of North America, 40
CIE Serv. Corp. v. W.T.P., 384
CIGA v. El Dorado Ins. Co., 468
City of Everett v. American Empire Surplus Lines Ins. Co., 393

City of Johnstown, N.Y. v. Bankers Standard Ins., 3
City of Laguna Beach v. Mead Reinsurance Corp., 392
City of Louisville v. McDonald, 393
City of Muncie v. United Nat'l Ins. Co., 391
City of Newton v. Krasnigor, 280
Clark v. Aetna Cas. & Sur. Co., 178
Clark v. John Hancock Mutual Life Ins. Co., 189
Clauder v. Home Ins. Co., 414
Claussen v. Aetna Cas. & Sur. Co., 365
Clements v. General Accident Ins. Co. of America, 78
Clements v. United States Fidelity and Guar. Co., 139
Clyburn v. Liberty Mut. Ins. Co., 114
Coffey v. State Farm Automobile Ins. Co., 88
Cohen v. Security Title and Guar. Co., 388
Cohen v. Washington Nat. Ins. Co., 189
Coleman v. Nationwide Life Ins. Co., 474
Collins v. Wilcott, 493
Colomb v. U.S. Fidelity and Guar. Co., 305
Colonial Amer. Life Ins. Co. v. Comm'r of Internal Revenue, 479
Colonial Ins. Co. of California v. Blankenship, 109
Colorado Civil Rights Comm'n v. Travelers Ins. Co., 78
Colorado Ins. Guarantee Ass'n v. Harris, 486
Comeau v. Maine Coastal Services, 438
Commercial Union Ins. Co. v. Ewall, 489
Commercial Union Ins. Co. v. Horne, 382
Commercial Union Ins. Co. v. Int'l Flavors & Fragrances, 325
Commonwealth Life Ins. Co. v. Davidge, 225
Community Credit Union of New Rockford v. Homelvig, 335
Compton v. Bunner, 73
Congleton v. National Union Fire Ins. Co., 373
Connolly v. Metropolitan Ins. Co., 126
Conrad v. Auto Club Ins. Ass'n, 160, 460
Consolidated American Ins. Co. v. Henderson, 283
Consolidated American Ins. Co. v. Mike Soper Marine, 311
Consumers Life Ins. Co. v. Smith, 220
Continental Assur. Co. v. Kourtz, 22
Continental Cas. Co. v. Fibreboard Corp., 12
Continental Casualty Co. v. Riveras, 159
Continental Corp. v. Aetna Casualty and Surety Co., 402
Continental Ins. Co. v. Bottomly, 491
Continental Ins. Co. v. Jaecques, 397
Continental Ins. Cos. v. Northeastern Pharmaceutical & Chemical Co., 300
Continental Oil Co. v. Bonanza Corp., 298
Continental Western Ins. Co. v. Klug, 136

TABLE OF CASES

Coolman v. Trans World Life Ins. Co., 64
Cooper Laboratories v. Int'l Surplus Lines Ins. Co., 427
Copeland Ins. Agency v. Home Ins. Co., 63
Cordaro v. Aetna Life Ins. Co., 213
Cotton v. Wal-Mart Stores, 205
Counties Contract & Construction Co. v. Constitution Life Ins. Co., 198
County Side Roofing v. Mutual Benefit Life Ins. Co., 196
Cranford Ins. Co. v. Allwest Ins. Co., 414
Crawford Chevrolet v. National Hole-In-One Ass'n, 350
Crawford v. Coleman, 228
Crawford v. Government Employees Ins. Co., 269
Crawford v. Safeco Title Ins. Co., 390
Creed v. Allstate Ins. Co., 16
Cresci v. The Yacht, "Billfisher," Official No. 517-614, 379
Criterion Ins. Co. v. Velthouse, 92
Crockett v. Great-West Life Assur. Co., 69
Crump v. State Farm Mutual Auto Ins. Co., 99
Crumpton v. Confederation Life Ins. Co., 242
Cruz v. Commonwealth Land Title Ins. Co., 387
Cullum v. Mut. of Omaha Ins. Co., 244
Cummings v. Farmers Ins. Exchange, 293
Curbee, Ltd. v. Rhubart, 287
Curry v. Fireman's Fund Ins. Co., 24

D

Daca, Inc. v. Commonwealth Land Title Ins. Co., 390
Dailey v. Royal Ins. Co., 453
Dairy Queen of Fairbanks v. Travelers Indem. Co. of America, 333
Darel v. Pennsylvania Mfrs. Ass'n Ins. Co., 113
Davidson v. Prudential Ins. Co. of America, 478
Davis v. Commercial Union Ins. Co. v. Continental Commercial Union Ins. Co. v. Continental Gin Co., 318
Davis v. Dep't of Consumer & Reg. Affairs, 113
Davis v. John Hancock Mutual Life Ins. Co., 188
Dayal v. Provident Life & Accident Ins. Co., 215
Degenhart v. Knights of Columbus, 17
DeJong v. Mutual of Enumclaw, 383
Delta Decks v. United States Fire Ins. Co., 327
Demonet Industries v. Trans America Ins. Co., 2
Denison v. Allstate Indem.Co., 89
Denny's Inc. v. Chicago Ins. Co., 308
DeRose v. Albany Ins. Co., 381

Deshotels v. SHRM Catering Services, 469
Devin v. United Services Auto. Assoc., 7
Devor v. Dep't. of Ins., 68
Dirks v. Farm Bureau Mutual Ins. Co., 30
District of Columbia v. Greater Washington Board of Trade, 472
Dockins v. Balboa Ins. Co., 124
Doe v. Rampley, 151
Dohanyos v. Prudential Ins. Co., 216
Donegal Mut. Ins. Co. v. Ferrara, 11
Donovan v. City of Buffalo, 465
Dorris v. INA Ins. Co., 446
Dossett v. Dossett, 227
Downey Savings & Loan Ass'n. v. Ohio Casualty Ins. Co., 26
Driskill v. American Family Ins. Co., 104
Ducote v. Audubon Ins. Co., 337
Duerksen v. Transamerica Title Ins. Co., 83
Duke Univ. v. St. Paul Mercury Ins. Co., 323
Duncan v. American Home Assur. Co., Inc., 234
Dunn v. State Farm Fire and Casualty Co., 334
Dyer v. Northbrook Property and Cas. Ins. Co., 355

E

E.A. Granchelli v. Travelers Ins. Co., 356
EAD Metallurgical, Inc. v. Aetna Casualty and Surety Co., 364
Easton v. Chevron Industries, Inc., 367
Ecktor v. Motorists Ins. Co., 136
Economy Fire and Casualty Co. v. Haste, 283
Edens v. Shelter Mut. Ins. Co., 148
Edmondson v. Pennsylvania National Mutual Casualty Ins. Co., 324
EEOC v. Cargill, Inc., 78, 205
Eichenseer v. Reserve Life Ins. Co., 21
Eisenberg v. Ins. Co. of North America, 84
Electric Ins. Co. v. Boutelle, 105
Ely v. Murphy, 385
Emasco Ins. Co. v. Waymire, 333
Emerson v. American Bankers Ins. Co., 29
Emmons v. Lake States Ins. Co., 264
Employers Mut. v. American Com. Mut., 126
Emscor, Inc. v. Alliance Ins. Group, 306
Engel v. Credit Life Ins. Co., 247
Enserch Corp. v. Shand Morahan & Co., 7
Equitable Life Assur. Society of the United States v. Anderson, 191
Erie Ins. Co. v. Foster, 115
Erie Ins. v. Insurance Commissioner, 114
Eris Ins. Exchange v. Stark, 277
Ertelt v. Emcasco Ins. Co., 95
Esker v. Nationwide Mutual Fire Ins. Co., 108
Estate of Belmar v. County of Onondaga, 394
Estate of Miller v. Principle Mutual Life Ins. Co., 237

xx

TABLE OF CASES

Eubanks v. Nationwide Mut. Fire Ins. Co., 282
Eureka Federal S&L v. Amer. Cas. Co. of Reading, 320
Eurick v. Pemco Ins. Co., 110
Evans v. Hartford Life Ins. Co., 214
Eveready Ins. Co. v. Hadzovic, 152
Eveready Ins. Co. v. Wilson, 123
Eyler v. Nationwide Mutual Fire Ins. Co., 261

F

F1 Aerospace v. Aetna Cas. and Sur. Co., 364
Fafinski v. Reliance Ins. Co., 169
Fanara v. Big Star of Many, Inc., 359
Farley v. Benefit Trust Life Ins. Co., 204
Farm Bur. Town & Country Ins. v. Franklin, 398
Farm Bureau Mutual Ins. Co. v. National Family Ins. Co., 494
Farm Bureau Mutual Ins. Co. v. Winters, 96
Farmers Alliance Mut. Ins. v. Reeves, 304
Farmers Ins. Co. Inc. v. Thomas, 120
Farmer's Ins. Co. of Oregon v. Stout, 165
Farmers Ins. Exchange v. Young, 121
Farnan v. NYS Dept. of Social Services, 439
Federal Ins. Co. v. Scarsella Bros., Inc., 39
Federated American Ins. Co. v. Granillo, 167
Federated American Ins. v. Strong, 98
Federated Mutual Ins. Co. v. Bennett, 71
Feliciano v. Waikiki Deep Water Inc., 384
Ferguson v. Union Mut. Stock Life Ins. Co. of America, 197
Fidelity & Guar. Ins. Co. v. Allied Realty Co., 350
Fine v. Bellefonte Underwriters Ins. Co., 340
Fireguard Sprinkler Systems v. Scottsdale Ins., 357
Fireman's Fund Ins. Co. v. Aetna Cas. & Surety Co., 407
Fireman's Fund Ins. Cos. v. Pearl, 87, 112
Fireman's Ins. Co. v. Wheeler, 347
Firestone Tire and Rubber Co. v. Bruch, 475
First American State Bank v. Continental Ins. Co., 401
First Financial Ins. Co. v. Rainey et al., 24
First State Bank of Denton v. Maryland Cas. Co., 330
Fittje v. Calhoun County Mutual County Fire Ins. Co., 336
Fitzpatrick v. American Honda Motor Co., 2
Flatiron Paving Co. of Boulder v. Great Southwest Fire Ins. Co., 404
Florida Patient's Comp. Fund v. Caduceus Ins., 426
Florists' Mut. Ins. Co. v. Tatterson, 347
FMC Corp. v. Holiday, 472
Foremost Ins. Co. v. Allstate Ins. Co., 18, 183
Forshee & Langley Logging v. Peckhan, 464

Foster v. National Union Fire Ins. Co., 401
Foxbilt Electric v. Stanton, 443
Frasher v. Life Investors Ins. Co., 239
Fraver v. North Carolina Farm Bureau Mut. Ins. Co., 73
Free v. Republic Ins. Co., 256
French American Banking v. Flota Mercante Grancolombia NA. SA., 328
Fricke v. Owens-Corning Fiberglas Corp., 450
Friendship Homes, Inc. v. American States Ins. Co., 354
Fryman v. Pilot Life Ins. Co., 241
Fuglsang v. Blue Cross, 251
Fulgham v. Union Central Life Ins. Co., 221

G

Gabor v. State Farm Mutual Automobile Ins. Co., 97
Gabrielson v. Warnemunde, 46
Galloway v. Guar. Income Life Ins. Co., 237
Galvan v. Cameron Mut.Ins., 294
Ganiron v. Hawaii Ins. Guar. Ass'n, 137
Gar-Tex Const. v. Employers Cas. Co., 366
Garcia v. Truck Ins. Exchange, 425
Gardner v. Aetna Cas. & Sur. Co., 429
Gargallo v. Nationwide Gen. Ins. Co., 116
Garneau v. Curtis & Bedell, Inc., 404
Garrison v. Fielding Reinsurance, Inc., 315
Garvey v. State Farm Fire and Cas. Co., 255
Gay & Taylor, Inc. v. St. Paul Fire & Marine Ins. Co., 422
Gehman v. Prudential Property and Cas. Ins. Co., 480
Gelder v. Puritan Ins. Co., 374
Gen. Acc. Ins. Co. of America v. Margerum, 354
General Accident Ins. Co. v. David C. Smith & Assoc., 65
General Accident Ins. Co. v. Namesnik, 415
General Casualty Co. of Illinois v. Sternberg, 100
General Electric Co. v. Industrial Comm'n, 445
Georgia Farm Bureau Mutual Ins. Co. v. Brown, 180
Gezendorf v. Washburn, 68
Gibraltar Financial Corp. v. Lumbermens Mut. Cas. Co., 339
Gibralter Casualty Co. v. Sargent & Lundy, 420
Gibralter Mut. Ins. Co. v. Hoosier Ins. Co., 59
Gieser v. Home Indem. Co., 135
Giles v. Nationwide Mutual Fire Ins. Co., 345
Gillespie v. Dairyland Ins. Co., 484
Glass v. Harvest Life Ins. Co., 62, 199
Glens Falls Ins. Co. v. Donmac Golf Shaping Co., 316
Glezerman v. Columbian Mutual Life Ins. Co., 54

TABLE OF CASES

Goldberg v. Nat'l Life Ins. Co. of Vermont, 176
Goodwin v. Investors Life Ins. Co., 186
Goodyear Atomic Corp. v. Miller, 464
Govar v. Chicago Ins. Co., 410
Government Employees Ins. Co. v. Oliver, 97
Grain Dealers Mut. Ins. Co. v. Pacific Ins. Co., 125
Granite State Ins. Co. v. Degerlia, 300
Graves v. Norred, 227
Great Cent. Ins. Co. v. Mel's Texaco, 447
Great Cent. Ins. Co. v. Tobias, 319
Great Global Assurance Co. v. Shoemaker, 393
Greater New York Mutual Ins. Co. v. Farrauto, 324
Green Construction Co. v. National Union Fire Ins. Co., 406
Gridley Associates v. Transamerica Ins. Co., 361
Griffin v. Calistro, 117
Grotelueschen v. American Family Mutual, 352
Grupo Protexa, S.A. v. All American Marine Slip, 378
Guaranty Nat. Ins. Co. v. Bd. of Educ., 314
Guaranty Serv. Corp. v. American Employers' Ins. Co., 181
Gust v. Pomeroy, 67
Guzman v. Allstate Ins. Co., 139

H

Hackethal v. National Casualty Co., 429
Hall v. Farmers Ins. Exchange, 73
Hall v. Time Ins. Co., 244
Hall v. Wilkerson, 103
Hallmark Ins. Co. v. Superior Court, 355
Halpern v. Lexington Ins. Co., 341
Hamidian v. State Farm Fire & Cas. Co., 90
Hammers v. Farm Bureau Town and Country, 119
Hammond v. Hunkele, 55
Hammons v. Prudential Ins. Co. of America, 252
Handel v. U.S. Fidelity & Guaranty, 179
Handler v. State Farm Mutual Automobile Ins. Co., 144
Hanson v. Prudential Ins. Co. of America, 209
Happy House Amusement, Inc. v. New Hampshire Ins. Co., 312
Harrigan v. New England Mut. Life Ins. Co., 206
Harris v. United States Liability Ins. Co., 326
Hartford Accident & Indem. Co. v. Ins. Comm'r, 162
Hartford Accident & Indem. Co. v. LeJeune, 140
Hartford Accident and Indemnity Co. v. Aetna Cas. and Surety Co., 119
Hartford Fire Ins. Co. v. Advocate, 490

Hartford Fire Ins. Co. v. Karavan Enterprises, 11, 12
Hartford Ins. Co. v. Blackburn, 137
Hartford Mut. Ins.Co. v. Jacobson, 6
Hartz v. Mitchell, 149
Harville v. Twin City Fire Ins. Co., 368
Havird v. Columbia YMCA, 446
Hawaiian Life Ins. Co. v. Laygo, 57
Health Ins. Ass'n of America v. Corcoran, 210
HealthAmerica v. Menton, 476
Hebeler v. Holland Co., 443
Helms v. Southern Farm Bureau Cas. Ins. Co., 449
Henderson v. Universal Underwriters Insurance Co., 160
Heredia v. Farmers Ins. Exchange, 116
Hickman v. Flood & Peterson Ins., 79
Hicks v. American Resources Ins. Co., 366
Higdon v. Ga. Farm Bureau Mut. Ins. Co., 258
Hill v. Citizens Ins. Co. of America, 140
Hillman v. McCaughtrey, 442
Hillman v. Nationwide Mut. Fire Ins. Co., 112
Hingham Mut. Fire Ins. Co. v. Heroux, 270
Hinners v. Pekin Ins. Co., 142
Hodge v. Continental Western Ins. Co., 177
Hodge v. U.S. Fidelity and Guar. Co., 465
Holly Hill Fruit Products v. Krider, 438
Holton v. McCutcheon, 15
Home Indem. Co. v. Shaffer, 355
Home Ins. Co. of Indiana v. Karantonis, 332
Home Ins. Co. v. Landmark Ins. Co., 407
Home Ins. Co. v. Owens, 24
Home Ins. Co. v. Southern California Rapid Transit Dist., 462
Home Ins. of Dickinson v. Speldrich, 62, 321
Horvatten v. Allstate Life Ins. Co., 245
Houlihan v. Fimon, 488
Howell v. Bullock, 120
Howell v. Colonial Penn Ins. Co., 294
Hoye v. Westfield Ins. Co., 264
Hubred v. Control Data Corp., 244
Hughes v. Blue Cross of Northern California, 21
Humana Health Care Plans v. Snyder-Gilbert, 212
Hunt Leasing Corp. v. Universal Underwriters Ins. Co., 165
Hutchinson v. J. C. Penney Ins. Co., 28

I

Iacovelli v. New York Times Co., 437
In re Death of Cole, 232
In Re Integrity Ins. Co., 486
In the Matter of Feliciano, 109
In the Matter of Injury to Spera, 463
Independent Fire Ins. Co. v. Lea, 45
Independent Fire Ins. Co. v. Mutual Assurance, Inc., 307

TABLE OF CASES

Inman v. Farm Bureau Ins., 121
Inman v. South Carolina Ins. Co., 144
Ins. Adjustment Bureau v. Pennsylvania Ins. Comm'r, 81
Ins. Co. of N. America v. Schultz, 399
Ins. Co. of North America v. Acousti Engineering, 489
Ins. Co. of North America v. Forrest City Country Club, 299
Insurance Services of Beaufort v. AETNA Casualty & Surety Co., 68
Integon Life Ins. Corp. v. Zammito, 84
Int'l Indem. Co. v. Smith, 120
IPCI Ltd. v. Old Republic Ins. Co., 315
Irion v. Prudential Ins. Co. of America, 203

J

J & S Enterprises v. Continental Casualty Co., 352
J & W Janitorial Co. v. Industrial Comm'n of Utah, 435
J. Kinderman & Sons v. United National Insurance Co., 39
Jackson National Life Ins. Co. v. Receconi, 191
Jackson v. Bogart Const., 456
Jackson v. Continental Cas. Co., 197
Jackson v. Leads Diamond Corp., 348
Jaffe v. Cranford Ins. Co., 423
Jakco Painting Contractors v. Industrial Comm'n of Colorado, 444
James B. Lansing Sound v. Nat'l Union Fire Ins. Co. of Pittsburgh, Pa., 326
James Graham Brown Foundation v. St. Paul Fire & Marine Ins. Co., 6
Jarvis v. Modern Woodmen of America, 56
Jefferson Insurance Co. of New York v. Sea World of Florida, 316
Jerry v. Kentucky Cent. Ins. Co., 340
Jimmy's Diner, Inc. v. Liquor Liability Joint Underwriting Ass'n of Massachusetts, 386
Johnson v. Allstate Ins. Co., 165
Johnson v. Blue Ridge Ins. Co., 104
Johnson v. Ins. Co. of North America, 284
Johnson v. South State Ins. Co., 175
Johnson v. Toro Co., 439
Jonax v. Allstate Ins. Co., 335
Jones v. Grewe, 53
Jones v. All American Life Ins. Co., 239
Jones v. Motorists Mut. Ins. Co., 168
Jones v. Valley Forge Ins. Co., 293
Joseph v. Utah Home Fire Ins. Co., 100
Joyner v. D.C. Dep't of Employment Services, 452
Jussim v. Massachusetts Bay Ins. Co., 260

K

K-W Industries v. National Sur. Corp., 405
Kadan v. Commercial Ins. Co., 215
Kane v. Royal Ins. Co. of America, 353
Kanne v. Connecticut General Life Ins. Co., 32, 473
Kassab v. Michigan Basic Property Ins., 341
Keetch v. Mutual Of Enumclaw Ins. Co., 346
Kelleher v. American Mutual Ins. Co., 94
Kelley v. Shelter Mut. Ins. Co., 48
Kemp's Case, 438
Kennedy v. Cochran, 461
Kennedy v. Washington Nat'l Ins. Co., 241
Kentucky Farm Bureau Mut. Ins. Co. v. McKinney, 134
Keyser v. Connecticut General Life, 238
Kirchstein v. Kentucky Central Life Ins. Co., 251
Kirkpatrick v. Boston Mut. Life Ins. Co., 213
Kirsh v. State Farm Mutual Automobile Ins. Co., 246
Klonowski v. Dep't of Fire, 464
Kloster Co., Inc. v. Michigan Mut. Ins. Co., 406
Knight v. United Farm Bureau Mut. Ins. Co., 76
Knowles v. United Services Automobile Association, 313
Krane v. Aetna Life Ins. Co., 221
Krause v. Pekin Life Ins. Co., 65

L

Laborde v. DeBlanc, 259
Laguna v. Erie Ins. Group, 131
Lake Charles Harbor & Term. D. v. Imperial Cas., 358
L'Allier v. Turnacliff, 157
Lamar v. Colonial Penn Ins. Co., 488
Lang v. Foremost Ins. Co., 267
Larocque v. Rhode Island Joint Reinsurance Ass'n, 267
Lasam v. Interinsurance Exchange of Auto Club of Southern California, 106
Lavanant v. General Accident Ins. Co., 299
Lawrence v. Chicago Title Ins. Co., 389
Lazer v. Metropolitan Life Ins. Co., 212
Lazzara v. Howard A. Esser, Inc., 52
Learfield Comm. v. Hartford Acc. & Indem., 360
LeBlanc v. Goldking Production Co., 448
LeDoux v. Continental Ins. Co., 14
Lee v. Aylward, 226
Lee v. Insurance Co. of North America, 130
LeFevre v. Westberry, 31
Lemmerman v. A.T. Williams Oil Co., 442
Lemoine v. Security Industrial Ins. Co., 200
Levine v. Lumbermans Mut. Cas. Co., 419
Lewis v. Rucker, 77

TABLE OF CASES

Liberty Mut. Ins. Co. v. Parkinson, 29
Liberty Mutual Ins. Co. v. Metzler, 322
Liberty Mutual Insurance Co. v. Aetna Casualty & Surety Co., 38
Liberty Nat. Life Ins. Co. v. Windham, 221
Liberty Transport, Inc. v. Harry W. Gorst Co., 25
Lick Mill Creek Apartments v. Chicago Title Ins. Co., 386
Life Ins. Ass'n of Mass. v. Com'r of Ins., 482
Life Ins. Co. of Georgia v. Lopez, 23
Life Ins. Co. of N. America v. Wollett, 226
Liimatta v. Lukkari, 19
Lincoln Nat'l Life Ins. Co. v. Commonwealth Corrugated Container Corp., 216
Lincoln Nat'l Life Ins. Co. v. Johnson, 241
Linder v. Prudential Ins. Co. of America, 76
Linick v. Employers Mutual Casualty Co., 69
Linthicum v. Nationwide Life Ins. Co., 32
Lipson v. Jordache Enterprises, Inc., 4
Lissmann v. Hartford Fire Ins. Co., 30
Lister v. American United Life Ins. Co., 212
Little Caesar's Pizza v. Ingersoll, 433
Lloyd v. First Farwest Life Ins. Co., 243
Loomer v. M.R.T. Flying Serv., Inc., 375
Lopez v. National General Ins. Co., 146
Loveridge v. Chartier, 266
Lucini-Parish Ins. v. Buck, 351
Lujan v. Houston Gen. Ins. Co., 437
Lujan v. Payroll Express, Inc., 457
Lumbard v. Western Fire Ins. Co., 327
Lumbermans Mutual Casualty Co. v. Belleville Industries, 362
Lumbermen's Mut. Cas. Co. v. August, 170
Lynburn Enterprises, Inc. v. Lawyers Title Ins. Corp., 387

M

Mackey v. Nationwide Ins. Cos., 74
MacLauchlan v. Prudential Ins. Co. of America, 198
Magnetic Data v. St. Paul Fire & Marine, 10
Magnum Marine Corp., N.V. v. Great American Ins. Co., 301
Mahan v. Safeco Title Ins. Co., 84
Mahoney v. Union Pacific Railroad Employees' Hospital Ass'n, 248
Maine Bonding & Casualty Co. v. Knowlton, 262
Maine Mut. Fire Ins. Co. v. Watson, 343
Malcom v. Farmers New World Life Ins. Co., 236
Malm v. Holiday Theatres, 455
Malta Life Ins. Co. v. Estate of Washington, 217
Manning v. First Federal Sav. & Loan, 217
Maravich v. Aetna Life & Cas. Co., 337

Market Ins. Corp. v. Integrity Ins. Co., 83
Marshall v. Donnelli, 47
Martin v. Commercial Union Ins. Co., 492
Martin v. Recker, 466
Maryland Casualty Co. v. Hayes, 286
Maryland Cup Corp. v. Employers Mut. Liability Ins. Co., 9
Massachusetts Indem. & Life Ins. Co. v. Texas State Bd. of Ins., 66
Massie v. Godfather's Pizza, 451
Matousek v. South Dakota Farm Bureau Mutual Ins. Co., 158
Matter of Compensation of Richmond, 438
Matter of Ideal Mutual Ins. Co., 307
Matter of Midland Ins. Co., 42
Mattheis by Vowinkel v. Heritage Mut. Ins., 317
Matthews v. New York Life Ins. Co., 75
Maurice Goldman & Sons v. Hanover Ins. Co., 347
Mauroner v. Massachusetts Indem. and Life Ins. Co., 49
Maxon v. Farmers Ins. Co., Inc., 129
Mayo v. National Farmers Union Property and Casualty Co., 166
Mays v. Transamerica Ins. Co., 362
Mazon v. Camden Fire Ins. Ass'n, 336
McAllister v. Avemco Ins. Co., 372
McCain v. Capital Veneer Works, Inc., 458
McCandless v. Equitable Life Ins. Co., 241
McCarthy v. Kemper Life Ins. Cos., 77
McCarthy's (Dependent's) Case, 458
McCloskey v. Republic Ins. Co., 286
McCollough v. Travelers Cos., 331
McCormick & Co. Inc. v. Empire Ins. Group, 359
McCrimmon v. North Carolina Mut. Life Ins. Co., 191
McCusker v. W.C.A.B. (Rushton Mining Co.), 457
McDill v. Utica Mut. Ins. Co., 28
McDonald v. State Farm Fire and Casualty Co., 289
McGee v. Equicor-Equitable HCA Corp., 210
McGinn v. Douglas County Social Servs. Admin., 440
McGory v. Allstate Ins. Co., 334
McGriff v. U.S. Fire Ins. Co., 10, 383
McIntosh v. State Farm Mutual Automobile Ins. Co., 144
McKee v. Federal Kemper Life Assurance Co., 35
McKinney v. Country Mut. Ins. Co., 156
McKleroy v. Wilson, 491
McLeod v. Continental Ins. Co., 33
McNeill & Associates v. ITT Life Ins., 82
Mead Corp. v. Tilley, 475
Meade v. Finger Lakes-Seneca Co-op Ins., 52

TABLE OF CASES

Medlin v. Medlin, 226
Meister v. Western Nat'l Mutual Ins. Co., 129
Melnick v. State Farm Mut. Automobile Ins. Co., 83
Members Mut. Ins. Co. v. Hermann Hospital, 145
Merchants Ins. Group v. Warchol, 312
Merchants Mutual Ins. Co. v. Maine Bonding & Casualty Co., 105
Meridian Mut. Ins. Co. v. Morrow, 272
Merin v. Maglaki, 178
Metalmasters of Minneapolis v. Liberty Mut. Ins., 346
Metropolitan Life Ins. Co. v. Barnes, 228
Metropolitan Life Ins. Co. v. Fogle, 242
Metropolitan Life Ins. Co. v. Lucas, 224
Metropolitan Life Ins. Co. v. Massachusetts, 202
Metropolitan Life Ins. Co. v. Taylor, 31, 472, 473
Metropolitan Property & Liability Co. v. Feduchka, 102
Metropolitan Property and Liability Ins. Co. v. Ins. Comm'r of Pennsylvania, 115
Meusy v. Montgomery Ward Life Ins. Co., 238
Meyer v. Norgaard, 44
MFA Mut. Ins. Co. v. Gov't. Employees Ins. Co., 93
Michigan Millers Mutual Ins. Co. v. Bourke, 108
Michigan v. Clifford, 332
Mid-Century Ins. Co. v. L.D.G., 282
Midamar Corp. v. Nat'l Ben Franklin Ins. Co. of Ill., 380
Midwestern Indemnity Co. v. Manthey, 281
Miles v. Aetna Casualty and Surety Co., 488
Millar v. State Farm Fire & Cas. Co., 291
Miller v. American National Fire Ins. Co., 395
Miller v. Northwestern Nat'l Life Ins. Co., 213
Miller's Mutual Ins. Ass'n v. Young, 458
Mills v. Comm'r of Ins., 67
Minnesota Mining and Mfg. v. Travelers Indem. Co., 483
Minton v. Tennessee Farmers Mutual Ins. Co., 258
Mollena v. Firemen's Fund Ins. Co. of Hawaii, Inc., 146
Mondelli v. State Farm Mut. Automobile Ins. Co., 137
Monroe v. Mutual of Omaha Ins. Co., 249
Montee v. State Farm Ins. Co., 291
Moore v. Commonwealth Life Ins. Co., 240
Moore v. Hartford Fire Ins. Co., 51
Moorman v. Prudential Ins. Co. of America, 248
Morehead v. Morehead, 231
Moss v. Protective Life Ins. Co., 222
Mott v. River Parish Maintenance, Inc., 449

Mounts v. Uyeda, 91
Munzer v. St. Paul Fire & Marine Ins., 5
Murray Ohio Mfg. Co. v. Continental Ins. Co., 5
Musselman v. Mountain West Farm Bureau Mutual Ins. Co., 345
Mutual of Enumclaw Ins. Co. v. Jerome, 90
Mutual of Omaha Ins. Co. v. Ruff, 107
Myers v. Ambassador Ins. Co., 27

N

Nancarrow v. Aetna Casualty & Surety Co., 270
Napper v. Schmeh, 229
Nappier v. Allstate Ins. Co., 292
Nasser v. Security Ins. Co., 436
Nat. Fidelity Life Ins. Co. v. Karaganis, 194
National Fire Ins. v. Valero Energy Corp., 353
National Union Fire Ins. Co. v. Hudson Energy Co. Inc., 370
Nationwide Mut. Ins. Co. v. Machniak, 169
Nationwide Mutual Ins. Co. v. Pasion, 146
Nationwide Mutual Ins. Co. v. Wright, 93
Nat'l Org. for Women v. Mut. of Omaha Ins. Co., 211
Nat'l Union Fire Ins. Co. v. Marty, 123
Nat'l Union Flyer Ins. Co. v. Zuver, 370
Natl. Union Fire Ins. Co. of Pittsburg v. Estate of Meyer, 372
Nawa v. Wackenhut Corp., 437
Nelson v. Becton, 377
Nelson v. Davidson, 47
New England Mut. Life Ins. Co. v. Caruso, 196
New England Reinsurance Corp. v. Nat'l Union Fire Ins. Co. of Pittsburgh, 420
New Hampshire Ins. Co. v. Power-O-Peat, Inc., 356
New Madrid School Dist. v. Continental Cas. Co., 299
New Market Investment Corp. v. Fireman's Fund Ins. Co., 379
New York Life Ins. Co. v. Palmer, 189
New York Property Ins. Underwriting Ass'n v. Primary Realty Inc., 8
Newhouse v. Laidig, 270
Newman v. Melahn, 66
Niagara Fire Ins. Co. v. Pepicelli, Pepicelli & Youngs, 422
Nickelberg v. W.C.A.B., 452
Nies v. Nat'l Automobile and Cas. Ins. Co., 118
Nikolai v. Farmers Alliance Mutual Ins. Co., 283
Nixon v. H & C Electic Co., 149
Norfolk Shipbuilding & Drydock v. Duke, 468
North Atlantic Life Ins. Co. v. Katz, 189
North Bay Schools Ins. Auth. v. Industrial Indem. Co., 302

xxv

TABLE OF CASES

North Carolina Farm Bureau Mutual Ins. Co. v. Stox, 276
North River Ins. v. ECA Warehouse Corp., 2
North Star Mut. Ins. Co. v. Holty, 398
Northbrook Excess and Surplus v. Proctor & Gamble, 368
Northern Ins. Co. v. Aardvark Assoc., 365
Northern Life Ins. v. Ippolito Real Est., 195
Northwestern Nat'l Ins. Co. v. Barnhart, 178
NOW v. Metropolitan Life Ins. Co., 254
Nunley v. Florida Farm Bureau Mut. Ins. Co., 310
Nunley v. Merrill, 309
Nyonteh v. Peoples Security Life Ins. Co., 175

O

Oakley v. City of Longmont, 454
O'Boyle v. Prudential, 460
Oestman v. National Farmers Union Ins. Co., 75
Ohio Cas. Ins. Co. v. Safeco Ins. Co., 103
Old Dominion Ins. Co. v. Elysee, Inc., 357
Old Line Life Ins. Co. of America v. Superior Court, 187
Olsen v. Federal Kemper Life Assur. Co., 218
O'Neill v. Illinois Farmers Ins. Co., 171
Opera Boats, Inc. v. La Reunion Francaise, 381
Osterdyke v. State Farm Mut. Automobile Ins. Co., 147
Overton v. Progressive Ins. Co., 182
Owens v. Coleman, 230

P

Pa. Nat'l Org. for Women v. Ins. Dep't, 162
Pabitzky v. Frager, 149
Pacific Indem. Co. v. Golden, 338
Pacific Mut. Life Ins. Co. v. Haslip, 20, 478
Pacific National Ins. Co. v. Superior Court, 82
Paige v. State Farm Fire and Casualty Co., 338
Pali Fashions, Inc. v. New Hampshire Ins. Co., 382
Palsce v. Guarantee Trust Life Ins. Co., 249
Parfrey v. Allstate Ins. Co., 147
Parker Solvents Co. v. Royal Ins. Companies, 300
Parks v. Workers' Compensation Appeals Board, 434
Parr v. Woodmen of the World Life Ins. Society, 76
Parris v. Pledger Ins. Agency, 377
Parrish v. Nationwide General Ins. Co., 156
Paxton Nat'l Ins. Co. v. Brickajlink, 121
Payne v. Safeco Ins. Co. of America, 275
Pearce v. U.S. Fidelity and Guar. Co., 81
Pearson v. Nationwide Mut. Ins. Co., 153
Peninsular Life Ins. Co. v. Wade, 59
Pennbank v. St. Paul Fire & Marine Ins. Co., 15

Pennsylvania Nat'l Mut. Cas. v. Fertig, 126
Penny v. Giuffrida, 377
People v. Marghzar, 176
People v. O'Boyle, 180
People v. Splawn, 182
Peoples Sec. Life Ins. Co. v. Currence, 231
Peoples Security Life Ins. Co. v. Hooks, 72
Perzik v. St. Paul Fire & Marine Ins. Co., 411
Phillips Products Co. v. Industrial Comm'n, 463
Physicians Ins. Co. of Ohio v. Grandview Hospital & Medical Center, 424
Pickrell v. Motor Convoy, 440
Pilot Life Ins. Co. v. Dedeaux, 31, 472, 473
Pinheiro v. Medical Malpractice Joint Underwriting Ass'n of Mass., 410
Planet Ins. v. Bright Bay Classic Veh., 106
Plohg v. NN Investors Life Ins. Co., 249
Poe & Assoc., Inc. v. Estate of Vogler, 419
Pollock v. Fire Ins. Exchange, 342
Pomerantz v. Nationwide Mut. Fire Ins., 88
Ponder v. Allstate Ins. Co., 337
Ponder v. Blue Cross of Southern California, 248
Portland Federal Employees Credit Union v. Cumis Ins. Soc., Inc., 400
Potomac Ins. Co. v. McIntosh, 411
Pratt v. Liberty Mutual Ins. Co., 465
Preferred Risk Ins. Co. v. Boykin, 71
Price v. State Employees Group Health, 211
Prince Check Cashing Corp. v. Federal Ins. Co., 327
Progressive Preferred Ins. Co. v. Williams, 168
Progressive Specialty Ins. Co. v. Easton, 317
Prokop v. North Star Mut. Ins. Co., 262
Protective National Ins. Co. of Omaha v. City of Woodhaven, 394
Provident Life and Accident Ins. Co. v. Waller, 477
Prudential Ins. Co. of America v. McCurry, 72
Prudential Ins. Co. of America v. Moorhead, 225
Prudential Ins. Co. of America v. NLRB, 79
Prudential Ins. Co. of America v. Superior Court, 34
Prudential-LMI Commercial Ins. v. Supreior Court, 407
Prudential Property & Cas. Ins. v. Pendleton, 485
Prudential v. Kollar, 276
Prudential. Prop. & Cas. Ins. Co. v. Bonnema, 257
Public Employees Mutual Ins. Co. v. James F., 278
Pullin v. Southern Farm Bureau Cas. Ins. Co., 117
Pyles v. Pennsylvania Manufacturers' Ass'n Ins. Co., 405

TABLE OF CASES

Q

Qualman v. Bruckmoser, 262
Quarles v. State Farm Mut. Auto. Ins. Co., 136
Quesada v. Director, Federal Emergency Management Agency, 378
Quinlan v. Liberty Bank & Trust Co., 482
Quinn v. Quinn, 231

R

R.L.B. Enterprises v. Liberty Nat'l Fire Ins. Co., 51
Randono v. CUNA Mut. Ins. Group, 188
Rashid v. State Farm Mutual Auto Ins. Co., 128
Rawlings v. Fruhwirth, 47
Ray v. Blue Alliance Mutual Ins. Co., 203
Reedon of Faribault v. Fidelity & Guar. Ins. Underwriters, 60
Reeves Trucking v. Farmers Mutual Hail Ins. Co., 396
Reinsurance Ass'n of Minnesota v. Patch, 289
Remedies v. Trans World Life Ins. Co., 220
Rensselaer Polytechnic Institute v. Zurich American Ins. Co., 302
Rentmeester v. Wisconsin Lawyers Mutual Ins. Co., 417
Republic Ins. Co. v. Jernigan, 266
Republic-Vanguard Life Ins. v. Walters, 195
Revis v. Automobile Ins. Fund, 160
Reyes-Lopez v. Misener Marine Const. Co., 376
Reznichek v. Grall, 358
Richardson v. Colonial Life & Accident Ins. Co., 235
Riffle v. State Farm Mutual Automobile Ins. Co., 147
Rivera v. Nevada Medical Liability Ins. Co., 410
RLI Ins. Co. v. Kary, 374
Roberts v. Country Mutual Ins. Co., 111
Robinson v. North Carolina Farm Bureau Ins. Co., 27
Rocky Mountain Cas. Co. v. St. Martin, 285
Rodriguez Diaz v. Mutual of Omaha Ins. Co., 232
Rodriguez v. American Standard Life and Accident Ins. Co., 440
Rogan v. Auto-owners Ins. Co., 34
Rohlman v. Hawkeye Security Ins. Co., 94
Roller v. Stonewall Ins. Co., 98
Rosenal v. Auto-Owners Mut. Ins. Co., 107
Rosenberg v. Equitable Life Assurance Society, 16
Rosenberg v. First State Ins. Co., 403
Rowe v. Farmers Ins. Exchange, 144
Rowe v. St. Paul Ramsey Medical Center, 494
Royal Ins. Co. v. Alliance Ins. Co., 64
Ruffin v. Sawchyn, 302
Russell v. Protective Ins. Co., 467
Ruwitch v. William Penn Life Assurance Co., 188

S

S.C. Medical Malpractice Liability Ins. Joint Underwriting Ass'n v. Ferry, 413
S.S. v. State Farm Fire & Casualty Co., 265
Saenz v. Family Security Ins. Co. of America, 58
Safeco Ins. Co. of Amer. v. Hirschmann, 292
Safeco Ins. Co. v. Howard, 286
Safeco Ins. Co. v. Seck, 167
San Jose Crane & Rigging, Inc. v. Lexington Ins. Co., 407
Sanderlin v. Allstate Ins. Co., 164
Sanford v. Ins. Co. of North America, 110
Sappington v. Covington, 49
Sarchett v. Blue Shield of California, 207
Saritenjdiam, Inc. v. Excess Ins. Co., Ltd., 348
Sawyer v. North Carolina Farm Bureau Mut. Ins. Co., 156
Scarborough v. Employers Cas. Co., 150
Schiff v. Federal Ins. Co., 317
Schiff v. N.D. Workers Comp. Bureau, 456
Schlosser v. Ins. Co. of North America, 406
Schmidt v. Prudential Ins. Co., 102
Schmoyer v. Church of Jesus Christ of Latter Day Saints, 434
Schneider v. Minnesota Mutual Life Ins., 192
Schneider v. Plainview Farmers Mut. Fire Ins. Co., 309
Schoenwald v. Farmers Cooperative Ass'n of Marion, 17
Schomber v. Prudential Ins. Co., 113
School District of Shorewood v. Wausau Ins. Co., 298
School Sisters of Notre Dame at Mankato, Minnesota v. State Farm Mutual Automobile Ins. Co., 100
Schroeder v. Board of Supervisors of Louisiana State Univ., 314
Schultz Management v. Title Guaranty Co., 388
Schwieterman v. Mercury Casualty Co., 133
Scott v. Bd. of Trustees Mobile S. S. Ass'n, 205
Scott v. Gunter, 66
Scottsdale Ins. Co. v. Van Nguyen, 359
Scouten v. Horace Mann Ins. Co., 161
Sears Mortgage Co. v. Rose, 390
Sears v. Grange Ins. Ass'n, 142
Secura Ins. Co. v. Pioneer State Mutual Ins. Co., 269
Security Ins. Co. v. Anderson, 371
Seegers Grain Co. v. Kansas City Millwright Co., 357
Sender v. State Farm Ins. Co., 171

TABLE OF CASES

Senn v. Merrill-Dow Pharmaceuticals, 369
Sequoia Ins. Co. v. Miller, 157
Sequoia Ins. Co. v. Royal Ins. Co. of America, 37
Shade v. U.S. Fidelity Guar. Co., 308
Shadle v. Amerisure Co., 81, 455
Shank v. Kurka, 101
Sharpley v. Sonoco Products Co., 492
Sheffield Ins. v. Lighthouse Properties, 383
Sheffield v. Stoudenmire, 71
Shelter Mut. Ins. Co. v. Smith, 399
Shelter Mutual Ins. Co. v. Littlejim, 104
Shteiman v. Underwriters at Lloyds of London, 349
Shults v. Griffin-Rahn Ins. Agency, 53
Shumaker v. Farm Bureau Mut. Ins. Co., Inc., 111
Sidney Binder v. Jewelers Mutual Ins., Inc., 328
Silver v. Garcia, 65
Simons v. Blue Cross and Blue Shield, 247
Simpson v. Travelers Ins. Co., 487
Sims v. Monumental General Life Ins. Co., 221
Sinopoli v. North River Ins. Co., 287
Skyline Harvestore Systems v. Centennial Ins. Co., 14
Slaby v. Cox, 173
Slater v. Lawyers' Mutual Ins. Co., 418
Smaul v. Irvington General Hosp., 90
Smith Land & Improvement Corp. v. Celotex Corp., 367
Smith v. Illinois Farmers Ins. Co., 133
Smith v. Nat'l Flood Ins. Program, 50
Smith v. Thompson Agency, 322
Smith v. Valley Forge Ins. Co., 149
Smithway Motor Xpress v. Liberty Mut., 303
Sonderegger v. United Investors Life Ins. Co., 236
South Carolina Farm Bureau Mut. Ins. Co. v. Windham, 164
South Carolina Farm Bureau Mutual Insurance Co. v. Mooneyham, 128
Southern County Mut. Ins. Co. v. First Bank & Trust of Groves, 64
Southern Farm Bureau Life Ins. Co. v. Burney, 233
Southern Farm Bureau Life Ins. Co. v. Moore, 223
Southern General Ins. Co. v. Thomas, 132
Southern Life and Health Ins. Co. v. Turner, 22
Southern Nat'l Bank of North Carolina v. United Pacific Ins., 328
Span, Inc. v. Associated International Ins. Co., 39
Spencer v. Floyd, 225
Sperry v. Maki, 87
Spilker v. William Penn Life Ins. Co. of New York, 175

Spirt v. Teachers Ins. & Annuity Ass'n, 254
St. Amant v. Mack, 415
St. Paul Fire & Marine Ins. Co. v. Albany Emergency Center, 412
St. Paul Fire & Marine Ins. Co. v. Asbury, 413
St. Paul Fire & Marine Ins. Co. v. Edge Memorial Hospital, 415
St. Paul Fire & Marine Ins. Co. v. Gilmore, 481
St. Paul Fire & Marine Ins. Co. v. McBrayer, 306
St. Paul Fire & Marine Ins. Co. v. Molton, 3
St. Paul Fire & Marine Ins. Co. v. Pensacola Diagnostic Center & Breast Clinic, 325
St. Paul Fire & Marine Ins. Co. v. Perl, 426
St. Paul Fire and Marine Ins. Co. v. Great Lakes Turnings, 54
St. Paul Fire and Marine Ins. Co. v. Lewis, 271
St. Paul Fire and Marine Ins. Co. v. Salvador Beauty College, 331
St. Paul Fire and Marine Ins. Co. v. Shernow, 413
St. Paul Fire and Marine Ins. Co. v. Vigilant Ins. Co., 416
St. Paul Fire Ins. Co. v. Afia Worldwide Ins., 40
St. Paul Ins. Co. of Illinois v. Armas, 419
St. Paul Mercury Ins. Co. v. Zastrow, 127
St. Paul Property and Liability Ins. Co. v. Nance, 494
Staff Builders v. Armstrong, 31
Stalnaker v. Boeing Co., 459
Starkman v. Sigmond, 344
State Comp. Health Plan v. Carper, 251
State Dep't of Transportation v. Houston Cas., 375
State Farm Auto. Ins. Co. v. Greer, 151
State Farm Automobile Ins. Co. v. Rose, 96
State Farm Fire & Cas. Co. v. Lawson, 271
State Farm Fire & Cas. Co. v. Stockton, 153
State Farm Fire & Cas. Co. v. Tringali, 98
State Farm Fire & Cas. Co. v. Victor, 281
State Farm Fire & Cas. Co. v. Von Der Lieth, 290
State Farm Fire & Cas. Ins. Co. v. Abraio, 11
State Farm Fire & Casualty Co. v. Elizabeth N., 257
State Farm Fire & Casualty Co. v. Guest, 139
State Farm Fire & Casualty Co. v. Johnson, 259
State Farm Fire & Casualty Co. v. Nycum, 282
State Farm Fire & Casualty Co. v. Wicka, 281
State Farm Fire and Cas. Co. v. Salas, 274
State Farm Fire and Casualty Co. v. Marshall, 280
State Farm Fire and Casualty Co. v. Walton, 263
State Farm Ins. Co. v. Seefeld, 273
State Farm Ins. Cos. v. Wood, 120
State Farm Life Ins. Co. v. Bass, 199
State Farm Mut. Auto Ins. Co. v. Nissen, 135

TABLE OF CASES

State Farm Mut. Auto Ins. Co. v. Seay, 124
State Farm Mut. Auto. Ins. Co. v. Khoe, 217
State Farm Mut. Automobile Ins. Co. v. Baldwin, 142
State Farm Mut. Automobile Ins. Co. v. Ochoa, 170
State Farm Mut. Automobile Ins. Co. v. Rechek, 88
State Farm Mut. Automobile Ins. Co. v. Wyant, 87
State Farm Mutual Auto Ins. v. Wolff, 96
State Farm Mutual Auto. Ins. Co. v. Estate of Braun, 133
State Farm Mutual Automobile Ins. Co. v. Cookinham, 94
State Farm Mutual Automobile Ins. Co. v. Simon, 369
State Farm v. Dep't of Ins., 158
State Farm v. Von Der Lieth, 256
State Mutual Ins. Co. v. Bragg, 310
State of Alaska v. Underwriters at Lloyds, London, 374
State of West Virginia v. Janicki, 424
State v. Wilson, 181
Statewide Ins. Corp. v. Dewar, 158
Staub v. Hanover Insurance Co., 141
Stecher v. Iowa Ins. Guarantee Ass'n, 482
Steele v. Statesman Ins. Co., 290
Stepho v. Allstate Ins. Co., 101
Stewart Title Guar. Co. v. Cheatham, 388
Stockton v. Shelter General Ins. Co., 45
Stone v. Seeber, 417
Stouffer Foods v. Industrial Comm'n of Utah, 443
Stoughton v. Mutual Enumclaw, 284
Strand v. Illinois Farmers Ins. Co., 89
Strategic Marketing Systems v. Soranno, 439
Strother v. Capitol Bankers Life Ins. Co., 187
Stuhlmiller v. Nodak Mutual Ins. Co., 123
Sturkie v. Erie Ins. Group, 150
Suazo v. Del Busto, 107
Sulser v. Country Mutual Ins. Co., 159
Suprenant v. City of New Britain, 454
Swain v. Life Ins. Co. of Louisiana, 114
Swerhun v. Guardian Life Ins. Co. of America, 476

T

Taisho Marine & Fire Ins. Co. v. M/V Sea-Land Endurance, 380
Tarmann v. State Farm Mut. Auto. Ins. Co., 18
Tate v. Industrial Claim Appeals Office, 461
Tatum v. Government Employees Ins. Co., 486
Taylor v. General Motors Corp., 245
Technicon Electronics v. American Home, 304
Thibodeaux v. Audubon Ins. Co., 292
Thomas v. General American Life Ins. Co., 203

Thomas v. Transamerica Occidental Life Ins. Co., 219
Thompson v. Mississippi Farm Bureau Mutual Ins. Co., 166
Thompson v. Nodak Mutual Ins. Co., 134
Thompson v. West American Ins. Co., 283
Thorco Leasing v. Lumbermens Mut., 356
Thornhill v. Houston General Lloyds, 382
Thornsberry v. Western Surety Co., 402
Thorton v. Allstate Ins. Co., 92
Threlkeld v. Ranger Ins. Co., 372
Title Ins. Co. of Minn. v. American Savings and Loan Ass'n, 8
Todd Shipyards Corp. v. Director, Office of Workers' Compensation Programs, 469
Todd v. Dow Chemical Co., 214
Tom Davis Ins. Agency Inc. v. Shivley, 70
Tomes v. Nationwide Ins. Co., 116
Torian v. Lumbermen's Mut. Cas. Co., 180
Totten v. New York Life Ins. Co., 238
Towne Realty, Inc. v. Safeco Ins. Co. of America, 38
Traders & General Ins. Co. v. Allen, 436
Tradewinds Construction v. Newsbaum, 441
Trammell v. Prairie States Ins. Co., 45
Trans World Maintenance v. Accident Prevention, 55
Transamerica Ins. Co. v. Doe, 143
Transamerica Ins. Co. v. F.D.I.C., 400
Transamerica Ins. Co. v. Sayble, 412
Travelers Indem. Co. v. Olive's Sporting Goods, Inc., 303
Travelers Indem. Co. v. Swearinger, 108
Travelers Ins. Co. v. Ty Co. Services, Inc., 312
Triangle Publications v. Liberty Mut. Ins. Co., 305
Trio's, Inc. v. Jones Sign Co., Inc., 359
Truck Ins. Exchange v. Ashland Oil Inc., 421
Truck Ins. Exchange v. Waller, 396
Truehart v. Blandon, 318
Trulove v. Woodmen of World Life Ins., 61
Trzcinski v. American Casualty Co., 179
Turner v. Estate of Turner, 242
Twin City Fire Ins. Co. v. Harvey, 294
Tzung v. State Farm Fire & Cas. Co., 313

U

U.S. Fidelity & Guar. v. Macon-Bibb, 403
U.S. Fidelity and Guar. Co. v. Edwards, 445
U.S. Fidelity and Guarantee Co. v. Citizens Electric Co., 364
U.S. Fire Ins. Co. v. Cowley & Assocs., 376
U.S. Fire Ins. Co. v. Goodyear Tire & Rubber Co., 481
U.S. Gypsum Co. v. Ins. Co. of North America, 329
U.S.A.A. Casualty Ins. Co. v. Torres, 122, 152

TABLE OF CASES

Ucuccioni v. USF&G, 272
Underwriters Subscribing to Lloyd's Ins. v. Magi, 351
Uniguard Security Ins. Co. v. North River Ins. Co., 42
United Equitable Life Ins. Co. v. TransGlobal Corp., 62
United National Ins. Co. v. Waterfront Realty Corp., 315
United Self Insured Services v. Faber, 466
United Services Automobile Ass'n v. Universal Underwriters Ins. Co., 41
United States Fidelity and Guaranty Co. v. McGlothlin, 260
United States v. Milwaukee Guardian Ins. Co., 163
Universal Reinsurance Corp. v. Greenleaf, 367
Universal Underwriters Ins. Co. v. Allstate Ins. Co., 106

V

Vacnin v. 20th Century Ins. Co., 27
Vali-Check v. Security-Connecticut Ins. Co., 194
Van Amerogen v. Donnini, 418
Vance v. Pekin Ins. Co., 335
Vereen v. Liberty Life Ins. Co., 46
Village Inn Apartments v. State Farm Fire & Cas. Co., 291
Village of Camden v. National Fire Ins. Co., 395
Virginia Farm Bureau Mut. Ins. v. Jerrell, 124
Vlahos v. Sentry Ins. Co., 112
Voorhees v. Preferred Mutual Ins. Co., 258

W

W. R. Grasle Co. v. Mumby, 444
Wachtell v. Metropolitan Life Ins. Co., 204
Wade Oilfield v. Providence Wash. Ins., 447
Wagner Enterprises, Inc. v. Brooks, 446
Waite v. Travelers Ins. Co., 271
Walker Rogge v. Chelsea Title & Guar., 389
Walker v. St. Paul Fire and Marine Ins. Co., 429
Wallace v. Huber, 316
Walt Disney World Co. v. Wood, 319
Walters by Walters v. Atkins, 263
Warren v. Dep't of Administration, 57
Warrilow v. Superior Court, 327
Washington v. Winn-Dixie of Louisiana, 204
Watkins v. Continental Ins. Co., 182
Watson v. Town of Arcadia, 392
Watson v. United of Omaha Life Ins. Co., 189
Watts v. Life Ins. Co. of Arkansas, 218
Webster v. State Farm Fire & Casualty Co., 334
Weir v. American Motorists Ins. Co., 143
Wengler v. Druggist Mutual Ins. Co., 459
Werner's Inc. v. Grinnell Mutual Reinsurance Co., 164
West American Ins. Co. v. Baumgartner, 363
West American Ins. Co. v. Lowrie, 258
West American Ins. v. Hinze, 4
West Bend Mut. Ins. Co. v. Milwaukee Mut. Ins. Co., 275
West v. Jacobs, 304
West v. Western Cas. & Sur. Co., 25, 451
Westberry v. State Farm, 92
Westchester Fire Ins. Co. v. City of Pittsburg, Kansas, 394
Western Assur. Co. v. Bronstein, 178
Western Cas. & Sur. Co. v. Sliter, 59
Western World Ins. Co. v. Stack Oil, Inc., 363
Westfield Ins. Co. v. Cahill, 135
Wexler Knitting Mills v. Atlantic Mut. Ins., 329
Wheeler v. Allstate Insurance Co., 101
Whitledge v. Jordan, 149
Whitmer v. Graphic Arts Mutual Ins. Co., 343
Whitmire v. Colonial Life & Accident Ins. Co., 219
Whitten v. Whitten, 229
Wilhite v. State Farm Fire and Cas. Ins., 273
Wilkens v. Iowa Ins. Commissioner, 80
Willett v. Blue Cross and Blue Shield of Alabama, 474
Williams Ins. Agency v. Dee-Bee Contracting Co., 50
Williams v. Galliano, 317
Williams v. Shell Oil Co., 449
Willis v. Tipton, 93
Wills v. State Farm Ins. Co., 87
Wilson v. American Standard Ins. Co., 134
Wilson v. Group Hospitalization and Medical Services Inc., 473
Wilson v. Rowlette, 198
Wilson v. Service Broadcasters, 459
Wilson v. State Farm Mut. Auto. Ins., 314
Wilson v. Western Nat'l Life Ins. Co., 190
Winans v. State Farm Fire and Cas. Co., 256
Windrim v. Nationwide Mutual Ins. Co., 122
Wine Imports v. Northbrook Property and Cas. Ins. Co., 31
Withrow v. Liberty Mutual Fire Ins. Co., 164
Wittcraft v. Sonstrand Health and Disability Group Benefit Plan, 206
Wolfe v. Employers Health Ins. Co., 208
Wood v. State Farm Mut. Ins. Co., 130
Woodhouse v. Farmers Union Mut. Ins. Co., 336
Woosley v. Transamerica Premier Ins. Co., 263
World Serv. Life Ins. Co. v. Bodiford, 253
Worldwide Ins. Group v. Klopp, 489
Worthington v. Modine Mfg. Co., 453
Wota v. Blue Cross and Blue Shield of Colorado, 243

TABLE OF CASES

Z

Zaharias v. Vassis, 344
Zeeb v. National Farmers Union Property and Casualty Co., 261
Zeigler v. South Carolina Farm Bureau Mut. Ins. Co., 148
Zimmerman v. American States Ins. Co., 200
Zuckerberg v. Blue Cross & Blue Shield of Greater New York, 246
Zurich Ins. Co. v. Uptowner Inns, Inc., 384
Zurich Ins. Co. v. Wheeler, 381

CHAPTER ONE

LIABILITY OF INSURERS

                                                                                           Page

I. THE DUTY TO DEFEND AND INDEMNIFY 1
    A. Duty Found 1
    B. Duty Not Found 7
    C. Coverage of Insureds' Punitive Damages 12
        1. Coverage Found 12
        2. Coverage Not Found 14
    D. Other Actions Against Insurers 16

II. PUNITIVE DAMAGE AWARDS AGAINST INSURERS 19
    A. Punitive Damages Awarded 19
        1. Life, Health, Accident and Hospitalization Policies 19
        2. Liability, Workers' Compensation, Casualty and Automobile
           Policies 23
    B. Punitive Damages Denied 29

III. EXCESS INSURERS 36

IV. REINSURANCE 41

I. THE DUTY TO DEFEND AND INDEMNIFY

    Generally, the courts hold that an insurer's duty to defend an insured in a lawsuit brought against the insured arises when any person makes a claim against the insured, and the facts *as alleged by the claimant* bring the incident within the purview of the policy covering the insured. The duty of an insurer to indemnify an insured arises after the facts clearly establish, or a court rules, that there has been a loss or an incident covered by the policy.

A. <u>Duty Found</u>

    A man was killed in a three-wheel all terrain vehicle accident. At the time, the man was working as an independent contractor and had borrowed the vehicle from a landscaping company. The man's wife brought a complaint against the principal of the landscaping company in his personal capacity, but did not name the company itself in the complaint because she misunderstood the principal's business relationship. The principal sought a defense from the company's liability insurer. The defense was denied because the complaint did not name the business, and because the principal was not a specifically named insured. Both the principal and the insurer's agent informed the insurer that the claim should be defended despite the wording of the complaint, but still the insurer refused. A suit was brought against it by the principal. The suit was successful, reversed on appeal, and then reached the Court of Appeals of New York. It is well settled that an insurer's duty to defend is broader than its duty to indemnify. The normal test to determine whether a duty to defend arises is whether the complaint's allegations could describe an occurrence covered under the policy at issue; if a duty arises, it is not defeated even though extrinsic evidence suggests that the claim is meritless or outside the scope of the policy. The insurer argued that this "four corners test" precluded a duty to defend and was the sole criteria. The policies underlying the development of this rule were examined by the court, and held not to allow such "wooden applications." The ruling specified that an insurer may not avoid its duty to defend when it has actual knowledge of facts which show that the suit involves a potentially covered occurrence. *Fitzpatrick v. American Honda Motor Co.*, 571 N.Y.S.2d 672 (Ct.App.1991).

The owners of a commercial property procured a blanket general liability policy from an insurer. The policy contained an endorsement which extended coverage to damages arising out of personal injury or advertising injury to which the insurance applied. The insurer had a duty to defend any suits which sought damages because of such injuries even if the allegations were groundless, false or fraudulent. The owners of the property then sold it, but continued to manage it for one year. The new owner subsequently filed suit against the insureds, alleging that they had interfered with its prospective economic advantage by refusing to provide rental information to potential tenants. The insurer denied coverage, and refused to provide a defense. This resulted in a lawsuit against the insurer for breach of contract. The trial court granted the insurer's demurrer, and the insureds appealed.
On appeal to the California Court of Appeal, First District, the insureds asserted that the endorsement was broad enough to cover liabilities potentially imposed in the underlying lawsuit. The appellate court agreed. It referred to *Bank of the West v. Superior Court*, 275 Cal.Rptr. 39 (Cal.App.1st Dist.1990), which broadly construed the phrase "unfair competition" to include all unlawful, unfair or fraudulent business practices. Because the advertising injury endorsement covered unfair competition within its provisions, and because unfair competition had been broadly defined as a general category in which a number of torts could be placed, the duty to defend was implicated here. The court of appeal reversed the trial court's decision, and allowed the insureds to amend their complaint against the insurer. *Demonet Industries v. Trans America Ins. Co.*, 278 Cal.Rptr. 178 (Cal.App.1st Dist.1991).

An insured warehouseman was sued for breach of contract when items under his control were lost. The insured then notified his insurer of the claim and lawsuit. His insurer contested the claim, stating that the breach should be excluded from coverage under the "mysterious disappearance" clause. The insurer filed a separate suit in a New York trial court seeking a declaration that it had no duty to defend or indemnify the warehouseman. The insurer was unsuccessful, and appealed to the Supreme Court, Appellate Division, of New York. The court stated that an insurer has a duty to defend when the allegations contained in the complaint against the insured fall within the scope of risks undertaken by the insurer. An insurer has no duty to defend only if the complaint against the insured excludes "every possible basis" which could require indemnification. It was ruled that the breach complaint could possibly be covered, and that the insurer had a duty to defend regardless of whether it would ultimately be required to indemnify. *North River Ins. v. ECA Warehouse Corp.*, 568 N.Y.S.2d 71 (A.D.1st Dep't 1991).

A New York city owned and operated a landfill in which industrial waste and sewage sludge was dumped. Evidence indicated that wastes leaking from the landfill had polluted surrounding groundwaters. The city was insured under several comprehensive liability insurance policies. The state of New York sued the city and others claiming that they were jointly and severally strictly liable for the cost of studying and remedying the environmental problems created by the landfill. The city notified its insurers of the claims. The insurers denied coverage claiming that their potential liability fell within various policy exclusions. The insurers denied any obligation to defend or indemnify the city. The city sought a declaration of the insurers' duty from a federal district court. The insurers moved to dismiss or, in the alternative, for summary judgment. The court granted summary judgment for the insurers, finding that the city had notice of the contamination and that the pollution damages were not covered by the policies. The city then appealed to the U.S. Court of Appeals, Second Circuit.

On appeal, the court noted that the insurers' policies specifically excluded losses or damages expected or intended by the city. The court held that under state law, evidence that the city had notice that the landfill was leaking into surrounding groundwaters did not relieve the insurers of their duty to defend. The insurers had failed to show that the alleged environmental damages were not accidental. Although the city was warned that the landfill was contaminating the local groundwaters, proof of any warning was not enough to show that as a matter of law the ultimate damages incurred were expected or intended. The insurers were required to defend the city and the lower court's decision was reversed and remanded. *City of Johnstown, N.Y. v. Bankers Standard Ins.*, 877 F.2d 146 (2d Cir.1989).

An insurance agency purchased an errors and omissions policy from an insurer. The agency then obtained ocean marine insurance coverage for nine different companies through another insurer, which became insolvent. The nine companies sued the agency for negligence, wantonness, fraud and breach of contract. The agency brought a declaratory relief action against its errors and ommissions insurer, seeking defense and indemnity. The insurer contended that coverage was excluded by a provision which precluded coverage resulting from "the inability of an insurance company, [] or any similar entity to pay all or part of insured claims." The trial court granted summary judgment to the agency, holding that the insurer had to defend on all counts except the ones alleging fraud and unpaid claims. The insurer appealed to the Supreme Court of Alabama. On appeal, the insurer asserted that the underlying lawsuits stemmed from the insolvent insurer's inability to pay claims. The court, however, disagreed. It stated that none of the lawsuits against the agency involved actual claims filed against the insolvent insurer. Basically, the suits were grounded in tort law; the sole breach of contract count did not concern the insolvent insurer's failure to pay actual claims. The court acknowledged that no defense had to be provided for the counts alleging fraud. The trial court's ruling in favor of the agency was affirmed. *St. Paul Fire & Marine Ins. Co. v. Molton*, 592 So.2d 199 (Ala.1991).

A commissioned sales representative for a clothing company brought suit against the company, after losing his job, for breach of contract, fraud, wrongful termination, personal harassment and emotional distress. The company tendered defense of the suit to its insurer, but the insurer denied coverage, primarily because any termination would be intentional and thus not an occurrence, and because of the employee status of the plaintiff. Two years after the suit was filed, and shortly before trial, an amended complaint was filed which included new causes of action for negligence and defamation. Again, the company requested defense, submitting by facsimile transmission approximately 700 pages of documents. When they did not get through, the defendant mailed the papers. The insurer received them on the Monday after the trial had taken place, and it then accepted tender of defense, unaware that judgment had already been rendered. The insurer then moved to set aside the judgment on the grounds of mistake, inadvertence, surprise and excusable neglect. The trial court denied the insurer's motion, citing its opportunity in the just-completed trial. The insurer appealed to the California Court of Appeal, First District, which reversed the superior court's decision. It found that the insurer had presented an adequate case for relief from the judgment due to the surprise of the amended complaint. The court held that the insurer should not necessarily have known of the new causes of action from the facts in its possession, and its offer of defense immediately after being informed of the amendments amounted to good faith. The court remanded the case for further proceedings. *Lipson v. Jordache Enterprises, Inc.*, 11 Cal.Rptr.2d 271 (Cal.App.1st Dist.1992).

An Illinois grandfather was babysitting his three-year-old grandson. They drove to a storage area and the grandfather left the car. It rolled into Lake Michigan and the grandson was killed. His estate sued the grandfather alleging negligent operation of an automobile and negligent supervision. The grandfather notified his homeowner's insurer which refused to defend him. The grandfather sued the insurer in an Illinois U.S. district court. The insurer argued that an automobile exclusion in the policy excluded coverage for any injuries arising "... out of the ownership, maintenance, use, loading or unloading of ... a motor vehicle owned or operated by ... any insured." The district court observed that the exclusion only applied to the claim for negligent operation of an automobile. Since one of the estate's allegations was not excluded, the insurer was required to defend the grandfather. The insurer appealed to the U.S. Court of Appeals, Seventh Circuit. The issue on appeal was how to determine the insurer's obligation to defend the grandfather. The insurer argued that the motor vehicle exclusion precluded coverage for all claims relating to a motor vehicle and that claims for coverage should not be considered without examining the instrumentality of the loss. Here, the instrumentality was a motor vehicle; therefore there should be no coverage. The court of appeals held that because the negligent supervision claim might be covered, the insurer had a duty to defend the grandfather. It was possible that liability would arise from his negligent supervision which was not excluded by the policy. Since the negligent supervision claim was not auto related, the insurer was obligated to defend the grandfather. *West American Ins. v. Hinze*, 843 F.2d 263 (7th Cir.1988).

A Rhode Island bicycle rider was injured as a result of a defective brake. The brake manufacturer had a products liability insurance policy which extended coverage to the company that put the brake on the bicycle. The rider sued the brake manufacturer, the bicycle assembler and the seller. The assembler sought a declaratory judgment from a U.S. federal district court to determine whether the insurer had a duty to defend it under the manufacturer's policy. The assembler argued that the insurer had a duty to defend it as the policy extended coverage to the distribution or sale of the brakes by the assembler. The insurer argued that the policy excluded damages caused by brakes that had been made a part of any other product and that the assembler had cut off its coverage when it put the brake on the bicycle.

The district court granted the declaratory judgment, stating that an insurer must defend when the complaint contains any allegations potentially covered by the policy. It also found the exclusionary clause language ambiguous. The court rejected the insurer's argument that the brake's attachment to the bicycle cut off the coverage, calling it utterly unreasonable given the assembler's use of the brake. The insurer had a duty to defend the bicycle assembler. *Murray Ohio Mfg. Co. v. Continental Ins. Co.*, 705 F.Supp. 442 (N.D.Ill.1989).

A Vermont mercury thermometer manufacturer experienced inadvertent breakage of thermometers and mercury spillage which resulted in mercury vapor contaminating its plant. Mercury also contaminated the walls and floor of the plant, and employees took mercury home on their clothing. A group of the plant's former employees sued the manufacturer for personal injury and property damage. The manufacturer sought a declaration from a New York trial court that its liability insurers had a duty to defend and indemnify it in the lawsuits. After the trial court held that the insurers had a duty to defend the manufacturer in the employees' lawsuits, the insurers appealed to the New York Supreme Court, Appellate Division. On appeal, one insurer argued that it had no duty to defend because the mercury contamination was not an occurrence within the policy's meaning. The manufacturer maintained that its liability in the employees' lawsuits had resulted from a series of unexpected or unintended events that constituted an occurrence triggering coverage. The court agreed, holding that the insurers had a duty to defend the manufacturer. It ruled that because the employees' complaints alleged personal and property damage, such allegations triggered a duty to defend. However, the court held that although the insurers had to defend the manufacturer, no duty to indemnify arose until the manufacturer proved that the policies provided coverage. The court affirmed the trial court's decision. *Munzer v. St. Paul Fire & Marine Ins.*, 538 N.Y.S.2d 633 (A.D.3d Dep't 1989).

A Vermont couple sold their home which had been insulated with urea formaldehyde foam. The buyers sued the sellers, claiming that the insulation was a noxious material which was abnormally dangerous to their health. The sellers owned a homeowner's policy, which provided coverage for claims made against them for bodily injury or property damage. The insureds notified their insurer of the lawsuit but the insurer refused to defend or indemnify them. The insureds then brought a declaratory judgment action against the insurer in a Vermont trial court to determine coverage under the policy. The trial court ruled that the claims brought by the buyers against the insureds did not come within the policy's coverage because they were not claims of bodily injury or property damage. The insureds appealed to the Supreme Court of Vermont. The supreme court held that the insurer was required to defend the insureds against claims for exposure to formaldehyde gas. The insurer was also required to indemnify the buyers for bodily injury and property damages, including exposure to toxic products and for diminution in property value. The court noted that the buyers suffered serious increased health risks from exposure to urea formaldehyde. This was sufficient to trigger coverage under the policy's bodily injury clause. The court also found that the buyers could no longer live in the house without injury and that the property's resale value was diminished. The supreme court reversed the trial court's decision and remanded the case for further proceedings. *American Protection Ins. Co. v. McMahan*, 562 A.2d 462 (Vt.1989).

An insured company faced an environmental cleanup order pursuant to the Comprehensive Environmental Response, Compensation, and Liability Act of 1980. The insured had full comprehensive liability policies, all of which provided coverage for an occurrence not expected or intended by the insured. The insurers defended the insured under a reservation of rights, and later brought an action against the company seeking a declaration that they had no duty to defend or indemnify. Despite conflicting evidence, a trial court granted summary judgment for the insurers on both issues. An appellate court affirmed, and the Supreme Court of Kentucky granted discretionary review. The first issue concerned the appropriateness of the summary judgment on the coverage issue. The policies at issue excluded coverage only when harm was expected or intended by the insured. Coverage would therefore be excluded only when the insured objectively intended the injury which gave rise to the harm. The second issue concerned the insurers' duty to defend. The duty to defend is separate from, and broader than, an insurer's duty to indemnify. When damage is not clearly outside the scope of a policy the duty to defend arises and is not later defeated by a finding that coverage does not exist. The summary judgment for each issue was reversed. *James Graham Brown Foundation v. St. Paul Fire & Marine Ins. Co.*, 814 S.W.2d 273 (Ky.1991).

In November 1983, a suit was filed on behalf of a child against a landlord's estate for lead paint poisoning. The estate sought coverage and defense from its liability insurer. The insurer discovered that the child was afflicted with lead poisoning in September 1982, and withdrew its defense. It stated that the poisoning did not arise during the policy period. The estate settled the suit for $32,000. The estate then sued the insurer in a Maryland trial court seeking reimbursement for settlement costs. The trial court held for the estate and the insurer appealed to the Maryland Court of Special Appeals. Issues before the court were whether the insurer had a duty to defend the estate and whether the claim was an "occurrence" under the policy. The court observed that the duty of an insurer to defend its insured is determined by the underlying claim. If the suing party alleged a claim covered by the policy, the insurer is obligated to defend. The estate argued that the claim was covered because the first notice it received of the poisoning occurred during the policy period. The insurer argued that the policy only provided coverage for bodily harm which occurred during the policy period. The court held for the estate. Because the poisoning could have occurred during the policy period, the insurer had the duty to defend the estate. The insurer should have sought to resolve the issue of whether the poisoning was an occurrence under the policy in court. Since it did not, the estate was also entitled to be reimbursed for the attorney's fees which arose from the settlement. *Hartford Mut. Ins. Co. v. Jacobson*, 536 A.2d 120 (Md.App.1988).

A corporation involved in the construction of a nuclear power generating station purchased two liability policies, each with a maximum recovery per claim of $25 million. The policies were "claims made" policies which provided coverage for prior acts, if the insured had no knowledge of any claims at the effective date of the policies. Subsequently, excessive costs forced a halt to construction of the facility. The holders of bonds which financed the project then brought suit against, among others, the insured. The corporation settled for $50 million, then sought coverage from its insurers. After they refused to provide a defense or coverage, the insured brought suit. A federal district court jury granted $50 million to the insured, and the judge reduced the coverage to $25 million. Both parties appealed to the U.S. Court of

Appeals, Fifth Circuit. On appeal, the court found that the parties had intended for the total coverage to be $25 million, partly because of the huge difference in premium payments between the two policies, but mostly because an employee of the corporation testified that the insured had only intended to purchase $25 million in coverage. The court also found that the insurers had breached their duty to defend the insured. Because of this, the insurers had no right to conduct discovery into the settlement to determine if it had been reasonable. The court affirmed in part the district court's decision. *Enserch Corp. v. Shand Morahan & Co.*, 952 F.2d 1485 (5th Cir.1992).

B. Duty Not Found

In the following cases the courts found no obligation to provide defense or indemnity.

A Huntington Beach couple owned a home which they later sold before moving to Carlsbad. Both residences were insured by the same insurer. The individuals who purchased the Huntington Beach residence sued the insureds two years after purchasing the home, claiming intentional and negligent misrepresentation. Their complaint alleged that the house was sliding, slipping, settling, sinking, fracturing, and buckling. They alleged that the insureds knew or should have known that the property had experienced continuing extensive subsidence damage. They sought damages for their home's decreased value, as well as for physical and emotional distress. The insureds tendered defense to their insurer. The insurer refused tender of defense, and the insureds sued for bad faith. The trial court awarded a motion for nonsuit to the insurer and the insureds appealed to the Court of Appeal, Fourth District.

The court stated that the duty to defend exists only when there is potential for the third party to assert a claim covered by the policy. First, there was no potential for the plaintiffs in the underlying case to assert a covered claim for property damage. The policy specifically limited coverage to occurrences causing property damage, with property damage defined as "physical injury to, destruction of, or loss of use of, tangible property." The plaintiffs alleged misrepresentation causing an economic loss — the lost fair market value of the home. Such an injury is not an injury to tangible property within the meaning of a liability policy, because damages for fraud are ordinarily limited to economic injuries. Put another way, the fraud caused only an economic loss, it did not actually damage the property. Second, there was no potential for the plaintiffs to assert a covered claim for bodily injury. Any emotional stress suffered by the plaintiffs could only have occurred after they took possession of the property. The policy on the Huntington Beach residence covered only liability for occurrences which resulted in bodily injury during the policy period. The policy on the Carlsbad residence covered only activities arising at the insured location. Therefore, neither provided coverage. Furthermore, damages for emotional distress are not recoverable for fraud. A separate claim for emotional distress which caused physical injury was not pursued in this case. Since no covered claims were alleged, no defense was necessary. *Devin v. United Services Auto. Assoc.*, 8 Cal.Rptr.2d 263 (Cal.App.4th Dist.1992).

After a New York insured realty company suffered fire loss to its premises, the insurer requested sworn proof of loss, as required under the policy. The insured submitted unsworn proof of loss forms and the insurer denied the claim. During discovery, the president identified but did not testify as to the accuracy of the forms' contents. The insured contended that there was substantial compliance with the requirements of the policy by virtue of its president's testimony given in an examination under oath. The trial court granted summary judgment to the insurer. The appellate court affirmed the trial court's decision stating that since the president did not verify the accuracy of the documents' contents, there could be no recovery under the policy. *New York Property Ins. Underwriting Ass'n v. Primary Realty Inc.*, 561 N.Y.S.2d 182 (A.D.1st Dep't 1990).

A California savings and loan association acquired deeds of trust on Colorado condominium units. The trust deeds were insured by standard title insurance policies. The policies excluded from coverage liens which were unenforceable due to failure by a creditor to comply with the "doing business" laws of the state in which the secured property was located. The savings and loan foreclosed on some properties and one of its subsidiaries sued the defaulting borrowers in a Colorado state court for the deficiency. Some of the borrowers filed third-party complaints against the savings and loan claiming that the loans were illegal under a Colorado statute which imposed criminal penalties against foreign savings and loans which originated loans in Colorado. The savings and loan requested defense and indemnification from its title insurer. The insurer denied coverage and sued the savings and loan in a federal district court for an order declaring that it had no duty to defend or indemnify.

The court found that the Colorado statute was not a "doing business" law under the policy exclusion, but was rather a criminal statute. The exclusion was inapplicable and the title insurer was obligated to provide defense in the state court action. The insurer appealed to the U.S. Court of Appeals, Tenth Circuit. The appeals court ruled that although the Colorado statute imposed criminal penalties against savings and loans violating the statute, it was still a "doing business" law. Despite using criminal sanctions, the law still regulated savings and loans. Because the illegal loans were within the terms of the policy exclusion, the insurer had no duty to defend or indemnify the savings and loan in the state lawsuit. The court reversed the district court's decision. *Title Ins. Co. of Minn. v. American Savings and Loan Ass'n,* 866 F.2d 1284 (10th Cir.1989).

A Texas corporation sought a declaratory judgment that its insurers must defend and indemnify it against a discrimination claim pending before the Equal Employment Opportunity Commission (EEOC), under provisions of general liability and excess coverage policies. The insured argued that the insurers should defend and indemnify it because the EEOC had already made a probable cause determination. A New Jersey trial court dismissed the claim, deciding that a reasonable cause determination by the EEOC was not "the functional equivalent of a suit so as to compel the insurers to defend the plaintiff." The trial court went on to decide that the insurer only has a duty to defend when the insured is involved in an adversarial proceeding. The EEOC's proceeding was not adversarial because the consequence was not a factual determination upon which legal liability could be imposed. The insured appealed this decision to the Superior Court of New Jersey. The appellate court affirmed the trial court's decision, but stated that the insured might be able to recover from its insurers if the EEOC's probable cause determination led to a subsequent federal action. The appellate court also stated that the duty of the insurers to defend could not be found before there was a claim setting forth specific acts of discrimination alleged by the EEOC or by the aggrieved employees. The court thus affirmed the trial court's decision, and dismissed the case. *Campbell Soup Co. v. Liberty Mut.*, 571 A.2d 969 (N.J.Super.A.D.1990).

A Maryland company purchased liability insurance policies from several insurers. Subsequently, three employees filed discrimination complaints with the Equal Employment Opportunity Commission (EEOC), and a fourth employee sued the company under Title VII of the Civil Rights Act of 1964. The company sought coverage from its insurers under its liability policies, and the insurers denied coverage. The company sued in a Maryland trial court, which ruled for the insurers, and the company then appealed to the Court of Special Appeals of Maryland. The appellate court held that the insurers were only liable for actual legal damages and not just for any claim involving monetary relief. If the insurers were liable for all monetary liability which the company had incurred, their use of the term "damages" in the contracts would become mere surplusage, because any obligation to pay would be covered. Since none of the four claims brought against the company sought legal damages as defined by the policies, but rather sought injunctive and other equitable relief, the court ruled that the insurers were under no obligation to defend, indemnify or reimburse the company. The court affirmed the trial court's decision. *Maryland Cup Corp. v. Employers Mut. Liability Ins. Co.*, 568 A.2d 1129 (Md.App.1990).

A man filed a civil rights complaint in a federal district court against an Illinois city and the police officers who arrested him. He alleged that the officers had used excessive force during the arrest and that the city had allowed the violations. When the city sought defense from its primary general liability insurer, the general insurer refused to defend either the officers or the city. The city then procured defense from its excess insurer which settled the lawsuit. The excess insurer then sought a declaration in a federal district court that the city's general liability insurer had to reimburse it for defending the police officers and the city. The district court found that the general liability insurer was not obligated to defend. The excess insurer appealed to the U.S. Court of Appeals, Seventh Circuit.

On appeal, the excess insurer pointed to an endorsement in the general liability insurance policy which covered employees acting within the scope of their employment. The general liability insurer maintained that the policy endorsement excluded any claim arising out of the willful misconduct of a policeman. The court of appeals affirmed the district court's decision, concluding that the man's injuries were expected or intended by the officers. The officers should have reasonably anticipated his injuries, and coverage under the general insurer's policy was therefore excluded. The court held that the general liability insurer also had no duty to reimburse the excess insurer for the city's defense. Since the arrested man's complaint alleged that the city had been reckless, his injuries were expected and therefore excluded by the policy. The court upheld the district court's decision, finding that the general insurer was under no duty to defend the police officers or the city. *Calvert Ins. Co. v. Western Ins. Co.*, 874 F.2d 396 (7th Cir.1989).

A Minnesota computer company which was in the business of inspecting and repairing computer disk cartridges was insured under a comprehensive general liability policy. The insured was hired to inspect cartridges for defects. While inspecting the cartridges, the insured's employees accidentally erased valuable client information. The client sued the insured for damages in a Minnesota trial court. The insured then requested the insurer to defend it in the lawsuit. Under the insured's policy, it was protected against accidental property damage. The insurer refused to defend the suit claiming the losses were not covered under the policy. The court found for the insured and the insurer appealed to the Minnesota Court of Appeals. The court of appeals held that the insured's liability policy covered the loss-of-use claims. The computer information erased constituted "property damage" which was "caused by an accidental event." The court found that the computer information encoded on the cartridges was tangible property, and loss of use of that property constituted property damage. The court of appeals affirmed the trial court's decision requiring the insurer to defend and indemnify the insured.

The insurer then appealed to the Supreme Court of Minnesota. The supreme court held that the policy did not cover the loss-of-use claim. The court noted that the policy did not extend coverage to intangible property. Even if the magnetically encoded data on the client's computer disk cartridges was deemed to be tangible property, coverage would have been excluded under the control of property exclusion. Under this exclusion, property damage while on the insured's premises to be worked on was excluded from coverage. Both the computer disk cartridge and the information encoded thereon were on the premises for work. The supreme court reversed the court of appeals' decision and ordered the trial court to enter judgment for the insurer. The insurer was not required to defend or indemnify its insured. *Magnetic Data v. St. Paul Fire & Marine*, 442 N.W.2d 153 (Minn.1989).

An uninsured South Dakota man became intoxicated and caused a car accident in which a girl was injured. The girl sued the fraternal lodge which had allegedly served alcohol to the man. The parties came to a settlement which called for payment of $359,000 by the lodge's liability insurer and two auto liability insurers. The two insurers that had paid out uninsured motorist benefits kept their subrogation rights. These insurers then sought a declaratory judgment in a South Dakota trial court that the lodge's comprehensive general liability insurer indemnify them. After the trial court dismissed the subrogated insurers' claim, they appealed to the Supreme Court of South Dakota. On appeal, the lodge's liability insurer maintained that its policy did not apply because it excluded coverage for bodily injury or property damage by organizations engaged in the business of selling or serving alcohol. The other insurers argued that the liability policy did apply, because the lodge was a nonprofit corporation, and therefore could not be "engaged in the business" of selling or serving alcohol. The supreme court held that the exclusionary clause in the policy was unambiguous and precluded coverage for the underlying lawsuit. The court noted that most of the lodge's income was generated by its alcohol sales, that it paid state sales tax on its bar operations and had state and city liquor licenses. The supreme court affirmed the trial court's decision that the lodge's liability insurer had no duty to indemnify the other insurers. *McGriff v. U.S. Fire Ins. Co.*, 436 N.W.2d 859 (S.D.1989).

A Pennsylvania insured kicked a police officer twice in the groin. The officer and his wife sued the insured for assault and battery, both of which required proof that the insured intended to do the acts. The insured's homeowner's insurer sought a declaratory judgment that it did not have to defend the insured because her acts were intentional. The policy contained a provision which excluded coverage for damage caused by the insured's intentional acts. A trial court directed the insurer to defend the insured in the lawsuit. The insurer appealed to the Superior Court of Pennsylvania. The court reversed the lower court's decision and granted the insurer's declaratory judgment. It held that an insurer must defend an insured if the complaint states a claim to which the policy potentially applies. Since the officer's complaint alleged that the insured's acts were intentional and because the insured could be substantially certain of the consequences of her actions, there was no duty to defend by virtue of the intentional acts exclusion. *Donegal Mut. Ins. Co. v. Ferrara*, 552 A.2d 699 (Pa.Super.1989).

A sixty-three year old California man was charged with the felony of molesting a child under fourteen. He pled guilty to a misdemeanor offense of molesting a child under the age of eighteen and was sentenced to a term of six months imprisonment. He later committed suicide. The child, through her guardian, sued the man's estate. The estate's homeowner's insurer sued the estate in a federal district court seeking a court declaration that it had no duty to provide a defense for or to indemnify the estate in the child's lawsuit. The homeowner's policy excluded coverage for "bodily injury or property damage which is expected or intended by an insured." The insurer contended that the deceased man's acts fell within both the exclusion and within the scope of California Insurance Code § 533. Section 533 provides that insurers are not liable for a loss caused by the wilful act of an insured. The man's estate argued that the insurer was liable because the man had acted out of affection for the child rather than trying to harm her. It also contended that the insurer was liable because the man was not convicted of a felony. The court granted the insurer's request for a declaration in its favor. The deceased man's intentional acts fell within the scope of § 533. The initiation of sexual activity by an adult with an eight year old was inherently harmful. Even though the man was found guilty of a misdemeanor rather than a felony, the insurer was not liable since "some acts are so extreme that public policy does not permit them to be insured." The insurer had no duty to defend or indemnify the deceased man's estate. *State Farm Fire & Cas. Ins. Co. v. Abraio*, 683 F.Supp. 220 (N.D.Cal.1988).

A U.S. district court in California has ruled that an insurer had no duty to defend or indemnify a business in a former employee's wrongful termination lawsuit. The employee's lawsuit contained two claims: 1) breach of employment contract and 2) breach of the implied covenant of good faith and fair dealing. In the second claim, the employee sought punitive damages for intentional infliction of emotional distress; the employee later informed the employer that he would seek damages for negligent infliction of emotional distress as well. Asserting that these claims should be covered under its general liability policy, the employer contacted its insurer. The insurer denied coverage. It pointed out that the liability policy, although providing coverage for employer liability based upon bodily injury or property damage caused by an "occurrence," required that such damages be "neither expected nor intended from the standpoint of the insured." The insurer requested a judicial declaration that it had no duty to defend or indemnify the employer against the employee's claims. The district court observed that it was undisputed that the employer acted intentionally when it terminated the employee. Therefore, the termination was not an occurrence as defined by the policy. Accordingly, the court issued a declaration that the insurer was bound to offer neither a defense nor indemnity to the employer. *Hartford Fire Ins. Co. v. Karavan Enterprises*, 659 F.Supp. 1075 (N.D.Cal.1986).

After the court issued its decision in the above case, the employer filed a motion asking the court to reverse its decision. The employer's motion was based on the fact that the employee had notified the employer that the wrongful termination lawsuit would be amended to include a claim based upon negligent infliction of emotional distress. The court held that "[f]or the purpose of insurance coverage the act of discharge is the determinative event.... [A]n intentional discharge cannot constitute an unintended or unexpected 'occurrence.' So, too, negligence claims based on the discharge fall within the ambit of the claim for wrongful discharge." The court continued: "Claims for negligent conduct must be treated analytically as an integral part of the assertedly wrongful discharge. Any alleged harm comes about as an intended or unintended consequence of the conduct of discharge, but in neither case constitutes an 'accident ... which results in bodily injury or property damage neither expected nor intended from the standpoint of the insured.'" The court therefore reaffirmed its earlier denial of coverage. *Hartford Fire Ins. Co. v. Karavan Enterprises*, 659 F.Supp. 1077 (N.D.Cal.1987).

C. Coverage of Insureds' Punitive Damages

Jurisdictions differ over whether indemnification should be available for punitive damages awarded against insureds. In jurisdictions where such indemnification is allowed, policy language often determines whether coverage exists.

1. Coverage Found

A California company manufactured asbestos and distributed it to many states. The manufacturer was sued by groups of people who developed health problems, and juries in Texas and West Virginia awarded punitive damages. A separate lawsuit later developed between the manufacturer and its insurer; the issue was whether the insurer would be required to indemnify the manufacturer for punitive damages. The laws of Texas, California and West Virginia vary on this issue, and the critical ruling in this case concerned determining which state law to apply. The case was heard in a federal district court.

The court was to apply California law if there would be no change in the outcome. If there would be a conflict in law, the court had to choose which law to apply based on a "government interest" test. California law allows punitive damages only to punish intentional conduct, and the liability may not be passed on to an insurer. West Virginia law allows punitive damages for either intentional or negligent conduct, and does allow liability to be passed on to an insurer. The verdict from West Virginia did not specify whether the award was for intentional or negligent conduct. The court ruled that since the award may have been for only negligent conduct the insurability of the award was allowable. The insurer was ruled to be liable for the West Virginia award. Texas law allows punitive damages only for intentional conduct, and does allow liability to be passed to on an insurer. A conflict of laws was present; the court thus examined the interest of the governments. Texas' interest in recovery for its citizens and limits on business liabilities was ruled to override California's interest in punishment. The insurer was found also to be liable for the Texas awards. *Continental Cas. Co. v. Fibreboard Corp.*, 762 F.Supp. 1368 (N.D.Cal.1991).

The New Mexico Supreme Court has held that insurance policies which cover liability for punitive damages are permissible. The case involved a motorist who was sued by the driver of another vehicle after a collision. After the driver of the other vehicle was awarded punitive damages the motorist sought a judicial declaration that the punitive damages award was covered by his insurance policy. The supreme court found two reasons to support coverage for punitive damages. First, the motorist's policy had no provision which excluded damages awarded to punish for driving in a grossly negligent manner. The supreme court did not accept the insurer's argument that punitive damages were for punishment, not for actual bodily injury or property damage, and therefore not covered. It reasoned that without bodily injury or property damage no punitive damages would have been awarded. Second, the motorist reasonably expected protection against claims of this kind for which he became liable. The supreme court would not find an exclusion of liability for punitive damages where there was nothing in the policy to forewarn the motorist that punitive damage awards were not covered. The insurer was liable for the punitive damage award. *Baker v. Armstrong*, 744 P.2d 170 (N.M.1987).

Avis Rent A Car System had an automobile insurance policy providing coverage for "all sums which the insured shall become legally obligated to pay as damages because of ... bodily injury" arising out of the ownership or use of an automobile. Under Connecticut law the owner of a rental car is liable for damages caused by its operation "to the same extent as the operator would have been liable if he had also been the owner." While intoxicated, one of Avis' renters caused a head-on collision which killed another car's driver. Damages awarded against Avis in the underlying lawsuit were augmented under a statute which provided for treble damages when an accident was caused by the grossly wrongful operation of a motor vehicle. Avis sought a judicial declaration that the insurer was required to pay. The Supreme Court of Connecticut ruled that under the policy, the treble damages arose out of the bodily injuries suffered by the victim. Avis' policy therefore provided coverage for the treble damages. The court declared that coverage for the treble damages did not violate the public policy against the providing of insurance to cover an insured's wrongdoing. This was because the rental car company was not a wrongdoer at all. Rather, its liability for the treble damages had been imposed vicariously. *Avis Rent A Car System v. Liberty Mut. Ins. Co.*, 526 A.2d 522 (Conn.1987).

After an Alaska couple was injured in an automobile accident, they filed a lawsuit against the driver of the other car. The couple sought punitive damages in their lawsuit, contending that the driver's conduct was "outrageous, of reckless indifference ... and demonstrated gross negligence." The driver was covered by an insurance policy covering any amount he became legally liable to pay "as a result of bodily injury or property damage" caused by accident. The driver sought a judicial declaration that the insurer would be liable for punitive damages in the couple's lawsuit if such damages were awarded. The insurer argued before a U.S. district court that punitive damages would be in excess of the couple's actual loss and therefore would not result from bodily injury or property damage. The court rejected this reasoning, concluding that punitive damages would be covered because the driver would become obligated to pay them as a "result" of the couple's bodily injuries and property damage. If the insurer had wanted to exclude coverage for punitive damages it could have expressly excluded such damages from coverage. The court went on to say that coverage of punitive damages in this case did not violate public policy because here, punitive damages would be based on negligence rather than intentional wrongful conduct. Under these circumstances the public interest served by imposing punitive damages upon the driver was not sufficiently strong to justify avoiding the clear terms of the insurance contract. *LeDoux v. Continental Ins. Co.*, 666 F.Supp. 178 (D.Alaska 1987).

The Supreme Court of Iowa, reversing a lower court, has held that an "all sums" insurance policy which obligated an insurer to pay all sums which the insured became legally obligated to pay because of bodily injury or property damage, includes coverage of punitive damages, and ruled that the public policy purposes of punitive damages (punishment and deterrence) do not preclude such a construction. The court cited prior case law wherein it had adopted the approach of construing "all sums" to include not only actual or compensatory damages, but punitive damages as well. This construction, said the court, comports with the rule that insurance contracts should be construed "from the standpoint of what an ordinary man would believe the contract to mean.... The insurer assumes a duty to define, in clear and explicit terms, any limitations or exclusions to coverage expressed by broad promises." The court went on to say that, while it did not repudiate the public policy purposes underlying punitive damages, it did not believe that public policy reasons for punitive damages could override other considerations favoring coverage of punitive damages in insurance policies.

It was noted by the court that its decision was based on the harmonization of two competing public policies: the freedom to contract and punitive damages. "We realize that the result of our decision is to elevate the public policy of freedom to contract for insurance coverage above the public policy purposes of punitive damages. We do so for two reasons. "First," said the court, "we doubt that ordinary potential tortfeasors make calculations to determine if the expected benefits of a harmful act are outweighed by the potential costs of punitive damages, insured or uninsured. Second, we do not view our decision as totally abrogating the sting of punitive damages. The sting will continue to be felt by the uninsured, the underinsured, and the poor risks who will experience substantial difficulty and high costs in obtaining such insurance." *Skyline Harvestore Systems v. Centennial Ins. Co.*, 331 N.W.2d 106 (Iowa 1983).

2. Coverage Not Found

After a Rhode Island couple was involved in an automobile accident with an intoxicated driver the couple sued him seeking both compensatory and punitive damages. They based their punitive damages claim on the driver's intoxication. A superior court held that the intoxicated driver's insurer was liable for the compensatory damages but not the punitive damages and the couple appealed. The question before the Rhode Island Supreme Court was whether the insurer was required to indemnify the couple for the punitive damages assessed against its insured (the intoxicated driver). The insurer relied on a policy provision which stated that it would "pay damages for bodily injury or property damage for which any covered person [became] legally responsible because of an auto accident." Observing that the insurer's obligation in the dispute was set forth in the simple and direct language of the insurance policy, the supreme court held that the insurer was not liable for the punitive damage claim for two reasons. First, punitive damages were awarded not to enrich the couple but rather to punish the intoxicated driver and serve as an object lesson both to him and to others who might be tempted to follow in his path. Second, the burden of satisfying the punitive damages award should remain with the intoxicated driver and should not be cast upon the blameless shoulders of other insureds who would eventually be required to help pay for the punitive damages award through increased premiums. The couple would have to seek their punitive damage award directly from the intoxicated driver. *Allen v. Simmons*, 533 A.2d 541 (R.I.1987).

An insured man's injuries were caused by the reckless driving of an uninsured motorist. The insured sued the driver for compensatory damages, and his own uninsured motorist coverage carrier for punitive damages for the uninsured's reckless driving. The insurer attained a dismissal of the suit, and the insured appealed to a Florida appellate court. The injured man argued that Florida law allows a punitive damage award, and in some instances does not require compensatory damages to have been assessed. The court distinguished those instances because they involved both compensatory and punitive claims against the same party. Further, another case made clear that an insured may not obtain punitive damages from his or her own insurer based on the negligent conduct of a third party. The dismissal was affirmed. *Holton v. McCutcheon*, 584 So.2d 50 (Fla.App.2d Dist.1991).

After a Pennsylvania company defaulted on its loans, the bank invited the company's officers to a meeting to discuss the delinquent loan account. While the officers were occupied in a conference room and cut off from incoming calls, the bank's agents took possession of the company's property, which had secured the defaulted loans. The company subsequently filed for bankruptcy. The bankruptcy trustee and the company's officers sued the bank for compensatory and punitive damages arising out of the repossession scheme. The bank was covered by a liability insurance policy with a limit of $500,000 per occurrence. The insurer contributed $275,000 to the settlement of the underlying lawsuits, and the bank sued it for additional funds that it expended in the settlements (over $700,000 had been paid by the bank to the company). The insurer maintained that under Pennsylvania law no coverage was allowed for punitive damages.

A U.S. district court noted that when a wrongful act is committed by a lowly functionary agent of a corporation, not pursuant to corporate policy, the corporation is entitled to insure against resulting punitive damages. In this case, however, the repossession plan was conceived, approved and implemented by the bank's upper management and was subsequently ratified by its board of directors. The court reasoned that where corporate management commits outrageous wrongful acts, punishment is appropriate and no insurance is available for punitive damages. *Pennbank v. St. Paul Fire & Marine Ins. Co.*, 669 F.Supp. 122 (W.D.Pa.1987).

In another Pennsylvania case, a boy was attacked and bitten by a dog. His parents sued the dog's owner who asked her homeowner's insurer to defend her in the lawsuit. The insurer informed the dog owner that its policy only provided protection against claims for personal injury and property damage and that it would not pay any portion of a verdict which would be attributable to punitive damages. The parents settled with the dog owner and her insurer for $102,000, with $101,000 being paid by the insurer for personal injury and $1,000 being paid by the dog owner to settle the claim for punitive damages. The settlement agreement provided that the parents released "all claims, including ... claims for punitive damages, ... under a certain policy ...

issued by ..." the insurer. The dog owner sued her insurer alleging that it had breached its contract of insurance by failing to pay the claim for punitive damages that it had allegedly agreed to pay in the settlement agreement. The Pennsylvania Superior Court noted that an insurer's duty to defend or indemnify is limited to claims covered by the policy, not settlement agreements. Here, the insurer had only agreed to indemnify the dog owner for bodily injury and property damage in the policy and therefore it had no obligation to provide indemnity for a punitive damages claim. *Creed v. Allstate Ins. Co.*, 529 A.2d 10 (Pa.Super.1987).

After a court awarded a pool construction firm $1.6 million in compensatory damages and $1 million in punitive damages against a business which sold defective swimming pool coatings, the pool coating business sought reimbursement for those damages from its excess liability insurer. The insurer denied coverage for both the compensatory and punitive damages awards and it sought a court declaration to that effect. A U.S. district court ruled that a trial was necessary to resolve whether the excess insurance policy's "intentional acts" exclusion applied to the compensatory damage award rendered against the pool coating business. The district court agreed, however, to dismiss the pool coating business's request that its insurer indemnify it for the punitive damages award. Although the policy agreed to provide indemnity for "all sums which insured becomes legally obligated to pay as damages," it did not expressly cover punitive damages. This factor, combined with the strong public policy in Illinois disfavoring the insurability of punitive damages, prompted the court to dismiss the pool coating business's claim regarding the punitive damages award. *Affiliated FM Ins. Co. v. Beatrice Foods Co.*, 645 F.Supp. 298 (N.D.Ill.1985).

D. Other Actions Against Insurers

A fifty-one-year-old diabetic, with a history of heart disease, applied for life insurance. The insurer sent him to a physician for an independent evaluation of his condition before issuing the policy. Apparently, the doctor performed a stress test on the applicant. One month later, the applicant died of a fatal heart attack at home. His widow brought suit against the insurance company, claiming first that it was vicariously liable for the doctor's negligence in administering the test, and second that it was negligent in ordering the stress test and in failing to get her husband's informed consent. She won at the trial court and appellate court levels, and the insurer appealed to the New York Court of Appeals. The court of appeals found that the insurer could only be vicariously liable in this case if the stress test was inherently dangerous, and the insurer recognized that danger. The court then held, however, that the stress test was not inherently dangerous. It was up to the doctor, ultimately, to determine whether the test should be performed on the applicant, and to decline to perform the test if it was not safe. Finally, the insurer had no duty to explain the risks of the stress test to the applicant. He was aware of the reasons for the test and could rely on the physician's explanation of potential health risks before taking the test. The court ruled in favor of the insurer. *Rosenberg v. Equitable Life Assurance Society*, 584 N.Y.S.2d 765 (Ct.App.1992).

A fraternal organization hired an insurance agent to procure life and health insurance applications for its members. The agent induced some members to invest in a personal business venture which benefited only the agent. The venture eventually failed, and the members sued the fraternal organization for their investment money. A master-in-equity granted the organization summary judgment. The members appealed to the South Carolina Supreme Court which upheld the decision, stating that the organization only owed the members a duty to supervise the agent within his capacity as an insurance agent for the organization. It had no duty to supervise the agent with respect to his own personal business ventures. *Degenhart v. Knights of Columbus*, 420 S.E.2d 495 (S.C.1992).

A liability insurer conducted periodic inspections of a grain elevator in order to determine future insurability and rates. After such an inspection, the insurer would sometimes make safety suggestions to the elevator operator. An explosion at the elevator killed three persons, and the estates of two of them brought suit against the insurer based on negligent inspection. The insurer denied that a duty of care extended to the elevator's employees, and successfully moved for summary judgment in a South Dakota court. The estates then appealed to the Supreme Court of South Dakota. A mere inspection does not give rise to a duty of care to third persons. Such a duty may arise only when an inspector has increased the risk, understood that it undertook such a duty, or when harm is suffered in reliance on such an inspection. The first and third factors were excluded, and the issue became whether the insurer undertook a duty to assist the elevator to provide a safe workplace. Other insurers have been found liable on this theory, but those cases involved insurers who had advertised or represented additional benefits of procuring insurance from them. There were no such extrinsic facts involved in this case, and the insurer thus owed no duty of care to the employees. The decision was affirmed. *Schoenwald v. Farmers Cooperative Ass'n of Marion*, 474 N.W.2d 519 (S.D.1991).

A bank developed a program to finance automobile insurance premiums for consumers who preferred to pay in installments. The program was not offered directly to consumers. Instead, the bank informed insurance agents that it was willing to lend money to finance premiums. The insurance agent would get a 20 to 30% down payment and the consumer's power of attorney. The agent would then apply for a loan in the consumer's name. The bank would not allow cancellation by prepayment and the loan terms included over 126% interest along with substantial fees and penalties. Many consumers were not even aware loans were being made until they received notice of approval from the bank. The consumers sued under numerous theories including the Unfair Business Practices Act. The consumers' federal claims were ultimately removed to federal court, while the Unfair Business Practices Act claims remained in state court.

The consumers were seeking restitution under § 17203 of the Unfair Business Practices Act when the case settled. The bank then sought restitution for the settlement amount from its insurer claiming that the settlement was damages for unfair competition that occurred in the course of the bank's advertising activities. The insurer refused restitution, stating that the policy covered the common law tort of unfair competition rather than practices prohibited by the Unfair Business Practices Act. The insurer also stated that insurance is not available for restitutionary relief under the act. Finally, the insurer stated that the consumers' claims had not occurred in the course of the bank's advertising policies. The trial court agreed with the insurer, but the court of appeal found coverage and reversed. The insurer was granted review by the California Supreme Court.

The supreme court reversed, finding no coverage. The policy promised to pay for damages because of advertising injury, if such injury arose out of unfair competition. The term "unfair competition" does not cover unfair business practices, but rather the common law tort of unfair competition, which is synonymous with the act of passing off one's goods as those of another. The term, although not defined in the policy, is not ambiguous since this interpretation conformed to the reasonable expectations of the insured. Further, insurance proceeds should not be available for violations of the act for public policy reasons. The insured should not be able to shift the loss to the insurer and retain its ill-gotten proceeds. *Bank of the West v. Superior Court*, 10 Cal.Rptr.2d 538 (Cal.1992).

A driver was involved in an auto accident with an insured motorist. The driver obtained an estimate of $3,200 to repair her vehicle, and the insurer allegedly authorized the repairs. The insurer did not immediately pay for repairs. Consequently, the repairs were held up for some time. Eventually, the driver and insurer settled for just under $3,500. The driver sued the insurer for fraud and negligent misrepresentation, claiming that the insurer had authorized the repairs with no intention of paying for them. She evidently did not know the names or identities of the individuals involved in authorizing the repairs and did not name them in her complaint. A trial court dismissed her claims for insufficient pleadings, and the driver appealed to the Court of Appeal, Sixth District.

The court of appeal noted that every element of a cause of action for fraud must be alleged in the proper manner and the facts constituting the fraud must be alleged with sufficient specificity to allow the defendant to understand fully the nature of the charge made. In this case, the driver did not know which of the insurer's agents made the allegedly false representations. Although the specificity requirement may be waived when a defendant necessarily possesses full information of the underlying events, that was not the case here. The insurer had no more reason to know who made the representations to the driver than did the driver herself. The court also held that the negligent misrepresentation claim failed because it did not deal with past or existing material facts. Predictions as to future action are deemed opinions and not actionable. Only a future promise made with the intention of not keeping it is actionable. But such an action must be pleaded as specifically as actual fraud. The court of appeal affirmed the dismissal. *Tarmann v. State Farm Mut. Auto. Ins. Co.*, 2 Cal.Rptr.2d 861 (Cal.App.6th Dist.1991).

A Michigan man secured a note for a motorhome. At the same time he entered into a contract with an insurer to provide motor vehicle insurance for the motorhome. The declaration sheet and the certificate of insurance designated the lienholder as having an interest in the motorhome. The insurer issued the lienholder a loss payable clause which provided that the insurance for the lienholder would not be invalidated by any act or negligence of the owner of the motorhome. Subsequently, the motorhome went up in flames. The insurer alleged arson and refused to pay the lienholder. The Michigan trial court and the Court of Appeals of Michigan held that the motorhome owner's acts of arson and misrepresentation did not preclude recovery by the lienholder under the loss payable clause. *Foremost Ins. Co. v. Allstate Ins. Co.*, 460 N.W.2d 242 (Mich.App.1990).

After the death of their son, a passenger, in an automobile accident, the parents sued the driver under the wrongful death act. The parents entered into an agreement with the automobile insurer in which they acknowledged that the insurer had tendered its policy limits to settle the claim. The parents demanded the policy limits plus interest from the date of filing the complaint. The insurer filed a motion asking the court for a declaration that it had no obligation to pay interest on the settlement. The trial court ruled for the insurer and the parents appealed to the Court of Appeals of Michigan. The parents based their claim on the insurer's duty to negotiate settlements in good faith which arise out of the language of the insurance contract. The court, however, determined that the duty to use good faith in attempting to settle the claim runs only to the insured, not to the injured party. The court affirmed the trial court's decision. *Liimatta v. Lukkari*, 460 N.W.2d 251 (Mich.App.1990).

II. PUNITIVE DAMAGE AWARDS AGAINST INSURERS

Generally, courts will allow an insured to recover punitive damages from an insurer where it is established that the insurer denied the insured's claim in bad faith or acted in careless disregard of the insured's rights under his or her policy. In some states, an award of double the policy limits constitutes punitive damages. In cases where an insured makes a successful claim for punitive damages, attorney's fees are often assessed against the insurer.

A. <u>Punitive Damages Awarded</u>

1. Life, Health, Accident and Hospitalization Policies

An Alabama insurance agent solicited Roosevelt City, Alabama, for health and life insurance for its employees. The agent prepared applications for the city and its employees for group health and life policies. The initial premium payments were taken by the agent and submitted to the insurers with the applications. An arrangement was made for the health insurer to send its premium billings to the agent at his office. The premium payments were then to be effected through payroll deductions and the city clerk would issue a check to the agent. The agent did not remit the premium payments but instead misappropriated most of the funds. However, the insurer did not send notices of lapsed coverage to the employees. Instead, these notices were sent to the agent. One of the employees was hospitalized and upon her discharge was required to make payment on her bill because the hospital could not confirm her health coverage. Her physician, when he was not paid, placed her account with a collection agency. The agency obtained a judgment against the woman and her credit was adversely affected. The city workers then filed this suit naming the insurer and the agent, asking for damages for fraud. The case was submitted to the jury and the jury returned a verdict against the insurer and the agent for over $1,000,000 which included a large sum for punitive damages. The Alabama Supreme Court affirmed this decision and the insurer appealed to the U.S. Supreme Court.

The issue, on appeal, was the constitutionality of certain punitive damage awards. The insurer contended that the award violated due process as the product of unbridled jury discretion. The Court noted that the punitive damage award did not violate due process. First, the trial court's instructions placed reasonable constraints on the exercise of the jury's discretion by expressly describing the purposes of punitive damages to be retribution and deterrence, by requiring the jury to consider the character and degree of the particular wrong, and by explaining that the imposition of punitive damages was not compulsory. Second, the trial court conducted a postverdict hearing which set forth standards to ensure the meaningful and adequate review of the punitive damages award. Third, the petitioner received the benefit of the appropriate review by the state supreme court which approved the verdict and brought in all relevant factors for ensuring that the punitive damages were reasonable. The Alabama Supreme Court's decision upholding the punitive damage award was affirmed. *Pacific Mut. Life Ins. Co. v. Haslip*, 111 S.Ct. 1032, 113 L.Ed.2d 1 (1991).

A Nevada insured suffered a stroke while undergoing an angiogram. The stroke left him permanently unable to walk or talk. The insured's wife attempted to collect benefits under two insurance policies. Their insurer had previously advised them that the policies would protect them in the event of any accident. The insurer's claims adjuster denied the claim, noting that the doctor's initial report indicated that the stroke might have been caused by disease rather than an accident. The claim totaled $9,600. During the following eighteen months, the insurer denied the insured's claim five times. Each time the claim was submitted, the insured added evidence and doctors' reports explaining that the injury was due to the accident during the angiogram. Because of the lack of funds for therapy at the appropriate time, the insured suffered permanent speech impairment.

The insured sued the insurer in a Nevada trial court. He sought benefits, compensatory damages and punitive damages. The jury awarded him $200,000 in compensatory damages and almost $6 million in punitive damages. The insurer moved for a new trial and judgment notwithstanding the verdict. The court denied the motion for a new trial but set aside the punitive damage award. The insured appealed to the Nevada Supreme Court. The supreme court noted that punitive damages were appropriate when the offending party was guilty of fraud, malice or oppression. The court also noted that there was substantial evidence that the insurer had deliberately ignored the insured's rights. The stroke was an unexpected result of the angiogram and therefore an accident. The financial position of the insurer was a factor in determining the amount of the punitive damage award. The $6 million award in this case amounted to only four-tenths of one percent of the insurer's 1985 total assets. The supreme court upheld the jury award of both compensatory and punitive damages. *Ainsworth v. Combined Ins. Co. of America*, 763 P.2d 673 (Nev.1988).

An insured was covered by group medical insurance offered by Blue Cross of California. The insured submitted claims for her son's hospitalization at the Belmont Hills psychiatric clinic. The claims totaled $23,698 but Blue Cross paid only $6,598. It disallowed the balance claiming that the hospitalizations were not medically necessary. After an arbitrator ordered payment the insured sued Blue Cross to recover damages for alleged breach of its implied covenant of good faith and fair dealing. The jury awarded her $150,000 in compensatory damages and $700,000 in punitive damages. Blue Cross appealed to the California Court of Appeal, First District. Blue Cross argued that the jury awards were unwarranted. However, the court of appeal upheld both jury awards.

The covenant of good faith and fair dealing places the burden on the insurer to seek information relevant to a claim. An insurer may breach the covenant when it fails to properly investigate a claim. The record indicated that Blue Cross' letters to the son's treating physician at Belmont Hills were not drafted in a manner calculated to elicit an informed response. This placed an undue burden of inquiry on the treating physician. The court of appeal observed that an award of punitive damages is justified where it serves to deter socially unacceptable corporate policies. Here, there was evidence that the denial of the insured's claim was the product of fragmentary medical records, a cursory review of the records, the consultant's disclaimer of any obligation to investigate, the use of a standard of medical necessity at variance with community standards and uninformative follow-up letters sent to the son's treating physicians. The jury reasonably inferred that these practices were all rooted in established company practice. This conscious disregard of the covenant justified the punitive damage award. *Hughes v. Blue Cross of Northern California*, 245 Cal.Rptr. 273 (App.1st Dist.1988).

Eighteen days after contracting for health insurance, a woman had a total hysterectomy. Her doctor mistakenly noted that she had experienced abdominal pain for two to three years, and should have noted 2 to 3 days. After a denial of her claim due to an alleged preexisting illness, the woman had extreme difficulty in correcting the doctor's error in the insurer's records. Her insurer repeatedly lost medical records and correcting affidavits, and eventually reaffirmed a denial of her claim despite its knowledge that important information had not reached her file. The woman filed claims for both contractual benefits and punitive damages. The contractual claim was settled, and the punitive damage claim was resolved in her favor for $500,000 by a federal district court. It then travelled through the federal courts and was remanded by the U.S. Supreme Court to the U.S. Court of Appeals, Fifth Circuit, to be reconsidered to determine whether the punitive damage award violated the Due Process Clause of the U.S. Constitution.
An analysis of the constitutionality of a punitive damage award includes, among other things, an examination of a function of two factors: 1) whether the circumstances of the case indicate the award is reasonable, 2) whether the procedure of review imposes a meaningful constraint on the discretion of the fact finder. The reasonableness prong of the test requires consideration of whether the award is grossly excessive in light of the conduct and the theory of punitive damages — which is to punish and deter. The court noted that the public had a great interest in discouraging insurers from trying to save money at the expense of an insured, and that a smaller award may have little effect on an entity of such magnitude. Further, this insurer had earlier received a smaller penalty for similarly egregious conduct with no apparent effect. The insurer argued that its conduct was not intentional and, therefore, was inconsistent with an award of punitive damages. This argument was unsuccessful, and the court noted that "some support was found that the award was reasonable." The second half of the analysis necessitated that the appellate review procedure provide a meaningful protection against a factfinder's impulsive reaction to wrongful conduct. The protections cited were that Mississippi case law provides guidelines to limit a court's discretion, and that a judge justify his decision in relation to these guidelines. The court upheld the punitive damages award. *Eichenseer v. Reserve Life Ins. Co.*, 934 F.2d 1377 (5th Cir.1991).

A woman brought a lawsuit against an insurer and an insurance salesman based on the salesman's fraud. A jury found in her favor and awarded $1,000 in compensatory damages and $5 million in punitive damages. Following a posttrial motion the trial court reduced the punitive damage award to $499,000. The appropriateness of that award was affirmed by the Alabama Supreme Court. The U.S. Supreme Court later vacated the decision and remanded the case for reconsideration. The first factor for consideration was whether the jury instructions sufficiently conveyed the purpose of punitive damages, the factual findings necessary, and the guidelines to consider in determining a dollar value. The Alabama justices unanimously agreed that the instruction met the standard established by the Court. The second factor involved the post trial procedures, and necessitated that the appellate court examine whether the appropriate factors were considered by the judge at trial. Again the justices held that the established standard had not been violated. The final factor requires adequate appellate review of the amount of the award, and some degree of uniformity of punitive damages awards. The insurer contended that some acceptable mathematical ratio should be established with respect to the compensatory damage award. The court rejected that argument, and affirmed the award of $499,000. *Southern Life and Health Ins. Co. v. Turner*, 586 So.2d 845 (Ala.1991).

A group health and accident insurer was sued by an Alabama woman for its alleged failure to pay a claim. The woman, who received a blow to the mouth during a robbery attempt, claimed that she had not been able to chew and eat normally and had other problems with her teeth. Relying on alleged representations by her insurance agent that the insurer would pay for necesssary oral surgery, the woman underwent extractions resulting in medical bills totaling $2,600. The insurer refused coverage on the ground that the woman's injuries had been made unduly severe by the preexisting condition of chronic periodontal disease, a condition causing deterioration of the gums. The woman brought suit against the insurer alleging breach of contract, false representation and bad faith. An Alabama trial court jury awarded the woman $23,000 in compensatory, bad faith and punitive damages and the insurer appealed. The Supreme Court of Alabama affirmed the trial court ruling, finding the evidence sufficient to prove that the woman's front teeth had been sound at the time she suffered injuries. Further, the woman had proven that the insurer intentionally failed to determine whether there was any lawful basis for denying payment, thus demonstrating a *prima facie* case of bad faith. Finally, there was evidence that the insurer acted with malice, wilfullness, and wanton and reckless disregard of the woman's rights. The trial court's award of punitive damages was ruled to be proper. *Continental Assur. Co. v. Kourtz*, 461 So.2d 802 (Ala.1984).

The Supreme Court of Florida was asked to decide whether an insurer issuing a life insurance policy can be liable to the insured, where the beneficiary attempts to murder the insured in order to collect the policy benefits and where the insurer had actual notice of the beneficiary's murderous intent. The insured claimed that his total family income was $9,000 per year. Nevertheless, he alleged, the insurance company issued to his wife insurance coverage on his life with a total face value of $130,000 and $260,000 for accidental death. The annual premiums were $7,464. The insured further alleged that he was not aware that his wife was purchasing life insurance; he claimed to have been tricked into signing the forms, believing his wife was purchasing a health insurance policy. Later, the insured overheard his wife and her brother plotting to kill him. He called his insurance agent immediately, informing him of the conspiracy but the insurance company made no inquiry into the matter. Subsequently, the insured's wife and brother-in-law abducted him and were attempting to drown him when a deputy sheriff intervened and rescued him. The insured charged the insurance company with negligence in failing to discover the disproportion of the coverage to the family's income and in failing to investigate the conspiracy to murder him after receiving actual notice. The case was certified to the Supreme Court of Florida because of its "great public importance."

The supreme court, affirming a decision by the state District Court of Appeal, held that the insured had a cause of action against the insurer. The court reasoned that to absolve the insurance company from any responsibility in the face of actual notice would permit the company to continue to collect premiums with the high probability of being able to avoid any payment on the policy. This would allow the company to gamble that the murder would occur and the company would benefit because it would not be required to pay the claim. Accordingly, the court denied the insurer's motion to dismiss and held that the insured was entitled to proceed with his suit against the insurance company. *Life Ins. Co. of Georgia v. Lopez*, 443 So.2d 497 (Fla.1983).

2. Liability, Workers' Compensation, Casualty and Automobile Policies

A farmer in Idaho sought to change his insurance coverage to include the contents of his barn. The insurer stated that the farmer must first increase the coverage on the barn, mentioning replacement costs. The farmer agreed to this. The insurer's representative later brought to the farmer the policy covering the barn's contents, and a bill (but no policy) for increased coverage on the barn. The farmer's barn and its contents were destroyed by fire. Since the policy was never delivered, a dispute arose about the amount of coverage on the barn. The farmer then filed suit in an Idaho trial court, which granted summary judgment on the insurance coverage question. A jury also awarded the farmer further damages on a bad faith claim. The insurer appealed both awards to the Court of Appeals of Idaho. The insurer disputed this award due to the question over the amount of coverage on the barn. The insured pointed out that even though the amount of coverage on the barn was debatable, there were other claims which were undeniably due that were not paid. The insured also noted the adjustor's unreasonable delay and the fact that the adjustor was not supervised. An expert testified at trial that this process could have been used as a tactic by the insurer to "starve out" the farmer. The insurer only offered the farmer the payment of undisputable claims on the condition that it was a final settlement. For the above reasons, the court found the insurer had acted in bad faith. The appeals court upheld the judgment against the insurer for bad faith. *Chester v. State Farm Ins. Co.*, 789 P.2d 539 (Idaho App.1990).

A Georgia boy was injured when a tree limb fell on the parked car he was sitting in. His grandfather, who owned the car, had the minimum no-fault coverage required and a $2,500 claim was subsequently filed under his policy. The insurer brought a declaratory judgment action seeking a determination that it was not liable for the child's injuries since they had not arisen "out of the operation, maintenance, or use of a motor vehicle." The insured counterclaimed for the $2,500 in medical benefits, as well as a claim for bad faith, attorney's fees and punitive damages. The trial court granted summary judgment on the $2,500 medical benefits counterclaim, but let the other claims go to the jury. The jury awarded a twenty-five percent bad faith penalty, attorney's fees and punitive damages in the amount of $50,000 to the insured. The insurer appealed.

The Court of Appeals of Georgia considered the question of whether the boy's injuries arose "out of the operation, maintenance or use of a motor vehicle." The insurer argued that this case presented a close question and there was no precedent squarely holding that an accident of this nature was covered. The court dismissed this argument citing prior holdings of the court which held that almost any causal connection or relationship would be sufficient. Accordingly, the court rejected the insurer's contention that it was acting in good faith when it decided to litigate this claim. Moreover, the question of whether an insurer is acting in good faith is one of fact for the jury. The jury's determination on this issue should be upheld on appeal if there is any evidence to support it. The fact which most strongly supported the jury's finding was the likelihood that the cost of litigating the declaratory judgment action would far exceed the $2,500 amount claimed. *First Financial Ins. Co. v. Rainey et al.*, 394 S.E.2d 774 (Ga.App.1990).

A Florida insured was horribly injured in an automobile accident where he was blameless. The insured tried unsuccessfully to receive personal injury protection benefits and uninsured motorist coverage. He then instituted this action which sought coverage under the policy and punitive damages due to bad faith refusal to provide coverage. The trial court entered judgment for the insured, which included punitive damages against the insurer, and the insurer appealed to the District Court of Appeal of Florida. Specifically, the insurer appealed the punitive damage award. On appeal, the insurer argued that its conduct never rose to the level of a bad faith action. Further, it argued that at most this conduct was merely an explained delay in payment by a carrier acting in good faith. However, the court noted that there was plenty of evidence to indicate bad faith on the part of the insurer and that there was no reversible error. Since the record supported a finding that the insurer acted in reckless disregard for the rights of the insured, the appellate court upheld the decision of the trial court. *Home Ins. Co. v. Owens*, 573 So.2d 343 (Fla.App.4th Dist. 1990).

A Kentucky couple sought a full coverage insurance policy when they opened a new business. The couple contacted an agent from the insurer and in due course a policy was issued. However, neither the agent nor the couple reviewed it. After obtaining the policy the couple's store was burglarized and $13,500 worth of merchandise was stolen. The couple made a claim against the insurer which it denied because the policy was not an all risk policy which would have provided theft coverage. After repeated requests for payment, the couple sued the insurance company for the value of the stolen merchandise and for lost profits which were caused by the failure to timely pay the claim. The couple also sought punitive damages for bad faith. A Kentucky trial court ruled in favor of the couple awarding them damages for lost profits and punitive damages for bad faith refusal to pay the claim. The insurer appealed successfully to the Kentucky Court of Appeals, and the couple then appealed to the Supreme Court of Kentucky. The supreme court overruled a law which would have disallowed recovery for bad faith claims. The court stated that the law would permit an insurance carrier to deny payment without any justification and to attempt unfair compromise by exploiting the policyholder's economic circumstance. The supreme court decided that this law was unjust and that the insureds should be allowed recovery under the policy. The court reversed the court of appeals' decision. *Curry v. Fireman's Fund Ins. Co.*, 784 S.W.2d 176 (Ky.1989).

An insured transport company's employee loaded a truck with produce intended for New York. The employee received a $1,000 advance for the trip. After departure, the tractor of the truck was found on fire in Texas (off the normal route to New York).

The trailer, cargo and driver were all missing. The company notified its insurer of the loss, and the insurer's agent began to process the claim. An investigation revealed that either the driver had been killed or abducted and the trailer full of goods sold, or the driver had burned the tractor and stolen the trailer and produce. There was no way to ascertain which had occurred. Since the policy issued to the insured excluded coverage for property stolen by an employee of the insured, the insurer decided to deny liability on the claim. However, this information was not communicated to the insured until fifteen months after the claim had been filed. Eventually, the insured brought suit against its insurer and the insurer's agent for bad faith. The jury returned a verdict for the insured, awarding both compensatory and punitive damages, and the insurer and its agent appealed to the California Court of Appeal, Second District.

On appeal, the court noted that the evidence supporting the jury's verdict was sufficient to uphold the awards against the insurer and its agent. The court stated that there was substantial evidence that the insurer and its agent unreasonably and unjustifiably delayed in communicating their denial of liability to the insured. This delay constituted bad faith. Further, even though no evidence of the insurer's wealth had been presented, the court upheld the punitive damages award, noting that evidence of the insurer's financial condition was not essential to an award of punitive damages. The court affirmed the jury's verdict in favor of the insured. *Liberty Transport, Inc. v. Harry W. Gorst Co.*, 280 Cal.Rptr. 159 (Cal.App. 2d Dist.1991).

An Illinois carpenter was rendered a paraplegic when he fell from a scaffold. At the time of the accident his employer was insured for $100,000 for workers' compensation and $300,000 for manufacturer and contractor coverage. The employer's insurer paid all the carpenter's medical bills up to the maximum amount available under the Illinois Workers' Compensation Act. A claims adjuster befriended the carpenter until the state Structural Work Act statute of limitations had expired. The Act allows an injured worker to recover for disability, pain and suffering, lost wages and earnings and reasonable medical expenses. The claims adjuster convinced the carpenter that the insurer would protect his legal rights. Upon learning that the adjuster was misleading him, he sued the insurer for fraud in an Illinois federal district court. It awarded him $3 million in compensatory damages and $2 million in punitive damages. The insurer appealed to the U.S. Court of Appeals, Seventh Circuit. In upholding the $5 million award, the appeals court held that the carpenter's recovery was not limited to workers' compensation. His injury from the alleged fraud arose from his relationship with the insurer, not out of the course of his employment. The insurer made false statements upon which the carpenter detrimentally relied. Because of the insurer's wilful and wanton conduct, the appeals court determined that the imposition of punitive damages was proper. It also determined that the punitive damage award was not excessive. The carpenter was entitled to the $5 million award. *West v. Western Cas. & Sur. Co.*, 846 F.2d 387 (7th Cir.1988).

A California savings and loan institution (S&L) was covered by a fidelity bond for losses up to a maximum of $3 million caused by the dishonest acts of any of its employees. The bond also promised to pay court costs and attorney's fees incurred by the S&L in defending lawsuits brought by third parties arising out of employees' dishonest acts. One of the S&L's branch managers was subsequently involved in a scheme whereby checks with insufficient funds were used to buy certificates of deposit, which were then pledged as security for loans from third-party lenders. A lender which issued a $100,000 loan because of the branch manager's dishonesty sued the S&L when the loan proved uncollectible. The S&L notified its insurer of the lender's lawsuit, but the insurer denied coverage. The insurer did not investigate the claim properly and concentrated its efforts on developing ways to avoid liability. Even after the branch manager was implicated by a co-conspirator at trial, the insurer steadfastly denied coverage under the bond. The S&L then sued the insurer in Superior Court, Los Angeles County, for indemnity and breach of the insurer's implied covenant of good faith and fair dealing. The court awarded the S&L $152,983 in compensatory damages and $5 million in punitive damages. Alleging that it should also have been awarded attorney's fees, the S&L appealed. The insurer cross-appealed, maintaining that the award of punitive damages for bad faith was excessive.

The California Court of Appeal, Second District, considered the insurer's argument that because the ratio between the punitive and compensatory damages was 32.7 to 1, the punitive damages were disproportionate to the compensatory damages and therefore excessive. The court noted that "[t]he purpose of punitive damages is to punish wrongdoers and thereby deter the commission of wrongful acts." Limiting punitive damages to a certain ratio above compensatory damages would thwart the purpose of punitive damages in cases where "a defendant's conduct is especially wanton or malicious but the plaintiff's actual damages are low." The court cited previous California cases where punitive damages were awarded with ratios to compensatory damages of up to 2000 to 1. The court ruled that the award of punitive damages was not excessive. With respect to the S&L's request for attorney's fees, the court ruled that such an award was required to give the S&L the benefits of the fidelity bond. It also declared that the S&L should recover its costs on appeal. The Superior Court's judgment was affirmed as to the award of punitive damages but reversed as to the denial of attorney's fees, and the case was remanded to the Superior Court for a determination of attorney's fees to be awarded to the S&L. *Downey Savings & Loan Ass'n. v. Ohio Casualty Ins. Co.*, 234 Cal.Rptr. 835 (App.2d Dist.1987).

A woman and her children were involved in an automobile collision while riding as passengers in one of the vehicles. The woman and her daughter died; her son became a quadriplegic. The woman's husband filed an uninsured motorist claim with his insurer, seeking to recover benefits under his automobile policy. Over a year later, when the insured had not received payment or rejection of his claim, he filed suit against his insurer for breach of contract and bad faith. The insurer sought summary judgment on the grounds that the insured had not complied with § 11580.2 of the California Insurance Code (as outlined by the policy). The code required that, within one year of the accident, the insured had to: conclude an agreement with the insurer regarding the amount due under the policy, formally institute arbitration proceedings, or commence an action against the uninsured motorist. The trial court granted summary judgment to the insurer, and the insured appealed. The California Court of Appeal, Second District, determined that the undisputed facts showed that the insured did not comply with § 11580.2's requirements. However, the court went on to hold that if the insured had failed to settle with the insurer because of bad faith on the insurer's part, the insured would not be barred from maintaining a suit against the insurer. Since bad faith would include unreasonable delay in settlement of the claim, there existed a triable issue of fact which required a reversal of the summary judgment. There was a question as to whether the insurer had deliberately waited until after the one-year period before requesting information necessary to effectuate the settlement. This could not be resolved without a trial. *Vacnin v. 20th Century Ins. Co.*, 284 Cal.Rptr. 400 (Cal.App.2d Dist.1991).

A businessman in Vermont who owned a number of taxicabs was sued by a pedestrian who was struck and injured by one of the cabs. The businessman notified his insurer, Ambassador Insurance Co., of the accident and the lawsuit. Ambassador, in turn, retained an attorney to represent both the businessman and the driver. Before trial, the attorney notified the businessman that the pedestrian's claim could exceed the $10,000 policy limit for bodily injury. Settlement negotiations became stalled when the pedestrian's demand for $9,000 was turned down by Ambassador. At trial, the court affirmed a jury verdict of $45,000 for the pedestrian and rendered judgment against the businessman. After paying the balance of the judgment in excess of his insurance coverage, the businessman sued Ambassador for the amount of his excess payment. He alleged that the insurer acted in bad faith in refusing to settle for less than the policy limit. The Vermont Supreme Court reasoned that an insurer has a fiduciary duty to act in good faith when handling a claim against the insured and must therefore take the insured's interest into account. If the plaintiff demands a settlement, the insurer must weigh all of the risks including the potential excess liability exposure to the insured. In addition, stated the court, the insurer must fully inform the insured of the results of its assessments of those risks and give accurate information as to possibilities of settlement. The court noted that the businessman was not notified of any of the developments in the lawsuit until he was informed of the $45,000 judgment against him. This failure to inform the businessman constituted an abandonment of the insurer's duty to represent the insured's interest "with all good fidelity," stated the court. The court therefore held that Ambassador was liable for the entire $45,000 judgment against the businessman. *Myers v. Ambassador Ins. Co.*, 508 A.2d 689 (Vt.1986).

The owner of a restaurant which was insured under a multi-peril policy requested full payment of the $100,000 policy limit on the loss of the building after it was destroyed by fire. The insurer denied that the building was damaged in excess of $100,000, offering instead $88,451. After the owner had his claim reviewed by an independent appraiser, the insurer paid the $100,000 building loss claim within the time specified under the policy. However, the owner sued his insurer alleging that the insurer's delay in paying the claim was unreasonable and evidenced bad faith. He requested compensation for loss of business and loss of the use of the money. He also sought punitive damages. The North Carolina Court of Appeals ruled that the insurer had a duty to deal in good faith and was not absolved from punitive damages because it later performed as it should. This was due to the fact that bad faith delay and aggravating conduct were present. Here, the insurer delayed payment because the restaurant owner had hired an independent appraiser. Also, the insurer had instructed a building contractor to produce a low estimate regarding the building repairs. The court of appeals held that this evidence established bad faith dealing and aggravating circumstances and remanded the case for further proceedings. *Robinson v. North Carolina Farm Bureau Ins. Co.*, 356 S.E.2d 392 (N.C.App.1987).

A Louisiana truck driver was injured in a collision which occurred when a car drove through a stop sign and broadsided his truck, causing it to flip over into the ditch and burst into flames. He barely managed to escaped from the burning cab, and afterward he complained of soreness in his ribs and neck. Nine months later he underwent surgery where a ruptured disk was removed from his back. He settled for the $10,000 policy limits of the other driver's insurance policy and then sought additional compensation under his employer's policy which provided underinsured motorist coverage. His employer's insurer, however, refused to advance any payment, claiming that satisfactory proofs of loss had not been submitted and that the man had been contributorily negligent. Suit was then brought in a state trial court, with the man claiming that the insurer had refused in bad faith to settle his claim. The trial court found the man to be free of contributory negligence and awarded him $250,000 in general damages, assessed $30,000 in punitive damages and awarded attorney's fees of $40,000.

The Supreme Court of Louisiana affirmed this award. There were absolutely no grounds for inferring from the police report that the man had been contributorily negligent. The insurer had been well aware of the claim and had known that the other driver had only $10,000 in liability insurance. The insurer had also been in contact with the man's doctors and should have known that his damages would greatly exceed $10,000; yet it still had refused to tender any payment to the claimant. Stated the court: "If the insured has shown that he was not at fault, the other driver was uninsured/underinsured and that he was in fact damaged, the insurer cannot stonewall the insured because the insured is unable to prove the *exact* extent of his general damages." Finding that the insurer should have tendered a "reasonable amount" to the claimant before a trial became necessary, the supreme court upheld the entire damage award. *McDill v. Utica Mut. Ins. Co.*, 475 So.2d 1085 (La.1985).

The Supreme Court of Ohio held that punitive damages and attorney's fees may be awarded for failure to settle an uninsured motorist claim in good faith. The claimant in this case was a young woman who was struck by an uninsured motorist. She was deemed to be a "covered insured" under the uninsured motorist provisions of foreign insurance policies her father carried with J. C. Penney Casualty Insurance Co. After sixteen months no settlement was in sight. The claimant decided to formally demand arbitration of the claim. Two years later the arbitration panel reached the following decision in favor of the claimant: $17,500 in compensatory damages, $35,000 in punitive damages and $17,500 in attorney's fees. After a series of appeals by the insurer, the Ohio Supreme Court substantially affirmed the arbitration panel's decision. Because uninsured motorist coverage must provide for "all damages for which a person is legally entitled to recover" from an uninsured motorist, which could include punitive damages and attorney's fees, it follows that the insurer must also be liable, where appropriate, for such items. The court further held that because punitive damages were appropriate in this case, attorney's fees were available as well. However, the case was remanded to the trial court for a more precise determination of attorney's fees. *Hutchinson v. J. C. Penney Ins. Co.*, 478 N.E.2d 1000 (Ohio 1985).

The Indiana Court of Appeals upheld a $40,000 punitive damages award against an insurer whose agent told an insured that her rates would go "skyhigh" if she made a claim for an automobile accident. The insured had been struck from behind by a hit-and-run driver as she waited at a stop sign. Fearful of high insurance rates, she made no claim on her policy and went without a car for several months. The court of appeals condemned the use of such "scare tactics" and approved the lower court's

$40,000 award. *Liberty Mut. Ins. Co. v. Parkinson*, 487 N.E.2d 162 (Ind.App.4th Dist.1985).

The owners of a standard bred stallion purchased a $50,000 livestock insurance policy on the horse. With his record as a trotter, the horse was important to the owners' horse breeding business. When the horse died, the insurer found a discrepancy between the application and the breeding reports with respect to the number of mares serviced by the stallion. The owners submitted a proof of loss based on the horse's value in the European market, but the insurer rejected it, offering only $25,000. The owners were awarded $40,000 in an arbitration proceeding, and they then sued the insurer for breach of the duty of good faith and fair dealing. A jury awarded them $45,000, and the insurer appealed. Before the Appellate Court of Illinois, the insurer contended that it had reasonably investigated and assessed the value of the horse, and that its refusal to pay the policy limits was not "vexatious, unreasonable, outrageous conduct." The court, however, determined that the evidence supporting the owners' claim of the horse's value was strong. The insurer's failure to take into account the overseas trotting market and the fact that its own agents had appraised the horse's value at $50,000 just a few months earlier were sufficient to support the jury's verdict. The court thus affirmed the award. *Emerson v. American Bankers Ins. Co.*, 585 N.E.2d 1315 (Ill.App.5th Dist.1992).

B. Punitive Damages Denied

In the following cases, the conduct of the insurance companies was found not to be sufficiently egregious to warrant awards of punitive damages.

An Iowa insured was seriously injured in a motorcycle accident. His wife reported the accident to their insurer which determined that no coverage existed. Later evidence showed that the insured had no coverage on the motorcycle but he did have insurance policies with the insurer which provided underinsured motorist benefits. The insured then sued the other driver. The suit was settled for $20,000 which was the limit of the liability insurance of the other driver. Following the settlement, the insureds sent their insurer a letter demanding coverage under the underinsured motorist provisions of their auto insurance policies. After receiving no response from their insurer they instituted this action in an Iowa trial court.

The insureds alleged bad faith and also sought recovery under their policy. The jury returned a verdict in favor of the insureds on the contract claim. It found that the insureds had sustained $1 million in actual damages and that the other driver was eighty percent at fault for those damages. The jury also found that the insurer had acted in bad faith in failing to fulfill its contractual obligations and awarded punitive damages. The trial court granted a motion for judgment notwithstanding the verdict on the bad faith claim. Both sides appealed to the Supreme Court of Iowa.

The court noted that the central issue in the case was whether the trial court erred in granting the insurer's motion for judgment notwithstanding the verdict on the bad faith claim. To prove a claim of bad faith denial of benefits, the insureds must prove the following: 1) that they made a claim for underinsured motorist coverage, 2) that the insurer denied their claim, 3) that there was no reasonable basis for denying the claim, 4) that the insurer knew that there was no reasonable basis for denying the claim or acted in reckless disregard of whether there was any reasonable basis for denial, and 5) that the denial was the reason that they did not receive their underinsured motorist benefits.

The court determined that there was a reasonable basis for denying the claim for underinsured motorist benefits. The claim was originally denied shortly after it was made. At that time, there were several factors providing a reasonable basis for denying the claim. First, it was unclear if the insurer was aware that the other driver was insured, or if he was insured, the amount of liability coverage he carried. Also, the insured did not indicate the amount of money necessary to fully compensate him for the injuries suffered in the accident. Therefore, since the insurer may not have been aware of the severity of the accident or the other driver's coverage, there was a reasonable basis for denying the claim. *Dirks v. Farm Bureau Mutual Ins. Co.*, 465 N.W.2d 857 (Iowa 1991).

A Virginia resort owner sought coverage for property damage caused by the collapse of a wall. Pending the outcome of a related suit the owner and insurer settled the property damage claim. The owner sought to have the settlement enforced but the insurer rebuffed all correspondence until the statute of limitations expired. It then notified the owner that it was denying the claim. The owner sued the insurer in a Virginia federal district court which found that the insurer had acted in bad faith and awarded the owner $54,000 in compensatory damages. It also awarded the owner $1 million in punitive damages. The insurer appealed to the U.S. Court of Appeals, Fourth Circuit. On appeal, the insurer argued that the punitive damage award was unwarranted. It asserted that the owner was required to show that the insurer had no intent to fulfill the agreement at the time of the settlement. The court held that although sufficient evidence had been introduced to support the compensatory award, the owner failed to present sufficient evidence to warrant the punitive damage award. No proof was presented which showed that the insurer did not intend to abide by the settlement when it was made. Since the owner failed to show fraudulent intent, the punitive damage award was unwarranted. The owner was only entitled to the compensatory damage award. *Lissmann v. Hartford Fire Ins. Co.*, 848 F.2d 50 (4th Cir.1988).

An Ohio woman was covered by a state employee retirement policy. The woman suffered a stroke which required hospitalization. After she was discharged she required home nursing care. The woman notified the insurer and it basically responded that there was nothing to worry about. The nursing service submitted a $25,000 bill to the insurer which rejected the claim. The nursing service sued the woman in an Ohio trial court. The woman then sued the insurer in an Ohio trial court for bad faith refusal to settle the claim. The trial court jury awarded the woman $85,000 for the insurer's breach of contract and failure to act in good faith. It also awarded the woman $125,000 in punitive damages. The trial court judge vacated the jury's decision and ordered a new trial. The woman appealed to the Ohio Court of Appeals which reinstated the total award. The insurer appealed to the Ohio Supreme Court. The supreme court noted that required care was covered under the policy. It held that the insurer breached the policy when it denied the claim. It also upheld the bad faith determination. The insurer had encouraged the woman's assumption that coverage would be provided but later denied coverage. Because the trial court did not give the jury clear instructions on the fact that a finding of bad faith did not necessarily warrant a punitive damage award, it overturned the punitive damage award. It found that the insurer had not acted in the requisite reckless manner

Sec. II   PUNITIVE DAMAGE AWARDS AGAINST INSURERS   31

necessary to justify a punitive damage award. The woman was only entitled to $85,000 for the breach of the policy and bad faith refusal to settle. *Staff Builders v. Armstrong*, 525 N.E.2d 783 (Ohio 1988).

A wine imports company had an insurance policy which covered fidelity losses. When the company had a claim and sought benefits under the policy, its insurer denied them. The company sued the insurer in a federal district court for the benefits and for an award of punitive and consequential damages. The company maintained that the insurer had acted in bad faith by refusing to pay the claim. The insurer sought dismissal of the punitive and consequential damages claim in the same court. The district court granted the insurer's dismissal motion. It concluded that an application of New Jersey law was appropriate. It noted that New Jersey appellate courts have refused to award punitive and consequential damages in several bad faith cases. Therefore, the company could not seek them in this case. *Wine Imports v. Northbrook Property and Cas. Ins. Co.*, 708 F.Supp. 105 (D.N.J.1989).

An Alabama insured was injured in an automobile accident when an uninsured motorist, who was speeding, crossed over the center line and collided head-on with his vehicle. His wife reported the accident to their insurer the next day. The insured had surgery on his foot and ankle, and his doctor indicated that he was doing fairly well. The insurer paid his medical bills under the uninsured motorist provision of his policy during this time. Some months later, the insured's doctor noted that continuing complications might require an amputation below the knee. Several months later, and fifteen months after the accident, the insurer offered to settle for the limits of the policy. When the insurer refused to pay interest on that amount, the insured sued. The trial court granted summary judgment to the insurer and the insured appealed. On appeal to the Supreme Court of Alabama, the court noted that, on the date of the claim, the insurer could not determine how much money the insured was entitled to receive. This was a case where the insured's injuries at first appeared to be nominal, but gradually worsened. The insurer here could not be charged with bad faith "for failing to anticipate what even the physicians did not predict." Accordingly, the court affirmed the trial court's grant of summary judgment for the insurer, holding that it only had to pay the policy limits. *LeFevre v. Westberry*, 590 So.2d 154 (Ala.1991).

The U.S. Court of Appeals, Ninth Circuit, has held that two U.S. Supreme Court decisions addressing ERISA preemption required that a lower federal court's damage award against an insurer be reversed. The case arose when a California couple's son was born two months prematurely while they were on vacation in Holland. The couple was insured by the husband's employer under a group medical insurance policy. The insurer refused to forward any medical expenses to the couple while they were in Holland and later delayed payment of the son's other medical expenses. Claiming bad faith, the couple sued the insurer and a U.S. district court awarded them $252,234 in compensatory damages and $500,000 in punitive damages due to the insurer's inexplicable delays and its failure to investigate their claims.

The court of appeals observed that the Supreme Court's decision in *Pilot Life Ins. Co. v. Dedeaux*, and *Metropolitan Life Ins. Co. v. Taylor*, made clear that where an insurance lawsuit relates to an employee benefit plan, the lawsuit is preempted by the federal Employment Retirement Income Security Act. Similarly, lawsuits alleging improper claims processing which are based upon state common law (rather than state statutory law) are also preempted by ERISA. Because in the present case the claims against the insurer arose under an employer's group medical insurance policy, the couple's state common law "bad faith" claims were preempted. The appeals court therefore reversed the damage awards levied against the insurer. *Kanne v. Connecticut General Life Ins.Co.*, 819 F.2d 204 (9th Cir.1987).

In September 1979, a man underwent an operation after being diagnosed as having a benign tumor. The man was required to continue to see his doctor and to receive medication to guard against reoccurrence. On April 1, 1980, his wife obtained medical insurance that covered the man as well, from Nationwide Life Insurance Company through a group policy issued to her employer. The policy provided that "eligible expenses do not include any charges incurred ... for an illness for which the insured person received medical care or treatment within the ninety days preceding the effective date of his insurance. ... The term 'treatment' includes the taking of any drug prescribed by a physician."

In July 1980, the man underwent another operation by a different doctor and was found to have extensive cancer of the parathyroid glands. After examining records from the original surgery, the doctor concluded that the 1979 tumor had been malignant. When the hospital bills were submitted to Nationwide, it examined the man's medical records and denied payment. Nationwide claimed that the expenses were for a preexisting condition that had been treated in the ninety days prior to the issuance of the policy. The woman found out about the denial only when she admitted her husband to the hospital in October 1980. The man died in February 1982. His wife sued Nationwide for bad faith and breach of contract in state court. She was awarded $14,951 for breach of contract, $150,000 for bad faith, and $2,000,000 in punitive damages. Nationwide appealed to the state court of appeals which reversed the punitive damages award. The woman appealed to the Arizona Supreme Court.

At issue was whether Nationwide had exhibited an "evil mind" mental attitude during the denial process so as to justify a punitive damage verdict. The court concluded that the "key is the wrongdoer's intent to injure the plaintiff or his deliberate interference with the rights of others, consciously disregarding the unjustifiably substantial risk of significant harm to them." Observing that Nationwide did construe its policy strictly in its own favor, the court stated that "clear and convincing evidence" did not demonstrate that Nationwide intended to harm the deceased or his wife. The insurer had sent a denial of claim letter to only the woman's employer, had been quick to examine his records without consulting his doctor and had not given the woman a copy of the policy but the court ruled these did not constitute actions upon which an award of punitive damages could be based. Nationwide's claims policy, although "tough," was not "aggravated, outrageous, oppressive or fraudulent" and therefore the punitive damage claim was denied. *Linthicum v. Nationwide Life Ins. Co.*, 723 P.2d 675 (Ariz.1986).

A Florida man had overlapping automobile coverage when his wife was killed in an accident. He sued the party at fault. He obtained a settlement with that party's insurer, and with one of his insurers, but the other insurer refused to settle. The wrongful death action then proceeded to trial. The verdict for the insured was $500,000 greater than what he had already received in the settlements. His second insurer then offered its policy limits of $300,000. The insured sued it for bad faith, and a jury awarded $100,000 more than the policy limits as compensatory damages.

Sec. II   PUNITIVE DAMAGE AWARDS AGAINST INSURERS   33

He appealed, asserting that he should have been awarded $200,000 above policy limits for the insurer's bad faith — the difference between all available insurance coverage and the wrongful death award amount. He was unsuccessful in his appeal. He then sought review from the Florida Supreme Court. On appeal, the court noted that this was not a third-party bad faith claim wherein the full $200,000 would be available because the insured was suing his own insurer. In a first-party claim, where punitive damages are not at issue, the only damages recoverable are those proximately caused by the insurer's bad faith. To allow greater recovery would violate public policy by, in effect, making the insurer liable for injuries that it did not cause. The court thus affirmed the award of $100,000 above the policy limits to the insured, but denied the allowance of punitive damages. *McLeod v. Continental Ins. Co.*, 591 So.2d 621 (Fla.1992).

In an Arizona case, a woman was issued a homeowner's policy by the Safeco Insurance Company of America. Dissatisfied with the amount of her renewal premium, she instructed her agent to place her insurance with the Home Insurance Company, and this was done. Her Safeco policy expired on December 8, 1980, and two days later, on December 10, her house was burglarized. She lost twelve pieces of jewelry. A friend who was a skilled insurance attorney sent proofs of loss to Home, but Home disputed whether all the items of jewelry were covered under the new policy. A few days after the burglary, Safeco informed the woman that company policy would allow her to reinstate her coverage retroactively to the date of expiration, if she acted within thirty-five days. She sent the renewal premium to Safeco within this period; Safeco was still unaware of the burglary. After initially denying coverage Safeco agreed to pay the woman's claim (about $7,000) but its employees were unable to perform the mathematical calculations necessary to apportion the claim between Safeco and Home. There was general confusion among the Safeco staff as to which draft check form to use and whether the entire claim would be released by tendering partial payment. After eleven months had passed since the burglary Safeco finally straightened out the woman's claim, but her attorney had already filed suit against Safeco for untimely failure to pay her claim. The trial court awarded the woman $70,950 in punitive damages, but Safeco appealed and won a reversal.

The Arizona Court of Appeals held that a punitive damages award must be supported by evidence of maliciousness or dishonesty. Here, the evidence merely showed that Safeco's employees had been careless, inexperienced and untrained. Furthermore, the woman's attorney had stood by and permitted Safeco to "fumble its way into difficulty" without attempting to assist in straightening things out. Because Safeco had lacked the "evil intent" necessary to support a punitive damages award, the lower court's ruling was reversed. *Borland v. Safeco Ins. Co. of America*, 709 P.2d 552 (Ariz.App.1985).

An employer told her insurance agent to add a 1971 trailer to her policy. The agent, however, mistakenly described the 1971 trailer as a tractor. Subsequently, when the employer met with the agent to pay the premiums, she noticed the mistaken description and requested by letter that it be changed. Based on this letter, the agent claimed to have sent the insurer a request to delete the tractor and add the trailer to the policy. The insurer contended that it never received that request. Subsequently, one of the employer's workers had an accident with the trailer, and the insurer denied coverage. The employer sued the insurer and the agent. The district court entered judgment against the insurer and agent in excess of the policy limits. The insurer appealed to the Arizona Court of Appeals, contending that it was only liable for $300,000, the amount of the policy coverage limits, not the $900,000 which the district court had awarded the insured. The appellate court agreed, noting that even though the insurer denied coverage in bad faith by refusing to provide coverage, it did not refuse a reasonable settlement offer because no offer of settlement was ever made for it to refuse. Thus, its actions could not be the cause of a judgment in excess of the policy limits. Accordingly, the court reversed the trial court's verdict against the insurer for $900,000, and required the insurer to pay only $300,000. *Rogan v. Auto-owners Ins. Co.*, 832 P.2d 212 (Ariz.App.Div.1 1991).

A California case involved a woman who was covered for major medical expenses under a group policy issued by her husband's employer. The policy defined "qualified dependent" as including an employee's wife, but excluding a "legally separated spouse." After the woman and her husband divorced she submitted claims to his employer for medical benefits under the group policy. The employer denied the claims on the ground that she was no longer covered. The insurer then confirmed the denial of coverage. Three years later she filed a lawsuit against the insurer for breach of the implied covenant of good faith and fair dealing. She alleged that her doctors had confirmed coverage with the insurer prior to her treatment. Under California law, complaints for breaches of the implied covenant of good faith and fair dealing can be based on either tort or contract theory. Punitive damages are available only under tort theory. The insurer asked the Superior Court, Los Angeles County, to declare that the woman could no longer recover punitive damages because the two-year tort statute of limitations had run. The Superior Court refused and the insurer appealed to the California Court of Appeal, Second District. The Court of Appeal noted that because the tort statute of limitations had run, the woman's lawsuit could only be based in contract. It then rejected the Superior Court's decision that lawsuits for the breach of the implied covenant of good faith and fair dealing "are a form of special contract action in which punitive damages are allowed, and are governed by the four-year statute of limitations." The court declared that it could "find no justification for this unwarranted extension of recovery of punitive damages to bad faith actions based solely on breach of contract." It concluded that the woman could not recover punitive damages. The Court of Appeal ordered the Superior Court to grant a declaration to that effect. *Prudential Ins. Co. of America v. Superior Court*, 237 Cal.Rptr. 425 (App.2d Dist.1987).

An Arkansas man purchased a life insurance policy worth $5 million. He was later killed in a car accident. Within two weeks, his beneficiary submitted a proof of loss to the insurer. Over the next two months, the insurer's representative contacted the beneficiary three times to inform her that the insurer was awaiting additional information. Payment was finally approved by the insurer and a check mailed to the beneficiary, which was received sixty-three days after the proof of loss was submitted to the insurer. However, the interest had been miscalculated and the check was for $12,000 less than expected. Arkansas law provided that payments shall not be made more than two months after receipt of proof by the insurer. Because the check was paid after it was due and was for an incorrect amount, the beneficiary returned it to the insurer, and sued it in state court for the proceeds plus punitive damages. The insurer removed the case to a federal district court and tendered a check for the correct amount with the court.

The beneficiary argued that Arkansas law provided a strict two month limit for payment of proceeds on a life insurance policy. She also argued that in all cases where the insurer failed to pay within the specified time, it would be liable for punitive damages and attorney's fees. However, the court noted that there was an exception to Arkansas law which allowed insurers to take a reasonable time to investigate claims. The court stated that the penalty nature of the law was "directed against unwarranted delaying tactics of insurers." The court further held that failure to comply with the two month limit did not automatically result in punitive damages against the insurer. In this case, the insurer had made a reasonable investigation, and made payment only a few days late. The court denied the imposition of punitive damages. *McKee v. Federal Kemper Life Assurance Co.*, 726 F.Supp. 245 (E.D.Ark.1989).

The U.S. Court of Appeals, Sixth Circuit, reversed a federal district court's finding of bad faith on the part of an insurer for failing to offer a policy limit settlement in a tort lawsuit. The tort lawsuit was the result of an automobile accident in which the insured was liable for the injuries of another driver. Before trial, the insured's attorney attempted to settle by offering less than the policy limit of $20,000 to the counsel of the injured driver. He responded that they would only accept the policy limit. At trial the insurer's attorney offered to settle at the policy limit but opposing counsel then demanded $25,000. The insurer's attorney refused the higher settlement amount but did not communicate the higher demand to the insured. After trial, the jury awarded the injured driver $175,000 in damages. The insured then brought this action against the insurer alleging that it had acted in bad faith in its handling of the settlement.

The appellate court's reversal was based on Michigan case law, which stated that simple negligence or bad judgment was insufficient for a showing of bad faith. Rather, a plaintiff must show a conscious doing of wrong because of dishonest purpose or moral obliquity. The court stated that the insurer's failure to settle at the policy limits before the trial was based on the insurer's opinion that the claim was not worth $20,000. While the insurer's failure to recognize the extent of the claim may have been bad judgment, the court held that it was not a showing of bad faith. Likewise, the insurer's failure to communicate the $25,000 settlement demand to the insured was at most a showing of simple negligence or bad judgment. The district court's judgment was reversed. *Awrey v. Progressive Cas. Ins. Co.*, 728 F.2d 352 (6th Cir.1984).

The Texas Supreme Court ruled that punitive damages cannot be assessed against a fire insurer who breached its contractual obligations by refusing to pay a claim. In this case, the owner of a building destroyed by fire was unable to show that he had suffered actual damages due to wrongful conduct by the insurance company. In other words, punitive damages would not be allowed unless the insurer had caused actual damages to the owner through a negligent or intentional wrongful act. An award of damages by a court for such a wrongful act is a necessary prerequisite to receiving punitive damages, according to Texas case law. The policyholder was, however, allowed to recover damages due to the insurer's breach of contract. This amount was the actual damage proceeds of the policy payable on the loss of the building. *Belefonte Underwriters Ins. Co. v. Brown*, 704 S.W.2d 742 (Tex.1986).

In an Alabama case, the state's supreme court approved a $3.5 million punitive damage award, but the U.S. Supreme Court threw out the award. The insurer in this case, Aetna, had appealed to the U.S. Supreme Court on the ground that one of the justices of the Alabama Supreme Court was unfairly prejudiced against insurance companies. Aetna argued that because Alabama's Justice Embry had filed a lawsuit against Blue Cross at the same time the case was pending before the Alabama Supreme Court, he could not have made an impartial decision in the case. Justice Embry's insurance lawsuit was nearly identical to the one before the state supreme court and involved identical legal issues. The lawsuit was later settled by the justice for $30,000.

The U.S. Supreme Court concluded that Aetna had been denied due process of law due to Justice Embry's then-pending lawsuit, which relied on the same legal theories as the case in question. The Alabama Supreme Court's decision had established a new precedent in that state, authorizing punitive damages in cases where partial payment of a claim had already been made. Also, the decision upheld a $3.5 million punitive damage award, which was 35 times larger than any punitive damage award against an insurer previously approved by the Alabama Supreme Court. Justice Embry, who had not disqualified himself from participating in the case and who had an identical lawsuit of his own pending in the state courts, had committed a breach of judicial ethics by participating in the decision.

The U.S. Supreme Court then turned to the question of what remedy should be granted to Aetna. Because the Alabama Supreme Court had decided the case by a 5 - 4 vote, with Justice Embry himself authoring the majority opinion, the decision was vacated and remanded. Although Aetna succeeded in obtaining Justice Embry's disqualification, the U.S. Supreme Court rejected the argument that merely because a justice is generally biased against the insurance industry he must disqualify himself from participating in any insurance case. Only where a justice has a direct financial interest in the outcome of a case must he be disqualified from participating in its decision. The U.S. Supreme Court remanded the case to the Alabama Supreme Court for further proceedings. *Aetna Life Ins. Co. v. Lavoie*, 475 U.S. 813, 106 S.Ct. 1580, 89 L.Ed.2d 823 (1986).

III. EXCESS INSURERS

Excess insurers are liable for amounts above the limits of an insured's primary policy. Actions often arise between excess and primary insurers with respect to who must provide coverage or defense. Further, insureds may try to obtain coverage from excess insurers by stacking policies.

A mechanic was test-driving a truck after performing some work on it. Another vehicle allegedly pulled out in front of the truck, and the driver, who was driving in excess of the speed limit, swerved and collided with a palm tree. A passenger in the truck was killed instantly. The vehicle's owner insured its truck with one insurer, and the driver, who was not the owner, held an insurance policy on his Winnebago recreational vehicle issued by another insurance company. The passenger's survivors brought a wrongful death action against the vehicle's owner and the driver. The owner's insurer rejected numerous offers to settle within its $500,000 policy limits. A jury awarded the survivors $700,000. The owner's (primary) insurer paid the judgment in full. A year and a half later, the primary insurer sought reimbursement

Sec. III   EXCESS INSURERS   37

for the excess from the driver's insurer. When the second insurer denied the excess claim, the primary insurer sued in federal court for declaratory relief, subrogation, and contribution. The excess insurer counterclaimed for equitable subrogation and a judicial declaration that it was not liable, based on the other insurer's bad faith failure to settle. The district court entered summary judgment for the primary insurer. The excess insurer appealed to the U.S. Court of Appeals, Ninth Circuit.

On appeal, the court affirmed the fact that the Winnebago policy provided excess coverage to the owner's policy. More importantly, the court stated that although a primary insurer owes no direct duty of settlement within policy limits to an excess insurer, California recognizes the right of an excess insurer who has fully paid the insured's claim to bring an action against the primary insurer for wrongful refusal to settle based on the theory of equitable subrogation. The court stated that it only made sense that an insurer could also raise this as a defense in an action by a primary insurer to collect. The facts indicated that the primary insurer knew that a defense judgment was in doubt since the driver had been speeding. It also knew that its expert's determination regarding the amount of damages or loss of future earnings alone exceeded the policy limits. Despite this information, the primary insurer set a settlement limit of $125,000 on the claim and went to trial rather than settle within its policy limits. Accordingly, a factual dispute existed over whether the primary insurer's failure to settle was a breach of its duty to protect its insured from a substantial likelihood of a judgment in excess of its policy limits. Therefore, summary judgment was improper. The court also noted that the primary insurer's failure to keep the excess insurer properly informed of the progress of the case raised an issue of whether such a breach of the policy (or its cooperation conditions) had a prejudicial effect on the excess insurer. Again, summary judgment was improper. The court of appeals reversed and remanded the case for further proceedings. *Sequoia Ins. Co. v. Royal Ins. Co. of America*, 971 F.2d 1385 (9th Cir.1992).

The driver of an automobile, while allegedly in her scope of employment, struck a bicycle rider causing over $1,100,000 in damages. The automobile was leased by the driver's employer from a lessor company. The injured party argued that four sources of insurance were available, but settlement negotiations with those insurers broke down because of disagreements concerning each insurer's liability. The four insurers involved were the driver's personal insurer, the driver's excess insurer, the employer's insurer, and the lessor's insurer, which insured the lessor for $1,000,000, and through the use of a "step down" provision in the same policy covered the lessee for $100,000. A state court held that the lessor's insurer was liable on behalf of both the lessor and the lessee, with the remainder of the judgment to be satisfied by the employer's insurer. The ruling was appealed to the Supreme Court, Appellate Division, of New York.

The primary issue was the order of liability. The personal insurer was successful in arguing a denial of coverage, which left the three remaining insurers to be ordered. The record of the earlier action concerning whether the driver was within her scope of employment was incomplete; therefore, a final judgment could not be given. Nonetheless, the court explained the results of each possible ruling. The order followed from an application of two guidelines: first, an insurer of an active tortfeasor (the driver and employer) should be considered primary to that of an inactive tortfeasor (the lessor) whose liability is purely derivative. Second, an inactive tortfeasor's insurer may seek indemnification from the party responsible. In the event that the driver's actions were in the scope of employment, the order would be as follows: 1) The lessor's insurer in its limited role as a lessee insurer, 2) the business' insurer because although it claimed to be excess coverage it did not negate *pro rata* contribution with other excess insurers, 3) the driver's personal excess insurer placed before the lessor's insurer because of the lessor's insurer's right to indemnification, and 4) the lessor's insurer. If found to be outside the scope of employment, the judgment should be satisfied by the driver's excess policy. The case was remanded for factual findings and treatment consistent with this opinion. *Liberty Mutual Insurance Co. v. Aetna Casualty & Surety Co.*, 571 N.Y.S.2d 735 (A.D.2d Dept.1991).

A Florida man was beaten and severely injured while delivering newspapers at an apartment building. The apartments were owned by a joint venture consisting of three individuals (the owners) and were managed by the insured. The injured man sued the owners and the insured in a state court. A settlement agreement was entered into by the insured and the injured man. At the time of the incident, both the owners and the insured were covered under a policy by Safeco. This policy provided $1 million of coverage for liability arising out of the ownership and management of the apartments. Safeco's policy coverage was contingent on the absence of other applicable insurance, except to the extent that the total liability facing the insured exceeded the combined coverage limits of all other insurance. The insured was also covered by policies issued by Commercial Union and Lexington. The Commercial Union policy provided $500,000 in liability coverage for properties owned or managed by the insured. The Lexington policy also provided $500,000 in liability coverage for the insured's various properties. As an umbrella liability policy it extended only excess coverage if there was other collectable insurance.

The insured sued the three insurers in the U.S. District Court for the Middle District of Florida. The court held that because the Commercial Union, Lexington and Safeco policies all covered the same property and were purchased within five days of one another there was a conflict regarding the primary insurer. After allowing evidence on the contracting parties' intent, the court concluded that the parties intended the Safeco policy to afford the primary coverage. The court found Safeco liable. Safeco appealed to the U.S. Court of Appeals, Eleventh Circuit. On appeal, the appeals court found that Safeco was not exclusively liable. Commercial Union's policy stated that it extended "primary insurance" to the insured. The Commercial Union policy also stated that the insurer would remain primarily liable if the only other applicable insurance was "on an excess or contingent basis." Neither Safeco's nor Lexington's policies stated that they were primary insurance. Because Lexington was responsible only for amounts in excess of the other insurers' coverage, the court found that Safeco's coverage must be extended before Lexington's. The district court's judgment was reversed and the case remanded for entry of judgment naming Commercial Union as the primary insurer and Safeco as the secondary insurer. *Towne Realty, Inc. v. Safeco Ins. Co. of America*, 854 F.2d 1264 (11th Cir.1988).

A federal immigration officer slipped and fell on insured premises. The insured was covered by a primary policy (to $500,000) and an excess policy which provided coverage in the event of reduction or exhaustion of an underlying policy by the primary insurer "by reason of losses paid thereunder." The officer sued the insured for his injuries. The primary insurer provided a defense for the insured, but did not notify the excess insurer of the lawsuit. Subsequently, while the action was pending, the primary insurer was placed in liquidation by the state of New York. The excess insurer, when notified of this, declined to defend the insured. At trial, the officer obtained a judgment against the insured for $1,276,000. The excess insurer then filed a declaratory relief action, claiming that it was not required to "drop down" into the primary insurer's position, claiming that it had received improper notice, and further claiming that the insured had acted in collusion with the federal officer in the underlying action. The trial court granted summary judgment in favor of the officer only for the amount over $500,000 and both parties appealed.

The California Court of Appeal, Second District, held that the trial court had properly determined that the excess insurer need not "drop down" to the position of the primary insurer. Because the excess policy required exhaustion of the primary policy only by payment of the underlying limits, the insolvency of the primary carrier was not sufficient to force the excess insurer to pay the first $500,000. The court then noted that the excess insurer had been placed on inquiry notice with respect to the underlying action and thus could not claim improper notice. That is, the insurer knew of the underlying lawsuit and should have further investigated to determine if it would be liable. Finally, the court determined that questions of fact existed regarding whether there had been collusive behavior on the part of the insured and the federal officer. It therefore remanded the case to the trial court for a determination of whether the excess insurer would be liable at all. *Span, Inc. v. Associated International Ins. Co.*, 277 Cal.Rptr. 828 (Cal.App.2d Dist.1991).

A business truck was involved in a collision which resulted in serious injuries. The truck was insured by three insurers; one provided primary coverage and the others supplied two tiers of excess coverage. A claim was made, which the first excess insurer was unable to pay because of insolvency. The second excess insurer then brought suit seeking a declaration that it was not required to "drop down" and cover the insolvency. A federal district court ordered coverage, and the insurer appealed to the U.S. Court of Appeals, Ninth Circuit. The excess policy provided that "coverage shall apply only in excess of and after all underlying insurance has been exhausted." The issue was whether insolvency amounted to exhaustion. The policy did not further define exhaustion, and the court ruled that the second excess insurer had assumed the risk of the solvency of the underlying insurers. The excess insurer was ruled liable. *Federal Ins. Co. v. Scarsella Bros., Inc.*, 931 F.2d 599 (9th Cir.1991).

A toy importer/distributor was sued as part of a products liability lawsuit brought about after the accidental choking death of a child. The importer had contracted for both primary and excess insurance, but the primary insurer had become insolvent. A separate suit was brought by the importer against the excess insurer, seeking a declaration that it was required to drop down and provide coverage below its minimum damage limit. The assertion was based on the theory that an excess insurer assumes the risk of the primary insurer's solvency. The importer was granted summary judgment, and the insurer appealed to the Superior Court of Pennsylvania. The policy specified that if the underlying insurance was not maintained, the excess insurance would be applied as if the underlying insurance had been in force. The court construed this to indicate that the parties did not intend to contract for "drop down" insurance, and reversed the trial court's judgment. *J. Kinderman & Sons v. United National Insurance Co.*, 593 A.2d 857 (Pa.Super.1991).

A primary liability insurer refused to settle a claim at an offer of $335,000, and did not inform the insured's excess insurer of the suit until after the trial had begun.

The trial resulted in an eventual judgment against the insured of $1.1 million, and the excess insurer was forced to pay over $300,000 in defense fees and contributions to the judgment. The excess insurer subsequently sued the primary insurer. Relying on subrogation, the excess insurer argued that the primary insurer breached a duty owed to the insured. A federal district court granted summary judgment dismissing the claim, and the outcome was appealed to the U.S. Court of Appeals, Fifth Circuit. The lower court relied upon a finding that the primary insurer owes no duty to the excess insurer when representing a common insured. However, since the action was brought as an assertion of subrogated rights, the question of duty to be examined is that of the primary insurer toward the insured. The presence of that duty was uncontested. Additionally, one year after the district court had entered its judgment, the Louisiana Supreme Court provided an authoritative decision allowing an excess insurer to maintain a subrogated rights action against a primary insurer to recover benefits paid. A trial was ordered to hear the excess insurer's claim. *St. Paul Fire Ins. Co. v. Afia Worldwide Ins.*, 937 F.2d 274 (5th Cir.1991).

Four medical malpractice cases arose concerning insured physicians who purchased primary malpractice insurance and excess insurance for the same policy period from the same two insurers. Each of the primary malpractice policies provided that the primary insurer agreed to defend the insured and pay damage awards up to the policy limit. They provided that defense costs were "payable by [the insurer] in addition to the applicable limit of liability of the policy." Each of the excess policies provided that the excess insurer would "not be obligated to assume charge of the settlement or defense of any claim or suit brought or proceeding instituted against the Insured...." The primary insurer appointed attorneys to defend the physicians and initially paid defense costs, but later, while litigation against the physicians was still pending, it contacted the excess insurer and demanded that the excess insurer take over responsibility for the physicians' defense in return for the surrender of the primary policy limits. The excess insurer refused this offer and denied that it had any duty to defend the physicians. The primary insurer continued to defend each physician until either the case was settled or lost. It then filed a lawsuit against the excess insurer claiming a right to reimbursement for defense costs incurred in each case after it requested the excess insurer to take charge of the defense. The four cases were consolidated for trial. The Superior Court, Los Angeles County, ruled against the primary insurer, and it appealed.

The California Court of Appeal, Second District, noted that the primary insurer made demands upon the excess insurer before the primary insurer's obligations under its policies had been satisfied. The primary insurer's obligation to pay damages on behalf of the physicians was not exhausted when it offered its policy limits to the excess insurer. That obligation could have been extinguished only by actual settlement or payment of the judgment. The court noted that if the primary insurer's position were adopted, any primary insurer which contracted to provide a defense in addition to policy limits could easily walk away from that obligation whenever the insured had excess coverage. The Superior Court's judgment was affirmed. The primary insurer was required to defend the physicians. *Chubb/Pacific Indemnity Group v. Ins. Co. of North America*, 233 Cal.Rptr. 539 (Cal.App.2d Dist.1987).

A North Carolina insured went to a car dealership to purchase a truck. He was given permission to test-drive a vehicle. While doing so, he struck another motorist's car, causing injuries. His insurer settled the claims against him, then brought suit against the dealership's liability insurer, seeking reimbursement. The dealer's policy stated that it would cover permissive users of the dealer's vehicles. Further, the insured's policy stated that any insurance it provided for a non-owned vehicle would be in excess of any other "collectible insurance." The trial court ruled that the insured's policy was an excess policy, and the dealer's insurer appealed. On appeal to the North Carolina Court of Appeals, the dealer's insurer claimed that it should be considered the excess insurer because the insured was required by law to be an insured under its policy, thus making the coverage excess. The court disagreed. It found that the dealer's policy was primary, and that the insured's policy was therefore excess. Since collectible insurance was provided by the liability insurer of the dealer, the insured's insurer was entitled to reimbursement. *United Services Automobile Ass'n v. Universal Underwriters Ins. Co.*, 408 S.E.2d 750 (N.C.App.1991).

IV. REINSURANCE

Reinsurance is a means by which insurers limit their liability for losses. By purchasing reinsurance, insurers can seek indemnification for certain types of risks they would not otherwise be able to insure.

A group of insurance companies provided reinsurance coverage to a primary insurer licensed in Colorado. The contracts between the insurers provided that, in the event of insolvency, the reinsurers would pay the receiver of the insolvent primary insurer on the basis of its liability. The contracts excluded an offset at the direction of the Colorado Commissioner of Insurance. Offset clauses allow a netting out between premiums owed to reinsurers and reinsurance recoverables. In this case, the primary insurer failed to pay premiums to the reinsurers for five quarters. Rather than terminate the reinsurance contracts, the reinsurers counted on having an equitable right to offset any payments they might have to make against the owed premiums they had not yet received. When the primary insurer was declared insolvent, the receiver sought to obtain more than $450,000 to compensate losses by the primary insurer's policyholders. The trial and appellate courts held that the reinsurers had to pay the full $450,000 without netting out the premiums owed to them. They appealed to the Supreme Court of Colorado. The supreme court held that, even if the reinsurers had an equitable right to offset premiums owed, they had freely entered into contracts from which an offset clause was deliberately excluded. Further, the insurance commissioner had the authority under the Colorado Insurance Code to regulate the reinsurance contracts so as to prohibit offset clauses. Therefore, the reinsurers could not reasonably have expected that the right to offset still existed. The lower courts' holdings were affirmed. *Bluewater Ins. Ltd. v. Balzano*, 823 P.2d 1365 (Colo.1992).

An insurer and its affiliates entered into a reinsurance treaty whereby the reinsurer agreed to reinsure certain lines of business. Some years later, the insurer entered into an excess products liability insurance contract with a corporation which contained an insolvency clause obligating the reinsurer to pay proceeds even if the insurer became insolvent. Two years after that, the insurer was placed into liquidation. The reinsurer attempted to set off the amount owed it by the insurer before paying on the contract with the insolvency clause. The New York Superintendent of Insurance objected. Suit was filed by the reinsurer, but the trial court ruled for the superintendent (acting as the liquidator for the insurer). The reinsurer successfully appealed to the Supreme Court, Appellate Division, and the superintendent appealed to the New York Court of Appeals.

On appeal, the superintendent asserted that the debts were not "mutual" because they did not arise out of the same contractual transaction; thus, they could not be offset against one another. The court of appeals, however, disagreed. First, allowing a setoff would not create a preference in favor of reinsurers in violation of public policy. Second, the debts were mutual because they were owed between the same parties and in the same right. Since the insurer unquestionably owed the premiums to the reinsurer before liquidation, the superintendent could not claim a better position just by being the insurer's liquidator. The right to setoff which existed before the liquidation continued after that event. Accordingly, the court of appeals affirmed the appellate division's order in favor of the reinsurer. *Matter of Midland Ins. Co.*, 590 N.E.2d 1186 (N.Y.1992).

Under New York law, in a contract of primary liability insurance, failure of the insured to give prompt notice of a potential claim operates to cut off coverage. The insurer need not show that it was prejudiced by the late notice before being freed from liability. Recently, a case came before the New York Court of Appeals wherein late notice was given to a reinsurer by an excess liability insurer. The question before the court was whether the "no prejudice" rule applied where late notice was given to reinsurers. The court first noted the reasons for allowing the "no prejudice" rule with respect to primary liability insurers: an insurer must have an opportunity to protect itself and to investigate a claim, and must be able to provide a sufficient reserve fund. For reinsurers, however, there is generally no difference between their interests and those of the primary insurers. Reinsurers can usually be protected without receiving prompt notice. Further, if they are prejudiced by the late notice, they may demonstrate in what way it was prejudicial and thus escape liability in those instances. The court of appeals answered the certified question before it and remanded the case. *Uniguard Security Ins. Co. v. North River Ins. Co.*, 584 N.Y.S.2d 290 (Ct.App.1992).

CHAPTER TWO

AGENTS, BROKERS AND EMPLOYMENT MATTERS

                                Page

- I. DUTY OF CARE 43
  - A. Agent's Duty of Care—Generally 44
    1. Duty of Care Satisfied 44
    2. Duty of Care Not Satisfied 48
  - B. Broker's Duty of Care—Generally 51
    1. General Rule 51
    2. Duty of Care Satisfied 52
    3. Duty of Care Not Satisfied 54
  - C. Misrepresentation, Fraud and Deceptive Trade Practices 56
  - D. Libel and Slander 59
  - E. Releases 60
  - F. Premiums 61

- II. BINDERS 63
  - A. Insurers Effectively Bound 63
  - B. Insurers Not Bound 64

- III. LICENSING 65
  - A. Constitutionality of Agent Licensing Statutes 65
  - B. Revocation and Suspension of Licensing 66

- IV. AGENCY/BROKERAGE AGREEMENTS 68
  - A. Breach of Contract—Generally 68
  - B. "No Competition" Agreements 71
  - C. Bonus Renewal Commissions 73
  - D. Redlining 73

- V. EMPLOYMENT MATTERS 74
  - A. Race, Sex and Age Discrimination 74
  - B. Collective Bargaining 79
  - C. Adjusters 80
  - D. Employment Contracts 82

I. DUTY OF CARE

    Generally, insurance agents and brokers have a duty to exercise the degree of reasonable skill and ordinary diligence which is commonly expected from the members of their professions. An insurance agent usually has a fixed and permanent relationship to the companies he represents. Strictly speaking, an agent owes a fiduciary duty primarily to the insurers he represents. The courts, however, have also placed a duty upon insurance agents to safeguard the interests of insureds. An insurance broker, unlike an agent, is generally regarded as acting exclusively on behalf of insured persons. Thus, a broker's duty of care and skill runs primarily to insureds rather than insurers.

A. Agent's Duty of Care—Generally

1. Duty of Care Satisfied

In the following cases, insurance agents were found to have satisfied the duty of care imposed upon them.

A Wisconsin man and his wife decided to upgrade their automobile insurance after they purchased a new car. The husband informed their insurance agent that they desired the "best coverage possible," and added underinsured motorist protection to their policy. The husband was later killed in an accident with an uninsured driver. The wife learned that higher underinsured limits were available, and alleged that in light of her husband's instructions their agent owed a duty to advise them of and obtain the higher limits. The wife sued in a state trial court, which dismissed her claims. She then appealed to the Wisconsin Court of Appeals.

The first issue concerned the extent of the agent's duty to advise. In general, an agent's duty is limited to acting in good faith and following instructions — the agent does not have an affirmative duty to advise. However, the duty to advise may be extended upon a showing of a special relationship. This ordinarily requires that the insured either paid more for the extra service, or that the agent knew the insured relied upon his expertise. The wife contended that a special relationship arose from the agent's practices of reviewing an insured's needs and then recommending coverage, combined with a periodic review of those needs. The court refused to infer a special relationship from these practices, and it also noted a lack of proof of reliance. The second issue concerned the wife's call for a reformation of the policy to include the higher limits. The wife would be required to show either a mistake or fraud. The court again ruled for the insurer and stated that a request for the "best possible insurance" does not mean the highest limits. The best insurance for an individual was ruled to require an insured's determination of whether an increased premium was justified. The dismissal of the claims was affirmed. *Meyer v. Norgaard*, 467 N.W.2d 141 (Wis.App.1991).

South Dakota required that automobile insurance policies be accompanied by an offer of supplemental accidental death coverage for any named insured. A South Dakota man contacted his insurance agent in order to add his daughter to his policy. The agent, without discussion of the possible supplemental coverage, added her as an additional insured for which the offer of supplemental coverage was not required. Three weeks later, the daughter died in a one car accident. The insured sued the agent and the insurer alleging that the agent had negligently breached his duty, and that coverage should be provided through the doctrine of reasonable expectations. A trial court granted summary judgment for the insurer and the agent. The man then settled with the insurer and appealed against the agent to the Supreme Court of South Dakota. The first issue questioned what duty was owed by the agent and whether it had been breached. The duty was found to be to "procure insurance of the kind and with the provisions specified by an insured's instructions." The agent thus had no duty to go beyond that standard to further inquire as to the scope of coverage. The last issue dealt with the doctrine of reasonable expectations. This doctrine had not been adopted by South Dakota courts, and was held to be inapplicable to a tort suit against an agent. The decision in favor of the agent was affirmed. *Trammell v. Prairie States Ins. Co.,* 473 N.W.2d 460 (S.D.1991).

An Iowa couple purchased a new residence and talked with their insurance agent about obtaining fire insurance. A fire damaged the new house. When the insureds sought coverage, they were notified that the agent had died, and that he had not written up a contract. Nine years later, they sued to recover the policy. The court ruled for the insurer, and the insureds appealed to the Iowa Court of Appeals. The court noted that the ten-year statute of limitations would apply just as if the policy had been written up. The court then remanded the case to determine whether the insurer had waived the one-year fire insurance defense, and whether the agent had been solely the insurer's agent. *Stockton v. Shelter General Ins. Co.,* 477 N.W.2d 872 (Iowa App.1991).

The owner of an apartment building contacted an independent agent and instructed him to obtain fire insurance. The agent unsuccessfully applied for insurance with an insurer but did not inform the owner that he was not insured. The owner later received a cancellation notice due to the insurer's clerical error. After fire damage, the owner sought coverage from the insurer to which the agent had applied. The owner alleged that the agent had either actual or apparent authority to bind the insurer. The insurer and the owner made cross motions for summary judgment in a federal district court. The actual authority of an agent depends on whether he is found to be an agent of the insured or of the insurer. This determination is made by viewing the "totality of the circumstances." The agent in this case was free to procure insurance from other insurers, and was not authorized by the insurer to bind it without approval. Therefore, the agent was found to be an agent of the insured and had no actual authority to bind the insurer. An agent may bind an insurer through apparent authority, but only if the insurer had given the insured a reasonable belief that the agent was acting on the insurer's behalf. The court rejected the apparent authority assertion for two reasons: first, Louisiana law limits the creation of coverage through this manner to that coverage which is set out in a policy, and in this case no policy was issued. Second, the only manifestation from the insurer to the owner was a cancellation notice, which had been received after the damage had occurred. The insurer was granted summary judgment. *Independent Fire Ins. Co. v. Lea,* 775 F.Supp. 921 (E.D.La.1991).

A South Carolina man conspired with an insurance agent to procure insurance on the life of another man. The insured never knew of the issuance of the policy. Three months later, the insured's body was found in a wooded area. The cause of death was a shotgun blast to the chest. The man who had conspired with the agent to obtain the policy was sentenced to life imprisonment as an accessory in the murder of the insured. The agent pleaded guilty to supplying false insurance information and unlawfully receiving part of the policy proceeds. The insured's estate then sued the insurer, seeking to hold it liable for the acts of its agent. The jury ruled for the insurer, and the estate appealed to the South Carolina Court of Appeals. On appeal, the estate contended that the insurer had given its agent apparent authority to write the policy.

The court dismissed this argument, noting that the insurer had not manifested to either the insured or anyone else that its agent had the authority to write the policy. Neither did the insured reasonably rely on the agent's position with the insurer, because the insured never knew that the policy existed. The court affirmed the jury's verdict, finding that the insurer was not liable for the agent's fraud. *Vereen v. Liberty Life Ins. Co.*, 412 S.E.2d 425 (S.C.App.1991).

A Minnesota man was injured in an accident involving a boat owned by an insured. The man brought a personal injury action against the insured. The injured man's homeowner's insurance policy did not cover the claim and the parties settled. The insured assigned to the injured man any claims which the insured might have against his insurance agent. The injured man then sued the agent in a Minnesota trial court for negligence in servicing the insured's insurance policy. Under the homeowner's policy, coverage was excluded for watercraft powered by motors exceeding twenty-five horsepower. The insured had not read the policy and the agent did not specifically advise him of the watercraft exclusion. The insured never told the agent about his newly purchased sixty horsepower boat and the agent did not ask if he had obtained a boat. The boat was never actually insured because the insured thought it was covered by his homeowner's policy. The trial court granted summary judgment for the agent. The court of appeals reversed, holding that summary judgment was inappropriate. The agent appealed to the Supreme Court of Minnesota.

The supreme court held that the agent had no affirmative duty to update the homeowner's policy at the time it was renewed or to inquire whether any changes had occurred to the insured's property which would affect coverage. The court noted that an agent's duty is ordinarily limited to acting in good faith and to following instructions. In this case, no special circumstances existed which would have given rise to a duty of care to make inquiries or to update the policy. The agent had neither actual knowledge nor any reason to know that the insured had acquired a boat. The supreme court reversed the court of appeals' decision and found for the agent. *Gabrielson v. Warnemunde*, 443 N.W.2d 540 (Minn.1989).

A Kansas couple purchased an umbrella liability policy which required them to have underlying automobile liability coverage of $250,000. The agency which sold them the policy also provided an automobile liability policy which met the necessary requirements. Later, the wife found coverage on an automobile liability policy for $400 less per year, and notified the agency of her desire to cancel her previous policy. The agency complied. It was later discovered that the new policy provided a limit of only $100,000 and left a gap in coverage of $150,000. The husband and another woman were subsequently killed in an automobile collision. When the other woman's husband sought coverage under the automobile liability policy and the umbrella policy, he was unable to recover the $150,000 that made up that gap. He then sued the agency in a Kansas trial court, asserting that the agency had negligently cancelled the automobile liability policy without first ascertaining that the other coverage obtained would comply with the umbrella policy's requirements. The court ruled for the insurer, and he appealed to the Court of Appeals of Kansas.

The appellate court ruled that the agency did not owe a duty to the couple to inquire whether their new automobile liability policy was compatible with their umbrella coverage. Had the couple sought advice from the agency, a duty would have resulted. In this case, however, the agency was merely told to cancel a policy because other coverage had already been obtained. The court held that the agency had not breached a duty to the couple, and affirmed the trial court's decision. *Marshall v. Donnelli*, 783 P.2d 1321 (Kan.App.1989).

Two Wisconsin insureds were involved in two separate accidents with underinsured motorists. They both instituted suits in Wisconsin state trial courts against their own insurers for the negligence of the agents who failed to inform them of the availability of underinsured motorist coverage. Both trial courts granted summary judgment to the insurers, concluding that the agents had no duty to inform the insureds about the availability of coverage. The Supreme Court of Wisconsin granted certification and consolidation of the two cases.

In Wisconsin, a plaintiff alleging negligence must show the four elements of tort: a duty on the part of the agent, a breach of that duty, a causal connection between the agent's conduct and the injury, and finally, actual damage as a result of the injury. Therefore, in order for liability to exist the insureds must show that the agents had an affirmative duty to advise them of the availability of underinsured motorist coverage. The court noted that the majority of other jurisdictions have held that an agent owes no obligation to advise of available coverage except where a special relationship exists. The relationship between the two insureds and their agents, the court determined, did not rise to the level of a special relationship because the insureds received the same services that all other clients received. The supreme court affirmed the trial courts' decisions granting summary judgment to the insurers. *Nelson v. Davidson*, 456 N.W.2d 343 (Wis.1990).

A North Dakota man purchased an automobile liability policy with a limit of $25,000 through an agent. He then obtained an umbrella policy through another agent which covered liability from $250,000 to $1,250,000. This resulted in a gap in coverage. Subsequently, he was involved in an automobile accident which resulted in the death of another. The lawsuit which arose out of that accident ended in a settlement, wherein the insured assigned his rights to the deceased's representative. The representative then sued both agents in a North Dakota trial court, alleging that they had negligently allowed a gap in the coverage to exist. The trial court dismissed the umbrella insurer's agent from the suit and the representative appealed to the Supreme Court of North Dakota.

The supreme court noted that without a showing of a special relationship between the insured and the umbrella insurer's agent, the agent would have no duty to procure insurance to fill the insured's gap. It noted that the agent and insured had discussed the gap in coverage and the agent had informed the insurer that he should fill the gap by obtaining coverage from someone else. Since the agent did not maintain a special relationship with the insured, he was under no affirmative duty to take action to protect the insured from gaps in his coverage. The court thus affirmed the trial court's decision to dismiss the agent from the case. *Rawlings v. Fruhwirth*, 455 N.W.2d 574 (N.D.1990).

A homeowner obtained fire insurance for her mobile home, but less than a month later the insurer canceled the policy. One week after the cancellation the mobile home was destroyed by fire. The homeowner sought coverage from the insurer, but the insurer refused. It stated that it had mailed the cancellation notice over one week before the fire. The homeowner sued the insurer in a Missouri trial court. She claimed that she had never received the cancellation notice and that the insurance agent was negligent for not notifying her of the cancellation. The trial court held for the homeowner and the insurer appealed to the Missouri Court of Appeals.

At issue was whether the agent was acting within the scope of employment when he failed to inspect the mobile home and notify the homeowner of the cancellation. The homeowner asserted that the agent was negligent for not doing what he had promised to do. She also asserted that his failure to notify her of the cancellation violated his duty to act with reasonable care. The insurer argued that the agent was acting on the insurer's behalf and thus only owed her a duty of reasonable care. Because the insurer had no duty to inspect the premises, the court of appeals held that the agent did not violate his duty to the homeowner. It also held that the agent was not required to provide the homeowner with a separate notice of cancellation. The insurer did not have to provide coverage. *Kelley v. Shelter Mut. Ins. Co.*, 748 S.W.2d 54 (Mo.App.1988).

2. Duty of Care Not Satisfied

In the following cases, insurance agents were found to have breached the applicable duty of care.

A Georgia man contacted an insurance agency's office and spoke with an agent about obtaining coverage for his trucking company. The agency processed the application and obtained a policy from an insurance company in Pennsylvania. The insured was sued in two lawsuits for injuries which arose from traffic accidents involving one of the insured's trucks. The insured testified that he spoke by telephone with the agent about these lawsuits and that the agent represented to him that he would take care of it. In fact, the agency did not forward the complaints to the Pennsylvania insurer until after the lawsuits were already in default. The insurer settled the lawsuits for $72,000 and incurred attorney's fees of $8,000. The insurer joined with the insured in bringing an action against the agent and agency alleging negligence and fraud. The trial court awarded compensatory and punitive damages and attorney's fees. The agency and agent appealed to the Court of Appeals of Georgia.

The defendants asserted that they were entitled to a directed verdict on the claim for the actual damages awarded to the insured because the insured did not pay any part of the settlement of the personal injury action. The court noted that although the insured failed to present evidence of actual damages, there were facts that supported the jury verdict in favor of the award. The court then stated that punitive damages may be awarded for wilful or negligent acts of an insurance agent. It ruled that under the circumstances the agency was negligent for its failure to use reasonable care to forward the suit in a timely manner. The judgment was affirmed. *Byrne v. Reardon*, 397 S.E.2d 22 (Ga.App.1990).

A New Mexico employee was hospitalized due to illness and incurred medical expenses of approximately $20,000. He submitted a reimbursement claim through his employer's insurance plan. However, the employer's insurance agents had selected a hospitalization insurer which was unlicensed to do business in New Mexico and which had become insolvent by the time of the employee's claim. The employee sued the agents, claiming that they had negligently failed to determine the insolvent and unlicensed insurer's status. The agents claimed that the employee was asserting a common law negligence claim relating to an employee benefit plan. They argued that the Employee Retirement Income Security Act (ERISA) expressly prohibits state common law actions against employee benefit plans because of Congress's intent to provide a uniform national law. A New Mexico trial court denied the agents' dismissal motion, and they appealed to the New Mexico Court of Appeals.

The appeals court noted that ERISA preempted only state law relating to employee benefit plans. State laws attempting to regulate employee benefit plans which "relate to" ERISA were generally preempted. However, where state laws did not directly relate to employee benefit plans, the laws were not preempted. In this case, the employee had alleged negligence by the agents in selecting an unlicensed and insolvent insurance company to provide hospitalization benefits. This did not "relate to" an employee benefit plan under ERISA. The insurance agents' conduct was at issue, not the employee benefit plan. New Mexico law provided that insurance agents and brokers may be held liable for failing to procure insurance for third party beneficiaries. The trial court had correctly ruled for the employee. *Sappington v. Covington*, 768 P.2d 354 (N.M.App.1988).

A Louisiana couple applied for life insurance on November 6, 1981. Their agent told them that the normal processing period for acceptance or rejection was four to eight weeks. The policy was not issued until February 11, 1982, because the agent made a mistake on the application. The policy contained a two-year suicide and contestability clause. The husband committed suicide on January 13, 1984. Because the death occurred three weeks prior to the end of the two-year suicide exclusion, the insurer refused to pay the proceeds of the policy. The widow successfully sued the insurer in a Louisiana trial court and the insurer appealed to the Louisiana Court of Appeal, Fifth Circuit.

On appeal the insurer argued that the trial court wrongly concluded that the extended delay between the application and issuance justified changing the date of issue to the date of application. It also argued that it was not negligent in the delay. The widow argued that a duty was imposed upon the insurer to issue the policy in a timely manner. She asserted that the insurer was negligent for delaying the date of issuance from the maximum of fifty-six days to ninety-two days. The court of appeal affirmed the trial court decision but disagreed with its reasoning. It held that the trial court wrongly substituted the application date for the policy issue date. Therefore it was inappropriate for the trial court to find that the two-year suicide exclusion had expired. However, it held that the insurer was negligent for delaying the date of issue past the maximum time stipulated. The insurer was required to provide the policy proceeds. *Mauroner v. Massachusetts Indem. and Life Ins. Co.*, 520 So.2d 451 (La.App.5th Cir.1988).

A minor bought some beer or wine at a convenience store, drank it and then drove his car into a motorcycle carrying two people. The motorcycle driver was injured and his passenger died. The motorcycle driver and the passenger's heir sued the minor and the convenience store claiming that its sale of alcoholic beverages to the minor caused the accident. The convenience store owner was covered by an insurance policy. His insurance agent had assured him when the policy was purchased that it covered him fully with respect to the store operation. The convenience store owner submitted the defense of the lawsuit to the agent who forwarded it to the insurer. The insurer undertook the defense under a reservation of rights, but sought a judicial declaration that the policy's liquor liability exclusion precluded coverage for damages arising from the "selling, serving or giving of any alcoholic beverage ... to a minor." The trial court ruled in favor of the insurer and the convenience store owner appealed.

The California Court of Appeal, Second District, ruled that "[i]n the case of standardized insurance contracts, exceptions and limitations on coverage that the insured would reasonably expect, must be called to his attention, clearly and plainly, before the exclusions will be interpreted to relieve the insurer of liability or performance." The court ruled that because the agent did not point out the exclusion, it could not be enforced. The court of appeal therefore ruled that the insurer was bound to defend and indemnify the convenience store owner. *Aetna Cas. & Sur. Co. v. Velasco*, 240 Cal.Rptr. 290 (App.2d Dist.1987).

An insured applied for additional flood coverage on his home and its contents through the National Flood Insurance Program on March 31, 1983. The agent mailed the application on the same day by regular mail and made the effective date April 1, 1983. Floodwaters damaged the insured's home on April 10, 1983. However, the program was declared not liable for damage totaling $8,243 due to the agent's negligence. The U.S. Court of Appeals, Fifth Circuit, ruled that the program was not liable because the agent did not send the application and premium by certified mail. The application provided that if the program received the application and payment more than ten days after the application date, and the information was not sent by certified mail within four days of the application date, coverage would be effective one day after receipt. When the application was sent by regular mail, the agent failed to avail himself of the only sure method of fulfilling his duty to provide protection. On this basis, the court ruled that the program was not liable, but that the agent was. The court also agreed that even though the original lawsuit by the homeowner was against the program, liability could be transferred to the agent since the claim against him arose out of the same facts as the claim against National. The agent was declared liable for the damages. *Smith v. Nat'l Flood Ins. Program*, 796 F.2d 90 (5th Cir.1986).

A South Dakota insurance agent was advised that he had understated the value of one of his insured's apartment buildings and immediately tried to contact the insured. Unable to reach him, the agent left on a trip and took no further action with respect to the letter. During the agent's absence the insured learned of the letter and attempted to contact the agent. The insured spoke to a secretary at the insurance agency who informed him of the agent's absence but told the insured that the matter would be taken care of. The insured took no further action. Fire destroyed the apartment building and an adjuster estimated the loss to be approximately $44,000, approximately $7,000 greater than the amount of insurance available to the insured. The insured sued the agency. A South Dakota trial court held that the agent had negligently failed to procure additional insurance but that the insured was contributorily negligent in failing to follow up on his request for additional coverage. The insured appealed to the South Dakota Supreme Court which affirmed that portion of the trial court ruling which found the agent liable for the underinsured property. It also held that the insured was not contributorily negligent for failing to follow up on his request for additional insurance because he had been assured by the agency's secretary that "the matter would be taken care of." *Williams Ins. Agency v. Dee-Bee Contracting Co.*, 358 N.W.2d 231 (S.D.1984).

B. Broker's Duty of Care—Generally

1. General Rule

An independent insurance agent, licensed to sell policies for six different insurers, was contacted by the owner of a music store who wished to obtain increased liability insurance and burglary insurance. He showed two plans to the owner, who chose the less expensive plan. The music store was burglarized, and the insured discovered that his policy did not include burglary coverage. He brought suit against the insurer, claiming that it had breached its contract to provide burglary insurance, and that its agent had represented that the policy included burglary coverage. The trial court found that the agent was not acting for the insurer, and the insured appealed to the Supreme Court of Nebraska. On appeal, the court noted that the independent agent was acting as a broker to provide coverage for the insured. Accordingly, any failure on his part to obtain burglary coverage for the insured could not be imputed to the insurer. The court affirmed the trial court's holding. *Moore v. Hartford Fire Ins. Co.,* 481 N.W.2d 196 (Neb.1992).

A Minnesota insurance broker convinced a business to change insurers. The broker prepared an insurance binder for fire coverage in the amount of $162,000. However, the binder was never transferred to the new insurer. In fact, the broker asked the new insurer's agent to write a policy providing coverage in the amount of $145,000. After fire destroyed the business, it sued the insurer claiming it was entitled to the amount of the insurance binder ($162,000) rather than the amount for which the policy was written ($145,000). The Minnesota Court of Appeals observed that its decision turned on whether the broker was acting as an agent for the insurer when he executed the insurance binder for $162,000. It noted that an agent acts on behalf of an insurance company, whereas a broker acts on behalf of the insured.

Here, the court of appeals held that the broker had no authority to bind coverage for the insurer. He was employed by an independent brokerage firm which had handled all of the business's insurance needs for two years prior to the fires. The insurer had only one authorized agent in the state of Minnesota, the agent with whom the broker had conversed when he obtained the $145,000 coverage. Further, the broker had prepared the insurance binder on a standard form rather than using the insurer's form. The insurer was only liable for $145,000. *R.L.B. Enterprises v. Liberty Nat'l Fire Ins. Co.,* 413 N.W.2d 551 (Minn.App.1987).

In 1974, an Illinois man instructed his insurance broker to acquire and maintain $1,000,000 in automobile insurance coverage for him. The broker acquired two policies from separate insurance companies. One policy provided primary coverage in the amount of $300,000. A second policy provided coverage in excess of $250,000 up to $1,000,000. The broker renewed both policies several times. In 1977, the primary coverage policy was issued with split limits of $100,000 per person and $300,000 per occurrence. This change resulted in a $150,000 gap in the man's coverage because the new primary policy covered only $100,000 per person and the second policy did not provide protection for any amount below $250,000. The broker renewed the policy but never advised the man of the gap in his coverage nor attempted to correct it. In August 1979, the man's daughter struck and killed a pedestrian while driving one of the man's cars. The pedestrian's estate sued for damages and was awarded $510,000. The secondary policy paid everything over $250,000. The primary split rate policy paid $100,000. A U.S. district court granted the man's request for judgment against his broker for the $150,000 gap. It also granted summary judgment to the insurance companies, dismissing an action the broker had filed against them for the same amount. The broker appealed.

The U.S. Court of Appeals, Seventh Circuit, observed that the broker's actions were directed by the insured. The broker was acting as the man's agent and had a duty to act in good faith and with reasonable care, skill and diligence in compliance with his instructions. The court found that the broker had breached this duty "because it failed to maintain the coverage that it had been instructed to maintain." The court of appeals concluded that the insurance company had a duty to exercise good faith, skill and diligence in writing and issuing policies for the insured. The broker was thus allowed to sue the primary insurance company alleging that the company had failed to issue requested coverage. *Lazzara v. Howard A. Esser, Inc.*, 802 F.2d 260 (7th Cir.1986).

2. Duty of Care Satisfied

A New York insured entered into military service and was forced to relocate. The insured alleged that he asked his property manager to inform his insurance broker of the change of address, but the broker failed to inform the insurer of the change of address. The insurer mailed a premium notice to the insured's last known address. The policy lapsed for nonpayment of the premium 15 days before a fire at the insured's home. The insured brought suit against the insurer, and the supreme court granted summary judgment to the insurer. The insured appealed. On appeal, the appellate division court held that the insured had failed to prove that the insurer did anything to cause the insured to believe that the broker was authorized to act on the insurer's behalf with respect to the premium contract. Because the oral notice to the broker was insufficient to put the insurer on notice of a change of address, the appellate division court affirmed the summary judgment. *Meade v. Finger Lakes-Seneca Co-op Ins.*, 584 N.Y.S.2d 937 (A.D.3d Dept.1992).

An Illinois man, insured under his parents' automobile policy, was involved in an accident with an uninsured motorist. The parents only had the statutorily required minimum uninsured motorist coverage of $30,000 and asserted that had their insurance agent informed them that the maximum coverage possible was $500,000, they would have gotten it because they had purchased liability insurance of $500,000 under the same policy. In their suit against the insurance company the parents alleged that the broker had breached an oral contract, that the insurer's broker was negligent in failing to advise them of the maximum coverage available to them, and that the insurance company had breached its fiduciary duty to them. The insurer filed a motion to dismiss, which the trial court granted.

On appeal, the appellate court held that the alleged contract was too vague to be enforced. The court further held that if a broker acts in good faith and with reasonable care he is not obligated to advise clients of disparities between liability and uninsured motorist coverage and the options of procuring uninsured motorist coverage in excess of the statutory minimum. Although the insurance company is required to inform clients upon issuance of the policy that they may obtain higher uninsured motorist coverage, a broker is under no duty to advise clients of this possibility again once the initial information is conveyed to the client. There being no evidence that the clients did not receive this information upon issuance of their policy, the appellate court affirmed the dismissal. *Shults v. Griffin-Rahn Ins. Agency,* 550 N.E.2d 232 (Ill.App.3d Dist.1990).

The owners of an apartment building were covered by a liability insurance policy with a coverage limit of $300,000. When a young child fell into the apartment building's swimming pool and was seriously injured, her parents filed a lawsuit against the owners for negligence. The owners agreed to a stipulated judgment which settled the case for $1.5 million. The child's parents agreed as part of the stipulated judgment not to seek the $1.5 million in court in return for a promise from the owners to pay a total of $200,000 and to transfer any legal right they had to sue their insurance broker. The parents then filed a cross-complaint against the insurance broker alleging that the broker breached its duty to provide the owners with liability insurance sufficient to protect the owners' personal assets and satisfy the $1.5 million stipulated judgment.

The Superior Court, Los Angeles County, dismissed the cross-complaint, and the parents appealed. The issue on appeal was whether the broker owed the owners a legal duty of care to provide them with a policy of liability insurance sufficient to cover any possible judgment against the owners arising out of their negligent acts. The California Court of Appeal, Second District, recognized that the broker had an obligation to use "reasonable care, diligence, and judgment in procuring the insurance requested by [the owners]." It was the owners' responsibility, however, to advise the broker of the insurance they wanted, including the limits of the policy to be issued. Because the cross-complaint did not allege that the owners had requested more insurance than the broker obtained, the broker had not breached any duty owed to the owners. The Superior Court's decision to dismiss the parents' cross-complaint was affirmed. *Jones v. Grewe,* 234 Cal.Rptr. 717 (App.2d Dist.1987).

A New York insurance broker was found to have satisfied the duty of care imposed upon him. The New York Supreme Court, Special Term, held that an insurance broker owes no continuing duty to advise, guide or direct an insured's coverage. A broker had handled automobile insurance for the insured for twenty-eight years. He had procured primary automobile insurance coverage with a combined single limit of $300,000 and an excess "umbrella" policy with a limit of $1,000,000. The excess policy required minimum primary coverage of $250,000. In 1980, the insured cancelled his primary insurance, and through another broker, obtained new primary insurance with a limit of only $100,000. This left a $150,000 gap between his primary and excess insurance coverage. The insured mailed a notice to his former broker which stated only that his primary coverage would now be handled by another company and included his new primary insurance policy number. The new policy coverage limit was not mentioned. In 1981, the insured was involved in an automobile accident; consequently he was sued. He settled the claim for $600,000. His new primary insurer paid its $100,000 policy limit and the excess insurer paid $350,000 pursuant to the requirement of a minimum primary coverage of $250,000. The insured then sued his former broker for the resulting $150,000 deficiency, claiming that the broker should have checked to ensure that there were no gaps in his coverage. The supreme court dismissed the suit against the insured's former broker, stating that a broker owes no continuing duty to advise a client after the broker complies with his initial duty to obtain proper coverage. *Blonsky v. Allstate Ins. Co.,* 491 N.Y.S.2d 895 (Sup.Ct.1985).

3. Duty of Care Not Satisfied

In the following cases, insurance brokers were found to have breached the applicable duty of care.

A New Jersey man purchased a life insurance policy from a broker who utilized a firm to service the policy. The insureds received the insurer's notification that a premium was due, but the servicing company told the wife "not to worry" because they still had ample time to pay. The insureds then received notice that the policy had lapsed. The broker and servicing company also received notice of the lapse, but allegedly failed to inform the insureds that a late payment with interest could reinstate the policy. The parties later sent a payment and request for reinstatement, without the required medical form indicating insurability. The broker then informed the insureds that the policy had been reinstated despite his knowledge to the contrary. The insured's health had made him uninsurable, and he died without coverage. The widow brought suit in a federal district court against the broker, servicing company, and insurer. Summary judgment was granted to all of the defendants, and the widow appealed to the U.S. Court of Appeals, Third Circuit. The initial dispute involved the extent of the duty owed by the broker to the insured. New Jersey courts will apply a duty greater than that normally associated with the broker-client relationship only if an insured can show that the relationsip was "something more," and included justified detrimental reliance. The question then became whether this heightened duty was breached. Because the insured could have utilized the late payment option, the court held that a breach claim could be based on the broker's failure to notify the insured of that option. The claim based on negligent misrepresentation failed because reliance on the broker's statements after the lapse statements were received could not have been justified. The summary judgment granted to the broker was reversed in part, and the disposition of the claim against the servicing company waas remanded for consideration of the duty owed to the insured. *Glezerman v. Columbian Mutual Life Ins. Co.,* 944 F.2d 146 (3d Cir.1991).

A shipping company contracted an insurance broker to purchase insurance. Following notification of a loss to the broker, the broker notified only two of the three insurers from which he had obtained coverage. The insurer which was not notified denied coverage due to improper notice, and brought a declaratory judgment action in federal district court against the insured. The insured then brought a counterclaim against the broker alleging breach of fiduciary duty, seeking indemnification in the event that the insurer effectively avoided coverage. The broker moved for a dismissal of the counterclaim. The court dismissed the motion and allowed the matter to continue to trial. It rejected the broker's arguments that the counterclaim was improper. *St. Paul Fire and Marine Ins. Co. v. Great Lakes Turnings,* 774 F.Supp. 485 (N.D.Ill.1991).

A New York maintenance company obtained a liability insurance policy which was to cover a one year period. It was cancelled by the insured. The insurer sued the insured to recover approximately $850,000 for past premiums due. The insured concluded that it had no defense to the lawsuit and settled by agreeing to pay the insurer $200,000. The insured brought an indemnity action against the broker seeking to recover the amount of the settlement, asserting negligence and misrepresentation in a New York trial court. At trial, the jury concluded that the broker was not obligated to indemnify the insured. The insured moved to either set aside the verdict or for a new trial.

Although the jury found negligence which proximately caused the insured's injury, the court also determined that there still remained a jury question as to whether the insured suffered damage because it had obtained needed coverage at or below prevailing market prices. Therefore, the court ordered a new trial on the issue of damages. *Trans World Maintenance v. Accident Prevention*, 560 N.Y.S.2d 914 (Sup.1989).

A New York man directed his broker to procure theft and auto collision coverage for his new automobile. With the broker's assistance, the insured entered into a contract with an insurer. When the insured reported his automobile stolen, the insurer denied his claim. The insured learned that the insurer was not licensed by New York to engage in the insurance business. He then sued his broker, alleging negligence, breach of contract, and fraud in a New York trial court. The trial court granted summary judgment to the insured on the issue of liability and the broker appealed. The appellate court affirmed the decision of the trial court. The insured had established the broker's negligence by showing that he had assisted the insured in obtaining a policy with a nonlicensed company. *Hammond v. Hunkele*, 566 N.Y.S.2d 69 (A.D.2d Dep't 1991).

A Colorado lounge owner procured liability insurance and was assured by his insurance agent that the lounge was "fully covered" for alcohol-related lawsuits. In fact, the policy obtained by the agent contained an exclusion for such lawsuits. The lounge was sued for permitting a minor to leave the lounge while intoxicated and causing an automobile accident. Citing the exclusion, the insurer refused to defend or indemnify the lounge in the lawsuit. After prevailing in the lawsuit, the lounge owner sued his insurance agent, the agent's brokerage firm and the insurer. He sought attorney's fees in defending the original lawsuit and a declaration that the agent, brokerage firm and insurer be held liable for any lawsuits arising out of the consumption of alcohol on the premises. A trial court concluded that the agent and the brokerage firm were negligent in failing to obtain liquor liability coverage. The trial court also held that the agent and the brokerage firm were responsible for all expenses incurred by the lounge in the original lawsuit and that the insurer was liable for the agent's negligence.

On appeal, the Colorado Court of Appeals held that the insurer was not liable because the policies it had issued clearly excluded coverage for alcohol-related activities. However, the court of appeals found that the agent and brokerage firm were liable for the costs of the original lawsuit and had to indemnify the lounge owner for further alcohol-related lawsuits. The agent and the brokerage firm appealed to the Colorado Supreme Court. The question for the court to consider was whether the lounge offered sufficient evidence at trial that liquor liability insurance was "generally available in the insurance industry when the broker or agent obtained insurance coverage" for the lounge. The supreme court held that the lounge had satisfied its burden of proof that such coverage was available at the time the policy was obtained. The evidence showed that the insurance agent had provided such coverage for a second lounge operated by the same owner. There was also testimony by a licensed insurance agent that liquor liability insurance had been available to lounges for a substantial period prior to July 1978, when the lounge had applied for liability insurance. The supreme court therefore upheld the ruling against the agent and brokerage firm. *Bayly, Martin & Fay v. Pete's Satire*, 739 P.2d 239 (Colo.1987).

C. Misrepresentation, Fraud and Deceptive Trade Practices

Agents and brokers have a duty not to misrepresent the scope of coverage available under an insurance policy nor to engage in any other deceptive trade practices.

A trucking company which specialized in hauling oversized cargo obtained an insurance policy which the agent represented would provide "full coverage." The company then suffered a loss when its cargo struck an overpass. The insurer denied coverage, claiming that a "collision of the conveyance" required contact by the truck. The insured asserted that coverage should apply, first because the language was ambiguous, and second because the insurer was prevented from denying coverage due to the agent's misrepresentation. A state trial court found the language to be unambiguous, but awarded coverage based upon the agent's misrepresentation. The court of appeals reversed the order of coverage, and the insured appealed to the Supreme Court of Tennessee. Historically, agents were held to bind an insurer even when acting beyond their authority. The court in this case noted that insurers could limit their exposure to potential liability through making conditions of coverage into limitations on coverage. The court then held that "[r]egardless [of] which language is selected by an insurer, the insured has a valid right to expect coverage as promised by the insurer's agent." The only limitation to this holding is that the agent's representation must have been justifiably relied upon. The decision of the trial court was reinstated. *Bill Brown Construction Co. v. Glen Falls Ins. Co.,* 818 S.W.2d 1 (Tenn.1991).

A parttime insurance salesman persuaded an insured to replace an incontestable policy with an extended term option in order to save money. The insured stated that he was a smoker and had stopped working due to mental problems. Despite this disclosure, the agent decided not to place the correct information on the application. The agent also paid the initial premium and set up an automatic deduction from his own checking account. The insured soon died. The agent delivered the letter which denied benefits, and was present when the insured's wife read it. The insured's wife informed the insurer that the agent was responsible for the misrepresentations, and sued the agent and insurer in a West Virginia trial court. The wife prevailed, and the insurer and agent appealed to the Supreme Court of Appeals of West Virginia. The court reviewed the agent's actions and agreed that they were sufficient to support the damage award because he had acted within the scope of his employment. The insurer was found to have acted with wilful or reckless negligence for its own actions in failing to properly investigate the matter. The court affirmed the trial court's decision. *Jarvis v. Modern Woodmen of America,* 406 S.E.2d 736 (W.Va.1991).

A woman from Guam underwent a thyroidectomy and then began cobalt treatments for cancer for undifferentiated carcinoma. Approximately six months later, the woman applied for life insurance. On the application, she denied receiving any cancer treatment. The insurer's medical examiner examined the woman and asked her questions about her medical history, and the insurer issued a life insurance policy. The insurer later sought declaratory relief in a federal district court to cancel the policy for material misrepresentations. The district court granted the insurer's motion for summary judgment, concluding that the woman had misrepresented her condition by failing to disclose her therapy and the possibility of cancer. The woman then appealed to the U.S. Court of Appeals, Ninth Circuit, alleging that she had not misrepresented the facts and that the insurer should be prevented from denying coverage because the company had reviewed her application and examined her before its acceptance. The court of appeals reversed the trial court's decision. There was evidence that the agent misrepresented the information on the application form. The case was remanded. *Hawaiian Life Ins. Co. v. Laygo*, 884 F.2d 1300 (9th Cir.1989).

A Florida man, employed by the state, sought to reverse his vasectomy. Since he could not afford the procedure, he decided he would undergo surgery only if he was covered by the state insurance plan. He had seen a brochure which excluded such procedures, but the brochure also directed that any questions concerning claims should be directed to the insurer's office, and not to the state. He contacted the insurer several times, and each time was told that the procedure would be covered. He underwent the surgery, relying on the insurer's assurance of coverage. His claim was initially paid, but the state later notified him that the surgery was not covered, and that he was required to pay the money back. A hearing was conducted, and the hearing officer ruled for the state. The man appealed to the District Court of Appeal of Florida.

The appellate court recognized that the master policy excluded the vasectomy reversal. However, since the insurer had repeatedly advised that the surgery would be covered, no claim could now be made that the surgery was not covered. The court ruled that the man had relied on the insurer's representation, and that he had undergone the surgery because of it. The court reversed the decision of the hearing officer, and granted the employee coverage. *Warren v. Dep't of Administration*, 554 So.2d 568 (Fla.App.5th Dist.1989).

An insurance agent in Louisiana visited a couple at their home to sell them medical insurance. The couple agreed to purchase two policies and the agent filled out their application as the couple responded to his questions. Although the wife informed the agent that she had suffered from several medical conditions the agent submitted a "clean" application listing no illnesses or pre-existing conditions for the wife or the husband. The couple subsequently filed six claims with the insurer, five of which were filed on behalf of the wife. Although these claims totaled over $10,000 only $1,400 was paid. After sending letters of demand to the insurer, the couple filed a lawsuit to recover the benefits due under the policies. A Louisiana district court ruled in favor of the insured couple. It awarded damages for the unpaid benefits as well as a 100% penalty and attorney's fees. The insurer appealed, and the couple requested an increase in the amount of penalties and attorney's fees awarded.

The Louisiana Court of Appeal first considered the insurer's argument that the insurance policy should be voided because its application contained misrepresentations about the wife's medical history. The court ruled that because the agent made the representations, and he worked for the insurer, the misrepresentations could not be used to void the policy. The court also addressed the issue of whether the statutory penalty should be assessed as twice the amount of benefits due in addition to the payment of the benefits, or simply twice the benefits due. Louisiana statutes provide that when an insurer is liable for a statutory penalty, its measure is "double the amount of the health and accident benefits due under the terms of the policy ... together with attorney's fees to be determined by the court...." Citing previous Louisiana decisions, the court decided that despite the wording of the statute, the couple should only be awarded a total of twice the amount of benefits due. *Bischoff v. Old Southern Life Ins. Co.*, 502 So.2d 181 (La.App.3d Cir.1987).

In 1980, an insured held an insurance policy which provided underinsured motorist coverage for him and residents of his household. When the insured's insurance agent changed his agency affiliation, the insured agreed to switch to an automobile policy issued by the new agency. Both he and the agent intended the new policy to include underinsured motorist coverage, but the agent failed to request it. In August 1981, the insured informed the agent that his son had been badly injured in a motorcycle accident. The agent then discovered that the policy lacked underinsured motorist coverage and requested the insurer to backdate such coverage to January 1981. The agent did not inform the insurer of the accident. The insurer, not knowing of the accident, backdated the coverage. When the insurer subsequently denied coverage, the insured filed a lawsuit against the insurer and the agent alleging breach of contract and negligence. The Minnesota Court of Appeals observed that both the insurer and the agent stipulated at trial that the agent was acting for the insurer and had the authority to bind it to provide underinsured motorist coverage. The record also indicated that the insurer would have provided the coverage had it been included on the initial application. The agent was not guilty of fraud when he requested backdating of the underinsured motorist coverage because the agent and the insured had agreed that underinsured motorist coverage would be part of the new policy as of January 1981, when the agent changed his agency affiliation. The insured was entitled to coverage, and the agent did not have to indemnify the insurer or contribute to the insured's recovery. *Anderson v. Minnesota Mut. Fire & Cas. Co.*, 399 N.W.2d 233 (Minn.App.1987).

An insurance agent convinced a Texas man to purchase a policy on the life of one of his employees. The two then tried to kill the employee in order to recover the insurance proceeds. The plot was discovered and both men were convicted of conspiracy to commit murder. The wife of the man who purchased the policy then brought suit against the agent's employer for intentional infliction of emotional distress, asserting that the insurance agent had been acting in the discharge of his employment when he devised the murder plan and the employer should be liable for the actions of the agent as a result. The trial court granted the insurer's motion for summary judgment. In upholding the lower court's ruling the court of appeals found it "inconceivable that an employee could plan and execute a fraud upon his employer and be in the furtherance of his employment." *Saenz v. Family Security Ins. Co. of America*, 786 S.W.2d 110 (Tex.App.-San Antonio 1990).

The question before the District Court of Appeal of Florida was whether a life insurer could properly deny full coverage where its agent misinformed the insured regarding such coverage and the insured relied on the misrepresentation. The policy issued to the insured contained a three-year limitation period after which the full face value of the policy would be paid at death. The insured questioned his agent about the limitation period and was told that very few understood this type of policy but that he did. He assured the insured that the policy would pay full benefits from the date of issuance. In reliance on these statements, premium payments continued. The insured died six months after issuance of the policy. The insurer refused to pay the $5,000 face amount of the policy, relying on the three-year limitation period. In upholding a lower court decision in favor of the insured for the full face amount of the policy, the District Court of Appeal held that the insurer could not deny full coverage notwithstanding the clear and unambiguous policy provision. Here, the insurer's agent held himself out as an expert on such policies and misinformed the insured as to the meaning of the limitation provision. *Peninsular Life Ins. Co. v. Wade*, 425 So.2d 1181 (Fla.App.1983).

A different result was reached in a Michigan case, however, in which an insured involved in a swimming pool construction business sued his insurer in a federal district court, seeking a declaratory judgment to determine the scope of coverage of an insurance policy. He sought a reformation of the policy to include products liability coverage not previously agreed to by the insurer. He contended that when he originally purchased the policy his agent informed him such coverage was included. Following a swimming pool accident in which a person was injured and the commencement of a suit against the insured for product liability damages, the insurer refused to defend, claiming it had not insured against such incidents. The insured moved for a summary judgment, which was granted.

The district court held that the law in Michigan is that an insurer "is not liable on erroneous representations by an agent as to the extent of coverage of a plainly worded policy, so as to entitle the insured to equitable relief, even though the latter failed to read the instrument." It went on to quote from a similar case: "Under the circumstances of this case, we think this plainly worded policy should be held to be something more than a mere scrap of paper. The policy is the contract between the insured and the insurer.... [T]he plain, unambiguous provisions of written or printed insurance contracts ought not to be less binding upon the respective parties than like terms of any other contract. Plaintiff's failure to read his contract does not excuse him." Summary judgment in favor of the insurer was thus granted. *Western Cas. & Sur. Co. v. Sliter*, 555 F.Supp. 369 (E.D.Mich.1983).

D. Libel and Slander

After an agent of Hoosier Insurance Company sent a letter to the Indiana Guaranty Association (a state regulatory agency) explaining that Gibralter Mutual Insurance Company was maintaining an inadequate surplus ($55,034 rather than the required $250,000), Gibralter sued for libel, claiming that the letter was a malicious attempt to induce Gibralter to settle an unrelated lawsuit. The circuit court entered summary judgment in favor of Hoosier and its agent, and Gibralter appealed. The Indiana Court of Appeals affirmed the lower court's ruling based upon the undisputed truth of Hoosier's letter to the Guaranty Association, rejecting Gibralter's contention that by enacting an unfair insurance competition statute (I.C. 27-4-1-1), the Indiana legislature had impliedly eliminated truth as a defense to libel. The time-honored common law defense of truth to a libel action could only be abolished by unequivocal legislative enactment, held the appellate court. *Gibralter Mut. Ins. Co. v. Hoosier Ins. Co.*, 486 N.E.2d 548 (Ind.App.2d Dist.1985).

An agent was held liable in the following case, in which a swimming pool company in Rhode Island brought suit against the homeowner's insurer of one of its customers, as well as the insurer's agent, to recover damages for slander. The customer reported to her agent damage from vandalism to her swimming pool liner and sought reimbursement under her homeowner's insurance policy. The customer told the agent that the pool had been supplied by a particular company. Upon learning this, the agent told the customer that the owner of the pool company "was a slippery character and that he was an arsonist, that he had blown up his bulldozer and set fire to his building on Warwick Avenue." Immediately following her conversation with the agent, the customer telephoned the pool company owner and advised him of the agent's remarks. The pool company owner brought suit for slander in a Rhode Island trial court, which held in his favor. The jury awarded punitive damages against the insurer and the agent and they appealed.

The Rhode Island Supreme Court held that there was sufficient evidence to support the jury finding that the agent was acting as an agent of the insurer within the scope of his authority at the time he allegedly slandered the president of the pool company. However, an award of punitive damages against the insurer was improper. The court stated that in a case where the proof does not implicate the principal and when the principal neither expressly nor impliedly authorizes or ratifies the act, "it is quite enough, that [the principal] shall be liable in compensatory damages.... Accordingly, the case was remanded to the lower court to decide the extent of the insurer's liability for compensatory damages. *AAA Pool Serv. & Supply v. Aetna Cas. & Sur. Co.*, 479 A.2d 112 (R.I.1984).

E. Releases

After a Minnesota motel was destroyed by fire it sued its insurer and agent for negligence in failing to provide adequate coverage. Before the trial the motel released the agent from liability. A trial court found the agent and the insurer each forty-five percent negligent and ordered the insurer to pay ninety percent by assigning to it the agent's forty-five percent liability. After the Minnesota Court of Appeals affirmed the decision the insurer asked the Minnesota Supreme Court to review the decision.

The issue before the supreme court was whether the release of the insurer's agent also released the insurer from liability for his negligence. The release agreement provided that for the sum of $15,000, the motel released the agent "from any claims, ... or any claim for loss or damage of any kind or nature whatsoever, which the undersigned now has, or may hereafter have, on account of, or in any way growing out of, ... the fire...." It also provided that the agent would credit and satisfy his portion of the damages. The motel claimed that the release only exempted the agent in his individual capacity and reserved all other claims against the insurer.

The supreme court reversed the lower court decisions because the agreement intended to release all claims "of any kind or nature whatsoever." No words in the release limited its effect to the agent's individual liability. Further evidence of intent to release all claims against the agent was the motel's agreement to indemnify the agent only for judgments obtained against him for contribution since the agent would have had no reason to agree to a release which left him open to a lawsuit by the insurer for indemnity. The effect of the release was simply to allow the motel to maintain its lawsuit against the insurer for the insurer's wrongdoing while relieving the insurer of any liability for the agent's negligence. *Reedon of Faribault v. Fidelity & Guar. Ins. Underwriters*, 418 N.W.2d 488 (Minn.1988).

F. Premiums

An insurance agent assured a customer that if he put $10,000 down on a policy, the money would be returned if the customer changed his mind. The customer paid a $10,000 deposit and signed the application for the policy. When he changed his mind, the insurer refused to refund the money because the customer failed to notify the agent within a 10-day period as stipulated in the policy. The insured sued for return of his deposit, but a district court granted the insurer a judgment notwithstanding the verdict. The insured then appealed to the Court of Appeals of Georgia. The appellate court upheld the decision because no special fiduciary relationship existed between the agent and the insured which would permit the insured to rely upon the agent's statements. *Trulove v. Woodmen of World Life Ins.*, 419 S.E.2d 324 (Ga.App.1992).

A New York insured was covered under an auto liability policy. He then changed insurance brokers and his new broker placed an auto liability policy with a new insurer. The policy was to go into effect on August 31, 1982. The insured had paid premiums to the first insurer through and including October 3, 1982. The first insurer sent the insured a notice that his policy would be canceled, effective October 3, 1982. On August 31, 1982, the insured's wife was involved in an accident in which a passenger was injured. A lawsuit ensued. Up until trial, the first insurer remained willing to contribute to the settlement. When the new insurer settled the passenger's claim, however, the first insurer disclaimed any liability under the policy. The new insurer sued the first insurer in federal district court to determine the insurers' obligations.

The court held that the insured's unexpressed intent to cancel his first policy and nonpayment of additional monthly premiums did not cancel that policy before expiration of the prepaid term. It noted that the insured did not demand a repayment of the unused premiums. The first insurer had neither canceled nor attempted to cancel the insured's policy and had not notified the insured's agent that the policy would not be renewed. The first insurer remained liable for accidents that occurred before expiration of the policy term, even though the insured had obtained a new policy from another insurer. The court granted the new insurer's motion for summary judgment. *Boston Old Colony v. Lumbermen's Mut. Cas.*, 710 F.Supp. 913 (S.D.N.Y.1989).

A North Dakota trucker purchased a business liability policy from an insurance agency. The following year, he placed his vehicles in his sons' names because he was unable to secure his own financing. The sons occasionally worked for the trucking business. The named insureds in the policy were changed from the trucker to his sons, his wife and the business itself. The trucker then defaulted on his premium payments. The agency canceled the policy and sued the trucker, his wife, sons and business for unpaid premiums and late charges. The trucker then filed bankruptcy, listing the agency as a creditor. The bankruptcy court discharged this debt. However, the court found that the agency's insurance services covered vehicles used by the trucking business, the family farm and personal vehicles. The court ruled that the sons commonly owned the vehicles and used the trucking business as a means to insure them. Because they had benefitted from the insurance services, the sons were liable for unpaid premiums for vehicles held in their names. The sons appealed to the North Dakota Supreme Court.

On appeal, the sons argued that they should not be liable for the payments because they had not contracted with the insurance agency. The supreme court agreed. There was no evidence that the father was acting as the sons' agent or that the business was operated as a partnership. Therefore, the sons were not liable for the unpaid premiums. *Home Ins. of Dickinson v. Speldrich*, 436 N.W.2d 1 (N.D.1989).

A Michigan insured died one day after his life insurance premium grace period expired. His insurance agent was notified of the death and he in turn notified his manager. The insured's widow mailed the premium in to the insurer who cashed the check and recorded the policy as current. The widow sought to recover the policy proceeds but the insurer denied coverage. She sued the insurer in a Michigan trial court which held for the insurer. The widow then appealed to the Michigan Court of Appeals which reversed the trial court decision. It held that the insurer waived its right to claim policy lapse by failing to return the premium upon learning that the death preceded payment. The insurer was required to provide the policy proceeds to the widow. *Glass v. Harvest Life Ins. Co.*, 425 N.W.2d 107 (Mich.App.1988).

An insurer entered into a sales agreement with two agents. The agents agreed to send completed applications for insurance and the first month's premium to the company. Each application contained a clause which certified that the applicant had paid the initial premium. The insurer advanced the agents seventy percent of the projected "annual" premium for each application. These advances were essentially loans to the agents. The agents began submitting applications and the insurer paid the advances. However, the agents did not collect the premiums from the applicants. The agents paid the premiums and collected the advances from the insurer. The agents fraudulently marketed the policies as "free insurance" to the applicants. One year later the insurer elected to discontinue the payment of the advances and pay commissions to the agents. The agents stopped paying the premiums which caused the policies to lapse. The insurer demanded that the agents pay the outstanding premium balances in full and the agents refused. The insurer terminated the agency agreements and sued the agents in an Illinois federal district court.

The insurer asserted that the agents failed to repay the advances when the insurer demanded. It also argued that the agents failed to remit premiums to the insurer which were collected from the policyholders. The agents argued that their contract contained a clause in which they agreed to repay the advances within eighteen months rather than on demand. The court observed that the agreement defined the advances as loans and specifically provided that they were due and payable on demand. Because full effect should have been given to the more specific intention, in this case repayment on demand, the court held that the insurer correctly terminated the agreement. Immediate termination was provided for if the agents committed certain misdeeds. The insurer was entitled to immediate reimbursement. *United Equitable Life Ins. Co. v. TransGlobal Corp.*, 679 F.Supp. 769 (N.D.Ill.1988).

Agents who collect premiums for insureds are liable for their payment to the insurer. A Florida insurance agent was president of an incorporated agency. He signed an agency agreement with an insurer which provided that the agency would collect premiums it solicited for the insurer and send the required sums to the insurer. The agency collected $75,000 in premiums but never paid this sum to the insurer. The insurer filed a lawsuit against the agent for the agency's failure to make payment and account for premiums it collected. A Florida circuit court ruled in favor of the insurer, and the agent appealed to the Florida District Court of Appeal.

Florida statutes provided that agents are fully liable and accountable for the wrongful acts of their employees when they are acting on behalf of an incorporated agency. On appeal, the agent alleged that this statute did not apply because the premiums were not wrongfully taken by him personally, and were not taken as a result of misconduct, diversion or appropriation from the agency. The appellate court noted that an intent to misappropriate premiums is not a necessary element to prove a violation of Florida agency statutes. "Liability arises upon a showing that a person has direct supervision and control over an agency and its employees, and that insurance premiums are collected by the agency, but not accounted for or turned over to the insurance company for whom the agency is acting." Because the agent's control over the agency and the premiums' disappearance were proven, the agent could be held liable as a matter of law. The circuit court's ruling was affirmed. *Copeland Ins. Agency v. Home Ins. Co.*, 502 So.2d 93 (Fla.App.5th Dist.1987).

II. BINDERS

The courts have generally upheld the authority of agents and brokers to bind insurers, provided there is contractual or statutory authority for doing so.

A. <u>Insurers Effectively Bound</u>

A Louisiana woman, desiring to purchase life insurance on the life of her father, informed the insurance agent of her father's poor health. The agent filled in negative responses to all of the questions on the application form concerning pre-existing illnesses and medical treatment. The agent said, "if he is alive and breathing, [he] is insurable." The agent then told the daughter to sign her father's name on the applications. When her father died, the insurer refused to pay and the daughter filed suit. The Louisiana Court of Appeal held that when an insurance agent falsely fills out an application form he binds the insurer. Since the insured and the applicant did not fill out the application, they had not made false representations with intent to deceive the insurance company. The daughter was allowed to recover on the policy. *Coolman v. Trans World Life Ins. Co.*, 482 So.2d 979 (La.App.3d Cir.1986).

A Texas truck driver purchased a truck on which his bank held a lien. He contacted his insurance agent. A binder was issued which identified Southern County Mutual (SCM) as the insurer and the bank as loss payee. The agent was later informed that SCM refused to provide coverage but that insurance could be procured through another insurer. The agent authorized the substitution but never relayed the information to the driver. When the truck was destroyed the driver learned that his agent had changed insurers. Before the insurer could pay the claim it was declared insolvent. Since the bank could not recover from the insolvent insurer it sought coverage from SCM. When SCM refused coverage the bank sued it in a Texas trial court. The trial court held for SCM and the bank appealed to the Texas Court of Appeals. It reversed the trial court decision and SCM appealed to the Texas Supreme Court.

At issue was whether the agent had the authority to cancel SCM's binder and obtain coverage with a different insurer. SCM asserted that because the driver had authorized the agent to obtain insurance, the agent was also authorized to accept

SCM's cancellation and obtain new insurance. The bank countered that the driver only authorized the agent to obtain insurance, not to accept cancellation. In holding for the bank the supreme court stated that the one who authorized an agent to obtain insurance did not necessarily give authority to accept cancellation. As lienholder, the bank was entitled to receive the policy proceeds. *Southern County Mut. Ins. Co. v. First Bank & Trust of Groves*, 750 S.W.2d 170 (Tex.1988).

In Tennessee a dispute arose between two insurance companies over which company was obligated to pay on a homeowner's policy. The insured had approached an agent for the purpose of insuring his home. The agent bound coverage for him but did not tell him the name of the insurer. A binder application was then sent to an insurer who declined to issue a policy due to high risk. Without consulting the homeowner, the agent then mailed a second binder application to an insurer which specialized in high risk policies. The day after the application was mailed the insured's house burned to the ground. The insured filed proofs of loss with both companies and both denied coverage. The company that had originally rejected the binder application filed suit in county court seeking a declaration that it was not liable for the loss. The court ruled that once the agent had placed the coverage with the first company a valid contract was formed between the insurer and the insured and the contract could not be altered or terminated by the agent. The insurer appealed and won a reversal from the Tennessee Court of Appeals.

That court noted that the agent possessed authority to bind either company. When the first company rejected coverage and the agent made a binder application to the high risk company, he had, in effect, terminated the first binder and then bound the high risk company. This was true regardless of the agent's failure to secure approval from the insured, because only binders were involved here, not actual policies of insurance. The appeals court held that the high risk insurer must bear the loss because its authorized agent had bound it to coverage. *Royal Ins. Co. v. Alliance Ins.Co.*, 690 S.W.2d 541 (Tenn.App.1985).

B. Insurers Not Bound

An agent for an insurer wrote a binder for fire insurance coverage for an applicant. However, the insurer discovered that there were too many risks involved. It told the agent to replace the policy immediately. The agent replaced the policy, but failed to reclaim the binder from the insured. A fire broke out, and the insurer became liable for coverage solely on the basis of the written binder. It then sued the agent to recover for the loss. The court held for the insurer, and the New York Supreme Court, Appellate Division, affirmed. The sole cause of the insurer's loss was the agent's breach of the agreement with the insurer to reclaim the binder. *General Accident Ins. Co. v. David C. Smith & Assoc.*, 584 N.Y.S.2d 900 (A.D.2d Dept.1992).

An Illinois man signed an application for disability insurance. The application provided a monthly disability benefit of $1,000. The insured was then injured and contacted the agent who gave the insured the necessary claim forms and a copy of the policy. The insured alleged that when he received the copy of the policy he noticed that the amount of the monthly benefit had been changed from $1,000 to $800. However, the agent assured him that a supplemental policy would be issued. The insured received no disability payments for the first two months. In the third month, however, he began receiving payments of $800 per month. The insurer testified that the agent did not have the power to bind the insurer to a policy. An Illinois trial court ruled in favor of the insurer. The insured then appealed to the Appellate Court of Illinois.

The appellate court agreed with the trial court that the insured had failed to produce clear and convincing evidence that the insurance policy was changed. The insured argued that since the agent was acting for the insurer, the insurer should be bound to the contract for disability benefits of $1,000 per month. The court decided that the agent was acting as a broker between the insured and the insurer. The broker solicits business from the public but is under no employment contract from a single insurer. Therefore, he had no authority to accept or enter into a contract on behalf of the insurance company. The appellate court then affirmed the trial court's decision that the plaintiff insured failed to produce evidence that there existed a contract for disability benefits of $1,000 per month. *Krause v. Pekin Life Ins. Co.*, 551 N.E.2d 395 (Ill.App.1st Dist.1990).

III. LICENSING

Insurance agents are required to be licensed under state legislation. The cases in this section involve legal challenges to the constitutionality of licensing statutes and license revocations.

A. Constitutionality of Agent Licensing Statutes

In 1974, the Commonwealth of Puerto Rico enacted a statute which established numerous requirements as prerequisites for licensing as an insurance consultant. One requirement was that all applicants for licensing must have resided in Puerto Rico for at least one year. Two consultants who operated an insurance consulting business in Pennsylvania attempted to obtain licensing in Puerto Rico, where they had also operated prior to the enactment of the statute. They were denied licensing because they failed to meet the residency requirement. One consultant was a charter member and past president of the Insurance Consultant's Society, and the other consultant had previously served as vice-president of the Society. After having been repeatedly turned down on their applications for licensing the consultants filed suit in a U.S. district court alleging that a denial of licensing on the basis of residency violated their constitutional rights. The district court agreed, holding that the statute was unconstitutional. The Commonwealth of Puerto Rico appealed.

The U.S. Court of Appeals, First Circuit, upheld the decision of the district court, stating that the Privileges and Immunities Clause of the U.S. Constitution "encourages a national economy by allowing persons to cross state lines freely in pursuit of economic gain." The government must advance important reasons in order to legitimately infringe upon this right. In this case, the discriminatory treatment of nonresidents was not justified by substantial reasons and therefore was constitutionally invalid. *Silver v. Garcia*, 760 F.2d 33 (1st Cir.1985).

A Florida statute requiring insurance agents to fulfill a one-year residency requirement before becoming licensed as general lines agents was also held in violation of the Privileges and Immunities Clause of the U.S. Constitution by the Florida District Court of Appeal. The suit was brought by an agent who had previously worked in Rhode Island. Because of the statute, the agent could not bind coverage, discuss questions about insurance policies with prospective insureds or write letters in regard to insured policies. In defense of the statute, it was argued that the statute tended to assure that agents are familiar with the special characteristics of Florida's insurance law before becoming licensed. The court stated that the residency requirement violated the privileges and immunities clause because newcomers to Florida were not convincingly shown to be a peculiar source of the problems. The lower court's decision to uphold the statute was reversed. *Scott v. Gunter*, 447 So.2d 272 (Fla.App.1st Dist.1983).

The constitutionality of a licensing statute was upheld in a Texas case where the statute was not linked to residency. An insurer doing business in Texas brought suit against the State Board of Insurance challenging a state statute which governed temporary life insurance agents' licenses. Under the statute, such licenses were issuable only upon certain conditions. The Court of Appeals of Texas upheld the constitutionality of the statute finding that the first condition, which required that an agent's application for a temporary license be accompanied by a certification executed by the insurer whom the agent would represent, assured the competence and training of agents.

The court also found that limiting temporary licensees to 250 in any calendar year, the second challenged condition, was presumptively constitutional and reasonable. The third condition provided that an agent holding a temporary license may not solicit or sell life insurance or annuity contract replacement policies. This condition was justified, in the court's view, by the Texas legislature's intent to minimize potential harm to holders of life policies that might be occasioned by ill-considered advice given by agents not yet sufficiently trained to analyze an existing policy. *Massachusetts Indem. & Life Ins.Co. v. Texas State Bd. of Ins.*, 685 S.W.2d 104 (Tex.App.3d Dist.1985).

B. Revocation and Suspension of Licensing

An insurance agent in Missouri was charged with fraudulently conducting insurance transactions by applying for loans to pay for one-year policies which were only in effect for six months. It was also alleged that he transacted insurance business through unlicensed persons. The division of insurance and the agent reached an agreement by which the agent's broker's license would be revoked, but not his agency license. The agent later pleaded guilty in federal court on charges of mail fraud. The insurance division director then suspended the agent's agency license for three years. The agent appealed to the Missouri Court of Appeals. On appeal, the director contended that the settlement entered into between the division and the agent did not prevent the director from suspending the agent's license at a later time. The court agreed. Public policy did not prevent the director from taking further action after the settlement, after a conviction was obtained. Protecting the public from a person who abused his rights under the license justified allowing the director this power. The court reversed the trial court's decision. *Newman v. Melahn*, 817 S.W.2d 588 (Mo.App.1991).

In 1985, a licensed life insurance agent in Montana was convicted of felony theft and ordered to pay a fine of $500 and serve 30 days in jail. Several months later, pursuant to a state statute governing occupations and following a hearing, the state insurance commissioner ordered that her license be revoked. A district court reversed the commissioner's decision and the commissioner appealed to the Montana Supreme Court. The commissioner challenged the district court's holding that he had to conduct an investigation provided for in a Montana licensing statute before revoking an insurance agent's license pursuant to a different statute governing occupations. The statute governing occupations provided that the insurance commissioner may suspend an agent's license if the agent was convicted of a felony involving moral turpitude. The supreme court observed that one of the problems faced by ex-felons was that the statute governing occupations automatically barred them from ever engaging in licensed occupations even though the offense may have had no relation to the occupation sought. Because the revocation of the agent's license was based solely on her conviction of felony theft, and no effort was made to find whether her conviction related to the public health, welfare and safety as it applied to selling insurance, the district court's decision in the agent's favor was affirmed. The case was remanded for further proceedings. *Mills v. Comm'r of Ins.*, 736 P.2d 102 (Mont.1987).

A North Dakota insurance agent sold an insured two insurance policies providing Medicare supplement coverage and nursing home coverage. At the time of the sale, the agent knew that the insured already had four other policies providing Medicare supplement coverage and two other nursing home policies. An administrative complaint was filed against the agent alleging that he sold unnecessary or excessive coverage to the insured. Following an administrative hearing, the commissioner determined that the agent had acted in violation of North Dakota law. The commissioner ordered the agent to pay a civil penalty of $600 and suspended his license to sell insurance for three months. The agent appealed to a North Dakota trial court which affirmed the commissioner's decision. The agent then appealed to the Supreme Court of North Dakota.

The agent asserted that the commissioner's finding that he sold unnecessary or excessive insurance coverage to the insured was not supported by the evidence. The court, however, disagreed and determined that the record clearly established that the agent sold the insured additional policies when he was admittedly aware that the insured already had sufficient coverage. The agent asserted that it was his intent to replace the insured's other policies. The court determined that if the agent had truly wanted to provide replacement coverage, he could have written the policies with a delayed effective date but since the policies took effect immediately, the agent guaranteed that there would be lengthy and costly overlaps in the insured's coverage. Therefore, the appellate court upheld the decision of the trial court. *Gust v. Pomeroy*, 466 N.W.2d 137 (N.D.1991).

An Illinois insurance broker's license was revoked. After an administrative hearing in which the hearing officer upheld the revocation, the broker appealed to an Illinois trial court which ordered additional depositions and eventually reversed the administrative order. The department of insurance appealed to the Appellate Court of Illinois. The appellate court noted that the trial court erred in allowing additional depositions that were not part of the administrative proceeding. The appellate court also stated that the trial court was without jurisdiction as the broker had not exhausted his administrative remedies. Further, the court found that since there was sufficient evidence to uphold the administrative hearing officer's decision, the license revocation would be upheld. The appellate court reversed the decision of the trial court and upheld the revocation. *Gezendorf v. Washburn*, 565 N.E.2d 1054 (Ill.App. 2d Dist.1991).

A Florida agent's license to sell insurance was revoked due to misconduct. The Florida Department of Insurance filed a ten-count administrative complaint against the insurance agent, alleging that he had directed his agency to sell accidental death and dismemberment policies to clients who thought they were only purchasing personal injury protection. An administrative hearing officer concluded that the agent had sold insurance without full disclosure and adequate explanation, and imposed the following penalties: license revocation (to be suspended for two years upon the payment of a $2,000 fine) and remission of the revocation upon a showing of no further violations after two years. However, the department of insurance later increased the penalty to unconditional revocation of all licensing. The agent appealed the department's action to the Florida District Court of Appeal. Finding that the department had based its conclusions on competent evidence, the court refused to disturb its revocation of the agent's licensing. The penalty imposed by the department was deemed to be within the scope of its statutory authority to regulate the business of insurance. *Devor v. Dep't. of Ins.*, 473 So.2d 1319 (Fla.App.1st Dist.1985).

IV. AGENCY/BROKERAGE AGREEMENTS

A. Breach of Contract—Generally

The following cases involve insurance agency agreements made with insurers.

An independent insurance agency in South Carolina represented an insurer in the sale of personal and commercial insurance lines. The agency agreements were cancelable upon written notice. The insurer gave notice to the agency that, because of overall unprofitability on the personal lines of insurance, it would terminate the agency agreement covering personal lines. The agency brought suit to compel the insurer to reinstate the agency contract. A federal district court found that the insurer had violated South Carolina law by canceling the agreement so as to reduce the volume of automobile insurance being sold. However, the court found inadequate evidence of damages, and refused to reinstate the agency contract because the insurer had withdrawn from the South Carolina auto insurance market. On appeal to the U.S. Court of Appeals, Fourth Circuit, the court agreed with the district court's ruling that the cancellation of the agency agreement was done to reduce the volume of auto insurance being carried. The court also found that the district court should have held a hearing on the issue of damages. The appellate court directed the district court to consider the agency's request for an injunctive order requiring the insurer to reinstate the personal lines division, minus auto insurance, which was properly cancelled. The court affirmed in part the district court's decision, and remanded the case. *Insurance Services of Beaufort v. AETNA Casualty & Surety Co.*, 966 F.2d 847 (4th Cir.1992).

An independent Iowa agent was very successful in selling a particular insurer's products and received substantial renewal commissions. In order to stimulate sales, the insurer developed a new life policy and encouraged current customers to replace their existing policy with the new product. It also hired an outside marketing team which solicited the independent agent's customer list, threatening his right to renewal commissions. The agent complained and his employment was terminated. He sued the insurer in an Iowa trial court, alleging that the distribution of his customer list was unlawful and deprived him of renewal commissions, and that the insurer was liable for tortious interference with business relations. At trial, the complaint was amended to seek punitive damages. A state court awarded both actual and punitive damages, and the insurer appealed to the Supreme Court of Iowa. The appellate court held that both agents and insurers were free to solicit customer lists absent an express agreement to the contrary, which was not found in this case. Evidence of industry custom did not establish a contract providing for renewal commissions. The remaining claims by the agent were that the insurer intentionally interfered with existing and prospective business relationships. The facts of this case supported both of the agent's claims, because the customer list was distributed prior to the agent's termination. The lower court's allowance of the amended complaint seeking punitive damages was held incorrect, and the case was remanded for an accurate determination of damages. *Burke v. Hawkeye National Life Ins. Co.*, 474 N.W.2d 110 (Iowa 1991).

An insurance company cancelled the agency agreement of a Texas agent. The agent filed suit against the insurance company in a state trial court for failing to comply with the Texas Insurance Code, and for refusing to renew policies or issue new coverage, contrary to the agency-insurer agreement. The trial court dismissed the complaint, and the agent appealed to the Texas Court of Appeals. The court of appeals stated that the agent had been bound to first pursue his complaint with the State Board of Insurance. Having failed to do so, his complaint had been properly dismissed. *Linick v. Employers Mutual Casualty Co.*, 822 S.W.2d 297 (Tex.App.1991).

Two insurance agents formed a partnership to sell insurance and sold a one year health policy to a business. The policy allowed the business to change the agent of record, and two years later the business renewed its policy and listed one of the agents as the sole agent. The other partner no longer received half of the renewal commissions. He sued the insurer seeking commissions, and added claims against the business and the other agent for intentional interference with the contractual relationship between himself and the insurer. A state court granted the defendants' motion for summary judgment and the partner appealed to the Supreme Court of Alabama.

The court noted that an agent in Alabama had no inherent right to renewal commissions. The right to such commissions must arise contractually. The agent's agreement stated that the insurer was obligated to the agent only as long as he was the designated agent of record. The partner argued that the business had waived its right to change the designation when it signed the designation on the original policy which remained effective "until termination of said contract." The court recognized that the policy was for only a single year, and held that the termination of the contract occurred at the end of that year. The right to change was not waived. The court further ruled that an absence of other changes upon renewal of the policy was irrelevant. The claim for contractual interference against the agent of record and the business also failed; again the court explained that the contract had ended. The lower court's decision was affirmed. *Crockett v. Great-West Life Assur. Co.*, 578 So.2d 1290 (Ala.1991).

A Missouri insurance agent entered into an oral agreement with the insurance agency wherein the agent was advanced a monthly payment to maintain his current standard of living. The parties contemplated that the agent would repay the advances through commission payments received from the sale of insurance. After the agent had been employed for thirteen months, all employees in the agency were terminated. The insurance agency brought suit against the agent seeking to recover the advance payments made to him. The trial court granted summary judgment in favor of the insurance agency and the agent appealed to the Missouri Court of Appeals.

The agent contended that the agency failed to prove breach of any contract or in the alternative that the agency failed in its obligations under the contract. The court noted that it was not necessary that there be an express agreement to repay the loan in this case because an agreement to repay could be implied from the circumstances. The court then addressed the agent's contention that the agency was required to provide him with three years of employment and had breached its obligation to do so. The court noted that the agent testified that he did not feel that he was obligated to stay for three years and that he would have to pay back the advances if he left before three years. Therefore, the court ruled that the agency was not prevented from collecting the advances because there was an agreement on the part of the agent to repay the advances. *Tom Davis Ins. Agency Inc. v. Shivley*, 799 S.W.2d 195 (Mo.App.1990).

In a case arising in Puerto Rico, an insurance agency brought suit against a Florida insurer alleging that the insurer breached its "General Agent's Agreement." The lawsuit was prompted by the insurer's termination of the agency agreement without cause. The Puerto Rican insurance agency claimed that it had acted as the exclusive general agent of the insurer in the issuance of insurance policies covering the borrowers of several small loan companies doing business in Puerto Rico. The agency further alleged that, after gaining a foothold on the Puerto Rico market through the agency, the insurer had conspired with companies to deflect the agency's business to other local insurers, afterwards selling them reinsurance. In this way, the argument continued, the agency had been gradually phased out until, as a final step, its contract was terminated without cause. The U.S. Court of Appeals, First Circuit, held in favor of the insurer, finding that the agent's agreement was null and void because of the agency's lack of a general agent's license. *Caribbean Ins. Servs. v. American Bankers Life Assur. Co. of Florida*, 754 F.2d 2 (1st Cir.1985).

In a Georgia case, an independent insurance agent and an insurance company entered into an agency contract. In the event the insurance company desired to terminate the agency contract, the following procedures were to be followed: consideration was to be given to a successor that the agent would nominate, provided that the successor was acceptable to the insurance company; the agent could then negotiate with his successor to receive the value of the good will of his customers. The contract also provided that if no successor were nominated, and if the company refused to purchase the agency at a specified price, the agent and company would each have the right to solicit the policyholders on their own behalf. The insurance company, however, failed to follow these procedures. It sent a notice to the agent which stated that his agency contract was being terminated immediately and that all his former customers had been contacted and assigned to another agent. The agent filed suit in state court, seeking money damages for breach of contract and interference with the implied contract with his customers. A jury awarded the agent

$40,000 in compensatory damages and $100,000 in punitive damages. The insurance company appealed to the Georgia Court of Appeals, which reversed the $100,000 punitive damage award. It held that an error in the jury verdict form rendered the punitive damage award null and void. However, the $40,000 award of compensatory damages for breach of agency contract was affirmed. *Preferred Risk Ins. Co. v. Boykin*, 329 S.E.2d 900 (Ga.App.1985).

B. "No Competition" Agreements

Courts will uphold "no competition" agreements between insurance companies and agents or agencies, but only if they are narrowly drawn and have a limited duration. If a court finds that a noncompetition agreement is unduly harsh or burdensome, or deprives a person of his or her livelihood, the agreement will not be enforced.

An agent signed a covenant not to compete in the same geographical area in which he practiced within two years after his separation from a business insurer. The agent resigned, and began to sell other types of insurance to his previous customers. The insurer brought an action to enforce the covenant not to compete. A trial court refused, and the issue came before the Court of Appeals of Arkansas. The restraint imposed on a former employee by a covenant not to compete must not be greater than reasonably necessary. The agent argued that the restraint was overbroad because it prohibited him from selling types of insurance which his previous employer did not offer. The insurer contended that it did not want competition even in types of insurance it did not now write. The court found that this restraint would stop the employee from selling insurance, and therefore found the clause to be overbroad. A severability clause in the employee's contract was ignored because a court will not rewrite a covenant not to compete in order to give a lawful effect. The decision in favor of the agent was affirmed. *Federated Mutual Ins. Co. v. Bennett*, 818 S.W.2d 596 (Ark.App.1991).

An Alabama agent entered into an employment contract with an insurance company. The contract contained a no compete clause, which stated that the employee agreed not to compete in any way with his employer for five years after his termination, within a radius of fifty miles. The employer terminated the agent's employment after one year. The employee had access to the company's customer list, but did not take it with him when he left. The employee then entered into a partnership to sell insurance with another company in the same city. The former employer sought an injunction in an Alabama trial court, attempting to enforce the no compete clause. The trial court denied the relief requested, and the case was appealed to the Supreme Court of Alabama.
The supreme court acknowledged that public policy generally disfavors contracts which restrain employment, but stated that courts will enforce them if the restrictions are reasonable and if the employer has a protectable interest. In this case, the court held that the company's interest was not substantial enough or unique enough to be protectable. It also ruled that the restriction imposed an undue hardship on the departing employee and therefore was unreasonable in relation to the company's interest. The court affirmed the trial court's decision denying the injunction. *Sheffield v. Stoudenmire*, 553 So.2d 125 (Ala.1989).

In December 1985, an insurer sued a former agent alleging that he had taken employment with another insurer and had induced several agents to leave the first insurer for the second. It further alleged that in doing so, the agent violated a no competition agreement. The North Carolina Court of Appeals held that North Carolina courts did not recognize claims based upon malicious interference with employment contracts terminable at will (employment agreements which can be terminated by the employer or employee at any time) within the context of a competitive business setting. It also observed that there was no evidence that the agent or those he allegedly induced to leave had solicited or serviced any of the first insurer's policy holders. The court of appeals held that the agent did not violate the no competition agreement. *Peoples Security Life Ins. Co. v. Hooks*, 357 S.E.2d 411 (N.C.App. 1987).

An insurance agency in Illinois which specialized in general aviation insurance filed suit in an Illinois circuit court to obtain an injunction preventing a former employee from using its confidential customer policy expiration lists to solicit accounts for his own insurance agency. The company alleged that while the employee was its vice-president and agency manager in charge of operations, he secretly compiled an extensive handwritten list of hundreds of its customers and pertinent information on each of the accounts. After he left the company and formed his own insurance agency, the majority of his new accounts were prior customers of the company. The circuit court issued an injunction precluding the former employee from soliciting the company's accounts for a period of one year. He appealed. The Illinois Appellate Court held that the evidence supported the circuit court's conclusion that the former employee was using the plaintiff's expiration lists to sell insurance in his own agency. The decision of the circuit court was affirmed. The former employee was ordered to stop soliciting the plaintiff's accounts. *Burt Dickens & Co. v. Bodi*, 494 N.E.2d 817 (Ill.App.1st Dist.1986).

Prudential Insurance Company brought suit against a former agent who had sold whole-life insurance policies. After he had worked for Prudential for seven years his employment was terminated. He then became affiliated with an insurance brokerage firm and acted as an agent for several other companies in the same region, often selling new life insurance policies to Prudential policyholders. As a result, several policyholders canceled their Prudential policies. Prudential alleged that the agent breached an implied covenant of good faith and had a duty to refrain from doing anything that would adversely affect Prudential's rights. Prudential claimed that the agent had "intentionally and maliciously" caused the premature termination of Prudential life insurance policies that he had either sold or serviced when he was employed with Prudential.

The Appellate Court of Illinois first observed that although the agent had signed an employment agreement when he was employed by Prudential, the agreement contained no covenant not to compete. The court stated that the obligations of good faith and loyalty generally do not apply after the termination of the agency relationship. The court then ruled that after the termination of an agency, an agent who has gone into the same business may lawfully solicit the future business of his former employer's customers. Prudential's claims were dismissed. *Prudential Ins. Co. of America v. McCurry*, 492 N.E.2d 1026 (Ill.App.3d Dist.1986).

C. Bonus Renewal Commissions

North Carolina insurance agents and agency managers brought suit against an insurer which employed them contending that they were entitled to bonus renewal commissions pursuant to their employment agreements. The insurer disagreed with the agents, saying that their employment contracts provided for the payment of a bonus renewal commission only if its loss ratio permitted. The agents and the agency managers sought judicial relief in a North Carolina trial court, which held for the insurer. They appealed.

The Court of Appeals of North Carolina affirmed the trial court ruling, holding that the insurer was under no obligation to pay a bonus renewal commission by virtue of the loss ratio provision. The loss ratio precondition was bargained for and understood. By entering into their respective agreements, the agents and the agency managers accepted the risk that the loss ratio might exceed sixty-three percent for a given year and that their bonus and renewal commissions would not be paid. The decision in favor of the insurer was upheld. *Fraver v. North Carolina Farm Bureau Mut. Ins. Co.*, 318 S.E.2d 340 (N.C.App.1984).

In an Oklahoma case, an insurance agent was terminated following several months of bitterness between the agent and his district manager. The district manager offered the agent a check for the contract value of the agency arrangement according to the terms of the agent's employment contract. The agent returned the check and sued for his right to future income from renewal premiums. The Oklahoma Supreme Court held that the agent's employer wrongfully terminated the agent for the purpose of depriving him of future income from renewal premiums. This act was a breach of the implied covenant of good faith. The company was held liable for damages in the amount of $225,000. *Hall v. Farmers Ins. Exchange*, 713 P.2d 1027 (Okl.1985).

D. Redlining

The following cases involve challenges to "redlining," the practice of territorial calculation of insurance rates based on the insured's place of residence.

Several parties including the Southern Christian Leadership Conference (SCLC), the city of Compton and several taxpayers sued the California Department of Insurance and the Farmers Insurance Exchange seeking a court declaration that California Insurance Code § 11628 was unconstitutional and that Farmers' redlining practices violated the state civil rights act and the state constitution.

The court of appeal observed that the purpose of § 11628 was the "eradication of discrimination between persons *within* a particular geographic area by licensed insurers." It upheld the superior court decision in favor of the department. Read together with § 1852, § 11628 was to be construed to prohibit insurers, the commissioner and the department from "differentiating" or discriminating" or permitting discrimination or differentiation on the basis of sex, race, language, color, religion, national origin, ancestry or wealth regardless of where the insured lived in California. The differentiation in rates between geographical areas was permissible solely when the rate differential was based on substantial, actual and verifiable loss experience in each geographical area. The act prohibited insurers from discriminating on the above criteria *within* such geographical areas. The superior court decision was affirmed. *Compton v. Bunner*, 243 Cal.Rptr. 100 (Cal.App.2d Dist.1988).

In an Illinois case, a black insurance agent challenged his employer's alleged redlining practice under the Fair Housing Act and Civil Rights Act. The agent claimed that the employer-insurer's practice of excluding sections of black community areas from hazard insurance coverage prevented him from selling property insurance to black friends and acquaintances. He sued the insurance company in a U.S. district court in Illinois, which held in the insurer's favor. The insurance agent appealed.

The U.S. Court of Appeals, Fourth Circuit, affirmed the district court's ruling, saying that the agent had no claim under the Civil Rights Act because, unlike the plaintiffs in the preceding case, he was not the appropriate person to bring the suit. He did not claim to be the victim of racial discrimination but only alleged that he lost opportunities to sell insurance to black friends and acquaintances. There was no impediment to a suit by any black individuals who were denied property insurance because of the insurer's alleged discriminatory practice. Further, there was no claim under the Fair Housing Act because that act makes it unlawful to discriminate in terms of the sale of residential buildings and in any services connected with the sale of houses. Thus, the agent's suit was properly dismissed. *Mackey v. Nationwide Ins. Cos.*, 724 F.2d 419 (4th Cir.1984).

V. EMPLOYMENT MATTERS

A. Race, Sex and Age Discrimination

Although the McCarran-Ferguson Act exempts insurers from many federal controls, insurers are nevertheless prohibited by federal civil rights legislation and state civil rights commissions from discriminating in employment on the basis of race, sex or age.

An insurance company lost several examiners in its medical claims department at the same time that its number of claims increased significantly. It interviewed and offered a position to a woman with limited experience. Upon making the offer the company explained that formal training took approximately six months, and that examiners generally required over a year to reach efficiency. On her first day of work the woman revealed that she was four months pregnant. The company then withdrew the offer of employment and explained that her required leave of absence would interfere with the training period. The woman claimed pregnancy discrimination and filed suit in a federal district court. The employer explained that the interruption in training decreased her value to the company. It testified that any leave of absence would have the same effect, and lead to the same action. This justification was examined in light of the U.S. Supreme Court's rule that the "dispositive issue is whether a challenged action serves, [in] any significant way, the employment goals of the employer." The woman failed to establish that the true reason for the action was to intentionally discriminate on the basis of pregnancy, and her claim failed. *Ahmad v. Loyal American Life Insurance Co.*, 767 F.Supp. 1114 (S.D.Ala.1991).

An insurer hired agents as independent contractors. They in turn hired employees of their own. A New York woman worked for one of the agents as a sales assistant and was allegedly raped by one of the independent agents. She then initiated demands for corrective action. Instead, she was fired approximately three months after the attack. She filed a discrimination charge with the Equal Employment Opportunity Commission (EEOC), alleging that the insurer had attempted to suppress her complaints against its agent and then had retaliated against her for refusing to drop her complaint by coercing the agent who employed her into firing her. She brought suit against the insurer under Title VII of the Civil Rights Act of 1964. The insurer moved for summary judgment. After finding that the employee had correctly filed a claim with the EEOC (a prerequisite to filing a Title VII action), the court turned to the question of whether the insurer could be liable under Title VII. The agent who employed the woman never had 15 employees and thus could not qualify as a Title VII employer. Further, the insurer was never the woman's employer. However, the court noted that, in the Second Circuit, the absence of a direct employment relationship does not bar a Title VII claim. In this case, if the insurer had "interfered with her employment opportunities," it could be liable under Title VII. The court denied the summary judgment motion, and allowed the case to proceed to trial. *Matthews v. New York Life Ins. Co.*, 780 F.Supp. 1019 (S.D.N.Y.1992).

An agent signed a contract with an insurer which allowed him to sell insurance as an independent contractor. The contract prohibited the agent from advertising the insurer's policies without written consent; it prohibited him from soliciting any other insurance without written consent; and it prevented him from modifying or waiving prescribed requirements in the insurance applications. The agent was paid on a commission basis, and filed his taxes as a self-employed individual. When the insurer terminated the contract, the agent filed suit under the Age Discrimination in Employment Act (ADEA). A federal district court ruled that the agent was not an employee for purposes of the ADEA, and he appealed to the U.S. Court of Appeals, Tenth Circuit. On appeal, the agent argued that the amount of control exercised by the insurer over him was sufficient to grant him employee status. The appellate court disagreed. It used a test which looked partly at economic realities, but mostly at "the employer's right to control the means and manner of the worker's performance," and determined that the agent was not an employee under the ADEA. The agent's performance was subject to virtually no restrictions. The court thus affirmed the holding in favor of the insurer. *Oestman v. National Farmers Union Ins. Co.*, 958 F.2d 303 (10th Cir.1992).

A man who had worked as a debit manager and as an insurance salesman sought work through an employment agency. The agency arranged an interview with a representative of a fraternal benefit society which sold insurance to its members. The man alleged that the representative said, "We do not sell to niggers, we do not hire niggers..." The man alleged that the benefit society's representative later told the employment agency that the man's employment as a commission-only salesman "just wouldn't work out" because he was married to a black woman. The man never turned in an application for the job. The representative, however, said he told the man that his interracial marriage would make success with the benefit society "very difficult," because he would have to work very closely with the membership to obtain leads to potential new members. The man sued the benefit society alleging that it had violated both Title VII and § 1981 for discrimination based on an interracial marriage. The case was remanded to the U.S. district court for trial.

On remand, the U.S. district court ruled that because the man failed to actually apply for the job, he had failed to establish a *prima facie* case of racial discrimination. Further, the court declared that even if the man had applied for the job and had been turned down, his lawsuit could not have succeeded because he would have been "nothing more than a test plaintiff" who could not have been damaged by the benefits society's failure to hire because he was not genuinely interested in the job. For these reasons the court ruled in favor of the benefit society. *Parr v. Woodmen of the World Life Ins. Society*, 657 F.Supp. 1022 (M.D.Ga.1987).

An agent brought suit against the insurance company she represented under Title VII of the Civil Rights Act of 1964, alleging that she had been discriminated against on the basis of her sex. The insurer filed a motion for summary judgment claiming that she was an independent contractor, not an employee and therefore not entitled to protection under Title VII. The federal district court denied the motion and proceeded to trial to determine the nature of the agent's employment relationship with the insurer. The employer's right to control is the most important factor in determining the employment status of an individual. Although the insurer limited the geographical area in which the agent worked, it did not place any restrictions on which customers the agent could contact. The agent was not required to account for her daily activities nor adhere to a specific work schedule. Also significant was the fact that the agent received no salary; her entire compensation consisted of commissions and incentive bonuses. The sole factor pointing in the favor of employee status was that the insurer provided office space, secretarial support and all necessary supplies. However, this was not sufficient to outweigh the other factors in favor of independent contractor status. *Knight v. United Farm Bureau Mut. Ins. Co.*, 742 F.Supp. 518 (N.D.Ind.1990)

A black Texas insurance agent had been one of the most highly successful and compensated employees in his district. After the agent indicated to the district manager that he wanted to be promoted to sales manager, the district manager offered him the promotion. The agent told the district manager that he would accept the position only on the condition that he would be guaranteed a substantial increase over the amount other sales managers received. The company refused to deviate from its policy and another applicant was given the job. At other times it was again made clear by the company that it wanted to promote the agent if he would accept a sales manager position under the same conditions as would be applicable to any other employee, but the agent refused. The agent then filed an action in a federal district court alleging employment discrimination based on race. The court determined that the insurance company had articulated a legitimate, nondiscriminatory reason for its action. It appeared that the insurance company did not promote the agent because the agent had indicated he would not accept the position under normal conditions applicable to all employees regardless of race. He wanted a higher compensation which the insurance company was unwilling to provide. The court held for the insurance company. *Linder v. Prudential Ins. Co. of America*, 743 F.Supp. 1237 (W.D.Tex. 1990).

An African American man worked for an Illinois insurance agency as a regional director of agency (RDA). As an RDA, the man served as a liaison between the insurer and independent insurance agents. In April of 1985, the employee filed a charge of discrimination against the insurer with the Equal Employment Opportunity Commission (EEOC) claiming that the insurer was paying him less than white RDAs. Without admitting liability, the insurer settled the EEOC charge by compensating the employee for the alleged disparity and raising his annual salary. The employee

Sec. V   EMPLOYMENT MATTERS   77

was later discharged in January of 1986. The insurer claimed that it discharged the employee solely because it found that he submitted numerous fraudulent expense reports. The employee, without denying that he defrauded the insurer on numerous occasions, argued that he was fired because of his race, and testified that he was the target of racial and ethnic jokes and remarks at the agency. The employee then filed a discrimination suit in a federal district court which granted summary judgment for the employer. The employee appealed to the U.S. Court of Appeals, Seventh Circuit. The appellate court noted that even if the employee had been able to make a *prima facie* case of discrimination, the record convincingly showed that he was fired because he committed expense account fraud and not because he was black. Therefore, the appellate court upheld the trial court's decision. *McCarthy v. Kemper Life Ins. Cos.*, 924 F.2d 683 (7th Cir.1991).

A black Ohio woman was employed at an insurance agency for approximately one and one-half years. The agency owner, also black, allegedly told the office manager that he wanted to expand his office to include white employees because they were good for business. The agency was in a predominantly white area. However, there was no evidence that business suffered because it was run by blacks. The agency's employee turnover rate was high and eventually the office manager was fired. A white man was hired to replace her. This office manager was put at a desk in view of the public, while the black employee was put at a desk not visible to the public. The office manager and the black employee did not get along and had many hostile confrontations. Finally, the office manager threatened to resign if something was not done. The agency owner tried to work the problem out, but finally fired the black employee. After this action, the owner continued to hire blacks. The former employee sued in a federal district court under 42 U.S.C. § 1981, which prohibits discrimination in the formation and enforcement of contracts.

The district court denied the employee's claim, stating that she had failed to prove that the employer had purposefully or detrimentally discriminated against her on the basis of race. A lawsuit could not be based on her own subjective belief that she was fired because of her race. She had failed to prove that white employees similarly situated to her were treated differently. The agency was not liable. *Lewis v. Rucker*, 721 F.Supp. 929 (S.D.Ohio 1989).

A 55-year-old insurance marketing representative was hired by a branch office in 1975. His duties consisted of acting as an intermediary between the insurance company and independent agents. The employee's supervisor became concerned about his effectiveness. Although the amount of business brought in by the employee rose by fifteen percent, the supervisor pointed out that the employee was not only required to meet dollar production goals, but was also required to meet goals concerning new agency appointments and sales of diverse types of policies. When the employee continued to fail to meet these goals, the supervisor fired him. The employee sued the insurer in a U.S. district court, winning a jury verdict of $68,223 for lost wages. The jury doubled that amount based on its finding that the supervisor had acted with discriminatory intent. The district court judge set aside the verdict. The U.S. Court of Appeals, Eighth Circuit, reversed the district court judge's action. It held that the employee's evidence was persuasive enough to support the verdict. The employee had been a high total dollar production achiever, and the supervisor's written evaluations of his work were contradictory and inconsistent. The court of appeals therefore reinstated the jury's verdict, including the award of double damages. *Clements v. General Accident Ins. Co. of America,* 821 F.2d 489 (8th Cir.1987)

The Age Discrimination in Employment Act (ADEA) makes it unlawful for employers to discriminate against individuals based upon age. The act extends to employment compensation, terms, conditions and privileges. An exception to the ADEA states that employers may operate employee benefit plans not enacted with intent to avoid the antidiscrimination provisions of the ADEA. A corporation maintained a group life insurance program providing life and disability insurance benefits to its employees. Employees also received life insurance benefits payable upon death. Unlike younger employees, corporate employees over age sixty were ineligible to receive disability benefits. The program had been instituted before passage of the ADEA. The Equal Employment Opportunity Commission (EEOC) sued the corporation in a federal district court, alleging that it violated the ADEA. It sought an order which would direct the corporation to remedy the age-based benefit disparity among its employees. The court dismissed the lawsuit. The EEOC appealed to the U.S. Court of Appeals, Tenth Circuit. The court ruled that the corporation's plan was exempt from the ADEA because it was not enacted to avoid the antidiscrimination law. Because the corporation had instituted the group life insurance program before the enactment of the ADEA, it was not required to present evidence to justify the disparate treatment between employees based upon age. The appeals court affirmed the district court's dismissal of the lawsuit. *EEOC v. Cargill, Inc.,* 855 F.2d 682 (10th Cir.1988).

A Colorado group insurance policy covered pregnancy complications but excluded normal pregnancy expenses. An employee filed a claim but the insurer denied coverage. She filed charges with the Colorado Civil Rights Commission alleging that the failure to provide a policy affording benefits for normal pregnancy constituted discrimination. The commission found the policy discriminatory and ordered the employer and insurer to pay medical expenses. The insurer appealed to the Colorado Court of Appeals which reversed the decision. The employee then appealed to the Colorado Supreme Court. The insurer asserted that it could not be held liable for aiding and abetting a discriminatory employment practice because its insurance form was approved by the state insurance commissioner. The supreme court held that the prohibition against discriminatory employment practices applied to the insurer. Thus, the insurer could not avoid responsibility for conduct aiding and abetting a discriminatory employment practice. The aiding and abetting prohibition reflected a recent legislative determination to decrease discrimination. Providing a comprehensive health insurance policy that excluded normal pregnancy costs was discriminatory. The insurer knew that provision applied only to female employees. Thus, the insurer was obligated to pay for the normal pregnancy costs. *Colorado Civil Rights Comm'n v. Travelers Ins. Co.,* 759 P.2d 1358 (Col.1988).

A female claims processor employed by a Colorado insurance company brought a sex discrimination suit in U.S. district court against her employer under Title VII of the Civil Rights Act. The woman had been employed as a claims processor for nine years. Although her duties were clerical in nature, she was required to obtain state licensing in several fields of insurance. During the course of her employment she made numerous requests for promotion to the position of insurance sales agent or broker. The district court concluded that the employer's decision not to promote the woman was justified. However, the court also found that the employer had retaliated against the woman for bringing suit and awarded damages and attorney's fees. The insurance company did not contest this finding. The woman appealed from the court's determination that the failure to promote her was not based upon her sex.

The U.S. Court of Appeals, Tenth Circuit, observed that all agents and brokers of the insurance company had extensive backgrounds in insurance work. Such experience was a necessary job requirement, and just because the woman had nine years of clerical experience did not qualify her to assume the duties and responsibilities of an agent. Because the insurance company had given legitimate, nondiscriminatory reasons for not promoting her, the court upheld the ruling that the woman was not entitled to a promotion. *Hickman v. Flood & Peterson Ins.*, 766 F.2d 422 (10th Cir.1985).

B. Collective Bargaining

Insurance company and agency collective bargaining and unionization matters are solely under the authority of the federal government by virtue of the National Labor Relations Act.

A union filed a petition with the National Labor Relations Board (NLRB) seeking to represent a unit of office employees at an insurer's Massachusetts district office. After the NLRB included the insurer's assistant district manager (as a prospective union member) in a pre-election hearing, the insurer contended that the assistant district manager's inclusion was improper because she was a confidential managerial employee, rather than an office employee. The NLRB concluded that the assistant district manager was not a confidential managerial employee and allowed her to participate in a secret ballot election. The insurer then asked the U.S. Court of Appeals, Fourth Circuit, to review the NLRB's determination.

One of the questions before the court of appeals was whether the NLRB was wrong in concluding that the assistant district manager did not assist or act in a confidential capacity to the district manager (who exercised managerial functions in the field of labor relations). The court of appeals held that the assistant district manager did serve in a confidential capacity and that therefore she should not have been included within the office bargaining unit. The insurer's job description questionnaire for the assistant district manager position described it as "confidential." The assistant district manager also testified that the insurer told her that her job was confidential. Furthermore, the assistant district manager had access to confidential correspondence between the insurer's home office and district office. The court of appeals remanded the case to the NLRB for it to determine whether a new election was necessary. *Prudential Ins. Co. of America v. NLRB*, 832 F.2d 857 (4th Cir.1987).

When an Illinois insurance agent who possessed a contract of employment with an insurance agents' association attempted to organize an agents' union, the insurance association allegedly retaliated against the agent. He sued in state court contending that the association had refused to give him quotes for insurance, among other things. He asserted that this amounted to a constructive discharge in retaliation for his union-organizing activities. The trial court dismissed his complaint and the Appellate Court of Illinois affirmed. Congress has stated that the National Labor Relations Board (NLRB) possesses exclusive jurisdiction over unfair labor practices such as these. A lawsuit thus could not be brought in state court because it would constitute a preemption of the power of the NLRB to regulate union matters. The dismissal of the agent's complaint was affirmed. *Beaird v. Miller's Mut. Ins. Ass'n of Illinois*, 479 N.E.2d 374 (Ill.App.5th Dist.1985).

Iowa law required insurance carriers to write policies through licensed resident agents. The law further required agents to countersign the carrier's endorsement. Until the mid-1980s, Allstate distributed its unrepresented policies to its agent closest to the insured interest. The agent would then countersign the policy and receive a commission. Allstate later instituted the practice of countersigning unrepresented policies under the computer-generated signature of a single agent. A group of Allstate agents filed a class action lawsuit against the carrier in an Iowa trial court. After transfer of the case to the state insurance commissioner and the filing of a second lawsuit, the case returned to the trial court which consolidated the cases and granted the carrier's summary judgment motion.

The agents appealed to the Iowa Court of Appeals. The agents argued that summary judgment was inappropriate because a fact dispute existed as to whether Allstate's procedure complied with Iowa law. They claimed that the computer-generated signatures were impermissible because they were not the writing or mark of the person whose signature was required and that they constituted a signature in blank. The court of appeals agreed with the carrier and the commissioner that the computer-generated signatures did not violate Iowa law. There was no evidence that the agent whose name was printed did not intend to be legally bound or intend to have his name affixed to the policies. There was no basis for the aggrieved agents to claim commissions because they had not performed any services. The court affirmed the trial court's grant of summary judgment for the carrier. *Wilkens v. Iowa Ins. Commissioner*, 457 N.W.2d 1 (Iowa App.1990).

C. Adjusters

The Pennsylvania Insurance Adjustment Bureau sued the Pennsylvania Insurance Commissioner in a state trial court. The bureau challenged a Pennsylvania law which prohibited insurance adjusters from soliciting disaster victims within twenty-four hours of a catastrophe. It argued that the twenty-four hour ban impermissibly restricted freedom of speech. The bureau also argued that property owners often failed to take necessary steps to protect their property which would lead to a prompt and fair settlement. The trial court held for the commissioner and the bureau appealed to the Pennsylvania Supreme Court.

The issue on appeal was whether the restriction was reasonably related to the state's interest in prohibiting insurance adjuster fraud. The bureau argued that the twenty-four hour restriction was improper because it was necessary to contact the property owners before they moved to a temporary location. The bureau also argued that anti-fraud laws sufficiently protected disaster victims from unscrupulous practices. The commissioner asserted that the state had the authority to regulate the time, place and manner in which adjusters could solicit business. He also asserted that adjusters who solicited within twenty-four hours may use fraudulent practices at a time when disaster victims were particularly vulnerable. Although the supreme court held that the state had an interest in protecting disaster victims, the regulation did not directly advance that interest. The regulation of misleading and fraudulent behavior could be more effectively accomplished through the enforcement of anti-

Sec. V   EMPLOYMENT MATTERS   81

fraud laws. The supreme court struck down the twenty-four hour restriction. *Ins. Adjustment Bureau v. Pennsylvania Ins. Comm'r*, 542 A.2d 1317 (Pa.1988).

An insurance claims adjuster fell out of his car and injured his elbow while in the course of his work. The elbow damage was severe, and the employee filed a workers' compensation claim. A Tennessee trial court determined that the employee had a vocational disability of eleven percent, but denied future medical benefits. The employee appealed to the Supreme Court of Tennessee. The supreme court ruled that there was no vocational disability. The employee had five years of college education and extensive special insurance training. He had returned to work only a few days after the injury and had worked regularly in the meantime. Ninety-five percent of his work was in the office, and because he was continuing to do satisfactory work, there was no evidence of vocational disability. However, there was no justification for the trial court's denial of future medical expenses. The insurer would be required to pay future medical expenses if the employee could prove they were related to his injury. *Shadle v. Amerisure Co.*, 764 S.W.2d 542 (Tenn.1989).

An insurance adjuster who had formerly been employed in the Fort Lauderdale, Florida, office of an insurance company sued the insurer and its claims superintendent for malicious prosecution. The adjuster had recently been acquitted of criminal fraud charges which alleged that he had falsified several insurance claims while employed as an adjuster. The county attorney had instituted the criminal proceedings against the adjuster after the state Division of Insurance received a report from the company stating that the latter had found suspicious-looking claims among his files. The District Court of Appeal of Florida upheld a lower court's dismissal of the adjuster's malicious prosecution complaint. State law required that an insurer report any instance of fraudulent claims to the Division of Insurance, and further provided that as a result of such reporting insurers were granted immunity from suit for libel or otherwise. The appeals court declared that "or otherwise" included malicious prosecution. Furthermore, even if the law did not grant immunity to the insurer, the malicious prosecution claim would fail since the insurer had not legally caused the criminal charges to be brought against the adjuster. The dismissal of the adjuster's malicious prosecution complaint against his former employer was affirmed. *Pearce v. U.S. Fidelity and Guar.Co.*, 476 So.2d 750 (Fla.App.4th Dist.1985).

A man's handbuilt, custom made vehicle was extensively damaged in an accident caused by the negligence of another driver. The man filed a lawsuit against the other driver to recover for the damage to his car. Estimates provided to the insurer for the repair of the car ranged from $35,000 to $40,000. The insurer initially offered only $10,000 to settle the claim and subsequently increased the offer to $20,000. At the time the $10,000 and $20,000 offers were made, the insurer was represented by a licensed independent adjuster. The claim was thereafter turned over for processing to an adjuster who was an unlicensed employee of the insurer. He notified the man that all previous offers were withdrawn and made a new offer to settle the claim for a total of $2,000. The man filed a lawsuit against the insurer which was settled for $25,000. The man then sued the insurer, its unlicensed adjuster, the licensed independent adjuster which made the first two offers, and the independent adjuster's employee who processed the claim. The man charged that the low settlement offers constituted a breach of the California Unfair Practices Act because they were not the result of a good-faith effort to settle the claim. The defendants moved for dismissal of the man's complaint which was denied by the Superior Court, San Bernadino County, and the defendants appealed.

The California Court of Appeal, Fourth District, ruled that a determination or admission of the insured's liability was a prerequisite to the maintenance of a third party lawsuit under the unfair practices act. The court decided that it was "unquestioned and unquestionable that a determination at some point that the insured was liable is a prerequisite to recovery by a third party claimant against a liability insurer." Because the insurer denied liability when it paid the $25,000 settlement, the lawsuit could not succeed. The Court of Appeal ordered the Superior Court to dismiss the case. *Pacific National Ins. Co. v. Superior Court*, 233 Cal.Rptr. 189 (Cal.App.4th Dist.1986).

D. Employment Contracts

A Minnesota man formed a corporation to serve as an insurance company's agent. The corporation agreed to service the company's accounts, which were owned by an affiliate of the insurer. After this agreement was terminated, the corporation purchased the affiliate. The purchase agreement provided for some payments, but did not state a purchase price. The insurer's representatives told the agent that his agency would not be terminated without cause. A few months later, the insurer sent the agent a new general agent contract, which he signed. The contract permitted termination upon sixty days' notice. Approximately one year later, the insurer notified the corporation that it still owed nearly all of the money for the affiliate purchase. The insurer withdrew consent for the purchase of its assets and would not release any more commissions to the corporation. The agent sued for conversion, breach of contract and intentional infliction of emotional distress in a Minnesota trial court. The court awarded damages for conversion and breach of contract, but denied the claim for emotional distress. The insurer appealed to the Minnesota Court of Appeals. The court reversed the trial court's decision regarding the conversion claim. It held that the corporation was unable to show that its property interest had been taken. The claim was really for breach of contract since the insurer had refused to give the commissions as promised. The court ruled that the insurer had wrongfully terminated the agency because the owner relied on the representatives' statement that it would not be terminated without cause. The court affirmed the dismissal of the emotional distress claim. *McNeill & Associates v. ITT Life Ins.*, 446 N.W.2d 181 (Minn.App.1989).

In two similar contracts an insurance agent agreed to represent an insurer as its general agent. Each contract contained complex formulas for calculating the agent's commissions on the basis of premiums collected and losses reported. Each contract provided that differences of opinion or interpretation would be submitted to arbitration. When disagreements developed over the payment of commissions the agent sued the insurer in the Superior Court, Los Angeles County, alleging breach of contract and breach of the covenant of good faith and fair dealing. The insurer filed a similar lawsuit against the agent in New Jersey, the location of the insurer's home office. It took no further steps, however, in pursuing that lawsuit. The insurer then petitioned for an order compelling arbitration of all disputes between the parties. The Superior Court denied the petition and the insurer appealed.

The California Court of Appeal, Second District, observed that California courts traditionally have maintained a strong preference for arbitration "as a speedy and inexpensive method of dispute resolution" and that arbitration agreements are to be accorded broad scope. The court noted that the arbitration provisions were broadly worded but were not ambiguous. The insurer and the agent were sophisticated in contract matters and easily could have limited the description of arbitrable issues had they chosen to do so. The Superior Court's order denying arbitration was reversed. *Market Ins. Corp. v. Integrity Ins. Co.*, 233 Cal.Rptr. 751 (Cal.App.2d Dist.1987).

State Farm canceled an agent's insurance agency contract and ordered him to close the agency. The agent was an at-will employee. The agent sued State Farm in a New Mexico district court. He asserted that State Farm broke an implied promise of good faith and fair dealing. After the agent presented his evidence State Farm moved for a decision in its favor. The judge granted the motion. The judge stated that even though there was a duty of good faith in contracts with at-will employees, here State Farm did not violate that duty. When the agent's motion for a new trial was denied, he appealed to the New Mexico Supreme Court. On appeal, State Farm argued that there was not a covenant of good faith and fair dealing in an at-will employment relationship. The court agreed with State Farm's argument. It stated that New Mexico does not recognize a claim for breach of contract for good faith and fair dealing in an at-will employment relationship. The two exceptions to this rule, retaliatory discharge and an implied contract that restricts the employer's power to discharge, did not apply in this case. In an at-will employment relationship, either the employee or the employer may terminate the contract for any reason, without liability. The court declined to impose an obligation on State Farm that was not found in the contract. The judgment granting State Farm's motion was affirmed. *Melnick v. State Farm Mut. Automobile Ins. Co.*, 749 P.2d 1105 (N.M.1988).

A California employee worked for a title insurance company for thirty years. He received various raises and bonuses and his job performance was never criticized. In October 1983, while serving as a major accounts manager, he was abruptly notified that he would be required to double his productivity. He was told in profane language that he would be fired if he did not fulfill the new requirements and that his thirty years with the company were "past history." He spent much of the next three weeks in oral and written discussions of the terms and obligations of his continued employment. The employee resigned in November 1983, and filed a lawsuit in the Superior Court, San Francisco County, seeking damages for wrongful discharge. The Superior Court granted summary judgment in favor of the title insurance company and the man appealed. The California Court of Appeal, First District, addressed the employee's allegation that the title insurance company had breached the covenant of good faith and fair dealing in causing his "forced retirement" or "constructive discharge" without good cause. The court cited previous decisions in holding that an employee cannot resign and then utilize his own resignation as the basis for recovering damages. The court concluded that allowing such a rule would "invite a flood of litigation and threats of litigation, creating a major new obstacle to efficient management." The Superior Court's decision to dismiss the employee's lawsuit was affirmed. *Duerksen v. Transamerica Title Ins. Co.*, 234 Cal.Rptr. 521 (Cal.App.1st Dist.1987).

An insurance agent and the insurer he worked for entered into an advance commission and loan agreement. The agreement gave the insurer the option of advancing commissions and loaning money to the agent. It provided that any funds advanced to the agent that were not later earned by him would be deemed a loan to be repaid by the agent. Subsequently, the agent assigned his right to all commissions, renewals, service fees, and any other remuneration due from the insurer to Marketing Services of America, Inc. After the agent and the insurer terminated their relationship the insurer sued the agent seeking to recover the amounts advanced and loaned to him. He claimed that because Marketing had failed to pay him under the assignment, he had not received any advances or loans and was therefore not obligated to pay anything to the insurer.

The Florida District Court of Appeal ruled that the fact that the insurer delivered funds to Marketing at the agent's request and that Marketing never paid the agent had no effect on the agent's obligation to repay the excess advances. The agent was found liable for repayment of the advances and loans. *Integon Life Ins. Corp. v. Zammito*, 506 So.2d 48 (Fla.App.2d Dist.1987).

A Sacramento insurance employee was fired for refusing to be transferred. She applied for unemployment benefits but her request was denied on the ground that she had voluntarily left work without good cause. An administrative law judge affirmed the denial of benefits. The employee appealed to a County Superior Court which granted the insurer's dismissal motion. She then appealed to the Third District Court of Appeal. While the appeal was pending the legislature passed Unemployment Insurance Code § 1960 which provided that administrative adjudications were not binding upon appeal. The only issue for the court of appeal to determine was whether § 1960 applied retroactively. If it did not, the administrative law judge's decision would be final, precluding her claim. The court of appeal determined that due to the unfairness that would be caused to the employee, § 1960 should apply retroactively. This allowed the employee to continue her fight for unemployment benefits. *Mahan v. Safeco Title Ins. Co.*, 245 Cal.Rptr. 103 (Cal.App.3d Dist.1988).

A claims supervisor was fired due to alleged economic considerations when the insurer he worked for eliminated two positions. The claims supervisor filed a lawsuit against the insurer alleging that the insurer had breached a covenant of good faith and fair dealing by discharging him in violation of public policy. He asserted that he had been terminated for his refusal to violate guidelines of the Insurance Department concerning the insurer's claim to employee ratio. He contended that although California Department of Insurance guidelines set a maximum case load of 250 claims per employee, the insurer's employees were required to manage as many as 800 cases. The supervisor produced two interoffice memos indicating that the insurer's management thought he was "uncooperative and troublesome." He claimed that the memos were written because he refused to violate the guidelines.

A U.S. district court dismissed the supervisor's claim on the ground that he had failed to present sufficient evidence to support his allegations. The supervisor appealed to the U.S. Court of Appeals, Ninth Circuit. The Court of Appeals noted that if all of the supervisor's allegations were true, a reasonable jury could conclude that he had proved his case. Furthermore, the court found that "termination in retaliation for failure to violate an Insurance Department Guideline is contrary to public policy." The court declared that the supervisor's lawsuit should be allowed to proceed to trial for a decision on its merits. It reversed the district court's dismissal of the case. *Eisenberg v. Ins. Co. of North America*, 815 F.2d 1285 (9th Cir.1987).

CHAPTER THREE

MOTOR VEHICLE INSURANCE

		Page
I.	SCOPE OF COVERAGE	86
	A. Arising out of the Use or Maintenance of a Motor Vehicle	86
	1. "Motor Vehicle" Defined	86
	2. "Arising out of" Defined	88
	a. Coverage Allowed	88
	b. Coverage Denied	90
	3. Parked Vehicles	93
	B. Accidents and Occurrences	95
	C. Intentional Harm	97
	D. Persons Eligible for Coverage	98
	1. Family Members and Household Residents	98
	2. Permissive Users	102
	E. Vehicles Eligible for Coverage	105
	1. Replacement and Rental Vehicles	105
	2. School District Vehicles	107
	3. Dealers	108
	4. Motorcycles	110
	5. Other Vehicles	111
	F. PIP Benefits	112
	G. Misrepresentation	114
II.	DUTIES OF INSURERS	115
III.	DUTIES OF INSUREDS	119
IV.	STATE AND FEDERAL REGULATION	121
	A. State Regulation	121
	B. No-Fault	125
V.	STACKING OF MULTIPLE POLICIES	126
	A. Stacking Allowed	127
	B. Stacking Precluded	129
VI.	UNINSURED/UNDERINSURED MOTORIST BENEFITS	131
	A. Scope of Coverage	132
	1. Insurers' Obligations	132
	2. Accidents and Events Covered	134
	3. Hit-and-Run Accidents	137
	4. Physical Contact Rules	138
	B. Individuals Entitled to Coverage	140
	1. Coverage Allowed	140
	2. Coverage Denied	142
	C. Interception of Benefits by Creditors	145

86   MOTOR VEHICLE INSURANCE   Ch. 3

        D. Insurers' Duty to Offer Coverage 145
           1. Duty not Satisfied 145
           2. Duty Satisfied 148
        E. Exclusions 149

VII.   POLICY CANCELLATION 151
        A. Cancellation Notices 151
           1. Inadequate Notice 151
           2. Adequate Notice 153
        B. Nonpayment of Premiums 155
           1. Coverage Valid 155
           2. Coverage Void 155
        C. Transfer of Ownership 156
        D. Binders 157

VIII. SETOFF 159

IX.   SEX-BASED RATE DIFFERENTIALS 161

X.   EXCLUSIONS 163
        A. Vehicles 163
        B. Persons 166
        C. Violations of Law 169

XI.   STATUTE OF LIMITATIONS 170

I. SCOPE OF COVERAGE

The courts characteristically employ a two-step approach when resolving motor vehicle coverage disputes. First, the courts ask whether an incident arose out of the use or maintenance of a covered motor vehicle. If so, the second inquiry is whether the resulting harm or injury falls within the terms of the insurance policy.

A. <u>Arising out of the Use or Maintenance of a Motor Vehicle</u>

In order for an injury to be considered as arising out of the use or maintenance of a motor vehicle, courts generally look for a close causal connection between the *contemporaneous* use of the motor vehicle *as a motor vehicle* and the resulting incident or injury. The term "motor vehicle" is usually defined by state statute or by the insurance policy under which a claim arises.

1. "Motor Vehicle" Defined

A Florida insured was involved in an accident while she was driving a rented golf cart. She sought liability coverage under her automobile insurance policy. Her insurer sought a declaratory judgment in a Florida trial court that it was not liable.

The insurer's request was denied. It appealed to the Florida District Court of Appeal, arguing that a golf cart is not ordinarily thought of as an automobile. The court of appeal affirmed the decision, finding that the term "auto" as used in the policy was ambiguous. It stated that the policy excluded coverage for any vehicle having less than four wheels, implying that four wheel vehicles were covered. Since the golf cart had four wheels, it was an "auto" within the policy's meaning. *Fireman's Fund Ins. Cos. v. Pearl*, 540 So.2d 883 (Fla.App.4th Dist.1989).

A Washington couple was riding in their car when it collided with an airplane that was making an emergency landing on a public highway. The couple's lawsuit against their own automobile insurer alleged that the airplane was a motor vehicle for purposes of underinsured motorist coverage. The Washington Court of Appeals noted that the term "motor vehicle" applied to a class of vehicles "that includes cars, trucks, buses, and the like." The Washington legislature did not intend an airplane to be covered by the term "underinsured motor vehicle." Furthermore, an ordinary purchaser of underinsured motorist coverage would not believe that such coverage would cover risks arising from a collision with an airplane. The couple's insurer was not required to provide underinsured motorist coverage to the couple. *Sperry v. Maki*, 740 P.2d 342 (Wash.App.1987).

A snowmobiler was killed after running into an unlighted parked car along a highway. The widow of the deceased brought suit to recover damages under the car's no-fault policy. The insurer was granted summary judgment by a state trial court, the decision was affirmed, and the widow appealed to the Supreme Court of Michigan. Michigan's no-fault act allows recovery of no-fault benefits if a vehicle is parked in an unreasonably dangerous manner which may lead to damage. Without such a showing, the accident is not deemed to involve a "motor vehicle." The court held that merely showing a parking violation does not imply an unreasonable danger. Parking the vehicle on the shoulder of the road was ruled not to be unreasonably dangerous as to those persons (like snowmobilers) who are not legally allowed to be on the shoulder. The vehicle was treated no differently than any other stationary object, and benefits were denied. *Wills v. State Farm Ins. Co.*, 468 N.W.2d 511 (Mich.1991).

In two Michigan cases, vehicles were found to be "motor vehicles" under state law. A farmer was driving his tractor, to which two flat haywagons were attached, for a 4-H Club hayride. A girl sitting on one of the wagons fell off and was run over by the wagon's wheels. The girl collected personal injury protection (PIP) benefits from her father's no-fault insurer, and the insurer then sued the farmer to recover the money it had paid. The Michigan Court of Appeals ruled that even though the tractor did not have to be registered, it was a "vehicle ... operated ... upon a public highway by power other than muscular power which [had] more than 2 wheels." It therefore was a motor vehicle under Michigan's No-Fault Act. Because the act precluded the insurer from seeking reimbursement for injuries arising from the operation of a motor vehicle, the insurer had no right to sue the farmer. *State Farm Mut. Automobile Ins. Co. v. Wyant*, 398 N.W.2d 517 (Mich.App.1986).

In the second case a minor was injured in an accident on a public road while operating a four-wheel go-kart powered by a one-cylinder, 2.5 horsepower engine. The minor was insured under two policies issued to his mother which provided personal injury protection (PIP). When PIP benefits were denied by the insurer on the ground that the go-kart was not a "motor vehicle," the minor sought a judicial declaration that it was. Under Michigan law, the definition of "motor vehicle" provides that a vehicle must be "operated or designed for operation upon a public highway." The Michigan Court of Appeals declared that the go-kart was a motor vehicle. It was being operated on a public highway when the accident occurred, and thus the question of whether it was designed for such operation did not have to be reached. *Coffey v. State Farm Automobile Ins. Co.,* 412 N.W.2d 281 (Mich.App.1987).

In a Wisconsin case, inoperable automobiles were excluded from the definition of "automobile." A man who was living with his parents was involved in an automobile accident. The man's father had automobile insurance coverage for relatives in the household who did not own a private passenger automobile. An automobile was defined as a "four wheel land motor vehicle designed for use principally upon a public road." The other driver's insurance company contended that the man was insured under his father's policy because he owned no automobile. However, the man did own a 1969 Dodge with a sprung frame, two flat tires and a bad motor, as well as a 1968 Plymouth that he had bought for $50 and which would not run. A Wisconsin trial court ruled that the inoperable and nearly valueless condition of these vehicles prevented them from being considered "automobiles" under the father's insurance policy. The man therefore possessed no automobile of his own and, as a resident of his father's household, he was covered under the policy. The Court of Appeals of Wisconsin affirmed this decision, noting that most jurisdictions similarly recognize that a vehicle can deteriorate to such an extent that it is no longer an automobile for insurance purposes. Because the man owned no "automobile," he was deemed to be a covered insured under his father's policy. *State Farm Mut. Automobile Ins. Co. v. Rechek,* 370 N.W.2d 787 (Wis.App.1985).

2. "Arising out of" Defined

a. Coverage Allowed

In the following cases the courts determined that the injuries or incidents arose out of the use or maintenance of a motor vehicle; coverage was therefore allowed.

A tree trimmer was loading an uninsured truck with branches when he missed the truck and struck another vehicle's windshield, causing injuries. The car's passengers sought uninsured motorist coverage in a Florida court. The court entered judgment in favor of the insurer, and the insureds appealed to the District Court of Appeal of Florida. That court explained that an uninsured motorist policy which provides coverage for damages resulting from the "ownership, maintenance, or use" of a motor vehicle must be interpreted in the same way that those terms are interpreted in an automobile liability policy; coverage must be provided for ordinary and customary uses of a vehicle. The court noted that trucks, by their nature, must be loaded and unloaded to be used in their customary manner. Therefore, coverage must be provided. *Pomerantz v. Nationwide Mut. Fire Ins.,* 575 So.2d 1311 (Fla.App.3d Dist.1991).

A Minnesota man was injured as a result of an explosion and fire in his garage caused by dripping gasoline from his car. He submitted a claim to his automobile insurer. The insurer denied the claim stating that the insured's injuries did not arise out of the use or maintenance of the automobile. After the automobile insurer denied the insured's claim, the insured's health insurer paid it and then settled with the auto insurer for half the amount it expended under a subrogation claim. Having paid the insured's medical expenses, the health insurer had subrogation rights against the auto insurer. The insured sued the insurer in a Minnesota trial court alleging that he was entitled to the medical expenses paid by his health insurer. The trial court denied the insured's claim. The insured appealed to the Minnesota Court of Appeals. On appeal, the auto insurer maintained that the insured's injuries did not arise out of the maintenance or use of an automobile. The insured argued that the insurer was benefitting from the insured's health insurance coverage and that he was entitled to the balance of unpaid medical expenses. The court of appeals held that economic loss benefits were payable for injuries which arose out of the maintenance or use of a motor vehicle. The insured's automobile was an "active accessory" in causing his injuries because the fire was caused by gasoline fumes leaking from it. The court found, however, that the insured was not entitled to the surplus resulting from the health insurer's decision to settle for an amount less than the claim. The appeals court affirmed the trial court's decision. *Strand v. Illinois Farmers Ins. Co.*, 429 N.W.2d 266 (Minn.App.1988).

The Georgia Supreme Court overruled a Georgia Court of Appeals decision that a widow could not recover for her husband's death. He died while sleeping in his van. An autopsy showed that he died of carbon monoxide poisoning produced by a propane heater that he had installed in the van. Benefits were denied because the insurer considered the use of the heater to be a substantial departure from the van's intended use. The court of appeals agreed with the insurer that it was not obliged to provide benefits to the widow. She then appealed to the Georgia Supreme Court. At issue was whether the use of the van as a vehicle ceased when the husband stopped and slept for the night. The court held that even though the van was not actively transporting him while he slept, the stop to sleep was a part of his journey. The fact that his death came as a result of the use of a heater did not alter the court's view. Because neither the overnight sleeping nor the modifications altered the use of the vehicle, their combination did not bring his death outside the vehicle's intended use. The insurer was required to provide benefits. *Denison v. Allstate Indem.Co.*, 367 S.E.2d 801 (Ga.1988).

A carpenter owned a truck which was covered under his mother's automobile insurance policy. The policy contained no-fault coverage for injuries "arising out of the ownership, maintenance or use" of the truck. As the carpenter directed a helper to stand on top of a scaffolding (which had been erected to install a wooden frame into the window of a building), the frame was hoisted into place by a rope and pulley. One end of the rope was attached to the frame, and the other end of the rope was tied to the side of the carpenter's truck. The carpenter moved the truck forward, and the wooden frame rose and struck the scaffolding, causing the helper to fall to the ground and be injured. The insurer declined coverage for the man's injuries, asserting that they did not arise out of the maintenance or use of the truck. A U.S. district court noted that a sufficient causal connection existed between the operation of the truck and the man's injuries to bring those injuries under the coverage of the policy. The court declared that the insurer was obligated to pay benefits to the injured helper. *Brack v. Allstate Ins. Co.*, 666 F.Supp. 703 (M.D.Pa.1986).

After a New Jersey driver stopped his car to ask for directions, two men approached his car and pulled him out. They stole the driver's cash, then attempted to take his car as well. When the driver resisted, one of the men cut him on the forehead with a knife and broke his ring finger. The men fled when another car approached. The driver's automobile insurance policy provided coverage if he sustained bodily injury "as a result of an accident involving an automobile." The driver sought PIP benefits from his insurer for the injuries he sustained and losses he incurred as a result of the incident, but his insurer refused payment. The insurer argued before the New Jersey Supreme Court that the driver's injuries and losses resulted from an assault and battery rather than an accident involving an automobile. The court noted that PIP coverage is not limited to instances in which an injury is directly caused by an automobile but extends to all situations in which there is a "substantial nexus" between an injury and the use of a car. In this case, the driver's car was directly involved in the incident. The driver had sought directions so that he could drive his car to his destination, he was sitting in his car when the assault occurred, and the purpose of the assault was to steal the car. The court ruled that coverage existed because the car played a central role in the incident. *Smaul v. Irvington General Hosp.*, 530 A.2d 1251 (N.J.1987).

b. Coverage Denied

A Kansas insured spent an evening with his family attending a musical performance. On the way home from the performance the insured's automobile was bumped by another vehicle. The insured stopped and got out to check for damage. While he was inspecting his car, the other motorist, an unknown man, walked over and fatally shot him. The unknown motorist then shot the insured's mother twice as she fled from the auto. The decedent's estate brought an action against the insurer to recover no-fault and uninsured motorist benefits. The district court denied recovery and granted the insurer summary judgment. The estate appealed to the Supreme Court of Kansas. On appeal, the decedent's estate argued that it was entitled to recovery because the collision between the two vehicles was the reason the decedent stopped his automobile and got out to inspect it. Kansas law requires drivers to stop after being involved in an accident and to give certain information. The court disagreed, finding that the mere use of the vehicles was not sufficient to trigger coverage. The shooting was an intentional act unrelated to the operation of either one of the motor vehicles. Because the decedent's estate failed to show that a significant nexus existed between the ownership, maintenance, or use of the vehicles and the resulting injuries and death, the supreme court denied recovery. *Hamidian v. State Farm Fire & Cas. Co.*, 833 P.2d 1007 (Kan.1992).

Three Washington youths were attempting to throw lit fireworks out of their car when a lighted firecracker dropped into a bag of fireworks. Unable to extinguish the fire, they left the car. The driver then attempted to remove the burning fireworks, but was severely burned in the process. The insurer maintained that the injuries did not result from the use of the vehicle and thus denied coverage. The Court of Appeals of Washington held that the term "resulting from use" did not require direct causation, but only a causal connection between the injuries and the vehicle. The court held for the insured. *Mutual of Enumclaw Ins. Co. v. Jerome*, 833 P.2d 429 (Wash.App.1992).

While a Louisiana woman was stopped at a railroad crossing, she was nudged from behind by a car containing two young men. One of the men got out of the car and motioned for the woman to get out of her car; she did. The other man stole her purse. When she protested, she was struck in the face and sustained injuries. After her insurer denied uninsured motorist benefits, she brought suit in a Louisiana trial court. The trial court found for the insurer and the insured appealed to the Court of Appeal of Louisiana. On appeal, the woman contended that the injury she received flowed directly from the use of the uninsured vehicle purposely utilized by the assailants. However, the court found that, in Louisiana, injuries caused by a battery have generally been found not to arise out of the operation, maintenance or use of a vehicle. Therefore, the appellate court affirmed the trial court's decision. *Byrne v. State Farm Ins. Co.*, 572 So.2d 728 (La.App.4th Cir.1990).

A New Jersey man drove his car from the right lane to the left lane and "cut off" an unidentified vehicle. While the man's car was stopped at the next intersection, the unidentified vehicle stopped beside him. A passenger emerged from it, punched the man and then fled. The man claimed personal injury protection benefits and uninsured motorist (UM) benefits under his policy and sued the insurer in a trial court. The parties settled the personal injury claim, and the court ruled for the insured on the UM claim. The insurer appealed to the Superior Court of New Jersey, Appellate Division. The appellate court overruled the trial court, holding that the injury did not arise out of the ownership, maintenance, or use of the uninsured motor vehicle. *Cerullo v. Allstate Ins. Co.*, 565 A.2d 1125 (N.J.Super.A.D.1989).

A passenger in an insured auto fired several shotgun blasts out the window of the moving car, one of which killed a sixteen-year-old girl. The car was being operated by the owners' son. After being sued, the owners of the vehicle sought coverage under their automobile insurance policy in a Michigan trial court, and on appeal in the Court of Appeals of Michigan. The lone issue was whether the shooting arose "out of the use of an automobile." The court ruled that a connection must be shown between the use of the auto and the shooting. That connection must be more than incidental; it was not enough to show that but for the use of the auto the shooting would not have happened. The court held that the shooting was not the forseeable use of an auto as described in the policy, and excluded it from coverage. *Auto Owners Ins. Co. v. Rucker*, 469 N.W.2d 1 (Mich.App.1991).

The question of insurance coverage arose in a case where a man allegedly waved or pointed a gun at a woman while they were both driving down the highway. She brought suit against him for infliction of emotional distress. The California Court of Appeal, First District, noted that the man's alleged conduct was independent of and unrelated to the operation of his motor vehicle. Accordingly, the woman's injuries did not arise out of the operation of a motor vehicle, and there was no insurance coverage. *Mounts v. Uyeda*, 277 Cal.Rptr. 730 (Cal.App.1st Dist.1991).

A father sought coverage under his automobile liability policy for dog bites he and his son suffered while riding in a neighbor's van. The dog had been chained in the back of the van but still managed to seriously injure them. The insurer denied coverage, stating the policy did not cover dog bites. The father sued the insurer in a Pennsylvania district court. The court held that the injuries did not arise out of the "use or maintenance" of the van. The father appealed to the Pennsylvania Superior Court. It upheld the district court decision observing that there must be some causal connection between the use of the vehicle and the injuries to hold the insurer liable for those injuries. *Alvarino v. Allstate Ins. Co.*, 537 A.2d 18 (Pa.Super.1988).

Two cases involving taxi drivers' gunshot injuries were decided similarly by courts in Michigan and Georgia.

A taxi driver was paralyzed from the neck down as a result of a gunshot wound inflicted during the robbery of his cab. The cab company was covered by an automobile insurance policy which provided first-party benefits and liability coverage. The Supreme Court of Michigan held that the insurance company was not liable under the policy because the gunshot wound did not arise out of the cab's "ownership, operation, maintenance or use as a motor vehicle." The court decided that "[t]he relation between the functional character of the motor vehicle and [the man's] injury was not direct — indeed, the relation was at most incidental." *Thorton v. Allstate Ins. Co.*, 391 N.W.2d 320 (Mich.1986).

A Georgia taxi driver was shot and killed during an armed robbery while sitting in the front seat of his taxi. When his wife's insurer denied her claim for maximum no-fault benefits, she appealed to the Court of Appeals of Georgia. The policy provided that the insurer would pay no-fault benefits "for bodily injury to an insured, caused by accident resulting from the maintenance or use of a motor vehicle as a vehicle...." The court denied the woman's claim because the injury did not originate from the use of the taxi as a vehicle. *Westberry v. State Farm*, 347 S.E.2d 688 (Ga.App.1986).

A truck owner who was "horsing around" picked up a loaded shotgun in his truck and pointed it at his friend. The truck owner believed that the gun was not loaded, but it discharged and seriously injured the friend. The truck owner had an insurance policy which covered injuries "arising out of the ... use" of his truck. The friend sued the truck owner claiming that the accident was caused by the man's negligence "in loading a charged shotgun into his vehicle and using his vehicle for transporting a charged shotgun" while carrying passengers. The insurer provided a defense for the man in his friend's lawsuit, but initiated its own lawsuit seeking a ruling that the incident was not covered by the policy. An Alaska superior court denied the insurer's request. The superior court ruled that because the truck owner had admitted liability in his friend's lawsuit against him, the insurer was liable for the damages arising from the incident. The insurer appealed.

The Supreme Court of Alaska noted that firearm discharges that occur while loading or unloading a vehicle are usually covered by automobile policies because the loading and unloading process itself constitutes a "use" of the vehicle. In this case, however, the shotgun was placed in the truck more than a week before the incident. The incident did not arise out of the loading and unloading process, but was caused by negligent handling of the shotgun. The court ruled that the "handling of the gun had no connection with the use of the vehicle," and thus no coverage was available. *Criterion Ins. Co. v. Velthouse*, 732 P.2d 180 (Alaska 1986).

A Colorado driver and his two passengers were injured when they stopped on the shoulder of an interstate freeway to change a flat tire. They were leaning into the

Sec. I SCOPE OF COVERAGE 93

trunk of the automobile, trying to remove a spare tire, when they were struck from behind by another automobile. Their insurer paid personal injury protection benefits to them and then sued the other insurer for reimbursement. The Colorado trial court found that the injured persons were occupants of the automobile and not pedestrians, and that their insurer was therefore solely liable for the personal injury protection benefits. The court of appeals affirmed this decision, and their insurer further appealed to the Supreme Court of Colorado.

The superior court held that the "vehicle oriented" test which had been applied by the lower courts was no longer good law. The test defined the injured persons as occupants of the vehicle if they "intended to continue their status as passengers of the vehicle until it reached its final destination." The supreme court, however, ruled that a person is an occupant of an automobile only when riding in or upon the vehicle, or when entering into or alighting from a vehicle. A pedestrian, the court held, was a person whose injuries have some causal connection to the use of a vehicle, but who is not an occupant. Since the injured persons in this case were merely leaning into the trunk of their vehicle, they were pedestrians at the time they were struck by the other car. The court reversed the lower court's decision, and ruled that the injured persons' insurer was not solely liable for coverage. *MFA Mut. Ins. Co. v. Gov't. Employees Ins. Co.*, 785 P.2d 128 (Colo.1990).

3. Parked Vehicles

Two thirteen-year-old Louisiana girls went on a double date. They argued while the car was parked. One of the girls raised a bottle to her mouth to drink and the other girl struck the bottle, breaking two of her companion's front teeth. The injured girl sued the owner of the vehicle and his insurer. A trial court ruled in her favor, and the owner and insurer appealed to the Court of Appeal of Louisiana. On appeal, the court noted that the incident clearly did not arise from the use of the vehicle; the vehicle was merely the place where the incident occurred. However, the medical payments section of the policy provided that such benefits would be paid for bodily injuries "caused by accident" while the person injured was occupying the vehicle. Even though this injury was intentionally inflicted, it was still an accident from the viewpoint of the injured girl. Therefore, the medical benefits had to be paid by the insurer, and it was also liable for statutory penalties. The court affirmed in part the trial court's decision. *Willis v. Tipton*, 593 So.2d 435 (La.App.2d Cir.1992).

An Ohio insured's automobile liability policy covered damages resulting from the "ownership, maintenance, use, loading or unloading" of the insured's vehicle. In a parenthetical phrase in the margin, the policy stated, "(for damage or injury to others caused by your auto)." After a hunting trip, the insured disembarked from the vehicle with a loaded gun which discharged, killing a passenger. The Ohio Court of Appeals held that coverage existed because the marginal language was not sufficient to limit the coverage provided in the main paragraph for damages resulting from use of the vehicle. *Nationwide Mutual Ins. Co. v. Wright*, 591 N.E.2d 362 (Ohio App.3d Dist.1990).

A New Hampshire woman and her friends gathered around a "mint condition" Camaro to examine it. She intended to ride home in the Camaro with its owner, the insured. While the woman was leaning against the Camaro, the insured spotted a car coming straight at them. He pushed her out of the way, but the car struck her anyway.

The woman attempted to collect on the insured's uninsured motorist policy because the other vehicle was uninsured. The insurer sued to prevent coverage and the court ruled in its favor. The Supreme Court of New Hampshire reversed, however, finding that the woman was "occupying" the Camaro at the time of the accident. *State Farm Mutual Automobile Ins. Co. v. Cookinham*, 604 A.2d 563 (N.H.1992).

An insured woman was towing a small trailer which broke loose and overturned. Her passenger was struck by an uninsured motorist during an attempt to right the trailer. The passenger sought uninsured motorist benefits from the woman's insurer, which were denied because he was not an "occupant" of the vehicle at the time of the injury. The man argued that the term "occupying" should be more broadly construed, and successfully pursued a lawsuit. The case was appealed to the Michigan Court of Appeals. The term "occupant" was explained by the court to be construed more narrowly than the term "occupying." The differing constructions were held not to be inconsistent because the former arises in no-fault cases, which are distinguishable from the private insurance cases in which the latter arises. This case involved the term "occupying," which was construed to include persons not immediately in contact with the vehicle in certain factual situations. The award of benefits was affirmed. *Rohlman v. Hawkeye Security Ins. Co.*, 476 N.W.2d 461 (Mich.App.1991).

A Massachusetts man drove home a car owned and insured by his employer. He parked the car across the street from his residence, got out of the car, locked the doors, and started across the street. When he was three to four feet from the vehicle, he was struck by a vehicle driven by an uninsured motorist. He attempted to recover uninsured benefits from the vehicle's insurer. The policy provided that coverage would be granted for persons "while occupying an insured automobile." Occupying was defined as "in or upon, entering into or alighting from." The insurer denied coverage. In the lawsuit which followed, the trial court ruled for the insurer, and the injured man appealed to the Appeals Court of Massachusetts. The man contended that his activity constituted "alighting from" the vehicle. However, the court determined that the facts did not support such an argument. Neither could he claim that he was "upon" the vehicle at the time of the accident. Clearly, he had left the vehicle at the time he was hit by the uninsured motorist. The appellate court affirmed the trial court's ruling in favor of the insurer. *Kelleher v. American Mutual Ins. Co.*, 590 N.E.2d 1178 (Mass.App.Ct.1992).

A North Dakota man drove his wife's car into his grain field located about three-eighths of a mile from his son's residence. Somehow, the car caught on fire. He ran the distance to his son's place to summon help, then ran back to the car to try to put out the fire. Near the car, he collapsed, suffering a fatal heart attack. His widow then claimed survivor benefits from her automobile insurer, which rejected the claim. It maintained that the man had not suffered an "accidental bodily injury" while "occupying" the car, which was required for no-fault benefits. In the lawsuit which followed, the trial court granted summary judgment to the insurer. The insured appealed to the Supreme Court of North Dakota. On appeal, the court agreed with the decision reached by the trial court. The heart attack did not occur while the man was in the car. Nor was he attempting to get into the car at the time of his heart attack. Since he was not "occupying" the vehicle at the time of the attack, the policy did not

Sec. I   SCOPE OF COVERAGE   95

provide coverage. Further, the heart attack was not "an accidental bodily injury arising out of the operation of a motor vehicle." The trial court's decision was affirmed. *Ertelt v. Emcasco Ins. Co.*, 486 N.W.2d 233 (N.D.1992).

A Michigan insured was injured while sitting on the bed of his truck, which was parked along a street waiting to be repaired. The truck was uninsured at the time of the accident, but the insured owned another vehicle which was insured. The insured sued his insurer in a Michigan circuit court for medical expenses and lost wages. The insurer denied liability and filed a motion for summary disposition claiming that the insured was not entitled to benefits because he was an occupant of an uninsured vehicle at the time of the accident. The circuit court denied the insurer's motion for summary disposition and the insurer appealed to the Court of Appeals of Michigan.

The court of appeals noted that under the state no-fault act a person is not entitled to personal protection insurance benefits for accidental bodily injuries if the person owned a motor vehicle involved in the accident. A parked vehicle is deemed to be involved in an accident when a person is injured while occupying the vehicle. The court found that the insured was injured while sitting in the back of the truck awaiting repairs. That activity was identifiable with the use of the truck as a motor vehicle. A person does not have to be seated in the passenger area of a motor vehicle to be considered an occupant. The court held that the insured was "occupying" the truck at the time of the accident and thus the provisions of the no-fault act precluded no-fault coverage. The court of appeals reversed the lower court's decision. *Childs v. American Com. Liability Ins.*, 443 N.W.2d 173 (Mich.App.1989).

B. Accidents and Occurrences

Most automobile insurance policies provide specific amounts of coverage for damages or injuries resulting from an "accident" or an "occurrence."

A two car crash resulted in injuries to the driver and passenger of one of the cars. The driver claimed bodily injury damages of approximately $12,000 and the passenger claimed in excess of $100,000. The applicable insurance coverage provided for $100,000 coverage for bodily injury "for each person" and $300,000 for "each occurrence." The injured parties claimed that, in an instance where more than one person was injured, this language allowed one person to collect more than $100,000, so long as the total liability was not greater than $300,000. The insurer disagreed and filed suit in a state court seeking a declaration that its liability to each person was limited to $100,000. The trial court granted summary judgment to the insurer, the court of appeals reversed, and the Kansas Supreme Court granted a petition for review.

In construing an insurance policy a court will construe any ambiguity in favor of the insured. The outcome of an ambiguity is determined not by what the insurer intended but what an ordinary insured would understand the language to indicate. The policy stated in its liability provision that "1) the bodily injury liability for 'each person' is the maximum for bodily injury sustained by one person in any one occurrence; 2) the bodily injury liability for 'each occurrence' is the maximum liability for bodily injuries sustained by two or more persons in any one occurrence."

Both the injured parties and the insurer provided outstate decisions which construed the language in their favor. The court was able to distinguish the policies involved in those cases, and ruled for the insured. It felt that an insured could reasonably read the policy to allow a $300,000 recovery when two persons were injured. The difference between this policy and others which had been construed to maintain the $100,000 limit was that this policy did not state that the occurrence limit was subject to the personal bodily injury limits. Since the limits were not referenced to each other they were ruled to be independent statements. The judgment of the court of appeals was affirmed. *Farm Bureau Mutual Ins. Co. v. Winters*, 806 P.2d 993 (Kan.1991).

An insured was involved in a collision which resulted in his death. His policy contained liability limits of $50,000 per person for all damages arising from bodily injury, and $100,000 per accident, subject to the per person limitations. The deceased's estate brought a wrongful death action against the driver, and agreed to accept the limit of the policy as found by a court. The insurer argued that the estate was entitled to recover only $50,000 because of the per person bodily injury limitation. The estate argued that a wrongful death action was legally separate from bodily injury claims, and that it should be allowed to collect the full $100,000. A declaratory judgment action was brought in a federal district court, which certified the question to the Supreme Court of Ohio.

Wrongful death actions permit claimants to have claims which are separate from those of the deceased. Further, an earlier Ohio case makes clear that an insurer may not disallow such claims by creating conflicting policy limitations. The policy limitations at issue in the present case, however, were not conflicting. Indeed, the court found them to be both clear and unambiguous. Premising an action as a wrongful death action was ruled to have "no consequence" on the coverage limitations of such a policy. The court answered the certified question by stating that an insurer may apply a single limit to all claims arising from an injury, provided that the limitation is clearly stated. *State Farm Automobile Ins. Co. v. Rose*, 575 N.E.2d 459 (Ohio 1991).

A North Dakota husband and wife were involved in a car accident in which both were injured and the wife was rendered a quadriplegic. The husband filed a personal injury action in a federal court for a variety of claims. All claims were eventually settled except for the husband's claim for loss of consortium. The insurer had denied coverage for his claim, taking the position that because it had already paid its $100,000 liability limit it had no further liability. The insurer then filed a declaratory judgment action asking the court to determine whether the policy covered the husband's claim for loss of consortium. The federal trial court ruled in favor of the insurer and the insured appealed to the U.S. Court of Appeals, Eighth Circuit.

On appeal, the husband contended that the insurer provided coverage for the loss of consortium claim under the liability section of the policy. The insurer contended that the each person limit of liability clearly applied because under the plain language of the policy, bodily injury included all injury and damages to others resulting from the underlying injury. The husband however contended that his loss of consortium claim came from his wife's accidental injury but was a wholly independent cause of action. The appellate court determined that in order to meet the each accident section for liability the injury must occur in the same accident. However, under North Dakota law, the injury giving rise to a loss of consortium claim occurs after the accident. Therefore, under the policy language the claim was subject to the each person limit of liability. The appellate court upheld the decision of the trial court. *State Farm Mutual Auto Ins. v. Wolff*, 926 F.2d 755 (8th Cir. 1991).

A California insured was injured in a multiple-vehicle accident while a passenger on a motorcycle. None of the drivers involved in the accident, including the motorcycle driver, were insured. The insured owned a policy which provided $15,000 per person uninsured motorist coverage. The insurer paid the $15,000 policy limit but allowed the insured to reserve the right to assert that the insurer's liability exceeded that amount.

The insurer then sought a ruling from the Superior Court, Alameda County, that its liability was limited to the amount it had already paid. When the Superior Court denied the insured's motion for summary judgment, she entered into a stipulated agreement with the insurer which provided that only one "accident" had occurred.

The insured then appealed to the California Court of Appeal, First District, where she argued that the insurer was liable for coverage up to the policy's liability limit for each negligently operated uninsured vehicle involved in the accident. The court of appeal noted that the policy limit applied to bodily injury sustained by one person as a result of one accident. It held that because the insured had stipulated that only one accident occurred, her recovery was limited to the policy's $15,000 uninsured motorist liability limit. *Government Employees Ins. Co. v. Oliver*, 237 Cal.Rptr. 174 (App.1st Dist.1987).

C. Intentional Harm

Insurers generally may exclude coverage for intentional misconduct on the part of insureds.

An insured reported his car as stolen. It was later found in a burned out condition. Since the insurance claim involved a possible arson, the insurer conducted an investigation. It asked the insured to submit tax records from the year before he had purchased the car. He refused. After the insurer denied the claim, and the trial court ruled for the insurer, appeal was taken to the Court of Appeals of Ohio. The appellate court held that the insured's refusal to submit his tax records resulted in a material and substantial prejudice to the insurer, justifying the claim denial. The judgment for the insurer was affirmed. *Gabor v. State Farm Mutual Automobile Ins. Co.*, 583 N.E.2d 1041 (Ohio App.8th Dist.1990)

A Washington man was intentionally struck by his estranged wife, while a passenger in an insured's car. The man then got out of the car to get her license plate number and she deliberately ran him down in the street, carrying him on the hood of her car. As a result, he sustained injuries. Neither the husband nor the wife had automobile insurance. The husband then sought to recover under the insured's uninsured motorist coverage. The insurer denied coverage stating that under the policy the man would have to have been using the car and the injury would have to have been the result of an accident. The man then brought a declaratory judgment action in a Washington trial court. After the trial court granted summary judgment to the insurer, the husband appealed to the Court of Appeals of Washington. The appellate court reversed, finding that the man was at all times a covered passenger who was using the insured's car. The insurer appealed to the Supreme Court of Washington.

The supreme court determined that the issue was whether the husband was "using" the insured vehicle at the time of the incident and whether the intentional act constituted an "accident." The insurer contended that the wife's actions were deliberate and intentional and therefore the collision was not "accidental." The court noted that the definition of accident was an unusual, unexpected and unforeseen happening and determined that an accident is never present when a deliberate act is performed. Therefore this act was not an accident. The court determined that it would deny coverage on the basis that there was no accident and also that when the husband exited the automobile and stood on the street, he was no longer "using" the insured vehicle. The supreme court reversed the court of appeals' decision. *Roller v. Stonewall Ins. Co.*, 801 P.2d 207 (Wash.1990).

After a woman in Washington intentionally collided with two other automobiles, her husband sought collision coverage under his automobile policy for the damages to his car. Although separated, the woman was using the car with her husband's permission at the time of the collisions. The insurer sought a court declaration that it was not obligated to pay on the claim. It argued that the damage to the car driven by the wife was not "direct and accidental" as required by the policy because it was the result of the wife's deliberate, intentional act. The Supreme Court of Washington reversed a trial court ruling in favor of the insurer and returned the case to that court. The supreme court found that separate insurance contracts existed between the insurer and the husband and wife, and that the acts of the wife did not bar coverage for the husband. Since the husband did not intend the damage to the car, the damage was "direct and accidental" as to the husband, and the policy afforded him collision coverage. The court further held that to the extent the car was community property, the insurer must reimburse the husband for only half the damages to the car, as his separate property. *Federated American Ins. v. Strong*, 689 P.2d 68 (Wash.1984).

The U.S. Court of Appeals, Ninth Circuit, said that the adoption in Hawaii of a compulsory scheme of automobile liability insurance very strongly suggested a legislative intent that there be no exclusion of intentional acts of the insured. Compulsory automobile insurance is adopted for the protection of the victims. From the viewpoint of the victim, the mental state of the insured is irrelevant. The common objection to insuring one's self against liability for deliberate wrongful acts has little validity in this context. Where compulsory automobile liability insurance statutes use the terms "accident" or "accidental" those terms should be read in such a way that does not exclude intentional acts of the insured. An event is accidental if it is neither expected nor intended from the viewpoint of the person who is injured. *State Farm Fire & Cas. Co. v. Tringali*, 686 F.2d 821 (9th Cir.1982).

D. Persons Eligible for Coverage

Recent court decisions have interpreted insurance policies to award coverage to persons wherever reasonably possible.

1. Family Members and Household Residents

A twenty-year-old Missouri boy was badly injured in a car accident while a passenger in a car driven by an uninsured motorist. At the time of the accident, he was attending the University of Missouri in St. Louis, where his parents resided. However, he was not living at his parent's house but was living temporarily with his

Sec. I SCOPE OF COVERAGE 99

brother in an apartment. The injured student brought suit against his mother's insurer which moved for declaratory relief claiming that the student was not insured since he did not qualify as a "relative." The mother's auto policy defined a "relative" as either a person related to the insured by blood, marriage, or adoption who lives with the insured or as a person who is an unmarried and unemancipated child "away at school." The district court agreed with the insurer and held that the student was excluded from coverage as a "relative" because he neither lived with his parents nor was he "away at school." On appeal, the Missouri Court of Appeals believed that the district court interpreted the phrase "away at school" too narrowly; its interpretation would afford coverage only to unemancipated and unmarried students who attend a "nonlocal school." Accordingly, the court held that the student was entitled to uninsured motorist insurance and reversed and remanded the case to the trial court. *Crump v. State Farm Mutual Auto Ins. Co.*, 961 F.2d 725 (8th Cir.1992).

A New York woman was injured when the car she was riding in hit a utility pole. After settling her claim against the driver, she demanded arbitration for underinsured benefits from her son-in-law's insurer. The insurer agreed to select an arbitrator, then sued to stay arbitration, contending that the woman was not a "family member" as defined by the policy because she did not reside in her son-in-law's household. The trial court dismissed the suit. The Supreme Court, Appellate Division, determined that the question of the woman's "family membership" had to be resolved prior to arbitration, and it reversed the trial court's decision. *Aetna Casualty & Surety Co. v. Cartigiano*, 577 N.Y.S.2d 314 (A.D.2nd Dept.1991).

A Wisconsin man and his girlfriend "sometimes lived together." When the couple was at a tavern, the woman took the keys to his car and caused an accident which killed three people. She did not have either the man's express or implied permission to use the car. The insurer of the auto denied any liability for the accident, but a jury trial found otherwise. The insurer appealed to the Court of Appeals of Wisconsin. The policy provided coverage for any person using the vehicle with the permission of the insured, or of a person living in the insured's household. In the earlier trial, the jury found that the woman was a member of the man's household. Therefore, coverage was required because the woman was deemed to have been using the car with the permission of a member of the insured's household — herself. The trial court's ruling was upheld. *Arps v. Seelow*, 472 N.W.2d 542 (Wis.App.1991).

A Minnesota religious organization required its members take a vow to be dependent upon the organization for the disposition of material goods. One of the members of the organization was employed as a high school principal. The organization received payment and benefits for her service. The principal was killed in an automobile accident. The insurer paid medical, hospital, and funeral expenses, but denied survivor's economic loss benefits. The organization filed a lawsuit. A trial court granted summary judgment to the insurer, and the dispute was then heard by the Minnesota Court of Appeals. Minnesota insurance law mandated that all automobile insurance policies include survivor's economic loss benefits. The benefits were payable to "surviving dependents" of the deceased. The issue in this case was whether a nonprofit corporation, such as a religious organization, could qualify as a surviving dependent. The court affirmed that the organization could not be considered a dependent in this context, resulting in a judgment for the insurer. *School Sisters of Notre Dame at Mankato, Minnesota v. State Farm Mutual Automobile Ins. Co.*, 476 N.W.2d 523 (Minn.App.1991).

A six-year-old girl was badly injured by an uninsured motorist while she was riding her tricycle outside her home. At the time she was injured, she lived with her biological mother and the insured. Although the insured was not the girl's biological father, he had reared her and lived with both her and her biological mother for several years. When the insurer denied coverage, the insured brought a declaratory judgment action, seeking a determination that the girl was entitled to uninsured motorist and personal injury protection coverage because she qualified as a "foster child" under his auto policy. A district court disagreed and granted the insurer summary judgment. The insured appealed, the court of appeals affirmed, and the insured further appealed to the Oregon Supreme Court. On appeal, the supreme court disagreed with the court of appeals' reasoning that a child can only be a "foster child," if the child forms a "legal relationship" to the foster parent. The supreme court construed the insurance policy's definition of foster child broadly; a foster child relationship also develops when a person nurtures, supports, and rears the child. Accordingly, the judgment was reversed and the case remanded to the district court for further consideration. *Joseph v. Utah Home Fire Ins. Co.,* 835 P.2d 885 (Or.1992).

An Illinois man purchased an automobile liability policy which provided coverage of $50,000 per person and $100,000 per accident. Further, the policy covered bodily injury (injury, sickness, disease, or death) "sustained by any one person in any one auto accident." After an accident resulted in injury to another, a two-count complaint was filed against the insured: one, for personal injuries to the driver and two, for loss of consortium to his wife. The insurer then brought a declaratory judgment action to determine if it had to pay out $50,000 or $100,000 under its policy. The trial court granted summary judgment to the insurer, and the couple appealed to the Appellate Court of Illinois. On appeal, the couple asserted that the loss of consortium claim was not merely derivative, but was an independent cause of action, for which coverage must be provided. The appellate court agreed with this contention, holding that the wife's claim was a separate bodily injury under the policy. Had the term "bodily injury" been more narrowly defined, no separate coverage would have been available. The trial court's ruling was reversed. *General Casualty Co. of Illinois v. Sternberg,* 581 N.E.2d 728 (Ill.App.5th Dist.1991).

A Georgia resident owned a pick-up truck which he insured with a policy excluding liability to any person related by blood to the insured and residing in the same household. The owner's adult son was a named insured on the policy and was authorized to use the truck. The owner's minor son was injured in an accident in which the adult son was driving. The owner, on behalf of his minor son, sued his adult son and the insurer. Disputing coverage on the basis of the family exclusion, the insurer moved for dismissal, which was granted. The owner then appealed to the Georgia Court of Appeals, which held that the intrafamily exclusion did not violate public policy and affirmed the trial court's decision. The owner then appealed to the Supreme Court of Georgia.

The supreme court stated that the state's public policy was to protect innocent victims from negligent motorists. It also stated that public policy mandated protection of the insured from unfair exposure to unanticipated liability. The court said that if either of these interests were left unprotected, the exclusionary clause in the policy violated public policy. It noted that there was no tort immunity between the adult and minor son. As a result, the adult son was exposed to liability for which he was not covered. It also meant that the injured son was left unprotected. The supreme court reversed, stating that the exclusion violated public policy. *Stepho v. Allstate Ins. Co.*, 383 S.E.2d 887 (Ga.1989).

An insured couple temporarily moved into the wife's parents' home. They had changed their address and given up their other residence. The daughter was then killed while using her parents' automobile, which was insured for any family member residing at the parents' address. The daughter was not listed on the policy as a resident and the insurer denied coverage on that basis. The policy called for arbitration of disputes but the insurer filed suit in a New York court seeking to stay arbitration and thereby avoid liability.

The insurer argued that the daughter was not a resident of the home because she was not listed on the policy and because of the temporary nature of her residence. The court noted that she had no other legal address, the policy did not exclude temporary residence, and the parents had not had time to add her to the policy. The insurer's motion to stay arbitration was denied and the daughter was ruled to be a resident family member. *Application of Aetna Life & Cas. and Schurr*, 568 N.Y.S.2d 299 (Sup.1991).

A Michigan insured struck and killed another driver while he was driving a borrowed car. The deceased's estate was awarded $500,000 in damages. The insured's and the owner's insurance companies provided partial payment. The estate then attempted to collect from the insured's father, grandmother and uncle, with whom he had resided. The trial court dismissed the action and the estate appealed to the Court of Appeals of Michigan. The court of appeals stated that coverage extended only to family members who resided with the insured. Family members were not covered if they owned a vehicle. Even though the insured's vehicle was inoperative at the time, coverage was precluded. *Shank v. Kurka*, 435 N.W.2d 453 (Mich.App.1988).

A woman caused the death of two persons while driving an uninsured vehicle belonging to a third person. A group of plaintiffs obtained judgments on wrongful death claims, and sought a declaration that the woman was insured through a policy which was issued to her mother. The insurer pointed out that she had not lived at her mother's residence for over one year, and denied coverage on that basis. A jury agreed with the insurer, and the plaintiffs appealed to the Colorado Court of Appeals.

The policy defined insured as "the named insured, and relatives living at the named insured's residence." Despite the policy's definition, the plaintiffs asserted that the jury should have determined the residency issue by a different set of factors, which had been established in an earlier case. The court held that when a definition is included in the policy it should be followed. It further held that the definition was not against public policy. The trial court's findings were upheld. *Wheeler v. Allstate Insurance Co.*, 814 P.2d 9 (Colo.App.1991).

Two New York men were injured in an automobile accident while passengers in a vehicle driven by an insured's son. The auto was not owned by a member of the insured's household, but was available for the son's regular use. The passengers sued the insurer seeking coverage under the policy. The trial court found for the passengers and the insurer appealed to the New York Supreme Court, Appellate Division, which held that the insurer was not required to provide coverage under the policy. The policy was never intended to provide coverage to a nonmember of the household while the insured's son had regular use of the automobile. Despite the insurer's failure to give timely disclaimers of coverage to the passengers, coverage was denied. *Schmidt v. Prudential Ins. Co.,* 533 N.Y.S.2d 614 (A.D.2Dep't 1988).

A New York insured's daughter was injured while riding as a passenger in an underinsured vehicle. The father's automobile insurance policy contained underinsured motorist coverage on "the named insured and, while residents of the same household, his spouse and the relative of either." The daughter, although listed as a driver on the policy at the time it was issued and at the time of the accident, was not living in the same household as her insured parents at the time of the accident. She sought coverage from her father's insurer. Coverage was denied because of her nonresidence in the father's household. She then sued the insurer in a New York trial court. The court found in favor of the insurer, a decision upheld by the New York Supreme Court, Appellate Division, Second Department. The appellate court pointed out that even though she was listed as a driver on her father's policy, she was not living with him and therefore was not legally entitled to recover under his policy. *Metropolitan Property & Liability Co. v. Feduchka,* 522 N.Y.S.2d 616 (A.D.2d Dept.1987).

2. Permissive Users

The son of an insured drove with a friend to the friend's father's home. The boys stated that they were going driving, and implied that the vehicle owner's son would continue to drive. The friend later drove and caused an accident which resulted in injuries. The injured parties brought suit against the friend's father's insurer. The claim was based on the contention that the father had given his son implied permission to drive the nonowned vehicle. A state court, on remand, held that the insurer had no duty to defend the father. The issue was then appealed to the Supreme Court of Montana. The insurer asserted that no permission had been granted. The father stated that the son may have believed that he had been given implied consent to drive. However, the son denied such a belief. The court agreed that no permission or implied consent had been granted, and affirmed the judgment for the insurer. *Allstate Ins. Co. v. Hankinson,* 815 P.2d 145 (Mont.1991).

A Missouri man purchased a pickup truck but failed to insure it. He later purchased an insurance policy on another vehicle that he owned. While that policy was in effect, a friend borrowed the pickup truck. The friend and a passenger were involved in a one-vehicle accident in which the passenger sustained personal injuries. The insurer brought a declaratory judgment suit seeking a holding that its policy did not provide coverage. The trial court granted summary judgment to the insurer. On appeal to the Missouri Court of Appeals, the court noted that the friend who was driving the pickup was neither related to the insured nor living in his household. Thus, he was not an insured under the policy. Further, the pickup was not a replacement vehicle for the insured vehicle because it was purchased prior to the insurance policy, and the insured vehicle remained in good working condition during the coverage. The court affirmed the summary judgment in favor of the insurer. *Atlanta Casualty Co. v. Stephens,* 825 S.W.2d 330 (Mo.App.1992).

A Pennsylvania driver was involved in a serious one-vehicle automobile accident while he was operating a vehicle owned by an insured. Two passengers were in the vehicle and were seriously injured as a result of the accident. At the time of the accident, the driver was residing at the insured's home. The insured granted the driver permission both to remain in her home and to operate her vehicle under certain prescribed conditions. The vehicle was insured under two policies, a general liability and a general umbrella policy. The general liability insurer brought a declaratory action in a federal trial court to determine its liability under the policy. The insurer claimed that the driver was not an insured under the terms of the policy covering the insured's vehicle because he was not a permissive user. The district court found that the driver was not an insured under the policy because his consumption of alcohol on the evening of the accident was a violation of the limited permission to use the vehicle. The driver then appealed to the U.S. Court of Appeals, Third Circuit.

The appellate court determined that there was ample evidence to support that the insured's permission to use the car was specifically circumscribed by the admonition not to use drugs or alcohol while driving the car. Therefore, the trial court's finding that the driver was under the influence of alcohol and precluded his being an insured under the policy was correct. The appellate court upheld the decision of the trial court. *Hall v. Wilkerson,* 926 F.2d 311 (3d Cir.1991).

A Missouri employee had taken his manager's vehicle on a pleasure excursion. Generally, the vehicle was used for business purposes. In the process of returning the vehicle, the employee was involved in an automobile accident. In a declaratory judgment action to determine coverage under the manager's policy, a Missouri circuit court held that the employee had implied permission to use the vehicle. The insurer appealed to the Missouri Court of Appeals. The court noted that the insured employer knew that the vehicle was used for personal purposes. Although she had requested that employees ask permission before using the vehicle for personal purposes, that procedure was not in writing. The court found that the employee had implied permission to use the vehicle and was covered under the insured's policy. *Ohio Cas. Ins. Co. v. Safeco Ins. Co.,* 768 S.W.2d 602 (Mo.App.1989).

A Missouri accident victim sued his automobile insurer in a federal district court to recover uninsured motorist benefits for injuries caused by a minor driver. The minor struck the insured while driving his parents' car without permission. The insurer in turn sued the parents' insurer. That insurer moved for a summary judgment in its favor. An exclusionary clause in the parents' insurance policy stated that the insurer would not cover any person using a vehicle without a reasonable belief that that person was entitled to do so. The insurer argued that this excluded people even specifically enumerated as covered by the policy — namely, family members residing in the household. The injured party's insurer argued that because the language was ambiguous, the court should construe the language in favor of the driver of the car and grant coverage. The court disagreed and granted the motion for summary judgment. The court concluded that the policy identified the persons it would cover and then stated that it would not provide coverage for certain identified persons in enumerated circumstances. The court noted that it would be illogical to conclude that the policy expressly excluded people from coverage who were never included in the first place. Even though the minor was a family member, he was operating the vehicle without a reasonable belief that he was entitled to do so and he was therefore not covered under his parents' policy. *Driskill v. American Family Ins. Co.*, 698 F.Supp. 789 (E.D.Mo.1988).

A boy's parents bought a car and loaned it to him to use while in college. They instructed him not to let anyone else use the car. The boy had been drinking and gave the car keys to a friend to hold. The friend drove the car and was involved in a three car crash resulting in injuries and death. The driver's insurer defended the driver, and later filed suit seeking a declaration that the car owner's insurance policy should provide coverage. A federal district court ruled against ordering coverage under the owner's policy, and the driver's insurer and the estate of the deceased appealed to the U.S. Court of Appeals, Tenth Circuit.

The owner's insurance policy specified coverage for the policyholder, his or her spouse, relatives, and those drivers with permission of a named insured or spouse. On its face, the policy did not provide coverage for the driver because the son was not a named insured. The plaintiffs argued that the denial of coverage would violate Oklahoma public policy and an Oklahoma statute which was enacted so that innocent victims could be protected. The court ruled that the applicable statute did place an obligation on the owner to insure the driver, but it did not require an insurer to provide coverage beyond the terms of the policy. Neither statute nor public policy required coverage, and a request by the plaintiffs to reform the contract failed because neither plaintiff was a party to the contract as required in reformation suits. Judgment in favor of the owner's insurer was affirmed. *Shelter Mutual Ins. Co. v. Littlejim*, 927 F.2d 1132 (10th Cir.1991).

A Georgia insured loaned his car to a friend so she could look for a job. However, the friend decided to pick up a twelve-year-old acquaintance and visit an out-of-town friend. While there, she allowed the twelve-year-old to drive the car. While driving, the twelve-year-old struck a pedestrian. The vehicle owner's insurer sought and obtained a declaratory judgment of no liability. The pedestrian appealed the decision to the Court of Appeals of Georgia. The court of appeals held that use of the insured vehicle had exceeded the scope of permission given by the insured, and that the twelve-year-old driver could not have had a reasonable belief that she was entitled to use the vehicle. The court of appeals affirmed the trial court's decision. *Johnson v. Blue Ridge Ins. Co.*, 376 S.E.2d 703 (Ga.App.1988).

In a New York case, a woman was driving her father's car accompanied by a friend. Upon recognizing someone he knew in another car, her friend pressed his foot upon her foot on the accelerator to speed the car up. As a result, she lost control of the vehicle and was seriously injured in the accident that followed. After she brought suit against her friend for her injuries, he sued her father's auto insurer, demanding that it defend him in the lawsuit. The New York Supreme Court, Special Term, denied the insurer's request to dismiss his case. On appeal by the insurer, the Supreme Court, Appellate Division, observed that the automobile policy excluded coverage of any person using the vehicle "without a reasonable belief that the person is entitled to do so." According to the evidence, the woman did not consent to her friend pressing his foot upon the accelerator but told him to stop and physically resisted him. Thus, the court concluded that the friend's "use" or exercise of control over the car was without permission. It therefore ruled that the insurer had no obligation to either defend or indemnify the man in the personal injury suit brought by the injured woman. The lower court's decision was reversed. *Electric Ins. Co. v. Boutelle*, 504 N.Y.S.2d 577 (A.D.3d Dept.1986).

E. Vehicles Eligible for Coverage

The courts have construed the terms of automobile insurance policies broadly to afford coverage for vehicles wherever reasonably possible.

1. Replacement and Rental Vehicles

A man owned and used two automobiles, of which only one was insured. The insured vehicle became inoperable due to fire damage, and the man was involved in a fatal accident in the uninsured car. The injured parties' insurer (subrogated insurer) brought an action against the insurer of the inoperable car. It argued that coverage should apply to the vehicle involved in the accident through a clause which provided coverage for a replacement automobile. A state court held that coverage existed, and the insurer appealed to the Supreme Judicial Court of Maine. The policy provided that it insured the described automobile, or another vehicle if it: 1) was acquired during the policy year and 2) was a replacement for the described automobile. The first requirement was undisputedly met. The insurer argued that even prior to the fire the insured typically used the uninsured vehicle, and that the occurrence of the fire should not create coverage for it. The court adopted the definition of replacement automobile to include a co-owned car if the insured auto was inoperable, and the insured was left with only one operable automobile. This rule maintained protection for other drivers, and did not force an insurer to insure two vehicles. The decision was affirmed. *Merchants Mutual Ins. Co. v. Maine Bonding & Casualty Co.*, 596 A.2d 1009 (Me.1991).

A man leased a vehicle to serve as a temporary substitute while his vehicle was being repaired. While driving the vehicle, the man struck a pedestrian who eventually died. The lessor owner's insurer negotiated and paid a settlement, and then sought contribution from the driver's personal insurer. Both insurers claimed to be responsible only as excess insurers. Accordingly, a state trial court ordered the driver's insurer to contribute to the settlement on a *pro rata* basis, and to share in the legal costs. The driver's insurer contended that the lessor owner's insurance was contrary to state law, and appealed to the Supreme Court of New Hampshire.

The state's financial responsibility law mandates a minimum of $25,000 liability coverage, and its purpose is to protect innocent injured parties. The driver's insurer contended that allowing the lessor owner's policy to contain a provision which provided only excess coverage violated that purpose and, therefore, the provision was invalid. The lessor owner's insurer argued that the injured party had been compensated, and that in such cases the provision did not violate the law. The court ruled for the driver's insurer. It stated that it was "not persuaded that violation of the clear language of the statute is permitted when the result adversely affects another insurance carrier rather than the insured." The second issue concerned the insurers' respective obligations to pay legal costs. The decision of the trial court was affirmed; a duty to provide a defense to an insured is shared equally between insurers, whether they be primary or excess. *Universal Underwriters Ins. Co. v. Allstate Ins. Co.*, 592 A.2d 515 (N.H.1991).

An insured included her son as a driver of her car under an automobile policy she purchased from an insurer. She owned another vehicle at the time (insured by another insurer) for which the son was specifically excluded as an insured. When the vehicle he was insured to drive broke down, his mother gave him permission to drive her other car. He was then involved in an accident. The son's insurer asserted that he was not covered. The son claimed that the second car was an additional insured automobile. The policy provided coverage when the son was using a car "not owned by or available for regular use" to the mother, the son *or* any resident of the same household. After the son was sued by the other party to the accident, the insurer cross-complained for declaratory relief, asserting that it had no duty to defend or indemnify the son. The trial court granted summary judgment to the insurer, and the son appealed to the California Court of Appeal, Second District.

The son argued on appeal that since the automobile was not available for his regular use, it fell within the policy's definition of an additional insured automobile. The insurer contended that since the car was owned by the mother and was available for her regular use, it could not be an additional insured automobile. The court of appeal agreed with the insurer. By using the word "or" in the policy, the insurer had clearly spelled out that coverage would be unavailable if the mother, the son or any other resident owned the vehicle involved in the accident. Coverage for the son could have been obtained on the second vehicle for an additional premium, but allowing such an increased risk without an increase in premiums simply was not fair. The court affirmed the lower court's grant of summary judgment for the insurer. *Lasam v. Interinsurance Exchange of Auto Club of Southern California*, 280 Cal.Rptr. 214 (Cal.App.2d Dist.1991).

A New York insured owned a fleet of automobiles, which were insured under a policy which covered automobiles "held by the insured for rental on a short-term basis (less than twelve months)." The insured leased a car to a man who authorized another to drive it. The written lease agreement specified a lease term of twenty-four months. When the driver was involved in an accident the insurer denied liability and the insured sued. A New York trial court held for the insured, and the insurer appealed to the Supreme Court, Appellate Division. The court held that the automobile leased by the insured for a twenty-four-month term was not a covered vehicle under the fleet automobile insurance policy. The lower court's decision was reversed. *Planet Ins. v. Bright Bay Classic Veh.*, 537 N.Y.S.2d 534 (A.D.1st Dept.1989).

A Georgia insured purchased airplane tickets and obtained an automatic flight insurance policy. While the insured was driving his rental car back to the airport he was involved in an accident. The policy provided coverage for accidents which occurred while the insured was riding as a passenger on a land common carrier such as a taxi or bus en route to the airport. The insurer sought a declaratory judgment as to the extent of its liability. A federal district court held that the insured's rental car was not a common carrier. The policy's listing of common carriers, when considered in conjunction with the requirement that the insured be a passenger, made it clear that coverage extended only to vehicles which were not operated by the insured. The policy clearly excluded coverage and the court granted the insurer's motion for summary judgment. *Mutual of Omaha Ins. Co. v. Ruff*, 711 F.Supp. 1112 (N.D.Ga.1989).

The Court of Common Pleas of Ohio has ruled that a "courtesy car" furnished by a garage when the customer's car was being worked on was not a rental vehicle. After a garage customer was injured in an accident while driving such a car, the customer and his insurer filed for a declaratory judgment to determine which policy provided primary coverage. The insurer for the garage denied liability on the grounds that the policy excluded coverage of rental vehicles. In holding that the courtesy car was not a rental vehicle, the court declared that the garage owner's insurer provided the primary coverage and would be required to fully indemnify the garage customer on any claim arising out of the accident. *Rosenal v. Auto-Owners Mut. Ins. Co.*, 489 N.E.2d 1086 (Ohio Com.Pl.1985).

2. School District Vehicles

A Florida boy was struck by a school bus owned and operated by a private school which provided an after-school program. The boy and the insurer of the bus agreed that he had suffered $25,000 in damages, but the policy issued by the insurer provided liability coverage of only $10,000 per person. The boy and his mother filed a lawsuit in a state court alleging that the contract was in violation of statutory coverage minimums, and that it should be construed to provide a minimum of $100,000 of coverage per person. The contract was ruled to be legal by a trial court, and the boy appealed to the Florida District Court of Appeal. The dispute required the court to construe the "awkward wording of the statutes pertaining to insurance coverage on nonpublic sector buses." Florida law provided that nonpublic sector buses must carry liability insurance with a minimum coverage of $100,000 per person. The school argued that school buses were exempt from that requirement. The court examined the possible exceptions, and determined that they were either inapplicable or otherwise failed to reduce the $100,000 minimum coverage requirement. Considerable statutory ambiguity led the court to request certification of the issue to the Florida Supreme Court. *Suazo v. Del Busto*, 587 So.2d 480 (Fla.App.3d Dist.1991).

Two persons were killed and two others severely injured when a school board's vehicle negligently caused an accident. The school board maintained liability insurance providing coverage of $200,000 per person and $325,000 per accident. At the time of his death, the driver of the private vehicle maintained uninsured motorist/bodily injury coverage for each of his two vehicles in the amount of $100,000 per person and $300,000 per accident. Because the policy permitted stacking, the amount of available uninsured motorist coverage was $400,000. The school board's liability insurance carrier paid the victims and their survivors a total of $325,000, the policy limit. However, the deceased driver's insurer denied claims for uninsured motorist benefits and filed a lawsuit in a Florida district court, asking it to resolve the question of whether uninsured motorist coverage benefits were available under the deceased's policy. If the amount available from the school board's insurer was less than the amount available from the driver's insurer, then uninsured motorist coverage would be available. The court ruled against the insurer finding that uninsured motorist benefits existed.

A Florida district court of appeal agreed and certified the question to the Supreme Court of Florida. The supreme court ruled that the insurer could not assert the school board's defense of sovereign immunity, because the immunity defense available under Florida statutes was not absolute. Florida's legislature permitted discretionary recovery through legislative claim bills and the resulting recoveries often exceeded limits under the sovereign immunity statute. State and agency subdivisions were permitted to settle claims within the limits of insurance coverage, even if they exceeded the statutory limitation on recoveries, which was $100,000 per person and $200,000 per accident. Because the school board might not be able to assert sovereign immunity as a defense to an action against it, the driver's insurer could not use the defense either. Thus, uninsured motorist coverage in the amount of $400,000 was available from the deceased driver's policy. *Michigan Millers Mutual Ins. Co. v. Bourke*, 607 So.2d 418 (Fla.1992).

A Florida insured was injured in an accident between a school bus and another vehicle. She was a passenger in the bus at the time. She sought personal injury protection (PIP) benefits from her insurer, which denied coverage. She sued in a Florida trial court, which ruled for the insurer. She then appealed to the District Court of Appeal, Second District. The appellate court found that PIP benefits were excluded for injuries incurred by insureds while riding as passengers in school buses. Not only did the policy exclude coverage for such injuries, but Florida law also excluded such coverage. The court of appeal affirmed the decision in favor of the insurer. *Esker v. Nationwide Mutual Fire Ins. Co.*, 593 So.2d 303 (Fla.App.2d Dist.1992).

A California high school student and her parents were selected by their local school board to be a host family for a member of a visiting basketball team. While the girl and her guest were driving to one of the basketball games in the host family's car they were involved in an accident. The school district's insurance company then sought and obtained a declaratory judgment which held that it was not liable for the girls' accident. The host family and the visiting student appealed. The California Court of Appeal reversed and held that the school district's insurance company would be bound to defend and/or indemnify the parties in any lawsuit arising from the accident. The appeals court reasoned that because the host family was expected to provide transportation to the visiting student, the school district had constructively "borrowed" their family car for that purpose. At the time of the accident, said the court, the host family's automobile was under the direction of the school district. Therefore, the school district's liability insurance company was responsible for any claims. *Travelers Indem. Co. v. Swearinger*, 214 Cal.Rptr. 383 (App.3d Dist.1985).

3. Dealers

A Pennsylvania minor approached a used car dealer about buying a car. The dealer contacted the minor's mother who told him that her son did not have permission to purchase the car. The dealer sold the car to the minor anyway, and also issued him a temporary registration card without confirming the existence of insurance. Approximately 30 minutes after the minor left the car dealership, he was involved in a car accident which resulted in serious injuries. A passenger injured in the accident sued him. The minor's parents' insurer brought a declaratory judgment action to determine whether it was required to defend or indemnify the minor. A

Sec. I　　　　　　　　　　　　　　SCOPE OF COVERAGE　　109

federal district court entered summary judgment in favor of the insureds. The insurer appealed to the U.S. Court of Appeals, Third Circuit. The minor's parents' insurance policy contained an exclusionary clause which denied coverage when any of the named insured's relatives owned another vehicle not covered by insurance. The appellate court determined that this exclusionary clause applied to the son because he owned the car when the accident occurred. The court refused to allow recovery for the passenger by accepting the minor's defense that he did not own the car because he was underage. Even though he was underage, the court believed that the minor still possessed all of the generally accepted attributes of ownership. For instance, he clearly had the exclusive right to use, enjoy and control the vehicle. The dealer, having taken the purchase price from the minor, was in no position to interfere with that use, enjoyment and control. Accordingly, the court reversed the lower court's decision and remanded the case. *Aetna Cas. & Sur. Co. v. Duncan*, 972 F.2d 523 (3d Cir.1992).

A Washington couple purchased a motor home from an automobile dealer. After paying for it in full, but before they went to pick it up, it was stolen off the lot. The couple sought to recover from their insurer for the theft but the insurer denied coverage on the ground that the dealer had not physically delivered the vehicle to them. In the lawsuit which followed, the trial court held that the insureds were the owners of the vehicle. On appeal to the Court of Appeals of Washington, the court affirmed, finding also that the insurer was also liable for the attorney's fees which the couple incurred in the litigation to recover their vehicle. *Brown v. State Farm Fire & Casualty Co.*, 831 P.2d 1122 (Wash.App.1992).

A Montana driver bought a car from an insured. The insured agreed to maintain coverage on the car until the driver could procure his own insurance. Even though the driver still owed him money, the insured transferred the title to the driver. Two nights later the driver was involved in an accident with a motorcyclist. The driver sought to require the insured's insurer to defend him and provide coverage for the motorcyclist's injuries. The case reached the Montana Supreme Court. The court held for the insurer. The insurer was not obligated to provide coverage for the accident since it had not agreed to insure the driver. The title had been transferred to the driver despite the monetary obligation to the insured. The insurer was not obligated to provide coverage. *Colonial Ins. Co. of California v. Blankenship*, 753 P.2d 880 (Mont.1988).

In a similar New York case an insured traded vehicles with an automobile dealer. They immediately transferred titles but the insured's insurer was not notified of the transfer until two days later. It immediately began the paperwork to cancel the coverage of the insured's old vehicle. A man drove the insured's previous vehicle without the dealer's permission and was involved in an accident in which the other driver was injured. The injured driver sought coverage for her injuries from the insurer but a New York appellate court held that coverage for the previous vehicle terminated upon transfer of title. The insurer had not consented to continue coverage and thus was not obligated to continue coverage. *In the Matter of Feliciano*, 528 N.Y.S.2d 653 (A.D.2d Dept.1988).

4. Motorcycles

A man was injured when the motorcycle on which he was a passenger slammed into a tree while fleeing from a police vehicle. The passenger sued the insurer of the police vehicle for benefits under the Michigan no-fault act. A state circuit court ruled for the insurer and the passenger appealed to the Court of Appeals of Michigan. The court observed that, while actual contact with the motor vehicle is not required, the injury should be "foreseeably identifiable with the normal use of a motor vehicle" [here the police vehicle]. In denying the passenger's claim, the court observed that fleeing from the police did not fit the "foreseeable and normal use" standard since only a small minority of traffic stops lead to flight and pursuit. *Sanford v. Ins. Co. of North America*, 391 N.W.2d 473 (Mich.App.1986).

When a boy died as a result of an accident that occurred while he was a passenger on a motorcycle covered by a policy that excluded him from coverage, his parents sued their own insurer for compensation. A Washington superior court ruled in favor of the insurer and the parents appealed. At issue was whether the parents could recover despite the following exclusion in the parents' policy: "this policy does not apply ... to bodily injury to an insured while operating, occupying or using a motorcycle...." Conceding that the boy was excluded, the parents sought compensation for damages they had suffered resulting from the boy's death. Based upon a state statute, the parents claimed to have a right of action against the driver whose negligence had caused their son's death. The insurer argued that the motorcycle exclusion was statutorily authorized, but the court observed that the scope of the exclusion was not fully explained. The court concluded that because this motorcycle exception statute was remedial, exceptions to the "general requirements of the statute should be narrowly confined." The court held that the motorcycle exception to the underinsured motorist statute permitted the parents' negligence claim against the driver of the motorcycle and entered summary judgment declaring the existence of coverage. *Eurick v. Pemco Ins. Co.*, 723 P.2d 554 (Wash.App.1986).

The father of a deceased motorcycle operator brought suit against his automobile insurer claiming that an "other vehicle" exclusion, precluding uninsured motorist coverage for an insured who is injured while operating his own vehicle not covered by liability coverage, violated the public policy underlying the Arizona uninsured motorist statute and thus was void. The son was killed when his motorcycle collided with an uninsured motorist. The father subsequently made a claim for $30,000 in uninsured motorist coverage, despite the fact that the motorcycle was not included under the liability coverage of his automobile policy. The Court of Appeals of Arizona held that the uninsured motorist statute was intended by the legislature to enable an insured to recover damages as though uninsured motorists were financially responsible. Accordingly, this statute protects persons insured who are legally entitled to recover damages from owners or operators of uninsured motor vehicles. The "other vehicle" exclusion, precluding coverage for the motorcycle, violated the public policy underlying the Arizona uninsured motorist statute, and thus was declared void. *Calvert v. Farmers Ins. Co. of Arizona*, 697 P.2d 707 (Ariz.App.1984).

Sec. I	SCOPE OF COVERAGE	111

5. Other Vehicles

An Illinois couple purchased an automobile policy with uninsured motorist coverage of $100,000 and medical payments coverage of $25,000. The policy defined "motor vehicle" as a "land motor vehicle designed for use principally on public roads." The insureds' son was then injured while riding as a passenger on an ATV. The insureds sought uninsured motorist benefits which the insurer refused to pay. It claimed that the ATV was not a motor vehicle under the definition in the policy. The insureds sued. The trial court found that the language of the policy which defined a motor vehicle was contrary to the statutory requirements of the Illinois Insurance Code. It thus ruled for the insureds. Appeal was taken to the Appellate Court of Illinois. On appeal, the court agreed with the trial court that an ATV was a motor vehicle for purposes of the uninsured motorists statute. The legislature had obviously chosen not to exclude ATVs from the definition of motor vehicles and, accordingly, the insurer could not limit coverage beyond that allowed by law. The appellate court affirmed the decision of the trial court in favor of the insureds. *Roberts v. Country Mutual Ins. Co.*, 596 N.E.2d 185 (Ill.App.3d Dist.1992).

At a family cookout in Alabama, the uninsured owner of an all-terrain vehicle (ATV) allowed the children to ride with him on the ATV, one at a time. During one riding trip, a girl fell off the ATV and broke her leg. The accident occurred just after the vehicle had crossed a road and entered the yard. The girl's mother sued her insurer, claiming benefits through the uninsured motorist provision of her policy. The trial court granted summary judgment to the insurer, and the insured appealed to the Supreme Court of Alabama. On appeal, the insured asserted that her daughter had been injured on a "public road" and that she was thus covered by the policy. The insured contended that a public road includes an eleven-foot right of way on each side of the paved area. The court disagreed. Even though "public road" had not been defined by the policy, the court determined that it included only the paved surface. Since the accident occurred in the yard just off the road, no coverage was available under the policy. The court affirmed the grant of summary judgment to the insurer. *Cannon v. State Farm Ins. Co.*, 590 So.2d 191 (Ala.1991).

A Kansas insured was injured while riding as a passenger in a friend's dune buggy. The dune buggy went out of control and crashed while off road on private property. It was neither licensed nor registered as an automobile and there was no insurance on it. After the accident, the insured filed a claim with his own automobile insurer. The insurer denied coverage because the policy excluded vehicles "designed mainly for use off public roads while not upon public roads." The insured sued successfully in a Kansas trial court, and the insurer appealed to the Court of Appeals of Kansas. The court of appeals held that since the vehicle had been off the road on private property, the insurer had properly refused coverage. It reversed the trial court's decision. *Shumaker v. Farm Bureau Mut. Ins. Co., Inc.*, 785 P.2d 180 (Kan.App.1990).

A Florida insured was involved in an accident while she was driving a rented golf cart. She sought liability coverage under her automobile insurance policy. Her insurer sought a declaratory judgment in a Florida trial court that it was not liable. The insurer's motion was denied. It appealed to the Florida District Court of Appeal, arguing that a golf cart is not ordinarily thought of as an automobile. The court of appeal affirmed the decision, finding that the term "auto" as used in the policy was ambiguous. It stated that the policy excluded coverage for any vehicle having less than four wheels, implying that four wheel vehicles were covered. Since the golf cart had four wheels, it was an "auto" within the policy's meaning. *Fireman's Fund Ins. Cos. v. Pearl*, 540 So.2d 883 (Fla.App.4th Dist.1989).

An Alaska couple possessed an automobile policy which stipulated that off-road vehicles were covered when used on public roads. The policy also stipulated that no coverage would be provided for an accident involving an uninsured vehicle. The couple's daughter was killed while crossing a highway on an off-road vehicle. The couple sought coverage from their automobile insurer. Coverage was denied. The couple sued the insurer in an Alaska trial court which held for the insurer. The couple appealed to the Alaska Supreme Court.

They asserted that the policy provided coverage because of the clause which called for coverage of off-road vehicles when used on public roads. The insurer argued that the daughter was operating an owned, but uninsured vehicle. Therefore the accident was expressly excluded under the policy. While the supreme court agreed with the insurer's argument, it held that that type of policy construction was narrower than that permitted by state law. Therefore it could not be given full effect. Once uninsured motorist coverage is purchased, the insureds have motorist protection under all circumstances. Although the supreme court held for the couple on this issue, it returned the case to the trial court for a determination of other issues. *Hillman v. Nationwide Mut. Fire Ins. Co.*, 758 P.2d 1248 (Alaska 1988).

F. PIP Benefits

Entitlement to personal injury protection (PIP) benefits generally depends on the status of the injured person in relation to a motor vehicle.

A Georgia business owner was involved in an automobile accident and claimed to be physically incapable of returning to work. She instituted a claim for personal injury protection benefits, but the insurer rejected her claim, maintaining that she could not recover lost income benefits because she had no income at the time of the accident. She brought suit in a Georgia trial court which ruled for the insurer, and she then appealed to the Court of Appeals of Georgia. The court of appeals noted that although the company books showed that the insured was accruing salary of three hundred dollars per week, she was not paid any money by the company in the year of the accident, or in the year preceding it. Because the business had been doing poorly, the "salary" was nothing more than an accounting practice. Accordingly, the insured could not establish with reasonable certainty that she had suffered lost income. The court affirmed the holding of the trial court in favor of the insurer. *Vlahos v. Sentry Ins. Co.*, 417 S.E.2d 180 (Ga.App.1992).

A New Jersey bicyclist rode off a sidewalk and into the path of an insured's car. Both the insured and the bicyclist swerved, so there was no collision. However, the bicyclist fell off the bike and was injured. She sued the driver's insurer in a New York trial court to collect personal injury protection (PIP) benefits, as provided by the state's no-fault act. The trial court found that the bicyclist's injuries were caused by the insured and awarded the bicyclist PIP benefits. The New Jersey Superior Court, Appellate Division, upheld the award. The insured then appealed to the New Jersey

Supreme Court. On appeal, the insurer argued that because the no-fault act was amended to require that bicyclists strike automobiles in order to collect PIP benefits, the legislature never intended to afford PIP benefits in no-contact cases. The court rejected this argument and upheld the PIP benefits award. It ruled that the legislature intended to award benefits in no-contact cases since it used the word "caused" instead of "struck" prior to the amendment. The court concluded that a "but for" test was appropriate for determining cause and that under that test the bicyclist qualified for PIP benefits. *Darel v. Pennsylvania Mfrs. Ass'n Ins. Co.*, 555 A.2d 570 (N.J.1989).

Nonresidents of the District of Columbia were injured in separate accidents in the District which were caused by uninsured drivers. The nonresidents filed claims for personal injury protection (PIP) benefits under the District of Columbia Compulsory No-Fault Motor Vehicle Insurance Act. The District of Columbia Department of Consumer and Regulatory Affairs denied the claims noting that the act disallowed PIP benefits if, at the time of the accident, the victims were not D.C. residents. The nonresidents petitioned for review to the District of Columbia Court of Appeals contending that the exclusion of nonresidents from benefits deprived them of their constitutional rights. The court held that the Act's provision excluding nonresidents from PIP benefits did not unconstitutionally burden the nonresidents' right to travel. Their rights under the privileges and immunities clause were also not violated. The nonresidents were denied benefits. *Davis v. Dep't of Consumer & Reg. Affairs*, 561 A.2d 169 (D.C.App.1989).

A New Jersey man was operating his pickup truck when he suffered a heart attack. The vehicle subsequently struck a utility pole, but the heart attack was the sole cause of his death. The pickup truck was covered by a policy which contained personal injury protection (PIP) coverage. The policy insured the man for bodily injuries sustained "as a result of an accident while occupying, entering into, alighting from or using an automobile." When the man's widow's claim for survivor benefits under this PIP coverage was denied, she filed a lawsuit seeking a declaration that the insurance covered her husband's death.

The New Jersey Superior Court considered the widow's argument that the man's heart attack constituted an accident under the New Jersey PIP statute and that it occurred while occupying an automobile. It noted that the language of the statute did not require a causal relationship between the use or operation of the automobile and the accident. It decided that the man's heart attack must be considered an accident because it was "an unexpected, unintended happening." Because the man's heart attack occurred while he was occupying an automobile, his death was covered. Summary judgment was granted in favor of the widow. *Schomber v. Prudential Ins. Co.*, 518 A.2d 1138 (N.J.Super.1986).

A passenger in a New York automobile left the car to examine it after a collision in New Jersey. While examining the automobile he was struck and injured by a New Jersey automobile insured by Liberty Mutual Insurance Company. Liberty contended that it was not liable since the passenger was "occupying" the New York car at the time of the accident. New Jersey state law provided that vehicle owners must possess insurance policies which provide PIP benefits to pedestrians but not "users" or "occupiers" of other cars. The passenger contended that he was a pedestrian and entitled to PIP benefits from Liberty Mutual. The New Jersey Superior Court, Appellate Division, ruled that although the passenger was "occupying" the New

York car in the sense that he was "using" it, he did not thereby lose his status as a pedestrian. He was therefore entitled to PIP benefits from Liberty Mutual. *Clyburn v. Liberty Mut. Ins. Co.*, 520 A.2d 829 (N.J.Super.A.D.1987).

G. Misrepresentation

Courts have applied traditional insurance law principles to instances of material misrepresentations made by automobile insurance applicants, voiding the policies where appropriate.

A Maryland man executed an application for automobile liability coverage in which he indicated that he had not received any tickets for speeding or other motor vehicle code violations within the past three years. A routine check of his driving record revealed that he had been convicted of two moving violations within the past three years. As a result of the man's misrepresentation the insurer sought to cancel his insurance contract by forwarding a notice of cancellation. The man protested and a hearing was held before the insurance division of the department of licensing and regulation. The hearing examiner determined that the nondisclosed information was not a material misrepresentation. The insurer appealed to a Maryland trial court. After the trial court affirmed the decision of the hearing examiner, the insurer appealed to the Court of Special Appeals of Maryland.

The appellate court noted that the question raised on appeal was whether the misrepresentation was material. It then stated that the misrepresentation made by the man concerned a matter that was clearly material to the contract of automobile liability insurance. The past driving history of a proposed insured has always been recognized as a factor properly considered by the insurer in assessing the proposed risk. The court held as a matter of law that the man had made a material misrepresentation on his insurance application and thus the insurance policy was voidable. The court reversed the trial court's decision. *Erie Ins. v. Insurance Commissioner*, 579 A.2d 771 (Md.App.1990).

A Texas couple purchased a car from a Louisiana car dealer. The dealer offered a credit life insurance policy which was to be financed with the car. The husband was on crutches, and did not even inspect the cars in the lot. However, the car salesman made no health inquiries when he offered the credit life policy. The husband was later diagnosed as having lung cancer and died within five months of the purchase. The credit life insurer refused the wife's benefit claim, stating that the husband had made a misrepresentation concerning his health when the policy was issued. The wife sued the insurer in a Louisiana trial court, which ruled for the insurer. The wife appealed to the Louisiana Court of Appeal, Second Circuit. The court stated that in order to avoid liability for misrepresentation, the insurer must establish that the applicant's statements were false and made with an intent to deceive. In this case, the car salesman, acting as the insurer's agent, made no inquiry despite the fact that the husband was on crutches. Although extensive evidence of the husband's poor health was presented at trial, none was immediately related to lung cancer, which was the eventual cause of death. Therefore, there was no evidence of a pre-existing condition which would preclude coverage. The court reversed the trial court's decision, ordering the insurer to pay the balance of the car loan plus interest. *Swain v. Life Ins. Co. of Louisiana*, 537 So.2d 1297 (La.App.2d Cir.1989).

A deaf Pennsylvania insured received notice from his automobile insurer of its intention not to renew his policy. The insurer had discovered that the insured had misrepresented his hearing impairment on a renewal form. The insured requested the state insurance department to review the insurer's nonrenewal notice. The department denied the request because the insurer's nonrenewal did not violate state law. An administrative hearing was held and the commissioner reversed the department's decision. He found the misrepresentations not knowingly false and not material to the risk, since the insured had a clean driving record for the previous four years. The insurer then appealed to the Commonwealth Court of Pennsylvania. The court held that nonrenewal of the policy due to the insured's misrepresentation did not violate state law prohibiting discrimination against disabled insureds. The insurer had refused to renew the policy not because of the insured's hearing impairment, but because he had blatantly attempted to conceal his impairment in an effort to benefit from lower insurance rates. The court further found that the insured's misrepresentation permitted the insurer to lawfully decline to renew the policy. The insured's hearing impairment was a condition that was material to risk, and was made knowingly and in bad faith. The court reversed the commissioner's decision and found for the insurer. *Erie Ins. Co. v. Foster*, 560 A.2d 856 (Pa.Cmwlth.1989).

A Pennsylvania woman applied for automobile insurance. She stated that she had a clean driving record and that her license had never been suspended or revoked. She paid her premium and a binder extending coverage was immediately issued. Less than a week later she submitted an $878 vandalism claim. While the insurer was reviewing the claim, it also reviewed her application. It obtained a report that indicated she had lied about her driving record and informed the applicant that due to the misrepresentations in her application it was rescinding her policy and returning the premium. She reported the cancellation to the Pennsylvania Insurance Department, which determined that the insurer's actions violated the Pennsylvania Automobile Insurance Act. The insurer appealed to the Pennsylvania Commonwealth Court which affirmed the decision. The insurer then appealed to the Pennsylvania Supreme Court. The supreme court observed that the act intended to balance the bargaining positions between insurers and insureds. It also noted that an insurer could cancel a policy due to misrepresentations. However, the court held for the applicant. The insurer could sue the woman for fraud and attempt to recover the damages incurred due to her misrepresentations. *Metropolitan Property and Liability Ins. Co. v. Ins. Comm'r of Pennsylvania*, 535 A.2d 588 (Pa.1987).

II. DUTIES OF INSURERS

Automobile insurers are obligated to settle legitimate claims promptly and must accept other responsibilities assigned to them by statute.

An Ohio insured was shopping at a grocery store when a shopping cart struck the side of his automobile parked in the store's lot. The insured contended that the wind propelled the cart into the car. The insurer argued that another force (a shopper or the parking lot grade) propelled the cart and that since the insured failed to prove what force put the cart in motion, he should only receive collision coverage. The district court agreed and granted the insured that coverage. The insured appealed. The Ohio Court of Appeals held that since the cause of the propulsion of the cart was unknown and because collision coverage was an exclusion from comprehensive coverage, the insured was entitled to comprehensive coverage with its lower deductible. Accordingly, the decision was reversed and the case remanded. *Gargallo v. Nationwide Gen. Ins. Co.*, 598 N.E.2d 1219 (Ohio App.10 Dist.1991).

After a Kentucky insured was involved in a one-car accident, he obtained two estimates for repairs. The insurer's adjuster estimated the damage to be almost $400 less, and the insurer paid the smaller amount. In the lawsuit which followed, the trial court held that the insurer could replace the damaged parts with used, rather than new, parts. The insured appealed to the Kentucky Court of Appeals which affirmed. Because the policy allowed used parts to be used, and because the vehicle was eight years old, the insured could not reasonably have expected the use of new parts. *Tomes v. Nationwide Ins. Co.*, 825 S.W.2d 284 (Ky.App.1991).

An insured driver, while driving his father's car, collided with a motorcycle and severely injured the motorcyclist. The insurer investigated and concluded that the accident was the insured's fault. It offered the motorcyclist the policy limits of $15,000 in exchange for a full release for the insureds (father and son). The offer was rejected. Subsequently, the motorcyclist sued the son for negligence and the father for negligent entrustment. The motorcyclist later offered to settle for $15,000 plus a defense for the insureds. However, he withdrew this offer before it could be accepted or rejected. After obtaining a judgment for $1.1 million dollars against the son, the motorcyclist and the insureds sued the insurer for statutory, tort, and contract claims which included breach of the implied duty of good faith and fair dealing. The trial court granted the insurer's motion for summary adjudication of issues, holding that the motorcyclist's offer to settle was not within policy limits, so the insurer did not have a duty to accept the settlement offer. The court then granted the insurer's motion for judgment on the pleadings. The motorcyclist and the insureds appealed to the California Court of Appeal, Sixth District. On appeal, the court noted that when there is a substantial likelihood of recovery in excess of policy limits, an insurer has an implied duty to settle a claim within the policy limits. However, in this case the motorcyclist's offer had been $15,000 plus defense costs, thus exceeding the policy limits. The court found the insurer had no duty to accept this offer. It went on to reverse the judgment on the pleadings, however, because the claims in the complaint had a basis in contract and tort law, and did not depend on a finding that the motorcyclist's offer was within policy limits. The court affirmed the summary adjudication of issues with respect to the insurer's duty to settle. *Heredia v. Farmers Ins. Exchange*, 279 Cal.Rptr. 511 (Cal.App.6th Dist.1991).

Two insured California residents were involved in an automobile accident. One driver suffered personal injuries and substantial damage to her automobile. Her insurer paid her for the damage to her car, and then filed a subrogation claim with the other party's insurer. That claim was paid. Six months later the injured party sued the insured who had hit her, claiming that he had been negligent. He proposed a settlement of $14,500 which the injured party accepted. His insurer, however, paid only $11,900 to the woman, claiming that it was entitled to subtract the subrogation payment it had made from the proposed settlement amount. The injured woman demanded full payment, and the insurer moved the trial court for an order enforcing the lower amount. The trial court granted the order. The injured woman appealed to the Court of Appeal, Second District. On appeal, she contended that the subrogation payment was not made as an accommodation to her, nor was it made on her behalf. It was made rather on her insurer's behalf because her insurer was the party with the legal claim. The court of appeal agreed. It noted that the payment did not in any way benefit the injured woman and thus the subrogation payment could not be deducted from the settlement amount. The court reversed the trial court's decision. *Griffin v. Calistro*, 280 Cal.Rptr. 30 (Cal.App.2d Dist.1991).

A Texas insured was involved in an automobile accident in which seven people were injured. The insured was covered under a policy which contained liability limits of $300,000 per occurrence and $100,000 per person. Two of the personal injury claims were promptly settled. The remaining claims belonged to five members of a family. Their injuries varied in severity. One member became a quadriplegic with injuries exceeding the $100,000 per person policy limit. The attorney for the family offered to settle with the insurer. His settlement demands overstated the amounts owing to family members other than the quadriplegic. All claims were finally settled except for the quadriplegic's, which went to trial and resulted in a $950,000 judgment. The insurer paid $100,000 of the judgment as required by its policy, and the insured agreed to contribute $250,000. The insured then sued the insurer in federal district court for failure to settle the claims in good faith. The insured contended that the insurer should have settled for inflated values for the four family members in order to make additional amounts available to cover the quadriplegic's claim, which would have avoided the excess judgment against the insured. The district court granted summary judgment for the insurer and the insured appealed to the U.S. Court of Appeals, Fifth Circuit. The court held that an insurer's duty of good faith did not require it to pay more than the policy limits. The insurer was not required to pay inflated amounts on some claims so that the more serious claim which exceeded the per person policy limit would receive additional compensation, thereby relieving the insured of the excess judgment. The court of appeals affirmed the district court's grant of summary judgment for the insurer. *Pullin v. Southern Farm Bureau Cas. Ins. Co.*, 874 F.2d 1055 (5th Cir.1989).

A New York insured and his companion were injured when their car hit a tree. The insured was charged with driving while intoxicated, although this charge was later dismissed. He then filed a no-fault claim under his automobile insurance policy. The insured told the insurer that there had been no police involved with the accident. However, the insurer did not make any inquiries of the police until two months later. The police notified the insurer of the insured's DWI charge four months after the incident. The insurer then denied the insured's claim. The insured sued the insurer in a New York trial court to enforce the policy. The New York Supreme Court, Appellate Division, upheld the trial court decision in favor of the insured. It held that the insurer had failed to diligently investigate the claim and to deny it properly. Under New York insurance law, an insurer has ten days to request verification of a claim, and the insurer in this case failed to do so. Nor did the insured's alleged misrepresentations prevent him from asserting a no-fault claim under the policy. *Bennett v. State Farm Ins. Co.*, 537 N.Y.S.2d 650 (A.D.3d Dept.1989).

A Texas woman was involved in an accident which caused her to miss work and rent a car until hers was fixed. The insurer of the other party agreed to pay the repair bill but would not pay for the rented car or the missed work. In fact, the insurer indicated that she would not receive any payment for the repair bill unless she signed a waiver. The woman and her attorney executed a release which held the driver and "all other persons, firms or corporations who might or could be claimed to be liable therefore, of and from any and all claims, demands, actions or causes of action or liabilities of any nature whatsoever going out of the accident." The woman sued the insurer alleging negligent and intentional infliction of emotional distress and gross negligence. The trial court entered summary judgment for the insurer. The woman appealed to the Court of Appeals of Texas.

On appeal, the court considered two issues: whether the release was effective against the insured and whether the insurer had a duty of good faith to the woman. The release did not name the insurer nor did it provide a specific description of the insurer. Therefore, the court determined that the release did not bar the woman's suit against the insurer. Next the court noted that there is a duty of an insurer to deal in good faith with its insured. However, the court noted that this policy was based on contract law. Since no contractual relationship existed between the parties, there was no duty of good faith. The appellate court upheld the decision of the trial court. *Bowman v. Charter General Agency, Inc.*, 799 S.W.2d 377 (Tex.App.1990).

An insured was struck by a dune buggy driven by an uninsured motorist. He suffered severe injuries and his expenses exceeded his insurance policy limits for uninsured motorist coverage and medical expenses. The insurer refused the insured's demand for payment because the policy limited uninsured motorist coverage to "highway vehicles." The insured filed a lawsuit for general damages of $500,000 plus punitive damages. Within ten days the insurer's attorney discovered that California law required insurers to pay insureds in this type of case. The insurer promptly issued a check to the insured for $30,000. The insured received the check within three and one-half months of the accident. The litigation entered a new phase as a bad faith and breach lawsuit. Over the next three years the insurer made several motions asserting the right to a refund of the $30,000. The insurer sought to exclude evidence of its actions following payment of the uninsured motorist benefits. The Los Angeles County Superior Court ruled in the insured's favor.

On appeal to the California Court of Appeal, Second District, Division 2, the insurer argued that use of its pleadings in the general damages phase of the lawsuit would prevent it from conducting a vigorous defense in the ongoing bad faith phase. The court noted that the insurer had an absolute right to defend its interests against the insured's claim. The insurer's claims manager had made a reasonable decision that the accident was not covered by the policy. The insurer mailed the check within ten days of discovering its incorrect legal position. The judgment for the insured was reversed and the insured failed to recover damages. *Nies v. Nat'l Automobile and Cas. Ins. Co.*, 245 Cal.Rptr. 518 (App.2d Dist.1988).

An Arizona insured was involved in an automobile accident while in the course and scope of her employment. The policy limit of her insurance was $25,000, but she had excess coverage available through a policy issued to her employer. After she reported the accident to her insurer, it made an investigation and determined that coverage was available. Prior to trial, the injured driver of the other vehicle made several settlement offers, the highest of which was $10,491. The primary insurer rejected the settlement offers and proceeded to trial. A jury awarded the injured driver $140,000 in damages which was reduced to $100,000, and the primary and excess carriers paid on the claim. The excess insurer then sued the primary carrier alleging that it had acted in bad faith by failing to accept settlement offers within its policy limits. It asserted that, under equitable subrogation, the primary insurer was obligated to pay the entire amount of the excess judgment. The trial court disagreed, holding that the primary carrier was only liable for the maximum amount of $25,000, and the excess insurer appealed to the Supreme Court of Arizona.

On appeal, the court noted that a number of jurisdictions had expanded the duty of good faith by recognizing a duty to an excess insurer by the primary carrier. Equitable subrogation was recognized as a means of encouraging fair and reasonable settlements of lawsuits. The court then stated that an excess insurer should not have to pay a judgment if the primary insurer caused the excess judgment by a bad faith failure to settle within its policy limits. Accordingly, under the theory of equitable subrogation, the excess insurer had the right to sue the primary insurer for bad faith failure to settle. The supreme court reversed and remanded the case for a determination of whether the primary carrier had exercised bad faith in refusing to settle within its policy limits. *Hartford Accident and Indemnity Co. v. Aetna Cas. and Surety Co.*, 792 P.2d 749 (Ariz.1990).

A Missouri woman was severely injured when the car in which she was a passenger was struck head-on by a car which had crossed the center line. The car was driven by an elderly woman. The injured woman filed a claim against the elderly driver's insurer, alleging that it was negligent in selling insurance to an "extremely senile" driver. The plaintiff argued that since automobile liability insurance is required in order to obtain a license, the insurer was in the best position to prevent an unfit driver from obtaining a driver's license. The insurer filed a motion to dismiss which was granted by the trial court. On appeal, the Missouri Court of Appeals focused on the question of whether an insurer owes a duty to refrain from selling insurance to obviously unfit drivers. The court held that it was unreasonable to place such a burden on insurers. *Hammers v. Farm Bureau Town and Country*, 792 S.W.2d 19 (Mo.App.1990).

III. DUTIES OF INSUREDS

In most states, an insured is required to notify his or her insurer as soon as reasonably practicable after an accident or a change of vehicles. An insured is also generally required to cooperate with and has certain obligations to his or her insurer.

An Arkansas motorcyclist sought liability coverage for passengers riding on his motorcycle. He contacted an insurance agent and purchased a "guest passenger liability insurance" policy. However, he expressly rejected medical coverage. The liability policy provided for bodily injury, property damage and passenger liability. Over a year after the policy was issued, the motorcyclist drove off the road and his wife, who was a passenger, was injured. The insurer denied the wife's medical benefits claim for lack of coverage. The insured insisted that her injuries were covered by the guest passenger liability policy. The insured and his wife sued the insurer and the agent in an Arkansas trial court. The court dismissed the complaint against the insurer, but awarded the insured and his wife over $38,000 for the agent's negligence in failing to provide correct insurance coverage. The agent appealed to the Arkansas Supreme Court.

The supreme court found that the insured sought a policy which would provide unlimited coverage, regardless of fault, to any passenger injured on his motorcycle. Such coverage was not offered by the insurer or any other insurance company. The court found that the insured had failed to read or understand his policy. Policyholders have a duty to educate themselves about their insurance coverage. If the insured had done so, he could have brought the lack of medical coverage to the agent's or insurer's attention. As no liability had been established in the trial court, there was no coverage under the liability policy. The supreme court reversed and dismissed the lawsuit. *Howell v. Bullock*, 764 S.W.2d 422 (Ark.1989).

An Ohio man entrusted his vehicle to his daughter without proof of financial responsibility as required under Ohio law. The daughter hit and damaged another vehicle. The other vehicle owner recovered from his insurer and the insurer then had subrogation rights against the daughter. She filed bankruptcy and the insurer sued the father in an Ohio trial court. The trial court granted the father's motion to dismiss and the insurer appealed to the Court of Appeals of Ohio. The appellate court affirmed the decision of the trial court stating that although the father violated an Ohio statute his entrustment of the vehicle was not the proximate cause of the damage suffered. *State Farm Ins. Cos. v. Wood*, 567 N.E.2d 1040 (Ohio App.1991).

The Georgia Court of Appeals has ruled that a policyholder's illiteracy was not a valid excuse for waiting over four years to notify his insurer of an accident. The man had been injured in 1979 while working on a truck. Although he received basic no-fault benefits from the owner of the truck and workers' compensation from his employer, he waited until 1983 to make a claim for optional no-fault benefits with his insurer. The court stated that if a policyholder cannot read the contract, it is his duty to find someone else to explain it to him. It held that the delay in notifying the insurer was "unjustified and unreasonable" and dismissed the man's lawsuit. *Int'l Indem. Co. v. Smith*, 342 S.E.2d 4 (Ga.App.1986).

An Oklahoma automobile passenger was injured in a car accident in which the driver of her vehicle was killed. The passenger sued the insurer of the deceased driver's former husband under an uninsured motorist clause in his policy. When a trial court held for the former husband's insurer, the injured passenger appealed to the Oklahoma Supreme Court. The supreme court upheld the trial court decision, noting that the former husband's insurable interest in the automobile ceased when it was awarded to his former wife (the deceased driver) in the divorce proceeding. The general rule in such cases was clear that liability coverage terminated upon a change of ownership unless the insurer approved an extension of coverage. Since there was neither notice to the former husband's insurer of the vehicle's change in ownership nor a corresponding transfer of the policy, the former husband's insurer could not be held liable to the injured passenger. *Farmers Ins. Co. Inc. v. Thomas*, 743 P.2d 1080 (Okl.1987).

An insured's truck was stolen while it was in the possession of a service station. After reimbursing the insured for his loss, the insurer requested that the insured sign a complaint against the service station so it could attempt to recover the amount paid to the insured. Despite three written requests by the insurer and further requests by the insurer's counsel, the insured refused to sign the complaint. The insurer then sued the insured, seeking to recover the amount it had paid. The policy under which the losses were paid provided that the insured was obligated to cooperate with the insurer and assist in making settlements, conducting suits, and enforcing the insurer's rights of contribution and indemnity against third parties who might be liable to the insured.

The Pennsylvania Supreme Court ruled that the insured's failure to cooperate was a material breach of the policy and that a return of the award paid under the policy was required. *Paxton Nat'l Ins. Co. v. Brickajlink*, 522 A.2d 531 (Pa.1987).

IV. STATE AND FEDERAL REGULATION

While the federal McCarran-Ferguson Act [15 U.S.C. §§ 1011,1012 (a, b)] granted the states exclusive control over the insurance industry, state automobile insurance regulatory statutes must nevertheless comply with federal and state constitutional requirements.

A. <u>State Regulation</u>

Indiana amended its law to require that auto insurers make uninsured/underinsured coverage with bodily injury limits equal to liability coverage for bodily injury. The requirement applied only to policies first issued after December 31, 1987. When an insured was struck by an uninsured driver, she sought to recover the amount listed in her liability coverage provision (which was higher than her uninsured coverage). After her insurer refused to pay the higher amount, she sued. The trial court held for the insurer, and the Indiana Court of Appeals affirmed. Because the policy had been issued before 1987, and had only been renewed after 1987, the new law did not apply. The insured was only entitled to the uninsured coverage amount. *Inman v. Farm Bureau Ins.*, 584 N.E.2d 567 (Ind.App.1st Dist.1992).

A Nevada insured held an insurance policy which excluded liability coverage for injury to another insured person. The exclusion stated that coverage would not apply to "liability for bodily injury to an insured person." The policy further stated that the insurer would provide coverage for "an insured person, other than a family member, up to the limits of the Nevada Financial Responsibility Law only." There was also a provision for permissive users which similarly limited liability coverage. The statutory minimum amount was $15,000 while the policy's limit to third parties was $100,000. The insured owner was then injured while riding as a passenger in her own car. A nonfamily member was driving at the time. Because the insured's injuries exceeded $15,000, she sued for coverage under the policy. The trial court held in her favor, and the insurer appealed to the Supreme Court of Nevada. On appeal, the court found that the language of the policy was clear and unambiguous, and that the trial court had erroneously ruled in favor of the insured. Further, the permissive user limitation in the policy, which also provided for minimum coverage, was plainly written and consistent with Nevada public policy. *Farmers Ins. Exchange v. Young*, 832 P.2d 376 (Nev.1992).

After an automobile accident, an insured demanded arbitration from his insurer on the ground that the insured's policy provided for arbitration when the other vehicle involved was uninsured. The insurer claimed that the other vehicle was still insured because a cancellation notice sent by the other insurer was invalid. A New York trial court stayed the arbitration. On appeal to the Supreme Court, Appellate Division, the court noted that the notice of cancellation had been defective because it failed to contain a clear statement to the insured that insurance must be maintained continuously throughout the registration of the vehicle. The court affirmed the stay of arbitration. *U.S.A.A. Casualty Ins. Co. v. Torres*, 577 N.Y.S.2d 408 (A.D.1st Dept.1991).

A Pennsylvania man was injured in an accident while driving his own car. He carried no insurance on the vehicle. As a result, he sought to recover uninsured motorist (UM) benefits under his mother's policy, asserting that he was a resident relative of her household. The insurer referred him to a policy exclusion which provided that UM benefits would not apply to injuries sustained while occupying a vehicle owned by a relative living in the insured's household — if the vehicle was not insured under the policy. In the lawsuit which followed, the insurer's counterclaim for a declaration that coverage was not available was dismissed, and the court ordered arbitration of the UM claim. The insurer appealed to the Superior Court of Pennsylvania. On appeal, the insurer contended that the trial court's dismissal of its counterclaim was erroneous because the passage of the Motor Vehicle Financial Responsibility Law (MVFRL) evinced a congressional intent to prevent uninsured motorists from using public highways by denying them insurance benefits. The appellate court disagreed. It noted that the MVFRL did not state that an uninsured owner of a vehicle could not receive UM benefits. Thus, even if an insured under one policy owned an uninsured vehicle, UM benefits could still be obtained after an accident involving the uninsured vehicle. The court affirmed the trial court's order compelling arbitration. Essentially, it held that Pennsylvania drivers only need to insure one of several vehicles to receive UM benefits. *Windrim v. Nationwide Mutual Ins. Co.*, 602 A.2d 1356 (Pa.Super.1992).

While a car was parked in a New York state office building, a fire began in a transformer which contained the chemical Pyranel. As a result, toxic chemicals contaminated the car. State officials ordered the destruction of the car, and the insurer (which had paid the car's fair market value to the insured) sued the state for conversion. The court of claims ruled for the insurer, and the state appealed to the New York Supreme Court, Appellate Division. The state contended that public necessity relieved it of any liability for the destruction of the car, but the court held that insufficient evidence had been presented that the car could not have been cleaned of the contaminants. The court held for the insurer. *Barton-Barnes Inc. v. State*, 583 N.Y.S.2d 547 (A.D.3d Dept.1992).

An Oregon man purchased two insurance policies. One was an automobile liability policy with a $500,000 limit and a $50,000 limit for underinsured motorist (UIM) benefits. The other was a $1 million multirisk, extra liability umbrella policy without UIM benefits. The insured was then involved in a car accident with another insured in which two passengers were injured. The other insurer paid the insured and his passengers its policy limits of $500,000. The insured and his passengers sought UIM benefits from the insured's insurer. It denied benefits and brought a declaratory judgment in an Oregon trial court. The court granted benefits under the umbrella policy, but denied them under the automobile policy. Appeals were taken by both parties to the Court of Appeals of Oregon. The court of appeals affirmed the trial court's decision. It noted that there could be no coverage under the automobile policy because it provided that UIM benefits would be reduced by amounts paid by those who were legally responsible. Since the limits on the two policies were the same, and the full amount had been paid under one, there could be no recovery under the

Sec. IV STATE AND FEDERAL REGULATION 123

other. With respect to the umbrella policy, however, since it was a motor vehicle liability policy for purposes of Oregon law, it had to be reformed to provide UIM benefits in the amount of bodily injury limits. *American Economy Ins. Co. v. Canamore*, 834 P.2d 542 (Or.App.1992).

A man was injured in an automobile accident in which his car was being driven by his son. Both the father and son were in the scope of their employment. The father sought liability and underinsured coverage from the son's policy. The insurer refused, and gained dismissal of a lawsuit which had been filed by the father in state court. The father appealed to the Supreme Court of North Dakota. The son's policy provided liability coverage when the insured was "legally obligated to pay," and underinsured coverage when the insured was "entitled to recover." The court held that workers' compensation was the sole remedy for the father. The son, as a co-employee, was immune from suit; the policy thus did not apply. The decision was affirmed. *Stuhlmiller v. Nodak Mutual Ins. Co.*, 475 N.W.2d 136 (N.D.1991).

An insurer covered a Ford automobile. Later, the Ford was deleted from coverage and another vehicle was substituted. The insurer never notified the Department of Motor Vehicles (DMV) that the Ford had been dropped from coverage. After an accident involving the Ford, the question arose as to whether it was an uninsured vehicle. The trial court held that it was, but the New York Supreme Court, Appellate Division, reversed. To effectively terminate coverage for third persons, a notice of termination must be filed with the DMV. *Eveready Ins. Co. v. Wilson*, 580 N.Y.S.2d 85 (A.D.2d Dept.1992).

A collision occurred in Florida involving a common carrier in which the plaintiff was injured. The plaintiff filed suit in a Georgia state court against the driver of the truck, who was a Georgia resident, the owner of the truck and its liability insurer. The insurer moved for summary judgment on the basis that Georgia law does not authorize direct causes of action when the accident occurs outside the state of Georgia. The trial court denied the summary judgment motion and the insurer appealed to the Court of Appeals of Georgia.

The court noted that the language of the direct action statutes authorized joint liability of the motor carrier's liability insurer in any suit. The statute did not state whether the suit could arise from an accident that occurred in another state. The court then looked to other provisions in the Motor Vehicle Code (MVC) which stated that the MVC came under regulation and registration of motor carriers on public highways of this state — meaning only in Georgia. Therefore, the court of appeals reversed the trial court's decision and granted summary judgment for the insurer. *Nat'l Union Fire Ins. Co. v. Marty*, 399 S.E.2d 260 (Ga.App.1990).

A Tennessee insured was injured in her husband's car while riding as a passenger. She had given permission to another person to drive the car. The driver's negligence caused a one-car accident. The insured's policy specifically excluded coverage for bodily injuries caused by a family-owned motor vehicle. The insured argued that because the driver carried no liability insurance their vehicle became uninsured at the time of the accident. She sued her insurer in a Tennessee county court, seeking uninsured motorist coverage. The court granted the insurer's summary judgment motion. The insured appealed to the Tennessee Court of Appeals, which reversed the trial court's decision. The insurer then appealed to the Tennessee Supreme Court.

The supreme court noted that a 1982 amendment to the Tennessee Code comprehensively defined uninsured motor vehicles. The 1982 amendments deleted the terms insolvency and underinsured "to require coverage by the insured's own insurer when the funds to which she is entitled from other policies, bonds, and securities cannot be collected." The 1982 enactment was not intended to transform uninsured motorist requirements into broad coverage resembling personal injury protection. The court concluded that the legislature intended to preserve exclusions such as the one in this policy. Therefore, the supreme court reinstated the trial court's summary judgment for the insurer. *Dockins v. Balboa Ins. Co.*, 764 S.W.2d 529 (Tenn.1989).

The Supreme Court of Virginia has dealt with several cases involving attempts to recover under the medical payments provisions of automobile liability insurance policies. In the first case the court decided whether an insured is entitled to coverage for injuries sustained while riding a motorcycle, notwithstanding a policy provision which limits coverage to injuries sustained while occupying an automobile. The court held that the injured motorcyclist was entitled to coverage because the policy provision conflicted with a state statute which requires coverage "while in or upon ... a motor vehicle." Therefore, the policy, under the statute, was required to include a motorcycle in motor vehicle coverage. *State Farm Mut. Auto Ins. Co. v. Seay*, 373 S.E.2d 910 (Va.1988).

The second case consolidated three cases involving motorcyclists and a fourth involving a truck collision. Again, the court held that there was coverage because of policy provisions which were in conflict with a state statute. The insurers argued that the State Corporation Commission mandated the use of the language in question in the policies and therefore that language was entitled to deference. They further argued that this language removed ambiguity in the statutory language. The court stated that as a result of its interpretation the commission had created an irreconcilable conflict between the policy provisions and the statute. In such a case, the statute prevails and supersedes the conflicting policy provisions. The court suggested that the result desired by the insurers could be obtained only by amending the statute. The commission was powerless to do that. The court therefore held in favor of the insureds. *Virginia Farm Bureau Mut. Ins. v. Jerrell*, 373 S.E.2d 913 (Va.1988).

An Arkansas couple was involved in a collision with an uninsured motor vehicle while riding in an Oklahoma couple's car. The Oklahoma couple's insurer was the primary insurer and the Arkansas couple's insurer was the excess insurer. The Oklahoma insureds' policy contained uninsured motorist limits of $10,000 per person which conformed to Oklahoma law. However, Arkansas law mandated coverage of $25,000 per person. The Arkansas insurer sought a declaration that the Oklahoma insurer was required to raise its coverage to the Arkansas limits. The trial court disagreed, and the Arkansas insurer appealed to the Supreme Court of Arkansas. The supreme court held that since the Oklahoma insurer's policy conformed to Oklahoma law, the policy limits would be upheld as written. The lower court decision was affirmed. *Automobile Club Inter-Ins. Exchange v. State Farm Mutual Automobile Ins. Co.*, 787 S.W.2d 237 (Ark.1990).

B. No-Fault

Two vehicles collided; one propelled the other vehicle into a group of nearby pedestrians. Even though the first vehicle never struck the pedestrians, they sought no-fault benefits from the vehicle's insurer. A district court entered summary judgment in favor of the pedestrians, and the insurer appealed. The Court of Appeals of Georgia upheld coverage even though the insured vehicle never actually came into physical contact with the pedestrians. The court held that the pedestrians were entitled to benefits because a collision was deemed to have occurred when one vehicle propelled itself into another vehicle, and the second vehicle struck a pedestrian. The court affirmed the lower court's grant of benefits to the pedestrians. *Atlanta Cas. Co. v. Tucker*, 420 S.E.2d 344 (Ga.App.1992).

An insured Hawaii driver was injured in a car collision and received more than $11,000 in no-fault insurance benefits from his insurer. The driver of the other vehicle was at fault, and the insured driver later settled a claim for $20,000 against the other driver's insurer. In return, the insured waived his rights to further claims. The other driver's insurer accepted the release, despite the fact that the no-fault insurer had previously informed it that having paid benefits to the insured, it was subrogated for fifty percent of the no-fault benefits paid. The no-fault insurer was unaware of the settlement negotiations between its insured and the other driver's insurer. The insured then vanished and the no-fault insurer unsuccessfully sought recovery of the no-fault benefits from the other insurer. Hawaii law expressly permitted no-fault insurers to recover fifty percent of the benefits paid when their insureds later obtained a tort recovery or settlement. The no-fault insurer sued the other insurer in a Hawaii court for the no-fault benefits. The trial court dismissed the complaint. It then appealed to the Hawaii Supreme Court. The supreme court rejected the other insurer's argument that no-fault insurer subrogation recovery lawsuits were limited to actions against their own insureds and were not allowed against tortfeasors or their insurers. The no-fault insurer was not precluded from seeking no-fault benefits from the other insurer. The insured had no authority to waive further recovery by his no-fault insurer. Thus the release he signed was ineffective. The no-fault insurer had timely notified the other insurer of its subrogation rights and had shown reasonable diligence to protect its equitable subrogation rights. The trial court's decision was vacated and the case was remanded. *Grain Dealers Mut. Ins. Co. v. Pacific Ins. Co.*, 768 P.2d 226 (Hawaii 1989).

A Michigan couple were injured in a car accident. They were insured under the husband's employer's health plan, a self-insured plan governed by ERISA. The plan specifically excluded benefits for injuries received in accidents involving a car for which a no-fault insurance policy was in effect. The couple's no-fault insurer sued the employer seeking reimbursement for medical expenses paid to the insureds. A Michigan circuit court granted summary disposition for the employer and the no-fault insurer appealed to the Court of Appeals of Michigan. The court of appeals affirmed the circuit court's decision. The Supreme Court of Michigan, in lieu of granting leave to appeal, remanded the case to the court of appeals for reconsideration. The court of appeals held that regardless of whether the employee's health plan was provided by the employer through an insurer or was self-funded, ERISA did not preempt the application of the state's no-fault act provision. The no-fault act provision made health insurance coverage primary and no-fault coverage secondary. The court noted that the state's no-fault coordination of benefits law was not preempted by ERISA simply because an uninsured ERISA plan was involved. The court of appeals reversed the grant of summary disposition and remanded the case to the trial court. *Auto-Owners Ins. v. Corduroy Rubber Co.*, 443 N.W.2d 416 (Mich.App.1989).

A Pennsylvania woman was insured under a policy issued in accordance with the Pennsylvania No-fault Motor Vehicle Insurance Act (no-fault act). The woman's husband elected Option B in order to receive reduced premiums which required that in the event of an accident, medical claims should be submitted to the insured's primary health insurer. After she was injured in an accident, the woman did not utilize her HMO coverage in obtaining medical treatment and the insurer refused to pay the outstanding medical bills. The woman filed a complaint which was submitted to arbitration. The panel of arbitrators found for the insurer and the trial court affirmed. The woman appealed to the Superior Court of Pennsylvania which determined that the woman was injured within the meaning of the no-fault act and thus bound by the named insured's election to coordinate benefits with a health insurer. *Connolly v. Metropolitan Ins. Co.*, 580 A.2d 35 (Pa.Super.1990).

A Pennsylvania insured became a quadriplegic when his vehicle was rear-ended. His health deteriorated until he was admitted into a nursing home. His automobile insurer sought a declaratory judgment that it did not have an obligation to pay for the insured's room at the nursing home. After a Pennsylvania trial court ordered the insurer to pay, it appealed to the Superior Court of Pennsylvania. The superior court held that the insurer was not obligated to pay for the insured's maintenance. The state no-fault act allowed recovery for rehabilitative services if they were necessary to reduce the insured's disability and to restore his functioning. The maintenance provided at the nursing home was therefore not recoverable. *Pennsylvania Nat'l Mut. Cas. v. Fertig*, 555 A.2d 208 (Pa.Super.1989).

A Michigan insured was injured in a car accident. He was insured under a no-fault policy containing a coordinated benefits clause. At the same time, he was also covered by a medicare policy. The no-fault policy insurer brought an action in a Michigan trial court, alleging that the medicare insurer was responsible for all of the insured's medical expenses. The trial court ruled in favor of the no-fault insurer and the medicare insurer appealed to the Michigan Court of Appeals. The appeals court affirmed the trial court's decision, holding that under Michigan law no-fault insurance was secondary to medicare health coverage. The court of appeals concluded that a federal law does not mandate that medicare be secondary to no-fault benefits. It said that making no-fault insurance secondary to medicare furthered the legislative intent of containing auto insurance and health costs. The medicare insurer was ordered to pay. *Employers Mut. v. American Com. Mut.*, 438 N.W.2d 275 (Mich.App.1989).

V. STACKING OF MULTIPLE POLICIES

The question of whether to allow the stacking of benefits under multiple automobile insurance policies or coverages is a matter of state law.

A. Stacking Allowed

An antique car collector in Wisconsin had two automobile insurance policies. One was the standard comprehensive policy; the other was an antique automobile insurance policy which had a substantially lower premium due to the fact that antique and collector vehicles are not driven on the highways with the frequency of regular cars. While both policies were in effect, the insured's wife and son were struck and killed by an uninsured motorist as they were walking along near their home. The insured obtained uninsured motorist benefits from his standard insurer. He then sought payment from the antique insurer. It denied coverage, asserting that since the wife and son were not occupying an insured antique vehicle when they were hit, no coverage had to be provided under the policy. The insurer sued for declaratory relief, and the trial court found that it did not have to provide coverage to the insured. The insured appealed to the Wisconsin Supreme Court. On appeal, the insured argued that the limitation in the insurer's policy served to prevent stacking in violation of Wisconsin law. The supreme court agreed. It stated that the law requires *every* policy of insurance to have uninsured motorist protection. Only the legislature could change this requirement. The court reversed the trial court's decision and held that uninsured motorist coverage was available under the antique automobile policy. *St. Paul Mercury Ins. Co. v. Zastrow*, 480 N.W.2d 8 (Wis.1992).

A girl, who resided in her father's home, was injured in an automobile accident. After receiving the policy limits of $50,000 from the driver's insurer, the girl sought to stack the underinsured motorist (UM) coverage from her father's three automobile policies. Each policy contained $50,000 of UM coverage. A state court granted summary judgment in favor of the insured, and the insurer appealed to the Court of Appeals of North Carolina. The insurer argued the girl was not entitled to collect any UM coverage because each of the UM limits were the same as the liability limit of the party at fault. It contended that the availability of UM coverage required that the party at fault had liability limits less than the limit of UM coverage. The court disagreed and specified that the aggregate total of the three policies was available to the girl, but that the exposure would be reduced by the amount received from the other driver's insurer. *Amos v. North Carolina Farm Bureau Mutual Ins. Co.*, 406 S.E.2d 652 (N.C.App.1991).

A New York couple purchased separate automobile liability policies from the same insurer for two vehicles which they owned. Both policies had a maximum limit of $75,000 for excess coverage and in both cases coverage extended to their son, who resided in their home. The policies' identical "other insurance" clauses provided "If there is any other applicable liability insurance we will pay only our share of the loss. Our share is the proportion that our limit of liability bears to the total of all applicable limits. However, any insurance we provide for a vehicle you do not own shall be excess over any other collectible insurance." A separate clause for "two or more auto policies" provided "If this policy and any other auto insurance policy issued to you by us applied to the same accident, the maximum limit of our liability under all the policies shall not exceed the highest applicable limit of liability under any one policy." The insured's son was involved in an accident while driving another insured's car. After exhausting the other owner's primary coverage limits, the insureds attempted to obtain excess insurance to the $75,000 limit on both policies. When the insurer refused to pay, the insureds sued in a New York trial court, which ruled that they were entitled to stack the policies for excess coverage.

The insurer appealed to the New York Supreme Court, Appellate Division, which reversed the decision. The insureds then appealed to the New York Court of Appeals. According to the court, the "other insurance" clause in the policies provided pro rata excess insurance under a New York statute. The court rejected the insurer's argument that the "two or more auto policies" controlled over the "other insurance" clause. Otherwise the policies would be in direct violation of the state law requiring excess insurance policies to contribute ratably. The "two or more policies" clause applied only where two or more policies covered the same loss and did not make either of the policies inapplicable to a particular accident. The court reinstated the trial court judgment for the insureds. *Carlino v. Lumbermens Mutual Cas. Co.*, 546 N.E.2d 909 (N.Y.1989).

A South Carolina woman was injured in an automobile accident and sought to stack and collect underinsurance benefits from three policies that she held. The insurer argued that she was not entitled to stack the coverages because her vehicle was covered by underinsurance benefits which exceeded the minimum limits required by the state. The woman appealed an adverse decision, and was heard by the South Carolina Supreme Court. South Carolina distinguishes between insureds who have a vehicle involved in an accident (class I insureds) and insureds who do not (class II insureds). The court noted that the woman was a class I insured, and determined that such insureds are entitled to stack underinsured coverage when carrying underinsurance above minimum limits. The stacking was limited, however, to allow recovery of benefits only up to the amount of coverage on the car involved in the accident. *South Carolina Farm Bureau Mutual Insurance Co. v. Mooneyham*, 405 S.E.2d 396 (S.C.1991).

A vehicle in which an insured was a passenger and a vehicle driven by an uninsured motorist collided. The "host" driver's insurance company provided uninsured motorist coverage of $50,000, but the insured's damages exceeded that amount. The insured passenger's own uninsured motorist coverage was $30,000. The driver's insurance company paid its limit to the insured passenger. The passenger's insurance company then refused to pay the balance of the damages by invoking its "other insurance" clause. The trial court found the passenger's other insurance provision void. The court of appeals reversed and the insured appealed to the Supreme Court of Arizona. The issue on appeal was whether the insurer could limit the mandatory coverage it provided when another policy had provided similar coverage to the passenger, or whether he had the right to aggregate his uninsured motorist limits with those covering the same loss and available from a primary policy. The supreme court concluded that aggregation was both equitable and desirable to permit recovery under more than one policy until the claimant was fully indemnified. The rule, however, does not allow a claimant to recover for more than out of pocket costs. The supreme court vacated the court of appeals' decision and affirmed the trial court's judgment. *Rashid v. State Farm Mutual Auto Ins. Co.*, 787 P.2d 1066 (Ariz.1990).

While a lodge employee was being driven to a nearby river by another employee in a company vehicle for his personal enjoyment, he was catapulted out of the bed of a pickup truck and severely injured. He sought benefits from his employer's comprehensive liability insurer and his father's no-fault insurer under which he was an insured. The no-fault insurer refused to pay the liability claim stating that the comprehensive liability insurer was the exclusive source of benefits. The employee then sued the no-fault insurer in a Minnesota trial court which granted summary judgment to the insurer. The employee/insured appealed to the Court of Appeals of Minnesota.

Minnesota had an antistacking law which did not allow stacking unless included under the policy. The court, however, determined that in this case the insured was not stacking the same coverage. Instead, the trial court had determined which policy covered the basic economic loss benefits. It had also given effect to additional protection that had been purchased by the employee's father. Requiring the insurer to pay benefits which it contracted to pay to covered members of the family (if they were seriously injured in an automobile accident) would not be stacking the coverage of the employer. Therefore, the appellate court reversed the decision of the trial court and found for the employee/insured. *Meister v. Western Nat'l Mutual Ins. Co.*, 465 N.W.2d 428 (Minn.App.1991).

A Missouri couple purchased two $100,000 automobile insurance policies which provided coverage for damages recoverable from the owner or operator of an uninsured motor vehicle because of an accident. Subsequently, they were involved in an accident when a negligent driver collided with their truck. The wife suffered extensive injuries; her damages far exceeded the $100,000 policy limits which the negligent driver possessed. The couple then sought coverage from their insurer, asserting that the policy provided coverage for underinsured vehicles the same as it did for uninsured vehicles. They also sought to stack their two policies to receive greater coverage. When the insurer denied the claims, they brought suit in a Missouri trial court which ruled in their favor. The insurer then appealed to the Missouri Court of Appeals.

The appellate court noted that the insurer had chosen in its policy to define uninsured as including underinsured. However, in another provision of the policy, it denied liability beyond the highest applicable limit available under any one policy. This clause would disallow coverage altogether because the negligent driver's policy had the same limit as the insureds' policies. Because there was an ambiguity, the court determined that the policies provided coverage. Further, the court noted that, with respect to uninsured provisions, there was a public policy allowing stacking. It thus affirmed the lower court's decision, and granted coverage to the insureds. *Maxon v. Farmers Ins. Co., Inc.*, 791 S.W.2d 437 (Mo.App.1990).

B. Stacking Precluded

An insured was seriously injured in an auto accident. He sued the other driver for negligence and received a $100,000 settlement from her insurer. The insured's policy contained "stacked" limits of $200,000 for each person and $600,000 for each accident. An arbitrator determined the amount of damages to be $337,000, plus $60,000 to the insured's wife for loss of consortium. After their insurer paid the insured $200,000, the husband and wife brought suit claiming that the wife was entitled to $60,000 for loss of consortium. The trial court certified the question of coverage to the Supreme Court of Rhode Island. The supreme court held that the wife's loss of consortium claim was derivative and not an independent action for bodily injury. Because the policy clearly limited liability for damages arising out of bodily injury to one person per accident, the loss of consortium claim could not succeed. The supreme court remanded the case to the trial court for judgment in favor of the insurer. *Allstate Ins. Co. v. Pogorilich*, 605 A.2d 1318 (R.I.1992).

An uninsured motorist collided with and killed a man operating a car owned by his employer. The deceased's wife sought to stack the underinsured coverage available in the employer's automobile insurance. The insurer contended that the coverage could not be stacked, and the woman filed suit in a state court. The trial court declined to resolve the dispute, and reserved the question for the Connecticut Appellate Court. Although stacking of underinsured coverage is generally allowed, Connecticut does not allow stacking when the insurance is a "fleet policy" because stacking in that context is beyond the parties' expectations. The wife argued that the policy should not be considered a fleet policy because it only insured two vehicles. In order to resolve the dispute, the court examined the coverage and premium charges. It then determined that it was unreasonable for the parties to the contract to have intended stacking. The insurer therefore prevailed. *Broderick v. Ins. Co. of North America*, 596 A.2d 18 (Conn.App.1991).

A Hawaii policeman was injured by an uninsured motorist while in his privately owned but city subsidized automobile. The automobile was insured under a single "business auto" policy providing uninsured motorist coverage in the amount of $25,000 per vehicle for 1,106 vehicles. The policy was not a "fleet" policy which would be a policy covering a number of vehicles owned by a business or government entity. Rather, the vehicles involved here were owned by individual police officers, not by the city. Also, unlike a typical fleet policy in which the employer is the named insured, here the city employees were also named insureds due to the unique practice in Hawaii of motor patrolmen using their own automobiles in performance of their official duties. The insurer paid the policeman the $25,000 policy limit on the uninsured motorist coverage but refused any further recovery based on stacking. An intermediate appellate court upheld the lower court. The policeman then appealed to the Supreme Court of Hawaii. The court stated that allowing injured persons to recover by stacking benefits under a group policy covering 1,106 unrelated vehicles for a total of $27 million dollars in uninsured motorist coverage would not serve to promote statutory purposes or public policy. It was noted that this was a narrow holding applying to the factual situation in this instance. The lower court decisions were upheld. *Lee v. Insurance Co. of North America*, 763 P.2d 567 (Hawaii 1988).

A Nevada insured caused an automobile accident and injured the occupants of another vehicle. The insured held third-party liability coverage on the vehicle he was driving. The insurer paid the policy limit. The insured owned two other vehicles each of which was covered by separate third-party liability policies. The occupants of the other vehicle claimed that the insurer should have paid them under all three policies since the anti-stacking provisions were not prominently displayed. A Nevada district court dismissed the case and the occupants appealed to the Supreme Court of Nevada. The supreme court noted that Nevada law did not apply to third-party liability coverage since it had already been determined that stacking coverage for bodily injury liability was inappropriate. Because such coverage was not stackable, a prominent notice would serve no purpose. The supreme court affirmed the trial court's decision. *Wood v. State Farm Mut. Ins. Co.*, 766 P.2d 269 (Nev.1988).

Sec. VI   UNINSURED/UNDERINSURED MOTORIST BENEFITS   131

A Pennsylvania man was a named insured in his automobile policy. A separate policy issued to his wife provided that he was covered as an insured. The wife's policy provided that her insurer would not pay benefits to an insured if there was another insurer at a higher level of priority. Under her policy the man's insurer was the first priority insurer. After he was injured in an automobile accident, his insurer paid him the limits of his policy. He then asked his wife's insurer to cover the remainder of his medical expenses. His request was denied and the man sued his wife's insurer in a court of common pleas. The court held in favor of the insurer and the man appealed to the Pennsylvania Superior Court. The superior court noted that the Motor Vehicle Financial Responsibility Law [75 Pa. C.S. §§ 1713(b), 1717(2)] provided in part: "the insurer [against whom a claim is asserted first] is ... entitled to recover contribution ... from any other insurer for the benefits paid.... First party benefits shall not be increased by stacking the limits of coverage of: ... (2) multiple motor vehicle policies covering the individual for the same loss." The wife's insurer argued that since the man was a named insured under his policy it had no obligation to pay benefits as a second level insurer. The man contended that he did not come within § 1717 since the same loss was not involved. The superior court upheld the decision in favor of the wife's insurer for two reasons. First, the medical bills covered by the man's policy and those which remained unpaid constituted the same loss. Second, the wife's policy, which excluded coverage where there existed coverage at a higher priority level, was fully enforceable. *Laguna v. Erie Ins. Group*, 536 A.2d 419 (Pa.Super.1988).

After a motorcyclist was killed when his motorcycle struck an illegally parked car, a Louisiana district court held that the motorcyclist's parents could stack their own uninsured motorist coverages on the motorcyclist's uninsured motorist coverage, thus collecting under both policies. The parents' insurer appealed and the Louisiana Court of Appeal reversed in favor of the insurer. It observed that the motorcyclist was the owner of the motorcycle when he was killed and that the motorcycle was insured by an insurer which paid the parents uninsured motorist benefits. Under these circumstances, the parents were prohibited by the provisions of Louisiana insurance law from stacking their uninsured motorist coverage on that of the motorcyclist. The law provided in part that "If the insured has any limits of uninsured motorist coverage in a policy of automobile liability insurance ... such limits of liability shall not be increased because of multiple motor vehicles covered under said policy ... and such limits of uninsured motorist coverage shall not be increased when the insured has insurance available to him under more than one uninsured motorist coverage provision or policy...." The court of appeal held that the insurance law clearly prohibited stacking since uninsured motorist coverage could not be increased when the insured had insurance available under more than one uninsured motorist coverage provision. *Belaire v. State Farm Mut. Automobile Ins. Co.*, 510 So.2d 1325 (La.App.3d Cir.1987).

VI. UNINSURED/UNDERINSURED MOTORIST BENEFITS

In most states automobile insurers are required either to offer or to provide uninsured and underinsured motorist coverage. This type of coverage provides benefits to the insured in the event that a person whom the insured is *legally entitled* to recover from is either uninsured or inadequately insured.

A. Scope of Coverage

The cases which follow deal with insurers' obligations to provide coverage for insureds' accidents involving uninsured or underinsured motor vehicles.

1. Insurers' Obligations

A North Carolina man owned a car, a truck and a motorcycle. He insured the car and truck under one policy, which provided $100,000 of underinsured motorist (UIM) coverage, and insured the motorcycle under another policy issued by a different insurer. This policy contained no UIM coverage. He was then permanently injured when a car struck his motorcycle. He obtained the $25,000 policy limits from the other driver's insurer, then sought payment from his car/truck insurer. The insurer denied coverage, and the insured sued. Eventually, the case reached the Supreme Court of North Carolina. The Supreme Court first noted that "liability insurance is essentially vehicle oriented, while [UIM] insurance is essentially person oriented." Here, the insured was the named insured of the car/truck policy. Thus, he was an insured "of the first class" under North Carolina law. As such, he was entitled to UIM benefits under his car/truck policy even though he had been injured while riding his motorcycle. The court granted coverage to the insured. *Bass v. North Carolina Farm Bureau Mutual Ins. Co.*, 418 S.E.2d 221 (N.C.1992).

After an insured Georgia man was injured in an automobile collision, he sued the other driver for damages. When the other driver failed to appear for the trial, a verdict was returned for the insured. The other driver's insurer then refused to pay the insured's judgment on the ground that the other driver had breached the cooperation clause contained in his policy. The insured filed a garnishment action against the insurer, but that proceeding proved to be unsuccessful. The insured then sought to recover the amount of the judgment pursuant to his own uninsured motorist policy. His insurer denied benefits and he sued in a Georgia trial court. The trial court granted summary judgment in favor of the insured. The insurer appealed to the Court of Appeals of Georgia.

The court noted that the uninsured motorist carrier would not be insulated from contractual liability to its insured simply because the liability carrier's subsequent denial of coverage was based upon its own insured's breach of a policy condition. The court also noted that when a tortfeasor behaved in such a way so as to make his policy unenforceable, the effect on his victim was very much the same as if the tortfeasor had never procured the insurance. The contractual result was that the tortfeasor was uninsured. Therefore, the injured party could recover from his own insurer under his uninsured motorist coverage. *Southern General Ins. Co. v. Thomas*, 397 S.E.2d 624 (Ga.App.1990).

Two Minnesota couples, while passengers in a taxicab, were involved in an automobile accident in Mexico. At least one of the involved vehicles was uninsured. Both couples submitted claims for uninsured motorist coverage to their respective insurers, which denied coverage, citing unambiguous territorial limitation provisions which excluded coverage for accidents occurring in Mexico. The couples then sued in a trial court which held for the insurers. The couples appealed to the Minnesota Court of Appeals. On appeal, they asserted that a territorial limitation on uninsured motorist coverage was in direct contravention to Minnesota law and therefore invalid. The court, however, disagreed. It stated that the law did not expressly prohibit an exclusion of uninsured motorist coverage for accidents occurring outside the United States. The court thus affirmed the trial court's decision. *Smith v. Illinois Farmers Ins. Co.*, 455 N.W.2d 499 (Minn.App.1990).

A Montana insured died as a result of a motor vehicle accident that occurred in Canada. The driver of the vehicle in which the insured was a passenger was found liable for the accident. He was insured by a Canadian insurer, with policy limits of $200,000; however, in wrongful death tort actions, Canadian law severely restricts the amount of damages payable. The insurer notified the deceased's estate that it would not pay any claims in excess of funeral expenses. Because the deceased's policy provided him with uninsured and underinsured motorist coverage, his estate sought coverage from his insurer, which brought a declaratory judgment action in a Montana trial court, asserting that coverage was unavailable. The trial court ruled for the insurer and the estate appealed to the Supreme Court of Montana.

On appeal, the insurer argued that the estate could not recover under the underinsured motorist provision of the deceased's insurance contract because the driver of the car had a $200,000 policy which had not been exhausted. The court, however, disagreed. It noted that because Canadian law restricted the damages recoverable on a wrongful death cause of action and because it had been demonstrated that the driver was at fault, the deceased's estate was legally entitled to damages. Further, since the insured's damages would certainly exceed the funeral expenses, and since the estate could not recover any further amounts from the Canadian insurer because of Canadian law, the deceased's insurer was obligated to provide coverage under the underinsured provision in its policy. The court reversed the trial court's decision. *State Farm Mutual Auto. Ins. Co. v. Estate of Braun*, 793 P.2d 253 (Mont.1990).

A California insured was injured along with several other individuals in an automobile accident. They settled with the insurer of the party responsible for the accident, and the insured received $10,000. He then demanded an additional $5,000 from his own insurer, claiming that the settlement amount was less than his underinsurance limits of $15,000. The insurer, however, maintained that the tortfeasor's policy was for the same amounts as the insured's limits and, thus, it need not compensate the insured. A lawsuit resulted in the grant of summary judgment to the insurer, and the insured appealed to the California Court of Appeal, Fourth District. On appeal, the court noted that § 11580.2 of the California Insurance Code defined an underinsured vehicle as being insured "for an amount that is less than the [victim's] uninsured motorist limits." The court then determined that the insured was not entitled to underinsured benefits because his underinsured limits were the same as the tortfeasor's liability limits. Even though the settlement was for an amount less than the limit, the potential liability was the same. The court thus held that the insured was not entitled to underinsured coverage, and the trial court's decision was affirmed. *Schwieterman v. Mercury Casualty Co.*, 280 Cal.Rptr. 804 (Cal. App.4th Dist.1991).

A North Dakota insured died as a result of injuries he suffered in an automobile accident with another vehicle. The other vehicle's insurer paid the estate its limit of $500,000. The estate's damages were in excess of $500,000 and it sought coverage under the deceased's automobile insurance policy. The court granted summary judgment to the insurer and the estate appealed to the Supreme Court of North Dakota. On appeal, the estate contended that it should be allowed to collect the underinsured motorist benefits to fully compensate for the loss caused by the accident. However, the court noted that the policy stated that underinsurance benefits were payable only when the amount of insurance carried by the tortfeasor was less than the applicable limit of underinsured coverage. Since the tortfeasor's coverage was $500,000 and was greater than the deceased's underinsured coverage limits, no further payment could be obtained from the insurer. The supreme court affirmed the decision of the trial court. *Thompson v. Nodak Mutual Ins. Co.*, 466 N.W.2d 115 (N.D.1991).

An insured driver and a passenger (plaintiffs) were injured in a collision with an uninsured driver. The plaintiffs settled with their insurer on the payment from the uninsured motorist portion of their policy. They then sought to recover their medical expenses. The insurer refused to pay the claim, and they filed suit in a Missouri trial court. The plaintiffs were granted summary judgment on both the insurance claim and an award for the insurer's vexatious refusal to pay. The insurer appealed both judgments to the Missouri Court of Appeals.

On appeal, the insurer argued that the plaintiffs were fully compensated from the uninsured motorist coverage settlement. The plaintiffs conceded full compensation. However, they claimed an exclusionary clause in the policy was void as against state law. The clause limited medical expenses coverage by the amount paid under the uninsured coverage of the policy. The court found the limitation in violation of the Missouri Uninsured Motorist Statute. This statute provides coverage to the insured driver to the level he would have been protected had he been in an accident with an insured driver. Since injured insureds would have been able to collect the medical coverage even though fully compensated in an accident with an insured driver, they must also be able to collect in an accident with an uninsured driver. Because this issue had not been addressed at the time the insurer refused to pay the claim, the summary judgment on vexatious refusal to pay was reversed. The court affirmed in part and reversed in part the ruling of the trial court. *Wilson v. American Standard Ins. Co.*, 792 S.W.2d 669 (Mo.App.1990).

2. Accidents and Events Covered

A pregnant truck driver was involved in a traffic accident and left her truck so she could flag away oncoming traffic. As she was directing traffic, another car struck and killed her. The estates of the decedent and her unborn child sought uninsured motorist coverage from the decedent's insurer. A state trial court granted coverage, and the Kentucky Court of Appeals affirmed. The insurer then appealed to the Kentucky Supreme Court. The supreme court upheld the decision because the decedent's presence at the point of impact was directly caused and necessitated by her disabled truck. Furthermore, the decedent was actively engaged in protecting her vehicle as well as protecting other vehicles. *Kentucky Farm Bureau Mut. Ins. Co. v. McKinney*, 831 S.W.2d 164 (Ky.1992).

An insured attempted to stop a thief from stealing her car by leaning across her car's windshield. The thief, however, proceeded to drive her car away with her on top of the hood. He struck another car head-on, injuring the insured. The insurer denied benefits to the insured claiming that the liability and uninsured motorist provisions did not permit recovery. The district court agreed that the liability provision did not permit recovery, but held that the uninsured motorist provision did provide coverage. The insurer appealed to the Court of Appeals of Colorado. On appeal, the insurer argued that because the insured's car was driven by a thief and the car was available for the insured's regular use, the car did not qualify as an uninsured vehicle. The insurer further argued that the insured was a passenger of her insured vehicle during the theft chase and therefore the uninsured motorist provision did not apply. The appellate court disagreed, noting that the purpose of Colorado's uninsured motorist statute was to compensate innocent victims for damages caused by irresponsible motorists, such as thieves. The statute was intended to compensate motorists for damages caused by an uninsured motorist whatever their status — passenger, driver, or pedestrian. Accordingly, the court of appeals held that the insured was entitled to uninsured motorist coverage and it affirmed the lower court's decision. *State Farm Mut. Auto Ins. Co. v. Nissen*, 835 P.2d 537 (Colo.App.1992).

An Ohio insured arranged to meet a woman friend. As the woman drove to meet the insured, her estranged husband followed her in a separate car. The estranged husband pulled up alongside the insured's motorcycle and fired a pistol at him, wounding him twice. The insured's vehicle was not involved. The insured sought uninsured motorist coverage from his automobile insurer. A district court held in favor of the insurer, and the insured appealed to the Ohio Court of Appeals. The appellate court denied coverage since the estranged husband's discharge of his pistol caused the insured's injury and the injury did not result from the ownership, maintenance, or use of the insured's vehicle. Thus, the trial court's decision was affirmed. *Westfield Ins. Co. v. Cahill*, 602 N.E.2d 339 (Ohio App.3d Dist.1991).

A Minnesota police officer arrived at the scene of an accident to direct traffic. He left his squad car running with its emergency lights flashing in an attempt to reroute traffic around the accident site. While he was 30 to 150 feet away from his car and directing traffic, a car struck him. The officer sought uninsured motorist coverage from his insurer. When coverage was denied, the officer sued in a state trial court. The court granted the officer coverage, and the insurer appealed to the Minnesota Court of Appeals. On appeal, the insurer argued that because the officer was not occupying his squad car within the meaning of the automobile policy he was not entitled to uninsured motorist coverage. The court agreed, stating that although he was using his squad car as a tool for directing traffic and had left the motor running and lights flashing, his connection with the vehicle was too remote. Furthermore, the officer was beyond the reasonable "geographic perimeter of the vehicle" to recover uninsured benefits. Accordingly, the court reversed the trial court's decision and held in favor of the insurer. *Gieser v. Home Indem. Co.*, 484 N.W.2d 256 (Minn.App.1992).

A Pittsburgh pedestrian was injured by an uninsured motorist driving a stolen car which was insured. The pedestrian first sued the driver, but dismissed his claim when he learned the driver was not covered under an automobile insurance policy. Then the pedestrian filed a claim against the insurance company insuring the stolen vehicle. The trial court ruled in favor of the uninsured pedestrian, and the insurer appealed the decision to the Superior Court of Pennsylvania. The insurer argued that it was not liable since both the victim and the driver were uninsured. It also argued that since the motor vehicle which injured the pedestrian was not uninsured as the

Pennsylvania statute requires, the pedestrian was not entitled to uninsured benefits. The superior court stated that if the statute was interpreted this way it would allow the pedestrian to recover only from uninsured motor vehicles. It decided that this was not the right interpretation. It also decided that a distinction could not be made between an uninsured victim and an uninsured motorist seeking uninsured motorist benefits from the insurer of the vehicle which injured the victim. For these reasons, the superior court held the insurance company liable and affirmed the trial court's decision. *Ecktor v. Motorists Ins. Co.,* 571 A.2d 457 (Pa.Super.1990).

A pedestrian was standing next to a pickup truck conversing with the vehicle's operator when a shotgun on a rack on the back of the truck cab accidentally discharged while the driver was attempting to unload it. The pedestrian was shot in the head and killed. The pedestrian's parents sought recovery under the truck owner's liability policy and their own uninsured motorist policy. When recovery was denied they sued. A lower court denied recovery. The District Court of Appeal of Florida reversed. It held that the accidental discharge of a shotgun which was in a gun rack permanently attached to the interior of the pickup truck evidenced sufficient causal connection to the use of the truck so as to come within policy coverages. It was noted that the transportation of firearms is an ordinary use of a motor vehicle, especially a pickup truck. Because the causal connection existed coverage was upheld. *Quarles v. State Farm Mut. Auto. Ins. Co.,* 533 So.2d 809 (Fla.App.5th Dist.1988).

In a Minnesota case, a man was driving home from work when another car driven by a coworker pulled up alongside of his. The coworker fired a shotgun, injuring the man's arm. The man filed a claim with his automobile insurer for no-fault and uninsured motorist benefits. The insurer sought a declaratory judgment that no coverage existed. After the declaratory judgment was awarded by a district court and affirmed by the court of appeals, the man appealed. The Minnesota Supreme Court ruled that the coworker's car was an "active accessory" to the assault; he had used it to keep up with the insured for over two miles in order to shoot him. Further, no act of independent significance occurred to break the causal link between the use of the coworker's car and the injury. Finally, the supreme court concluded that the coworker was using his car for transportation purposes; he used his car to maneuver himself into position to shoot the insured. The court declared that coverage existed. *Continental Western Ins. Co. v. Klug,* 415 N.W.2d 876 (Minn.1987).

A Hawaii motorist, who was insured by no-fault and uninsured motorist coverage, was injured when he was struck by a bullet fired from another vehicle on a freeway. The other vehicle and the person firing the gun were never identified. After he claimed benefits under his no-fault and uninsured motorist coverages his insurer denied coverage. He sued his insurer, seeking no-fault and uninsured motorist coverage. A Hawaii circuit court held for the motorist, and his insurer appealed to the Hawaii Supreme Court. The insurer contended that there was an absence of no-fault coverage since the gunshot was not accidental but was the result of either reckless or intentional conduct. It also contended that there was no uninsured motorist coverage since the gunshot did not result from the operation, maintenance or use of a motor vehicle as required under Hawaii's uninsured motorist statute. The supreme court held for the motorist with respect to both coverages. He was entitled to no-fault coverage due to the fact that both the gunman and the motorist were occupying motor vehicles traveling on the highway when the incident occurred. From the motorist's standpoint the injuries were accidental. The supreme court reasoned that if the gunman had rammed the motorist's car with his car, instead of shooting him, coverage would have existed. The motorist was entitled to uninsured motorist coverage since he could legally recover for his injuries from the owner or operator of the vehicle from which he was shot. Furthermore, a literal reading of Hawaii's uninsured motorist statute suggested that the injury resulted from the "operation, maintenance or use" of a motor vehicle. *Ganiron v. Hawaii Ins. Guar. Ass'n*, 744 P.2d 1210 (Hawaii 1987).

3. Hit-and-Run Accidents

A Pennsylvania insured's car was hit by another car while parked in a lot. The insured obtained the other driver's name and a license plate number, but the other driver drove away before the insured could get more information. The insured did not call the police. When he contacted his attorney, he had forgotten the other driver's name and the license number given by the woman turned out to be fake. The insured sought uninsured motorist benefits from his automobile insurer. The insurer refused to pay and sought a declaratory judgment in a federal district court that it was not liable under the uninsured motorist policy because the insured had not been involved in an accident with an uninsured motorist. The district court refused to grant the insurer's declaratory judgment. The court found that the insured's policy did not require him to question the driver nor could the insurer deny coverage because the insured had failed to call the police. It held that under Pennsylvania law, the driver whose vehicle struck the insured's had a legal obligation to supply him with the information. The insurer could not refuse coverage on the ground that the insured was unsuccessful in attempting to do something that his insurance policy did not require him to do. *Hartford Ins. Co. v. Blackburn*, 702 F.Supp. 1199 (E.D.Pa.1989).

A New Jersey man brought suit against his girlfriend's uninsured motorist insurer after he was injured in a hit-and-run accident. The plaintiff was injured while standing in a roadway and leaning against his girlfriend's car. The uninsured motorist policy afforded coverage to any person injured while occupying the vehicle. The issue, therefore, was whether the plaintiff was occupying his girlfriend's vehicle so as to be entitled to the protection of the policy. The Superior Court of New Jersey, Appellate Division, after reviewing the extensive case law on this matter, concluded that if an injured person was not in an insured vehicle and was not in the process of entering or leaving it when the accident occurred, he was not an occupant unless he was on or near the vehicle in connection with his immediate use of it as a means of transportation. Here, the plaintiff had no intention of entering the vehicle. Using the roof of the vehicle as an armrest while talking to someone inside, the court stated, did not constitute occupying the vehicle. In holding for the insurer, the court stated that its conclusion was consistent with the reasonable expectations of a person buying uninsured motorist coverage. *Mondelli v. State Farm Mut. Automobile Ins. Co.*, 475 A.2d 76 (N.J.Super.A.D.1984).

In Oklahoma an automobile passenger who was injured in a hit-and-run collision brought suit against her insurer, seeking no-fault benefits. The insurer refused to pay the passenger's claim on the ground that the vehicle causing the accident was followed by another motorist and subsequently identified. The name of the owner of the vehicle causing the accident was ascertained, but the name of the driver who caused the accident had not been established. The insurer contended that because the owner of the vehicle was identified, the vehicle ceased to be a hit-and-run vehicle for purposes of uninsured motorist coverage. The Supreme Court of Oklahoma, which had been asked by a U.S. district court to resolve the case, held that a vehicle is a hit-and-run vehicle for purposes of uninsured motorist coverage so long as the identity of the operator has not been ascertained. A hit-and-run driver is still a hit-and-run driver, said the court, even if the vehicle and the vehicle's innocent owner can be identified. *Brown v. United Services Automobile Ass'n*, 684 P.2d 1195 (Okla.1984).

4. Physical Contact Rules

The Court of Appeals of New York, New York's highest court, ruled on two cases interpreting a state statute which governed the application of insurance coverage in the minimum amount required by laws of other states. The cases both involved New York drivers who were injured in automobile accidents in New Jersey. In the first case, a New York insured demanded arbitration when his insurer refused to cover an accident involving an uninsured vehicle. His policy contained standard language limiting uninsured motorist coverage to "accidents which occur within the state of New York." The supreme (trial) court granted the insurer's motion to stay arbitration, then reversed itself and denied the stay. The Appellate Division, Second Department, affirmed. In the second case a New York resident was cut off by a vehicle while driving in New Jersey, causing his car to leave the road and overturn. There was no contact between the cars. The driver owned a New York policy containing standard uninsured motorist endorsements covering hit and run accidents. While New York insurance law required "physical contact" for uninsured motorist coverage, New Jersey's rule expressly required that uninsured motorist coverage be provided even without showing physical contact. The driver demanded arbitration when his claim was denied. The supreme court granted the insurer's stay of arbitration and the Appellate Division, First Department, affirmed. The insured appealed to the Court of Appeals of New York.

The court of appeals noted the split in appellate division rulings and consolidated the cases. It held that New York Insurance Law § 5103(e) and state insurance department regulations supported the insureds' claims for coverage. The law provided that insurance coverage for every liability policy shall also provide insurance coverage for the covered vehicle at least in the minimum amount required by the laws of vehicles operated in any other state. The result was that New Jersey requirements for uninsured motorist coverage were incorporated into the New York insurance contracts being considered. The court rejected the insurers' argument that older case law controlled, noting that § 5103(e) was adopted after the cases cited by the insurers. *American Transit Ins. Co. v. Abdelghany; Atlantic Mutual Ins. Co. v. Finker*, 589 N.Y.S.2d 842 (Ct.App.1992).

A woman's vehicle was struck by a tire and rim which had become disengaged from an unidentified vehicle. The tire crashed through her windshield, and resulted in her death. Her insurer refused uninsured benefits because there was no physical contact with the unidentified vehicle. The deceased's estate demanded arbitration, but a state court agreed with the insurer and granted a stay of arbitration. The stay was originally upheld, and the estate further appealed to the Court of Appeals of New

Sec. VI   UNINSURED/UNDERINSURED MOTORIST BENEFITS   139

York. New York insurance law followed a policy of discouraging fraudulent claims for uninsured coverage which result from claiming that an accident was caused by a hit and run vehicle by imposing a physical contact requirement. This requirement was held in previous cases to preclude coverage for cars struck by snow, hubcaps, tires and rims. The court expressed concern over these results and then "clarified" the rule to allow coverage upon collision with an "integral part" of an unidentified vehicle. The new standard allowed coverage upon proof that the detached part of the vehicle caused the accident through an unbroken chain of events. The estate was ruled to be entitled to arbitration. *Allstate Ins. Co. v. Killakey*, 574 N.Y.S.2d 927 (Ct.App.1991).

A Georgia insured sustained injuries after her car struck a tire assembly lying in the center of a highway. She filed a "John Doe" action against her insurer, alleging that the assembly had been left there by an unknown truck driver. The insurer sought summary judgment because there had been no actual physical contact with an unknown motor vehicle as required by Georgia law. The motion was denied, and on appeal to the Court of Appeals of Georgia, the court adopted the "indirect physical contact" doctrine to allow recovery where a vehicle comes into contact with an integral part of another vehicle. The summary judgment was properly denied. *State Farm Fire & Casualty Co. v. Guest*, 417 S.E.2d 419 (Ga.App.1992).

A Kansas insured was injured when her car struck a utility pole. She claimed that another vehicle forced her off the road. She sought coverage under her uninsured motorist coverage. Her insurer denied coverage based on a Kansas statute which allowed insurers to exclude coverage when there is no physical contact with the uninsured vehicle. The insured sued the insurer in a state trial court, claiming that the statute violated her constitutional due process and equal protection rights. The trial court held for the insurer and the insured appealed to the Kansas Supreme Court. The supreme court held for the insurer. The statute did not restrict the insured's right to purchase insurance coverage for accidents caused by an unidentified vehicle and where there was no physical contact with the unidentified vehicle. Therefore the statute did not violate her equal protection or due process rights under the Constitution. The insurer was not required to provide coverage. *Clements v. United States Fidelity and Guar. Co.*, 753 P.2d 1274 (Kan.1988).

A Texas man was injured in an automobile accident while riding with the insured. The insured was blinded by the lights of an oncoming vehicle and forced to turn right, sliding into a post, to avoid a head-on collision. The passenger sought to recover uninsured motorist benefits from the insurer in a Texas trial court. The trial court granted summary judgment to the insurer and the passenger appealed to the Court of Appeals of Texas. The appellate court affirmed stating that under the policy an uninsured vehicle is defined as a vehicle which hits your vehicle. Since there was no physical contact the court ruled that there were no uninsured motorist benefits available. *Guzman v. Allstate Ins. Co.*, 802 S.W.2d 877 (Tex.App.1991).

Two Illinois men were injured in an accident while driving a station wagon owned by their employer. While driving east on a Chicago highway, an unidentified vehicle struck the rear of another automobile, causing it to strike the station wagon. The men filed a claim with their employer's insurer under the uninsured motor vehicle provision of the policy. The insurer denied coverage of the claims because the automobile was not "hit" by an uninsured motor vehicle as defined in the insurance policy. The insurer filed a lawsuit seeking a declaratory judgment that it was not required to cover the men's injuries. The circuit court, holding that the station wagon was not "hit" by the hit-and-run vehicle as required by the policy, granted the summary judgment. The men appealed, and the Appellate Court of Illinois affirmed the circuit court's decision. They appealed again.

The Illinois Supreme Court noted that when an unidentified vehicle strikes one vehicle which in turn collides with the insured's vehicle, uninsured motorist coverage usually applies. The court noted that the contact requirement of the policy exists to prevent motorists from blaming accidents on nonexistent vehicles. It agreed with a previous Illinois decision that "where there is a direct causal connection between the hit-and-run vehicle and the plaintiff's vehicle, which connection carries through to the plaintiff's vehicle by a continuous and contemporaneously transmitted force from the hit-and-run vehicle, recovery [should be] allowed." The court decided that even though the "hit" in this case was indirect, it triggered coverage under the employer's policy. It further noted that because a "hit" must be proven, the decision did not enhance the ability of insured motorists to blame accidents on "phantom" motorists. The judgments of the appellate and circuit courts were reversed and the case was remanded for further proceedings. *Hartford Accident & Indem. Co. v. LeJeune*, 499 N.E.2d 464 (Ill.1986).

A couple was traveling in their car on a Michigan highway when a camper-truck approached from the other direction. As the camper-truck passed the couple's car, a large rock crashed through their windshield and killed the husband who was driving. The wife filed a lawsuit against the couple's insurer, seeking no-fault survivor benefits and the policy limits of the uninsured motorist provisions of their policy. The insurer paid the survivor benefits but declined payment of the uninsured motorist policy limit. The couple's policy covered bodily injury arising out of the "physical contact" of a hit-and-run automobile with an insured person or with an automobile that an insured person is occupying. The insurer claimed that because the two vehicles did not come into contact, no "physical contact" had occurred under the policy. After a Michigan circuit court ruled in favor of the insurer, the wife appealed.

The Michigan Court of Appeals noted that the physical contact requirement is meant to preclude "claims by a driver who negligently loses control of his car and thereafter claims that he was forced off the road by an unknown vehicle," which can easily be done in cases where no contact occurs. The court pointed out that "where indirect contact occurs, the possibility of fraud is substantially diminished by the tangible physical evidence of the intermediate object," in this case the rock. It concluded that the physical contact requirement of the couple's policy was met when the rock propelled by the camper-truck collided with the couple's car. The decision of the circuit court was reversed. *Hill v. Citizens Ins. Co. of America*, 403 N.W.2d 147 (Mich.App.1987).

B. Individuals Entitled to Coverage

1. Coverage Allowed

A man purporting to be a prospective customer asked a used car dealer's employee if he could test-drive a car. The car dealer's manager okayed the test-drive. Accompanied by the employee during the test-drive, the driver picked up another man, who he claimed was a mechanic. These two men then physically overpowered the employee, and forced him onto the floor of the back seat. They subsequently dragged him from the car and shoved him into the trunk, hitting him repeatedly. The men used the car to rob a bank. The employee managed to escape from the moving car, but was injured in the process. The two men were never apprehended. After the employee sought coverage under the used car dealer's uninsured motorist policy, the insurer brought a declaratory judgment action, and a district court granted summary judgment in favor of the employee. The insurer appealed to the Court of Appeals of Ohio.

On appeal, the insurer claimed that the employee was excluded from uninsured motorist coverage because the car was stolen. However, the court found that the exclusionary clause did not apply since the driver initially drove with the used car dealer's permission. The insurer further argued that coverage did not apply since the employee's injury and the use of the car did not have a significant causal connection. The court, however, noted that the employee's injuries occurred when he was a passenger of the car and that the assault by the driver and his accomplice was in furtherance of the use of the car to rob a bank. Thus, the court believed that the causal connection was not severed. Accordingly, the court affirmed the trial court's decision and granted summary judgment in favor of the employee. *Buckeye Union Ins. Co. v. Carrell*, 602 N.E.2d 305 (Ohio App.10th Dist.1991).

An insured man with liability limits of $100,000 per accident caused an accident injuring four people. The $100,000 was split among the injured parties. One injured man received $53,000 less than his damages, and sought to recover underinsured (UIM) motorist coverage from his insurer. His policy had UIM limits of $100,000 per person and $300,000 per accident. A state court granted judgment for the insurer, and the man appealed to a New Jersey appellate court. All previous cases defining underinsured were distinguished because they dealt with policies having one type of limit — either per person or per accident. The court held that where either the tortfeasor or the injured party has "double limits" it becomes necessary to consider whether more than one person was injured. Here, since more than one person was injured, the claimant's insurance controlled. The earlier decision was reversed. *Staub v. Hanover Insurance Co.*, 596 A.2d 1096 (N.J.Super.A.D.1991).

An Iowa man was severely injured in South Carolina by an uninsured vehicle. His wife was living with her parents in Iowa at the time of the accident. Her father had an insurance policy which provided uninsured motorist protection for "a person related [to the named insured] by blood ... who is a resident of [the named insured's] household." The wife claimed loss of her husband's consortium as a result of the accident and sought proceeds under her father's policy. After the insurer refused to pay she sued it in an Iowa trial court. Following a denial of a motion for summary judgment, the insurer appealed to the Supreme Court of Iowa.

The supreme court noted that language in the policy appeared to include the wife as a covered person but the policy then provided that the company would only pay damages which a covered person was legally entitled to recover from the owner or operator of an uninsured motor vehicle because of bodily injury sustained by a covered person and caused by an accident. This language excluded coverage of her claim because her husband was not a resident of her father's household and thus not a covered person under the policy. However, an Iowa statute, which overrides policy provisions if there is a conflict, states that to recover for damage caused by an uninsured motorist it must be shown that bodily injury resulted from ownership or operation of the uninsured vehicle. The court held that the wife was a covered person under the statute and that the statutory term "bodily injury" included injury to a noncovered person causing damage to a covered person. The supreme court affirmed the trial court's decision for the insured. *Hinners v. Pekin Ins. Co.*, 431 N.W.2d 345 (Iowa 1988).

A Washington man was injured in an automobile accident while a passenger. He sought to recover under the driver's underinsured motorist coverage. The insurer denied coverage claiming that the passenger was not exercising control over the vehicle. Thus he was not "using" the vehicle within the policy definition of insured. A Washington trial court found for the passenger and the insurer appealed. The Court of Appeals reversed the lower court's decision and the passenger petitioned for review. The Supreme Court of Washington held that because there was no definition of "use" in the policy it would not be interpreted to have a unique meaning. The term "using" included passive use by a passenger entitling the passenger to coverage as an insured. *Sears v. Grange Ins. Ass'n*, 762 P.2d 1141 (Wash.1988).

An Alabama man was struck by a government vehicle as a result of the negligence of its driver, a government employee. The injured man possessed three vehicles, each having uninsured motorist coverage of $10,000. The man contended that the insurer was therefore obligated to provide him with $30,000 worth of uninsured motorist coverage. However, the injured man's insurance policies stated that such coverage would be granted only "for bodily injury an insured is legally entitled to collect" from the driver of the other vehicle. This clause was patterned after Alabama's Uninsured Motorist Act. Because the Federal Tort Claims Act precludes a negligence suit against the government and its employees, the insurer disclaimed liability, contending that the injured man was not "legally entitled" to damages from the negligent driver of the government vehicle. A declaratory judgment action was brought in a U.S. district court, which ruled that the insurer was liable on the policy.

On appeal, the U.S. Court of Appeals, Eleventh Circuit, affirmed the decision in favor of the injured man. Noting that this question had never been addressed before by an American court, the appellate court held that although, strictly speaking, government immunity barred the injured man from suing the negligent driver of the other vehicle, he was nevertheless legally entitled to collect from him under the Alabama Uninsured Motorist Act. To hold otherwise would be to contravene the legislature's goal of providing compensation to innocent victims. The court ordered the insurer to provide policy coverage as required by the Act. *State Farm Mut. Automobile Ins. Co. v. Baldwin*, 764 F.2d 773 (11th Cir.1985).

2. Coverage Denied

An insurer issued an automobile policy to a corporation which was owned by a woman and her father. The corporation was listed as named insured and the two shareholders were listed as insured drivers. The woman was riding a bicycle when she was struck by an underinsured motorist. She then sought to collect underinsured coverage from the policy which had been issued to the corporation. The insurer contended that only the corporation, as named insured was entitled to underinsured benefits. A trial court found in favor of the insurer, and the woman appealed to the

Sec. VI   UNINSURED/UNDERINSURED MOTORIST BENEFITS   143

Court of Appeals of North Carolina. The woman contended that her status, as majority shareholder and insured under the policy, in effect made her one and the same as the corporation which was the only named insured. No case law supported this assertion, and the court held that the denial of coverage was appropriate. *Busby v. Simmons*, 406 S.E.2d 628 (N.C.App.1991).

Two Arizona medical professionals witnessed a single car accident and rushed to the passengers to help. One of the passengers did not survive, and it was determined that he had AIDS. The medical professionals underwent a year of testing because they had used CPR. Neither tested HIV positive, but the two medical professionals sought uninsured motorist benefits since the driver of the car involved in the accident had not been insured. A district court granted summary judgment in favor of the insurer, and the medical professionals appealed to the Arizona Court of Appeals. On appeal, the medical professionals contended that their exposure to the passenger and the testing for AIDS constituted "bodily injury" under the terms of the policy. The court, however, held that the medical professionals could not claim damages for the threat of contracting AIDS in the future without demonstrating any bodily injury. *Transamerica Ins. Co. v. Doe*, 840 P.2d 288 (Ariz.App.Div.1 1992).

A woman was killed in an automobile accident during which she was a passenger in a car owned by her employer. Her estate brought suit against her employer's insurer seeking underinsured motorist benefits. Although the policy contained a waiver of such coverage, the estate asserted that the waiver was insufficient for two reasons: 1) the waiver had been signed only by the employer's broker and not a "named insured," and 2) the procedure utilized to waive such coverage did not constitute a "writing." A Washington court held for the insurer, and the estate appealed to the Court of Appeals of Washington. Washington allows a "named insured or spouse" to reject underinsured coverage. However, Washington courts have long accepted an agent's authority to act when an insured so intended. The court ruled that the agent's authority had not been changed in the underinsured context. The insured's intentions then became the focus, and the evidence was held to indicate a clear desire to waive such coverage. The final dispute concerned the law's requirements that the waiver be in writing. Other states have required a separate document and signature, but the court rejected a proposal for adoption of these requirements in Washington. The writing was held to have sufficiently reflected a desire to waive the coverage. The decision of the trial court was affirmed. *Weir v. American Motorists Ins. Co.*, 816 P.2d 1278 (Wash.App.1991).

A patron at a lounge in Torrance, California, became ill and unable to drive around 1 p.m. An employee of the lounge asked two other customers to take the sick customer home. They agreed and one drove the sick patron's insured 1979 Cadillac and the other customer followed in her own uninsured vehicle. After arriving at a certain intersection, the two left the sick patron in the back of his vehicle and departed. Thereafter, the patron died of hyperthermia. The decedent's wife filed a claim under the uninsured motorist provision of the Cadillac's policy. The insurer refused to pay stating that the claim did not arise out of the ownership, maintenance or use of an uninsured motor vehicle. The widow sued, but the trial court granted the insurer's motion for judgment on the pleadings. The widow appealed. The Court of Appeal, Second District, affirmed the judgment. It stated that uninsured motorist coverage is not intended to act as a substitute for general liability coverage for tortfeasors who, by chance, also happen to be uninsured motorists. The court stated that the injury did not arise out of the use of an uninsured motor vehicle. Any act of negligence was independent and remote from the use of the uninsured vehicle which the customer had driven to the intersection. *Rowe v. Farmers Ins. Exchange*, 9 Cal.Rptr.2d 314 (Cal.App.2d Dist.1992).

A New Jersey man purchased the minimum coverage for underinsured motorist injuries from an insurer. He was then involved in an auto accident which severely injured him. After collecting from his insurer, he sought recovery from his former daughter-in-law's insurer. Although divorced from his oldest son, she was engaged to marry his second oldest son, and she and her children resided in his home. Her insurer denied coverage because the former father-in-law was not a "relative" under the policy. The Superior Court of New Jersey, Appellate Division, upheld the insurer's definition of "relative" and denied coverage. *Handler v. State Farm Mutual Automobile Ins. Co.*, 602 A.2d 796 (N.J.Super.A.D.1992).

A Minnesota insured was confronted by her former boyfriend, who began to chase her down the highway. He pulled his car up alongside hers and began shooting at her, hitting her once. Since he was uninsured, she attempted to recover benefits under the uninsured motorist clause of her automobile policy. The insurer denied coverage. She sued unsuccessfully in a state trial court and appealed to the Minnesota Court of Appeals. The court stated that she could not recover because, first, the shooting had been an intentional act and, second, the shooting was not causally connected with the insured's use of her car. The court affirmed the judgment for the insurer. *McIntosh v. State Farm Mutual Automobile Ins. Co.*, 474 N.W.2d 227 (Minn.App.1991).

A South Carolina woman lived in an insured's household. She was not related to anyone in the family. While walking home from work, she was killed by an uninsured motorist. The insured filed a claim on the woman's behalf under the uninsured motorist provisions of his policy, which the insurer denied. The insured then sued in a South Carolina trial court which held for the insurer, and the insured appealed to the Court of Appeals of South Carolina. The appeals court held that in order for the woman to have been covered under the insured's policy, the woman must have been a "relative" within its meaning. Since the woman was not related to the insured, she was not a "relative" and thus coverage was denied. Accordingly, the court affirmed the trial court's decision. *Inman v. South Carolina Ins. Co.*, 389 S.E.2d 173 (S.C.App.1990).

A Florida man was killed in a car accident while driving his own vehicle. At the time, he was a fifty percent owner of a partnership. The partnership had an automobile insurance policy covering three business vehicles. The man's estate argued that he should be deemed a Class I insured under the business policy so he could recover under it. After a Florida trial court refused to allow coverage, the estate appealed to the District Court of Appeal of Florida. The appellate court affirmed the trial court's decision, concluding that the policy specifically indicated that only the partnership was intended to be the named insured. In order for the man to have been covered under the partnership's policy, it was necessary that he himself be listed as a named insured. *Burnsed v. Florida Farm Bureau Cas. Ins.*, 549 So.2d 793 (Fla.App.5th Dist.1989).

New York's highest court decided to follow the majority of states, ruling that a business automobile policy issued to a corporation does not provide uninsured motorist coverage for the family members of corporate officers or shareholders. The plaintiff here was a college student who lived with his parents, who were the officers and sole shareholders of a real estate corporation. A business automobile policy had been issued to the corporation which contained an uninsured motorist endorsement for "you or any family member." After being struck by a hit-and-run driver while riding his bicycle the plaintiff sought uninsured motorist benefits under the corporation's automobile policy. The Court of Appeals ruled that a corporation, due to its status as a "legal fiction," cannot have personal injuries or a family. Coverage was therefore denied. *Buckner v. Motor Vehicle Accident Indem. Corp.*, 495 N.Y.S.2d 952 (1985).

C. Interception of Benefits by Creditors

At least one state supreme court has ruled that creditors may not attach a lien on uninsured motorist benefits.

In this case a Texas hospital, which had provided care for a man severely injured in an accident with an uninsured motorist, attempted to attach a lien to the uninsured motorist's benefits paid to the patient's heir after his death. The Texas Court of Appeals affirmed a lower court's decision to allow the lien and appeal was taken to the Texas Supreme Court. Texas law allows the existence of hospital liens to encourage hospitals to provide immediate care for persons injured in accidents. The statute provides, however, that liens are allowed to attach only to public liability insurance.

The question before the supreme court was whether uninsured motorist coverage is included in the term "public liability insurance." The court stated that public liability insurance insures against damage claims for which the insured might become liable. In contrast, uninsured motorist coverage protects insureds against negligent, financially irresponsible motorists. The court concluded that the insured's uninsured motorist coverage did not fit within the definition of public liability insurance. The court of appeals' decision was reversed and the creation of the lien was not permitted. *Members Mut. Ins. Co. v. Hermann Hospital*, 664 S.W.2d 325 (Tex.1984).

D. Insurers' Duty to Offer Coverage

Generally, in states where uninsured or underinsured motorist coverages are optional, 1) an insurer must make a valid offer to provide such coverage to the insured, and 2) the insured must make a valid rejection of that offer.

1. Duty not Satisfied

A passenger in an automobile driven by a Connecticut insured was injured in a collision. The driver was insured with limits of $100,000 for liability and $50,000 for underinsured coverage. Under Connecticut law, an insured must sign a waiver of equal underinsured coverage in order to obtain underinsured limits lower than liability limits. The driver's husband had signed such a waiver upon making his application. The passenger contended that the waiver was ineffective because it was not signed by both named insureds. An arbitration panel and a trial court ruled in her favor, and the Connecticut Supreme Court granted direct appeal. Connecticut General Statutes § 38-175C (A)(2) grants the right to equal liability and underinsured limits, and provides that unequal limits are illegal "unless the insured in writing requests" a lower underinsured limit. The insurer contended that the term "insured" requires a signed waiver only by the initial purchaser. The passenger argued that "insured" meant all named insureds. The term was ruled to be ambiguous. The court held that all named insureds must sign the waiver, and that the waiver in this case was insufficient. The passenger was allowed to collect the higher limits. *Nationwide Mutual Ins. Co. v. Pasion*, 594 A.2d 468 (Conn.1991).

The state of Hawaii amended its insurance law to require an offer of underinsured motorist (UM) coverage. In an attempt to comply, an insurer mailed a letter to all of its Hawaii policy holders which informed them of the coverage and the premium. The letter suggested that in order to purchase such coverage insureds should contact their agent or broker. Two Hawaii insureds who did not purchase UM coverage were injured in separate mishaps. Each brought suit alleging that they did not receive the letter, and that the letter did not satisfy statutory notice requirements. The injured parties lost their respective suits, and they were consolidated on appeal to the Supreme Court of Hawaii. The court adopted a four part test which is used in many states with similar legislation: "1) If made other than face-to-face, the notification process must be commercially reasonable; 2) the limits of optional coverage must be specified and not merely offered in general terms; 3) the insurer must intelligibly advise the insured of the nature of the optional coverage and 4) the insurer must apprise the insured that the optional coverage is available for a relatively modest increase in premium." After applying this test, the court held that the letter was insufficient. The second and fourth parts of the test were not met because the limits of coverage were found to be unclear. The letter failed the third part of the test due to a lack of examples or description of coverage. The suggestion of contacting an agent or broker also impermissibly placed a burden on the insured. The court further held that the offer was required for each issuance, delivery, or renewal of a policy; the duty was thus found to be applicable to this case, and breached. Lastly, the court ruled that the statute imposed a written rejection requirement on the offer of UM coverage. The prior judgment was reversed. *Mollena v. Firemen's Fund Ins. Co. of Hawaii, Inc.*, 816 P.2d 968 (Haw.1991).

A South Carolina couple purchased an automobile insurance policy. The insurer made an offer of underinsured motorist coverage by placing an insert (with several other inserts) in the insureds' renewal premium notice envelope. The couple did not elect to buy such coverage. The wife was then killed in an automobile accident with an insured who carried only minimum liability limits. The husband sued his insurer for failing to make a meaningful offer of underinsured motorist coverage. The case reached the Supreme Court of South Carolina which held that the insurer's premium renewal notice, which merely referred to the availability of underinsured coverage, was not sufficient to allow an informed decision by the insureds. *Lopez v. National General Ins. Co.*, 417 S.E.2d 864 (S.C.1992).

A Colorado couple was involved in an accident with an uninsured motorist. The insureds alleged that they were unaware that their underinsured motorist (UM) limits were at the same level as their liability limits. The couple brought suit against their agent and insurer contending that the defendants had breached a statutory duty to offer higher limits. A state court granted summary judgment to the insurer, and the decision was appealed to the Colorado Court of Appeals. Three issues faced the court: what duty did the statute create for the insurer, did that duty arise upon a change in a policy, and would the breach of that duty give rise to a cause of action against the agent and/or the insurer. Colorado law requires a written rejection of equal UM and liability limits. The court found the intent of the law to be to ensure that consumers were aware of the availability of UM coverage. The extent of the duty was held to be "an affirmative duty to inform" so that a consumer could make an intelligent decision. The court ruled that the duty arises when any material alteration is made. In this case, both the addition of a vehicle and the change of policy limits were found to be "material alterations." The earlier judgment was reversed, and the case was remanded. *Parfrey v. Allstate Ins. Co.*, 815 P.2d 959 (Colo.App.1991).

Four separate automobile policies were issued to a couple with liability limits of $25,000/$50,000, and no underinsured (UIM) coverage. A fifth policy was issued with the same liability limits and UIM limits of $100,000/$300,000. The couple's son was injured in an accident with an underinsured driver. The insurer refused coverage so the insured sued. A jury found that the waiver of UIM coverage on the four policies without UIM coverage was not "knowing and informed" as required by statute. The offer which had been made by the insurer on those policies was for UIM limits of $100,000/$300,000. The trial court was unsure whether to impute coverage by law with the statutorily created minimum limits, or with the limits which had been offered by the insurer. The question was certified to the Supreme Court of Appeals of West Virginia. The court held that the statute required an effective waiver of *statutorily required* coverage. In absence of the effective waiver, it is that minimum coverage which was imputed by law. A holding otherwise, the court stated, would encourage insurers to avoid potential losses by offering only the minimum coverage at all times. Underinsured coverage was imputed at the statutorily required minimum. *Riffle v. State Farm Mutual Automobile Ins. Co.*, 410 S.E.2d 413 (W.Va.1991).

After being injured in an automobile accident, an insured sued his insurer seeking to obtain underinsured motorist benefits equal to the liability limits of the policy. The insurer had failed to make a mandatory offer of underinsured motorist coverage pursuant to Minnesota insurance law. The insurer contended that underinsured motorist coverage should be imposed only in an amount equal to the minimum statutory coverage allowed. However, the Minnesota Court of Appeals agreed with the insured, holding that the insurer's failure to offer underinsured motorist coverage resulted in a court imposed amount equal to the liability limits of the insured's policy. *Osterdyke v. State Farm Mut. Automobile Ins. Co.*, 410 N.W.2d 892 (Minn.App.1987).

After a South Carolina insured was involved in a collision with an underinsured motorist, she brought an action in a state trial court seeking a determination that her automobile policy included underinsured motorist coverage. The trial court determined that the insurer had made an effective offer of underinsured motorist coverage which the insured refused. She appealed to the Supreme Court of South Carolina. The insurer contended that the insured had received an insert with the renewal notice explaining underinsured motorist coverage. The court determined that since the renewal policy did not contain any language directing the insured to read the insert, it did not constitute an effective offer of underinsured motorist coverage. The supreme court reversed the trial court's decision. *Zeigler v. South Carolina Farm Bureau Mut. Ins. Co.*, 393 S.E.2d 166 (S.C.1990).

2. Duty Satisfied

An Arkansas man was injured while a passenger in his own car which was being driven by his son. The insured's automobile was struck by another vehicle and he sustained serious injuries. The insured obtained a $25,000 settlement from the other driver's insurer but that was insufficient to compensate him for his injuries. He then instituted this suit against his insurer claiming that he was entitled to underinsured motorist benefits under the policy. The insurer acknowledged that the insured had an insurance policy but stated that he never purchased underinsured motorist coverage. The insurer submitted copies of various documents showing the renewal of coverage and demonstrated that underinsured motorist protection was never elected. The trial court found that the insurer had complied with an Arkansas statute that required insurers to make available underinsured motorist's coverage to policyholders. The passenger then appealed to the U.S. Court of Appeals, Eighth Circuit. Arkansas law provided that every insurer writing automobile liability policies covering liability arising out of any motor vehicle shall make underinsured motorist coverage available to the named insured. There were no reported Arkansas decisions that had interpreted this statute. The court noted that the legislature could better address the issue than a federal court. It therefore held that the insurer complied with the Arkansas statute and made available underinsured motorist coverage. The court upheld the trial court's decision denying coverage. *Edens v. Shelter Mut. Ins. Co.*, 923 F.2d 79 (8th Cir.1991).

While on vacation, a man rented a vehicle through an agreement which provided liability insurance. An intoxicated driver hit his vehicle, killing him and injuring certain family members. After recovering from the drunk driver, the family members sued the car rental company and its insurer, asserting that they had violated Nevada law by failing to offer underinsured motorist coverage. The court ruled for the defendants. The family appealed to the Nevada Supreme Court, which held that the law in question only applied to "insurance agents." Since the rental company was not an insurance agent, it had no duty to offer underinsured motorist coverage. Further, the insurer had offered such coverage to the company, which had rejected it. The ruling for the defendants was affirmed. *Hartz v. Mitchell*, 822 P.2d 667 (Nev.1991).

A woman was killed in an accident with an uninsured motorist. Although she did not purchase underinsured coverage, her estate contended that coverage should be imputed because she was not offered underinsured coverage as required by Arkansas law. The insurer contended that her policy was renewed before the effective date of this requirement. A trial court granted summary judgment for the insurer, and the estate appealed to the Supreme Court of Arkansas. Although the statute which imposed the requirement stated only that the offer should be made, and failed to specify an effective date, the insurer argued that it was required only upon issuance or renewal of a policy. The insurer pointed out that the statute was later

Sec. VI   UNINSURED/UNDERINSURED MOTORIST BENEFITS   149

amended to require a written rejection of coverage, and that the amendment was applicable only to issuances or renewals. The court held this to be indicative of legislative intent. The judgment in favor of the insurer was affirmed. *Nixon v. H & C Electric Co.*, 818 S.W.2d 251 (Ark.1991).

Insured automobile owners in California brought suit against an insurance agent and their insurer, alleging that the agent had breached a duty to them by not advising them to carry uninsured motorist coverage in an amount greater than the statutory minimum. The plaintiffs were severely injured in an automobile collision with a vehicle driven by an uninsured driver. The California Court of Appeal affirmed a trial court ruling in favor of the insurer and the agent. The court observed that the purpose of the uninsured motorist statute is not to provide full compensation for all drivers for accidents with uninsured drivers, but to make sure that drivers injured by such drivers are protected to the extent that they would have been protected had the driver at fault carried the statutory minimum of liability insurance. In addition, there is no duty on the part of an insurance agent to do more than to call the attention of his customer to the availability of the statutory provision and, unless expressly told to omit it, to see that the policy complies with the statute. Since the agent owed the plaintiff no duty other than to secure for him a policy meeting the statutory requirement, the trial court properly dismissed the plaintiff's lawsuit. *Pabitzky v. Frager*, 210 Cal.Rptr. 426 (App.2d Dist.1985).

E. Exclusions

An Indiana man was using an automobile owned by his mother. A liability insurance policy had been issued on the car. While it was parked at the son's place of employment, two people attempted to steal it. The son tried to stop them, became entangled in the shoulder safety belt, and was injured. He then sought uninsured motorist coverage from his mother's insurer. When the insurer denied coverage, he brought suit in a state trial court. After a grant of summary judgment to the insurer, he appealed to the Court of Appeals of Indiana. On appeal, the son asserted that one of the thieves was an uninsured motorist driving an uninsured vehicle because he did not have permission to drive the car. However, because Indiana law defined an uninsured motor vehicle as one without liability insurance, and because the vehicle was covered by liability insurance, the car was insured. Further, the policy contained an exclusion for family members with respect to bodily injury. Thus, the court held that summary judgment had been properly granted to the insurer. It affirmed the trial court's decision. *Whitledge v. Jordan*, 586 N.E.2d 884 (Ind.App.1st Dist.1992).

A Florida insured was injured in a car accident while riding as a passenger in her own car. Her adult daughter, who lived elsewhere and had no liability insurance, was driving at the time. When the insured sought coverage under the liability and uninsured provisions of her policy, the insurer rejected her claim. In the subsequent lawsuit, which reached the Florida Supreme Court, it was held that since the car was owned by the insured, coverage was excluded by the clause which excepted vehicles "owned by or furnished or available for the regular use of you or any family member." *Smith v. Valley Forge Ins. Co.*, 591 So.2d 926 (Fla.1992).

A Texas woman was injured when the car her husband was driving jumped the median into oncoming traffic. She was a passenger at the time. After their insurer settled with the other driver, the woman sued for uninsured/underinsured benefits. The trial court ruled for the insurer, and the woman appealed to the Texas Court of Appeals. The court noted that a clause in the policy expressly stated that uninsured vehicles did not include vehicles available for regular use by a family member. Since her husband was driving a family car, uninsured coverage could not apply. The court affirmed the trial court's ruling for the insurer. *Scarborough v. Employers Cas. Co.*, 820 S.W.2d 32 (Tex.App.1991).

A teenage driver was involved in an automobile collision and his passenger sustained injuries. She collected the limits of his liability coverage, and then also sought to collect underinsured motorist benefits from his insurer. The passenger unsuccessfully brought suit against the driver's insurer, and appealed to the Superior Court of Pennsylvania. The passenger argued that the driver's policy did not expressly exclude the recovery of both liability and underinsured motorist benefits. She attempted to distinguish the policy from policies in earlier cases denying such recovery. The court noted that underinsured motorist coverage operates in much the same way that uninsured coverage operates; the liability limits of the tortfeasor's policy must be insufficient, and a claim must then be made against the insurer of the party seeking the benefits. The exclusion was unnecessary. The ruling was affirmed. *Sturkie v. Erie Ins. Group*, 595 A.2d 152 (Pa.Super.1991).

An insured driver could not start his automobile, and while temporarily borrowing his mother's car was severely injured in an accident with an uninsured driver. His mother's car was insured under a policy issued to his parents which had an uninsured motorist coverage limit of $60,000. His car was insured under a separate policy from the same insurer having uninsured motorist coverage of $300,000. The insured sought uninsured coverage under his policy through the "temporary substitute provision." The insurer argued that he should be limited to coverage under his parents' policy, and contended that his policy excluded uninsured motorist coverage for automobiles owned by a family member and not listed on the policy. A suit was brought by the insured in state court. The issue was whether the uninsured motorist coverage exclusion for a vehicle owned by a family member applied when the vehicle was being used as a temporary substitute. The question was certified to the Supreme Court of Rhode Island.

The temporary substitute vehicle provision allowed an insured coverage for a borrowed vehicle in the event of breakdown, repair, servicing, loss, or destruction of the insured auto while maintaining for the insurer a reasonable definiteness of which vehicles are insured. The uninsured motorist clause excluded coverage when an insured occupied, or was struck by, an automobile owned by a family member and not listed in the policy. Its purpose was found to be to preclude insuring all autos in a household while receiving a premium for only one. The insured argued that the clauses were ambiguous. The court agreed, and explained that "even though the exclusionary clause at issue in our present case is not ambiguous by itself, we find that the two possible interpretations arise when the exclusionary clause is read together with the definition of a temporary substitute vehicle ... a policy holder should not be required to engage in such rigorous analysis to learn that there is no coverage." The ambiguity was construed in favor of the insured. *Bartlett v. Amica Mutual Ins. Co.*, 593 A.2d 45 (R.I.1991).

An Oklahoma man was insured under four automobile policies which provided for uninsured motorist coverage. Under the policies the definition of uninsured motor vehicle excluded any land motor vehicle owned by any government or its political subdivisions or agencies. The insured's daughter was injured while a passenger in a vehicle owned by an Oklahoma university. The daughter sued the insurer claiming she was entitled to uninsured motorist coverage. The insurer brought a declaratory judgment action in a federal district court, seeking a determination that the vehicle in which the daughter was a passenger was not an uninsured motor vehicle as defined in the policy. The federal district court certified a question to the Supreme Court of Oklahoma to determine whether the policy's definition of an uninsured motor vehicle was against public policy. The state supreme court held that the policy's definition of an uninsured motor vehicle was against public policy. The court noted that Oklahoma had clearly mandated the inclusion of uninsured motorist coverage in automobile insurance policies. The primary purpose of the inclusion was to protect insureds from the effects of personal injury resulting from an accident with an uninsured/underinsured motorist. The policy's language was a blatant attempt to limit the inclusion of uninsured motorist coverage in automobile policies and was ruled void and unenforceable. *State Farm Auto. Ins. Co. v. Greer*, 777 P.2d 941 (Okl.1989).

A man was killed when an unknown motorist negligently drove into the path of a truck the man was driving. The man's employer provided the truck for his regular use. The man was covered by his son's automobile insurance policy. The policy provided uninsured motorist coverage with an exclusion precluding recovery for injuries incurred while occupying a motor vehicle "owned by or furnished for your regular use and not insured under this insurance...." The man's widow sued the insurer when it denied coverage under this exclusion. The Georgia Supreme Court observed that statutorily mandated uninsured motorist coverage was required to indemnify the insured for "all sums which he shall be legally entitled to recover as damages from the owner or operator of an uninsured motor vehicle." The exclusion was invalid because it reduced the man's uninsured motorist coverage below the legal standard. The son's insurer was liable for damage resulting from the man's accident. *Doe v. Rampley*, 351 S.E.2d 205 (Ga.1987).

VII. POLICY CANCELLATION

Limitations have been placed upon insurers' rights to cancel automobile insurance contracts, including giving adequate notice to insureds and allowing a reasonable period of time in which insureds may pay overdue premiums.

A. Cancellation Notices

1. Inadequate Notice

After an automobile accident, an insured demanded arbitration from his insurer on the ground that the insured's policy provided for arbitration when the other vehicle involved was uninsured. The insurer claimed that the other vehicle was still insured because a cancellation notice sent by the other insurer was invalid. A New York trial court stayed the arbitration. On appeal to the Supreme Court, Appellate Division, the court noted that the notice of cancellation had been defective because it failed to contain a clear statement to the insured that insurance must be maintained continuously throughout the registration of the vehicle. The court affirmed the stay of arbitration. *U.S.A.A. Casualty Ins. Co. v. Torres*, 577 N.Y.S.2d 408 (A.D.1st Dept.1991).

The mother of a four-year-old boy injured in an auto accident made a demand for arbitration according to her policy's uninsured motorist endorsement. The insurer claimed that the owner of the vehicle which had struck the boy was not uninsured. A New York trial court disagreed, and the insurer appealed to the Supreme Court, Appellate Division. The higher court found that the renewal notice which had been sent out was not in the proper form required by law. It did not state the amount needed for renewal, and it did not inform the insured that he could pay either the broker or the insurer. Thus, the cancellation was ineffective and insurance was in effect, precluding uninsured motorist coverage. The arbitration was stayed. *Eveready Ins. Co. v. Hadzovic*, 582 N.Y.S.2d 508 (A.D.2d Dept.1992).

A Rhode Island automobile insurer issued an automobile liability insurance policy to a couple. The couple's son was in an accident but the insurer denied coverage, claiming that the policy lapsed or expired prior to the accident. The policy was originally issued to the parents alone. When renewing the policy, the mother requested that their son be added to the policy as a regular driver. The insurer then forwarded a revision billing notice asking for an additional premium. It stated a due date which was also an expiration date but it did not further explain the meaning of these terms. Shortly before the date in question, the insurer sent a final revision notice, again warning that the policy would expire unless payment was made. A check was sent but it was returned due to insufficient funds. The insurer informed the insureds that their coverage had lapsed. A few days later their son was involved in a collision. The insureds demanded that the insurer defend them in an ensuing lawsuit. The insurer then asked a trial court to determine its rights and obligations under the policy. The issue involved was whether the insurer effectively canceled the policy. The trial court held that it had not and, on appeal, the Supreme Court of Rhode Island affirmed. The court noted there are specific prescribed methods of cancelling an automobile insurance policy in Rhode Island. The purpose of providing notice of cancellation is to notify the insured that the policy is being terminated and to afford the insured the time to obtain other insurance prior to termination of the existing policy. In order for a notice of cancellation to be sufficient, it must be clear, definite and unequivocal, and specify a termination date. Therefore, the insured parties were covered. *Automobile Club Ins. Co. v. Donovan*, 550 A.2d 622 (R.I.1988).

An Arkansas woman obtained an auto loan from a bank. She then obtained auto insurance and paid for three months of a six month policy. She failed to make the second payment and was notified that the policy would be canceled if she did not make payment by the stipulated date. She did not make the payment and the day after the stipulated date her son totaled the car. The following day she gave a check to her agent for the second half of the premium. She sued the insurer in a state trial court seeking a declaration that she was insured and requiring the insurer to defend a claim against her son. The bank entered the suit against the insurer because the insurer refused to pay the bank, as loss payee, under the policy. The case was transferred to a circuit court which held for the insured and the insurer appealed to the Arkansas

Supreme Court. At issue was whether the insurer had to notify both the insured and the bank for an effective cancellation. The insurer asserted that other states had held that notifying the insured was sufficient. The insured argued that the court should follow the plain language of state law which stated that cancellation notice would not be effective unless delivered by the insurer to the named insured and to any lending institution having a lien on the named insured's automobile. The supreme court held for the insured because the statutory language was clear. The insured's son was entitled to defense of the claim and the bank was entitled to the policy proceeds. *State Farm Fire & Cas. Co. v. Stockton*, 750 S.W.2d 945 (Ark.1988).

A North Carolina insured purchased an automobile insurance policy and paid for three months of a six month premium. When she failed to pay the balance the insurer mailed her a cancellation notice which specified when cancellation would be effective. One month after the proposed cancellation the insured's car was involved in an accident in which a passenger in her car was injured. The passenger obtained a judgment from the insured and then sought coverage from the insurer. The insurer denied coverage asserting cancellation due to nonpayment. The passenger sued the insurer in a North Carolina trial court which granted the insurer's dismissal motion. The passenger then appealed to the North Carolina Court of Appeals.

The passenger asserted that the insurer's cancellation notice was ineffective because it did not conform with state law. The law provided for fifteen days between the date the cancellation notice is mailed and the effective cancellation date. Here, the insured was only provided twelve days. According to the court of appeals, failure to comply with the statute meant that the cancellation was ineffective. An insurer's mid-term cancellation of compulsory insurance due to nonpayment is ineffective unless and until the insurer has strictly complied with the law. The policy remained in effect for the full six months and the insurer was required to satisfy the judgment against the insured. *Pearson v. Nationwide Mut. Ins. Co.*, 368 S.E.2d 406 (N.C.App.1988).

2. Adequate Notice

A Florida resident purchased PIP coverage through his agent and arranged to pay premiums through a finance company. After making a downpayment, he made no further payments, alleging that he had not received a payment book. He also alleged that he never received a cancellation notice. The insured was then involved in an accident and submitted a claim, although the insurer had canceled the policy by notifying the finance company. The insured sued the insurer in a Florida trial court, which ruled in the insured's favor stating that the insurer had failed to strictly comply with Florida insurance law cancellation procedures. The Florida District Court of Appeal reversed the lower court's decision, finding that the insurer had not violated the cancellation procedures. The notice it had given the finance company was sufficient, and the insurer had no liability for failure to notify the purchaser. *Bankers Ins. Co. v. Pannunzio*, 538 So.2d 61 (Fla.App.4th Dist.1989).

An insurer issued a noncertified assigned risk automobile insurance policy to a North Carolina insured. The policy provided coverage for a six month period. Prior to the expiration of the policy, the insurer offered to continue the insured's coverage. The insured declined to continue and the policy was terminated. However, the insurer did not notify the Division of Motor Vehicles (DMV) that the policy had been terminated. Such notification is required under North Carolina law. Later, the insured was in an accident while driving the previously insured vehicle and two of his passengers were injured. The insurer filed a declaratory relief action, seeking a judgment that its failure to notify the DMV had not extended the policy.

The insurer argued that it was not required to notify the DMV since the commissioner of the DMV had issued regulations requiring notification only on auto policies of less than six months in duration. The insured and the passengers argued that the commissioner had overstepped his authority by issuing regulations which completely nullified the notification provision, since almost all auto policies are issued for six months or more. The trial court entered summary judgment for the insured and the court of appeals affirmed. The insurer then appealed to the Supreme Court of North Carolina. The supreme court agreed that the commissioner had exceeded his authority. The statutory notification requirement could not be overridden by the commissioner, whose regulatory authority extended only to the manner by which the notification would be carried out. However, the court held that the failure to notify the DMV did not extend the policy coverage. Only faulty notice to the insured would extend coverage, and the insured was adequately notified in this case. The DMV could assess a civil penalty for failure to give termination notice. There was no legislative intent for such a failure to extend coverage. *Allstate Ins. Co. v. McCrae*, 384 S.E.2d 1 (N.C.1989).

A New York case addressed the question of what constitutes an effective cancellation notice by an insurance company. A brother and sister who had been living together at the same address each owned their own automobile and both were insured by Prudential Property & Casualty Insurance Company under the same policy. In order to cancel the policy for nonpayment of premiums, Prudential sent one cancellation notice to both insureds at the address on the policy. Three months later, one of the automobiles in question was involved in a five-car collision. The accident resulted in four separate lawsuits which were consolidated for trial. The issue was whether the single cancellation notice was sufficient to terminate the insurance policy on the automobile owned by the brother and sister. The trial court held that it was not, stating that although they lived at the same address and were both named as insureds in the same policy, they should have received separate cancellation notices. Prudential appealed.

The New York Supreme Court, Appellate Division, observed that at all relevant times, the insureds occupied the same dwelling place and were not living apart. The address appearing on the policy was the only address that the brother and sister had ever provided to Prudential and all written communication from Prudential was sent to this address. In addition, the court found that the cancellation was in strict compliance with the New York Vehicle and Traffic Law which requires fifteen days notice from an insurer for cancellation of a policy for nonpayment of premiums. Since Prudential mailed the cancellation notice over three months prior to the accident and since the insureds did not oppose the cancellation in timely fashion, the court held that the brother and sister had waived their right to contest the validity of the cancellation. The Appellate Division reversed the decision of the trial court and ruled in favor of Prudential. *Allstate Ins. Co. v. Prudential Property & Cas. Ins. Co.*, 502 N.Y.S.2d 446 (A.D.1st Dept.1986).

B. Nonpayment of Premiums

1. Coverage Valid

A man mailed a check for renewal of his automobile insurance. His insurer received the check after the termination deadline, but attempted to cash the check and extended the man's coverage. The coverage commenced two days after the deadline for renewal. The check was dishonored and resubmitted for payment. The man's wife was then killed in an auto accident. The check was again dishonored and the insurer denied coverage for the accident due to nonpayment. A lawsuit arose, and a state trial court granted summary judgment for the insurer. The man then appealed to the Court of Appeals of Georgia. The court distinguished between a renewal of coverage and the issuance of a new policy. Since the coverage was extended beginning two days after the deadline, the coverage was ruled to be a new policy. That policy must then be canceled as per statutory requirements, which the insurer had not done. The court ruled that the man's policy was in effect at the time of the accident and reversed the judgment of the trial court. *Brown v. Progressive Preferred Ins. Co.*, 402 S.E.2d 303 (Ga.App.1991).

2. Coverage Void

An insured couple received two notices that their automobile insurance premium was due. They also received a late notice, but alleged that they did not receive a cancellation notice before suffering injury in an accident. A dispute arose over the effectiveness of a cancellation notice which was mailed but never received. The insured urged that actual receipt was not required, and that only proof of mailing was required. In this case that proof was shown by the automobile lien holder and local agency having received notice. The trial court agreed that actual receipt was not necessary, and review was granted by the Court of Appeals of Kansas. Cancellation for nonpayment of a premium was treated differently than other cancellations; Kansas law required no notice when cancelling for nonpayment. Also, the policy language required only proof of mailing—not receipt. The trial court's decision was affirmed. *Bell v. Patrons Mutual Ins. Association*, 816 P.2d 407 (Kan.App.1991).

An insured in Illinois was notified by his automobile insurer that his policy would lapse on September 4, 1984, but that if payment of the premium amount was received by that date "and approved by the company," his coverage would continue uninterrupted. He mailed a check which was received and cashed by the insurer before the termination date. He received a letter on September 8, 1984, however, which stated that the insurer declined his "request for reinstatement." Enclosed with the letter was a check for the premium amount that the insured had just paid. The next day, the insured's car was involved in an accident. The insured sued the insurer seeking to recover under the policy for damages to his car, but an Illinois circuit court ruled that no coverage existed. The insured appealed to the Appellate Court of Illinois. The insured argued that the insurer approved his offer to extend the coverage period when it cashed his premium check. The court declared that insurers should be allowed a reasonable amount of time under the circumstances "to decide whether or not to accept or approve a late premium payment which constitutes an offer to purchase insurance." It stated that acceptance occurs only when an insurer retains a premium payment for an unreasonable length of time "or otherwise manifests an intention to approve a late payment." Because the insurer in this case notified the insured promptly of its decision not to provide further coverage, and because it did not retain the premium payment for an unreasonable length of time, no coverage existed at the time of the accident. The decision of the circuit court denying coverage was affirmed. *McKinney v. Country Mut. Ins. Co.*, 507 N.E.2d 940 (Ill.App.4th Dist.1987).

A Tennessee woman procured an automobile liability policy covering April 1, 1981, to October 1, 1981. On August 21, she was notified that her policy would be cancelled unless payment for the April to October term was received before September 3. The insurer received a payment from the insured on September 24, which was credited to her account and a refund (which would have covered September 3 to October 1) was sent to her. After she was involved in an auto accident on November 1, she sued the insurer to recover under the policy. The Tennessee Court of Appeals held that the policy expired by its own terms on October 1, 1981, and that acceptance of the insured's check did not reinstate her policy. *Parrish v. Nationwide General Ins. Co.*, 731 S.W.2d 547 (Tenn.App.1987).

The North Carolina Court of Appeals has held that an insurer was not liable to an insured who failed to make his premium payment within the grace period allowed by the insurer. The insured, who had failed to pay his automobile insurance premium payment on time, was extended a seventeen-day grace period on condition that the insurer receive the insured's premium payment within the grace period. The insurer would then reinstate the policy retroactively to the date the premium was due. In past dealings with the insurer, the insured had paid his premiums within the grace period and had his policies reinstated retroactively. However, in this instance, the insurer received the insured's payment after the grace period had expired. It therefore opted to reinstate the policy effective upon receipt of the insured's premium payment and not retroactively. The insured, whose car had been destroyed by fire during the lapse period of his policy, brought suit seeking to have his policy reinstated retroactively to cover his loss. The North Carolina appellate court reversed a trial court ruling in the insured's favor, holding that where the insurer did not receive timely payment, it was within its right in refusing to renew the insured's policy retroactively, even though the insurer had previously renewed the insured's other policies retroactively. *Sawyer v. North Carolina Farm Bureau Mut. Ins. Co.*, 323 S.E.2d 450 (N.C.App.1984).

C. Transfer of Ownership

A New Mexico man possessed an automobile policy which provided automatic coverage if he purchased a new vehicle. The policy required him to inform the insurer of the purchase within thirty days. The policy also stipulated that the vehicle would be deemed to be owned by the insured on the date that the insured took possession. The insured went to California and purchased a used Porsche. Even though he did not have the vehicle's title, he was permitted to take the car back to New Mexico. He made his first payment a week later and one week after that he received the title to the vehicle. Three weeks after he received the title and five weeks after he took possession of the car the insured was involved in a collision which injured another man. The insured sought coverage from the insurer but it refused. It stated that the insured had failed to inform it of the purchase within the required time. The insured appealed to the New Mexico Supreme Court. It rejected the insured's assertion that he did not have an insurable interest in the vehicle until he received the vehicle's title. It determined that delivery, and hence an insurable interest, occurred at the time the insured took possession of the vehicle. Therefore automatic insurance coverage need not have been provided because of the expiration of the thirty-day period. *L'Allier v. Turnacliff*, 758 P.2d 796 (N.M.1988).

The California Court of Appeal has held that an insurer was not bound to extend insurance coverage to the buyer of a car where the insurer failed to cancel the seller's auto policy after the car was sold. In this case the buyer took possession of the car and had an accident resulting in the death of a woman. The accident occurred before the seller's insurance was cancelled. After learning of the accident the insurer retroactively cancelled the policy to a date prior to the accident. After the new owner of the car made a claim with the seller's insurer, the insurer sought a declaration from the courts that it was not liable for the accident. The Court of Appeal upheld a lower court decision in favor of the insurer, saying that the insurance policy language clearly indicated that coverage was to last only so long as the named insured owned the specified covered vehicle. The court found that no legitimate construction of the policy would make the new owner of the car a "named insured" or a "permissive user" protected by the policy. *Sequoia Ins. Co. v. Miller*, 202 Cal.Rptr. 866 (App.5th Dist.1984).

A California man whose daughter struck a pedestrian while driving an automobile given to her by her father sought a court declaration that his insurer was obligated to defend him in the resulting personal injury action brought by the pedestrian. The insurer had denied coverage, claiming that the insured had requested that the car driven by the daughter be deleted from insurance coverage. Sometime prior to the accident the insured gave the vehicle to his daughter for her permanent use. The insured also delivered the car's title to his daughter, releasing his interest in the vehicle. However, at the time of the accident, ownership had not been transferred on the records of the Department of Motor Vehicles; thus the insured was still the registered owner of the car. The question before the California Court of Appeal was whether the insured "owned" the car at the time of the accident within the meaning of an exclusionary clause in the insurer's policy for noncovered persons or automobiles. The court held that the exclusion in the policy precluded liability coverage for the car because the insured had caused it to be deleted from his policy. The insured could have had no reasonable expectation that coverage for the car would continue after he specifically deleted it from the policy. *Bohannon v. Aetna Cas. & Sur. Co.*, 212 Cal.Rptr. 848 (App.3d Dist.1985).

D. Binders

A Pennsylvania teenager was convicted of underage drinking. His driver's license was suspended for ninety days. After his license was reinstated, he disclosed the suspension and obtained an automobile insurance binder from an agent. The insurer later sought to cancel the binder. However, the Pennsylvania Insurance Commissioner determined that the insurer did not have grounds for cancellation. The insurer appealed to the Commonwealth Court of Pennsylvania. The commissioner argued that the state criminal code did not allow an insurer to raise the premiums or cancel the insurance of someone convicted of underage drinking. Therefore, the binder effectively disallowed any adverse action against the boy because he had become a policy holder upon the issuance of a binder. The court agreed with the commissioner and affirmed his decision. *State Farm v. Dep't of Ins.*, 598 A.2d 1344 (Pa.Cmwlth 1991).

A South Dakota man, employed as a semi-truck driver, sought full insurance coverage on an automobile that he had purchased. He had previously obtained a similar policy from the same insurer. Four days after the man's wife had paid the premium and signed the application, the man was killed while driving his semi. The man's wife sought supplementary death benefits from the insurer because the binder had been issued and did not contain any exclusionary terms. The insurer stated that the death occurred outside the scope of the policy, and denied coverage. The wife sued unsuccessfully in a South Dakota trial court, and appealed to the Supreme Court of South Dakota. The supreme court noted that the insurer's standard contract, at the time of the insured's death, excluded coverage when the insured was driving a commercial vehicle. It also found that because the man had previously purchased a similar policy with the same exclusions, the policy would be enforced with the same exclusions, even though they were not mentioned in the binder. The court further noted that certain definitions in the policy concerning supplementary coverage paralleled the state statutory language, leading the court to conclude that the policy terms were "standard and usual." The court affirmed the trial court's decision, denying coverage. *Matousek v. South Dakota Farm Bureau Mutual Ins. Co.*, 450 N.W.2d 236 (S.D.1990).

The Arizona Supreme Court was asked to decide whether a binder for automobile insurance creates coverage prior to an applicant's formal notice of rejection. This case arose after an applicant had completed an application for automobile insurance and submitted a check to cover the first two months' premium. The check was thereafter returned to him for insufficient funds. The applicant was involved in an automobile accident on a date prior to receiving the insurer's notice that the policy would not issue due to the return of the check.

The insurer sought a court declaration that it was not liable for the accident. At trial, the applicant argued that coverage had been effected under the binder issued by the agent at the time the check for the premium payment on the policy was delivered to the agent. He also argued that such coverage did not terminate until the day after the accident, when the agent received the message from the insurer informing him of the dishonor of the check and consequent rejection of his application for insurance. Further, the agent expressly represented that the execution of the binder would make coverage effective immediately and, according to the applicant, the agent did not state that coverage would be conditioned upon the premium check being honored.

The Arizona Supreme Court held that in light of the agent's express representations, the binder was effective immediately and was not conditioned upon the check being honored. In addition, an insurer's notice of rejection was effective only when received by an applicant. Here, since he had not received notice of rejection prior to the accident, the applicant was insured for the agreed limits of the binder. *Statewide Ins. Corp. v. Dewar*, 694 P.2d 1167 (Ariz.1984).

VIII. SETOFF

Automobile insurers generally can "set off" benefits from other sources only when state statute and policy language provides for a setoff.

An Illinois man was killed in a motor vehicle accident involving an underinsured motorist. His policy provided for underinsured motorist benefits in the amount of $100,000. His wife received $50,000 from the underinsured motorist and then sought $50,000 from his own insurer. However, she had stipulated with her insurer that she had received more than $50,000 in workers' compensation benefits. The insurer stated that it had no further obligation under the policy, and the wife sued. The trial court ruled for the insurer, the appellate court reversed, and the insurer appealed to the Supreme Court of Illinois. The supreme court determined that the legislature had enacted laws relating to underinsured motorist coverage with the same underlying purpose as for uninsured motorist coverage laws. Accordingly, insurers would be allowed to set off their underinsured motorist benefits against workers' compensation benefits, provided they clearly stated so in their policies. Here, the policy clearly provided for such a setoff. Thus, the court reversed the appellate court's decision and ruled for the insurer. *Sulser v. Country Mutual Ins. Co.*, 591 N.E.2d 427 (Ill.1992).

A bus driver for a public school was injured while driving. He suffered $90,000 in damages, and received partial indemnification from the other driver's insurer and through workers' compensation. A dispute then arose as to whether the school's underinsured motorist (UM) carrier was entitled to reduce benefits paid by the amount received from workers' compensation. A trial court held that the setoff was void as against public policy, and the insurer appealed to the Supreme Court of Nevada. The driver contended that allowing the reduction would permit the insurer to escape paying benefits for which premiums have been paid. The court held that public policy was not violated by the setoff for two reasons: first, the school chose insurance with the setoff provision and thus probably paid less for that coverage. Second, the school was not required to purchase UM coverage. In such an instance, allowing the setoff should lower insurance costs and increase the availability of coverage for public employees. *Continental Casualty Co. v. Riveras*, 814 P.2d 1015 (Nev.1991).

A minor was injured in a car wreck, and collected personal injury protection (PIP) benefits from his father's insurer. He later reached a settlement with all parties, including the father's insurer, on a claim for underinsured motorist benefits. Liabilities for attorney's fees later became disputed, and a Kansas trial court ordered that the father's insurer assume a percentage of the fees. The court went on to hold that the insurer was not liable to pay the judgment which resulted from the settlement, because it was entitled to a setoff of the PIP benefits which it had previously paid. The setoff decision was appealed to the Court of Appeals of Kansas. The minor argued that the policy allowed a setoff only for benefits which were "payable," not those which were paid. Kansas law regarding underinsured coverage, however, allows a setoff when PIP benefits "apply". A provision in the policy did not change that. *Bardwell v. Kester*, 815 P.2d 120 (Kan.App.1991).

An automobile accident resulted in over $75,000 damages for an Arkansas man. The injured party settled with the other driver for his policy limit of $25,000. He then sought to collect the full amount of his underinsurance coverage, which was $50,000. The insurer and insured disagreed over whether the insurer was entitled to a reduction of benefits due to the earlier settlement. A federal district court heard the dispute, and resolved it by looking at a 1987 amendment to the Arkansas Underinsured Motorist Coverage Act. The amendment provides that an insurer is entitled to reduce benefits payable only to the extent that the insured party would receive compensation in excess of his damages. The insured was entitled to $50,000 from his insurer. *Henderson v. Universal Underwriters Insurance Co.*, 768 F.Supp. 688 (E.D.Ark.1991).

A Michigan insured was employed at a carwash when she was pinned between two automobiles and injured. The insured was covered under a no-fault automobile liability policy that specifically provided for noncoordinated personal protection insurance (PIP) benefits. The insured received workers' compensation benefits and also filed a claim with the insurer for PIP benefits. The insurer paid the claim, but deducted a setoff equal to the amount of workers' compensation benefits. The insured sued the insurer in a Michigan circuit court to recover the setoff. The circuit court found for the insured, and the insurer appealed to the Court of Appeals of Michigan. The court of appeals noted that the insured's policy provided that the insurer could subtract benefits provided under the laws of any state or federal government from benefits otherwise payable under the policy. The court found that this provision clearly and unambiguously authorized the insurer to deduct workers' compensation benefits, which were required under Michigan law, from PIP benefits. Nothing in the policy indicated that this provision only applied where the insured had elected to coordinate benefits. Under Michigan's no-fault automobile insurance act, workers' compensation benefits must be subtracted from PIP benefits in order to eliminate double recovery. The court of appeals reversed the circuit court's decision. The insurer was entitled to deduct the insured's workers' compensation benefits from PIP benefits. *Conrad v. Auto Club Ins. Ass'n*, 442 N.W.2d 762 (Mich.App.1989).

A Maryland pedestrian was struck by an uninsured motorist. The pedestrian was insured under an automobile policy which provided both uninsured motorist (UM) and personal injury protection (PIP) coverage. His employer's workers' compensation insurer partially compensated the man and he sought the remainder of his damages from his automobile insurer. Maryland law allowed a reduction of auto insurance benefits by the amount recovered under workers' compensation. The insurer sought to subtract the amount of the workers' compensation recovery from both the PIP and the UM benefits. A lawsuit developed over the issue and reached the Court of Appeals of Maryland.

The court agreed that the reduction allowance was designed to avoid a duplication of benefits, but noted that the legislature did not intend to avoid all duplication. Indeed it expressly allowed the recovery of both UM and PIP benefits. The court ruled that the insurer must total the benefits from UM and PIP coverage and subtract the workers' compensation recovery from the total — not from each type of coverage separately. *Revis v. Automobile Ins. Fund*, 589 A.2d 483 (Md.1991).

A Delaware woman was seriously injured in an accident with an uninsured driver, while operating her mother's car. The mother's insurance policy provided uninsured motorist coverage in the amount of $300,000 per accident. After the insurer denied coverage, the insured mother brought an action in a Delaware trial court, seeking payment of insurance benefits. Delaware statutes provided that the

Sec. IX   SEX-BASED RATE DIFFERENTIALS   161

insurer make full recovery available for accidents with uninsured motorists. After the insured had filed the suit, she received a $100,000 settlement from the uninsured motorist responsible for the accident. The trial court decided that the insurer must provide $300,000 worth of uninsured motorist coverage even if the insured received a settlement payment. The insurer appealed this decision to the Supreme Court of Delaware. The supreme court stated that the clauses of the policy must be read in the context of the whole policy. It decided the policy was not ambiguous. The clause in the contract stated "any amount otherwise payable for damages under this coverage shall be reduced by all sums paid because of bodily injury by those who may be legally responsible." The greatest amount that the insurer would be obligated to pay was $300,000 less $100,000, the amount already paid to the insured. The court reversed the trial court's decision, stating it would be contrary to public policy to allow the insured to recover more than the maximum protection under the policy. *Aetna Cas. and Sur. Co. v. Kenner*, 570 A.2d 1172 (Del.1990).

An insured purchased five separate automobile policies from the same insurer, each with stackable underinsured motorist protection of $25,000. His daughter was injured in an automobile accident and her damages exceeded $225,000. $100,000 was received from the tortfeasor, and the insured sought to stack his underinsured motorist coverage and collect $125,000 from his insurer. His insurer refused payment, arguing that it was entitled to offset the amount received by the tortfeasor and was thus only liable for $25,000. The insured then brought suit. A federal district court first found that the policy was ambiguous. Equally important was that allowing an offset against underinsured coverage was ruled contrary to the reasonable expectations doctrine and to Montana's demonstrated public policy strongly favoring underinsured coverage. The court ruled in favor of the insured. *Scouten v. Horace Mann Ins. Co.*, 765 F.Supp. 639 (D.Mont.1991).

IX. SEX-BASED RATE DIFFERENTIALS

While it is well-settled under the U.S. Constitution that employer offered life insurance plans may not establish different premium schedules for males and females (*see* Chapter Five), it is unclear whether the courts will uniformly agree to extend this nondiscrimination logic to automobile insurers.

An insured Pennsylvania man sought to prevent the state insurance commissioner from enforcing an amendment which would permit automobile insurers to base actuarial rates on sex. The insured was charged a higher premium than similarly situated females. He sought to have the amendment declared unconstitutional and to order the commissioner not to enforce the amendment. The commissioner argued that the amendment was constitutional because gender-based rates were founded upon sound actuarial principles. The insured sued the commissioner in the Pennsylvania Commonwealth Court.

At trial, the insured argued that the amendment violated the Pennsylvania Equal Rights Amendment (ERA). The ERA was passed to ensure equality of rights under the law and to eliminate sex as a basis for distinction of legal rights. The commissioner argued that the ERA only prohibited sex discrimination by the state, not private companies. The commissioner also asserted that the amendment did not create sexual classifications. It merely permitted insurers to structure rates on gender classifications only if such classifications were sound. The commonwealth court determined that there was no requirement of state action under the ERA. The only types of sexual discrimination that were permissible in Pennsylvania were those which were "reasonably and genuinely based on physical characteristics unique to one sex." In granting the insured's motion, the court declared that gender classifications pertaining to insurance rates were unconstitutional. Therefore, the commissioner was obligated to reject any proposal which based rates on gender classifications. *Bartholomew v. Foster*, 541 A.2d 393 (Pa.Cmwlth.1988).

The Pennsylvania National Organization for Women (NOW) claimed that the Pennsylvania Insurance Commissioner ignored evidence of automobile insurers' discriminatory practices against women by using rate structures which were not based on mileage. Pennsylvania law required insurers to give due consideration to mileage in setting rates. The commissioner had concluded that, regardless of sex, the insurers' practice of charging uniform rates was permissible. NOW argued that although women drove only half as much as men on the average, rate discounts for women given by insurance companies ranged from zero to twenty percent. Therefore, the rates did not adequately reflect the mileage factor and insurers used higher women's premiums to subsidize men's risks. NOW claimed that this violated women's equal protection rights under the Fourteenth Amendment and the Pennsylvania Equal Rights Amendment. The commissioner argued that since the risk of loss was not directly proportional to miles driven, the discounts adequately considered mileage as a factor. NOW asked the Pennsylvania Commonwealth Court to decide the matter.

The court noted that it would not interfere with the commissioner's decision unless it was clearly in violation of the law, or was arbitrary or was a violation of constitutional rights. It determined that the decision was not arbitrary since there was ample evidence to support the commissioner's findings and that the decision was not a clear violation of the law. Federal equal protection rights did not apply to private conduct, such as insurance filing rates. The decision did not violate the Pennsylvania Equal Rights Amendment because the insurers established that there was no direct correlation between mileage and insurance costs. The court affirmed the commissioner's decision. *Pa. Nat'l Org. for Women v. Ins. Dep't*, 551 A.2d 1162 (Pa.Cmwlth.1988).

A male automobile insurance policyholder in Pennsylvania filed a complaint with that state's Commissioner of Insurance contending that his obligation to pay $148 more in annual premiums than would a similarly situated female insured for identical coverage was discriminatory. The insurance company argued that its actuarial data indicated that male policyholders in the plaintiff's age group were more likely to incur accident losses than female policyholders in the same age group. The commissioner, in light of Pennsylvania's public policy against sex discrimination, concluded that the insurer's sex-based rates were unfairly discriminatory and therefore invalid. The insurer sought review of the commissioner's decision in the Commonwealth Court of Pennsylvania, which affirmed that decision. The insurance company, along with another automobile insurer, appealed further to the Pennsylvania Supreme Court, which held that under the Pennsylvania Constitution's Equal Rights Amendment, sex-based automobile insurance rates were unacceptable. The commissioner's decision, found the court, was therefore an appropriate exercise of statutory authority. *Hartford Accident & Indem. Co. v. Ins. Comm'r*, 482 A.2d 542 (Pa.1984).

X. EXCLUSIONS

Exclusionary clauses in automobile insurance contracts are strictly construed by the courts against the insurer, and any ambiguity in an exclusionary clause will usually result in coverage being awarded.

A. Vehicles

A postal employee delivering mail on a rural route drove his privately owned vehicle into another car, killing a passenger and injuring the driver. A lawsuit was brought against the United States under the Federal Tort Claims Act, alleging negligent driving by the postal worker. The United States then sought indemnity from the employee's automobile insurer. The insurer denied coverage under an exclusion in the policy which provided no coverage where a vehicle is used to carry persons or property for a charge. A federal district court ruled for the insurer, and the United States appealed to the U.S. Court of Appeals, Eighth Circuit. On appeal, the court noted first that the government was an insured under the omnibus clause of the policy. However, the exclusion was sufficient to deny coverage in this case. The postal service was paid a fee by those who used its delivery service and the employee here was carrying out the deliveries. Clearly, the employee was carrying property for a charge. Thus, the policy excluded coverage and the insurer did not have to indemnify the United States. The district court's decision was affirmed. *United States v. Milwaukee Guardian Ins. Co.*, 966 F.2d 1246 (8th Cir.1992).

An Illinois woman asked her boyfriend, an owner and operator of a service station, to repair her car. He loaned her his car so she could drive to work. After her car was repaired for no charge, the boyfriend got a phone call from his ex-wife asking him if he could come to her house to check her sump pump which was malfunctioning. As he drove to her house in the repaired car, he was involved in an accident. The vehicle's insurer brought a declaratory relief action seeking to determine whether it had to cover the accident. A circuit court ruled in the insurer's favor, and the garage owner appealed to the Appellate Court of Illinois. On appeal, the garage owner argued that either his personal insurance policy or the automobile's liability policy had to indemnify him. The appellate court noted that both policies contained automobile business exclusions. The garage owner, however, argued that the exclusions did not apply because the primary purpose of his trip was not to test-drive the car, but to check on the sump pump. The court disagreed, finding that the owner took the opportunity of the test-drive to complete the personal favor for his ex-wife. Thus, the court denied the garage owner coverage, and affirmed the trial court's decision. *Allstate Ins. Co. v. Hutcheson*, 596 N.E.2d 1357 (Ill.App.5th Dist.1992).

An Iowa couple insured their vehicle for "full coverage." While on vacation in Mexico, their vehicle was stolen and never recovered. Their insurance agent told them that their policy provided coverage but the adjusters later advised them that their loss was excluded because it occurred in Mexico. An exclusion in the policy provided that only losses which occurred within the United States or Canada would be covered. The insureds filed suit against their insurer, seeking recovery under the policy. A trial court granted summary judgment to the insurer, and the insureds appealed to the Court of Appeals of Iowa. On appeal, the appellate court noted that the exclusionary clause in the policy did not defeat the insureds' reasonable expectations of coverage. Since the loss occurred in Mexico, they could not have reasonably expected coverage. Further, the language of the policy was clear and unambiguous. Finally, public policy favored denying coverage because the risks abroad could be higher than at home, and it would be unfair to impose that extra burden on insurers. The court affirmed the grant of summary judgment to the insurer. *Werner's Inc. v. Grinnell Mutual Reinsurance Co.*, 477 N.W.2d 868 (Iowa App.1991).

An Ohio insured had a policy which excluded liability coverage for nonowned vehicles which were furnished or available for the insured's regular use. The insured drove his employer's van on a daily basis, had his own set of keys, and was allowed to take the van to his home on numerous occasions, sometimes for personal use. While driving the van home from a bar one evening, the insured was involved in an accident. The insurer denied coverage, but a trial court granted it. On appeal to the Court of Appeals of Ohio, the court found that the van had been furnished for the insured's regular use. The court reversed the judgment for the insured. *Withrow v. Liberty Mutual Fire Ins. Co.*, 595 N.E.2d 529 (Ohio App.1991).

A South Carolina boy was injured while driving a car owned by his mother. At the time of the accident, he owned an insured van. His insurer denied coverage for the accident due to an exclusion in its policy for the regular use of nonowned vehicles. The insured then filed a claim in a South Carolina trial court which found for the insured because the mother's car was not available for regular use by the son. The insurer appealed to the South Carolina Court of Appeals.

On appeal, the court noted that the policy excluded liability coverage for nonowned vehicles. The exclusion applied to autos "available for the regular use, of the insured." The insurer argued that since the boy lived in a trailer on the same property as his mother's house, since his van had been disabled for a few weeks, and since his mother had several automobiles including the car at issue, the car was available for regular use. The record did not specifically indicate how many times the boy used the car before the accident. He would seek permission to use the car and there was no indication that he had his own set of keys. Therefore, the appellate court ruled that the insurer failed to prove the use of the car was steady or regular as opposed to casual or infrequent. Therefore, the court affirmed the trial court's decision and held for the insured. *South Carolina Farm Bureau Mut. Ins. Co. v. Windham*, 400 S.E.2d 497 (S.C.App.1990).

A Georgia insured lent her van to several men so that they could drive to North Carolina to pick up some tractors and drive them back to Georgia. On the way to North Carolina, the van collided with a semi. One of the passengers sued the driver of the van and the driver demanded that the woman's insurer defend him. The insurer sued in a trial court, seeking a declaration that it was not liable because its policy excluded coverage for vehicles used in the auto business. The trial court agreed and the insured then appealed to the Court of Appeals of Georgia. The court ruled for the insurer because the van had been used to transport drivers to a place where they would pick up tractors and drive them to Georgia for resale. The van's use was thus an integral part of the auto business and therefore not covered. The court affirmed the trial court's decision. *Sanderlin v. Allstate Ins. Co.*, 386 S.E.2d 707 (Ga.App.1989).

Sec. X   EXCLUSIONS   165

A leasing corporation leased an automobile to a taxi service. The leasing corporation's automobile liability policy contained an exclusion for damages arising out of the use of a vehicle as a "public or livery conveyance." When a taxi customer who was allegedly assaulted by a taxi driver while riding in the leased automobile sued the leasing corporation, the leasing corporation sought coverage from its insurer. The insurer refused to provide coverage and stated that the public conveyance exclusion precluded coverage. A New York trial court ruled that a trial was necessary to determine whether the exclusion applied, and the insurer appealed. The New York Supreme Court, Appellate Division, reversed this ruling and ordered that the insurer be absolved of liability. The appellate court stated that a trial would be wholly unnecessary because given the nature of the exclusion, there could be no possible legal basis for holding the insurer liable. *Hunt Leasing Corp. v. Universal Underwriters Ins. Co.*, 506 N.Y.S.2d 886 (A.D.2d Dept.1986).

A day care center offered a daily pickup service to parents who wanted their children transported to and from the center. Parents who wanted their children to use the transportation service were charged $1 for each child transported to or from the center. The van used by the center to transport children was involved in an accident in which several children were injured. The president of the day care center had put the van on an individual policy which also covered his personal vehicles. The individual policy provided that coverage did not apply while the van was "used to carry persons or property for a charge," but provided coverage for injuries arising from the use of the van in "shared expense car pools." The center's president sought a ruling that his individual policy covered claims arising out of the van's accident. When an Alabama circuit court ruled that no coverage existed, he appealed to the Alabama Supreme Court.

The center's president asserted that the $1 per trip charge was used only to defray the van's operating expenses and therefore constituted a car-pool contribution rather than a fee for transportation. The court noted that the children using the service "were not friends or relatives engaged in an isolated pleasure trip and had no common interest other than reaching a common destination." Because the amount collected by the center was a set fee rather than an amount proportionate to the expense of the trip, the service could not be considered a car pool. Thus no coverage existed under the president's individual policy and the circuit court's ruling was affirmed. *Johnson v. Allstate Ins. Co.*, 505 So.2d 362 (Ala.1987).

A man lived with a woman in her mobile home from January to May 1983. He paid half of the mortgage payments during that time and half of all other living expenses. They kept their finances separate, and each insured his or her own car. In May 1983, the couple was involved in an accident while he was driving her car. He was killed, and she suffered serious injuries. She made claims under both his insurance policy and her own, both of which were denied. The man's insurer obtained a court declaration that no coverage existed under his policy. On appeal, the Oregon Court of Appeals noted that the man's policy excluded coverage for damages arising out of the use of an automobile owned by "any resident of the same household." It further noted that substantial evidence existed indicating that the couple were members of the same household. The lower court's decision that the man's insurance did not cover their accident was affirmed. *Farmer's Ins. Co. of Oregon v. Stout*, 728 P.2d 937 (Or.App.1986).

B. Persons

A Colorado couple purchased an automobile liability insurance policy which contained a household exclusion clause. The clause excluded coverage for claims asserted by a member of the insured's household against another member of the same household. While the policy was in effect, the husband and wife were involved in an accident; the husband was behind the wheel. The wife sued her husband to recover for her injuries, and the insurer filed a declaratory judgment action against both insureds, seeking a ruling that no coverage had to be provided. The trial court granted summary judgment to the insurer, and the court of appeals affirmed. On further appeal to the Supreme Court of Colorado, the insureds contended that the exclusionary clause violated the Equal Protection Clauses of the U.S. and Colorado Constitutions. They asserted that the statutory authorization for the exclusion significantly burdened their fundamental right to travel. The court, however, upheld the constitutionality of the exclusion. At most, it inhibited the insureds' decisions to travel together by automobile, but it did not place a limitation on either interstate or intrastate travel. The right to drive an automobile on state highways is not a fundamental right. Therefore, since there was a rational basis for the statute and the exclusion, the insureds' appeal failed. The court affirmed the summary judgment for the insurer. *Mayo v. National Farmers Union Property and Casualty Co.*, 833 P.2d 54 (Colo.1992).

A divorced Mississippi resident purchased an automobile liability insurance policy which provided that there would be no coverage for bodily injury to any member of the insured's family residing at the same household. The insured's minor daughter lived with her. However, she wanted to attend school in Florida and travelled there to live with her father. Before they reached the insured's ex-husband's house they were involved in an auto accident. The insurer brought a declaratory judgment action to determine whether it had to provide coverage for the daughter's injuries. The trial court found for the insurer, and appeal was taken to the Supreme Court of Mississippi. On appeal, the court noted that although the intent to change domicile had been formed, the move had not come into fruition at the time of the accident. The daughter had not yet made contact with her father, nor had any of her belongings been transferred to his residence. Accordingly, since she still resided with her mother, she was still covered by the policy and thus unable to recover under the liability provision in the policy. The court affirmed the trial court's decision in favor of the insurer. *Thompson v. Mississippi Farm Bureau Mutual Ins. Co.*, 602 So.2d 855 (Miss.1992).

An Arkansas man had an insurance policy which covered accidental death by motor vehicle accident. However, at the time of the accident, the insured had to be wearing a seatbelt, or benefits would not be paid. The insured then suffered fatal injuries in a car accident. When the investigating police officer arrived at the scene of the accident, paramedics were already transferring the insured to an ambulance. It was never determined whether the insured had been wearing his seatbelt. The insurer denied coverage. After a trial court granted coverage, the Supreme Court of Arkansas affirmed. It found that the seatbelt provision was an exclusion rather than a condition precedent. Accordingly, the burden of proof was on the insurer, and coverage had to be provided. *Arkansas Farm Bureau Ins. Fed. v. Ryman*, 831 S.W.2d 133 (Ark.1992).

Sec. X   EXCLUSIONS   167

A Nevada man contacted his insurer for auto coverage. The insurer offered him a lower rate of $552.00 per year if his son was excluded from coverage. However, if the insured wished to cover his son also, the premium was $1,170.00 per year. The insured accepted the lower premium, but allowed his son to drive the auto. Subsequently, his son caused an accident in which another driver was injured. The insurer of the injured driver sought reimbursement from the father's insurer contending that the exclusion for the son was invalid. The father's insurer refused to pay, and brought a declaratory judgment action to determine whether the exclusion was valid. A Nevada district court ruled the exclusion invalid, and the father's insurer appealed to the Nevada Supreme Court. On appeal, the court held that public policy favors providing its residents who are injured in accidents with at least minimum compensation for their injuries. Therefore, irrespective of whether the father allowed his son to drive his car aware of the exclusion, the insurer was required to provide at least minimum coverage to the father. This was so despite the express exclusion in the policy. The court held that reimbursement was available for the injured driver's insurer. *Federated American Ins. Co. v. Granillo*, 835 P.2d 803 (Nev.1992).

A husband and wife were involved in an auto accident in Illinois. The wife sued her husband for personal injury damages. The husband's insurer then filed for declaratory relief, but the trial court held that the family exclusion clause in the policy was void as against Illinois public policy (because of the abrogation of interspousal immunity). The Appellate Court of Illinois reversed, holding that the family exclusion clause did not violate public policy. It held, however, that uninsured motorist coverage might be available under the policy even though no liability coverage could be had. *Safeco Ins. Co. v. Seck*, 587 N.E.2d 1251 (Ill.App.2d Dist.1992).

A California man owned an uninsured truck. He allowed no one to use it without his permission and retained the keys himself. His son was a covered person under the man's wife's policy. On certain occasions the son would drive his father around in the truck. One July night, after taking his father to a fireworks display, the son drove his father's truck without asking for permission. The son ran the truck into a tree, killing one passenger and injuring two others. The son's insurer then brought a declaratory relief action, asserting that no coverage existed. Even though the policy stated that the insurer would "pay damages for bodily injury or property damage for which any covered person [became] legally responsible because of an auto accident," the insurer maintained that it need not provide coverage. It argued that its exclusions section disallowed liability coverage for persons using vehicles without a reasonable belief that they were entitled to do so. The trial court granted the insurer's summary judgment motion, and appeal was taken to the California Court of Appeal, Fourth District.

On appeal, the court first noted that Insurance Code § 11580.1 enumerated the permissible exclusions to automobile liability insurance policies. However, the court then stated that if an insurer provides coverage greater than the statutorily mandated minimums (as the insurer here had done), the insurer could "tailor such additional coverage by drafting [appropriate] exclusions." This would not violate the insurance code. Accordingly, the limitation with respect to nonowned vehicles was a valid exclusion, and the insurer was not required to provide coverage. The trial court's decision was affirmed. *Canadian Ins. Co. v. Ehrlich*, 280 Cal.Rptr. 141 (Cal.App.4th Dist.1991).

A Georgia insured lent his truck to a friend's daughter who in turn lent it to an unlicensed fifteen-year-old driver. The truck was then involved in an accident in which the driver and two passengers were injured. The insured's policy excluded bodily or property damage caused by the insured vehicle if driven by an unlicensed person or person under the minimum age to obtain a license. The insurer filed a lawsuit in a federal district court for a declaration of its duty to defend or provide coverage. The court granted the insurer's motion for summary judgment and the driver appealed to the U.S. Court of Appeals, Eleventh Circuit. The appeals court held that the injured party was not an innocent victim, because the accident was caused by her own unlicensed driving. The appeals court affirmed the district court's decision. *Progressive Preferred Ins. Co. v. Williams*, 864 F.2d 110 (11th Cir.1989).

A Missouri man purchased an automobile liability insurance policy which excluded coverage for bodily injury to persons related to and residing in the same household with the insured while he was operating the car. Subsequently, the insured was involved in a multi-car accident, and his wife, traveling as a passenger, sustained bodily injuries in the collision. Several lawsuits were brought by the involved parties, and the insured's insurer was joined as a defendant in the wife's suit for damages. The insurer then filed a declaratory relief action, asserting that the family exclusion clause relieved it not only of a duty to pay the wife's damages, but also relieved it of any obligation to contribute toward damages attributable to the insured's negligence. The trial court ruled for the insurer, and the case was subsequently transferred to the Supreme Court of Missouri. On appeal, the insured argued that the family exclusion clause violated public policy because Missouri's Safety Responsibility Law was designed to permit all people injured in accidents to recover from those who caused the injuries. The supreme court, however, disagreed. It noted that, at the time of the accident, the procurement of automobile liability insurance was voluntary. Further, the exclusionary clause was unambiguous and unequivocal; it was not subject to construction or interpretation. Since it was reasonable and had been fairly bargained for, the supreme court determined the exclusion to be valid, and it thus affirmed the lower court's decision. *American Family Mut. Ins. Co. v. Ward*, 789 S.W.2d 791 (Mo.banc 1990).

The Supreme Court of Appeals of West Virginia has held that the "named driver exclusion" endorsement in auto policies is only effective after the "limits of financial responsibility required by" West Virginia law have been met. The case involved a woman who had listed her son under the "named driver exclusion" policy provision. Her insurer had refused coverage in a third party lawsuit after her son had been involved in a car accident in which he was driving her car. The court concluded that the legislature intended (under the law) to provide a minimum level of financial security to third parties who suffer damages from negligent drivers. Therefore, the woman's insurer had to settle or defend the lawsuit against her for property damage and personal injuries to the third party up to the limit of mandatory coverage under state law. *Jones v. Motorists Mut. Ins. Co.*, 356 S.E.2d 634 (W.Va.1987).

C. Violations of Law

Two men began fighting over a mutual girlfriend. During the fight, one man drove off in his car with a passenger while the other man chased him. During the car chase, the passenger tried to escape from the vehicle and fell to the ground. The other man's car pulled around and ran over her left arm. The second driver was convicted of felonious assault. In the lawsuit which followed for insurance benefits, a district court granted the convicted driver's insurer summary judgment because of the intentional injury exclusion in the policy. The convicted driver appealed to the Ohio Court of Appeals. The appellate court noted that to avoid coverage on the basis of the intentional injury exclusion, the insurer had to demonstrate that the injury itself was expected or intended. The convicted driver testified that the fight had nothing to do with the injured passenger, and that he never intended to harm her. Because he did not intend to harm the passenger, coverage ought to apply. The court vacated and remanded the case since the driver's conviction for felonious assault did not conclusively establish the intent required for the policy exclusion. This had to be established before coverage could be awarded or denied. *Nationwide Mut. Ins. Co. v. Machniak*, 600 N.E.2d 266 (Ohio App.8th Dist.1991).

A man was rendered comatose after an automobile accident. His blood alcohol content at the time was above .10 percent. His guardian sued the man's insurer for PIP and a jury awarded coverage. The New York Supreme Court, Appellate Division, reversed the jury's decision, noting that the trial judge should have instructed the jury that a finding that intoxication contributed to the man's injuries entitled the insurer to exclude coverage pursuant to an exclusion in the policy. A new trial was therefore granted. *Baron v. Nationwide Mut. Ins. Co.*, 516 N.Y.S.2d 382 (A.D.4th Dept.1987).

A New York man possessed an automobile insurance policy which excluded from coverage any person injured "as a result of operating a motor vehicle while in an intoxicated condition." Intoxication was defined by reference to the traffic laws dealing with drunk driving. The man was involved in an automobile accident after which his blood alcohol content was found to be .276 percent. However, he was never convicted of the criminal offense of driving while intoxicated. He sought benefits under his automobile insurance policy, but his insurer denied coverage due to the policy exclusion for intoxication. The man filed suit in state court, arguing that the exclusion was inapplicable because he had not actually been convicted of driving while intoxicated. The New York Court of Appeals upheld the insurer's denial of benefits. The language of the policy exclusion tracked a state insurance code provision which allowed the denial of benefits due to driving while intoxicated, and the court stated that the insurer must prove only that the insured had done this. The insurer was not required to prove that the insured had been convicted of the offense. Because the evidence established that the insured had a blood alcohol content of .276 percent, the denial of benefits was upheld. *Fafinski v. Reliance Ins. Co.*, 484 N.E.2d 121 (N.Y.1985).

XI. STATUTE OF LIMITATIONS

A state statute setting a maximum time period after an event takes place within which a claim must be filed is known as a "statute of limitations." All states have one or more statutes of limitations governing automobile insurance claims. If a claim is filed after the limitations period has expired (or "run") then the courts are without jurisdiction to hear the claim and it will be dismissed.

A Massachusetts insured was involved in an auto accident with an uninsured motorist in Florida. Her policy provided mandatory uninsured motorist coverage. Almost five years after the accident, the insured sued her insurer in a Florida trial court for uninsured motorist benefits. The insurer moved to dismiss the matter, claiming that Massachusetts law allowed only three years to bring such an action. The court ruled that Florida's law applied, because the accident had occurred in Florida. Under Florida law, the insured had five years to bring her action and the claim was still valid. On appeal, the Florida Supreme Court ruled that because the insurance contract had arisen in Massachusetts, Massachusetts law applied. Thus, the insured's claim was barred. *Lumbermen's Mut. Cas. Co. v. August*, 530 So.2d 293 (Fla.1988).

A California insured was involved in an automobile accident with an uninsured motorist on May 20, 1985. The insured notified her insurer of the accident on June 10, 1985. The insurance policy provided that in the event of disagreement concerning the amount of damages, the disagreement would be resolved by arbitration. The insured sued the uninsured motorist on April 2, 1986. The insurer was not notified then of the lawsuit. The insured sent the insurer a copy of the lawsuit documents on July 1, 1986. The insured then asked the Los Angeles County Superior Court to order an uninsured motorist arbitration hearing. The superior court dismissed the insured's request and the insured appealed to the California Court of Appeal, Second District, Division 5, which reversed the superior court decision. California Insurance Code § 11580.2(i) was unclear concerning the one-year notice requirement. This ambiguity involved public policies favoring coverage for the insured if notice had been given within a reasonable time and the insurer had not been harmed by the delay. Here, there was no harm to the insurer. The insurer was notified of the claim soon after the accident. Furthermore, the insurer notified the insured that it was investigating the accident. This demonstrated that the insurer had notice. The insured complied with the provision of § 11580.2(i) by filing a lawsuit against the uninsured motorist within one year of the accident. The superior court's dismissal was reversed. *State Farm Mut. Automobile Ins. Co. v. Ochoa*, 244 Cal.Rptr. 838 (App.2d Dist.1988).

In July 1978, a Pennsylvania insured was injured in an automobile accident. She received medical treatment from a physician who was authorized by the insured to collect payment from her insurer. On October 27, 1981, the insured sued the insurer for further benefits allegedly attributable to the accident. The insurer asserted that because its last payment of benefits was made on February 9, 1979, the insured's lawsuit (instituted more than two years later) was time-barred. A common pleas court dismissed the insured's lawsuit and a superior court affirmed the decision. The insured appealed to the Pennsylvania Supreme Court. The issue on appeal was whether a settlement between the insurer and the insured's physician constituted a payment of benefits to the insured within the meaning of Pennsylvania's insurance law. The October 26, 1981, settlement provided that the physician would receive payment for three hundred outstanding medical bills. The bills represented multiple patients, one of whom was the insured. The insurer contended that the payment to the physician was payment to him, not the insured. The insured argued that the settlement embodied a payment of benefits to her renewing the statute of limitations. The supreme court reversed the two lower court decisions, holding that the settlement constituted a payment of benefits by the insurer to the insured. The settlement named the insured as one of the multiple patients to whom payments were due. Furthermore, there was no basis to conclude that the insurer did not intend to pay a benefit to her. Since the insured's lawsuit was instituted within two years after the settlement was reached, her lawsuit against the insurer was timely. *Sender v. State Farm Ins. Co.*, 535 A.2d 65 (Pa.1987).

The statute of limitations for no-fault insurance cases was an issue before the Minnesota Supreme Court. On October 18, 1979, a minor was injured in an auto accident. Over six years later, she and her father sued the father's liability insurer for underinsured motorist benefits. At the time of the accident, her father's policy did not expressly include underinsured motorist coverage. According to the Minnesota No-Fault Act, underinsured motorist coverage would be added to the policy by operation of law if the insurer had failed to prove that a mandatory offer of underinsured motorist coverage had been made when the policy was sold. The court ruled that the statute of limitations in such a case runs for six years beginning on the date of the injury. The claimant's cause of action was barred because the six-year period had passed before the action was filed. The case was dismissed. *O'Neill v. Illinois Farmers Ins. Co.*, 381 N.W.2d 439 (Minn.1986).

CHAPTER FOUR

INSURANCE FRAUD BY CONSUMERS

                                                                                  Page

I. INSURANCE FRAUD FOUND 173

II. INSURANCE FRAUD NOT FOUND 178

I. INSURANCE FRAUD FOUND

In most states, fraudulent behavior on the part of an insured will generally render the policy void and may result in criminal charges against the insured.

A Kansas man's son was operating one of his vehicles while a friend was riding on the hood of the car. The friend slid from the hood and was seriously injured. About three hours later, the Kansas man met with an insurance agent to obtain automobile insurance for his vehicles. He made no mention of the accident in the application. Thus, when the agent signed the application to make it into a binder, it became effective as of 12:01 AM that day. When the insurer learned of the claim against it, it notified the insured that it considered the policy to be void from the outset due to the insured's fraud. A Kansas trial court held that the policy could not be rescinded, and ordered the insurer to pay the innocent injured third party. The insurer appealed. On appeal to the Kansas Supreme Court, it was noted that an insurer cannot retrospectively avoid coverage under a financial responsibility law to escape liability to a third party on the ground of fraud by the insured. However, the court went on to say that under the Kansas Automobile Injury Reparations Act — which requires liability insurance on all motor vehicles registered in the state — it would be improper to provide coverage here. In this case, there had been no coverage at the time of the accident. Thus, the insurer was not attempting to remove coverage it had previously granted. The correct result, then, was to reform the insurance policy to provide coverage only from the time the binder was executed. The court reversed the lower court's decision. *Slaby v. Cox*, 827 P.2d 18 (Kan.1992).

When an Illinois insured applied for life insurance, she represented that she had had a cancerous polyp removed, but that her prognosis was excellent. Two months later, the insured signed a form validating the policy. The form contained a clause which stated that the answers given on the application form were still true and accurate. The insured failed to reveal that she had suffered a recurrence of her cancer since the application had been filled out. Two months later the insured died of cancer. Her husband sought benefits under the policy. The insurer denied the benefits, maintaining that the insured had fraudulently induced the policy. The husband sued the insurer in a federal district court and the insurer moved to dismiss the suit.

The district court upheld the dismissal motion. It rejected the husband's contention that the policy was ambiguous and that the insured believed that she was simply attesting to the truthfulness of her original application by signing the form. The district court concluded that no genuine issue of fact existed relating to the insured's omissions about her recurring cancer. It stated that no reasonable jury could find that the insured's health remained the same after her prognosis changed. The insured had an obligation to reveal the change, and since she failed to do so, the policy was invalid. The district court dismissed the husband's suit. *Brackin v. Metropolitan Life Ins. Co.*, 708 F.Supp. 206 (N.D.Ill.1989).

In 1972, an Ohio man underwent gallbladder surgery. By 1981 he was diagnosed as having diabetes, hypertension, hardening of the arteries, and several other illnesses. In 1983, he applied for health insurance. The application contained numerous questions about his medical history. He revealed the gallbladder surgery but failed to mention his other ailments. He signed the application and placed his initials next to the phrase "No Other Medical History." The man also returned a verification form confirming the application's truthfulness. He later sought coverage for over $37,000 in medical bills under the policy. The insurer returned the man's premium and notified him that it had canceled the policy because of the undisclosed medical background. He then sued the insurer in an Ohio trial court which dismissed his claim.

The man appealed to the Ohio Court of Appeals arguing that the case should not have been dismissed without a trial. The insurer argued that it would not have issued the policy had it been aware of the man's medical history. The court noted that the insurer issued the policy placing total reliance on the information gathered from the insured. This required the parties to act in good faith. Here, the application was wilfully and fraudulently made. The misrepresentations materially affected the acceptance of risk assumed by the insurer. The dismissal was upheld. *Buemi v. Mut. of Omaha Ins. Co.*, 524 N.E.2d 183 (Ohio App.1987).

A homeowner sued his homeowner's insurer. He sought coverage under a homeowner's policy for fire damage to his house and personal property. A Georgia superior court held for the insurer, finding that the homeowner "acted fraudulently or failed to comply with the conditions of the contract of insurance," thereby voiding the policy. The homeowner appealed to the Georgia Court of Appeals. The court of appeals noted that the homeowner refused to provide the insurer with complete copies of his income tax returns upon request. The record also indicated that, although damage to the homeowner's home and personal property amounted to only $25,000, he asserted a claim of $120,137.58. Also, the homeowner included in his claim items that were primarily insured by a third-party insurer. This evidence persuaded the court of appeals to support the superior court's decision that the homeowner either acted fraudulently or failed to comply with the insurance policy provisions. Coverage was denied. *Barber v. Wausau Underwriters Ins. Co.*, 362 S.E.2d 109 (Ga.App.1987).

In February 1988, a man applied for and was issued life insurance. He fraudulently failed to disclose that he had undergone recent medical treatments and had a fever and chills of unknown origin. The man died from AIDS in June 1988. In March of 1990, the insurer refused to pay benefits because the insured had made material misrepresentations. The insured's estate argued that because the insurer did not refuse to honor the policy until more than two years after its issuance, it had become incontestable. A trial court agreed, and the insurer appealed to the Superior Court of New Jersey, Appellate Division. New Jersey statutory law provides that a policy becomes incontestable "after it has been in force during the life time of the insured for a period of two years." Based on this language, the court held that the statute did not limit the contestability period to the lifetime of the insured. Therefore, if an insured dies before the policy has been in force for two years, the incontestability clause becomes irrelevant and does not bind the insurer. The trial court's decision was reversed. *Spilker v. William Penn Life Ins. Co. of New York*, 598 A.2d 929 (N.J.Super.A.D.1991).

A Virginia man was hospitalized and diagnosed as suffering from leukemia. He was told that he had only a short time to live. Four months later, he and his ex-wife applied for life insurance on his life. They fraudulently concealed his terminal condition. Ownership of the policy was transferred to the ex-wife. When she was late in paying her premiums, the policy lapsed. She then reinstated the policy. After the insured died, his ex-wife sought to recover under the policy. A federal district court held that the policy was void and unenforceable due to material misrepresentations in the application, and the ex-wife appealed to the U.S. Court of Appeals, Fourth Circuit. On appeal, she asserted that she had had no knowledge of her ex-husband's illness and that she did not instruct the agent on how to fill out the application. However, the agent testified that he had filled out the reinstatement application by asking the ex-wife questions. Further, the evidence presented allowed an inference that the ex-wife knew of the insured's condition. Also, the reinstatement application was filed less than two years before the suit was brought. Thus, the incontestability clause did not bar the insurer's defense of fraud. The district court's decision was affirmed. *Nyonteh v. Peoples Security Life Ins. Co.*, 958 F.2d 42 (4th Cir.1992).

In 1977, fire destroyed the house and possessions of a South Carolina man. The insurer refused to pay the claim, contending that the claim for the contents of the house was fraudulent. The homeowner sued. At trial, the insurer argued that fraud in the contents claim voided the entire contract including loss of dwelling and living expenses. The trial judge, however, ruled that the contract was severable. Although fraud would void the contents claim, he held that it would not void the other claims.

On appeal from the Court of Appeals, which reversed the trial court's decision, the South Carolina Supreme Court noted that under South Carolina law, forfeitures of insurance are not favored. In agreeing with the trial court, the supreme court acknowledged that its decision had been reached in only a minority of jurisdictions. In the overwhelming majority of states, any fraud or misrepresentation under an insurance policy will void the entire policy. Nevertheless, the homeowner was allowed to recover on his claims for loss of dwelling and living expenses. *Johnson v. South State Ins. Co.*, 341 S.E.2d 793 (S.C.1986).

After suffering a series of business reverses a thirty-nine-year-old businessman took out disability policies with two insurers, each of which provided $2,000 per month in benefits. On both applications he made misrepresentations as to his income, other disability insurance (he had four other such policies) and his prior receipt of disability benefits. On the day after one of his policies became incontestable for fraud he claimed that he was mugged and pistol whipped by two blacks. He drove himself to the hospital where the attendant nurse found no visible trauma. Undaunted, he claimed that the mugging had left him totally disabled and notified all his insurers, requesting disability forms. One of his insurers, National Life, began making the $2,000 per month disability payments.

National Life became suspicious of the claim and arranged for an examination by one of its physicians. The businessman appeared for the examination in a disheveled state, appearing to be "haunted." He was unshaven and his clothes were baggy. He was obsessed with imaginary black men hiding in closets, and had plastic straws in his mouth "to keep his airway open." The physician concluded that the man was indeed disabled, but National Life hired an investigator to observe him. He behaved in a normal fashion at all other times and was well-dressed and well-groomed.

Upon learning these facts the physician decided he could have been deceived, and another examination was arranged, this time with a psychologist. The psychologist concluded that he was "conning" them, and National Life decided to discontinue benefits. The man sued, but not only did the federal court rule against him, it ordered that he reimburse National Life for the $33,628 in benefits paid. He appealed unsuccessfully to the U.S. Court of Appeals, Second Circuit. The court of appeals held that the mistake of fact by National Life that the man was psychiatrically disabled justified its recovery of benefits. *Goldberg v. Nat'l Life Ins. Co. of Vermont*, 774 F.2d 559 (2d Cir.1985).

A California man obtained a $30,000 bank loan for the purchase of a particular 1984 Porsche 911. The loan officer inspected the car and entered its vehicle identification number (VIN) on a form. When the man applied for automobile insurance, a check of the VIN indicated that the car was actually a 1983 Porsche 944, a less expensive car than the 911. The man indicated that there had been a mixup and accepted an automobile insurance policy providing only $20,175 coverage. The man then reported the car stolen. When police found the car, with the VIN removed, at the address next door to the man's residence, he denied that it was his. He then filed an affidavit of loss with the insurer and accepted a draft from the insurer for the policy limit. The man was arrested and convicted of presenting a fraudulent insurance claim by a state superior court. He appealed, alleging that his conviction was not supported by sufficient evidence.

The California Court of Appeal, Second District, pointed out that intent to defraud is an essential element of the offense of presenting a fraudulent insurance claim. It stated that a person who "willfully submits a claim, knowing it to be false, necessarily does so with intent to defraud." The court noted that many of the man's personal belongings had been in the car when it was found by the police. These possessions included pictures of his girlfriend who later identified the car as his. Also, the man told police that they could not prove the car was his because it did not have any "ID numbers on it" before they told him that its VIN had been removed. Finally, the man's ownership and registration documents were filled with inaccuracies and inconsistencies including a listing of previous owners who could not be located. The Court of Appeal concluded that there was substantial evidence supporting the finding that the man knowingly presented a false or fraudulent claim to the insurer with intent to defraud. His conviction was affirmed. *People v. Marghzar*, 237 Cal.Rptr. 808 (App.2d Dist.1987).

Sec. I   INSURANCE FRAUD FOUND   177

An insurer issued a fire insurance policy on a house for $40,000 after having it inspected by an agent. In 1981, the insured contacted the agent and requested an increase in the policy limits. The insured told the agent that he had made substantial improvements to the house and that he had obtained a written appraisal stating that the replacement cost of the house was $70,000. The agent increased the insured's coverage to $70,000 on the basis of this representation. The house and its contents were subsequently totally destroyed by fire. Because substantial evidence indicated that the fire had been set deliberately, the insurer refused to pay for the loss. The insured then sued. When a circuit court ruled in favor of the insurer, the insured appealed, claiming that Missouri statutes precluded the insurer from using errors in the home's evaluation as a defense.

The Missouri Court of Appeals noted that under Missouri law, "the valuation listed in the policy is conclusive unless the valuation set is the result of fraud, misrepresentation, or collusion." The insured in this case had made positive statements regarding the cost and extent of improvements allegedly made to the house and stated that he had a written appraisal that the replacement cost of the house was $70,000. Such a statement could reasonably have been considered fraudulent by the jury. The defense of fraudulent misrepresentation was therefore properly allowed and the circuit court's decision was affirmed. *Hodge v. Continental Western Ins. Co.*, 722 S.W.2d 133 (Mo.App.1986).

On June 22, 1981, Aetna issued to a Mississippi farmer a fire insurance policy which covered seventeen pieces of farm equipment valued at $38,000. It stated that "[t]his entire policy shall be void if, whether before or after a loss, the Insured has concealed or misrepresented any material fact or circumstance concerning this insurance or the subject thereof, or the interest of the Insured therein, or in case of any fraud or false swearing by the Insured relating thereto." Two months later a fire destroyed all seventeen pieces of equipment, the farmer having bunched them under an open shed. The farmer reported the loss to Aetna the next day, and Aetna sent out a claims representative to investigate.

In response to the investigator's attempt to verify the farmer's original $38,000 valuation of the equipment, the farmer vaguely asserted that he could not identify exactly from whom he had obtained the equipment. Later, Aetna informed the farmer that bills of sale for each piece of equipment were necessary before they would reimburse him. He produced the bills of sale and gave them to Aetna, which noticed that most of them were from family or friends. One particularly suspicious bill of sale showed a purchase price of $16,000 and a purchase date of May 12, 1981 (only three months before the fire). The numeral "1" in the $16,000 figure was written in blue ink, while the "$6,000" was in black ink. Nonetheless, Aetna offered to settle the farmer's claim for $20,000. The farmer, however, counteroffered for $26,000. Aetna then exercised its right to take the farmer's sworn statement. In his statement he revealed that he had secured all the bills of sale after the fire and that he had made approximately $12,500 in profits in 1981 from selling cattle, hauling hay and hauling pulp wood. His federal income tax return, however, showed no profits for these activities in that year.

After the statement was taken, Aetna discovered that one bill of sale was completely false and that another overstated the sale price by $5,000. The farmer was informed that his misrepresentations had voided the policy. He sued in federal court, lost, and appealed to the U.S. Court of Appeals, Fifth Circuit, which also ruled against him. Applying Mississippi law, the court of appeals held that the farmer's statements to Aetna were 1) false, 2) material and 3) knowingly and wilfully made. The farmer's policy was ruled void due to his fraudulent misrepresentations. *Clark v. Aetna Cas. & Sur. Co.*, 778 F.2d 242 (5th Cir.1985).

A New Jersey man submitted a fraudulent claim to his insurer, seeking to recover $300,000 in accidental death benefits for the death of his wife. He claimed that she had died in a car accident in the Philippines. In fact, she was still alive. He submitted six falsified documents in support of his claim. Eventually, he pleaded guilty to third degree attempted theft by deception. The commissioner of insurance then filed a civil suit against him, seeking to impose a $5,000 penalty for each fraudulent document submitted in support of his claim. The trial court determined that the insured's action constituted a single violation of New Jersey law, and the appellate court affirmed. On appeal to the Supreme Court of New Jersey, the commissioner asserted that each false document had been a separate violation of the statute. The supreme court agreed. It stated that the law made "any written or oral statement as part of, or in support of *** a claim for payment or other benefit pursuant to an insurance policy" a violation. Here, each false statement enhanced the fraudulent claim, making the danger of payment more likely. The court found that the law clearly made each false statement a violation, allowing a separate penalty to be assessed for each false document submitted. The lower courts' decisions were reversed. *Merin v. Maglaki*, 599 A.2d 1256 (N.J.1992).

A Colorado case resulted in the insurer's reimbursement for a fraudulent claim already paid. The insurer sued to recover the amount paid on a theft loss claim. It had paid the claim after the insured's business was burglarized and a substantial loss was sustained. Subsequently, the man admitted "padding" the claim in order to recover significantly more insurance money than the actual amount of his losses. The Colorado Court of Appeals followed the rationale of *Western Assur. Co. v. Bronstein*, 236 P. 1013 (Colo.1925) which held that a fraud clause would render a policy void under the contract if there is some proof of a "false statement by [the] insured as to some material matter made for the purpose and with the intention of deceiving the insurer and inducing it to pay more insurance than the amount of the loss sustained." The insured was ordered to pay back the entire amount of the insurance proceeds to the insurer. *Northwestern Nat'l Ins. Co. v. Barnhart*, 713 P.2d 1360 (Colo.App.1985).

II. INSURANCE FRAUD NOT FOUND

In the following cases the insureds' conduct did not amount to fraud so as to result in nonliability for insurers, or in convictions for criminal insurance fraud.

An Illinois woman purchased a homeowner's insurance policy. Her main source of income was rent from an automobile business which her late husband had owned with another man. She had a fifty percent interest in the business. The business began encountering financial difficulties, and the insured undertook to save it by guaranteeing a loan personally. She also suffered other financial problems; a bond indemnity company purchased her home at a public auction for delinquent real estate taxes. Subsequently, her home was destroyed by fire, and she sought recovery under her homeowner's policy. The insurer refused to provide coverage, alleging that the insured had committed fraud by failing to reveal the tax sale of her home or the

Sec. II   INSURANCE FRAUD NOT FOUND   179

personal liability she was subject to as a guarantor. The insured brought suit in a federal district court. A jury found that she had not intended to defraud the insurer when she failed to reveal the information it had eventually discovered. Appeal was taken to the U.S. Court of Appeals, Seventh Circuit. There, the court decided that the question of the insured's intent to defraud the insurer had been properly left to the jury. A question also arose as to an inflated repair estimate that the insured had submitted; but again, since the jury had not found fraud, the court refused to do so. It affirmed the decision of the district court in favor of the insured. *Trzcinski v. American Casualty Co.*, 953 F.2d 307 (7th Cir.1992).

A rug retailer filed a burglary and theft loss claim under its fire insurance policy. Burglars apparently entered the business premises by breaking a small hole through a brick wall. The rug retailer first reported that fifteen rugs valued at about $153,000 had been stolen, but after an inventory check it reported 109 rugs stolen at a total cost of $471,519. Sheriff's deputies and the insurer's investigators suspected that the allegedly stolen rugs could not have been removed through the small hole in the wall. Evidence indicated that 109 rugs could not have been removed during the time in which the burglary allegedly took place. Also, an adjuster hired by the insurer found the rug retailer's inventory records "inadequate, incomplete or nonexistent for the rugs listed on the proof of loss." The insurer never expressly denied or paid the claim. When the rug retailer sued to recover damages, the insurer filed a cross complaint for fraud on the part of the rug retailer. The Superior Court, Los Angeles County, found for the insurer and the rug retailer appealed to the California Court of Appeal, Second District.

The court noted that a finding of fraud must be established by proof of justifiable reliance on intentional misrepresentations and resulting damage. In this case, the insurer began its investigation into the burglary before the rug retailer filed its proof of loss. The Court of Appeal noted that because the Superior Court found that a burglary and theft had occurred, the damages it awarded to the insurer could only be based on misrepresentations as to the value of the rugs stolen. Evidence indicated that the insurer never believed the amount of loss to be that which the rug retailer claimed. Thus, the costs of the insurer's investigation had not been incurred in reliance on the truth of the proof of loss. The insurer had produced no evidence indicating that its decision to investigate or the extent of its investigation depended on the amount of the loss claimed. There was therefore no reliance by the insurer on the rug retailer's misrepresentations. In absence of such reliance the Superior Court's finding of fraud was unfounded. Its decision was reversed. *Handel v. U.S. Fidelity & Guaranty*, 237 Cal.Rptr. 667 (App.2d Dist.1987).

A Georgia man inherited a piece of property from his parents and renewed the farm owner's policy which had been issued covering the property. He then conveyed the property by warranty deed to his brother to conceal his ownership of the land from the Farmers' Home Administration, to which he owed a debt. The insured's brother then reconveyed the property to the insured by another deed. Subsequently, a fire occurred and, upon investigating the loss, the insurer discovered the insured's conveyance to his brother and denied coverage. It asserted that the conveyance was a change in interest such as would void the policy by its terms. The insured then sued the insurer in a Georgia trial court and the jury returned a verdict in his favor. The insurer unsuccessfully appealed to the Georgia Court of Appeals and further appealed to the Supreme Court of Georgia.

On appeal, the court noted that although the insured's actions might have been reprehensible, he was still entitled to coverage under the policy. Merely because the insured had violated a condition of the policy, the law would not void the contract of insurance when the violation did not affect the loss nor contribute to it. If the insurer had been harmed by the insured's alleged fraud, it could perhaps have voided the policy. However, since the fire was not contributed to by the conveyance, the policy was still in effect. The court affirmed the lower court's decision and required the insurer to pay on the claim. *Georgia Farm Bureau Mutual Ins. Co. v. Brown*, 390 S.E.2d 586 (Ga.1990).

On November 4, 1981, an insured submitted a proof of loss statement to his insurer claiming that art had been stolen during a burglary of his office. The insurer paid the insured the full amount claimed. Several months later, after the art was recovered, it was found that the insured had submitted a fraudulently inflated appraisal to the insurer and that the insured had been involved in the burglary. On December 11, 1986, the insured's attorney entered into an agreement with the district attorney which extended the statute of limitations for any crimes the insured might have committed in connection with the insurance claim until March 31, 1987. After the insured was indicted for the crime of insurance fraud on February 27, 1987, he asked a New York supreme court to dismiss the indictment on the ground that the statute of limitations had expired.

The insured argued that the crime of insurance fraud is complete upon the filing of a fraudulent insurance claim. Thus, since he filed the claim on November 4, 1981, and the extension agreement was executed on December 11, 1986, the indictment was barred by New York's applicable five year statute of limitations. The supreme court held for the insured, observing that it was the commission of the fraudulent insurance act itself which completed the crime of insurance fraud. The presentation to the insurer of the proof of loss by the insured, when he knew that it contained materially false information, was the criminal activity. Therefore, the agreement to extend the statute of limitations was ineffectual. The insured's request for dismissal was granted. *People v. O'Boyle*, 519 N.Y.S.2d 524 (Sup.Ct.1987).

In another New York case, a doctor was injured in an automobile accident. Unable to practice medicine for approximately one month, he collected no-fault insurance benefits for lost earnings. In addition, he filed suit against the owner and operator of the other vehicle involved which was insured by Lumbermen's Mutual Casualty Company. Meanwhile, one of the doctor's patients who had been injured in a separate automobile accident submitted claims to her insurer, Allstate Insurance Company, for treatment that she claimed to have received from her doctor during the month that he was receiving lost earnings benefits. Allstate and Lumbermen's turned the matter over to the Insurance Crime Prevention Institute (ICPI), a nonprofit organization established by the property/casualty insurance industry to investigate allegations of insurance claim fraud. The ICPI determined that either the doctor or the patient had committed fraud and reported its findings to the district attorney's office. That office initiated a grand jury proceeding but the grand jury ended its investigation due to insufficient evidence. The doctor then sued Lumbermen's and ICPI charging malicious prosecution, negligence, violation of civil rights and intentional infliction of emotional distress. The Supreme Court, Appellate Division, however, dismissed the doctor's lawsuit. *Torian v. Lumbermen's Mut. Cas. Co.*, 502 N.Y.S.2d 105 (A.D.3d Dept.1986).

A hurricane struck an apartment complex on the Mississippi gulf coast, causing extensive damage. The owner sought a repair estimate for its insurer. After the insurer received the estimate, it requested a more detailed accounting, which the insurance contract permitted. The owner then submitted two further estimates which the insurer rejected, stating that they were mere damage summaries instead of required detailed cost estimates. The insured then sued its insurer in a federal district court, asserting that it had refused in bad faith to pay the claim. The insurer alleged that the insured had refused to submit a properly detailed repair estimate, had misrepresented repair costs and had concealed a lower estimate. The jury determined that the insured had willfully and knowingly misrepresented material facts about the claims to the insurer, and the insured's claim was dismissed. The court then dismissed the insurer's claim for punitive damages because of the misrepresentation, but allowed the insurer to retain $13,000 in unearned premiums paid by the insured. Both parties appealed to the U.S. Court of Appeals, Fifth Circuit.

The court of appeals held that the question of misrepresentation had properly gone to the jury, and that the evidence had been sufficient for the jury to return a verdict for the insurer. Also, there had been no bad faith on the part of the insurer because it had not refused to pay the claim. It had merely requested a more detailed damage estimate than the one which had been provided. However, the court ruled that the insurer was not allowed to keep the $13,000 in unearned premiums because no fraud on the part of the insured had been shown. The court affirmed the trial court's decision in part, and reversed in part. It denied coverage to the insured due to misrepresentation, but did not allow the insurer to retain the unearned premiums. *Guaranty Serv. Corp. v. American Employers' Ins. Co.,* 893 F.2d 725 (5th Cir. 1990).

"Every person who presents, or causes to be presented, any false or fraudulent claim" is guilty of insurance fraud under Utah law (U.C.A.1953, 76-6-521). The Utah Supreme Court held that telephoning in a false claim does not constitute presenting a false claim within the meaning of the statute. In upholding a lower court's decision to set aside an insurance fraud conviction, the supreme court held that the defendant had not caused a false claim to be "presented" because the insurer required more extensive documentation prior to the payment of a claim. *State v. Wilson,* 710 P.2d 801 (Utah 1985).

A California undercover officer received a telephone call from a man responding to a contrived newspaper ad placed by a local sheriff's department which solicited buy-sell transactions. The man said he wanted to sell his Camaro Z-28, report it stolen, and collect the insurance proceeds. The man and the officer planned a scheme whereby the officer would pay the caller $900 and then hide the car until the insurance money was collected. The $900 changed hands in a grocery store parking lot. At this point the officer gave a cue word to other policemen monitoring the events. As the arresting officers moved in, the man threw the money into the air.

A California trial court convicted the man of disposing of insured property with intent to defraud and he appealed, arguing that the evidence was insufficient to support his conviction. The California Court of Appeal, Fourth District, agreed. The appellate court found that where the man had not given the car keys or the car to the officer and was still seated behind the steering wheel of the car when he was arrested, the evidence was insufficient to convict him of the offense. At most, this was evidence to show that the defendant was guilty of an *attempted* disposal of property with intent to defraud. *People v. Splawn*, 211 Cal.Rptr. 638 (App.4th Dist.1985).

The owner of a vehicle and his wife suffered the loss of an automobile due to fire, and submitted a claim to their automobile insurer. A Florida jury found that the husband had intentionally started the fire and had filed a false claim, but that the wife was unaware of his actions. The court ruled that the wife could not recover because the policy provided coverage only for acts which were "direct and accidental." The wife appealed to the District Court of Appeal of Florida. Traditionally, courts have held that fraudulent acts by one coinsured were imputed to and barred recovery for the other innocent insured. The imputation has sometimes been avoided upon a finding that the policy provides "several" coverage — that is, each insured is covered separately. Accordingly, the court sought to determine whether the policy afforded joint or several coverage. The policy was silent; it was thus found to be ambiguous and construed against the insurer (several). Therefore, an examination of what was intended by the parties had to be done from the viewpoint of the insured seeking coverage; the damage was found to be unintended from the viewpoint of the wife. The insurer argued that the wife should not be allowed to recover because she had no ownership interest in the vehicle. The court focused not on ownership, but on an insurable interest, and ruled in favor of the wife. The denial of benefits for the wife was reversed. *Overton v. Progressive Ins. Co.*, 585 So.2d 445 (Fla.App.4th Dist.1991).

In a Mississippi case, after a homeowner's dwelling was destroyed by fire he sought compensation from his insurer. The insurer refused payment, citing incorrect statements regarding the homeowner's whereabouts on the day of the fire made by the homeowner in the course of the investigation. A U.S. district court granted a motion for a directed verdict to the insurer. The homeowner appealed to the U.S. Court of Appeals, Fifth Circuit. The statement in question was that the homeowner had spent the entire day of the fire in a tavern near the Mississippi-Tennessee border drinking beer and playing pool. In actuality he had left the tavern for a period of time to make a court appearance regarding another matter. The homeowner conceded the inaccuracy of his statement but denied it was either material or knowingly and wilfully made with the intent to deceive. The appellate court agreed stating that under Mississippi law an insurer seeking to defeat a policy on the basis of a "concealment" clause must establish that statements made by the insured were false *and* material *and* knowingly and wilfully made. Here the materiality of the misstatement was far from conclusive and was for a jury to determine. There was also a question as to wilfullness of the misstatement. Therefore, the appellate court concluded that the granting of a motion for a directed verdict was inappropriate and it remanded the case to the district court for further proceedings. *Watkins v. Continental Ins. Co.*, 690 F.2d 449 (5th Cir.1982).

A Michigan man purchased a motor home, executing a note with a credit union which was secured by the motor home. The credit union was named as a lienholder on the title to the vehicle. The man then purchased motor vehicle insurance wherein the credit union was made a loss payee. Subsequently, while the policy was in effect, the insured committed arson upon the motor home in an effort to defraud the insurer. The insurer denied coverage. The credit union then filed suit to recover under the policy. A trial court ruled for the credit union and the court of appeals affirmed. The case then came before the Michigan Supreme Court. The court first noted that the clause in question was a standard loss payable clause, under which a lienholder is not subject to the exclusions available to the insurer against the insured. Under this type of policy, a separate contract of insurance exists between the lienholder and the insurer (apart from the one between insured and insurer). Accordingly, the lienholder/credit union was entitled to recover under the loss payable clause even though the insured was precluded from recovering under the same policy by his act of arson. The court affirmed the lower courts' decisions in favor of the credit union. *Foremost Ins. Co. v. Allstate Ins. Co.*, 486 N.W.2d 600 (Mich.1992).

CHAPTER FIVE

LIFE AND HEALTH INSURANCE

		Page
I.	MISREPRESENTATION	186
	A. Application Misrepresentations Precluding Coverage	186
	B. Alleged Misrepresentations Not Precluding Coverage	191
	C. Incontestability Clauses	195
II.	NONPAYMENT OF PREMIUM	197
	A. Policies Voided	197
	B. Policies Not Voided	199
III.	GROUP LIFE AND HEALTH INSURANCE	201
	A. Scope of Coverage	201
	1. Types of Claims and Individuals Covered	202
	2. Regulation of Practice	210
	3. Injuries	211
	4. Policy Dates and Limitations Periods	211
	B. The "Actively at Work" Requirement	214
IV.	DELIVERY OF POLICY	216
V.	DOUBLE INDEMNITY AND ACCIDENTAL DEATH BENEFITS	219
VI.	PAYMENT OF PROCEEDS	223
	A. Rival Claimants	223
	B. Change-of-Beneficiary Disputes	228
	C. Missing Persons	232
VII.	EXCLUSIONS FROM COVERAGE	233
	A. Life Insurance	234
	1. Coverage Precluded	234
	2. Coverage Allowed	239
	B. Health and Medical Insurance	242
	1. Coverage Precluded	243
	2. Coverage Allowed	246
	3. Preexisting Conditions	250
VIII.	SEX-BASED MORTALITY TABLES	253

I. MISREPRESENTATION

Generally, when an insured makes a material misrepresentation of fact on an application for life or health insurance, the courts will declare the policy null and void. Often the misrepresentation must have been intentional and it must involve a fact material to the risk which is being insured.

A. Application Misrepresentations Precluding Coverage

In the following cases the misrepresentations or false application statements by insureds were deemed sufficient to preclude insurance coverage.

A North Carolina married couple applied for a life insurance policy on the life of the husband. The agent asked the couple questions, filled out the application form and had the couple sign it. Since it was for a life insurance policy, the form included questions concerning driver's license suspension, moving violations, and accidents. The couple, however, failed to inform the agent that the husband's driver's license had been suspended and that he had two moving violations and two accidents within the previous two years. The wife later alleged that the subject never came up during the application process and that she unknowingly signed the insurance form. After the insurer issued the policy, the husband was killed in an accident while driving seventy miles per hour in a thirty-five mile per hour zone. The insurer investigated the accident, discovered the traffic violations, and consequently rescinded the policy. The wife filed suit against the agent and insurer. The district court returned a verdict against the insurer and denied the insurer's motions for a directed verdict and judgment notwithstanding the verdict. The insurer then appealed to the court of appeals which affirmed. The Supreme Court of North Carolina granted review.

On appeal, the court noted that the insured is not responsible for false answers on an application if the insured is justifiably ignorant of the untrue answers or has no actual or implied knowledge. It was presumed that the wife knew the contents of the application when she signed it; she had never asserted anything to justify her ignorance of her husband's traffic violations. Moreover, the law presumes that the insured knows what is in an insurance agreement and is bound by it when signed. Thus, because the representation made regarding the decedent's driving record was false, and because there was no finding of fraud on the part of the agent or insurer, the court of appeals' decision was reversed. *Goodwin v. Investors Life Ins. Co.*, 419 S.E.2d 766 (N.C.1992).

A California woman applied for life insurance. She represented to the broker who sold the policy that she had not smoked cigarettes for the preceding twelve months. In fact, she had been a long-time smoker and had smoked during the previous year. She then signed a "Non-Smoking Declaration" in which she checked the box indicating that she smoked pipes or cigars. This declaration was not forwarded to the insurer. A nonsmoker's policy could still issue so long as the insured did not smoke cigarettes. The broker then informed the applicant that if she had misrepresented that she was a nonsmoker, the policy would be void. After the policy was issued, the insured died. An investigation revealed that the insured had been a smoker and had misrepresented this to obtain a nonsmoker's policy. When the insurer refused to pay under the policy, the beneficiary brought suit. The insurer sought summary judgment, which the court refused. The insurer then sought a writ of mandate from the California Court of Appeal, First District.

The beneficiary asserted before the court that because the insurer would still have issued a life insurance policy if the insured had admitted she was a smoker, the policy could not be rescinded. The insurer admitted it would have issued a smoker's insurance policy, with premiums about twice those required for a nonsmoker's policy. However, it asserted that the policy actually issued would not have been issued had the insured told the truth. The court of appeal determined that even though the misrepresentation affected only the premium, it was material and allowed the insurer to rescind the policy. The court also stated that the declaration signed by the insured (admitting that she smoked pipes or cigars) was not sufficient to put the insurer on notice that the insured smoked cigarettes. Thus, the insurer had had no duty to investigate further. The court issued the writ to grant the insurer's motion for summary judgment. *Old Line Life Ins. Co. of America v. Superior Court*, 279 Cal. Rptr. 80 (Cal.App.1st Dist.1991).

A Colorado man applied for life insurance shortly after receiving four medical examinations from an internist. A battery of tests was performed, and he was referred to a cardiologist. Nevertheless, he only indicated to the insurer that he had seen a general practitioner for a headache. When he died two months later, his widow was denied benefits. She sued in a state court, but the action was removed to a Colorado federal district court. On the insurer's motion for summary judgment, the court determined that the insured had materially misrepresented his condition and that the insurer did not have sufficient notice to investigate his true medical condition. The court granted summary judgment to the insurer. *Barciak v. United of Omaha Life Ins. Co.*, 777 F.Supp. 839 (D.Colo.1991).

A Washington businessman bought a life insurance policy for $250,000. Within a year, a second life insurance policy was purchased. However, the application for the second policy contained misrepresentations; it indicated that the insured (an avid mountain climber) had not climbed within the last 3 years, that the insurance was not intended to be a replacement policy and that the insured's preexisting policy was $40,000 rather than $250,000. The insured then discontinued paying premiums on the first policy. Within a year the insured died in a mountain climbing accident, and the second insurer refused to cover the claim due to material misrepresentations contained in the application. The decedent's wife sued the insurer, and a Washington district court ruled in her favor. The insurer appealed. On appeal, the court rejected the district court's conclusion that the insurer could not raise a misrepresentation defense. The appellate court noted that when the life insurance policy was issued to the decedent, he had had an opportunity and a duty to read the application in order to correct any misrepresentations. Moreover, the insured ratified the misrepresentations concerning his mountain climbing by his signature. However, the insurer might have breached a duty to the insured because the insurance agent knew or should have known that the policy was a replacement policy. Accordingly, the court reversed and remanded the case to determine whether the insurer's "negligence" caused the insured to cancel his old policy. *Strother v. Capitol Bankers Life Ins. Co.*, 834 P.2d 1111 (Wash.App.Div.1 1992).

A husband and wife applied for life insurance. Unaware of the fact that she was suffering from acute lymphocytic leukemia (a malignancy involving the bone marrow), the wife certified that she was in good health. Shortly thereafter, she was diagnosed and treated; however, she died less than two years later. When her husband sought benefits, the insurer denied his claim. The lawsuit reached the Georgia Court of Appeals, which stated that since the wife was not in good health at the time she applied, recovery was precluded. Her good faith intent in completing the application was irrelevant. Coverage was denied. *Davis v. John Hancock Mutual Life Ins. Co.*, 413 S.E.2d 224 (Ga.App.1991).

A Missouri man decided to purchase a life insurance policy, and filled out an application stating that he had never had cancer. The policy contained a "good health" clause which said that the insurance would not take effect unless the insured was actually in the state of health he represented himself to be in. Unbeknownst to the insured, he had incurable colon cancer and died less than a year after the policy was issued. The insurer claimed that the policy never took effect because of the good health clause. The U.S. Court of Appeals, Eighth Circuit, agreed with the insurer. Even though the insured had not deliberately misled the insurer, his health was not as he represented it. *Ruwitch v. William Penn Life Assurance Co.*, 966 F.2d 1234 (8th Cir.1992).

A Nevada insured purchased a $50,000 term life policy. In his application, the insured falsely stated that he had not been treated for high blood pressure. If the insured had fully disclosed his history of serious hypertension, the insurer would have required a premium three times higher than actually charged. The insured died of stomach cancer within a year of purchasing the policy and his beneficiary requested a lump sum payment of the death benefit. Upon investigation, the insurer discovered the insured's history of hypertension, cancelled the policy and returned policy premiums with interest. The beneficiary sued the insurer in a Nevada trial court, which granted summary judgment to the insurer under a Nevada statute permitting policy cancellation in cases of fraudulent or material misrepresentation. On appeal to the Nevada Supreme Court, the beneficiary argued that the statute relied on by the trial court should not apply because the insured's death was unrelated to hypertension. Under that theory, failure to disclose the insured's medical history was immaterial. The insurer argued that the statute permitted cancellation. The state supreme court agreed with the insurer, finding that the statute's intent was clearly to make insurance policies voidable when misrepresentations were made on policy applications. The lower court had properly granted the insurer's motion for summary judgment. *Randono v. CUNA Mut. Ins. Group*, 793 P.2d 1324 (Nev.1990).

A New York man falsely answered specific questions about his wife on a health statement in his application for insurance under a group policy issued by his employer. He failed to disclose his wife's recent medical visits to doctors. Her complaints led to testing which revealed cancer. The insurer established that had it known of the wife's ailments it would have denied her coverage in accordance with the guidelines established in its medical manual. The court granted the insurer's motion for summary judgment. On appeal, the appellate court determined that it did not matter whether the defendant had made those representations innocently because the law is clear that material misrepresentations which induce the insurer to extend coverage may later be used to rescind the insurance contract. *New York Life Ins. Co. v. Palmer*, 565 N.Y.S.2d 192 (A.D.2d Dep't 1991).

Two years after a New York man was issued a life insurance policy, the insurer solicited him for a second policy. It relied on the medical information contained in his first policy. The insured, however, had had a recurrence of lymphoma which required chemotherapy, which he did not disclose to the insurer. After the insured's death the trial court denied the insurer's motion to rescind the policy. On appeal, the appellate division of New York reversed the trial court's order and rescinded the policy because of the material misrepresentation. The court determined that the deceased had a duty to review and correct any incorrect or incomplete answers on the policy. *North Atlantic Life Ins. Co. v. Katz*, 557 N.Y.S.2d 150 (A.D.2d Dep't 1990).

A Louisiana woman applied for a $50,000 term life insurance policy. In her application, she indicated that she had no present health problems, and the insurer issued a policy. Nine months later, the insured died from respiratory failure resulting from a brain tumor. Upon the beneficiary's claim under the policy, the insurer conducted an investigation, concluded that the woman had materially misrepresented her medical condition and rescinded the policy, refunding the premiums. The beneficiary then sued the insurer. A district court noted that the woman's doctor had diagnosed and treated the woman for cancer just prior to her application for insurance. It also stated that the insured had been aware of the seriousness of her condition. Thus, the court held that the insurer was entitled to void the insurance contract it had issued. *Watson v. United of Omaha Life Ins. Co.*, 735 F.Supp. 684 (M.D.La.1990).

A Michigan man who had experienced epilepsy during his childhood purchased a disability policy from an insurer. The insured did not admit to epilepsy in his medical history. He then suffered injuries in a table saw accident and submitted a claim to his insurer. When the insurer denied coverage the insured sued it in a Michigan trial court, which ruled for the insurer. The insured appealed to the Court of Appeals of Michigan, which affirmed the trial court's decision. Even though the insured's disability was not "due to his undisclosed epilepsy," the insurer had retained the right to void the policy for misrepresentation. *Clark v. John Hancock Mutual Life Ins. Co.*, 447 N.W.2d 783 (Mich.App.1989).

A health insurance applicant was asked on an application form if she had ever been treated for a mental or emotional disorder or had consulted any physician or practitioner. She answered no to this question and the insurer issued the policy. She later sought reimbursement for hospitalization for psychiatric treatment. The insurer then learned that prior to applying for her insurance she had been to over 130 sessions with a psychologist. The insurer refused payment and declared the policy void for the material misstatements made on her application. The insured then sued for a declaratory judgment in an Illinois trial court which found in the insured's favor. The insurance company appealed to the Appellate Court of Illinois, First District. That court reversed the trial court's decision. The court concluded that the word "practitioner" as used in the insurer's application was not ambiguous and should include the term "psychologist" in its meaning. *Cohen v. Washington Nat. Ins. Co.*, 529 N.E.2d 1065 (Ill.App.1st Dist.1988).

An insurance agent visited a couple who wished to purchase a life insurance policy. After having them fill out an application, he gave them a conditional receipt showing payment of the first month's premium. Two days later, the husband died from a drug overdose. Two months later, the wife received the life insurance policy and a copy of the application. She then called the agent to start a claim for the policy's death benefits. The insurer refused to pay, claiming that the husband failed to disclose treatment for a heroin overdose several months before the application. The treatment should have been reported on the application. The wife sued for coverage and a superior court granted summary judgment for the insurer. The wife then appealed to the Court of Appeal, Fifth District.

On appeal, the wife argued that the insurer could not rely on the misrepresentations in the application since a copy of the application was not attached to the receipt. She argued that California law requires the application to be attached to the policy for an application's provisions to be effective. She also argued that the misrepresentations were not intentional, and even if they were, coverage was irrevocable during the interim period between acceptance of the application and delivery of the policy. The court disagreed with all her arguments. The court stated that since the receipt was not the policy itself, a copy of the application did not need to be attached for the insurer to rely on it. Further, the policy, when it was eventually delivered, did have a copy of the application attached to it. In addition, the misrepresentations were material. The fact that the insurer demanded answers to specific questions is usually in itself sufficient to prove materiality. Finally, the court stated that, as a general rule, interim life insurance arises at the time a purchaser pays the initial premium and coverage exists if the insured dies before the company issues a policy. However, a misrepresentation allows rescission. The court affirmed the judgment. *Wilson v. Western Nat'l Life Ins. Co.*, 1 Cal.Rptr.2d 157 (Cal.App.5th Dist.1991).

In 1982 an Arizona man obtained a major medical policy. A question on the application asked if he had been a habitual user of narcotics, barbiturates, amphetamines, or halucinatory drugs during the past ten years. He answered no. A month later, the man was admitted to a hospital emergency room for treatment of a heroin overdose. The man told the doctor that he had once been a heavy user of drugs and had withdrawn from heroin eight years before. He later testified that he had stopped using heroin in 1974 and had started using it again in 1978. He said that between 1978 and 1982 he took heroin or dilaudid approximately five times a year. He testified that he did not feel his usage was habitual during that ten-year period. The man submitted a claim for insurance benefits to cover the hospital costs resulting from his heroin overdose. His insurer denied liability because he had failed to disclose his past history of drug addiction. The insurer then filed a lawsuit seeking to rescind the health policy. A superior court granted the policy rescission and the man appealed.

On appeal, the man argued that the question on the insurance application asked for his opinion as to whether he was a habitual drug user. The court rejected this argument, deciding instead that the question "elicited a factual answer." The Arizona Court of Appeals noted that "[u]nder these circumstances, no reasonable person could view this drug usage as susceptible to an opinion that it was not habitual." The court agreed with the superior court's decision that the man had provided a false answer to the question. Because evidence was admitted indicating that no policy would have been issued if he had answered truthfully, the superior court's decision to allow the insurer to rescind the policy was affirmed. *Equitable Life Assur. Society of the United States v. Anderson*, 727 P.2d 1066 (Ariz.App.1986).

A North Carolina case involved an applicant who procured a life insurance policy on his son. The applicant represented to the insurance agent that his son did not have a defect and had not consulted a doctor within the last five years for any condition not set out in the application. In reality, the six-year-old child had been born with brain damage and had been sick most of his life. The insurance agent, who was aware of the child's condition, filled out the application for the insured. The applicant signed the application but did not read it. After the boy died of pneumonia the applicant sought to claim the insurance proceeds. The insurer denied recovery on the ground that the material misrepresentation in the application voided coverage. The applicant brought suit against the insurer in a North Carolina trial court, which held in the applicant's favor. The insurer appealed to the Court of Appeals of North Carolina which reversed the trial court's ruling. It relied on a case which held that if an application for insurance containing material misrepresentations is filled in by the agent before being signed by the applicant, the misrepresentations are made by the applicant and bar his recovery. Thus, the court of appeals dismissed the applicant's claim. *McCrimmon v. North Carolina Mut. Life Ins. Co.*, 317 S.E.2d 709 (N.C.App.1984).

B. Alleged Misrepresentations Not Precluding Coverage

An insurance agent sold life insurance policies to a minister and his wife. He later recommended that they change insurers, so they submitted applications to do so. The agent used information from previous applications to fill out the applications with regard to certain health-related questions. The application contained certain misstatements and omissions as a result, due to the minister's changed health. On the day the insurer approved the application, the minister was in the hospital with viral pneumonia. Nine days later the minister died. The insurer brought a declaratory relief action against the minister's wife, asserting that the minister's health had been materially misrepresented on the application. The court held for the minister's wife, and the insurer appealed to the Supreme Court of New Mexico. On appeal, the court noted that even though the minister had not signed the application, this did not render the policy void from the outset. Further, any misrepresentation made on the application was made by the agent, not the minister. The court thus held that the policy was enforceable. However, the insurer could seek indemnification from its agent for his breach of duty. Finally, the court noted that the beneficiary was not entitled to punitive damages because the insurer's refusal to pay was neither frivolous nor unfounded. *Jackson National Life Ins. Co. v. Receconi*, 827 P.2d 118 (N.M.1992).

The widow of a New York insured sought benefits under his life insurance policy. The insurer denied benefits, stating that it would not have issued the policy had it known of the insured's long-time drug abuse. The widow then sued the insurer in a New York trial court. The insurer moved for dismissal. The court denied the insurer's motion and the insurer appealed to the New York Supreme Court, Appellate Division. The appellate court affirmed the lower court's decision. It held that a jury must determine whether the insured had suffered from an "impairment" to his health as defined in the policy because he used drugs. It refused to hold as a matter of law that a life insurance policy is void when the insured fails to disclose drug use. The insurer's motion was denied and the case continued to trial. The Supreme Court, Appellate Division, held that the insurer had not established that the insured was an intravenous drug user. There was also no proof that the insured was suffering from an "impairment" to his health because of his drug use. The court further held that the insurer did not establish that the insured's failure to disclose his alleged drug use on the application provided a basis for denying benefits. The insurer had failed to adequately describe exactly what its underwriting practices were with respect to applicants who were drug users and it remained unclear as to what degree the insured's drug use would have influenced the insurer's decision to issue a policy. The supreme court affirmed and modified its previous decision. *Botway v. American Int'l Assur. Co. of New York*, 543 N.Y.S.2d 651 (A.D.1st Dep't 1989).

A man had a life insurance contract, and sought to obtain another life insurance policy with the same insurer in order to cover a debt. The man answered "no" to two questions on the policy application: *Have you consulted a physician or been hospitalized during the last three years*, and *have you had any of the diseases specified on the application*. He later died of an accidental gunshot wound. The insurer paid the man's first life policy but invoked a period of contestability on the second policy. It later found that the man had failed to disclose a series of visits to a physician which resulted in a diagnosis of alcoholism and depression, and denied his claim based on the misrepresentation. His widow successfully sued in state court, and the insurer appealed to the Supreme Court of Montana.

Under Montana law, an insurer may deny a claim if a material representation affected the insurer's acceptance of the risk, was fraudulent, or would have affected the policy limits accepted or premium charged. The widow contended that the insurer would not have denied coverage even if it had known of the consultations. After finding an absence of fraud, the court examined the insurer's underwriting procedures and application. The underwriting manual included procedures to be followed concerning alcohol use, but did not call for an automatic denial of coverage. The trial court found that the insurer should have followed its written procedures and could have issued the policy with knowledge of the man's health. The supreme court ruled that substantial evidence supported this finding. The court also upheld a finding that the insurer had not denied the claim in good faith. It noted that the insurer failed to follow its own procedures, which called for an additional investigation of alcohol use, when the claim was submitted. Judgment for the widow was affirmed. *Schneider v. Minnesota Mutual Life Ins.*, 806 P.2d 1032 (Mont.1991).

Two separate life insurance contracts were obtained by a man who died shortly thereafter. The insurer found that the man had made material misrepresentations, and denied payment of benefits on those grounds. The estate of the deceased argued that the denial was unwarranted because the misrepresentations were unrelated to the death. A state trial court granted summary judgment to the estate, and the insurer appealed to the Court of Appeals of South Carolina. A distinction was made between related and unrelated misrepresentations; an insurer must establish a causal connection between a misrepresentation and the death of the insured when it attempts to void a policy following a death. Therefore, proceedings to void a policy on unrelated misrepresentations must be brought during the lifetime of the insured. The judgment was affirmed. *Carroll v. Jackson National Life Insurance Co.*, 405 S.E.2d 425 (S.C.App.1991).

A New York man applied for and received a life insurance policy. Upon his death, his wife claimed the proceeds. However, the insurance company refused to compensate her because her husband had made material misrepresentations on his application. He had failed to disclose that he drank a pint of alcohol daily and that his drinking was directly related to heartburn. The trial court decided in favor of the wife, holding that an applicant cannot be required to answer questions about the past and present condition of his health with the skill of a trained physician. It stated that the insurer failed to prove that this nondisclosure was a material misrepresentation by the decedent. The insurer appealed to the Supreme Court, Appellate Division. On appeal, it argued that a new trial was mandated so that the insurer could provide evidence that the nondisclosure by the decedent would have led it to refuse to issue the policy. The New York Court of Appeals affirmed the trial court's decision that the insurer failed to prove a material misrepresentation. The court of appeals rejected the insurer's contention that evidence was not allowed at trial to establish a material misrepresentation. The decedent's wife was allowed to recover the life insurance proceeds. *Chase v. William Penn Life Ins. Co.*, 552 N.Y.S.2d 772 (A.D.4 Dep't 1990).

A Louisiana insured died of cancer. His wife sought coverage under his life insurance policy. The insurer refused to pay the proceeds, contending that the insured had purposely concealed on his application form that he was a diabetic. The insured's wife sued the insurer in a Louisiana trial court which found for the wife but denied her petition for statutory penalties and attorney's fees. Both parties then appealed to the Court of Appeal of Louisiana, Fifth Circuit. The court held that the evidence failed to establish that the insured had intentionally concealed his diabetes when he completed the application. None of the insurer's witnesses could say with certainty that the insured knew of his diabetes before the policy date. Because there was a question of coverage, the insurer was allowed to deny payment without being statutorily arbitrary. The trial court's decision was affirmed. *Chifici v. Riverside Life Ins. Co.*, 546 So.2d 811 (La.App.5th Cir.1989).

A Virginia insured accidentally shot and killed his wife. He was then admitted to a hospital for depression. He was soon discharged and in a later therapy session he told the doctor that he thought of committing suicide. The insured then borrowed money from the Standard Federal Savings and Loan Association (Standard) to finance his home. As additional security for the loan, the insured applied for a decreasing term credit life insurance policy. The application inquired as to whether the man had been treated by a physician within the last five years for "epilepsy or nervous disorder." The man answered no. He did not disclose his previous hospitalization. The insurer issued the policy and the insured paid the required monthly premiums. Within the two-year contestability period, the insured was murdered. The insurer declined to pay the policy proceeds to Standard because of the insured's failure to disclose his treatment. The Virginia Supreme Court noted that the phrase "nervous disorder" was a general term which could include physical or mental disorders, or both. The phrase, as used in the application question, was ambiguous since it could have referred to physical disorders only. Thus the insured had not answered the question untruthfully when he failed to disclose his depression. The insured's answer did not give the insurer grounds to rescind the policy and the lower court's decision was affirmed. *Andrews v. American Health & Life Ins.*, 372 S.E.2d 399 (Va.1988).

A life insurance policy was issued to three officers of an Iowa corporation. The policy stipulated that the policy should not take effect "if the insured's health as shown in the application has changed so as to increase the mortality rating or class of risk before delivery and payment ... are complete." At the time of the application the insurer knew the medical history of all three officers. The policy was issued on November 7, with a policy date of November 15. When the policy was delivered the insurer's agent was notified that one of the officers had been in the hospital. On November 22, the officer in question had exploratory surgery. Two weeks later he died due to surgical complications. The surviving officers sought coverage but the insurer refused. They sued the insurer in an Iowa trial court which held for the insurer. The officers appealed to the Iowa Court of Appeals which reversed the decision. It held that the insurer had sufficient information to put it on notice to investigate the officers' health. The insurer could not blind itself from ascertaining the truth and then claim wilful misrepresentation to avoid payment. The insurer's vice-president had admitted that had the surgery been a success, the officer would have fallen within the same rating. The insurer failed to present evidence that the deceased officer's medical condition had increased the mortality rate or the class of risk. The court of appeals reversed the trial court decision and held that the insurer must provide coverage. *Vali-Check v. Security-Connecticut Ins. Co.*, 423 N.W.2d 556 (Iowa App.1988).

In October 1983, a man submitted an application to an insurer for a life insurance policy in the amount of $250,000. Under "plan applied for," the man requested a nonsmoker policy. One month later, he submitted a medical examination report which was labeled "Supplement to Application." After another month passed, the man signed a "smoking statement" which read: "I do not now smoke cigarettes nor have I smoked any cigarettes for at least the past twelve months." The life insurance policy contained a clause indicating that "[t]his policy and application make up the entire contract." When the man died, his insurer filed a lawsuit to rescind the policy alleging that the man knowingly provided false answers on the smoking statement because he smoked regularly at the time of and within twelve months prior to the date of the smoking statement. A U.S. district court ruled in favor of the policy's beneficiary, and the insurer appealed. The U.S. Court of Appeals, Seventh Circuit, considered the insurer's allegation that the smoking statement was part of the application. It noted that if a policy provision is ambiguous, it would be strictly construed against the insurer because the insurer drafted the policy. The court observed that, unlike the medical examination report, the smoking statement did not indicate that it was part of the application. Because ambiguity existed as to whether or not the smoking statement was part of the application, the insurer could not rely on misrepresentations made in the smoking statement to rescind the policy. The district court's ruling in favor of the policy's beneficiary was affirmed. *Nat. Fidelity Life Ins. Co. v. Karaganis*, 811 F.2d 357 (7th Cir.1987).

A Texas man applied for a mortgage protection life insurance policy. He stated on the application that he did not know himself to be suffering from any physical ailments but that he had visited a doctor during the previous two years for back treatment. In a physical examination requested by the insurer he told the examiner that he had been wounded in Viet Nam and had gained 50 pounds in the previous year "due to beer drinking." He indicated that he had no mental illness and provided the names of two hospitals and two doctors who had previously treated him. The insurer issued the policy with a death benefit of $42,900. Thirteen months later the man violently attacked his wife and she shot him to death. The insurer contested the wife's claim for the policy's death benefit when it discovered that the man had been treated several times for depression. It declared the policy void because of misrepresentation. The Texas Court of Appeals declared that although the man had intentionally misrepresented facts and the insurer had relied on those misrepresentations, the insurer could not void the policy because it would have discovered the misrepresentations if it had made a reasonable further inquiry. Had the insurer examined the records of the two doctors and hospitals that the man gave the examiner it would have discovered his history of mental problems. *Republic-Vanguard Life Ins. v. Walters*, 728 S.W.2d 415 (Tex. App.1st Dist.1987).

In 1982, two brothers each obtained life insurance policies naming the businesses they owned as the beneficiaries. Three years later, one of the brothers completed five more life insurance applications. In each of these applications, he disclosed that he suffered from hemophilia. While the five policies were being considered for approval, the insured underwent a physical exam which determined that he had lost 20 pounds and had a sinus infection. The examining doctor was concerned that he had AIDS but refrained from telling the insured. Within a month of this exam, the insured verified on an "amendment to application" for each policy that he was in good health. The insured then decided to obtain a sixth life insurance policy. When he filled out this application, he disclosed that he had hemophilia but failed to disclose his weight loss and sinus infection. Two days later, he was hospitalized and diagnosed with AIDS. The insurance agent presented him with a sixth policy and its "amendment to application." The insured verified that he was in good health and had not suffered any sickness. After the insured died as a result of his AIDS condition, the insurer conducted an investigation. It denied coverage and brought suit to rescind the life insurance policies. The insurer moved for summary judgment on all six policies. A district court granted summary judgment to the insurer on the sixth insurance policy, but denied summary judgment as to the first five. The beneficiaries appealed to the Appellate Court of Illinois.

The appellate court stated that the connection between AIDS and hemophilia was not so great that the insurer would be put on notice that the insured had contracted AIDS. The beneficiaries argued that the insured's misrepresentations did not materially affect the insurer's risk. The court rejected this argument since the insurer relied upon the insured's representations made in the amendment. If the insured had disclosed that he had AIDS, the insurer would have declined coverage. Because the insured's undisclosed AIDS diagnosis was a material risk to the insurer, the appellate court granted the insurer summary judgment on the sixth policy. The trial court's decision was affirmed. *Northern Life Ins. v. Ippolito Real Est.*, 601 N.E.2d 773 (Ill.App.1st Dist.1992).

C. Incontestability Clauses

A man contracted to replace a life insurance policy with a second policy which provided virtually the same benefits at exactly half the cost. The man owned a business, and listed the business as the owner of the policy. The agent who sold the replacement policy had told the man that the policy was "a lot better." The disadvantages of changing policies were allegedly not discussed, but the man executed a notice which explained applicable changes and specifically addressed the contestability period. The contestability period had not yet expired when the man died from a gunshot wound to the head. The man's business was irritated by the insurer's investigation, and brought fraud and bad faith claims against the insurer. The claims were dismissed through summary judgment, and eventually reached the Supreme Court of Alabama. The first fraud claim alleged that the agent's statement that the replacement policy was "a lot better" was unlawful. Alabama law requires that the person alleging fraud based on misrepresentations be the same person to whom any misrepresentation was made. The claim, therefore, could neither survive the insured's death nor be brought by his business. The second fraud claim alleged a fraudulent failure to disclose the disadvantages of changing policies. The notice which the man had executed specifically addressed the disadvantages, and was ruled to sufficiently provide disclosure. The last claim by the business sought damages for bad faith refusal to pay. The court held that a payment received roughly five months following death was not unlawful. The decision of the lower court was affirmed. *County Side Roofing v. Mutual Benefit Life Ins. Co.*, 587 So.2d 987 (Ala.1991).

A New York insured obtained a life insurance policy and named his business partner as the owner and sole beneficiary of the policy. The partner was not related to the insured. However, the two men financed their restaurant operations by securing a loan with the partner's assets. The policy on the insured's life was acquired to protect the partner in case of default. Two years later the insured died. The partner then claimed the proceeds of the life insurance policy. The insurer sought a declaratory judgment in a New York trial court that it was not obligated to pay the life insurance benefits because the partner had no insurable interest in the life of the insured. The partner argued that the insurer was barred from asserting the invalidity of the policy because the statutory incontestability period had expired before the insured died. The trial court held for the insurer. However, an appellate court reversed, holding that the insurer's claim was barred after expiration of the incontestability period. The insurer appealed to the Court of Appeals of New York.

On appeal the insurer argued that the life insurance policy was void from its inception because it was issued to a person who lacked an insurable interest in the life of the insured. Therefore, it argued, since no contract existed, the expiration of the incontestability period could not operate to create a contract. The court rejected the insurer's arguments. It held that to enforce the incontestability ruling would result in a forfeiture to the partner and an unnecessary advantage to the insurer by enabling it to avoid a claim it previously accepted. The two-year incontestability period served a public service by encouraging the insurer to investigate the insurable interest of its policyholders promptly. Therefore, the court dismissed the insurer's declaratory judgment action. *New England Mut. Life Ins. Co. v. Caruso*, 535 N.E.2d 270 (N.Y.1989).

The application of an incontestability clause in a disability insurance policy formed the issue in a case appealed to the U.S. Court of Appeals, Eighth Circuit. An insurance applicant made incorrect statements regarding the existence of other disability policies when he applied for the policy contested here. When the policy was issued, it contained a clause stating that after two years statements made in the application would become incontestable. Eighteen months following issuance of the policy the insured fell and became totally disabled. The following day he instructed his insurance agent to submit disability claims under all his policies. After doing so, the agent noticed that the insured had not listed the other policies on his application. He notified the insured, advising him that since two years had not elapsed the insurer would be permitted to contest the claim. The insured thus delayed the claim until the two years had expired. After the insurer denied his claim the insured sued the insurer. A U.S. district court held for the insurer and he appealed to the U.S. Court of Appeals, Fifth Circuit. The court of appeals observed that under ordinary circumstances incontestability clauses bar specified defenses. Here, however, the conduct of the insured in withdrawing his claim during the two year contestability period, then advising the insurer no claim would be filed and subsequently refiling the claim after the expiration of the period was not an ordinary circumstance. Recovery was denied. *Ferguson v. Union Mut. Stock Life Ins. Co. of America*, 673 F.2d 253 (8th Cir.1982).

The Louisiana Supreme Court, reversing two lower courts, has held that life insurance benefits are payable to a surviving "spouse" even though the couple was not legally married. State law provided that the validity of a policy shall not be contested after it had been in force for two years from the date of issue, except for nonpayment of premiums. The supreme court rejected the lower courts' finding that the defense of ineligibility was not barred by an incontestability clause. The supreme court stated that eligibility can be contested only if allowing coverage extends the risk beyond that contemplated by the insurer. Here, the insurer's risk was not increased simply because the couple's thirty-five-year union was not blessed by the sacrament of matrimony. One who is for all practical purposes a spouse should not be denied recovery by an irrelevant legal status. *Jackson v. Continental Cas. Co.*, 412 So.2d 1364 (La.1982).

II. NONPAYMENT OF PREMIUM

An insured's nonpayment of premiums usually renders an insurance policy void and bars any later claim brought under the policy, unless the insurer waives its right to collect premiums, or unless it reinstates the policy following the insured's tender of the amount of premiums due. Additionally, insurers and insureds must comply with state laws regulating policy cancellation and reinstatement.

A. Policies Voided

An Indiana man applied for a $5 million life insurance policy, intending to replace an existing policy which also insured him for $5 million. The insurer requested financial and medical information so that it could evaluate the risks of insuring him. He failed to provide this information. He subsequently died of an accidental gunshot wound while the application was still pending and before any premiums had been paid. After receiving the policy proceeds from the other insurer, the insured's widow brought suit against the second insurer for its delay in processing her husband's application. A federal district court granted summary judgment to the insurer, and the widow appealed to the U.S. Court of Appeals, Seventh Circuit. On appeal, she contended that the insurer should be promissorily estopped from asserting that the policy premiums had not been paid because of its delay in handling the application. The court, however, noted that the insurer had not made any promises to the applicant so as to induce him not to seek insurance elsewhere. Further, the applicant had kept his other policy current up through his death. Thus, he had not relied on any representations by the insurer to his detriment. The court then stated that, even if the delay in processing the application was unreasonable, the widow had no recognizable claim because the insurer had not been under any legal duty to act. The court affirmed the grant of summary judgment for the insurer. *MacLauchlan v. Prudential Ins. Co. of America*, 970 F.2d 357 (7th Cir.1992).

A Pennsylvania construction company purchased a life insurance policy on one of its employees. The policy provided a thirty-one day grace period for premium payments. Several years passed before the company failed to make a payment when due. Two weeks after the premium was due the company filed for bankruptcy. Two days later the insurer mailed a late premium notice to the company. Three months after the premium was due the insurer sent another notice which stated that the insured had an additional thirty-one days in which to make the payment before the policy would be canceled. The insured died before the expiration of that time period. The company informed the insurer of the death and requested the policy proceeds. The insurer denied coverage and the company sued the insurer in a Pennsylvania federal district court. The district court held for the insurer and the company appealed to the U.S. Court of Appeals, Third Circuit. The issue before the appeals court was to determine at what point, if any, the company's failure to pay the premium extinguished its right to the policy proceeds. It held that U.S. bankruptcy law granted a sixty day extension from the time the bankruptcy petition was filed. If the company had paid the amount due before the expiration, coverage would have been provided. Because no payments were made, coverage ceased to exist when the sixty day time period expired. To hold otherwise would effectuate an indefinite grace period. The appeals court affirmed the district court determination. The company was not entitled to recover the policy proceeds. *Counties Contract & Construction Co. v. Constitution Life Ins. Co.*, 855 F.2d 1054 (3rd Cir.1988).

The Virginia Supreme Court reversed a lower court decision which recognized a widow's right to recover under her deceased husband's group life insurance policy. The lower court had held that as trustee of a group life insurance policy, the deceased's labor union was liable for failure to notify the husband of his rights and obligations under the policy. The husband had terminated his employment because of total disability. The supreme court held that the union had fulfilled its obligation because it gave the husband a booklet describing his rights under the policy. He had failed to pay premiums in accordance with the booklet and the insurer discontinued coverage. The union had no separate duty to notify the deceased of his obligations other than providing him with the booklet. *Wilson v. Rowlette*, 369 S.E.2d 194 (Va.1988).

In 1974, an Arkansas company purchased a life insurance policy for one of its employees. The company then assigned its interest in the policy to a bank. The bank utilized the automatic premium loan provision of the policy to make premium payments. In June, 1980, the bank defaulted on its premium payments when the cash value of the policy could no longer be used to pay premiums. The insured employee became disabled in May, 1980, due to a heart attack. The insurance company notified the bank in January, 1981, that the policy had lapsed. In June, 1981, the bank discovered that the employee was disabled. It contacted the insurance company in July demanding reinstatement of the policy based on the man's total disability and the premium waiver disability benefit provision in the policy. The insurance company refused to reinstate the policy because the bank had not provided "written notice and proof of disability within one year of the due date of the first premium in default," as the policy required. The bank sued, arguing that the man's disability, not notice of that disability, created the insurer's duty to waive premiums. It also pointed out that notice and proof of disability were given as soon as reasonably possible. A trial court ruled in favor of the bank and the insurer appealed.

The Court of Appeals of Arkansas agreed with the trial court that the insurance company's duty to waive premiums was triggered by the disability, not notice of the disability. The court disagreed, however, with the trial court's finding that notice and proof of disability were given as soon as reasonably possible. The court said failure to give timely notice and proof of disability "has been excused only in those cases where there were grave and extenuating circumstances prohibiting timely notification." No evidence was presented proving that the man was unable to notify the insurance company of his disability. The appellate court reversed the lower court's decision and entered a judgment for the insurance company. *American General Life Ins. Co. v. First American Nat'l Bank*, 716 S.W.2d 205 (Ark.App.1986).

B. Policies Not Voided

A Florida woman and her son applied for life insurance through their agent. The agent subsequently contacted the proposed insureds informing them that the policies would be delivered to them that evening. At this time, the agent told the woman that she would have to pay an increased premium because of her medical condition; she agreed to pay it when the policy was delivered. However, the agent failed to deliver the policy as promised. The insureds contacted the agent and asked that the policies be delivered. Two weeks later, the agent finally delivered the policies. However, the son had died the previous day. The insurer denied coverage. The woman sued the insurer for breach of an oral and a written contract to deliver the policy and for negligence. A circuit court entered judgment in favor of the woman, and the insurer appealed to the District Court of Appeal of Florida. On appeal, the insurer argued that it was not liable since the insureds did not include a payment premium with the insurance application. The appellate court, however, disagreed because the insurer owed the insureds a duty to act within a reasonable time, regardless of whether the premium was tendered. Because the insureds relied on the agent's representations and refused competing offers from other insurers, the court held the insurer was liable. Accordingly, the court affirmed the lower court's decision. *State Farm Life Ins. Co. v. Bass*, 605 So.2d 908 (Fla.App.3d Dist.1992).

A Michigan insured died one day after his life insurance premium grace period expired. His insurance agent was notified of the death and he in turn notified his manager. The insured's widow mailed the premium into the insurer who cashed the check and recorded the policy as current. The widow sought to recover the policy proceeds but the insurer denied coverage. She sued the insurer in a Michigan trial court which held for the insurer. The widow then appealed to the Michigan Court of Appeals which reversed the trial court decision. It held that the insurer waived its right to claim policy lapse by failing to return the premium upon learning that the death preceded payment. The insurer was required to provide the policy proceeds to the widow. *Glass v. Harvest Life Ins. Co.*, 425 N.W.2d 107 (Mich.App.1988).

A man entered into a life insurance contract in February of 1979 and paid the premiums regularly until December of 1984. He then wrote to his insurer explaining that he wished to surrender the policy in exchange for its cash value. The policy stated that it would terminate coverage after the expiration of a thirty-one day grace period following the nonpayment of a premium. It also specified that a surrender must be in a form acceptable to the insurer. The insurer mailed the insured a letter which enclosed such a form, and explained that the policy would remain in effect until the company received the returned form and the policy. The insured mailed the form and policy, but died before the insurer received it. The deceased's estate filed an action in a federal district court seeking the full death benefit.

The insurer first argued that the policy expired at the end of the thirty-one day grace period following the unpaid premium. The court felt that coverage would have ordinarily terminated at that time, but needed to determine whether the insurer's letter changed the termination date. The court found that it had. The letter stated that the policy would remain in force absent the return of the form and the policy. The issue then became whether the insured had accepted the surrender offer. The insurer argued that the insured's acceptance of the offer was effective when it was mailed. The estate argued that acceptance of the offer was effective only upon receipt. The letter had established what form was acceptable, and thus also determined when acceptance was effective. The court ruled that receipt of documents was required in order to terminate coverage, and entered judgment for the estate. *Zimmerman v. American States Ins. Co.*, 763 F.Supp. 228 (S.D.Ohio 1990).

A Louisiana man died of a self-inflicted injury in November 1984. The deceased had purchased an annual renewable life insurance policy in September 1981. The policy allowed for payment of premiums on an annual, semi-annual, quarterly or monthly basis with a thirty-one day grace period from the due date during which the policy remained in effect. The record showed that all premiums were paid through November 1984, and late payments were made for the months of August and October 1984. The insurer sought to deny coverage due to the late payments. The beneficiary successfully sued in a Louisiana trial court. The insurer then appealed to the Court of Appeal of Louisiana.

The court determined that the policy was governed by Louisiana Statute § 22:177 which required that certain notices be given to the insured before the insurer could declare forfeited or lapsed any policy issued or denied. Section 22:177 also prohibits the lapsing of any life insurance policy for nonpayment of premiums within one year of a default in payment in the absence of written notice to the insured except in the case of policies issued upon payment of weekly or monthly premiums. The insurer contended that the policy in question was for a term of one year or less and was therefore exempted from the notice requirements. The court, however, determined that the policy was an annual renewable policy. By its terms the policy provided for annual premium payments but afforded the insureds the option of paying the annual premiums on a monthly basis. The insurer attempted to prove that it mailed timely written notices to the insured, but failed to introduce any document from its business records which would indicate that the written notices were actually mailed to the insured. The appellate court affirmed the decision of the trial court. *Lemoine v. Security Industrial Ins. Co.*, 569 So.2d 1092 (La.App.3d Cir.1990).

A Nebraska insured was covered by a life insurance policy upon which a premium of $33.92 was payable on the 22nd day of each month by preauthorized check. Each premium paid for coverage through the 22nd of the following month. The policy contained a 31-day grace period during which the policy remained in effect if a payment was not made on time. The preauthorized check for the April 22, 1980, premium was returned to the insurance company because of insufficient funds. The insurer requested a replacement check by June 6, 1980, to keep the policy in force. A replacement check was received in time but was also returned because of insufficient funds. Meanwhile, however, the preauthorized check for the May 22, 1980, premium was drawn from the man's account and deposited by the insurer. This check cleared on June 25, 1980. The check contained the following language: "this check when paid is receipt for amounts due on the policies listed. The date of this check indicates the premium due month." The man died the same day that this check cleared. The insurer denied the policy beneficiary's claim for the proceeds of the policy due to an alleged lapse of the policy for nonpayment of the April 22, 1980, premium. The beneficiary filed a lawsuit against the insurer for the proceeds of the policy, but a Nebraska district court ruled for the insurer and dismissed the lawsuit. The beneficiary appealed.

The Nebraska Supreme Court observed that the insurer, having noticed that the April premium had been returned for insufficient funds, could have withheld the drawing and depositing of the May premium, but did not do so. "By drawing the May premium before it determined whether the April premium would be paid, the [insurer] did an act amounting to a recognition of the continued validity of the policy as a binding obligation upon it." The supreme court reversed the lower court's decision and held that the beneficiary of the life insurance policy should receive the policy's proceeds. *Bohannon v. Guardsmen Life Ins. Co.*, 400 N.W.2d 856 (Neb.1986).

III. GROUP LIFE AND HEALTH INSURANCE

Employers often purchase group life and/or health policies on behalf of their employees. The terms of these policies vary. For example, some policies provide for automatic employee participation upon hiring, while others retain the requirement that employees must apply and be individually approved by the insurer.

A. Scope of Coverage

The following cases involve scope-of-coverage disputes, types of claims covered and policy limitations.

The types of coverages which must be provided under a group health policy has been the subject of a decision by the U.S. Supreme Court. The Supreme Court upheld a Massachusetts law requiring that minimum mental health care benefits be provided to any person who is insured under a health care policy, including employer-provided group health and life policies. The case arose when the Massachusetts Attorney General sued two insurers who refused to provide the mandatory coverage. The insurers claimed that 1) the federal Employment Retirement Income Security Act (ERISA) superseded the state law requirements of minimum mental health benefits, and 2) insofar as the state requirement removed the topic of mental health care benefits from the collective bargaining process, the law conflicted with the National Labor Relations Board's (NLRB) jurisdiction over collective bargaining procedures.

The Court held that the state statute was a law generally regulating insurance, not a law aimed at pensions, and thus it was upheld. The requirement of minimum mental health care insurance impacted only tangentially on pensions and other employee plans. Thus it fell within the ERISA "insurance exemption." The court further held that the state law did not infringe upon the NLRB's jurisdiction over the collective bargaining process. Although admittedly the law set a minimum standard for employee health insurance plans, states are allowed to set such minimum standards. The insurance companies were therefore ordered to meet the mental health care requirements. *Metropolitan Life Ins. Co. v. Massachusetts*, 105 S.Ct. 2380 (1985).

1. Types of Claims and Individuals Covered

Two Maryland women were diagnosed as having breast cancer which was in an advanced stage of development. They were insured through their spouses' employment benefit plans with Blue Cross/Blue Shield of Maryland Inc. (Blue Cross). Both were told by their physicians that the best treatment for them would be High Dose Chemotherapy with Autologous Bone Marrow Transplant. Due to the high expense of the treatment the women sought preapproval of coverage from Blue Cross. Blue Cross denied coverage, even following appeals, because it felt the treatment was experimental and therefore excluded. The women filed suit in a federal district court seeking a declaration that coverage should be provided under their policies.

The policies excluded experimental treatments, and defined experimental as "any treatment ... not generally acknowledged as accepted medical practice ... in Maryland." The doctor in charge of determining the eligibility of a treatment for coverage testified that he based his decision on a 1988 report done by Blue Cross, and an independent review. Blue Cross also provided a nationwide sample of doctors who testified that the procedure was experimental. Each was shown, however, to have used a definition of experimental which was different from that used in the policy. The term experimental was found not to exclude coverage for treatments which may still be in a stage of development and research; it excluded coverage only for treatments not generally accepted. The court noted that even though all effects of the treatment were not conclusively known, physicians must evaluate all factors in determining if the treatment is the best available. The women provided testimony from groups of Maryland physicians, and the court ruled that the practice was generally accepted in Maryland. It further noted that it disagreed with a finding of experimental even using Blue Cross' definition. The court entered judgment for the insureds. *Adams v. Blue Cross/Blue Shield of Maryland, Inc.*, 757 F.Supp. 661 (D.Md.1991).

An Illinois child was afflicted with lop ear syndrome. He received bilateral autoplasty surgery to alleviate the problem. The child's father was insured under a group medical insurer and sought coverage. The insurer denied coverage claiming that the surgery was cosmetic and the insured filed this action in an Illinois trial court. The court entered summary judgment in favor of the insured and the insurer appealed to the Appellate Court of Illinois. The insured alleged that the alteration of the external ear may have therapeutic value and that the variation of the external ears may be characterized as a congenital deformity. The appellate court found that the evidence overwhelmingly showed that the trial court's decision was not supported by the record and must be reversed. The evidence at trial demonstrated that the surgery performed was cosmetic. The purpose of the surgery was to improve the child's appearance. Even the treating doctor admitted the purpose of the surgery was aesthetic or cosmetic in nature. Therefore, the appellate court reversed the decision of the trial court and found for the insurer. *Thomas v. General American Life Ins. Co.*, 568 N.E.2d 937 (Ill.App.3d Dist.1991).

A Texas woman suffered from Alopecia Areata Totalis which resulted in a total loss of hair on her head. After her doctor prescribed an $850 wig, her insurer refused to pay the cost. She brought suit in federal district court under the Employee Retirement Income Security Act, which governed the policy, seeking a clarification of her rights under the policy. The court found that hair is a "limb" and thus awarded coverage for the wig as an artificial limb. The insurer appealed to the U.S. Court of Appeals, Fifth Circuit. The appellate court disagreed with the district court's characterization of the wig as an artificial limb. Since a limb was either an arm or a leg, wigs could not be artificial limbs. Further, even though the insurer had provided for such things as artificial ears and noses, and penile and breast prostheses, it had specifically excluded coverage for wigs, thus limiting its expanded coverage. The court reversed the district court's decision, and held for the insurer. *Irion v. Prudential Ins. Co. of America*, 964 F.2d 463 (5th Cir.1992).

When policies exclude coverage for treatment which is not "medically necessary," disputes often arise over treatment which has not been traditionally extended. However, due to the rapid increases in medical technology, many treatments that are initially considered "experimental" eventually come to be recognized as necessary.

An insured couple suffered from osteoarthritis. Treatments provided by a doctor produced no relief, and the couple sought and received acupuncture. The acupuncturist was not a medical doctor. The insurer denied coverage because it considered the treatment to be experimental, and also because the policy limited the coverage to treatments listed therein and performed by a licensed doctor. A small claims court awarded judgment to the insureds, but that decision was reversed by a trial court. The insureds then appealed to the Supreme Judicial Court of Maine. The policy specifically listed covered services, and excluded "all other services." The court held that even a liberal construction of the policy could not afford coverage for a service which was not listed. Further, the services were not performed by a licensed doctor. The court held for the insurer and expressed no opinion on whether the treatment was experimental. *Ray v. Blue Alliance Mutual Ins. Co.*, 594 A.2d 1110 (Me.1991).

A Missouri woman was diagnosed with skin cancer which later spread to her lungs and brain stem. She was covered under a group health insurance policy furnished by her husband's employer. A cancer specialist at a university school of medicine recommended high-dose chemotherapy and an autologous bone marrow transplant. The insurer regarded the treatment as "investigational/experimental." The couple nonetheless decided to obtain the treatment. The woman died six months later and the insurer denied payment for related hospital bills. The husband sued the insurer in a Missouri state court alleging common-law causes of action including breach of contract, bad faith, outrage and unfair claims settlement practices. The insurer removed the case to the U.S. District Court for the Eastern District of Missouri, which dismissed all common-law claims but allowed the husband to amend his claim under ERISA, since the health insurance policy was an employee welfare benefit plan under federal law. The court determined that according to the insurer's policy, the treatment was not "medically necessary." It dismissed the husband's claim.

On appeal to the U.S. Court of Appeals, Eighth Circuit, the husband alleged that the policy provision defining "medically necessary" treatment was not a part of the policy because it was contained in an amendment which was not signed by his employer and which modified policy language which referred only to "necessary care." The court of appeals rejected this and other arguments by the husband, reasoning that because the unsigned amendment was sent as part of a package which was endorsed, there was substantial compliance with the contract requirements for endorsement. The policy defined "medically necessary" treatment as non-experimental, investigational or educational procedures which were not furnished in connection with medical research, and that were approved for reimbursement by the Health Care Financing Administration, the federal agency with responsibility for approving Medicare payments. The court of appeals affirmed the district court's decision for the insurer. *Farley v. Benefit Trust Life Ins. Co.*, 979 F.2d 653 (8th Cir.1992).

A New York insured's wife suffered from multiple sclerosis and benefits were paid for a motorized wheelchair. A claim was then submitted for a nonmotorized wheelchair for use based upon the wife's religious beliefs. The claim was denied by the insurer as not being medically necessary. A New York trial court found the policy to be ambiguous and ordered the claim paid. On appeal, the Supreme Court Appellate Division of New York found the insurance plan clear and incapable of another construction. While there was a need for a non-motorized chair, it was not medically necessary. The need was completely religious and not called for under generally accepted medical standards. The appeals court reversed the judgment of the trial court. *Wachtell v. Metropolitan Life Ins. Co.*, 559 N.Y.S.2d 85 (Sup.1990).

A Louisiana insured suffered a spinal fracture dislocation which rendered him quadriplegic. The insured was employed by a company which provided him with a group health insurance plan. Two months after his accident, the insured sought coverage under the plan for hyperbaric oxygen therapy which was recommended by his doctor. The insurer denied the request because hyperbaric treatment was not an established treatment. The insured sued his insurer in a Louisiana trial court and the insurer had the case removed to a federal district court. The district court stated that the insured's plan provided coverage for major medical expenses that were necessary. However, the insured alleged that his policy did not indicate whether experimental or investigative treatments were covered under his plan. The court stated that the insured must establish that the medical expense was recommended by a qualified physician and that the expense was reasonably necessary. It found that the investigative treatment was not necessary because it was not recognized by the medical profession and because the insured did not seek the treatment until months after his accident. The district court awarded summary judgment for the insurer. *Washington v. Winn-Dixie of Louisiana*, 736 F.Supp. 1418 (E.D.La.1990).

An Alabama insured lived with a woman for thirty-one years as her common-law spouse. He was insured under a welfare plan which provided group health insurance. The policy extended coverage to qualified dependents of participants. The insured's common-law spouse was hospitalized. The welfare plan rejected her claim for spousal benefits. The insured sued the insurer in a federal district court seeking an order to compel the insurer to extend coverage. The district court found for the insurer and the insured appealed to the U.S. Court of Appeals, Eleventh Circuit. The court of appeals certified the question to the Alabama Supreme Court. The supreme court found that insurance companies had the right, in the absence of statutory provisions to the contrary, to limit their liability through exclusion clauses as long as they did not conflict with public policy. The court found that common-law marriages as well as traditional marriages were recognized in the state. A valid distinction could not be made between common-law and traditional marriages. The fact that a marriage created in one manner was easier to prove than a marriage created in another could not alone justify the distinction. The U.S. Court of Appeals held that contractual provisions denying common-law marriages the same status as traditional marriages were void as violative of the public policy of Alabama. The district court's decision was reversed and the case was remanded to the district court for further proceedings. *Scott v. Bd. of Trustees Mobile S. S. Ass'n*, 859 F.2d 872 (11th Cir.1988).

The Age Discrimination in Employment Act (ADEA) makes it unlawful for employers to discriminate against individuals based upon age. The act's coverage extends to employment compensation, terms, conditions and privileges. An exception to the ADEA states that employers may operate employee benefit plans which were not enacted with intent to avoid the antidiscrimination provisions of the ADEA. A corporation maintained a group life insurance program providing life and disability insurance benefits to its employees. Employees also received life insurance benefits payable upon death. Unlike its younger employees, corporate employees over age sixty were ineligible to receive disability benefits. The program had been instituted before passage of the ADEA. The Equal Employment Opportunity Commission (EEOC) sued the corporation in a federal district court, alleging that it violated the ADEA. It sought an order which would direct the corporation to remedy the age-based benefit disparity among its employees. The court dismissed the lawsuit, noting that the corporation's policy was exempt from the ADEA because it was not intended to avoid the statute. The EEOC appealed to the U.S. Court of Appeals, Tenth Circuit. The court ruled that the corporation's plan was exempt from the ADEA because it was not enacted to avoid the antidiscrimination law. Because the corporation had instituted the group life insurance program before the enactment of the ADEA, it was not required to present evidence to justify the disparate treatment between employees based upon age. The appeals court affirmed the district court's dismissal of the lawsuit. *EEOC v. Cargill, Inc.*, 855 F.2d 682 (10th Cir.1988).

An employee, insured through her employer's health plan, sought treatment for her temporal mandibular joint syndrome (TMJS). A dentist provided her with an acrylic appliance that covered her teeth, which temporarily relieved her TMJS. The dentist then permanently adjusted her bite by capping her teeth, curing the TMJS. The employer's health plan denied coverage, claiming that capping her teeth was a dental procedure rather than medical and was not covered under the policy. She sued her employer to recover benefits. The trial court ruled in favor of the employee, and the employer appealed to the Louisiana Court of Appeals. The court of appeals affirmed, holding that under the employee's health plan, the capping of her teeth was an accepted form of medical treatment for TMJS. *Cotton v. Wal-Mart Stores*, 552 So.2d 14 (La.App.3d Cir.1989).

A New York insured was covered under his company's group long-term disability policy. Under the policy, totally disabled employees became entitled to monthly benefits until age sixty-five. Following a twenty-four month waiting period employees were deemed "totally disabled" if injuries or sickness prevented them from engaging in any occupation or employment for which they were qualified. The insured worked without any complaint of illness until his voluntary resignation. At his exit interview the insured chose not to convert his group insurance coverage to individual coverage. Two months later, the insured underwent testing which revealed a brain tumor. He then had surgery to remove the tumor. The tumor had been present for a considerable period of time before its discovery. The insured submitted a long-term disability claim to the insurer. The insurer denied the claim. The insured sued the insurer in a federal district court, seeking long-term disability benefits. The court held that despite the tumor, the insured was not totally disabled at the time of his resignation. Thus, the insured could not recover under the disability policy. The court entered judgment for the insurer. *Harrigan v. New England Mut. Life Ins. Co.*, 693 F.Supp. 1531 (S.D.N.Y.1988).

An Iowa couple covered by a group health policy were infertile. They had a child after undergoing treatment and their health insurer covered all costs. The couple underwent several similar treatments in an unsuccessful attempt to conceive another child. These treatments were also paid for by the insurer. The couple's doctor suggested a more complex and expensive treatment for which the insurer denied coverage. They sued the insurer in a small claims court which held for the insurer. The couple appealed to an Iowa district court which held for the couple. The insurer appealed to the Iowa Supreme Court. At issue was whether the couple's infertility was an illness. The insurer argued that the condition of nonpregnancy was not an illness; therefore the treatment to change that condition was not a treatment of an illness. The couple argued that infertility was covered because they both had a disorder that could only be treated with the particular treatment they underwent.

The supreme court observed that "illness" could be defined as a condition of the body which deviates from the normal function of the body. Evidence showed that the couple suffered from an incorrect functioning of their respective reproductive systems. Therefore, the treatments to correct those dysfunctions should be covered. Failure to explicitly exclude artificial insemination and other treatments could reasonably be interpreted to mean that the policy covered the treatments. That failure, along with past payments for similar treatments, furnished further reasons to support the district court decision. The insurer was required to pay for the treatments. *Wittcraft v. Sonstrand Health and Disability Group Benefit Plan*, 420 N.W.2d 785 (Iowa 1988).

A man insured under a group medical insurance policy was rendered a quadriplegic in an automobile accident. His insurer notified him that his insurance would be terminated in one year. The insurer entered into a reinsurance agreement with California Life Insurance Company (Cal Life) pursuant to a state directive. Cal Life assumed all of the insurer's rights and liabilities. The insured's approval was never sought nor was he notified of the change. When complications arose which required his hospitalization, he was forced to seek coverage from Cal Life which refused to pay the claim. Soon after the denial Cal Life was declared insolvent. The insured then sued the original insurer in a Los Angeles County Superior Court seeking coverage. The superior court granted the insurer's dismissal motion and the insured appealed to the California Court of Appeal, Second District, Division 4.

On appeal, the insured argued that the reinsurance agreement was invalid because his approval was not sought and he did not receive notice. The insurer asserted that notice was given and that by submitting his claim to Cal Life, he implicitly gave his approval. At issue was whether an insurer which withdraws coverage in response to a state directive is released from future liability. The court noted California Civil Code § 1457 which provides that "[t]he burden of an obligation may be transferred with the consent of the party entitled to its benefit, but not otherwise...." The court held for the insured because changing insurers is predicated on consent and the insurer never sought the insured's consent. Consent could not be implied where the insured had no opportunity to consent. Even though the insured submitted a claim to Cal Life, he had no alternative. This did not reach the level of approval needed to constitute a change of insurers. The insurer was required to provide coverage. *Bare v. Associated Life Ins. Co.*, 248 Cal.Rptr. 236 (App.2d Dist.1988).

In January 1976, a man insured under a group policy was hospitalized for three days by his family doctor. The insurer paid the man's medical and testing bills, but refused to pay for the hospital stay. Its denial was based on an exclusion for "[s]ervices when hospitalized primarily for diagnostic purposes or medical observation" and an exclusion for services which were not medically necessary. The policy provided that "[b]enefits will be provided under this contract only for such services ... as are reasonably intended, in the exercise of good medical practice, for the treatment of illness or injury." The man, his doctor, and the hospital's utilization review committee protested the denial of coverage. The insurer repeatedly denied the man's claim without advising him of his contractual right to impartial review and arbitration. The superior court found that under the policy the insurer had no right to review the medical necessity of a procedure ordered by an insured's physician. It also ruled that the insurer broke the covenant of good faith by not informing the man of his rights under the policy. The insurer appealed.

The California Supreme Court ruled that the policy provided unambiguously that disputes concerning the justification for hospitalization would be settled through arbitration. The insurer therefore had not breached the covenant of good faith and fair dealing by challenging the doctor's decision to hospitalize. The court found, however, that the nature of the insurer-insured relationship required "each contracting party to refrain from doing anything to injure the right of the other to receive the benefits of the agreement." It stated that when an insured's lack of knowledge might result in a loss of benefits, an insurer is required to bring to the insured's attention information that will enable him to secure his rights under the policy. The court held that the insurer had acted in bad faith by not informing the man of his rights under the policy. The issue of whether the man's hospitalization was reasonably intended for the treatment of his illness or injury had not been considered at trial. The Supreme court reversed the superior court's decision and remanded the case for a ruling on this issue, so that the man's damages could be properly determined. *Sarchett v. Blue Shield of California*, 729 P.2d 267 (Cal.1987).

While a Missouri child was hospitalized, her parents sued the hospital for medical malpractice. The parents and the hospital settled the case by agreeing that the hospital would waive its right to be reimbursed for the cost of the child's medical care. The settlement also provided that any insurance benefits paid to the hospital by the father's group health insurer would be returned to the parents and would not prevent the parents from collecting from the insurer. After the parents received a bill from the hospital stamped "charges waived" they sued the group health insurer seeking a court ruling that the group health insurer had a duty to pay for the medical expenses incurred by their daughter despite the fact that they were not legally obligated to pay for those expenses. Before the Missouri Court of Appeals, the parents focused on phrases in the policy such as "an expense shall be deemed to be incurred upon the date the medical care is received [and] benefits ... shall be payable ... for the covered expenses incurred...." They contended that had they made a claim under the policy before entering into the settlement agreement, they would have been entitled to payment. However, the court of appeals held for the group health insurer, observing that payment for unsustained expenses was contrary to the intent of the insurance contract and would unnecessarily contribute to inflated medical insurance costs. The parents were not entitled to payment of the medical expenses from the group health insurer. *Bloebaum v. General American Life Ins. Co.*, 734 S.W.2d 539 (Mo.App.1987).

Three months after a Michigan couple was informed by their doctor that the wife was pregnant, the husband was terminated from his job. Subsequently, the employer's insurer canceled the husband's health insurance policy and offered them a conversion policy to meet their expenses from the child's birth. The couple refused the conversion policy claiming it was too expensive and filed a complaint for declaratory relief against the insurer. The insurer moved to have the claim dismissed. Both the trial court and court of appeals denied the summary judgment and the court of appeals held that the married couple was entitled to coverage for pregnancy expenses. On appeal, the Supreme Court of Michigan remanded the case to the court of appeals for reconsideration.

On remand, the married couple argued that the insurer violated public policy because coverage would have been provided had the insurance policy not been terminated. The court disagreed and held the insurer was not liable since the husband's employer rather than the insurer canceled the policy. Furthermore, the insurer did not render the married couple uninsurable; it offered them a conversion policy for their anticipated child birth expenses after the employer terminated their coverage. Accordingly, the court of appeals reversed its earlier holding and granted summary judgment to the insurer. *Wolfe v. Employers Health Ins. Co.*, 486 N.W.2d 319 (Mich.App.1992).

A California case involved the definition of the term "hospital." Here a child who suffered from a functional nervous disorder was admitted to the Clear Water Ranch Children's House, a residential treatment facility which specialized in the treatment of such disorders. The staff at the facility consisted of one registered nurse, who worked days only, child care workers who were present twenty-four hours per day, and licensed clinical social workers. A psychiatrist supervised this staff. The child's stepfather, who was issued a group medical insurance policy by his employer, submitted a claim to his insurer for the cost of the child's treatment at the facility. The insurer denied the claim and stated that the facility did not qualify as a "hospital," which was defined in the policy as "an institution ... primarily engaged in providing on an in-patient basis for the medical care and treatment of sick and injured persons through medical, diagnostic and major surgical facilities, all of which facilities must be provided on its premises under the supervision of a staff of Physicians with twenty-four hour a day nursing service."

The U.S. Court of Appeals, Ninth Circuit, awarded coverage. The term "nursing service" was not defined in the policy. The insurer's argument that coverage could be provided only for facilities with twenty-four-hour staffing by registered nurses was rejected by the court, which found that the child care workers who were on duty twenty-four hours each day satisfied the policy requirements. Furthermore, the fact that the treatment facility possessed no "major surgical facilities" presented no bar to coverage, since it was the insurer's admitted practice to disregard this policy requirement for facilities which treat mental illnesses. *Hanson v. Prudential Ins. Co. of America*, 772 F.2d 580 (9th Cir.1985).

Where a mutual mistake occurs (e.g., a clerical error which leads both parties to believe coverage is other than contracted-for) the policy will be reformed to reflect the actual intent of insured and insurer.

A couple borrowed money to finance the purchase of a travel trailer. When the husband was turned down for credit life insurance, the wife sought coverage. However, a clerical error resulted in the insurance being placed in the husband's name. The wife called to correct the mistake. Although the correction was made internally, the insurer did not send a corrected version to the couple. When the husband died, the wife sought payment under the policy. The insurer denied payment, and the wife sued. The trial court ruled for the insurer, and the Missouri Court of Appeals affirmed. Here, no contract had actually been formed between the insurer and the husband due to the parties' mutual mistake. *Brand v. Boatmen's Bank*, 824 S.W.2d 89 (Mo.App.1992).

On December 1, 1970, a man applied for a $30,000 life insurance contract. In 1984 he applied for a duplicate policy because the original was lost. He was delivered a policy stamped DUPLICATE, which stated that the new policy replaced the old policy which was now void. Sometime later he wished to surrender the policy for the cash value. The insurer then discovered that the guaranteed value table on the replacement policy was inflated and not a duplicate of the original. The insured sued seeking the inflated limit, and a trial court held that the duplicate should be reformed to contain the original values. The insured appealed to the Court of Appeals of Georgia. The duplicate policy's language was held by the appellate court to actually create a new policy. The consideration for the new policy came from the surrendering of rights under the old policy. The insurer and insured intended, however, that the duplicate policy contain the same terms as the original. Because the duplicate policy contained a term assented to through mutual mistake, reformation was proper. The judgment was affirmed. *Brannen v. Golf Life Ins. Co.*, 410 S.E.2d 763 (Ga.App.1991).

A young woman sustained severe head injuries in an automobile collision. Her father was a participant in a welfare benefit plan governed by the Employee Retirement Income Security Act. Medical benefits coverage was provided under the plan by a health maintenance organization (HMO). During the young woman's recovery, disputes arose between the treating physicians and the insured. The insured then unilaterally moved his daughter to a facility which specialized in head injuries. The facility was outside the HMO coverage area, but had been recommended by one of the treating physicians at various times during the first few months of the young woman's recovery. However, at the time the insured moved his daughter to the facility, neither of the treating physicians believed that particular placement was medically necessary. The HMO refused to provide coverage for the 25 month stay at the rehabilitative facility. The insured sued. A federal district court found that the HMO had to pay for the first two months at the rehabilitation facility, but did not have to reimburse the insured for the remaining 23 months. The court also awarded attorney's fees to the insured. Both parties appealed to the U.S. Court of Appeals, Tenth Circuit. On appeal, the court determined that the district court had reached a correct result. Here, the agreement did not automatically limit coverage to 60 days. However, it did require that the "plan physician" prescribe the medical services in dispute for each 60 day period of rehabilitation. Since the initial placement of the young woman in the head injury facility was pursuant to the treating physicians' original recommendation, the HMO was required to pay for the first 60 days. However, when the insured severed relations with the treating physicians by unilaterally placing his daughter in the outside facility, he lost his entitlement to coverage beyond the initial 60 day period. Finally, the court found no abuse of discretion in the district court's award of attorney's fees to the insured. The court affirmed the lower court's decision. *McGee v. Equicor-Equitable HCA Corp.*, 953 F.2d 1192 (10th Cir.1992).

2. Regulation of Practice

Several New York insurance trade associations and companies selling individual and small group health insurance brought this action challenging a regulation relating to human immunodeficiency virus (HIV) testing. HIV testing is used to help determine an individual's risk of developing AIDS. The regulation at issue banned insurers from considering HIV test results in determining insurability. The State Superintendent of Insurance, arguing for the regulation, stated that the tests were limited predictors of mortality and of whether a person would actually develop AIDS. He feared that unauthorized disclosures of seropositive test results would result in discrimination against HIV carriers. The insurance companies, on the other hand, argued that the superintendent exceeded his authority in enacting the regulation and further alleged that it violated the antidiscrimination and full disclosure policies underlying insurance law. The appellate court agreed with the latter viewpoint and declared the HIV testing ban invalid. The state superintendent appealed. The New York Supreme Court, Appellate Division, held that HIV testing was a sound risk detecting underwriting practice, and by virtue of this was not "unfair, unequitable, discriminatory, or deceptive." Whether to enact such a ban was a question for the legislature to decide. Consequently, the court directed the insurance companies to institute a declaratory judgment action to have the law declared invalid. *Health Ins. Ass'n of America v. Corcoran*, 551 N.Y.S.2d 615 (A.D.3d Dep't 1990).

The National Organization for Women (NOW) sued Mutual of Omaha Insurance Co. claiming that Mutual's practice of charging higher health insurance premiums for women violated the District of Columbia Human Rights Act. A superior court dismissed the case and NOW appealed to the District of Columbia Court of Appeals. The court of appeals held that the human rights act did not prohibit actuarial rating practices since it contained no language claiming to regulate insurance premium practices. The court of appeals observed that if the District of

Columbia had intended to effect such a dramatic change in insurance rate-setting practices it would have made specific reference to it in the human rights act or within the act's legislative history. Reference was present in neither. *Nat'l Org. for Women v. Mut. of Omaha Ins. Co.*, 531 A.2d 274 (D.C.App.1987).

3. Injuries

A woman purchased a limited travel accident insurance policy for coverage during a cruise. "Injury" was defined as an accidental bodily injury arising solely from accident and not contributed to by sickness or disease. On the day after she boarded the ship, she fell in the bathroom of her cabin and broke her right hip. She was taken to a hospital for surgery, and suffered a fatal heart attack during the operation. This was caused in part by her arteriosclerosis. When her beneficiary sought to recover benefits under the policy, the insurer denied coverage. A federal district court granted summary judgment to the insurer, and the beneficiary appealed to the U.S. Court of Appeals, Third Circuit. On appeal, the beneficiary contended that the insured's death was a "loss resulting from injury" rather than an injury itself. The court agreed. The injury here was the broken hip, and the death which resulted from that was a "loss resulting from injury" which was covered under the policy. The exclusions in the policy concerning sickness and disease applied only to injuries and did not extend beyond those to losses which resulted from them. The court reversed the summary judgment and ruled in favor of the beneficiary. *Allison v. Nationwide Mutual Ins. Co.*, 964 F.2d 291 (3rd Cir.1992).

An Oklahoma woman was employed by the state. As a state employee she was covered by a group health insurance policy. It extended benefits for twelve months after termination as long as the insured was totally disabled. Her son was seriously injured in an accident and required extensive medical care. When he was released from the hospital his activities were severely limited. Although he was still able to attend school, his mother resigned her position so she could provide the home care her son required. Several months after the mother's resignation her son required reconstructive surgery for which the insurer denied coverage. She then sought an administrative hearing to determine the insurer's liability. The hearing examiner recommended payment of insurance benefits. The case was appealed to several boards and courts and eventually to the Oklahoma Supreme Court. The insurer asserted that because the son attended school, he was not totally disabled under the policy. The court rejected this argument noting that the son had to put forth considerable effort to attend school. It also noted a policy provision which defined total disability as "[one] unable to engage in his regular customary activities and is not engaged in any occupation...." The definition did not require an insured to be totally restricted to the home. As a matter of policy, students should be encouraged to attend school. The insurer was required to continue to provide benefits until the expiration of the twelve month time limit. *Price v. State Employees Group Health*, 757 P.2d 839 (Okl.1988).

4. Policy Dates and Limitations Periods

A psychologist with an Indiana county school system enrolled herself (at $1 per month) and her husband (at $150 per month) in the county health insurer's plan. The premiums were deducted from her paycheck. Due to a clerical error, the husband's coverage was begun and ended on the same day. When the husband received minor medical treatment at facilities approved by the insurer, his claims were denied. However, since they only totaled $69, the insureds did not dispute the denial. Later, they discovered that the clerical error had been made. The insurer then mailed them a check for $69, but the wife filed suit to recover the premiums paid — $1800. A trial court ordered the insurer to return the premiums, and the insurer appealed to the Court of Appeals of Indiana. On appeal, the court noted that if an insurer has been put at risk on behalf of the insured, a court cannot award a refund of premiums. Here, the insurer had accepted the offer to provide coverage for both insureds. It was only a clerical error which had resulted in the denial of coverage. Since the insurer was at risk for the claims the husband had submitted after the insurer accidentally terminated his coverage, the premiums were not refundable. Had the husband incurred large medical expenses during this time, the insurer would have been liable for coverage. Accordingly, the trial court's decision was reversed, and the premiums did not have to be returned. *Humana Health Care Plans v. Snyder-Gilbert*, 596 N.E.2d 299 (Ind.App.4th Dist.1992).

A woman became pregnant in October 1984. She was covered by a major medical insurance policy obtained through her husband's work. The woman entered upon a course of treatment and agreed with her doctors in November 1984, that she would pay them $1,700 for treatment during her pregnancy and the birth. The woman's husband left his employment in March 1985. The insurer denied coverage for the wife's treatment because the child was born after that date, on July 19, 1985. A New York district court observed that the policy provided that when coverage ended the insurer would be liable for any claim incurred during the husband's employment. Because the couple's claim arose before the husband left work the insurer was liable. *Lazer v. Metropolitan Life Ins. Co.*, 509 N.Y.S.2d 243 (Dist.Ct.1986).

A Colorado man sustained a severe and disabling brain injury in an automobile accident. On the date of the accident, his mother was insured under a group policy. The policy extended coverage for the benefit of her dependent son and provided for major medical benefits that had a maximum lifetime benefit of one million dollars. Shortly after the accident, the employer terminated the group policy. The mother then filed a complaint seeking a declaratory judgment that the insurer was obligated to pay major medical lifetime benefits up to one million dollars. After the trial court ordered that the mother was entitled to the benefits, the insurer appealed to the Colorado Court of Appeals. The insurer contended that the group policy provided for termination of benefits three months from the date when the employer terminated the policy. When an insurer seeks to restrict coverage, the limitation must be clearly expressed. The court determined that the policy unambiguously expressed that if the group policy was terminated then benefits would only continue for at most three months. The court of appeals reversed the trial court's decision. *Lister v. American United Life Ins. Co.*, 797 P.2d 832 (Colo.App.1990).

In a similar case, a New York man worked for Tandy Corp. for just over four months. During this time he and his wife were covered under a group health insurance policy. Eight months after he left his job, his wife gave birth. The man filed a claim for her medical expenses with Tandy's insurer claiming that the pregnancy had commenced while he still worked at Tandy. When the insurer denied coverage, the man sued. A lower court granted the man's motion for summary judgment, declaring that under state law the insurer could not disclaim the man's entitlement to reimbursement for the medical expenses. The insurance company appealed. The New York Supreme Court, Appellate Division, noted that New York law provides only that policies "may" provide for child birth expenses which arise after termination of coverage as a result of pregnancies commencing during the policy period. Such coverage is not required by law and was not provided in the man's policy. The lower court's judgment was reversed. *Cordaro v. Aetna Life Ins. Co.*, 507 N.Y.S.2d 426 (A.D.2d Dept.1986).

A California man became totally disabled in 1983. At that time, he was covered primarily under his employer's insurance plan and secondarily as a dependent under his wife's insurance. When the insured's primary insurance proved inadequate, he sought benefits under his wife's policy. That insurer was then replaced by another insurer, and a dispute arose as to which insurer was required to provide benefits. The insured brought suit against his wife's prior and current insurers, and the prior insurer paid over $300,000 in benefits to the man. It then sought reimbursement from the current insurer in a federal district court. The court concluded that the current insurer was required to reimburse the former insurer. The current insurer appealed. On appeal to the U.S. Court of Appeals, Ninth Circuit, the court noted that California law was not completely clear as to which insurer was required to provide coverage and benefits. It then stated that its interpretation was that replacement carriers would provide coverage to totally disabled individuals, but benefits for the disabling condition would be provided by the previous carrier. As long as prior insurers' payments were made during the statutorily mandated extension of benefits period, replacement insurers did not have to reimburse the former insurers for these payments. The court thus reversed the district court's decision. *Miller v. Northwestern Nat'l Life Ins. Co.*, 915 F.2d 1391 (9th Cir.1990).

A former employee of a manufacturing company in Massachusetts sued an insurer for long-term disability benefits pursuant to an employer-furnished group policy. The employee was hospitalized and subsequently terminated from employment due to a continuing disability. During his hospitalization, the employee received a group insurance certificate through his employer. At the top of the first page of the certificate, the employer filled in an erroneous effective date for the employee's long-term disability coverage. However, according to the terms of the group policy which the employee never received, the effective date was approximately two months later. The employee brought suit in a Massachusetts trial court contending that the earlier effective date on the certificate served to cover his disabilities. The court held in favor of the insurer. On appeal, the employee argued that the employer was acting as an agent of the insurer in filling out his certificate and, therefore, the insurer should be bound by the erroneous effective date appearing on the certificate. Further, the employee contended that a conflict in terms between an individual certificate and a group policy should be resolved in favor of the employee. The Supreme Judicial Court of Massachusetts agreed, holding that a conflict between a certificate and policy should be resolved to provide the broadest coverage to the insured. It remanded the case to the lower court to determine whether the employer was an agent of the insurer. *Kirkpatrick v. Boston Mut. Life Ins. Co.*, 473 N.E.2d 173 (Mass.1985).

In an Oklahoma case, the beneficiary of a deceased construction worker was denied recovery on a life insurance policy. She sued the insurer and was awarded recovery by a U.S. district court. The insurer appealed to the U.S. Court of Appeals, Tenth Circuit. The construction company where the deceased had worked retained a number of laid-off workers as employees. Even though the deceased had not received a paycheck for over a year, he was still considered an employee until his death. The group life insurance policy that the employer had negotiated with the insurer contained a rider extending coverage to the laid-off workers retained as employees, provided their leaves of absence did not extend beyond twelve months. The beneficiary sought recovery on the group policy or, in the alternative, recovery based upon an alleged oral contract between the employer and the insurer to cover workers laid off for long periods of time. The lower court reformed the policy to reflect this alleged oral understanding.

On appeal the insurer maintained that no agreement had existed to extend coverage, and that the lower court was wrong in reforming the policy. It further maintained that the deceased was not covered by the terms of the written policy. The court of appeals reversed the decision of the lower court. It stated that in order for a reformation to take place, there must be proof that an agreement between the parties was reached, and that when the agreement was reduced to writing a provision was omitted or a mistake inserted into the contract through mutual mistake or fraud. No such proof was presented. The case was reversed and remanded to the district court. *Evans v. Hartford Life Ins. Co.*, 704 F.2d 1177 (10th Cir.1983).

B. The "Actively at Work" Requirement

The cases in this section involve the general requirement that an employee must have been "actively at work" at the time of an injury or mishap in order to qualify for coverage under an employer-provided group life or health insurance policy.

An employee at a chemical corporation who subsequently died of leukemia was insured under a group life insurance plan for $72,000. In early 1981 a new group plan was negotiated with the same insurer which provided that all employees who were currently covered by the old plan and were "actively working" on July 1, 1981, would automatically be insured under the new group plan for $100,000. If a currently covered employee was not working on July 1, 1981, then he or she would continue to be insured under the old plan. This case arose when the leukemia victim, who was permanently hospitalized on May 29, 1981, died on August 18, 1981. From the time he left work until his death he received full pay and was listed on his employer's computers as an active employee. The mother of the deceased, who was his beneficiary, was paid $72,000 by the insurance company. She then brought suit in a U.S. district court claiming that her son had been actively at work on July 1, 1981, and that she was therefore entitled to $100,000 under the new plan. However, the district court refused to agree that a hospitalized employee could be actively at work for the purposes of a group life policy. The decision was upheld by the U.S. Court of Appeals, Eighth Circuit, which stated that being actively at work on July 1, 1981, was a condition precedent to the $100,000 coverage under the new policy. The employee's mother was only entitled to $72,000 under the old policy. *Todd v. Dow Chemical Co.*, 760 F.2d 192 (8th Cir.1985).

In a North Carolina case, an injured man who was a covered dependent under his wife's employer-furnished group health policy sought reimbursement for $18,000 in medical expenses. The husband owned and operated a store, and during summer hours at the store he would take afternoon naps in a back area while his son tended to the business. While napping one afternoon, the insured was struck in the head by a falling ceiling fan. He suffered severe injuries. The wife's group health insurer denied coverage based upon a policy exclusion which precluded coverage for "treatment of bodily injuries arising from or in the course of any employment." The couple filed suit in a North Carolina trial court which held in favor of the insurer. The couple appealed to the Court of Appeals of North Carolina.

The appellate court held that the accident did not occur "in the course of" nor did it "arise from" the insured's employment, and thus did not fall within the policy's exclusion clause. It found that the insured had left his work area for another area, totally unused in his business, for forty-five minutes. The insured, having completely abandoned his employment for a substantial period, was not engaged in employment at the time of the accident. The controlling test of whether an injury arises out of employment, found the court, is whether the injury is a natural and probable consequence of the nature of employment. The case was reversed and remanded to the lower court for a determination of damages. *Dayal v. Provident Life & Accident Ins. Co.*, 321 S.E.2d 452 (N.C.App.1984).

In January 1984, a medical doctor procured disability insurance from an insurer. The doctor's eligibility for this policy was conditioned on her status as a physician actively engaged in the medical profession on a full-time basis. She renewed the policy over the next four years. In June 1988, she suffered an injury which was covered by the policy. She received benefits under the policy until July of 1989 when the insurer discovered she had been suspended from the practice of medicine in December 1987. The insured physician sued for benefits under the policy in a federal district court. The insurer argued that the insured could not recover under the policy since she had been suspended and therefore no longer actively engaged in her occupation. The court agreed that the insured fell within the nonrenewal provision of the policy since she had violated the law by practicing medicine after her license had been revoked. However, the court determined that the insurer only had a right to refuse to renew the policy, not to terminate it. Since the insurer did renew the policy by accepting the insured's premiums, the policy was in effect when the injury occurred. The court rejected the insurer's defense that the insured's failure to notify it of her suspended license rescinded the policy. The insurer failed to investigate the insured's status before it renewed her policy. The court entered judgment in favor of the insured and ordered a federal magistrate to determine the amount of damages. *Kadan v. Commercial Ins. Co.*, 800 F.Supp. 1392 (E.D.La.1992).

The widow of a Virginia employee was denied life insurance proceeds after the death of her husband. The employee was in the hospital with an illness at the time his employer acquired a group life policy. The insurer claimed that the employee was ineligible for coverage because he was not actively at work within the meaning of the policy. The terms of the policy required employees to be actively at work when the policy became effective in order to qualify for policy benefits. The Virginia Supreme Court held that the widow was entitled to the proceeds due to the fact that the employee participated in business decisions while at home and in the hospital.

Lincoln Nat'l Life Ins. Co. v. Commonwealth Corrugated Container Corp., 327 S.E.2d 98 (Va.1985).

IV. DELIVERY OF POLICY

Most life insurance policies provide that the policy is not in force until 1) the insurer approves the application for coverage, 2) the insurer receives the premium, 3) the insurer delivers the policy to the insured, and 4) the insured (or his or her agent) actually receives delivery of the policy.

A Michigan man completed an application for life insurance which was to begin on July 1, 1990. According to the application, the policy would not become effective until the first full premium was paid and the contract was delivered. The insured was to pay his premiums out of payroll deductions. The payroll deductions started on June 8. In late June, the policy was mailed by the insurer to its agent, who did not deliver it to the insured because the agent was on vacation. The insurer, apparently unaware that the payroll deductions had begun, also notified the insured that he had until July 19 to pay the first premium. The insured died in a work-related accident on July 2. His parents then attempted to pay the full premium before July 19. The insured's employer also attempted to pay the insured's premium. The insurer returned the checks and denied coverage. In the suit which followed, the federal district court ruled for the parents, and the insurer appealed to the U.S. Court of Appeals, Sixth Circuit.

On appeal, the court noted that the insurer was estopped (prevented by its own acts) from relying on the delivery requirement because its agent had been on vacation when the policy should have been delivered, and it failed to make other arrangements for the timely delivery of the policy. Further, the insurer's notice to the insured that he had until July 19 to pay the premium was sufficient to waive the payment requirement in the application. Because payment was twice tendered to the insurer prior to July 19, the payment requirements of the contract were satisfied. The court thus affirmed the district court's ruling, and ordered the insurer to pay the policy proceeds. *Dohanyos v. Prudential Ins. Co.*, 952 F.2d 947 (6th Cir.1992).

An insurance agent went to the home of a California couple to complete a health insurance application. The application contained a conditional receipt clause which stated that no insurance would be effective unless a policy was issued. The couple claimed the agent never read and explained the conditional receipt to them. They also stated that the agent told them that if they paid their premium immediately, they would receive coverage beginning that day. A policy was never issued and the insurer attempted to return the premium to the couple. Eventually, the couple submitted a claim for $22,000 in hospitalization costs. The insurer then brought a declaratory judgment action in order to determine if a contract had been formed. A federal district court determined that no contract had been formed. The insureds appealed to the U.S. Court of Appeals, Ninth Circuit.

The court of appeals noted that under California law, a contract of temporary insurance may arise from completion of an insurance application and payment of the first premium, if the language of the application would lead an ordinary lay person to conclude that coverage was immediate. The policy in this case clearly and unambiguously indicated that there would be no coverage until the policy was issued. However, the court stated that there was a triable issue of fact as to whether the clause actually was called to the applicant's attention and adequately explained. It noted that in California exclusions and limits on coverage must be called to the insured's attention before they will be given effect. The court stated that if the exclusion had not been explained adequately, a contract for temporary insurance did arise. Therefore, the court of appeals remanded the case to the district court for a determination of whether the clause was in fact explained to the insured. *State Farm Mut. Auto. Ins. Co. v. Khoe*, 872 F.2d 1427 (9th Cir.1989).

A Mississippi man took out a loan for $53,000 from a bank, which obtained a life insurance policy on him for that amount. The policy limit was $50,000, but the insurer authorized the policy. Less than a year later, the man took out another loan for $41,000 and again the bank obtained a policy on the man's life through the same insurer. The bank told the man it would have to obtain approval of the higher amount from the insurer, but issued a certificate of insurance and also collected an insurance premium. Seventeen days later, the man died and the insurer paid the bank only $50,000, the maximum amount it provided for in its policies for one debtor. The bank sued the man's estate for the balance in a Mississippi trial court, and the estate brought the insurer into the suit. The court held the insurer liable for the balance of the loan due the bank. The insurer appealed to the Supreme Court of Mississippi.

The insurer argued that the coverage was only tentative, and that the policy clearly established a maximum of $50,000 for one debtor. The court, however, ruled that because a certificate of insurance was issued to the man, it was not a conditional receipt, but an insurance policy. The bank, which issued the policy to the man, was an authorized agent of the insurer and had the apparent authority to issue the policy. The court held that it was reasonable for the man to believe he was insured because a policy had been issued to him. The court affirmed the trial court's decision and held the insurer liable for the loan balance. *Malta Life Ins. Co. v. Estate of Washington*, 552 So.2d 827 (Miss.1989).

A South Dakota couple obtained a home loan from a bank. They executed several loan documents, including a settlement statement which required the husband to obtain credit life insurance. The husband applied for the insurance but failed to answer a follow up question on the application. The bank sent the application to the insurer which received it and labeled it incomplete. No premiums were paid and no policy was issued. Eight years later the husband was killed in a plane crash. His wife filed a claim with the bank to have his credit life insurance pay the remaining loan balance. The bank stated that the policy had never been issued. The wife sued the bank for breach of contract for failing to provide the requested insurance coverage. The bank filed a third-party claim against the insurer for indemnity and contribution. A South Dakota circuit court granted the insurer's motion for summary judgment and the bank appealed to the Supreme Court of South Dakota. The supreme court held that the insurer owed no duty to the bank to act upon the incomplete credit life insurance application. The insurer was not required to indemnify the bank for any damages it was required to pay because of its failure to obtain the requested coverage. Because the insurer owed no duty to the husband or his agent to act upon an incomplete application form, indemnification did not apply. The supreme court affirmed the trial court's decision granting summary judgment for the insurer. *Manning v. First Federal Sav. & Loan*, 441 N.W.2d 924 (S.D.1989).

In an Oregon case, a man completed an application for life insurance and mailed it to the insurer on December 2, 1980. His wife was named as beneficiary on the application. The application contained the following provision: "The Company shall incur no liability under this application until it has been received and approved, a policy issued and delivered and the full first premium specified in the policy has actually been paid to and accepted by the Company, all while the health, habits and any other condition relating to each person proposed for insurance are as described in this application." The man learned that he had cancer on January 2, 1981, but did not inform the insurer. The policy, which contained a "policy date" of January 1, 1981, was delivered to the man on January 16, at which time he made the first full premium payment. He died of cancer on February 14, 1981.

The man's widow requested the proceeds on the policy but the insurer denied her request, contending that the policy never became effective because the man's health had changed before actual delivery of the policy. The wife sued the insurer and a state trial court ordered the insurer to pay; the insurer appealed. The Oregon Court of Appeals reversed the trial court decision and the woman appealed to the Oregon Supreme Court, which upheld the decision in favor of the insurer. No contract had been formed between the insured and the insurer because the policy application explicitly stated that in order for coverage to become effective, the policy must be delivered while no change has taken place in the applicant's health. The general rule that when a policy contains an effective date, that date is controlling, was inapplicable because no policy had ever come into effect. *Olsen v. Federal Kemper Life Assur. Co.*, 700 P.2d 231 (Ore.1985).

An insurer provided group accident life insurance to Arkansas public schools. A woman, employed by one of the schools, applied for an individual life insurance policy, naming her brother as the beneficiary. The policy stated that individual insurance would become effective "on the first day of the month next following the date the application is received." She applied for the policy on September 3, and was murdered on September 18. When her brother filed a claim, the insurer returned the premium and denied benefits, asserting that the insurance had not yet become effective. The brother sued the insurer in an Arkansas trial court, which ruled for the insurer. He then appealed to the Court of Appeals of Arkansas. On appeal, he argued that because the effective date on the application had been left blank, the policy was ambiguous as to its effective date, and the woman might have had a reasonable expectation that coverage was in force when she submitted a premium with the application. The court disagreed, holding that the policy clearly stated the effective coverage date. Because the woman died prior to that date, there was no insurance coverage available. The court further stated that this had been a freely entered into agreement, and that if the woman had not liked the terms of the policy, she could have refused to enter into the contract with the insurer. The court denied coverage to the beneficiary and affirmed the trial court's decision. *Watts v. Life Ins. Co. of Arkansas*, 782 S.W.2d 47 (Ark.App.1990).

In a Georgia case, the state court of appeals held that an insurer was not liable to the parents of a deceased dependent child. The parents had met with the insurer's agent and had applied for two separate policies of insurance, one for life insurance and one for accident and health insurance. The application for life insurance included coverage for the couple's child under a dependent child rider. The application, which was forwarded to the insurer, stated that the child had undergone surgery for cancer of the colon earlier that year. According to the couple, the agent assured them that the child's life insurance coverage would not be precluded by his medical condition. The child died shortly after the applications were submitted to the insurer. The insurer refused to pay benefits and the couple sued the insurer.

The court of appeals affirmed a trial court ruling in favor of the insurer. The court found that the application for life insurance for the dependent child had not been accepted when he died. An underwriting manager for the insurer testified that no life insurance policy had been issued and would not have been issued for two reasons. First, the maximum age of an insurable dependent is eighteen years of age (the child was nineteen years old). Second, the child was uninsurable under any rating due to the fact that he had undergone treatment for cancer during the year preceding the application. Thus, the insurer was not liable for death benefits. *Whitmire v. Colonial Life & Accident Ins. Co.*, 323 S.E.2d 843 (Ga.App.1984).

V. DOUBLE INDEMNITY AND ACCIDENTAL DEATH BENEFITS

In interpreting insurance contracts providing double indemnity and/or accidental death benefits, the courts have applied traditional insurance law principles and generally have strictly construed the terms of such provisions against insurers.

A man was working in extreme heat as a painter and sandblaster when he died of a heart attack. The autopsy showed that he had suffered from coronary artery disease and that it had led to his death. His wife claimed that she was entitled to recover under an accidental death life insurance policy and sued in a federal district court. The policy defined accidental as "independent of sickness or other cause." Under Oregon law, a heart attack could be considered accidental only when the work being performed was "abnormal and unusual." The court refused to find the death to be accidental due to extreme heat, and noted that the man's duties regularly required working in heat. The court granted the insurer's motion for summary judgment. *Thomas v. Transamerica Occidental Life Ins. Co.*, 761 F.Supp. 709 (D.Or.1991).

A Louisiana woman died as a result of multiple injuries from a two-vehicle collision. At the time of the accident the woman had a blood alcohol content of .14 percent. The woman had been issued a life insurance policy by the insurer which named her two minor children and husband as beneficiaries. The policy had a face value of $5,000 with a provision for double indemnity in cases of accidental death. The insurer paid the beneficiaries the $5,000 face value of the policy but denied the claim for double indemnity. The insurer relied on a policy provision which excluded double indemnity benefit payments where a death resulted directly or indirectly from injuries incurred while the insured was intoxicated. The beneficiaries sued the insurer in a Louisiana trial court. The trial court entered judgment for the beneficiaries in the sum of $10,000. The insurer appealed to the Court of Appeal of Louisiana, Third Circuit.

The court of appeal held that the insurer had not established intoxication by a preponderance of the evidence so as to exclude the beneficiaries' claim for double indemnity under the intoxication exclusion. The court noted that the only evidence submitted by the insurer to prove intoxication was the coroner's statement that the woman's blood alcohol content was .14 percent. Since there is no legal presumption of intoxication in civil cases, the insurer had failed to prove the woman's intoxication by a preponderance of the evidence. The court found that the beneficiaries were entitled to recover $5,000 of additional death benefits. The court of appeal affirmed the award of double indemnity benefits to the beneficiaries. *Remedies v. Trans World Life Ins. Co.*, 546 So.2d 1380 (La.App.3d Cir.1989).

A Maryland insured was killed in a single car accident when the car he was driving left the roadway, struck a telephone pole, and overturned. The postmortem examination revealed that the insured had a .2% blood alcohol concentration, indicating he was intoxicated while operating his vehicle. The insured had an accidental death and dismemberment policy which provided that the insured would receive benefits for an accidental bodily injury which resulted independently of all other causes. However, there were some risks that were excepted; they included suicide, infection, disease or war. The beneficiaries sued the insurer seeking double indemnity benefits. The trial court entered judgment for the beneficiaries and the insurer appealed to the Court of Special Appeals of Maryland.

The insurer contended that as a matter of public policy the beneficiaries should not recover because the Maryland legislature has acted to deter a person who has consumed alcohol from driving. The court noted that unless a statute, regulation or public policy is violated the first principal of construction of insurance policies in Maryland is to apply the terms of the contract. The court did not find anything in the enactments of the general assembly relative to insurance to indicate that the court was expected, as a matter of public policy, to deny recovery to a beneficiary of an accident insurance policy because the insured drove a vehicle while intoxicated. If insurers desire to avoid liability on such a ground, they are free to insert a clause to that effect in their policies. Such a clause would be valid and binding. Therefore, the court held that the insurer was liable and affirmed the trial court's decision. *Consumers Life Ins. Co. v. Smith*, 587 A.2d 1119 (Md.App.1991).

In a similar case in Kentucky, an insured was killed when his car struck a tree. The subsequent investigation revealed that he had a blood alcohol level of .20%. One month previously, the man had purchased an accidental death policy and named his mother as the beneficiary. The insurer refused to pay benefits, relying on the policy exclusion which excluded coverage for death which occurs during the commission of a crime. The mother brought this action in a federal trial court which granted her summary judgment motion. The insurer appealed to the U.S. Court of Appeals, Sixth Circuit. On appeal, the insurer argued that the insured was violating a Kentucky law which prohibits driving while under the influence of alcohol and thus was killed during the commission of a crime. The court, however, determined that the policy language was sufficiently ambiguous because in reading crime, the insured is more likely to understand it to mean burglary, armed robbery or murder than drunk driving. The term "crime" should have been more clearly defined by the policy if the insurer wished to include driving under the influence in its grasp. Thus, the appellate court upheld the decision of the trial court. *American Family Life Assur. Co. v. Bilyeu*, 921 F.2d 87 (6th Cir.1990).

A Louisiana man purchased a group insurance policy which contained a provision for accidental death benefits. He named his sister as the beneficiary. Subsequently, he was found in his home, apparently the victim of an ill-fated attempt at autoerotic asphyxiation. His sister sought coverage under the policy, but the

Sec. V   DOUBLE INDEMNITY/ACCIDENTAL DEATH BENEFITS   221

insurer rejected her claim. She then brought suit in a Louisiana federal district court. Both parties moved for summary judgment. The court held that no coverage existed because the policy excluded loss resulting from an "intentionally self-inflicted injury." Even if the death was accidental, the insured had clearly intended to "injure" himself by his actions. The court granted summary judgment to the insurer. *Sims v. Monumental General Life Ins. Co.*, 778 F.Supp. 325 (E.D.La.1991).

An Alabama man was a beneficiary under a life insurance policy issued on the insured which included a double indemnity provision for accidental death caused by external means. The insured had been drinking and complained about having trouble breathing. Shortly after the insured vomited, he was found dead. The insurer paid the beneficiary the face amount of the life insurance policy. The beneficiary then sued the insurer for additional benefits. An Alabama circuit court found for the beneficiary and the insurer appealed. The Alabama Supreme court reversed the lower court's decision, noting that the insured's death occurred when he choked on food that he had regurgitated. The insured's accidental death was not caused by external means as required under the double indemnity provision of the policy. *Liberty Nat. Life Ins. Co. v. Windham*, 529 So.2d 967 (Ala.1988).

A woman was anesthetized in preparation for an operation. The initial results of the operation were good and the woman was removed to a recovery room. However, upon her arrival she had no heartbeat or blood pressure. She died nine days later. The woman had been insured under a group life policy which paid double indemnity for accidental death. The insurer paid primary benefits, and the estate sought double indemnity in state court. Summary judgment was granted for the insurer because of a medical/surgical treatment exclusion. On appeal, the Court of Appeals of Ohio affirmed the judgment. Even though doctors could not explain the death, the court ruled that a reasonable jury could only find that it was caused by the medical treatment. *Fulgham v. Union Central Life Ins. Co.*, 578 N.E.2d 483 (Ohio App.1st Dist.1989).

A Colorado man was insured under an accidental death and dismemberment policy. The policy stated that no benefits would be paid for losses resulting from medical or surgical treatment. The insured entered a Denver hospital for exploratory surgery. He died approximately two hours into the procedure. The official cause of death was noted as cardiac arrest of unknown cause while under general anesthesia. His children sought a declaratory judgment in a U.S. district court that the insurer was obligated to pay benefits for the insured's death. The insurer moved for summary judgment which was granted. The court disputed the children's contention that the physician's negligence caused the insured's death and ruled that the exclusion was applicable. The court stated that other courts which have considered similar exclusionary clauses have all held that such provisions exclude from coverage death caused by mishaps that occur during medical treatment. The policy unambiguously stated that no benefits would be payable for any loss attributable to medical or surgical treatment unless the treatment was itself necessitated by a covered accident. Since it was undisputed that the decedent's death was attributable to surgical treatment and the surgical treatment was not itself necessitated by an accident, the court concluded that the children were not entitled to recover benefits under the policy. *Krane v. Aetna Life Ins. Co.*, 698 F.Supp. 220 (D.Colo.1988).

Two police officers arrived at an insured's home in response to a call by his wife. They asked the insured to step outside. Without provocation, he suddenly came out with a loaded pistol and immediately shot one of the officers. He turned and fired a second shot at the other officer. Both officers returned his fire, killing him. His wife then sought to collect on a group accidental death insurance policy which insured her husband. She brought suit in a state trial court which granted summary judgment to the insurer. She appealed to the Court of Appeals of Georgia. The question on appeal was whether the insured's death was accidental. Here, the police officers' depositions showed that the shooting by the insured was sudden and without provocation. Whether the insured appreciated that his conduct could reasonably result in his death would normally be a question for a jury to decide. However, here, there existed no triable issue of fact. Even though the wife had presented evidence that her husband was intoxicated at the time of the shooting, she had not shown that he did not understand that deadly force would likely be used on him. The grant of summary judgment was affirmed. *Moss v. Protective Life Ins. Co.*, 417 S.E.2d 340 (Ga.App.1992).

An Iowa insured had a prosthetic aortic heart valve surgically implanted in April 1982. Seven years later, the value malfunctioned. The insured was taken to a hospital, where he died three days later. The insured's two life insurance policies paid face benefits of $10,000 with double indemnity provisions in the case of accidental death. To be eligible for such benefits, death had to be "the result of bodily injury caused directly and independently of all other causes by external, violent and purely accidental means." The insurer brought suit to determine whether it was liable for the double indemnity amounts. The trial court ruled for the insurer, and the beneficiaries appealed to the Supreme Court of Iowa. On appeal, the court noted that even though the prosthetic heart valve never actually became part of the insured's body tissue, it did become a functional part of the body. As such, it was no longer an "external" object; it had been internalized within the insured's body. Accordingly, the cause of death was not by external means, and double indemnity benefits did not have to be paid. The court affirmed the trial court's decision for the insurer. *Century Companies of America v. Krahling*, 484 N.W.2d 197 (Iowa 1992).

An Illinois man obtained a certificate of insurance on his life which contained an accidental death benefits provision in the amount of $60,000. The insured was a former correctional officer with a history of playing Russian Roulette. He had also threatened to take his own life on other occasions. While the policy was in effect, and during a quarrel with his live-in girl friend, the insured shot himself by playing Russian Roulette. His mother, the beneficiary, sought the accidental death benefits, maintaining that her son's death was unintended. A federal district court granted summary judgment to the insurer, and the beneficiary appealed to the U.S. Court of Appeals, Seventh Circuit. On appeal, the argument was made that this was not the typical Russian Roulette case because the insured believed that the bullet would automatically fall to the bottom when the cylinder was spun (due to its weight), and thus the gun would not fire. The court, however, stated that as long as the insured knew that there was one live cartridge in the cylinder, the beneficiary had no right of recovery. The insured knew that death was a foreseeable result of Russian Roulette and therefore his death was not accidental. The court of appeals affirmed the district court's decision in favor of the insurer. *Arnold v. Metropolitan Life Ins. Co.*, 970 F.2d 360 (7th Cir.1992).

Sec. VI PAYMENT OF PROCEEDS 223

A Mississippi man was insured under an accidental death policy when the automobile he was driving crashed into a building and burst into flames. The insurer denied coverage, asserting that even if the insured's death had been immediately caused by the crash and fire, the accident would not have occurred but for a brain tumor which caused the insured to black out while driving. A policy exclusion stated that a loss contributed to by a disease or infirmity of the mind or body was not covered "even though it was caused by an accidental bodily injury." In federal court, a jury found for the beneficiary, and the insurer moved the court for judgment as a matter of law or for a new trial. The court held that the policy did not unambiguously bar recovery where bodily infirmity or disease was merely a remote cause and not a direct cause. Accordingly, since the evidence presented had shown that death was caused solely as a result of injuries suffered in the accident and not by virtue of the disease or infirmity itself, the insurer could not refuse coverage. The court denied the insurer's motions and allowed the jury's verdict to stand. *Southern Farm Bureau Life Ins. Co. v. Moore*, 793 F.Supp. 702 (S.D.Miss.1992).

A 1982 helicopter crash in Ireland took the life of an oil company executive. The decedent was insured under a policy containing a clause providing double indemnity for accidental death sustained while a fare paying passenger in a public conveyance being operated as a licensed common carrier for passenger service. The insurer argued that the double indemnity clause did not apply and refused to pay on it. The U.S. Court of Appeals, Eleventh Circuit, ruled that the helicopter service was a common carrier and had been used by the decedent on the terms and conditions available to the general public. The insurer was ordered to pay the double indemnity claim. *Brill v. Indianapolis Life Ins. Co.*, 784 F.2d 1511 (11th Cir.1986).

VI. PAYMENT OF PROCEEDS

The courts have devised rules governing the payment by insurers of proceeds under insurance policies. These rules are designed to further the dual purposes of 1) protecting the legitimate expectations of insureds and beneficiaries, and 2) protecting insurers from making payments to undeserving claimants.

A. Rival Claimants

In determining which of two or more rival claimants to the proceeds of an insurance policy should recover under the policy, the courts will usually adhere to the language of the policy as tempered by state law.

A corporation purchased a life insurance policy on a corporate officer, who also owned twenty percent of the corporation's stock. Three months later the man sold his stock and resigned his position. Upon his death, his estate brought suit against the trustee of the then bankrupt corporation for the benefits of the policy. His estate argued that the corporation lacked an insurable interest, and that the benefits should thus be paid to the man's estate. A bankruptcy court ruled for the trustee, and was upheld by a bankruptcy appellate panel. The man's estate appealed to the U.S. Court of Appeals, Ninth Circuit. As an initial matter, the trustee asserted that only an insurer may complain of a lack of insurable interest. Arizona statutory law, however, has altered that general rule; if a beneficiary receives payment, Arizona law allows an insured or the insured's estate to bring suit based on a lack of an insurable interest. A corporation does, however, have an insurable interest in its officers, key employees, and principal stockholders. The severance of their relationship does not destroy that interest so long as the purchase was made in good faith. The estate presented no evidence of bad faith, and the ruling was upheld. *Al Zuni Trading Co., Inc. v. Penick*, 947 F.2d 1403 (9th Cir.1991).

A retired federal employee died, and several individuals made a claim for the benefits of his life insurance policy. One claimant was his ex-wife, from whom he had been divorced for fifteen years. Another was his daughter. The last claimant was a woman with whom he had lived since his divorce, owned joint property with, had granted power of attorney to, had relocated to another state with, and had held out to be his wife. The claims were heard by the U.S. District Court for the Middle District of Georgia. The court held that the proceeds of a Federal Employees Group Life Insurance policy are paid in the following order: first to any listed beneficiaries, second to the widow or widower, and then to the child or children of the employee. The ex-wife's claims were based on the fact that she paid funeral expenses. A creditor has no such rights and the court eliminated consideration of her claim. The issue then became whether the woman he lived with was considered his widow. The court applied the laws of their resident state (Florida) which provided that the state will recognize a common law marriage if the state where it took place would recognize it. The "marriage" took place in Georgia, which will recognize a common law marriage if competent parties agree to a contract which is consummated. The evidence presented showed that the two considered themselves married but chose to dispense with formalities. Therefore, the woman was ruled to be the deceased's widow and entitled to the insurance proceeds. *Metropolitan Life Ins. Co. v. Lucas*, 761 F.Supp. 130 (M.D.Ga.1991).

Congress established the Servicemen's Group Life Insurance Act (SEGLI) to make group life insurance available to current and former members of the armed forces. When an insured servicemember dies, SEGLI requires that the private insurer pay the proceeds to the beneficiary. If the insured fails to designate a beneficiary before his death SEGLI provides the order of precedence of beneficiaries as: the insured's spouse, the insured's children, the insured's parents, the executor of the insured's estate, or the next of kin under the law of the state in which the insured was domiciled at the time of death. SEGLI defines children to include illegitimate children. A child illegitimate as to his father is a potential beneficiary if it can be shown that the putative father is the real father.

An active duty member of the U.S. Navy, a Louisiana man, was told by his girlfriend that she was pregnant with his child. Eleven days later the man died from injuries sustained in a motorcycle accident. Seven months after his death his girlfriend gave birth to a daughter. At the time of his death, the insurer brought an interpleader action to determine who was the rightful beneficiary under the life insurance policy. The court granted summary judgment in favor of the insured's parents. The illegitimate daughter's representative appealed to the U.S. Court of Appeals, Fifth Circuit. The court noted that the problems associated with proving paternity are well known. The proof relied on is often sketchy and strongly contested, frequently turning upon conflicting testimony from only two witnesses. Since the insured died before any DNA testing was done the court had to rely on other evidence.

Sec. VI   PAYMENT OF PROCEEDS   225

Because none of the judicially recognized conditions for illegitimate children were met, the court held that the child could not recover. The appellate court affirmed the trial court's decision. *Prudential Ins. Co. of America v. Moorhead*, 916 F.2d 261 (5th Cir.1990).

The primary beneficiary of an insurance policy intentionally murdered the insured, an Arkansas man. The insurance policy also named a contingent beneficiary. In an interpleader action in an Arkansas trial court, the chancellor disqualified the primary beneficiary due to public policy. The chancellor awarded the insurance proceeds to the contingent beneficiary as opposed to the insured's estate. The insured's daughter then appealed to the Court of Appeals of Arkansas. The issue on appeal was whether contingent beneficiaries should receive insurance proceeds when the primary beneficiary is still living or if the proceeds should pass to the insured's estate. This case was one of first impression in Arkansas. The court decided that the purpose of interpreting a testamentary document is to arrive at the testator's intention. It looked at the express language of the instrument. The policy provided that the insured's estate should only recover if no beneficiary survived the insured. Since the contingent beneficiary survived the insured, the court of appeals affirmed the decision of the chancellor, and granted benefits to the contingent beneficiary. *Spencer v. Floyd*, 785 S.W.2d 60 (Ark.App.1990).

A Louisiana man purchased two life insurance policies, listing his wife as the primary beneficiary on one and the sole beneficiary on the other. Subsequently, he died of a gunshot wound, and his wife was convicted of manslaughter. The insurer then filed an action seeking to determine the ownership of the proceeds of the two policies. The trial court disqualified the widow as the beneficiary under both policies, and further excluded her from recovering one-half of the proceeds of the policies from the former community property. The widow appealed to the Court of Appeal of Louisiana, contending that she should at least have been given a one-half interest in the policy proceeds. The appellate court, however, stated that it would be illogical and against public policy to grant the wife recovery of half the proceeds when the whole had been denied to her. The court thus affirmed the trial court's decision. *Commonwealth Life Ins. Co. v. Davidge*, 559 So.2d 2 (La.App.1st Cir.1990).

A Missouri man was insured under a group life insurance policy. He named his wife as the primary beneficiary and named three other relatives as contingent beneficiaries. His wife then shot and killed him, after which she pleaded guilty to manslaughter. Because of her conviction, she was disallowed any proceeds from the life insurance policy. A lawsuit was brought to determine whether the proceeds should be paid to the contingent beneficiaries or to the insured's estate. The trial court held in favor of the estate, and appeal was taken to the Supreme Court of Missouri.

On appeal, the beneficiaries of the insured's estate argued that the contingent beneficiaries had no interest in the policy unless the primary beneficiary died before the insured. Here, the primary beneficiary was still alive, but unable to collect the proceeds because of her illegal action. The court, however, disagreed. It determined that the insured had given a clear indication that he preferred the contingent beneficiaries to collect on the policy rather than his next of kin. He expressly designated the contingent beneficiaries without regard to his next of kin, so the contingent beneficiaries were entitled to the policy proceeds. The court reversed the trial court's decision. *Lee v. Aylward*, 790 S.W.2d 462 (Mo.banc 1990).

A Nevada woman shot and killed her husband. She was originally charged with murder, but as a result of a plea bargain agreement, she pled no contest to charges of involuntary manslaughter. The wife was the primary beneficiary of three life insurance policies on her husband. Two of the insurers paid the benefits to the wife; however, the third asked a Nevada court to determine the proper distribution of benefits under the policy given the circumstances surrounding the insured's death. The family's children then sued the first two insurance companies to recover the benefits that had already been paid to the wife. The lawsuits were filed in a federal district court, but the district court asked the Nevada Supreme Court whether a person who has wilfully taken the life of an insured person may receive the insurance proceeds under Nevada law. The supreme court noted that under Nevada law life insurance benefits cannot be paid to a person convicted of murder and who is a beneficiary of the decedent's policy. The court also stated that it construed the language of the law very narrowly so that only a criminal conviction of murder precluded an individual from succeeding to an estate. Since the wife was not convicted of murder, she was entitled to the life insurance benefit despite the fact that the killing was wilful, intentional and unlawful. *Life Ins. Co. of N. America v. Wollett*, 766 P.2d 893 (Nev.1988).

A Texas man purchased a group life and accidental death policy which named as beneficiaries his wife and mother, each to receive fifty percent of the proceeds. Subsequently, the insured and his wife were murdered by their daughter and her boyfriend (who later killed themselves). Since the insured's mother was listed as only a fifty percent beneficiary, a question arose as to who was entitled to the remaining half. The insured's children by a previous marriage claimed entitlement in opposition to the insured's mother. The trial court found for the children, and an appeal was taken to the Court of Appeals of Texas. On appeal, the court ruled that the insured's mother was entitled to the full amount of the policy proceeds. The addition of the fifty percent notation by each beneficiary's name was held to be mere surplusage; it was not a specific provision which denied the survivorship right to the insured's mother. Because the co-beneficiary did not outlive the insured, the policy proceeds should have been paid according to the survivorship clause of the policy. The court reversed the decision of the trial court. *Medlin v. Medlin*, 830 S.W.2d 353 (Tex.App.1992).

Two Alabama businessmen entered into an oral partnership agreement. Each partner took out life insurance in which the other partner was designated as beneficiary. Premiums were paid from partnership funds. When one of the partners died a dispute arose over the intended purpose of the policy. Before the Alabama Supreme Court, the surviving partner contended that the proceeds were to be used to pay off partnership debts incurred by him (the surviving partner) because the partnership had been discontinued. The deceased partner's spouse argued that the proceeds were to go to the deceased partner's estate to pay for his interest in the partnership. The supreme court concluded that the surviving partner was entitled to the proceeds. It noted that a partner has an insurable interest in the life of another partner. This interest continues even though the partnership is discontinued prior to the death of one of the partners, as in this case. It also noted that it is entirely

Sec. VI   PAYMENT OF PROCEEDS   227

permissible for a partner to select another partner, and not a spouse or an estate, as beneficiary. The supreme court concluded that here, the spouse's evidence that her husband intended that the proceeds go to his estate consisted solely of oral testimony from the insurance agent (her brother) and a mutual friend. Since no ambiguity existed as to the designation of the surviving partner as beneficiary, the supreme court held that he should receive the proceeds from the life insurance policy. *Graves v. Norred*, 510 So.2d 816 (Ala.1987).

After a Tennessee man died by accidental drowning, his two daughters brought suit against his second wife for the proceeds of a life insurance policy. When the daughters' parents were divorced fours years before his death, the divorce decree incorporated a property settlement agreement requiring the man to maintain a $20,000 life insurance policy upon his life with the daughters as beneficiaries. At the time of the divorce, he held one known insurance policy, a group insurance plan for Tennessee state employees issued by Provident Life & Accident Insurance Co. Although a state court ruled in favor of the daughters, the Tennessee Court of Appeals reversed, stating that the actual policy was not introduced into evidence. The daughters appealed. The Supreme Court of Tennessee disagreed with the court of appeals. The document presented was actually a pamphlet describing a group insurance plan for state employees and a letter from Provident, but the court noted that such a pamphlet and a certificate are usually all that are furnished to an employee under a group insurance plan. The evidence also showed that the value of the group life benefit had risen to nearly $26,000 in addition to a $50,000 special accident benefit. Since the man's effort to change the beneficiary of the policy to his second wife was without court approval, the court ruled that the change was ineffectual. The daughters were held to be the actual beneficiaries of the entire $76,000 proceeds of the policy. *Dossett v. Dossett*, 712 S.W.2d 96 (Tenn.1986).

In a Texas case, a wife was stabbed to death by her husband. The wife's life was insured under four insurance policies which all designated her husband as the primary beneficiary. The contingent beneficiaries under two policies were the wife's parents. The husband's son from a prior marriage was the contingent beneficiary of the other two policies. The Texas Insurance Code provides that when a beneficiary wilfully causes the death of an insured "the nearest relative of the insured shall receive [the] insurance." This provision has been interpreted by the Texas courts to affect the distribution of benefits only when both the primary and contingent beneficiaries are disqualified. When the insurers sought a ruling as to who should receive policy benefits, the trial court disqualified the husband and awarded the benefits of the four life insurance policies to their respective contingent beneficiaries. The proceeds of two of the policies went to the wife's parents, and the proceeds of the other two went to the wife's stepson. The wife's parents appealed this distribution of benefits. When the distribution was affirmed by the state court of appeals the wife's parents appealed to the Texas Supreme Court arguing that as the wife's nearest relatives they should be awarded the proceeds of all four life insurance policies. The supreme court noted that the provision of the insurance code mandating that when a life insurance policy's beneficiary is disqualified the proceeds should go to the "nearest relative of the insured" is "as much a part of the insured's contract as if it [had] been incorporated in the policy." The court declared that the interpretation of this provision which had previously been established by the Texas courts was "inconsistent with the explicit language" of the insurance code. The court overruled the previously applied interpretation which failed to disqualify contingent beneficiaries and awarded the benefits of all four policies to the wife's parents as her nearest relatives. *Crawford v. Coleman,* 726 S.W.2d 9 (Tex.1987).

B. Change-of-Beneficiary Disputes

In order to effect a valid change of beneficiary under a life insurance policy, an insured must 1) comply with policy provisions and 2) comply with state law and prior court orders relating to the insured (e.g., a divorce decree).

A group life insurance policy insured a man who was involved in a tumultuous marriage. The man's wife also experienced problems in her relationship with his daughters. The insurance benefit representative had become aware of these difficulties, partly through the man's proper change of beneficiary from his wife to his daughters. The wife (seeking to be reinstated as the beneficiary) later was unable to procure a change of beneficiary form from the benefit representative, but was successful in obtaining one from another of the insurer's employees. The form was returned to the benefit representative in the wife's handwriting, but was not accepted. The benefit representative stated that she would need to be contacted by the husband. No contact was made by the man before his death. The insurer received competing claims for the benefits, and filed an interpleader action in a federal district court which allowed the court to determine the legal recipient.

It was undisputed that the man had not changed his beneficiary according to the terms of the policy. That fact did not end the inquiry, however, as an insurer may waive strict compliance with a term of the policy. The insurer's filing of an interpleader action operated as such a waiver, and the court next needed to determine whether the doctrine of substantial compliance had been met. This doctrine allows a change in beneficiary despite technical noncompliance if it can be shown that the insured intended a change. The intent must be shown beyond question. Because of the relationships present and the benefit representative's knowledge of them, the court would not allow a change without the insured having contacted the benefit representative. Both the insured and the wife were aware of this requirement, and the wife had no explanation for noncompliance. The court awarded the benefits to the daughters. *Metropolitan Life Ins. Co. v. Barnes,* 770 F.Supp. 1393 (E.D.Mo.1991).

A Colorado insured named his wife as beneficiary of a life insurance policy. The couple later separated and entered into a separation agreement. Each party agreed to maintain his or her own life insurance policies and retain their present beneficiaries until they entered into a final decree of dissolution. At that time, each party was to become the sole owner of their respective life insurance policies. Each spouse would waive any interest in the other spouse's policy and would become free to change beneficiaries. After the final decree was issued, the insured requested his insurer to change his policy beneficiary to his mother. However, he failed to return the beneficiary forms and policy to the insurer. The insured remarried and his mother later died. The insured then died intestate, leaving his second wife as sole heir.

The insurer filed an interpleader action in a Colorado trial court which found that the insured's widow was entitled to the policy proceeds. The insured's former wife then appealed to the Colorado Court of Appeals which reversed the trial court's decision and ordered the policy proceeds to be paid to the former wife as the named beneficiary. The Supreme Court of Colorado then granted certiorari. The supreme

Sec. VI   PAYMENT OF PROCEEDS   229

court held that the former wife had waived her interest as a beneficiary in the insured's life insurance policy by entering into the separation agreement. The parties intended the agreement to be a full and final settlement of all interests, including any interest they may have had as beneficiaries. At the time of the final decree, the former wife's interest or expectancy as the beneficiary expired. The supreme court reversed and remanded the court of appeals decision with directions to reinstate the trial court's decision. *Napper v. Schmeh*, 773 P.2d 531 (Colo.1989).

A Colorado insured owned a $60,000 life insurance policy with his wife named as beneficiary. The couple was divorced. The divorce decree provided for each to receive their own personal effects, savings, bonds and retirement benefits. Both later remarried. The insured died intestate without having changed the named beneficiary on his insurance policy to his surviving spouse. The spouse sued the ex-wife in order to get the policy proceeds. A Colorado trial court held for the ex-wife, and the Colorado Court of Appeals affirmed the decision. The surviving spouse then appealed to the Supreme Court of Colorado. The supreme court stated that a divorce decree does not automatically terminate a spouse's expectancy as named beneficiary of a life insurance policy. It also stated that the divorce decree did not manifest the intention that the ex-wife's expectancy be extinguished. The court also held that the ex-wife's interest was not extinguished by the addition of the term "wife" onto her given name on the policy. The supreme court affirmed the lower court's rulings. *Christensen v. Sabad*, 773 P.2d 538 (Colo.1989).

An Alabama man purchased a life insurance policy. His wife later divorced him in a default proceeding while one of his children was still a minor. He designated his minor son as the beneficiary of his insurance policy, according to the court's order. He then moved in with his brother and sister-in-law, who took care of him — he was suffering from cancer. Approximately one year before his son reached the age of majority, he amended his insurance policy to designate his siblings as the beneficiaries of the policy. Three months after his son reached majority, the insured died. When a dispute over the policy proceeds arose, the insurer filed an interpleader action, conceding liability. The insurer also sought attorney's fees and an injunction against further actions by the "beneficiaries." The trial court awarded the policy proceeds to the insured's son, granted attorney's fees to the insurer, and issued the injunction. The siblings appealed to the Supreme Court of Alabama. On appeal, the court stated that there was no equitable problem with the insured changing beneficiaries. Even though it was done while his son was still a minor, the insured had been free to change the policy after his son reached majority. Clearly, the insured had wanted his siblings to take the proceeds under the policy, so the court reversed the trial court's decision and remanded the case. *Whitten v. Whitten*, 592 So.2d 183 (Ala.1991).

A Washington insured purchased a life insurance policy. He divorced his first wife and later remarried. Upon his death, a conflict arose between his second wife and the children from his first marriage over the policy proceeds. The deceased had agreed to name the children as irrevocable beneficiaries of the policy under a divorce decree. He had agreed to maintain that policy for them as long as they were his dependents. The insurer filed a motion with a Washington circuit court to determine who should receive the proceeds. The court granted the children's motion to award them the proceeds. The widow appealed to the state court of appeals which affirmed the decision. She then appealed to the Washington Supreme Court.

The widow asserted that she, as the surviving spouse, was entitled to one-half of the proceeds and that her status as designated beneficiary entitled her to the remaining half of the proceeds. The children argued that their father was required to abide by the decree and that they were entitled to the full policy proceeds. The supreme court held that the deceased was not allowed to change the beneficiaries in violation of the decree. The subsequent marriage did not relieve him of his support obligations. Therefore, the policy proceeds were to go to the children. *Aetna Life Ins. Co. v. Bunt*, 754 P.2d 993 (Wash.1988).

An insured's fiancee brought an action to collect the proceeds of a life insurance policy in which she was named the beneficiary. The insured had exercised his conversion rights (granted by the policy) at the time of his divorce from his former wife by changing his beneficiary to his fiancee. The insured died before he married his fiancee, and the wife and children successfully sued for the proceeds of the policy. The fiancee appealed. The Supreme Court of South Dakota reversed in part, holding that the children were entitled to the equitable rights in the life insurance policy as beneficiaries and the fiancee was entitled to the remainder of the proceeds. *Bentley v. New York Life Ins. Co.*, 488 N.W.2d 77 (S.D.1992).

In February 1977, an Alabama man was diagnosed as having a brain tumor. He designated his daughter as beneficiary of his bank account and insurance policy in May 1977. In August, he changed the life insurance beneficiary to his sister. He executed a will in September leaving all his property to his sister. The next month he directed that his life insurance proceeds go to his children. When the man died in November his sister offered the September will for probate. His children and ex-wife contested the will. An Alabama trial court declared that all of the actions bearing on the disposition of the estate were void because of undue influence. It then ordered the proceeds to be paid to the children. The sister appealed to the Alabama Supreme Court, arguing that the children could not attack the change of beneficiary solely on grounds of undue influence. The children argued that the trial court had amended the order declaring that the beneficiary designations were void due to mental incompetence, not undue influence. The supreme court stated that the man was mentally incompetent. Thus, the beneficiary designations could properly be declared void by the trial court. It was also proper for the trial court to amend the order stating that the changes were made due to mental incompetence rather than undue influence. The trial court decision to award all proceeds to the children was upheld. *Owens v. Coleman*, 520 So.2d 514 (Ala.1987).

An employee filed a beneficiary designation card with his employer which named his son as sole beneficiary under the employer's group policy. The employer changed to a new insurer which issued a new group life insurance policy. The employee died and at the time of his death the new policy was in effect but a new beneficiary designation card had not been executed. The new insurer asked a Texas district court for a determination as to who should be awarded the insurance benefits. It held that the beneficiary designation card did not apply to the new policy and awarded the policy proceeds to the representative of the employee's estate, rather than his son. The son appealed to the Texas Court of Appeals.

Sec. VI PAYMENT OF PROCEEDS 231

The son contended that the trial court wrongly refused to admit into evidence information supplied by the new insurer. The information would have shown that the new insurer was obligated to accept the old insurer's beneficiary designation cards, thus waiving its regular policy requirements for designating beneficiaries. The representative of the employee's estate argued that the information was properly excluded since it would have contradicted the terms of the written insurance contract. The court of appeals held for the son, concluding that the information should have been admitted. It observed that requirements for designating or changing the beneficiary of a policy are primarily for the benefit of the insurer and compliance may be waived by the insurer during the lifetime of the insured. The trial court's decision was reversed and the case was remanded for a new trial. *Morehead v. Morehead*, 738 S.W.2d 42 (Tex.App.1987).

An Indiana man purchased a life insurance policy in 1975, naming his wife as beneficiary. The policy provided that a change of beneficiary became effective "when a written request for such change satisfactory to the [insurer] is received at its home office." In May, 1985, the man's wife filed for divorce. In June he went to the insurer's office and completed a change of beneficiary form, naming his mother as sole beneficiary. He committed suicide less than an hour later. The man's mother and wife both filed lawsuits against the insurer for the life insurance proceeds. The Indiana Court of Appeals decided that even though the man had not complied with the policy requirements concerning a change of beneficiary, he had "done everything within his power to effect such a change." This "substantial compliance" with the requirements of the policy was sufficient to change the policy beneficiary. A lower court's decision to award life insurance proceeds to the man's mother was affirmed. *Quinn v. Quinn*, 498 N.E.2d 1312 (Ind.App.1st Dist.1986).

A West Virginia man obtained a life insurance policy designating his wife as the beneficiary. Sometime later, the insured obtained a second life insurance policy again designating his wife as the primary beneficiary. He also designated his daughter by a prior marriage as the contingent beneficiary in the event his wife failed to survive him. Subsequently, the insured changed the beneficiary in the first insurance policy from his wife to his daughter. On that same day, he shot and killed his wife and one of her children by a prior marriage. He then committed suicide. Both insurers brought a declaratory judgment proceeding to determine who was entitled to the life insurance proceeds. The court held that the wife's estate rather than the daughter was entitled to the proceeds. The daughter appealed to the Supreme Court of Appeals of Virginia. The appellate court disagreed with the district court's interpretation of a state statute which mandated that one who feloniously kills another should not be able to deprive the one killed of property. The district court had ruled that the wife's estate was entitled to the benefits so that the decedent could not profit by the killing of his own wife (by denying her estate the proceeds). The court of appeals, however, disagreed and interpreted the state statute to apply only when the death of the person killed created the property corpus which was in dispute. Here, the father's suicide, not the killing of his wife, gave rise to the corpus of the money in dispute, and therefore the daughter was entitled to the proceeds since she was the only legally designated surviving beneficiary. Accordingly, the appellate court reversed the trial court's decision and held for the daughter. *Peoples Sec. Life Ins. Co. v. Currence,* 420 S.E.2d 552 (W.Va.1992).

C. Missing Persons

The cases in this section involve the relationship between insured individuals who "disappeared" and the proceeds of life insurance policies.

Two men went on a fishing trip off the coast of Puerto Rico. When they did not return, the wife of one of the fishermen notified the U.S. Coast Guard, and a search began. The boat was found capsized but no bodies were found. The wife sued her husband's life insurer in federal district court. The insurer argued that recovery was barred because the policy stated that the death of an insured would only be presumed if after seven years no evidence was found that the insured had survived. The court disagreed, noting that the policy did not state that the beneficiary was excluded from making a claim before the seven year period. The wife did not have to prove beyond a reasonable doubt that her husband had died. Accordingly, the court ruled that the wife was entitled to the policy proceeds. *Rodriguez Diaz v. Mutual of Omaha Ins. Co.*, 803 F.Supp. 575 (D.Puerto Rico 1992).

An Idaho man disappeared in March 1978. His wife, who was the beneficiary of his life insurance policy, continued to pay premiums on the policy for seven years, then filed a "Statement of Disappearance" with the insurer in May 1985. She was told by the insurer that a judicial declaration of death was required before it would pay the policy's death benefit. The wife waited over thirty days and filed a lawsuit seeking a declaration that her husband was dead and that she was entitled to the policy proceeds along with attorney's fees. The trial court ruled in favor of the wife but did not award attorney's fees and the wife appealed the denial of such fees.

The Idaho Court of Appeals observed that under Idaho law an insured is entitled to attorney's fees only if he or she provides proof of loss, the insurance company fails to pay the amount due under the policy within thirty days and the insured "thereafter" has to file a lawsuit to recover under the policy. If the "Statement of Disappearance" in this case constituted a proof of loss under Idaho law, the woman would be entitled to attorney's fees. The law did not set out standards for determining what constitutes a "proof of loss," but the following rules applied to the legal determination of death: "A person who is absent for a continuous period of five (5) years, during which he has not been heard from, and whose absence is not satisfactorily explained after diligent search or inquiry is presumed to be dead." The court held that since these criteria were established in the wife's "Statement of Disappearance," it sufficed as a proof of loss. Because the insurer did not pay the death benefit within thirty days after the statement was submitted and since the wife had to file a lawsuit to receive the benefit, the court declared that the wife was entitled to attorney's fees. *In re Death of Cole*, 741 P.2d 734 (Idaho App.1987).

In a case arising in Arkansas, a U.S. district court held that an insurer could not collect life insurance proceeds paid to the beneficiaries under two policies, even after it was discovered that the insured was actually alive. Several years prior to the lawsuit, the insured became the president of a corporation formed for the purpose of storing grain harvested by local farmers. Due to several years of bad management, the corporation became unable to pay its debts. The farmers who had stored grain and suffered losses due to the corporation's inability to meet its obligations brought lawsuits against the president of the corporation. Subsequently, the president, who had formerly been a well respected individual in the community, disappeared. His abandoned truck was found parked on a bridge spanning a river, but his body was not found. The nature of the situation and the bleakness of the president's future in the community left little doubt that he had committed suicide, despite the fact that no body was found.

After five years, there being no evidence that the president was alive, the insurer entered into settlement agreements with his wife and the corporation, each of whom had been issued insurance policies on the president's life. The insurer paid the wife $90,000 and the corporation $380,000. Both the wife and the corporation agreed to forego any further claims against the insurer and agreed that if the president's death was found to be accidental, the insurer would not be obligated to pay the double indemnity amount.

Approximately one year later it was discovered that the president was alive and had established a new identity in Florida. He had remarried without divorcing his first wife, had falsified government documents to conceal his true identity, and had otherwise designed every relevant phase of his life to deceive everyone, including his insurers. The life insurer asserted that due to the insured's blatant fraud, the beneficiaries under the life insurance policies should be required to return the insurance proceeds they received. The district court disagreed saying that the insurer, believing the insured dead, had entered into a legally binding "business agreement" with the insureds. The insurer made a business decision to settle the case. In fact, the insurer had settled the wife's claim for less than the face value of the policy. The court found, therefore, that if anyone was liable to the insurer it was the president. *Southern Farm Bureau Life Ins. Co. v. Burney,* 590 F.Supp. 1016 (E.D.Ark.1984).

A woman in Tennessee asked a trial court to declare her husband legally dead so as to enable her to collect under his life insurance policy. The court held in favor of the insurer and the husband's wife appealed. The Tennessee Court of Appeals had to decide whether a 1941 statute displaced the common-law rule that a disappearance of seven years created a presumption of death. The statute provided that death could not be presumed from mere absence. It allowed proof that the insured was exposed to peril of death but treated a seven-year absence as only one factor in proving the husband's alleged death. The insurer presented evidence that the husband, who was known in Tennessee as a deeply religious and devoted family man, left Tennessee with a woman with whom he had been having an extramarital affair. The insurer reasoned that it was probable that the husband was still living elsewhere with a new identity. The court agreed with the insurer, holding that the wife had not proven that her husband had been exposed to a peril of death. Additionally, the wife had made no effort to locate him until at least six years after he had disappeared, and she never contacted the police. The trial court's holding was affirmed. *Armstrong v. Pilot Life Ins. Co.,* 656 S.W.2d 18 (Tenn.App.1983).

VII. EXCLUSIONS FROM COVERAGE

As with other kinds of insurance, life and health insurance policy exclusions are usually subjected to rigorous judicial scrutiny in an effort to provide coverage wherever possible. In other words, exclusions from coverage are "strictly construed" by the courts against insurers and ambiguous language in exclusionary clauses will nearly always result in coverage being awarded.

A. Life Insurance

The cases which follow deal with exclusionary clauses in life insurance contracts.

1. Coverage Precluded

An Alabama man died after jumping from the tenth floor of a New Mexico hotel. He had entered into a disability insurance contract which provided for payment of $60,000 upon his accidental death. The policy did not cover any loss from suicide, however, while sane or insane. His wife's claim was denied and she brought an action in a federal trial court alleging that Alabama law prohibited this type of exclusion in a life insurance policy. The defendant moved for summary judgment. The Insurance Code of Alabama, § 27-15-24, limits the exclusion of benefits for suicide to two years from the date the policy was entered into. However, § 27-15-24(c) states that this section shall not apply to disability insurance which includes insurance against death by accident. The court determined that the accidental death policy was a type of disability insurance specifically excepted from the requirements of Alabama law. The exclusion provision of the policy was therefore applicable and barred recovery due to the undisputed act of suicide. The court granted the summary judgment motion. *Duncan v. American Home Assur. Co., Inc.*, 747 F.Supp. 1418 (M.D.Ala.1990).

An Oregon insured was afflicted with multiple myeloma. He developed pulmonary problems and was being treated in a hospital. His doctors decided to perform a bronchoscopy in order to detect any infection. The insured died when the bronchoscopy caused cardiopulmonary arrest. The insured's life insurer refused to pay the policy's beneficiary. It argued that the insured's death fell within the exclusion in the policy for losses resulting from sickness, disease or medical treatment. It also argued that previous judicial authority held that the word "treatment" in an insurance contract included diagnostic procedures. The beneficiary then sued the insurer in an Oregon circuit court which dismissed the beneficiary's claim for benefits. The beneficiary then appealed to the Court of Appeals of Oregon.

On appeal, the beneficiary contended that the word "treatment" was ambiguous and therefore required a trial to determine whether the word was intended to apply to diagnostic procedures. The court agreed with the insurer and upheld the lower court's decision. It stated that "treatment" as used in the policy must be given a reasonable scope. Treatment should not merely include the actual operation in a surgical case, but also the preliminary examination, including exploratory examinations. It pointed out that in this case the diagnostic procedure was performed as part of an ongoing intensive treatment program. Therefore, the diagnostic procedure performed on the insured was encompassed in the word "treatment" and excluded from the policy. *Beveridge v. Hartford Acc. and Indem. Co.*, 770 P.2d 943 (Or.App.1989).

A New York insured sought benefits under her husband's life insurance policy when he died in a white-water rafting accident. The policy provided insurance against loss from an accident, but excluded coverage for death caused by disease or sickness. The insurer denied the benefits, contending that the husband had been suffering from arteriosclerotic heart disease before the accident. It argued that his

Sec. VII EXCLUSIONS FROM COVERAGE 235

death did not result solely and independently from the accident. The insurer sought a declaratory judgment in a federal district court that it was not liable to the insured. The district court held that the insured had the burden of proving that her husband's death was due to an accident and not the result of a pre-existing condition. The court said that there are four factors that determine whether justice is served by placing the burden on the insured: 1) whether the plaintiff objects to assuming the burden of proof; 2) which party asserts the affirmative issue; 3) which party will lose in the absence of any evidence on the issue; and 4) what sort of relief is sought. The court held that because the insured was asserting affirmatively that the life insurance policy covered her claim, she had the burden of proving that her husband died from the accident. The mere fact that the insurer had instituted the declaratory judgment action did not mean it should bear the burden of disproving the insured's right to the policy benefits. The burden of proof was placed on the insured. *Barker v. Goldberg*, 705 F.Supp. 102 (E.D.N.Y.1989).

A Missouri man insured under a life insurance policy took part in the armed robbery of a shoe store. During the robbery, he and the other robbers were photographed by a security camera. They fled to a residence where the insured argued with another robber over the money they were dividing up. The insured started pushing the other robber and the other robber shot him to death. The life insurance policy excluded coverage if death occurred while an insured was committing a crime. When the insurer refused to pay the policy's beneficiary, the beneficiary filed a lawsuit seeking the policy's death benefit. A state circuit court ruled for the insurer, and the beneficiary appealed. The Missouri Court of Appeals considered the beneficiary's argument that evidence of the robbery including photographs taken by the security camera should not have been admitted into the trial since the robbery was not related to the insured's death. The court noted that if not for the robbery the two robbers would not have been dividing stolen money and the argument which resulted in the insured's death would never have happened. The admission of the security camera photographs was proper because they identified the insured as a participant in the robbery which ultimately led to his death. The court of appeals sustained the circuit court's ruling that death benefits were not payable. *Richardson v. Colonial Life & Accident Ins. Co.*, 723 S.W.2d 912 (Mo.App.1987).

An insurer issued two $100,000 policies on an insured's life. Each policy contained a clause providing: "Suicide, whether sane or insane, will not be a risk assumed during the first two policy years. In such a case we will refund the premiums paid." Less than two years after the policies were issued, the insured committed suicide. The beneficiaries filed claims seeking each policy's $100,000 benefit. The insurer refused payment, citing the suicide exclusion. The beneficiaries sued, but the trial court granted summary judgment to the insurer, holding that the suicide exclusion was conspicuous, bold, clear, and unambiguous. The beneficiaries appealed. On appeal, the beneficiaries argued that the exclusion was unclear because the words "risk assumed" are a term of art in the insurance industry. They also argued that the exclusion was unclear in not specifying whether risks were assumed by the insured or by the insurer. Finally, they argued that the insurer owed the insured an affirmative duty to point out the suicide exclusion and explain its limiting effect on coverage. The Court of Appeal, Fourth District, disagreed. It held that none of the words in the exclusion were beyond the working vocabulary of lay persons. It also clearly identified the insurer as the party not assuming risk of loss for such suicides.

Further, the insurer had no duty to point out and explain the suicide provision. Even though the insured asked what effect his treatment for depression might have on his application, this did not give rise to an affirmative duty. In addition, there was no evidence suggesting that the insurer knew the insured had entered the transaction under a mistaken belief that the policies would cover suicide-related death. The court affirmed the summary judgment. *Malcom v. Farmers New World Life Ins. Co.*, 5 Cal.Rptr.2d 584 (Cal.App.4th Dist.1992).

A Kansas woman was the owner and beneficiary of a $50,000 life insurance policy covering her husband. The policy contained a two-year suicide exclusion clause. Ten years after the policy was in effect, the husband and wife were given the opportunity to convert the policy into another type (e.g., term insurance) without a new contestablity period. They sought a $100,000 policy to replace their old policy. The new policy also had a two-year suicide exclusion clause. The husband then committed suicide. When the wife sought payment of $100,000, the insurer contended that only $50,000 was not subject to the exclusion. In the lawsuit which followed, the trial court ruled for the insurer. The beneficiary appealed. On appeal to the Court of Appeals of Kansas, the court noted that the conversion allowed by the insurer was only for policies of an equal or lesser amount. Here, the new policy was for twice the amount of the old policy. Since the risk of liability was increased by $50,000 of coverage, and since the insurer had clearly allowed only conversions of equal or lesser amount to be incontestable, the new policy was subject to the exclusion to the extent its value exceeded the old policy's value. Accordingly, the insurer did not have to pay the beneficiary the additional $50,000 benefit. The lower court's ruling was affirmed. *Sonderegger v. United Investors Life Ins. Co.*, 829 P.2d 605 (Kan.App.1992).

A fifty-five-year-old man fell down a set of stairs and sustained a laceration on his forehead. The man died eight days later and an autopsy disclosed that the cause of death was advanced nutritional cirrhosis of the liver caused by the man's alcohol consumption. The man's estate sued his three life insurers after each insurer disclaimed coverage. Each policy had an exclusionary clause which provided that payment would not occur if death resulted from a disease or illness of any kind. The U.S. Court of Appeals, Sixth Circuit, noted that the testimony of the estate's own witnesses confirmed that the man's death was caused by his cirrhosis of the liver. The three insurers did not have to provide life insurance coverage to the man's estate. *Ann Arbor Trust Co. v. Canada Life Assur. Co.*, 810 F.2d 591 (6th Cir.1987).

A New Mexico man executed a life insurance policy in 1983, insuring his life for $500,000 and naming his wife as owner of the policy and beneficiary. The policy contained a standard suicide clause which stated that "[i]f the insured commits suicide, while sane or insane, within two years from the policy date, the liability of the company shall be limited to the amount of premiums paid." The man shot himself through the head less than one year later. His widow filed suit against the insurance company for the face value of the policy. A state district court ruled in favor of the insurance company, and the widow appealed. The widow argued before the Supreme Court of New Mexico that her husband's action was not a "suicide" because he never formed the deliberate intent to kill himself. She presented evidence that on the night of his death he set out his things in preparation to get up the next morning. She also alleged that he was taking medication which rendered him unable to clearly realize the moral and physical consequences of his act.

The supreme court, finding no definition of "suicide" in the insurance policy or in applicable statutes, adopted the dictionary definition: "the deliberate termination of one's existence." The court noted that many past cases held that self destruction while insane was not "suicide." These cases found that an insane person could not "form a conscious intention to kill himself and do so realizing its moral and physical consequences." Insurance companies were prompted by these cases to include the phrase "sane or insane" in the suicide exclusion clauses of their policies. Citing decisions of other jurisdictions, the court found that "the applicability of a 'suicide, sane or insane' clause is not dependent on the insured's clear realization of the physical nature and consequences of his act." The suicide exclusion clause was thus found to apply to the husband's action whether or not he realized what he was doing. The widow could recover only the value of premiums paid. *Galloway v. Guar. Income Life Ins. Co.*, 725 P.2d 827 (N.M.1986).

A Florida man, employed by a construction company as a project superintendent, was insured under a group life insurance policy issued to his employer. The policy was governed by the Employee Retirement Income Security Act of 1974. It provided $35,000 in life insurance benefits and $35,000 in accidental death benefits. However, it excluded the latter where a contributing cause was flying or other aeronautic activities, "except as a passenger on a commercial aircraft." The employee was then killed in an airplane accident when a plane owned by the owner of the construction company crashed. His widow sought both benefits under the policy, but the insurer refused to pay the accidental death benefits. It contended that the plane was not a commercial aircraft. A lawsuit was filed and the case came before the U.S. District Court for the Middle District of Florida. The district court found that the term "commercial aircraft" was not ambiguous, and that the policy excluded coverage for the accidental death benefits here. The plane was not used to transport passengers or property for hire, and was not registered with the FAA as a common carrier. The court granted summary judgment to the insurer. *Estate of Miller v. Principle Mutual Life Ins. Co.,* 791 F.Supp. 858 (M.D.Fla.1992).

On August 20, 1983, an Illinois man and his adult son, both licensed pilots, were killed when their biplane plunged into Lake Michigan. The man's widow possessed an insurance policy on the son's life in the amount of $50,000. A rider was payable in case the son died "as a result of bodily injury effected directly ... through external, violent and accidental means." An exclusion, however, stated that "death caused by ... travel or flight in any aircraft while the Insured is a pilot or member of the crew of such aircraft" would preclude recovery under the accidental death rider.

The insurer paid the widow the basic $50,000 benefit for her son's death but refused to pay the accidental death benefit, citing the pilot or crewmember exclusion. The widow then sued the insurer, claiming that it could not prove that her son had not merely been sitting passively in the biplane while his father piloted it. A federal district court ruled in favor of the insurer, holding that the deceased son had been a crewmember at the time of his death. The biplane had two seats, each of which had a readily operable set of pilot's controls, but the rear seat had better visibility and held the ignition switch. The son had occupied this seat at the time of the crash. Furthermore, witnesses stated that the crash had resulted from an attempted aerobatic stunt; the son was an expert aerobatic flyer while his father detested such maneuvers.

While recognizing the high probability that the son had been piloting the craft, the court stated that even if the father had been at the controls, the son had been a crewmember under the accidental death rider's exclusion. The son owned the biplane, he had been active on the radio immediately prior to the crash, and he had determined the day's flight plans. The critical inquiry was whether the son exercised the duties of pilot or crewmember at some point in the flight. It was irrelevant whether he had actually been at the controls at the time of the crash. The court held that because at several times during the flight it was "virtually inescapable" that the son had functioned as a crewmember or pilot, the accidental death rider's exclusion prevented the widow from recovering more than basic death benefits. *Keyser v. Connecticut General Life*, 617 F.Supp. 1406 (N.D.Ill.1985).

In Oregon a beneficiary of a life insurance policy sought the policy's accidental death benefits after her husband drowned when his hang glider landed in the ocean. The insurer refused to pay accidental death benefits, stating that the policy specifically excluded any death that was contributed to, or caused by, travel in any aircraft if the insured acted in any capacity other than as a passenger. In her suit against the insurer, the beneficiary argued that a definition of "aircraft" in the Oregon Revised Statutes specifically excluded hang gliders. The Oregon Court of Appeals stated that the statute cited by the beneficiary existed solely to regulate aeronautics in the state and did not concern insurance or the general usage of the term "aircraft." The test applied by the court in interpreting the policy exclusion was what a reasonable person in the position of the insured would have understood the words of the exclusion to mean. It stated that a reasonable reading of the exclusion supported the conclusion that the policy was intended to exclude accidental death benefits from death resulting from the operation of an aircraft, such as a hang glider, when the insured was acting in any capacity other than as a passenger. The Oregon Supreme Court upheld this decision ruling that the term "aircraft" should be given its ordinary dictionary meaning. Judgment was entered for the insurer. *Totten v. New York Life Ins. Co.*, 696 P.2d 1082 (Ore.1984).

A man was involved in an automobile accident which left him permanently disfigured and suffering from headaches and bouts of depression. The man had been a recovering alcoholic, but began to drink again and three months after the accident shot and killed himself while drunk. His wife claimed that the auto accident had effectively caused his death, and made claims against his insurer. The insurer contended that the death was suicide, and denied benefits. The widow successfully brought suit in a federal court, and the insurer appealed to the U.S. Court of Appeals, Ninth Circuit. The widow relied on an earlier case which allowed benefits for self-inflicted death following a construction accident. That case involved a man who had suffered both organic and psychological brain damage which was ruled to have led to an uncontrollable impulse which resulted in death. Another case, decided in 1894, also allowed benefits for self-inflicted death. In that case, a physician suffered an accident which left him susceptible to convulsions, and he later cut his throat with a scalpel. The court compared the injuries from both cases to the case at bar, and held that the car accident did not lead to the man's death. Injury to appearance, as opposed to brain damage, does not lead to an uncontrollable impulse for self-destruction. The effects of alcohol had no bearing on the outcome. The decision of the district court was reversed. *Meusy v. Montgomery Ward Life Ins. Co.*, 943 F.2d 1097 (9th Cir.1991).

In North Carolina the beneficiary under a life insurance policy sued an insurer to recover the proceeds of the policy after the insured died. The insurer refused to pay the proceeds on the ground that there was substantial evidence that the beneficiary murdered the insured to recover under the policy. The evidence suggested, among other things, that the insured had been killed at the beneficiary's house and that his body had been removed in her car. Despite the evidence, the beneficiary was never charged with a criminal action in connection with the killing. She contended that the absence of a criminal conviction barred the insurer from using the "slayer" defense to her action for the insurance proceeds. The North Carolina Court of Appeals affirmed a trial court ruling in the insurer's favor, finding that although the beneficiary did not fit the statutory definition of "slayer" because she had not been convicted of a killing, she nonetheless was barred from receiving the proceeds. It was persuaded by the transcript of the criminal proceedings that the beneficiary in all likelihood killed the insured. The court of appeals held in favor of the insurer. *Jones v. All American Life Ins. Co.*, 316 S.E.2d 122 (N.C.App.1984).

2. Coverage Allowed

A Missouri resident purchased a car in Kansas. He received credit life insurance available through the car dealer. The man subsequently died of a self-inflicted gunshot wound. The insurer tendered only the premiums which were paid contending that a policy exclusion was applicable. The policy provided that if "an insured or spouse dies by self-destruction within one year from the effective date of coverage, whether sane or insane, the death benefits payable shall be limited to the amount of premium paid." The man's estate brought a lawsuit asserting that Missouri law was applicable and the suicide exclusion was disallowed as a policy defense. The trial court granted summary judgment in favor of the insurer determining that Kansas law governed as the place of making the contract. The man's estate appealed to the Court of Appeals of Kansas. The court of appeals determined that the insured in the credit life policy referred to the buyer rather than the dealer. Because the buyer resided in Missouri, Missouri law governed the construction of the policy. Therefore, the Missouri statute barring suicide as a defense to nonpayment of life benefits applied and the insurer was required to pay benefits following the buyer's suicide. Accordingly, the court determined that the policy's suicide exclusion was invalid. *Frasher v. Life Investors Ins. Co.*, 796 P.2d 1069 (Kan.App.1990).

A Texas insured died after consuming a large amount of alcohol. He had a life insurance policy which included a $100,000 accidental death rider. However, the accidental death benefit would not be paid if the death was caused, directly or indirectly, by the use of any drug. The insurer refused to pay the additional accidental death benefits, claiming the death was not an accident under the policy. The insured's beneficiary sued the insurer for the disputed benefits. The insurer moved for summary judgment and the federal district court granted it. The court first stated that since the consequences of excess alcohol consumption are well known, the death was not an accident. Secondly, the court found that alcohol is considered to be a drug and the policy excluded coverage for deaths caused by drugs. The beneficiary appealed to the U.S. Court of Appeals, Fifth Circuit.

The appeals court first examined the lower court's determination that the insured's death was not an accident. Under Texas law, a death is accidental if, from the viewpoint of the insured, the injuries are not the "natural and probable consequence of the action." The court rejected the insurer's argument that, since it is common knowledge that drinking too much alcohol may cause death, the insured should have reasonably anticipated that his actions would result in death. The court noted that engaging in inherently dangerous activities does not automatically rule out accident as a cause of death, if the person reasonably believed that death would not be a result of those activities. Thus, the appeals court held that the insured's death was accidental. The court next examined the question of whether alcohol is a drug for purposes of the exclusion clause in the insured's policy. Because the term "drug" was not defined in the policy, the court was obligated to construe the term in a light most favorable to the insured. Since in common usage alcohol is not considered a drug, the court held that the drug exclusion did not apply to alcohol. *Chen v. Metropolitan Ins. and Annuity Co.*, 907 F.2d 566 (5th Cir.1990).

A Kentucky woman held a cancer policy. She died after incurring medical expenses in excess of $18,000. The administrator of her estate sued in a Kentucky trial court for medical expenses following the refusal of the insurer to pay those expenses voluntarily. The insurer claimed that a provision in the policy stating that cancer must be positively diagnosed by a bioptic examination performed by a registered pathologist precluded recovery because no biopsy was ever made. The administrator claimed that the decedent would probably have died from such a procedure. This claim was supported by medical testimony by the decedent's physicians. A lower court held in favor of the insurer. The administrator then appealed to the Court of Appeals of Kentucky.

The court of appeals stated that it was certainly reasonable for the insured to believe that the policy would insure her and her family against the costs of treating cancer. However, it noted that under the language of the policy, even an autopsy confirming cancer as the cause of death would not allow her recovery of benefits. To require a biopsy to be performed as proof of cancer where the patient's life would be endangered would be ludicrous. The court held that the insured was excused from furnishing the biopsy pathology report required by the policy because of the risk involved to the patient. The appellate court reversed the trial court's decision. *Moore v. Commonwealth Life Ins. Co.*, 759 S.W.2d 598 (Ky.App.1988).

A Wisconsin doctor was covered by a life insurance policy which provided a life insurance benefit of $50,000 and an additional accidental death benefit of $50,000. The doctor engaged in an autoerotic sexual act in the basement bathroom shower of his home. Before engaging in this act, he placed a rope around his neck to reduce the supply of oxygen to his brain in order to heighten the sexual pleasure during masturbation. As a result of this conduct the doctor died from strangulation. Investigating authorities initially suspected suicide, but after further examination they concluded that the death was accidental. The doctor's insurer paid the $50,000 life insurance benefit to the doctor's wife, but declined payment of the additional accidental death benefit on the ground that the doctor's death was not accidental because he voluntarily exposed himself to a known and unnecessary risk of death. A Wisconsin circuit court ruled that the doctor's death was accidental and the insurer appealed. On appeal the insurer argued that the autoerotic asphyxiation in this case would be similar to a case where death results because an insured engaged in Russian roulette with a loaded weapon. Courts in other jurisdictions have reasoned that death resulting from such "reckless abandon and exposure to a known and obvious danger cannot be said to have been accidental." The Wisconsin Court of Appeals rejected this reasoning, declaring instead that "the intentional or unnecessary exposure to risks, as well as the negligent creation of risks to one's own safety, does not prevent the result from being accidental." The court ruled that "there is no evidence that [the doctor's] death was highly probable, expected, or a natural result" of the autoerotic act. Because no circumstances surrounding the incident indicated that the doctor intended to commit suicide, his death was an accident and the insurer was liable for the accidental death benefit. *Kennedy v. Washington Nat'l Ins. Co.*, 401 N.W.2d 842 (Wis.App.1987).

A man was fatally shot in the head while attempting to make a deal for some drugs. He was covered by two insurance policies, each of which provided that if he died by accident, the insurers would pay an additional $10,000 to the beneficiary. Each policy excluded the accidental death benefits if death resulted from "participating in a riot or committing an assault or felony." The insurers refused to pay the accidental death benefits, claiming the man was participating in a felony when he was killed. A trial court held in favor of the insurer and the policies' beneficiary appealed.

The Tennessee Court of Appeals noted that under state law it is a felony "for two or more persons to conspire to manufacture, deliver, [or] sell" drugs. Simple possession of drugs, however, is a misdemeanor. The court held that the insured was engaged in a conspiracy to commit a crime but that the crime was not a felony. His intent was to help his friend purchase drugs for his friend's personal use. "One purchasing for his own use is not in a conspiracy to distribute a controlled substance with the seller." The court determined that because the man was not committing a felony at the time of his death, his beneficiary was eligible for the accidental death benefits of his policies. The decision of the trial court was reversed. *McCandless v. Equitable Life Ins. Co.*, 721 S.W.2d 809 (Tenn.App.1986).

In an Illinois case, a man's life insurance policy provided that half its death benefit would be paid to his daughter and half to his son. After the man was killed by his son, the son was found not guilty of murder by reason of insanity. The insurer sought a judicial ruling on whether the son could collect his half of the policy's proceeds. A U.S. district court ruled that "'the long-established policy that one may not profit by his intentionally committed wrongful act' has no application where the killer did not have felonious intent — as he could not if he were insane." Because the son had already been declared not guilty by reason of insanity, and because no evidence was presented that the son was actually sane at the time of the killing, the court awarded him his share of the life insurance policy's proceeds. *Lincoln Nat'l Life Ins. Co. v. Johnson*, 669 F.Supp. 201 (N.D.Ill.1987).

The Kentucky Supreme Court ruled that the death of a motorcyclist, which occurred as a result of speeding while having a blood alcohol content of .20 percent, was "accidental" within the meaning of a double indemnity life insurance provision. General insurance contract principles should be applied to determine whether a death is accidental, held the court. The argument that the death was not accidental because a reasonable person should have foreseen a high probability of death when riding a motorcycle at excessive speeds while intoxicated, was rejected by the court. Tort law principles were held to be inapplicable to the construction of an insurance contract insofar as determining the meaning of the term "accidental death." *Fryman v. Pilot Life Ins. Co.*, 704 S.W.2d 205 (Ky.1986).

A Texas woman, beneficiary of an accidental death policy on her father's life, sued an insurer for the benefits under the policy. Her father had been shot by a neighbor whom he had allegedly beaten and raped a week earlier. The insurer declined to pay, saying the death was not accidental but should have been anticipated. The beneficiary denied that the rape occurred but said even if it had, the father could not have anticipated being shot and killed. The U.S. Court of Appeals, Fifth Circuit, affirmed a lower court ruling after examining two alleged errors in that ruling. One was that the lower court improperly allowed into evidence testimony regarding the character of the insured father. The issue of character was unquestionably part of the case. The second alleged error was that a motion by the insurer for a decision in its favor had been improperly denied. In rejecting this allegation, the court said that there was sufficient testimony given regarding the alleged rape to leave doubt in the minds of the jurors as to whether it actually occurred. This testimony included inconsistencies in the alleged victim's story as well as medical evidence which left the rape story inconclusive. This was sufficient to allow reasonable jurors to conclude that the rape never occurred and that the father would have had no reason to anticipate his death. Accidental death benefits were allowed. *Crumpton v. Confederation Life Ins. Co.*, 672 F.2d 1248 (5th Cir.1982).

A South Carolina woman shot and killed her husband because he physically and mentally abused her and their two children. Subsequently, the children sued their mother claiming she was not entitled to their deceased father's life insurance policy proceeds. A district court granted the mother summary judgment. The children appealed, arguing that their mother did not kill in self-defense; she intentionally placed herself in a position to continue receiving the physical abuse from their father so she could have the opportunity to kill him and claim justification. The South Carolina Court of Appeals disagreed, citing how the facts undisputedly established self-defense. The summary judgment was affirmed. *Metropolitan Life Ins. Co. v. Fogle*, 419 S.E.2d 825 (S.C.App.1992).

In an Indiana case, a son who had shot and killed his parents was acquitted in a criminal prosecution by reason of insanity. His sisters filed a petition in an Indiana trial court to prevent him from inheriting his intestate share of his parents' estate and to prevent him from receiving a share in the proceeds of their mother's life insurance policy. A lower court ruled that the son must serve as a constructive trustee of his intestate share of the estate and precluded him from receiving the life insurance proceeds. The son appealed to the Indiana Court of Appeals, which reversed the trial court ruling. The court of appeals held that because the son lacked any wrongful intent in the killing of his parents he could not be subjected to punishment by being deprived of his intestate share. Further, he had been incorrectly precluded from receiving the life insurance proceeds because, legally speaking, he had committed no wrong. *Turner v. Estate of Turner*, 454 N.E.2d 1247 (Ind.App.1st Dist.1983).

B. Health and Medical Insurance

The cases which follow deal with exclusionary clauses in health and medical insurance contracts.

1. Coverage Precluded

A Colorado insured under a group health plan received major medical-surgical and hospital benefits coverage according to the terms of his policy. He contacted his insurer prior to undergoing heart transplant surgery and was informed that his policy did not cover the procedure. The policy stated that only corneal, kidney and bone marrow transplants would be covered. The insured went ahead with the operation, and when coverage was denied, he sued his insurer for bad faith and breach of contract. The trial court ruled for the insurer, and the court of appeals affirmed. The insured appealed to the Supreme Court of Colorado. On appeal, the court noted that the policy clearly set forth the types of transplant procedures which were covered, and that heart transplant procedures were not listed in the contract. The insured's argument that a specific exclusion was necessary for the denial of heart transplants was rejected. Only if there were an ambiguity about the types of transplants covered by the policy would a specific exclusion be necessary. The court thus affirmed the lower courts' decisions and denied coverage to the insured. *Wota v. Blue Cross and Blue Shield of Colorado*, 831 P.2d 1307 (Colo.1992).

A Washington insured suffered a ruptured cerebral aneurysm caused by deliberate, nonmedical cocaine inhalation. The insured's health insurance policy covered bodily injury caused by accident but excluded loss due to sickness, disease, or disorders. The insured sued the insurer to recover benefits for the ruptured aneurysm. A Washington trial court found that the ruptured aneurysm was not a bodily injury caused by an accident, and therefore was not covered. The court granted the insurer's summary judgment motion. The insured then appealed to the Court of Appeals of Washington. The appeals court noted that an accident is never present when a deliberate act is performed unless an additional unexpected, independent and unforeseen event occurs which produces injury or death. The court found that the insured's injury was the natural consequence of a deliberate act. Increased blood pressure is a primary cause of aneurysm rupture and medical research indicates that cocaine increases a user's blood pressure twenty to forty percent. The court noted that the insured's injury was not the product of an unusual intervening event. The court found that the rupture of the insured's aneurysm was the natural consequence of cocaine inhalation. Because the insured produced no evidence of an intervening event, the trial court's summary judgment motion was affirmed. *Lloyd v. First Farwest Life Ins. Co.*, 773 P.2d 426 (Wash.App.1989).

A Minnesota insured was injured while working at his place of business. The insured was not covered by workers' compensation. However, he was covered under his wife's healthcare plan through her employer. The insured submitted medical claims to the insurer, which it paid. The insurer then stopped making payments, relying on an exclusion in the wife's employee handbook, which described medical expenses not covered as those necessary because of an injury or disease which occurred during employment for wages or profit at or outside of the company, or covered by the workers' compensation act. The insured sued the insurer in a Minnesota trial court. The trial court held for the insurer, and the Minnesota Court of Appeals affirmed. The insured then appealed to the Supreme Court of Minnesota. The supreme court held that the plan's exclusion for injuries incurred while employed for wages or profit was not ambiguous and applied to the insured's injuries. The court noted that the insured was an employee of his own corporation and was injured during the course of his business. His injuries fell within the policy exclusion. The court also found that the insured had presented no facts which would have justified a reasonable expectation of coverage under the policy. The supreme court ruled that the employer had no obligation to pay benefits to the insured. *Hubred v. Control Data Corp.*, 442 N.W.2d 308 (Minn.1989).

Pursuant to a divorce decree a Georgia man purchased medical insurance for his child. Although he was not aware of it, his ex-wife had also obtained a policy for the child. On his application for coverage he stated that the child was not covered by any other policy. A few months after the policy was purchased the child suffered a cerebral hemorrhage. The ex-wife's insurer provided coverage. The man's insurer refused to provide coverage because the child was covered under the other insurance policy. The insurer returned the premiums to the man along with a letter explaining that it was canceling the policy because of his misrepresentations. A check was then tendered to the man for all premiums. The man sued the insurer in a Georgia federal district court for failing to provide coverage. The district court held for the man and the insurer appealed to the U.S. Court of Appeals, Eleventh Circuit. On appeal, the insurer argued that by depositing the refund check for the premiums, the man discharged his claim. The insured contended that he was never informed that by cashing the refund check he would release the insurer from its liability under the policy. The court found that the letter that had accompanied the check sufficiently notified the man that the insurer was disputing the claim. The insurer had clearly expressed its intent to refund the premiums rather than honor the contract and it had stated that it would not have issued the policy had it known of the double coverage. The district court's judgment was reversed. The insurer was not required to provide coverage. *Hall v. Time Ins. Co.*, 854 F.2d 440 (11th Cir.1988).

A South Dakota college student sought coverage from his college's health insurer for medical expenses associated with his daughter's premature birth. The insurer denied coverage and the student sued the insurer in a U.S. district court. The insurer was granted a summary judgment on the basis of an exclusion in the policy. The policy did not cover claims for the first thirty days after birth. The student appealed to the U.S. Court of Appeals, Eighth Circuit. The student argued that South Dakota law included newborn children under family coverage. He then argued that the students at his college were a group. Therefore, the policy should be construed as a "group health policy," not a "blanket health policy." The insurer argued that although the student was a member of a group, the college only offered its students the "blanket health policy." The law upon which the student relied only applied to "group health policies." Therefore, it should be able to limit coverage. The court of appeals upheld the district court decision. It stated that the South Dakota legislature made specific differentiations between the two types of policies. "Group health" policies were required by law to provide infant coverage from the moment of birth while "blanket health" policies were not. Based on the language of the law, it was reasonable for the district court to grant the summary judgment. *Cullum v. Mut. of Omaha Ins. Co.*, 840 F.2d 619 (8th Cir.1988).

An insured motorcyclist became paralyzed from the waist down after an accident. His policy provided benefits for loss of life, hands, feet, or sight. It covered loss to a hand or foot if it was "severed" at or above the wrist or ankle joint. The insured sought coverage for the lost use of his feet because his spinal cord was severed. The insurer denied coverage claiming that the policy only covered the actual amputation of the feet. The insured sued the insurer but a federal court determined that there was no coverage. The insured appealed to the U.S. Court of Appeals, Ninth Circuit. In holding for the insurer the court of appeals determined that the paraplegia was not covered by the policy because severance of the spinal cord did not constitute amputation of the feet. Although this was a question of first impression for California, holdings in most other states went against coverage in these types of cases. The court of appeals observed that California state courts would likely condition coverage on actual amputation of the feet rather than construe "loss" to encompass severance of the spinal cord. The policy explicitly required "severance" and the court would not hold the insurer liable for a risk which it had not assumed. *Horvatten v. Allstate Life Ins. Co.*, 848 F.2d 1012 (9th Cir.1988).

An insurer issued two insurance policies containing disability income benefits to an insured. These policies contained identical provisions as follows: "REHABILITATION. If the insured is receiving monthly benefits for total disability, the company, ... will consider a rehabilitation program for the insured. The extent of the company's participation in the program shall be determined by mutual agreement. ..." The insured became disabled within the meaning of the policies, suffering from a mixed personality disorder with prominent narcissistic features. The insurer paid the insured the maximum disability benefits allowable under the two policies. The insured twice asked the insurer to fund his enrollment in a Ph.D. program in a Louisiana university. When the insurer refused the insured sued. A U.S. district court held for the insurer and the insured appealed.

The insured argued before the U.S. Court of Appeals, Fifth Circuit, that the use of the words "shall" and "will" in the rehabilitation clause indicated an obligation on the part of the insurer to do more than merely consider a rehabilitation proposal by the insured; actual implementation of such a proposal was required. The court of appeals upheld the district court decision. Although "shall" and "will" were words of mandate, the question was not whether they mandated something, but what they mandated. The word "will" only mandated that the company *consider* a rehabilitation program for the insured. Similarly, the word "shall" simply imposed an obligation on the insurer to seek agreement with the insured on the extent of its participation, if and when a rehabilitation program was selected. These obligations did not amount to an obligation to fund a rehabilitation program. *Boudreaux v. Unionmutual Stock Life Ins. Co. of America*, 835 F.2d 121 (5th Cir.1988).

After a Michigan employee was terminated by his employer he sued the employer's disability insurer. He claimed that alleged emotional and work-related back problems entitled him to receive disability benefits. A U.S. district court denied coverage and the U.S. Court of Appeals, Sixth Circuit, affirmed. The court of appeals observed that the insurer's contract with the employer provided for disability benefits only when an employee was "wholly and continuously disabled" from performing "any and every" job duty. Furthermore, the employee had to be under the care of a legally licensed physician. Because the employee was under the care of a psychologist (not a medical doctor) and because two medical doctors failed to find the employee "wholly and continuously disabled" within the meaning of the insurance policy, the employee was not entitled to disability benefits. *Taylor v. General Motors Corp.*, 826 F.2d 452 (6th Cir.1987).

The New York Supreme Court, Appellate Division, was presented with the question of whether a health facility, which specializes almost exclusively in an unorthodox and scientifically unproven treatment of cancer, can be considered a "hospital" with services subject to reimbursement pursuant to a health insurance policy. A lower court had concluded that "Gerson therapy," a nutritional therapy for cancer patients, while not in the medical mainstream, complied with the provisions of the health insurance policy and therefore was covered under the insured's policy. The court also held that the facility providing the therapy was within the policy definition of a hospital. The appellate division reversed the lower court's ruling. It found that the facility at which the insured underwent nutritional therapy did not meet the major medical policy's definition of a hospital. The policy defined hospital as a facility for both medical and surgical care. The institution in question, which primarily treated cancer patients, merely had facilities for bandaging minor wounds, lacked an operating room or facilities for anesthesia and was not equipped to perform surgery; thus it did not meet the policy definition. Further, nutritional therapy for cancer patients was "experimental" for purposes of a policy exclusion for medically unrecognized treatments. *Zuckerberg v. Blue Cross & Blue Shield of Greater New York*, 487 N.Y.S.2d 595 (A.D.2d Dept.1985).

2. Coverage Allowed

A thirty-six-year-old California woman purchased a hospital-surgical policy with a catastrophic medical expense rider from an insurer. The policy allegedly cost her over $400 per year more than it would have cost a man of the same age. Further, the policy apparently excluded coverage for the costs of normal pregnancy and childbirth, but did not exclude coverage for any care, treatment or surgery required solely by men. Although a maternity rider could have been purchased, it would have cost an additional $1,200 per year, according to the insured. She brought suit against her insurer in a California trial court, claiming that the insurer's practices constituted arbitrary discrimination in violation of the Unruh Civil Rights Act. The insurer moved for summary judgment, arguing that the Insurance Code specifically allowed gender-based premiums, and that the Unruh Act did not apply to the life and disability insurance business. The trial court granted summary judgment to the insurer, and the insured appealed to the Court of Appeal, Second District.

The court of appeal stated that the Unruh Act did apply to the insurance business generally; however, the specific provisions of the Insurance Code allowed different treatment based on sex in the issuance, cancellation and pricing of life and disability insurance. This disparate treatment did not extend to terms of the policies, however. The Unruh Act controlled with respect to the types or conditions of coverage available. This meant that the insurer's refusal to provide coverage for the costs of normal pregnancy and childbirth constituted sex discrimination in violation of the Unruh Act. The appellate court reversed the lower court's grant of summary judgment, and held in favor of the insured. *Kirsh v. State Farm Mutual Automobile Ins.Co.*, 284 Cal.Rptr. 260 (Cal.App.2d Dist.1991).

An Arkansas woman was insured under her husband's group policy. She underwent heart bypass surgery and against medical advice discharged herself. The insurer denied coverage based upon the following exclusion in the policy: "no benefits are provided for inpatient services where you terminate such inpatient admission against medical advice." The woman and her husband filed suit to force payment of benefits by the insurer. The case was presented to the jury which determined that the exclusion was ambiguous. The insurer appealed to the Court of Appeals of Arkansas. The appellate court noted an Arkansas Supreme Court decision, *Arkansas Blue Cross & Blue Shield v. Long*, 792 S.W.2d 602 (1990), in which a similar situation arose involving the exact policy language at issue here. The supreme court held that the provision was against public policy. Since this opinion of the Arkansas Supreme Court was handed down after the briefs on appeal were filed in the instant case, the public policy issue had not been raised. The court determined that it could properly raise the issue on its own motion. Therefore, the court found that the policy exclusion would divest the insured of benefits already accrued, without a reasonable basis. Therefore, the appellate court upheld the decision of the trial court granting group health benefits to the insured. *Arkansas Blue Cross & Blue Shield v. Brown*, 800 S.W.2d 724 (Ark.App.1990).

A New York insured's daughter was hospitalized to alleviate her poor physical condition which was the result of anorexia nervosa. The father then sought benefits under his health insurance policy to pay for her hospital stay. The insurer refused, quoting policy provisions which prohibited additional coverage for psychiatric care. The New York Supreme Court, Appellate Division, ordered the insurer to pay the benefits. It recognized that while anorexia nervosa is a psychiatric disorder, the treatment was for malnutrition, a medical problem. Physical condition, and not the reason for the condition, was the crucial determination. *Simons v. Blue Cross and Blue Shield*, 536 N.Y.S.2d 431 (A.D.1st Dept.1989).

A Michigan case involved an injured parachutist and an "aircraft" exclusion. Here an insurer issued a group student accident policy which contained the following policy exclusion: "No benefits are payable under the policy for ... [i]njuries sustained while in or on, or entering or leaving any kind of aircraft, except as a passenger in a duly licensed passenger aircraft provided by a scheduled airline and flown by a pilot duly licensed to operate such aircraft." The injured parachutist, a student at Michigan State University, was an insured under this policy. The student underwent surgery after he broke his leg upon striking the ground after an otherwise successful parachute jump. The insurer denied the plaintiff's claim for medical expenses and contended that the exclusionary clause barred recovery. The Michigan Court of Appeals reversed the lower court's ruling and held that the phrase "while ... leaving any kind of aircraft" did not include exiting an airplane by parachute, thus declaring that the exclusion was inapplicable. In order for the "entering or leaving" clause to exclude coverage, the injury must have taken place contemporaneously with entering or leaving, and it must have been in close proximity to the aircraft. The appeals court explained that in so interpreting the policy, its goal was to prevent the insurer from expanding the meaning of "entering or leaving an aircraft" beyond its ordinary meaning. The court also noted that "entering" was not distinguished in the policy from "leaving." Since entering must be done on the ground, reasonable individuals could believe that leaving must be done on the ground as well. After further ruling that a parachute was not an "aircraft" under the policy, the appeals court remanded the case to the lower court for resolution of the question whether the policy was in effect at the time of the injury. If it was, coverage would be awarded. *Engel v. Credit Life Ins. Co.*, 377 N.W.2d 342 (Mich.App.1985).

A woman suffering from temporomandibular joint syndrome was denied insurance coverage for treatment on the grounds that this treatment was excluded from a health policy she carried which was advertised as a "High Option Performance Plan." She sued her insurer and the California Court of Appeal held in her favor because the language of the exclusion was not plain, clear and conspicuous as required. Further, an exclusion must be in words which are part of the working vocabulary of average laypersons. The court also said that policyholders could reasonably expect coverage because under a policy labeled "High Option Performance Plan," it would be reasonable to expect coverage for any condition which impairs one's health, and temporomandibular joint syndrome is such a condition. *Ponder v. Blue Cross of Southern California*, 193 Cal.Rptr. 632 (App.2d Dist.1983).

An insured fell down a flight of stairs at a local VFW club and suffered extensive permanent injuries. She was transported to a hospital which found that she had a blood-alcohol content of .20%. Her health insurer denied coverage because her policy excluded payment for injuries which "were caused, or contributed to, by intoxication exceeding the legal limits of the state." The insured sued in a state court and was granted summary judgment. The insurer then appealed to the Supreme Court of Nebraska. The disputed term in the contract concerned the legal limits of intoxication for the state. The insurer argued that the court should adopt the state's DWI limit. The court declined; it found that the state had no legal limit for nondriving intoxication. It affirmed the award of medical expenses and attorney's fees to the insured. *Mahoney v. Union Pacific Railroad Employees' Hospital Ass'n*, 471 N.W.2d 438 (Neb. 1991).

The question before the Ohio Supreme Court was whether charges for the crowning of teeth as part of the treatment for a jaw disorder were excluded from coverage under a medical insurance clause which excluded coverage for mouth conditions. The definition of mouth conditions in the exclusion included any treatment of the teeth. The insurer argued that since crowning of the teeth is treatment of the teeth, such costs were not covered. The insured contended that costs of crowning the teeth were covered by the policy because such service constituted treatment of the jaw disorder, a medical condition covered under the policy. The court held that because the exclusionary clause was susceptible of a number of constructions it would be construed narrowly and in favor of extending coverage. Indeed, said the court, nothing mentioned in the exclusionary clause dealt with the treatment of a jaw condition which necessitates treatment to the teeth. The court noted that the crowning of the insured's teeth was not an end in itself and would not have been necessary were it not for the jaw disorder. *Moorman v. Prudential Ins. Co. of America*, 445 N.E.2d 1122 (Ohio 1983).

A couple purchased a group health insurance plan to cover them and their business. They apparently asked the agent about the exclusions, and he showed them the exclusions page. Nothing on the page dealt with intoxicants or narcotics. However, elsewhere in the policy, there was an exclusion for losses sustained by an intoxicated insured. After the policy was in effect, the husband was seriously injured in an automobile accident. When the couple attempted to collect medical benefits under their policy, the insurer denied coverage, contending that the husband had been intoxicated at the time of the accident. A trial resulted in a jury verdict for the insureds for compensatory damages only, and they appealed to the Court of Appeals of

Indiana. On appeal, they asserted that they should have been granted punitive damages also. The court, however, noted that the evidence failed to show more than mere negligence on the part of the insurer's agent; he might simply have forgotten about the intoxication provision when he was asked about exclusions. He could have unknowingly just turned to the exclusions page to review its contents without any intent to misrepresent the policy's scope. The court thus affirmed the trial court's decision. *Plohg v. NN Investors Life Ins. Co.*, 583 N.E.2d 1233 (Ind.App.3rd Dist.1992).

An Indiana boy brought home a brochure from school which offered a student accident insurance policy through the school. The brochure stated that $25,000 was the maximum amount available for each accident. It also detailed the costs that would be covered for medical expenses and contained many specific exclusions and limitations. At the bottom of the brochure, the insurer noted that the master policy was on file at the school, and that the brochure was not a contract. The boy's mother purchased coverage, but never attempted to read the master policy. Subsequently, the boy was involved in an accident which resulted in permanent blindness to his right eye. Injury costs exceeded $10,000, but the insurer stated that the policy limited coverage to $1,000. A lawsuit followed. After summary judgment was granted to the insurer, the mother appealed. Before the Court of Appeals of Indiana, the mother asserted that she had reasonably relied on the brochure she had received. The court agreed, noting that a prominent trend had developed wherein insurers were being held to brochures and other material they handed out for prospective insureds to read. Since the policies are often practically unintelligible and generally never read, it makes sense to enforce the representations made by insurers in their promotional material. The court reversed the trial court's decision. *Palsce v. Guarantee Trust Life Ins. Co.*, 588 N.E.2d 525 (Ind.App.3d Dist.1992).

An Oklahoma insured suffered a heart attack at the age of thirty-two. Three years later, he switched jobs and discussed obtaining health insurance from the insurer which had previously covered him. He bought three policies, two of which excluded medical and hospital expenses resulting from disease or disorder of the heart or coronary artery. The insured then suffered another heart attack. His insurer paid benefits under the policy which had not excluded coverage for heart disorders, but he sued for coverage under the other two policies, because the single policy had not covered all his expenses. He claimed breach of contract, breach of the duty to act fairly and in good faith, and fraud and deceit (for not telling him his heart condition wasn't covered). The court let the fraud and deceit claim go to the jury which found in the insured's favor for $5,500. He appealed to the U.S. Court of Appeals, Tenth Circuit. On appeal, he argued that his two other claims should have gone to the jury. The court, however, agreed with the insurer's assertion that even if all three claims had been submitted to the jury, the insured was only entitled to "one recovery." Since he had been awarded his damages on the third claim, he could not recover more. Further, he was not entitled to an award of punitive damages because, even if the insurer had not told him his heart condition was *not* covered, it had never told him his condition *was* covered. Therefore, punitive damages were unavailable. The court affirmed the jury's decision. *Monroe v. Mutual of Omaha Ins. Co.*, 953 F.2d 1210 (10th Cir.1992).

A Tennessee teenager worked for a truck company which provided him with employee health coverage. He had to stop working for a two-year period, so he could undergo cancer treatment, but then resumed working for the company. Subsequently, the truck company shut down its operation and dissolved its corporate charter, but it still sold parts as a sole proprietorship. Within a month of the company's dissolution, the company's insurer received a disability form from the company which did not contain information about when the employee's disability originated. The insurer then realized that the company had been out of business for months, and that it had paid out approximately $59,000 in disability benefits for the employee after the truck company's policy was terminated. The insurer sought recovery for benefits paid after the policy terminated in the U.S. District Court for the Middle District of Tennessee. The court noted that the insurer had established that none of the truck company employees worked 40 hours a week, 48 weeks a year (which the policy required) after the corporation was dissolved. Moreover, several of the insurance claim forms signed by the truck company after its dissolution indicated that the employee was "employed and covered by the employer health plan." Although the insurer established that it mistakenly paid out benefits to a shut-down company's employee, the court held for the insured under an implied contract theory. The insurer failed to establish that the truck company knowingly made any misrepresentations. The employee had no knowledge of whether he was "employed" within the insurance policy's meaning, and he probably assumed he was covered. Because the employee was mistaken about the coverage and relied upon the benefit payments for his cancer treatments, the court granted judgment for the insured and its employee. *Association Life Ins. Co. v. Jenkins,* 793 F.Supp. 161 (M.D.Tenn.1992).

3. Preexisting Conditions

A Florida woman was receiving periodic treatment for asthma from April 1985 through December 1988. In April 1989, she was hospitalized for her asthmatic condition because her body was exposed to heavy environmental smoke caused by wildfires in the Everglades. She sought to recover her medical expenses pursuant to a group health policy, but the district court granted the insurer summary judgment. The insured appealed. On appeal to the District Court of Appeal of Florida, the insured conceded that her hospitalization occurred within the preexisting condition exclusionary period of the policy. She argued, however, that she was still entitled to coverage because the pollution from the Everglades wildfires, not her preexisting condition, caused her to be hospitalized. Although the court found the insured's argument persuasive, it denied coverage because the policy expressly excluded coverage for the insured's preexisting asthma. Even if the hospitalization had resulted from the Everglades wildfires, the policy expressly excluded any bodily injury or sickness for which the insured received medical treatment within 12 months before the effective policy date, until a continuous period of 12 months had elapsed during which the insured received no treatment for her condition. Accordingly, the court denied the insured coverage and affirmed the summary judgment in favor of the insurer. *Bartolina v. NN Investors Life Ins.*, 600 So.2d 535 (Fla.App.4 Dist.1992).

In January 1989, a Nebraska woman complained of difficulty when swallowing, chewing or moving her tongue, and weakness of the muscles in her arms and legs. Her family physician diagnosed her condition as being thyroid related and treated her accordingly. The woman apparently felt fine until late June 1989. In the meantime, she had become insured through a group health insurer. In July she sought another opinion at which time she learned that she had myasthenia gravis, a condition which results in muscle weakness but not pain. The group health insurer refused to pay for her medical expenses stating that the condition was preexisting and therefore not covered. The insured then sued in a Nebraska trial court which found in favor of the insured and the insurer appealed to the Supreme Court of Nebraska. On appeal, the insurer contended that the instruction to the jury concerning the preexistence of her disease was erroneous. The jury instruction read "a disease, condition or illness exists within the meaning of a health insurance policy excluding preexisting conditions only at such time as the disease, condition or illness becomes known to the insured or is capable of being diagnosed by a physician." Specifically, the insurer contended that the condition was preexisting if it manifested itself to the insured, and since the disease manifested itself in January 1989, it existed before she had obtained the insurance policy. The court, however, rejected this reasoning, stating that since the insured sought medical help and received an erroneous diagnosis the disease did not manifest itself until she received a proper diagnosis in July. The supreme court affirmed the trial court's decision and granted the insured medical expenses. *Fuglsang v. Blue Cross,* 456 N.W.2d 281 (Neb.1990).

A Florida woman enrolled in a group health insurance plan which excluded coverage for sicknesses within ninety days of becoming insured. Within the ninety day period, the insured received treatment for a breast abscess. Several months later, an abnormal finding in a chest X-ray prompted surgery because of a fear of lung cancer. However, the problem was merely lung inflammation caused by the breast abscess. The insured sought coverage, which her insurer denied. She sued unsuccessfully in a Florida trial court, and appealed to the District Court of Appeal of Florida. The appellate court held that the sickness for which the insured had received treatment was excluded under the policy because it resulted from the breast abscess. The court affirmed the trial court's decision. *Kirchstein v. Kentucky Central Life Ins. Co.*, 556 So.2d 1190 (Fla.App.4th Dist.1990).

A Mississippi insured was employed by an organization which provided comprehensive health insurance. The plan excluded benefits for any pre-existing condition unless the insured had prior coverage for a period of twelve consecutive months. It also excluded congenital conditions. Prior to being accepted for employment, the insured was required to submit to a complete physical examination and yearly examinations thereafter. The insured's initial and one-year examinations did not reveal any problems. One month after her first annual exam she began experiencing headaches, shortness of breath, dizziness and blackouts. She was hospitalized and treated for a congenital heart condition. The insurer refused to pay medical expenses relating to her heart condition. The insured sued the insurer in a Mississippi trial court, which found the contract ambiguous and held for the insured. The insurer appealed to the Supreme Court of Mississippi. The supreme court found that the insured's congenital heart condition had not manifested itself prior to the plan's effective coverage date. The congenital conditions exclusion did not apply. The court noted that on the date the insured was hired she had no known heart problems. The insured's heart condition had to manifest itself prior to the policy's effective date in order for the insurer to deny coverage. The supreme court affirmed the trial court's decision. *State Comp. Health Plan v. Carper,* 545 So.2d 1 (Miss.1989).

In a 1974 preemployment physical exam a man was diagnosed as having diabetes. Between 1975 and 1979 he had several other exams which confirmed this diagnosis. In April 1979, he received group credit life insurance without indicating on the application that diabetes was a preexisting condition. When he died of an acute codeine overdose in March 1981, the insurer launched an investigation of his death, found diabetes in his medical history and denied the wife's claim. The wife sued and when a district court ruled that the insurer had properly denied the wife's claim, she appealed to the Utah Supreme Court. At issue, among other things, was whether diabetes had caused the man's death. The relevant Utah statute stated that concealment of facts will not prevent recovery unless the facts were "material either to the acceptance of the risk, or to the hazard assumed by the insurer...." The court observed that even though the man's death was not caused by diabetes, there was substantial evidence to support the jury's verdict that the man's diabetes was material to his insurability and to the acceptance by the insurer of the risk of death. The court ruled that because the fact that the misrepresentation was related to the insurer's willingness to initially accept the risk, the ultimate cause of death was irrelevant. Because the evidence was unrebutted that a truthful representation by the man concerning his diabetes would have caused rejection of the credit life policy, the insurer did not have to pay the wife's claim. *Berger v. Minnesota Mut. Life*, 723 P.2d 388 (Utah 1986).

An Arkansas man had a life insurance policy through his place of employment. The man's truck jackknifed on an icy Oklahoma road and he suffered a fatal heart attack shortly thereafter. The man's widow filed a claim for accidental death benefits which the insurer denied. The insurer argued that the man's death was not caused by the accident, but by his existing heart condition. When the widow sued, a circuit court granted the insurer's motion for summary judgment dismissing her claim. The widow appealed. The state court of appeals decided that under Oklahoma law "the insurance contract alone is the measure of liability." The policy provided for accidental death benefits only when the death arose from an accidental injury "directly and independently of all other causes." All parties agreed that the man's death resulted at least in part from his heart condition. The circuit court's summary judgment for the insurer was affirmed. *Hammons v. Prudential Ins. Co. of America*, 717 S.W.2d 819 (Ark.App.1986).

An insured man in Akansas sought coverage under his medical insurance policy for a tonsillectomy performed on him. The insurer denied coverage on the ground that the hospitalization and surgery were caused by a condition which existed prior to the effective date of coverage to the insured. Preexisting conditions, claimed the insurer, were expressly excluded from coverage. The insured sued the insurer to recover for the cost of his operation. The Arkansas Court of Appeals reversed a trial court ruling in the insured's favor, finding that the insured's condition had, in fact, existed prior to the effective date of the policy. The insured's physical report, which contained a summary of his medical history, indicated that the insured had known of his "chronic hypertrophic tonsilitis" for years. Thus, the court held that the insurance policy did not provide coverage for the insured's tonsillectomy. *Arkansas Blue Cross & Blue Shield v. Fudge*, 669 S.W.2d 914 (Ark.App.1984).

In November 1980, a Florida man executed a credit life insurance policy in connection with his purchase of a new car. The preprinted application/policy contained a declaration directly above the applicant's signature space certifying that the man had no serious existing diseases or disorders. The man died less than one month later during emergency surgery to repair a ruptured abdominal aortic aneurysm, the result of an ongoing condition. The man's wife testified that the signing of the insurance application took only two to three minutes, and the insurance agent had said "sign here" without mentioning the clause. The insurance company denied coverage, and the man's estate sued. The Florida District Court of Appeal held that the jury should have been told "that a representation ... will not void the policy unless made with conscious intent to deceive." Since the instructions given had been incorrect, the case was remanded for a new trial with these modified instructions. *World Serv. Life Ins. Co. v. Bodiford*, 492 So.2d 457 (Fla.App.1st Dist.1986).

An insured under a group health insurance policy sued an insurer to recover benefits for his child's soft palate operation, performed to correct a congenital defect. The insurer refused to pay for the operation on the ground that the child had not complied with a policy provision regarding preexisting conditions. The policy stated that preexisting diseases and bodily injuries were excluded from coverage unless the insured, while covered under the policy, completed a ninety-day period during which the insured received no medical, surgical or nursing services, and used no prescription medicine to treat the disease or injuries. The insurer alleged that the child's visit to a surgeon during this ninety-day period specified in the policy precluded coverage for the operation.

The Georgia Court of Appeals disagreed, finding that the cursory diagnostic examination of the child's condition which lasted no more than fifteen minutes and consisted merely of the surgeon's looking briefly into the child's mouth, did not constitute "medical services" for purposes of the policy exclusion. Because the court was compelled to construe the policy language due to its lack of clarity, it construed the policy in favor of the insureds. Accordingly, the court reversed a trial court ruling which had held in favor of the insurer. The court was persuaded that the child had completed a ninety-day "treatment free" period during coverage and thus the operation was not excluded from coverage under the preexisting condition provision. *Beggs v. Pacific Mut. Life Ins. Co.*, 318 S.E.2d 836 (Ga.App.1984).

VIII. SEX-BASED MORTALITY TABLES

Title VII of the federal Civil Rights Act of 1964 (42 U.S.C. § 2000e *et. seq.*) prohibits any employer from discriminating against an employee on the basis of sex. As the first case illustrates, the courts have consistently held that the use of sex-based mortality tables (even if statistically accurate) by employer-provided life insurance plans violates this prohibition. Where the insurance is not employer provided and where the insurer makes distinctions based upon sex in terms and conditions of its insurance, the result may be different as the second case illustrates.

The use of sex-based mortality tables by a university in two retirement annuity plans formed the basis of this civil rights lawsuit brought by a female college professor. The professor claimed such use discriminated against female employees since they actuarially live longer and therefore were required to contribute more to the funds than males in order to receive the same retirement benefits. The U.S. Court of Appeals, Second Circuit, partially upholding a lower court, agreed with the professor and held such use of sex-based mortality tables to be in violation of Title VII of the Civil Rights Act of 1964. The court said that, regardless of any actuarial soundness, the plan was in violation of the law. Title VII's "focus on the individual is unambiguous. It precludes treatment of individuals as simply components of a racial, religious, sexual, or national class." Even a true generalization does not apply. Because there is no way of knowing prior to or at the time of retirement which *individual* female retirees will fulfill actuarial predictions as to longevity and in fact live longer than the average male retiree, a requirement that *all* female employees make larger contributions than *all* male employees penalizes female retirees who do *not* actually live longer than the average male retiree. Such a result violates Title VII because it does not "pass the simple test of whether the evidence shows 'treatment of a person in a manner which but for that person's sex would be different.'" The court therefore remanded the case to the distict court for further proceedings in accordance with its decision. *Spirt v. Teachers Ins. & Annuity Ass'n*, 691 F.2d 1054 (2d Cir.1982).

The National Organization for Women (NOW) sued the Metropolitan Life Insurance Co. alleging that Metropolitan's refusal to sell life and disability insurance to women on the same terms as men was discriminatory in violation of the New York Human Rights Law. Specifically, NOW argued that Metropolitan should not distinguish between men and women in determining who qualifies for life and disability insurance protection. Metropolitan moved to dismiss the complaint but a New York trial court denied the motion. Metropolitan appealed to the Supreme Court, Appellate Division.

The appellate court observed that although New York insurance law did not permit distinctions based on sex in the offering of life and disability insurance, distinctions were permitted when based upon the terms and conditions of the insurance. The Human Rights Law provided that it was unlawful for any "place of public accommodation, resort or amusement ...to refuse, withhold from or deny to [any] person any of the ... advantages ... thereof ... on the basis of sex. The appellate court noted that when a special statute is in irreconcilable conflict with a general statute covering the same subject matter, the special statute will control. It concluded that the Human Rights Law, which generally prohibited sex discrimination in the offering of services or privileges, "would not override the later, more specific legislation in the Insurance Law [which expressly permits] use of some gender classifications with regard to the terms and conditions of life and disability insurance policies." The trial court decision was reversed and Metropolitan was permitted to make distinctions based upon sex in the terms and conditions of its insurance. *NOW v. Metropolitan Life Ins. Co.*, 516 N.Y.S.2d 934 (A.D.1stDept.1987).

CHAPTER SIX

HOMEOWNER'S INSURANCE

                                                       Page

I. SCOPE OF COVERAGE 255

II. RESIDENCE AND DOMICILE MATTERS 267

III. POLICY EXCLUSIONS 272
    A. Motor Vehicle Exclusions 272
    B. Intentional Acts Exclusions 275
    C. Business Pursuit Exclusions 284
    D. Earth Movement Exclusions 289

IV. MISREPRESENTATION 292

I. SCOPE OF COVERAGE

The following cases involve disputes over the scope of the coverage provided under homeowner's insurance policies.

A Malibu couple owned a home in the Big Rock Mesa area. That area had experienced massive landslides for several years. The couple held an all-risk homeowner's policy which specifically excluded damage caused by earth movement. The policy included coverage for losses caused by the negligence of third parties. The family's home was damaged when excessive groundwater levels caused shifting and settling. The insurer paid for the damage, but filed a declaratory action. The insured argued that the damage was caused by the negligence of third parties, and was therefore covered under the policy. Specifically, the insureds claimed that the state, county, and the homeowners' association were negligent for taking actions which caused the groundwater level to rise. The jury found that third party negligence was the efficient proximate cause of the damage and was, therefore, a nonexcluded risk. The Court of Appeal reversed and the case was appealed to the California Supreme Court.

    The supreme court held for the couple. The court stated that when a loss is caused by a combination of covered and specifically excluded risks, the loss is covered if the covered risk was the efficient proximate cause of the loss. Expert testimony supported the jury's determination that third party negligence was the predominating cause of the loss. By developing the hillside with septic tanks instead of sewers and failing to properly dewater the hillside, it was inevitable that the ancient landslide would be reactivated. The court also stated that its suggestion in *Garvey v. State Farm Fire and Cas. Co.*, 257 Cal.Rptr. 292 (1984), that there might be a narrow category of exclusion in third party negligence cases where the negligence is in the preparation of protection against the operation of specifically excluded risks, was inapplicable. That would be the case where a builder seeks to protect a home from an excluded risk but, because of negligent construction, the home is damaged anyway. Here the negligence was not in taking counter measures to protect the home, but rather in actually precipitating the slide. The court reversed the verdict for the insured and remanded the case for further proceedings. *State Farm v. Von Der Lieth*, 2 Cal.Rptr.2d 183 (Cal.1991).

A married couple made a claim under their homeowner's insurance policy after noticing cracks and separation in footings, slabs, walls, and ceilings in their home. Their insurer hired subsurface exploration experts to investigate the cause of the damage. Preliminary investigations indicated that the cracks might be due to soil settlement. Subsequently, more extensive investigation revealed that the damage was caused by the builder's failure to remove loose alluvial soil before the house was built. The insureds claimed coverage for third party negligence, but the insurer refused, citing the latent defect exclusion in the policy. The insureds sued in federal court. The insurer made a motion for summary judgment which was denied. It appealed the denial to the U.S. Court of Appeals, Ninth Circuit. The court of appeals held that a defect which is not apparent upon reasonable inspection, but only after an intensive postfailure expert examination, is a latent defect for the purposes of a latent defect exclusion. In this case, the negligent construction of the house was not readily discoverable. It was not even until the second, more thorough, examination that the true cause was known. The preliminary investigation revealed nothing about the negligence. Therefore, since it was only discoverable through intensive investigation, the negligence was a latent defect and excluded by the policy. *Winans v. State Farm Fire and Cas. Co.*, 968 F.2d 884 (9th Cir.1992).

A California homeowner purchased a policy of insurance on his residence which had a policy limit of $141,000. When his home was completely destroyed by fire, he discovered that the policy proceeds were insufficient to replace his residence. He sued his insurer and its local agency, alleging that he had inquired every year as to whether his insurance would cover rebuilding his home and had been told each time that the coverage limits were adequate. He asserted that the defendants had breached their duty to provide him with accurate information. The superior court dismissed his lawsuit, and he appealed to the Court of Appeal, Second District. On appeal, the court noted that the defendants were not required, under the general duty of care owed to the insured, to advise the insured of the sufficiency of his liability limits or the replacement value of his residence. However, if they once elected to respond to his inquiries, a special duty would have arisen which would require them to exercise reasonable care. Here, even though the insured might not be able to prove his theory at trial, he had properly alleged the existence of an expanded duty of care and was entitled to the opportunity to prove his case. The court reversed the lower court's dismissal of the complaint. *Free v. Republic Ins. Co.*, 11 Cal.Rptr.2d 296 (Cal.App.2d Dist.1992).

An insurer issued a homeowner's policy which had a liability limit of $100,000 per occurrence. The policy stated that all bodily injury resulting from continuous or repeated exposure to the same general conditions would be deemed the result of one occurrence. The insured provided child care services at her home. When she occasionally ran errands (for example, taking some of the children to and from school) her husband or daughter would look after those left behind. Later, it was discovered that the insured's husband had sexually molested several of the children.

Sec. I   SCOPE OF COVERAGE   257

The parents involved sued the insured on behalf of their children. In negotiations with the insurer, it was agreed that any claims of the parents would not be separate from the children's claims, and that the insurer would waive coverage defenses and limitations except as to its per occurrence liability limit to each of the children. It was assumed by the parties that the insured had been negligent in caring for and supervising the children. The insurer then brought suit in a state trial court, seeking a declaration of its rights and obligations regarding the indemnification of its insured. The trial court held that the insured's acts and omissions were one occurrence under the policy as to each child. The parents appealed to the California Court of Appeal, First District, which affirmed the lower court's holding. Here, the repeated molestation of the children was "repeated exposure to substantially the same general conditions." Accordingly, the injuries to each child were the result of one occurrence, and the insurer's liability was $100,000 at the most for each child. *State Farm Fire & Casualty Co. v. Elizabeth N.*, 12 Cal.Rptr.2d 327 (Cal.App.1st Dist.1992).

An insured boat owner and her mother were involved in a boating accident and the mother suffered injuries. The insurer brought suit against the insured to determine whether she could recover under her homeowner's policy for the resulting injuries. The district court granted the insured summary judgment and the insurer appealed. On appeal, the insured argued that the insurer intentionally designed its policy so the insured could not find the family exclusion. Nowhere was the term "family exclusion" used in the policy; the policy used endorsements to amend it and consequently the family exclusion endorsement was referred to as the "Amendatory Endorsement." Although the court could empathize with the insured's argument that the exclusion was not easy to find, the court did not agree that the exclusion was buried in endorsements and amendments and therefore not susceptible to discovery by the insured. Accordingly, the case was reversed and remanded. *Prudential. Prop. & Cas. Ins. Co. v. Bonnema*, 601 So.2d 269 (Fla.App.5th Dist. 1992).

An eight-year-old Michigan boy was bitten by a dog. He sued his mother and stepfather, and they sought liability coverage under their homeowner's policy. Their insurer accepted the defense of the lawsuit under a reservation of rights, but contended that liability coverage was unavailable because the boy was an "insured person." The policy defined an insured person to include "any relative and any dependent person." The insurer sought dismissal of the suit for lack of coverage, which the trial court denied. The insurer then appealed to the Court of Appeals of Michigan. The insureds argued that the boy was not an insured person because he was not the natural or adoptive son of his stepfather and the policy required insureds to be relatives and dependents. The court disagreed, finding that the policy language must be interpreted according to its commonly understood meaning. Because the boy would have been an insured person if he had caused an injury to another, the court ruled that he must be an insured, even though the injury was to him. Though a broad reading would exclude coverage in this case, the court held that, in most instances, it would provide greater coverage. The appellate court reversed the trial court. *Allstate Ins. Co. v. Tomaszewski*, 447 N.W.2d 849 (Mich.App.1989).

An insured parent made certain public comments questioning a teacher's competency and fitness. The teacher sued the insured for emotional distress and the case eventually was settled. The insured then sued her insurer to recover for the defense costs as well as for breach of contract. The case reached the Supreme Court of New Jersey which held that a homeowner's policy providing for bodily injuries will cover liability for emotional distress resulting in physical harm. Further, even if the actions of the insured were intentional, coverage had to be provided if the actions were not intentionally injurious. The court held for the insured. *Voorhees v. Preferred Mutual Ins. Co.*, 607 A.2d 1255 (N.J.1992).

A Georgia man died, naming his eldest son as executor and leaving his estate equally to his sons. The eldest son took title to the house and renovated it for resale. Subsequently, the house burned down and the sons sued the homeowner's insurer for coverage. A Georgia district court granted the insurer summary judgment, and the sons appealed. On appeal, the sons claimed they were entitled to coverage because the eldest son was a "legal representative" under the policy. The appellate court disagreed, stating that because the will had not been probated at the time of the fire, there was no legal representative (no one with an insurable interest in the house). Accordingly, the insurer did not have to pay the policy proceeds to the sons. The court affirmed the summary judgment in favor of the insurer. *Higdon v. Ga. Farm Bureau Mut. Ins. Co.*, 419 S.E.2d 80 (Ga.App.1992).

An insured, while attempting to fill her waterbed, broke the containment mattress, causing water damage. The homeowner's policy covered "accidental discharge or overflow of water ... from within a household appliance." The trial court ruled in favor of the insured, and the insurer appealed to the District Court of Appeal of Florida. The appellate court held that a waterbed is not a household appliance and accordingly denied coverage to the insured. The trial court decision was reversed. *West American Ins. Co. v. Lowrie*, 600 So.2d 34 (Fla.App.3d Dist.1992).

A Tennessee insured under a homeowner's policy obtained coverage in the amount of $6,759 for a ring. When she lost a stone from the ring, she notified her insurer. She insisted on sending the ring back to the jeweler in Alabama where she had purchased it. The ring was lost in the mail. The insurer then denied coverage because she had neglected to use all reasonable means to protect the ring. The trial court held for the insured, and granted her an additional 25% for the insurer's refusal to pay in good faith. The Tennessee Court of Appeals affirmed the lower court's decision, holding that the mailing of the ring did not constitute neglect. *Minton v. Tennessee Farmers Mutual Ins. Co.*, 832 S.W.2d 35 (Tenn.App.1992).

A Florida man purchased a homeowner's policy which excluded coverage for personal liability (bodily injury or property damage) arising out of the ownership, maintenance or use of a watercraft "designated as an airboat, aircushion, jet ski or similar type of craft." The insured then purchased two Yamaha Wave Runners (which are operated from a sitting position rather than a standing position). An accident resulted in personal injuries, and the insurer denied coverage. The trial court found that coverage had to be provided because the wave runner was not similar to a jet ski. The insurer appealed. On appeal to the District Court of Appeal of Florida, the court noted that the evidence produced at trial conclusively established that the wave runner was a similar craft to the Kawasaki Jet Ski. The term "jet ski" is often used as a generic term (like "Xerox") despite the fact that it is a registered trademark. The two watercraft were similar in appearance; they were powered alike; and they were driven alike. Accordingly, they were similar, and the exclusion applied to bar

Sec. I   SCOPE OF COVERAGE   259

coverage. The trial court's ruling was reversed. *State Farm Fire & Casualty Co. v. Johnson*, 596 So.2d 1162 (Fla.App.4th Dist.1992).

A Louisiana man owned a watercraft and installed a generator before selling the boat. The purchaser took an overnight fishing trip during which carbon monoxide gas allegedly leaked from the generator's exhaust system. Two persons died and two persons suffered personal injury. The former owner subsequently faced claims, and his homeowner's insurer and general liability insurer filed suit to determine their respective liability. A trial court found that the damage was not excluded by a "watercraft exclusion" which was contained in the homeowner's policy, and ruled the homeowner's insurer to be primarily liable. The decision was appealed to the Court of Appeal of Louisiana. The watercraft exclusion in the homeowner's policy made the policy inapplicable to claims "arising out of the ownership, maintenance, or use of any watercraft owned or rented by the insured." The liability insurer asserted that the exclusion did not encompass former ownership and that coverage should therefore be provided. The court disagreed. The second argument by the liability insurer was that the damage was caused by the generator and not the boat. Again the court disagreed; the generator was found to be an "integrally related component" such that in determining the cause of harm a litigant may not ignore the entity of the boat. All claims were found to be derivative of ownership, and excluded from coverage under the homeowner's policy. The liability insurer was held to be primarily liable. *Laborde v. Deblanc*, 587 So.2d 58 (La.App.4th Cir.1991).

After a seventeen-year-old New Jersey boy struck another vehicle and caused the death of two persons and injury to two others, four actions were instituted against him and his mother. One claim asserted against the mother was that she failed to exercise sufficient control and supervision of her son in the operation of his automobile. The mother then instituted this action against her homeowner's insurer for defense and indemnity. The insurer filed a declaratory judgment to determine coverage. After the trial court granted summary judgment to the mother, the insurer appealed to the appellate division. The homeowner's policy expressly precluded coverage for claims asserted against the mother for bodily injury or property damage arising out of entrusting any motorized land vehicle or trailer. The court held that the policy plainly and unambiguously excluded coverage for the negligent supervision claim against the mother. The appellate court reversed the decision of the trial court and held that the insurer need not defend or indemnify. *Allstate Ins. Co. v. Moraca*, 581 A.2d 510 (N.J.Super.A.D.1990).

A Virginia insured owned a camper trailer which was destroyed by a sudden windstorm while parked near his residence. The insured had a homeowner's insurance policy at the time which provided coverage for damage to a dwelling, other structures and personal property. The general policy limit for damage to personal property was $7,560, and the insured claimed that he was entitled to this sum. The insurer, while admitting that the loss was covered, asserted that it need pay only $1,000 because of a "special limits of liability" provision in the policy. The policy clearly stated that there was a $1,000 limit on trailers. The insured sued the insurer in a Virginia trial court, asserting that it had breached its contract with him by denying liability for any sum in excess of $1,000. The trial court ruled for the insured, and the insurer appealed to the Supreme Court of Virginia.

On appeal, the insurer argued that the trial court had incorrectly decided that the property damaged was not a trailer within the meaning of the special limits of liability clause. The court agreed, noting that the Virginia statute which dealt with motor vehicles defined "trailer" so as to clearly include the camper trailer that had been destroyed. Because it could find no ambiguity in the policy with regard to the trailer, the supreme court held that the $1,000 limitation on the amount of recovery available under the policy was controlling. It thus reversed the decision of the trial court. *United States Fidelity and Guaranty Co. v. McGlothlin*, 392 S.E.2d 814 (Va.1990).

A Minnesota insured suffered an epileptic seizure and caused a car accident in which one person died. The insured's failure to take his medication caused the seizure. The victim's family brought a wrongful death action against the insured. The insured's automobile insurer acknowledged coverage and tendered its policy limit. The insured's homeowner's insurer then brought a declaratory judgment action that its policy did not cover the automobile accident. A Minnesota trial court found that the homeowner's policy was applicable. The insurer then appealed to the Minnesota Court of Appeals. The court reversed the trial court's decision, concluding that the insured's failure to take his medication was not a divisible concurrent cause of negligent driving. The court noted that the cause of the accident did not qualify as an independent, nonvehicle-related act of negligence which would have been covered under the homeowner's policy. It stated that failure to take medication which causes an automobile accident would not reasonably be contemplated as a risk covered by a homeowner's insurance policy. *Auto-Owners Ins. Co. v. Selisker*, 435 N.W.2d 866 (Minn.App.1989).

As a result of negligence, some heating oil was spilled onto a yard in Massachusetts, and it eventually contaminated an adjacent insured's property. The insured brought a declaratory judgment action against his homeowner's insurer for coverage. After both parties moved for summary judgment, the district court denied the insurer's motion. The insurer appealed to the Appeals Court of Massachusetts arguing that its "contamination or pollutants" exclusion barred the insured's claim. The appellate court, however, disagreed, noting that the discharge of the pollutants from the oil tank next door was not the cause of the loss to the insureds, but rather the cause was the neighbor's negligence, a covered risk. Accordingly, the court affirmed the summary judgment in favor of the insured. *Jussim v. Massachusetts Bay Ins. Co.*, 597 N.E.2d 1379 (Mass.App.Ct.1992).

Two Kentucky men were partners in a business which intended to sell used tires to the Chinese government. The tires were stored on a piece of property which was owned by one of the partners. He sought to improve one of the buildings on the property so that it could be rented as an apartment; he thus hired a man to clean up the area by rolling the tires down a hill away from the building. One of the rolling tires struck and injured a woman, and she sued the partner for his negligence. He assigned his rights under his homeowner's insurance policy to the injured woman, who recovered a judgment against the insurer. On appeal, the court of appeals reversed, holding that an "other premises" exclusion defeated coverage. The woman appealed to the Supreme Court of Kentucky. The supreme court noted that the other premises exclusion invalidated coverage for occurrences which *arose out of* other owned premises of the insured, and which caused the injuries. Here, even though the injury had occurred on uninsured property, it did not arise out of the property, but rather out of the negligent act of rolling tires down a hill. Next, the court held that the business pursuits exclusion would not preclude coverage in this case because the insured was merely an investor — his partner had done all the work in acquiring the tires and negotiating the sale with the Chinese. The court reversed the court of appeals' decision and held for the injured woman. *Eyler v. Nationwide Mutual Fire Ins. Co.*, 824 S.W.2d 855 (Ky.1992).

A woman experienced pain in her neck after a boat in which she was a passenger struck a wave. The owner of the boat took her to an emergency room, where the staff instructed her to take Tylenol and discharged her. The boat owner requested that she contact him if she had any further problems. Two and one-half years later, the man was sued by the woman and immediately gave notice to his insurer. The insurer contended that the coverage had been waived due to the insured's failure to comply with the requirement to give written notice as soon as possible. Summary judgment was granted to the insured, and the insurer appealed to a New York appellate court. A delay by an insured in giving notice may be excused when it was based on a reasonable good faith belief of nonliability. The court noted that neither the manner of the injury nor the medical treatment provided to the woman led the man to expect liability. The decision in favor of the insured was affirmed. *Briggs v. Nationwide Mutual Ins. Co.*, 575 N.Y.S.2d 413 (A.D.3d Dept.1991).

A South Dakota farmer owned a house in town and a mobile home located on a farm. Each dwelling was insured through a separate homeowner's policy. The farmer's family had begun to move their belongings to the farm when a lightning strike caused a fire which destroyed the mobile home and its contents. The insurer of the mobile home later discovered that the contents of the mobile home were also insured by the policy on the farmer's house, which contained a clause providing temporary coverage to items moved to a new structure. An "other insurance" clause in the mobile home policy specified that if other coverage was available, the policy became null and void. A federal district court ruled that no coverage existed under the mobile home policy, and the insured appealed to the U.S. Court of Appeals, Eighth Circuit. The purpose of an other insurance clause is to minimize the incentive for an insured to defraud insurers, or to ignore the existence of a hazard. The two policies of insurance in this case covered two entirely separate properties. The only overlap of coverage arose due to a "moving provision." If respected, the clause would remove coverage not only on the personal property, but also on the structure. This result was held to be beyond the scope and purpose of the other insurance clause, and to be unconscionable. The district court's decision was reversed. *Zeeb v. National Farmers Union Property and Casualty Co.*, 946 F.2d 601 (8th Cir.1991).

An insurer mailed a homeowner's insurance cancellation notice to an insured. Roughly four months later, an incident occurred which gave rise to potential liability for the insureds. They claimed that the cancellation was ineffective under Maine law because it was not received at least 20 days prior to the specified cancellation date. A trial court held that the cancellation thus became effective 20 days following receipt of the notice. The insureds appealed to the Supreme Judicial Court of Maine. The applicable statute states: "no notice of cancellation of a policy shall be effective unless received by the named insured at least 20 days prior to the effective date of cancellation." The court found that the legislature intended strict compliance with the statute, and reversed the trial court's decision. The cancellation was held to be ineffective. *Maine Bonding & Casualty Co. v. Knowlton*, 598 A.2d 749 (Me.1991).

The buyer of a home discovered that it had cracked basement walls as well as defective kitchen pipes, and alleged that the seller either intentionally or negligently failed to disclose the defects and had thus breached the contract. A suit was brought against the seller and the seller's homeowner's insurer. The insurer denied coverage, refused to defend the insured, and moved for summary judgment against the buyer. A trial court agreed that the insurer had no duty to defend the seller and granted summary judgment against the buyer. The buyer and seller appealed the ruling to the Wisconsin Court of Appeals.

The complaint against the seller alleged pecuniary damages. The insurer asserted that such losses were not covered under the policy, which only covered property damage which was defined as "injury to or destruction of tangible property, including the loss of use." The seller argued that the damage should be covered because the complaint implied a "loss of use" of the property. Even though the condition of the home was an element of the complaint, the court ruled that the condition was not the cause of the damage at issue — the seller's misrepresentations were. The court stated that "simply because the underlying facts deal with defects in the property does not change the nature of the claim asserted ... nor does it change the risks the policy insured against." The decision of the trial court was affirmed. *Qualman v. Bruckmoser*, 471 N.W.2d 282 (Wis.App.1991).

South Dakota homeowners purchased an insurance policy with a policy limit of $27,500 which provided property coverage when the insureds moved permanently to another location. A clause in the policy stated that property in transit was covered to $2,750 against direct loss. The insureds accepted employment in California and moved there. Because they had no other living arrangements, the insureds stayed in a motel and parked a trailer full of their property in the motel parking lot. The trailer was stolen and the insureds filed a claim with their insurer for the $27,500 liability limit. The insurer refused to pay the liability limit, stating that the $2,750 amount applied as the claim was for property in transit. The insureds sued the insurer in a South Dakota trial court, which granted the insurer's summary judgment motion.

On appeal to the South Dakota Supreme Court, the insureds argued that the policy's change in location clause required payment of the liability limit. They stated that the clause was ambiguous because it referred to "another location where [the insureds] intend to permanently reside." They claimed that in that context, "location" could refer to either a specific residence or the new city or metropolitan area of residence. The court agreed with the insurer's narrower interpretation of the word "location." This was because the term was used in the policy to describe houses or dwellings. "Location" was never used to describe a city or metropolitan area. As the insureds did not intend to permanently reside at the motel, the in-transit clause applied. The supreme court affirmed the trial court's decision in favor of the insurer. *Prokop v. North Star Mut. Ins. Co.*, 457 N.W.2d 862 (S.D.1990).

The owners of a mobile home insured their personal effects. The policy contained an extension of personal effects coverage which provided for payment of up to ten percent of the policy limits for losses occurring off the premises. The couple then initiated a move to another city. Personal effects were lost or destroyed at the new location before the insureds moved their mobile home there. When the insurer paid only ten percent for the loss, the insureds sued for full coverage, which they obtained. The Court of Appeals of Oregon reversed, however, holding that the limitation in the policy was valid. *Woosley v. Transamerica Premier Ins. Co.*, 826 P.2d 1054 (Or.App.1992).

Four Virginia teenagers started a fire in a partially completed house which they had illegally entered. After they left, the fire destroyed the house and its contents. The homeowners referred the claim to their insurance carrier, whose investigator determined the identity of the four teenagers. The insurer's attorney wrote to the parents of two of the teenagers to advise them to contact their homeowner's carriers about the loss. One of the teenager's parents responded but the other did not. This teenager, who was an honor student, had enlisted in the U.S. Navy. The honor student's parents' homeowners' insurer filed a lawsuit to determine coverage in the matter. Because the honor student had joined the navy, he was absent for some time and was not served with process until three years after the fire. Statements taken by the investigator indicated that the honor student admitted building the fire and running from the site when a car approached. Evidence also indicated that the honor student was aware of the insurer's attorney's letter, and that the honor student's mother did not report the matter to her insurer because her "child had not been convicted of anything ...." The court ruled against the insurer and it appealed to the Supreme Court of Virginia.

The supreme court agreed with the insurer that the honor student's parents had failed to notify it of potential liability as soon as practicable, which was a duty prescribed by its policy. The policy unambiguously required insureds to perform listed duties and required them to cooperate in seeing that the additional insureds' duties were performed. The court rejected the honor student's and parents' argument that notice had been given as soon as practicable after being served with process. The occurrence which gave rise to the duty of notice was the fire, and not the advent of the lawsuit and service of process three years later. The supreme court reversed the lower court's decision. *State Farm Fire and Casualty Co. v. Walton*, 423 S.E.2d 188 (Va.1992).

A New York man owned an all-terrain vehicle (ATV). A minor was operating the ATV, struck a tree, and was injured. Four days later, the minor's father called the owner of the ATV and requested that the owner contact his insurer. He was told that the insurer had already been notified. A negligence action was then brought against the insured owner of the ATV. The plaintiff's attorney repeatedly urged the insured to notify his insurer, but without response. Eventually, a default judgment was entered against the insured. A year after the accident, the minor's attorney discovered the name of the insurer. When the insurer disclaimed coverage, the minor sued. The trial court ruled for the minor, and the insurer appealed to the New York Supreme Court, Appellate Division. On appeal, the court noted that an injured party has an independent right to provide written notice to an insurer, and cannot be bound by an insured's late notice. Here, the minor had acted reasonably in notifying the insurer, once the insurer's identity had been disclosed. Accordingly, the judgment in favor of the minor was affirmed. *Walters by Walters v. Atkins*, 579 N.Y.S.2d 525 (A.D.4th Dept.1992).

A Michigan insured hired a construction worker to work on his home. The insured became dissatisfied with the worker's performance. He told his wife to tell the worker to finish the job as soon as possible and then payment for the work would be discussed. After talking to the worker, she left to pick up her husband. When the couple arrived home, the worker was gone along with 25 of their household items including tools and hardware. The insured spoke to an employee of his insurance agent who told him the loss was covered under his homeowner's insurance policy, and that the insured could buy new items for which he would be reimbursed. The insured did so and submitted a claim totaling $3,970. Subsequently, the worker and the couple resolved their financial dispute over the missing property at a pre-trial conference. The couple, however, still attempted to recover under their homeowner's policy for the "theft." When coverage was denied, the insured sued the insurer for breach of contract and the insurer's agent alleging equitable estoppel (i.e., that they had changed their position in reliance on the agent's statement; thus, the agent could not disclaim liability for the statement). The district court granted summary judgment for the insurer and its agent, and the insured appealed to the Court of Appeals of Michigan.

The appellate court held that the worker's actions did not constitute theft because he did not possess the specific intent to permanently deprive the couple of their tools. The worker only took the tools as "collateral" to ensure payment for his work. On the issue of equitable estoppel, the insurance agent argued that it was not liable because its employee only explained the claims procedure to the couple rather than stating that the claim was covered. Although the court believed the insured could not recover damages for equitable estoppel, it noted that a factual dispute existed as to whether the insurance agent's employee's statement was made. The court affirmed the lower court's decision which denied the insured coverage for theft but remanded the case so the insured could amend his pleadings to allege fraud or negligence for the agent's employee's statement. *Hoye v. Westfield Ins. Co.*, 487 N.W.2d 838 (Mich.App.1992).

An insured under a homeowner's policy had her home partially destroyed by fire. She later defaulted on the note which was secured by a mortgage on the property. The mortgagee foreclosed on the property and, after the redemption period had expired, sold it. The insured then challenged the appraisal award and asserted that the mortgagee was not entitled to the insurance proceeds because the assignment clause in the mortgage did not survive foreclosure. A Michigan trial court ruled against her on both counts, and she appealed to the Court of Appeals of Michigan. On appeal, the court noted that the assignment clause provided that the mortgagee's interest in the insurance proceeds vested at the time of the fire. However, by purchasing the property at the foreclosure sale for the full amount of the debt, the debt became satisfied, and the mortgagee's interest then expired. Since the foreclosure purchase price equaled the full amount of the debt, there was no deficiency and thus no valid claim against the insurance proceeds. This was true regardless of the amount the mortgagee received upon resale of the property. The court reversed the trial court's decision on this issue, but affirmed the appraisal award, holding that it was not in error. *Emmons v. Lake States Ins. Co.*, 484 N.W.2d 712 (Mich.App.1992).

A man and a woman had consensual sexual relations which resulted in the man transmitting genital herpes to the woman. The woman submitted a claim to his homeowner's insurer for damages. The man's insurer denied the claim but intended to defend the man in legal proceedings. The man refused the defense provided by the insurer, agreed to a settlement with the woman, and brought a bad faith claim against his insurer (part of the bad faith claim had been assigned to the woman). A Texas trial court granted the insurer summary judgment on all claims. The man and the woman then appealed to the Court of Appeals of Texas.

Due to the procedural setting the court was limited in its resolution of the dispute. The court did, however, provide an answer to two important issues: does an insured's active participation in sexual intercourse when he knew or suspected that he had genital herpes cause an inference which precludes coverage under an "intentional injury" exclusion clause, and does allowing indemnification for the negligent transmission of a sexual disease violate public policy. In order to avoid liability, the insurer would need to show that the man intended harm, not merely that he intended to engage in sexual relations. The record did not show such an intent, and the court reversed the summary judgment on that issue. The court held that engaging in sexual contact under these circumstances does not infer an intent to harm. The insurer then argued that an indemnification would violate public policy because it would remove personal liability and personal responsibility thereby encouraging the spread of the disease. The court disagreed. It analogized this situation to no fault automobile insurance and held that such a theory does not remove personal liability but instead "insures that the injured are not left without recourse." The court answered these important questions, and remanded the case to resolve the remaining issues. *S.S. v. State Farm Fire & Casualty Co.*, 808 S.W.2d 668 (Tex.App.-Austin 1991).

A sixteen-year-old girl began to have consensual sexual relations with a forty-four-year-old man who was her supervisor at work. The relationship continued for approximately eight months and resulted in the girl contracting herpes, which the man did not know that he had. The girl then sued the man and his homeowner's insurer for the bodily harm which was the result of the disease. A Wisconsin jury awarded both compensatory and punitive damages. The Wisconsin Court of Appeals affirmed in part and reversed in part, and the case reached the Wisconsin Supreme Court.

The first issue was whether the transmission of herpes should be excluded from coverage by the intentional acts clause. The court first ruled that the evidence did not show that the man wished to harm the girl. The insurer argued that coverage should be excluded on other grounds. The sexual contact violated Wisconsin law because the girl was a minor, and the insurer argued that the court should infer intent to harm from this violation of the law. The court refused, and noted that the inference would be proper only if intent to injure was an element of the crime or if the act carried a substantial risk of harm. Sexual contact with a sixteen or seventeen-year-old was distinguished from contact with a minor of "tender" years, and was ruled not to carry a great risk of injury.

The court also refused to infer intended harm from the exposure to a risk of pregnancy because the man had used birth control. Without making a factual finding, the court held that a loss of virginity is not a harm. The court noted that the contact was consensual, that no threats or misrepresentations had been made, that the transmission of the disease was not intentional, and ruled that coverage was not excluded under the intentional acts clause. The insurer then argued that allowing coverage would violate public policy. The court disagreed. It stated that it would not rewrite a policy after a loss and mentioned that the insurer was free to add an applicable exclusion to its policies. The court lastly turned to the issue of punitive damages. It found that the transmission was not wilful, wanton, or reckless, and that no evidence suggested that harm was substantially certain to result. The court affirmed the judgment which allowed coverage, but disallowed the award of punitive damages. *Loveridge v. Chartier*, 468 N.W.2d 146 (Wis.1991).

A high school girls' softball coach became involved in a sexual relationship with a member of the team. Their relationship continued for eighteen months until the young woman, then a college student, attempted suicide. The student and her parents then sued the teacher/coach for damages arising from the sexual relationship. The teacher's homeowner's insurer brought a declaratory relief action in a Washington trial court, asserting that its policy did not provide coverage. The trial court agreed and appeal was taken to the Court of Appeals of Washington. The appellate court noted that an intent to injure the student could be inferred from the teacher's conduct. Because of this, coverage was unavailable under the policy. The court affirmed the trial court's decision. *Allstate Ins. Co. v. Calkins*, 793 P.2d 452 (Wash.App.1990).

An insured suffered damages due to fire. Her homeowner's insurer requested that she submit to an examination under oath prior to suit being filed, as specified in the policy. The insured felt that the exam would "accomplish nothing" and agreed to be examined only subsequent to suit being filed. The request for indemnification was refused. The insured unsuccessfully sued, and then appealed to the Court of Appeal of North Carolina. The court explained that the policy required an insured to comply with its terms, which included examination under oath, prior to bringing suit. It was undisputed that the insured refused, and it was held that an offer to be examined subsequent to a suit being filed could not meet the requirement. The trial court's decision was affirmed. *Baker v. Independent Fire Ins. Co.*, 405 S.E.2d 778 (N.C. App.1991).

A married Colorado couple purchased a homeowner's insurance policy. The policy stated that an insured could be examined under oath regarding a claim. Two months later the house sustained substantial fire damage. Following an examination the insurer rejected the couple's claim stating that the husband set the fire. The couple sued the insurer in a Colorado trial court which determined that the husband set the fire. However, it held that the wife was a separate insured and entitled to coverage. The insurer appealed to the Colorado Court of Appeals which held that the wife was entitled to coverage. The insurer then appealed to the Colorado Supreme Court. On appeal the insurer asserted that because the couple was named as joint insureds, they had joint responsibility to abide by the policy. The wife argued that her personal interest in the property was separate from that of her husband and that she was entitled to full value. She then asserted that her husband would not directly profit from his illegal act. The wife would only recover what she already owned and insured. The insurer argued that if she was entitled to separate coverage, a policy clause limited recovery to one-half of the property value. The supreme court agreed with the wife and stated that her property interest was separate and distinct from her husband's. However, it determined that the wife could not recover a greater interest than she held in the property. She could only recover one-half the value of the damage sustained. *Republic Ins. Co. v. Jernigan*, 753 P.2d 229 (Colo.1988).

A Rhode Island homeowner applied for and received an increased amount of fire insurance on his home subject to an inspection by the insurer. After the homeowner failed to keep an appointment to have the home inspected by his homeowner's insurer, it notified him that a cancellation would issue if he did not return the letter within five days to arrange for an inspection. The homeowner did not respond to the letter. The insurer then sent by certified mail, return receipt requested, a notice of cancellation to the homeowner. His wife refused to accept its delivery although she did retain a postal notice-of-delivery slip identifying the insurer as the sender. The homeowner did not pick up the certified letter and it was returned to the insurer unsigned. After the home was destroyed by fire the insurer denied liability. The homeowner sued the insurer and a superior court held for the homeowner. The insurer appealed to the Rhode Island Supreme Court.

Rhode Island insurance law required the insurer to give notice of cancellation to the homeowner before termination of the policy. The homeowner maintained that the insurer's cancellation was improper due to lack of notice. The insurer contended that it gave "implied actual notice" when the homeowner's wife retained the postal notice-of-delivery slip for her husband, the homeowner. The supreme court held for the homeowner observing that "implied actual notice" was not sufficient. Public policy dictated that the homeowner receive actual notice of cancellation. Since neither the policy nor Rhode Island insurance law stipulated the form of notice, actual receipt of notice of cancellation by the homeowner was required. By attempting to ensure delivery of notice through the more certain means of certified mail the insurer actually incurred a greater danger of nondelivery. Fundamental fairness required that the insurer should have done more to ensure that the homeowner was properly notified of the cancellation. The superior court decision was upheld. *Larocque v. Rhode Island Joint Reinsurance Ass'n*, 536 A.2d 529 (R.I.1988).

II. RESIDENCE AND DOMICILE MATTERS

The cases below involve problems often encountered in determining who is an insured under a homeowner's policy and whether the location of certain accidents precludes recovery.

An Oregon couple's grandchild started a fire on their property which spread and seriously damaged a neighbor's property. The couple was insured under a homeowner's policy which limited coverage to actions by members of the insureds' family. The grandchild and his family had left their home in Texas due to unemployment and had arranged to stay with the insureds until they found work. The family stayed for three weeks and did not unpack their belongings. The neighbors brought a declaratory judgment action in an Oregon trial court seeking coverage under the insureds' homeowner's policy. The trial court found that the insureds' policy did not provide coverage for the grandchild and his family. The insured then appealed to the Court of Appeals of Oregon.

The court of appeals held that the insureds' relatives were not members of the insureds' family under the policy. The court noted that the insureds' relatives were only staying with the insureds due to the son-in-law's unemployment. Although the stay was to be of an indefinite length, it was not permanent. The property damage was not covered under the homeowner's policy. The court of appeals affirmed the trial court's decision. *Lang v. Foremost Ins. Co.*, 778 P.2d 510 (Or.App.1989).

A man was forced by a court order to move out of his marital home and away from his wife and two sons. He later returned and vandalized the home, then shot and killed his two sons and himself. The wife brought a wrongful death claim against the husband's estate, which tendered its defense to the homeowner's insurer. The wife and the insurer were then parties to a declaratory judgment action to determine coverage. A trial court ruled that a household exclusion precluded coverage, and was affirmed by the court of appeals. The wife argued that coverage was proper due to a severability clause, and was granted appeal to the Supreme Court of Minnesota. The household exclusion precluded liability for bodily injury to any insured. "Insured" was defined as "any named insured or any resident of your household." The insurer argued that although the children were not residents of the father's household, they were "insureds" because they were residents of a named insured's household — the mother's. Therefore, coverage was precluded. The severability clause stated that the insurance applied separately to each named insured. The wife claimed that whether the children were to be considered insureds depended upon which named insured was invoking coverage. She argued that they were not "insureds" when the father invoked coverage because they were not residents of his household. The court agreed with the mother; it stated that to find otherwise would ignore the policy's language and the doctrine of severability. Despite a dissenting opinion, the decision was reversed. *American National Fire Ins. Co. v. Estate of Fournelle*, 472 N.W.2d 292 (Minn.1991).

An Indiana woman obtained a homeowner's policy which excluded coverage for intentional acts and for bodily injury to an insured person (including any relative residing in the named insured's household). She then allowed her nephew's three children to move in with her while he looked for work and a new home. There was no predetermined length of time for the children's stay. Subsequently, the insured's son molested the children. The nephew then sued the insured for negligent supervision, and the insurer sought a declaration that it was not liable under the homeowner's policy. Before a federal district court, the insurer contended that the children were not covered under the policy because they were relatives residing with the insured. Accordingly, the policy exclusion prevented recovery for injuries to them. The court agreed with the insurer. The children were not transients, and they manifested more than a mere physical presence in the household. They were completely dependent on the insured for food, clothing, shelter, medicine and parental care. Thus, under a reasonable interpretation of the term "resident," the children were insureds and the nephew could not recover for his injuries. *Allstate Ins. Co. v. Shockley*, 793 F.Supp. 852 (S.D.Ind.1991).

Georgia insureds rented out their home for approximately nineteen years. The last tenant had moved out one month before the home was damaged by fire. The insureds sought recovery of their damages from their homeowner's insurer. The policy provided coverage for the home so long as it was "used principally as a dwelling." Because of this clause and the one month vacancy, the insurer contended that it was not liable. The insureds brought suit in state court seeking a determination of coverage, and the insurer removed the case to a federal district court where it made a motion for summary judgment. The phrase "used principally as a dwelling" was argued by each party to have a different meaning: the insurer asserted that it meant that the structure was occupied as opposed to vacant; the insureds argued that it meant habitually used as a place of abode as opposed to being used for commercial purposes. Both definitions were deemed to be plausible by the court, and the policy's ambiguity was construed in favor of the insureds. Further, the policy did not contain a vacancy provision under the fire loss peril such as it did for other perils. The vacancy was held not to preclude coverage, and the insurer's motion was denied. *Crawford v. Government Employees Ins. Co.*, 771 F.Supp. 1230 (S.D.Ga.1991).

Parties to a purchase agreement for a home agreed that the sellers of the home would remain as tenants for thirty days following the closing. During this tenancy period, the home was damaged by fire. The purchaser of the home had obtained a homeowner's policy, and that insurer paid for the entire loss. The purchaser's insurer then brought suit against the sellers' insurer seeking a contribution. The sellers had not terminated their policy before the fire. They had, however, a month after the fire, terminated the policy retroactively. The retroactive termination was effective to the date of the closing. A Michigan trial court entered summary judgment for the purchaser's insurer, and the sellers' insurer appealed to the Court of Appeals of Michigan.

The sellers' insurer argued that the sellers had no insurable interest in the home subsequent to the closing, and that under Michigan public policy such coverage is void. A determination of whether a party has an insurable interest is made by ascertaining whether the insured will suffer a direct pecuniary loss as a result of damage to the property. The purchaser's insurer argued that the sellers held an insurable interest either based on a leasehold theory or a contract theory. Under the leasehold theory, it was argued that the interest arose because the sellers might not be able to locate alternative housing or because alternative housing might be more costly. The court ruled, however, that this possibility gave rise to a breach of contract action against the landlord, and that no insurable interest was present. Under the contract theory, the sellers' insurer argued that the interest arose because the tenants were parties to the contract for sale. It could not, however, show that the seller had a duty to surrender the possession of the home in the same condition as at closing. The sellers were ruled not to have an insurable interest because they would suffer no direct pecuniary loss in the event of damage to the home. The decision of the trial court was reversed. *Secura Ins. Co. v. Pioneer State Mutual Ins. Co.*, 470 N.W.2d 415 ([Mich.App. 1991).

A Louisiana child was bitten by a dog owned by the daughter of a homeowner. The daughter was leasing the home from her mother. The child's parents filed suit for personal injury against the daughter, mother, and the mother's homeowner's insurer. The daughter brought a third party action seeking a declaratory judgment that she was an insured under the mother's homeowner's policy. The trial court awarded coverage to the daughter and the insurer appealed to the Court of Appeal of Louisiana. The appellate court reversed, noting that the policy defined insureds as the named insured and any person in the residence of the household if they were a relative or a dependent. Since the daughter was leasing, she was not a member of the named insured's current household and was not insured within the meaning of the policy. *Cain v. Parent*, 574 So.2d 497 (La.App.3d Cir.1991).

A Rhode Island couple stabled horses on property which was not covered by their homeowner's policy. One of the horses escaped from the stables and collided with a motor vehicle on a neighboring roadway. The insurer refused to pay for damages since the horse had been stabled on property which was not covered by the policy. A Rhode Island trial court was unable to make a determination of policy coverage and certified the question to the Supreme Court of Rhode Island. The supreme court ruled that the policy unambiguously covered injuries caused by an animal owned by or in the care of any insured. The fact that the horse had been stabled on uninsured property was immaterial and coverage applied. *Hingham Mut. Fire Ins. Co. v. Heroux*, 549 A.2d 265 (R.I.1988).

A man had lived in a home for fourteen years before becoming married and moving into an apartment. He had plans to renovate and reoccupy the home. The man left some belongings in the home, shut off some utilities, and left a forwarding address at the post office. Family emergencies and a death led the man to purchase a different home. The man continued his insurance policy on the unoccupied home, and it was later burglarized. The insurer then learned of the disrepair of the home and canceled the policy, but the man did not receive the notice because his forwarding address had expired. The home was subsequently destroyed by fire and the insurer denied coverage due to a lapsed policy and non-occupancy. The man unsuccessfully sued to recover benefits in a federal court, and then appealed to the U.S. Court of Appeals, Eighth Circuit.

The court focused on the defense of non-occupancy. The man contended that the insurer had waived that defense when it renewed the policy with knowledge that the man had a forwarding address. The court disagreed. The policy renewal could not be considered a waiver of the necessity that the home be occupied. The man's claim that the evidence showed that the home was his primary residence also failed. Evidence cited by the court included the home having not been lived in for over three years and its obvious state of disrepair. Judgment for the insurer was affirmed. *Nancarrow v. Aetna Casualty & Surety Co.*, 932 F.2d 742 (8th Cir.1991).

A Wisconsin farmer possessed a homeowner's policy which excluded coverage for accidents which occurred on the insured premises. The farmer's son was injured when he became entangled in a silo unloader which was located on an uninsured parcel of land owned by the farmer. A state trial court granted the insurer's dismissal motion but the farmer appealed. The court of appeals held that the injuries did not occur on property excluded from coverage. The exclusion only precluded coverage for an occurrence on insured premises. The appeals court ordered the insurer to provide coverage. *Newhouse v. Laidig*, 426 N.W.2d 88 (Wis.App.1988).

A Mississippi woman, while attempting to burn down her house for the insurance proceeds, became trapped by the flames and died. Her husband, who was not involved, attempted to recover accident insurance benefits. The insurer denied coverage. He sued in a federal district court which held that even though the woman was committing arson, her death had been an accident because she did not expect to die, and her expectation was reasonable. Had the insurer included a felony exclusion provision in the policy, it could have denied coverage. Since it failed to do so, summary judgment for the insured was proper. *Brown v. American Intern. Life Assurance Co.*, 778 F.Supp. 912 (S.D.Miss.1991).

An insured man carried a $1 million umbrella liability policy which provided coverage for persons "living with" the insured. An adult son of the insured was involved in an automobile accident which resulted in damages exceeding his automobile liability insurance limits. The umbrella insurer contended that the son "lived" elsewhere and brought suit seeking a declaration that the son was not covered under the umbrella policy. A federal district court directed a verdict in favor of the insurer, and appeal was taken to the U.S. Court of Appeals, Third Circuit.

The dispute concerned the construction of the term "living with." The son had used his parents' address for his driver's license, tax return forms, personal checks and deposit tickets, and job applications. He also frequently visited his parents' home to eat, visit, and celebrate holidays. Immediately following his accident, the son gave his parents' address as his home address, and resided there during his recovery. The court ruled that these facts did not constitute "living with." It stated that Pennsylvania law requires "regular personal contacts" with the insured's home to create coverage. The son's contacts did not meet that standard, and the court affirmed the directed verdict which had been granted for the insurer. *St. Paul Fire and Marine Ins. Co. v. Lewis*, 935 F.2d 1428 (3d Cir.1991).

A woman asked her father if she and her children could stay in his home in order to save money. Although the father had a strained relationship with his daughter he agreed to let her stay in the house for one month. During the stay, her five-year-old boy was injured by a shotgun blast while playing in the basement of the home. The father's insurer asked the Minnesota Court of Appeals to declare the boy a resident of the home and, therefore, excluded from coverage. The court of appeals observed that the policy excluded coverage for insureds who were listed in the policy as "your relatives" or "any other person under the age of 21 who is in the care of any person named above." It also noted that in Minnesota, "residency in a household" is established if a person is "1) living under the same roof; 2) in a close intimate and informal relationship; and 3) where the intended duration is likely to be substantial...." Because the father was in Texas at the time of the injury and because there was no substantial duration to his daughter's stay at the home, there was no residency, held the court of appeals. *State Farm Fire & Cas. Co. v. Lawson*, 406 N.W.2d 20 (Minn.App.1987).

The Court of Appeals of Wisconsin held that a foster child under a one year dispositional order of placement is a resident of the household for homeowner's insurance purposes. The case arose when a foster child placed in a home for a one-year period suffered injuries due to the negligent discharge of an air rifle by one of the biological children in the household. Suit was brought against the homeowner, her son and the insurance carrier which provided homeowner's insurance. Like most homeowner's insurance policies, this policy was designed to cover liability for injury to third parties and excluded coverage for liability to residents of the household.

The court, in holding that the foster child in this case was a resident and thus was excluded from coverage, noted that persons unrelated by blood, marriage or adoption who are living together under the same roof can be considered residents of the same household for policy exclusion purposes. The relationship will depend on the circumstances of each case. However, where, as in this case, the placement was for a one-year period and the foster child was expected to receive the same physical and emotional support of the family as would a natural child, the facts warranted a finding that he was a resident at the time of the injury. The court further noted that its decision was a two-edged sword in that it would now be very difficult for an insurer to avoid defending an insured foster child on the ground that the child is not a resident of the household in cases where a foster child commits a tortious act against a third party. *Waite v. Travelers Ins. Co.*, 331 N.W.2d 643 (Wis.App.1983).

III. POLICY EXCLUSIONS

Incidents involving motor vehicles, intentional acts and other types of occurrences are frequently excluded from homeowner's insurance coverage.

A. Motor Vehicle Exclusions

Three Michigan boys were riding together on a motorcycle when they struck a mailbox and were thrown off, killing one of the boys. The insureds had purchased the stripped down motorcycle with the intent to use it as an off-road vehicle. They never obtained no-fault insurance or registered it with the Secretary of State. The insureds owned a basic homeowner's policy which excluded liability arising out of the ownership, maintenance, or use of a recreational land motor vehicle owned by them. The exclusion did not apply to vehicles designed exclusively for off-road use. The insureds had also obtained a separate recreational vehicle endorsement to insure the motorcycle. The endorsement did not apply to recreational motor vehicles subject to motor vehicle registration. The insurer brought a declaratory judgment action in a Michigan circuit court claiming that it was not required to defend the insureds in a suit brought by the deceased boy's estate. The circuit court granted summary disposition for the insureds and the insurer appealed to the Court of Appeals of Michigan. The court of appeals held that the exclusionary language in the recreational motor vehicle endorsement did not apply to the motorcycle. The court noted that the motorcycle had been stripped down and was not intended for use on streets or roadways. The insureds had specifically purchased coverage for the vehicle by purchasing the recreational motor vehicle endorsement. The insureds had a reasonable belief that the motorcycle was covered under their homeowner's policy. The court found that the exclusionary language in the endorsement was ambiguous and construed it against the insurer. It affirmed the circuit court's decision. *Meridian Mut. Ins. Co. v. Morrow*, 443 N.W.2d 795 (Mich.App.1989).

An insurer issued a homeowner's policy to a couple who owned an all-terrain vehicle. The policy contained an exclusion for motorized vehicles "designed for use off public roads, while off an insured location." A guest of the couple was killed while operating the vehicle on a private roadway which was part of the couple's housing complex. The deceased's estate brought suit against the insureds, and their insurer sought a declaration that it had no duty to defend the insureds. A state trial court ordered coverage, and the insurer appealed to the Superior Court of Pennsylvania. The policy defined "insured location" as the residence premises or any premises used in connection with the residence premises. The court affirmed that this definition was broad enough to include the privately owned roadway. The decision in favor of the deceased's estate was affirmed. *Ucuccioni v. USF&G*, 597 A.2d 149 (Pa.Super.1991).

An Alabama insured found that his four-wheeled all terrain vehicle (ATV) had been stolen from his home. He sought coverage for the ATV under his homeowner's policy. His insurer denied coverage, pointing to a policy exclusion for theft of any motor propelled vehicle. After an Alabama trial court upheld the policy exclusion, the insured appealed to the Alabama Court of Civil Appeals. The insured contended that the ATV was not included in the definition of motor vehicle and was thus not excluded by the policy. The appeals court rejected his argument and held for the insured. It concluded that the policy exclusion unambiguously precluded coverage for theft of any motor propelled vehicle. The court held that it could not create an ambiguity and rewrite the parties' contract. *Wilhite v. State Farm Fire and Cas. Ins.*, 541 So.2d 22 (Ala.Civ.App.1989).

A Minnesota man, insured under a mobile homeowner's policy, designed and built a two-wheel utility trailer. His daughter and a friend hooked the trailer up to an ATV and went for a joyride on a township road. Because the trailer was attached to the ATV by a bolt rather than a cotter pin, it separated from the ATV when the bolt worked its way free. The friend, who was riding in the trailer, was injured. She and her father sued for negligent design and construction of the trailer, and for negligent driving of the ATV. The insurer brought a declaratory action against its insureds, and the trial court ruled against it. The insurer appealed successfully to the court of appeals, and further appeal was taken to the Minnesota Supreme Court. The supreme court first noted that an individual may recover under both an automobile and a homeowner's policy where two independent acts (one vehicle-related and one nonvehicle-related) combined to cause injury. However, in this case there was only a remote possibility that the friend's injuries could have been caused without the use of a motor vehicle. Accordingly, even though the trailer had been negligently designed and constructed, any injury arising out of this negligence could only have occurred through the use of a motor vehicle, which was excluded by the policy. The court affirmed the appellate court's ruling for the insurer. *State Farm Ins. Co. v. Seefeld*, 481 N.W.2d 62 (Minn.1992).

A Maryland insured bought a skeleton car for restoration. The insured then obtained show tags and whenever he took it to a show he pulled it on a trailer. While working on the car one day a fire started and the car was completely destroyed. The insurance policy provided that it did not cover property damage arising out of the use of an automobile but did cover a stored vehicle. The insurer filed a declaratory judgment action seeking a declaration that the homeowner's policy did not cover the loss due to the automobile exclusion. The court held that the automobile exclusion did not apply and the insurer appealed to the Court of Appeals of Maryland.

On appeal, the insurer contended that the vehicle was not in dead storage. The insurer argued that dead in this context means totally inoperable, incapable of any function whatsoever, while storage means that which is put beyond use, beyond any handling or dealing with in the ordinary course of things. Thus, the insurer determined that the car was not in dead storage as it was fully operable and was in fact driven from the yard to the garage to be regularly repaired and maintained. The court disagreed, and determined that the car was a collectible item, not a means of transportation. Just because the car was operable and occasionally moved from one part of the property to the other did not change the status of the car. The court further stated that had the insurer wished it could have incorporated into the policy the very restrictions on the meaning of dead storage which it asked to find applied in the language that it actually used. Therefore, the court held for the insured and affirmed the decision of the trial court. *Allstate Ins. Co. v. Geiwitz*, 587 A.2d 1185 (Md.App.1991).

A California man purchased a homeowner's policy which insured him for "damages because of bodily injury or property damage." However, the policy contained an exclusion for injuries which arose out of the ownership, maintenance or use of a motor vehicle owned by the insured. The insured purchased three new tires from a tire store for his car. Two of the tires developed slow leaks, so he purchased a can of tire leak sealant which he injected into one of the tires. It was ineffective. He then brought the two tires to a welding shop so that the wheel rims could be repaired. During the welding process, the tire which had been injected with sealant exploded and seriously injured the welder. The welder sued the insured who sought coverage from his insurer. It brought a declaratory relief action, however, asserting that the automobile maintenance exclusion applied to preclude coverage. The trial court granted summary judgment for the insured, and the insurer appealed to the California Court of Appeal, Third District.

On appeal, the insurer asserted that the insured had clearly been involved in attempting to keep his vehicle in a state of repair. The appellate court agreed, noting that the insured's entire purpose both in using the sealant and in hiring the welder was to maintain his tire's air pressure. Thus, his car was not the mere "passive site of negligence divorced from the vehicle's maintenance." Accordingly, the court determined that the motor vehicle maintenance exclusion applied, and it reversed the trial court's decision. *State Farm Fire and Cas. Co. v. Salas*, 271 Cal.Rptr. 642 (Cal.App.3d Dist.1990).

An Arizona man possessed and lived in a mobile home. He obtained a liability policy on the mobile home in the amount of $25,000. It covered damages from bodily injury or property damage, but contained an exclusion for bodily injuries "arising out of the ownership, maintenance, operation, use, loading or unloading of ... [a]ny motor vehicle." The insured man and a friend participated in slaughtering a steer on the mobile home property. After the steer was slaughtered, it was placed under a tripod. The steer was to be pulled into a vertical position by a rope which was attached to the trailer hitch of the insured's vehicle. As the steer was being pulled off the ground, the tripod collapsed and injured the friend who sued the property owner. The friend filed a personal injury lawsuit against the man, and his homeowner's insurer sought a declaratory judgment that it was not liable to pay any damages because of the automobile exclusion. When a trial court granted summary judgment for the insurer, the man and his friend appealed. The Arizona Court of Appeals addressed the issue of whether the automobile exclusion clause in the man's homeowner's policy precluded coverage for the accident. The court noted that a mere connection between an injury and an automobile is insufficient to allow the application of an automobile exclusion to a homeowner's policy. A causal connection between the injury and the automobile is required before such an exclusion may be given effect. Because the truck involved in the accident had not been negligently driven, no causal connection between it and the injury existed. The policy exclusion therefore did not apply, and the trial court's decision was reversed. *American Modern Home Ins. Co. v. Rocha*, 729 P.2d 949 (Ariz.App.1986).

A Montana couple owned several antique vehicles, only one of which was licensed for road use. When the garage containing the vehicles burned, the couple's homeowner's insurer denied coverage on the vehicles. The couple then sued in a state district court. When the court granted the insurer's request to dismiss the case, the couple appealed. Before the Montana Supreme Court, the couple argued that the exclusionary clause upon which the insurer based its denial was ambiguous. The policy stated: "This coverage excludes ... Motorized vehicles, except such vehicles pertaining to the service of the premises and not licensed for road use...." The couple argued that the provision could refer to two types of vehicles, vehicles to service the premises or vehicles unlicensed for road use. The court disagreed. The grammatical structure of the provision, explained the court, was such that "pertaining to the service of the premises" and "not licensed for road use" modified the same word, "vehicles." According to the court, the policy clearly and unambiguously covered only vehicles that met both the requirements listed in the provision. The court therefore ruled that the policy did not provide coverage for the couple's antique vehicles. The ruling of the lower court was affirmed. *Payne v. Safeco Ins. Co. of America*, 720 P.2d 1197 (Mont.1986).

In a Minnesota case, a man's girlfriend, riding as a front seat passenger with him in his automobile, grabbed the steering wheel in an attempt to induce him to stop the vehicle so they could settle a misunderstanding. The car then rolled over, severely injuring the driver. He later sued the woman, alleging that her negligence contributed to his injuries. The woman lived with her parents, who had a homeowner's policy and an automobile policy. After the injured driver sued the woman, the homeowner's insurer brought suit to determine which insurer, if either, was responsible for payment of the claim against the woman. A state trial court held that the homeowner's insurer was liable and it appealed.

The Minnesota Supreme Court pointed out that the woman would be covered under the homeowner's policy unless an automobile exclusion in the policy applied. The exclusion would deny coverage if the injury arose out of the use of a motor vehicle operated by an insured person. According to the court, if the woman's act of grabbing the steering wheel is considered "operating" the vehicle, then the exclusion would apply. After observing that a vehicle normally has only one operator unless the driver invites the passenger to share in that operation, the supreme court ruled that the woman's action was a disruption of someone else's operation of the vehicle rather than an act of operating the vehicle herself. The homeowner's insurer was ordered to pay the claim of the injured driver. *West Bend Mut. Ins. Co. v. Milwaukee Mut. Ins. Co.*, 384 N.W.2d 877 (Minn.1986).

B. Intentional Acts Exclusions

A seventy-year-old North Carolina woman worked for a shoe store as a sales clerk. She began speaking to a customer's mother while a sixty-eight-year-old fellow employee was assisting the customer. The younger employee became upset with her for "invading his territory" and gave her a push. Because she was not expecting it, she fell to the floor and broke her arm. She then brought suit against the younger employee for her injury. His homeowner's insurer sought declaratory relief in a state trial court, asserting that its insured was not entitled to coverage for his act in shoving his fellow employee. The court found coverage, but the court of appeals reversed. Appeal was then taken to the Supreme Court of North Carolina. On appeal, the insured contended that he did not intend to knock the woman to the floor or cause any other injury to her. The insurer asserted that even if there was no intent to harm, there was an intentional act on the part of the insured which precluded coverage. The court agreed with the insured. Here, the term "accident" was not defined by the policy. Accordingly, coverage had to be provided for an intentional act which "accidentally" resulted in injury. The court reversed the appellate court's decision and held that the insured was entitled to coverage. *North Carolina Farm Bureau Mutual Ins. Co. v. Stox*, 412 S.E.2d 318 (N.C.1992).

A man was awakened from sleep, and fired a handgun at what he perceived to be a dog in his garbage. The supposed dog was actually a garbageman, who suffered injuries and sued the man in a Tennessee trial court. The court held that an intentional acts exclusionary clause did not preclude coverage by a homeowner's insurance policy. The insurer appealed to the Court of Appeals of Tennessee. The policy excluded coverage for acts intended by an insured person. The issue was whether the unexpected result of an intentional act was also precluded from coverage. Prior Tennessee cases have made clear that an insured person is not protected against intentional acts even though the resulting injury may have been accidental. The court declined to distinguish the earlier cases on the grounds that they dealt with other types of coverage, and reversed the judgment in favor of the insured. *Allstate Ins. Co. v. Brooks*, 814 S.W.2d 737 (Tenn.App.1990).

To conceal a burglary, one of three burglars started a fire to damage the home they had burglarized. The perpetrators were caught and pled guilty to aggravated arson among other charges. The home's insurer filed a subrogation suit against the perpetrators, one of whom was possibly covered under his father's homeowner's policy. The father's insurer then brought suit against the owner of the damaged home and the perpetrators seeking a declaration that it was not responsible for defending or indemnifying the father's son. A New Jersey trial court found that since the son had pled guilty he was precluded from arguing otherwise in a different proceeding. The father and son then appealed to the Superior Court of New Jersey, Appellate Division.

The insurer pointed out that the son had pled guilty to aggravated arson, which is intentional arson, and that it was not responsible for intentional acts of additional insureds, such as the son. The father and son argued that the son's pleading was part of a plea bargain, and that he should be able to relitigate his intent in another trial. The appeals court found that a plea bargain is not the same as a factual finding by the jury. While the plea may be presented as evidence in a later trial, it does not preclude another trial. The court of appeals reversed the summary judgment granted in the lower court and ordered the father's insurer to prove the son's intent in order to remove its liability to defend or indemnify. *Prudential v. Kollar*, 578 A.2d 1238 (N.J.Super.A.D. 1990).

A man was killed when another man accidentally discharged a shotgun which he was attempting to clean. The man who discharged the gun was insured through his parents' homeowner's policy. The deceased's estate brought a wrongful death action against the insured, who had pled guilty to a criminal charge of second degree manslaughter. His insurer denied coverage because the policy contained an exclusion for losses which could be reasonably expected from criminal acts. It then brought suit requesting a declaration that it had no duty to defend the insured. A trial court denied the insurer's motion for summary judgment, and the insurer successfully appealed. The Court of Appeals of New York then granted review.

Facts which were established in a criminal proceeding may be given a preclusive effect in a later civil proceeding only if the party had a full and fair opportunity to litigate the identical issue in the criminal proceeding. In this case, the lower court correctly had found that the deceased died as the result of a criminal act. However, the inquiry had to proceed beyond that point. The second prong of the exclusion clause requires that the loss — death — must have been reasonably expected from the act — negligent discharge of the shotgun. This issue had not been litigated, and the court ruled that the insured must be granted an opportunity to contest that issue. The trial court's denial of the insurer's summary judgment motion was reinstated. *Allstate Ins. Co. v. Zuk*, 571 N.Y.S.2d 429 (Ct.App.1991).

Some Iowa boys were playing a game named "lob ball." One boy quit playing because the others would not let him pitch. Another boy became irritated and threw a baseball at the quitter's head which tragically killed him. The deceased youth's parents sought proceeds from the homeowner's policy of the parents of the boy who had killed their son. A district court ruled that the insurer had to provide coverage. The insurer appealed to the Supreme Court of Iowa arguing that the policy's intentional injury exclusion barred coverage. The supreme court, however, disagreed, since the insurer could not prove that the boy should have known that his friend would die when he threw the baseball at him. Thus, the trial court's decision was affirmed. *Amco Ins. Co. v. Haht*, 490 N.W.2d 843 (Iowa 1992).

Trying to cope with the death of his son, a father became very drunk and spread gasoline around his house. He ignited it, and suffered second and third degree burns. The insurer brought a declaratory action to determine whether its homeowner's insurance policy provided coverage for the house fire. A Maryland federal district court granted the insured summary judgment and the insurer appealed. The U.S. Court of Appeals, Fourth Circuit, found that the homeowner's policy required actual intention to cause a loss before coverage could be denied. The court believed that the insured's "insanity" and suicidal purpose might prevent him from forming the requisite intent. Thus, a fact question existed as to the insured's intention. Accordingly, the court vacated the summary judgment in favor of the insured and remanded the case for further consideration. *Erie Ins. Exchange v. Stark*, 962 F.2d 349 (4th Cir.1992).

A Michigan insured embarked on a killing spree in a restaurant. After the insured was sued by an injured party, the insurer brought an action seeking a declaratory judgment that the homeowner's policy excluded coverage for the damages sustained. The policy stated that the insurer did not cover any bodily injury or property damage which could reasonably be expected to result from the intentional or criminal acts of an insured person or which were in fact intended by the insured. The trial court granted summary judgment for the insurer and the insured appealed to the Court of Appeals of Michigan.

On appeal, the court noted that the Michigan Supreme Court has enumerated a two part test to determine whether an insurer may obviate its duty to indemnify under an exclusion. Coverage will be excluded when 1) the insured acted either intentionally or criminally and 2) the resulting injury was either reasonably expected or actually intended to result from such criminal or intentional conduct. The court noted that insanity may preclude a person from forming a specific criminal intent and therefore such a person may not have acted intentionally as the term is used in insurance policies. Thus, the court noted that the presence of expert testimony to the effect that the plaintiff's insured was either not aware of what he was doing or was unable to control his actions while he was embarking on his killing spree was needed to determine whether the plaintiff acted intentionally. Summary disposition was improper. The court remanded the case. *Allstate Ins. Co. v. Miller*, 460 N.W.2d 612 (Mich.App.1990).

A woman left a bar with some men. She was seen by a man who mistakenly believed that the woman was his estranged wife. The man followed the woman outside the bar and kicked her, thereby causing serious injuries. The woman was granted a judgment in a personal injury lawsuit, and the man's homeowner's insurer brought suit seeking a declaration that it had no duty to indemnify the man. A state trial court granted judgment for the insurer, but was reversed on appeal. The Supreme Court of Colorado subsequently agreed to hear the case. The primary issue was whether the coverage was precluded by an intentional acts exclusion. The specific language provided that coverage did not apply to harm "which is expected or intended by any insured." The man argued that coverage should be available because the harm to this particular woman was unexpected and unforeseen. The insurer countered that the man had intended bodily injury, and that it was irrelevant that he intended to harm someone other than the person actually injured. The court dismissed the theory that an examination should be made as to whether the conduct constituted a reasonable mistake; "[I]ssues germane to intentional torts litigation and to exclusionary clause insurance contract litigation 'involve two fundamentally different areas of the law, each founded on separate and distinct legal theories and principles.'" The correct focus, decided the court, was whether the harm was intended. The court reversed the appellate court's decision and reinstated the judgment for the insurer. *American Family Mutual Ins. Co. v. Johnson*, 816 P.2d 952 (Colo.1991).

A Washington couple purchased a homeowner's insurance policy which excluded liability coverage for acts by an insured which were expected or intended to result in bodily injury, including death. Thereafter, the wife decided she wasn't a very good mother; she then proceeded to strangle and drown her two-and-a-half year old son to stop his suffering. The state charged her with first degree murder. The court acquitted her by virtue of a finding of insanity. The husband then filed a claim with the insurer for liability coverage for his son's death. The insurer filed a declaratory judgment action to determine if coverage had to be provided. The trial court granted summary judgment to the husband and the insurer appealed to the Court of Appeals of Washington. The insurer argued on appeal that the wife's acquittal by reason of insanity did not preclude a finding that she expected or intended her son's death so as to exclude coverage under the policy. The appellate court agreed. However, it then stated that the question of whether a person is capable of forming intent is one of fact. Here, the husband had provided affidavits from three experts who all stated that the wife did not appreciate the nature and quality of her actions at the time of the incident. Since the insurer presented nothing other than the wife's statements to police, it had failed to raise a material issue of fact regarding the wife's ability to perceive the nature and quality of her act. The court affirmed the entry of summary judgment, and also affirmed the award of costs of the wife's guardian *ad litum*, against the insurer. *Public Employees Mutual Ins. Co. v. James F.*, 828 P.2d 63 (Wash.App.1992).

A sixteen-year-old boy visited a friend's home and was given cocaine to inject, which caused his death. The friend was insured under his parents' homeowner's policy. The insurer brought suit seeking a declaration that the incident be excluded from coverage due to a clause which excludes coverage for injuries which were

Sec. III   POLICY EXCLUSIONS   279

"expected or intended" by an insured. A trial court ruled for the insured, the insurer successfully appealed, and the case reached the Supreme Court of Missouri.

The issue was whether a court should infer an intent to harm. Case law from other states showed a division over when to infer an intent to harm. Certain states allow an inference upon a showing that some harm was intended, and hold it irrelevant that the harm realized was different than that intended. Other states require that the harm realized must have been intended, never allowing an inference. Missouri chose the latter approach. Though the court recognized injecting cocaine as a dangerous activity it refused to infer an intent to kill. Reckless activity alone was ruled not to exclude coverage. The evidence did not show that the friend intended death, and the decision of the trial court was reinstated. *American Family Mutual Ins. Co. v. Pacchetti*, 808 S.W.2d 369 (Mo.1991).

A Colorado ten-year-old vandalized an elementary school, causing substantial property damage. The school district's insurer reimbursed the school district for the property damage incurred, then filed suit against the boy's parents. A state statute allows a school district to recover damages from the parents of a minor child who willfully damages property belonging to the district. The court found for the insurer. The boy's parents then filed a loss claim related to the damages caused by their son's vandalism under their homeowner's policy. After coverage was denied, the boy's parents sued the insurer. The trial court found that the parents were barred from recovery by the intentional act exclusion of the policy. The court of appeals affirmed. The boy's parents then appealed to the Supreme Court of Colorado.

The issue on appeal was whether the exclusion provision clearly and unambiguously denied coverage. The parents contended that the policy created a separate insurance status for each insured and that the exclusion clause could be independently applied to each insured. The boy would then be excluded but not his parents. The Supreme Court, however, ruled that the policy was a contract and should be enforced in a manner consistent with the intentions of the parties. The court construed the exclusion to represent the parties' agreement to deny coverage when damage was intended by any of the insureds. The supreme court affirmed the lower courts' decisions. *Chacon v. American Family Mut. Ins. Co.*, 788 P.2d 748 (Colo.1990).

A Florida man rented the master bedroom in the home of his ex-wife. He was awakened one night by his ex-wife's son, who broke a window, climbed through the opening, and advanced on him, wildly swinging his fists. The man, fearing for his life, grabbed his pistol and fired a warning shot. When the son continued to advance, the man placed the gun flat in the palm of his hand and struck the son. The gun accidentally discharged, injuring the son. The son sued the man, alleging that the shooting was intentional. The man's insurer also sued, asserting that it had no duty to defend or indemnify the man because the shooting was intentional. The trial court ruled for the insurer, and the man successfully appealed to the court of appeals. The insurer then appealed to the Supreme Court of Florida.

The insured conceded that intentional acts were excluded under his policy, but contended that public policy supported coverage because he had been acting in self-defense. The court, however, held that insurance companies set their rates based on random occurrences, and indemnification for intentional acts would encourage people to commit wrongful acts. The court stated that people who wished to insure themselves against liability for lawfully defending themselves must bargain for such coverage and pay for it. It refused to rewrite a policy to provide coverage where the clear language of the policy did not. The court reversed the appellate court's decision, and denied coverage to the insured. *State Farm Fire and Casualty Co. v. Marshall*, 554 So.2d 504 (Fla.1989).

Three Massachusetts youths broke into a junior high school and started several fires which resulted in extensive damage to the school. The city sued the youths for the damage, and a homeowner's insurer for one of the youths' parents intervened in the action. The insurer contended that its policy excluded coverage for expected or intended property damage by the insured. A jury in a Massachusetts trial court determined that the insureds' son intended to start the fire but did not intend the substantial damage that resulted. The trial court declared that the policy's exclusion did not apply to the son's activities and held that the policy provided coverage. After a series of appeals, the case reached the Supreme Judicial Court of Massachusetts. On appeal, the insurer argued that the jury's finding that the son intended to start the fire at the school implied that he harbored the intent to cause property damage. The court agreed, stating that the policy's exclusion applied when there is a showing of a deliberate setting of a fire with the intent of causing some property damage. It was not necessary that the son did not intend to cause the exact extent of the damage which resulted. It noted that the son had started several separate fires in the school and had made no effort to extinguish them before he left. The court ruled that the jury's finding that the son deliberately intended to set the fires implied as a matter of law that he intended to cause some property damage. Therefore, the exclusion for intended property damage applied to the son's activities and the insurer did not have to pay. *City of Newton v. Krasnigor*, 536 N.E.2d 1078 (Mass.1989).

A Nebraska insured hosted a party where money was believed to have been taken by one of the guests. The insured visited the guest's home to ask him about the missing money, and took two loaded guns with him. After a confrontation with the guest's father, the insured fired his gun at the guest's car. When the insured reached his own car he heard a shot, turned back to the house and saw a person silhouetted in the doorway. The insured fired towards the doorway. The guest was struck in the head and died. The insured was convicted of manslaughter and the personal representative of the guest's estate filed a wrongful death action against the insured. The insured referred the suit to his homeowner's insurer. Under the homeowner's policy, coverage did not apply to bodily injury or property damage which was expected or intended by the insured. The insurer defended the insured, but reserved the right to deny coverage. The insurer then brought a declaratory action to determine whether the insured was covered under the policy. A Nebraska district court granted summary judgment for the insurer and the insured appealed to the Supreme Court of Nebraska.

The supreme court held that the policy did not cover the insured's liability to the guest's estate. The court noted that an injury is expected or intended if the reason for the insured's act is to inflict bodily injury or if the character of the act is such that the intention to inflict injury can be inferred as a matter of law. The insured had admitted that he shot at the doorway, knowing there was a person standing in it. He knew the weapon he used was powerful and capable of causing serious damage. At the time he fired the fatal shot, the insured believed the person standing in the doorway was the guest. From the insured's actions it could only be concluded that the insured expected or intended to injure the guest. The supreme court affirmed the lower court decision. *State Farm Fire & Cas. Co. v. Victor*, 442 N.W.2d 880 (Neb.1989).

A man burst into the home of his ex-girlfriend, chased the man she dated into the street, and shot him several times. The injured man then heard his assailant whimper, and take his own life. Upon his recovery, the injured man brought suit against the deceased's estate. The estate tendered its defense to the deceased's father's homeowner's insurer. The insurer denied coverage under an intentional act exclusionary clause, and the estate argued that the shooting should not be ruled to be an intentional act because the insured was insane. A trial court granted summary judgment for the insurer, was reversed on appeal, and the issue was reviewed by the Supreme Court of Minnesota. The issue involved articulating a standard of intent necessary for an act to be ruled intentional for the purposes of liability insurance. Standards from foreign jurisdictions were examined, and the court expressed a desire to establish a new measure which would fall between the two existing rules. Two aspects of intent to act were recognized: cognitive and volitional. Criminal law in Minnesota exclusively applies the cognitive element—a person must understand the nature and wrongfulness of an act. The court adopted the cognitive element as a portion of its test and, despite a dissent, the court held that for the purposes of liability coverage a standard of intent must also include a volitional element — a person must have the ability to control his actions. Unless both elements are met the act may not be deemed to be intentional. The case was remanded for consideration with respect to the newly adopted standard. *State Farm Fire & Casualty Co. v. Wicka*, 474 N.W.2d 324 (Minn.1991).

An Ohio man, suffering from Alzheimer's disease, shot and killed a woman at her home, then committed suicide. He held a homeowner's insurance policy at this time. However, coverage did not extend to bodily injury which was either expected or intended by the insured. When the woman's estate sued the insured's estate, the insurer brought a declaratory judgment action, seeking a declaration that it had no duty to defend or indemnify the insured's estate. The trial court held for the insurer, and the two estates appealed to the Court of Appeals of Ohio. The court of appeals noted that the burden of proof was on the insured's estate to show that the insured was insane at the time of the shooting. Here, there had been expert testimony on both sides of this question, and the trial court had chosen to side with the insurer's expert. Thus, the ruling that the insured was capable of formulating the intent to injure was upheld, and the judgment for the insurer was upheld. *Midwestern Indemnity Co. v. Manthey*, 589 N.E.2d 95 (Ohio App.6th Dist.1990).

A Georgia man, insured by a homeowner's policy, became delusional and psychotic after weeks of sleep deprivation while he was caring for his dying wife. He engaged in an argument with another man in a shopping center parking lot and eventually pulled out a gun, shooting the man five times and killing him. The widow sued the insured for damages, and he sought defense and indemnification from his insurer under his homeowner's policy. It filed a declaratory judgment action, however, seeking to resolve whether coverage was available under the policy. At trial, it was conclusively established that the insured was mentally ill, but the jury nevertheless returned a verdict in favor of the insurer, finding that the insured expected or intended bodily injury to result from his acts. The insured and the widow appealed to the Court of Appeals of Georgia.

On appeal, they argued that a mentally incompetent person was incapable of intent as a matter of law and, in the alternative, they asserted that the court should have applied the doctrine of transferred intent, holding that the insured accidently shot his victim while intending to shoot a third person even though there was no actual third person present at the time of the shooting. The court, however, disagreed. It stated that the question of the insured's intent had been properly submitted to the jury. Further, it held that the defense of transferred intent had been presented to the jury and decided adversely. It was not required that the trial court judge decide this issue. The court thus affirmed the trial court's decision and held that the insurer was not liable under the policy. *Eubanks v. Nationwide Mut. Fire Ins. Co.*, 393 S.E.2d 452 (Ga.App.1990).

An insured under a homeowner's policy allegedly touched a three-year-old girl in the anal or vaginal area when she was at a child-care center in the insured's home. He maintained that he didn't touch her; she stated that he did. No other information was available, and thus no criminal charges were brought against the insured. A civil action was then initiated against the insured on theories of both intentional harm and negligence. The case went to the jury which returned a general verdict in favor of the child and her parents. The insurer filed an action in federal district court seeking a declaration that it need not indemnify the insured for the damages resulting from the underlying action based upon an intentional acts exclusion. The court granted the parents' motion for summary judgment, finding that they had met their burden of showing that the touching was negligent, and that the insurer had failed to show that the touching was wilful. The insurer then appealed to the U.S. Court of Appeals, Ninth Circuit.

On appeal, the insurer contended that § 533 of the California Insurance Code precluded coverage here because the case involved "digital anal or vaginal penetration." The insurer argued that such touching was intentional as a matter of law and that nothing more had to be shown to relieve it of liability. The court, however, stated that it was possible for the child to have been touched accidentally or negligently. The underlying case had not proven intentional child molestation. Because a general verdict had been returned, the jury might have found negligence. Since the insurer had not presented evidence that the touching in question was intentional molestation, the court affirmed the district court's grant of summary judgment. *State Farm Fire & Casualty Co. v. Nycum,* 943 F.2d 1100 (9th Cir.1991).

A Missouri couple purchased homeowner's insurance. While the policy was in effect, the mother left their two-year-old daughter alone with her husband who then raped her. Following this sexual contact, the daughter contracted the sexually transmitted disease chlamydia. A claim was made to the homeowner's insurer which then sued for a declaratory judgment to determine whether it was liable for this claim. The circuit court granted the insurer summary judgment. The child's parents appealed, arguing that the intentional act exclusion in the policy did not bar recovery because the insured was unaware that he was a chlamydia carrier at the time of the rape. The court of appeals, however, denied coverage, citing the chlamydia as a reasonable and foreseeable consequence of the insured's intentional act. Accordingly, the court affirmed the summary judgment in favor of the insurer. *Mid-Century Ins. Co. v. L.D.G.*, 835 S.W.2d 436 (Mo.App.W.D.1992).

Sec. III   POLICY EXCLUSIONS   283

A Colorado homeowner was insured for personal liability coverage. The policy excluded coverage for intentional torts. While the policy was in effect, the insured was sued by his niece, who alleged that he had sexually assaulted her. His insurer denied coverage and a trial court agreed that neither defense nor indemnification was required. He appealed to the Colorado Court of Appeals, which held that it did not matter if negligence was alleged in the complaint against the insured because intent to harm was presumed from sexual misconduct. Accordingly, it affirmed the ruling in favor of the insurer. *Nikolai v. Farmers Alliance Mutual Ins. Co.*, 830 P.2d 1070 (Colo.App.1991).

Two individuals filed a civil action against an insured Kentucky man for his alleged acts of sexual molestation. The insured requested his homeowner's insurer to defend and indemnify him against any damages awarded. The insurer brought suit for a declaration of rights. A Kentucky district court granted summary judgment in favor of the insurer, and appeal was taken to the Court of Appeals of Kentucky. The appellate court noted that courts broadly construe the meaning of "occurrence" under a homeowner's policy to grant coverage to insureds. However, the court believed it was inconceivable that a criminal act of sexual molestation could be classified as an occurrence which would create a loss under the policy. It was not an accident. The court denied coverage, and affirmed the trial court's decision. *Thompson v. West American Ins. Co.*, 839 S.W.2d 579 (Ky.App.1992).

A girl was subjected to sexual abuse while at the home of a Florida insured. The insured's son committed the abuse. In the lawsuit which was brought against the insured and her son, the insurer paid over $250,000 for the insured's negligence in failing to prevent the abuse. Another $750,000 was at issue with respect to the son's liability. The trial court granted the award, and the insurer appealed to the Florida District Court of Appeal. That court determined that there could be no coverage for the intentional acts of the son in abusing the child. The $750,000 award was reversed. *Consolidated American Ins. Co. v. Henderson*, 590 So.2d 1050 (Fla.App.3rd Dist.1991).

A Missouri man, insured under a homeowner's policy, abducted four people, subjecting them to physical, psychological and sexual torture. All four victims died. The insured tied a plastic bag over the head of one victim, intentionally causing suffocation. The other three victims died either as a result of drug injection, asphyxiation from being gagged, bleeding or infection. The families of all four victims brought suit against the insured for wrongful death, and for the abusive actions of the insured prior to the victims' deaths. Because the insured had pleaded guilty to one count of first degree murder and three counts of second degree murder, the homeowner's insurer charged that the insured intended all four deaths. The trial court agreed, granting summary judgment. The families appealed to the Missouri Court of Appeals. On appeal, the court noted that there was clear evidence in the record confirming that the insured had intended to *harm* his victims by torturing them. However, with respect to the three victims for whom the insured had pleaded guilty to second degree murder, there was a question as to whether the insured had intended their deaths. It was possible that he only intended to torture them, and that they had died accidentally. Thus, the summary judgment had to be reversed for those three wrongful death claims. In all other respects, the judgment was affirmed. *Economy Fire and Casualty Co. v. Haste*, 824 S.W.2d 41 (Mo.App.1991).

In February 1982, a Virginia man believed that the voice of God commanded him to kill his friend. The man searched his house for a gun, found a .22 caliber pistol, loaded it with bullets and went to the victim's house. The man started talking to the victim, and then, without warning fired six shots at the victim from close range, injuring him severely. The man was insured under his parents' homeowner's policy. The victim filed a lawsuit seeking damages against the man and his parents. The insurer sought a declaratory judgment, saying that the shooting was not covered by the policy and that the insurer had no duty to defend in the victim's lawsuit or to pay any damages arising from it. A trial court ruled that the shooting was excluded from coverage because the man "was aware of what he was doing and intended the resulting injury." The victim appealed.

The Virginia Supreme Court ruled that although the man did not know right from wrong, he knew that he was firing the pistol at the victim. He also knew that the victim would be wounded as a result. It ruled that he "did have this minimal degree of awareness of his actions." The shooting was therefore intentional and thus was excluded from coverage under the policy. The trial court's decision was affirmed. *Johnson v. Ins. Co. of North America*, 350 S.E.2d 616 (Va.1986).

C. Business Pursuit Exclusions

A number of cases deal with the question of what is a "business pursuit" rendering coverage excludable under a homeowner's policy.

A retired man worked at various odd jobs to supplement his income. He worked as a handyman at a particular ranch for approximately three months, arriving for work every morning and working from twelve to twenty hours per week. A coworker was injured by a splinter of wood which flew from the wall of a barn which the man was repairing. The coworker sued both the man and the ranch, both of whom were insured through homeowner's policies. The man's insurer denied a duty to defend or indemnify because of a "business pursuits" exclusion. A Washington trial court granted summary judgment for the coworker, and the man's insurer appealed.

The Court of Appeals of Washington explained that a business pursuit exclusion applies if the activity in question was performed on a "regular and continuous basis" and was profit motivated. Parttime employment may satisfy the regular and continuous test, and the employment does not need to consist of a single trade or occupation. The man had performed handyman type work for two successive years, and had advertised his services on a bulletin board. The work was found to be regular and continuous. The insured argued that the work was not profit motivated because he did not need the money. The court held that the activity does not need to be performed as a "major source of livelihood" in order to exclude coverage. The work was thus also found to have been profit motivated. The appellate court reversed the lower court's decision and held that the business pursuit clause excluded coverage. *Stoughton v. Mutual Enumclaw*, 810 P.2d 80 (Wash.App.1991).

A Georgia farmer's cow escaped from its fenced enclosure on the property and collided with a car. The driver and passenger filed tort actions against the farmer. The farmer sought coverage under his homeowner's policy and the insurer sought a declaratory judgment to determine its obligations under the policy. The policy excluded coverage for any personal liability and medical payments to others resulting from activities in connection with the insured's business. The policy then defined business as a trade, profession, or other occupation including farming, all whether full or part time. The trial court found for the insurer and the farmer appealed to the Court of Appeals of Georgia.

The farmer contended that the exception covering activities in conjunction with business pursuits which are ordinarily considered nonbusiness in nature applied because an escaping cow was nonbusiness in nature. The policy contained no definition of nonbusiness in nature. The farmer further relied on the fact of the insurer's agent's visit to his home and the observance of his cows as proof of the insurer's intention to be bound by the terms of the policy. The court, however, found that keeping cows fenced was an activity related to the business of cattle farming. And it naturally followed that an escaping cow was an activity incident to normal farming activities. Therefore, the court upheld the business pursuits exclusion and denied coverage. *Alewine v. Horace Mann Ins. Co.*, 398 S.E.2d 756 (Ga.App.1990).

An eleven-month-old Washington child fell against an iron woodburning stove at his babysitter's home, severely burning his right hand. At the time of the accident, the babysitter had been providing childcare in her home for four children on a regular basis for three months. She was paid a regular stipend per day per child. Her homeowner's insurance policy specifically excluded liability coverage for personal injury "arising out of business pursuits of any insured." Excepted from that exclusion, however, were activities which were ordinarily incident to nonbusiness pursuits. The insurer refused to provide coverage and the woman sued in a Washington trial court. The trial court found for the insurer and the insured appealed to the Court of Appeals of Washington.

The court noted that this issue was of first impression in Washington. It determined that babysitting was a business pursuit if conducted on a regular and continuous basis for compensation. The proper focus in analyzing the incident activities exception should not be on the activity, but on the babysitter's alleged negligence. In this case, the babysitter admittedly had to heat her house. Her negligence was not in doing that, but in failing to keep the child away from the stove. This was related to the insured's business of operating a daycare facility. Therefore, the court upheld the business pursuits exclusion and denied coverage. *Rocky Mountain Cas. Co. v. St. Martin*, 802 P.2d 144 (Wash.App.1990).

A Missouri woman, insured under a homeowner's policy, was engaged in the business of providing home day care services. She went to a couple's home three days a week to watch their two children. While in the kitchen, preparing lunch for them and tea for herself, she spilled boiling water on herself and the younger child. Suit was brought against her for negligence. Her insurer also filed a declaratory relief action, asserting that the business pursuits exclusion negated coverage. The trial court ruled in the insurer's favor, and the insured appealed to the Missouri Court of Appeals. The insured argued on appeal that there was an exception to the exclusion for "activities which are usual to nonbusiness pursuits." She asserted that the activity which formed the basis for liability was the pouring of boiling water to make tea and that this was an activity which was usual to a nonbusiness pursuit. The court, however, found that the activity occurred upon the employer's premises and was in furtherance of her work duties to her employer. The injury occurred as a result of a failure to supervise and because of food and drink preparation. Thus, the business pursuits exclusion applied, and the ruling in favor of the insurer was affirmed. *Maryland Casualty Co. v. Hayes*, 827 S.W.2d 275 (Mo.App.1992).

A fifteen-month-old girl was fatally injured while in the care of a Maryland insured. The insured received weekly compensation for providing home daycare services for seven children Monday through Friday. The insured was covered under a homeowner's liability policy which covered damages for bodily injury. The policy excluded coverage for bodily injury or property damage resulting from business pursuits. This exclusion did not apply to activities which were ordinarily nonbusiness pursuits. The infant's mother sued the insured in a Maryland circuit court alleging that the infant's death was caused by the insured's negligence. In response to the insured's request for a defense and indemnification, the insurer filed an action in a Maryland circuit court, seeking a declaration that the death arose out of a business pursuit. The court granted the mother's motion to intervene in the declaratory judgment action. The mother and the insurer filed cross motions for summary judgment. The court granted the insurer's motion and the mother appealed to the Court of Special Appeals of Maryland.

The court held that the insured's home daycare service was a business pursuit under the policy's exclusion. It noted that business pursuit denotes a continued, extended or prolonged course of business or occupation. The court found that the insured provided childcare for compensation on a regular basis and the business pursuit exclusion applied. The insurer had no obligation to defend or indemnify the insured in connection with the underlying tort action. *McCloskey v. Republic Ins. Co.*, 559 A.2d 385 (Md.App.1989).

A Missouri woman ran a baby-sitting service out of her home for ten years. She supervised approximately six children at a time, aged from two months to six years old. All her own children were considerably older than the ones she watched. Her oldest son was charged with molesting several young children and he pled guilty to the offenses in a criminal action. The parents of the children sued the woman in a Missouri trial court, asserting that she had negligently failed to supervise her son. Her homeowner's insurer also filed an action against her, asserting that its policy did not cover the negligence claim. The policy excluded bodily injury "arising out of business pursuits of any insured." There was, however, an exception to the exclusion for "activities which are ordinarily incident to non-business pursuits." The trial court ruled that the woman's homeowner's policy did cover her and the insurer appealed to the Missouri Court of Appeals.

The appellate court ruled that the alleged failure to supervise unquestionably arose out of the business pursuits of the insured. This was a day-care service which was merely being run out of the home. Except for the fact that she ran her service at home, the insured's family responsibilities were wholly unconnected with her work. The court thus found that her failure to supervise her son was not "ordinarily incident to nonbusiness pursuits," but was related to her business. The court reversed the trial court's decision, and disallowed coverage under her homeowner's policy. *Safeco Ins. Co. v. Howard*, 782 S.W.2d 658 (Mo.App.1989).

A New Jersey child was severely injured when he came into contact with an open container of sulfuric acid in a shoe store. The child brought suit against the store and two corporate stockowners each owning forty-nine percent of the stock. Their wives each owned one percent. The liability coverage for the store had a policy limit of

$500,000. The child claimed that his damages exceeded this amount and refused to settle. Faced with a claim in excess of the corporation's liability policy, one of the owners commenced a declaratory judgment action against his homeowner's insurer. The homeowner's policy provided an exclusion for any loss under its personal liability coverage for bodily injury or property damage arising out of any business activities except those within the term business pursuits. Business pursuits was defined as occupation as a salesperson. The policy, however, excluded bodily injury arising from any business "owned or financially controlled" by the insured. The trial court granted summary judgment to the insurer and the insured appealed to the appellate division.

The insured contended that his occupation was as a salesperson employed by the corporation, an occupation which qualified as a business pursuit. The court, however, determined that the insureds (as husband and wife) controlled fifty percent of the stock and therefore financially controlled the business, thus falling within the business exclusion. The appellate division affirmed the trial court's decision. *Sinopoli v. North River Ins. Co.*, 581 A.2d 1368 (N.J. Super.A.D.1990).

A restaurant held an employee appreciation dinner at another location to which the owners of the restaurant brought wine to be served with the meal. One of the employees was later involved in a multifatality accident. The owners and their restaurant subsequently faced wrongful death actions brought by the estates of the deceased. The owners sought a defense, and filed a declaratory judgment action against both the restaurant's liability insurer and their homeowner's insurer. The Court of Common Pleas ruled that neither insurer was required to defend the owners; the liability policy excluded damages arising from the consumption of alcohol, and the homeowner's policy did not apply because of a business pursuits exclusion clause. The owners appealed to the Superior Court of Pennsylvania.

The liability policy clearly excluded coverage for the events contained in the complaint. Specifically, an exclusion addressed the "sale, serving or gift of alcoholic beverages ... which causes or contributes to the intoxication of any person." The homeowner's policy contained an exclusion for liability arising out of business pursuits. An exception to the exclusion was available for "activities which are ordinarily incident to nonbusiness pursuits." The court held that the correct inquiry then became not whether the insured was engaged in a business pursuit, but "[r]ather it is whether the particular activity at the time of the accident ... was nevertheless ordinarily incident to nonbusiness pursuits." The employee dinner was held not to be a normal part of the restaurant business, and the homeowner's insurer was ordered to defend the owners in the wrongful death action. *Curbee, Ltd. v. Rhubart*, 594 A.2d 733 (Pa.Super.1991).

Insured California homeowners utilized a real estate agent for several transactions, including purchase of their home and some rental properties. The agent contacted them to make a $10,000 investment which was to yield a quick profit. The agent disappeared with the $10,000. The homeowners later learned that the agent had forged their names on a promissory note and deeds of trust for investment property. The noteholders contacted the homeowners for nonpayment of the promissory note and then foreclosed on the deeds of trust. The homeowners tendered defense to their homeowner's insurance carrier. However, the insurer invoked the policy's bodily injury and business pursuits exclusions, refusing to defend. It sued the homeowners in a California trial court for declaratory relief.

At the same time, the noteholders testified in the underlying litigation that they had suffered anxiety and concern about their loss. The homeowners then argued in the declaratory relief action that these claims amounted to emotional distress. Under that theory, a bodily injury damage claim was possible. The court agreed that the homeowners were potentially liable for tortious conduct by their agent, and that the homeowners' investment dealings did not constitute business pursuits. The insurer appealed to the California Court of Appeal. According to the court of appeal, the trial court had correctly determined that the noteholders had a potential tort claim for bodily injury and the bodily injury exclusion was inapplicable. However, the business pursuits exclusion was unambiguous, clearly defining business as a trade, profession or occupation. The agent and homeowners' activities were business pursuits and fit into the exclusion. The homeowners were not insulated from liability under agency principles. Despite the lack of an ongoing partnership agreement, the homeowners worked with the agent for two years on two or three rental property investments. This was sufficient to constitute a parttime business pursuit. The court of appeal reversed the trial court's decision. *California Mut. Ins. Co. v. Robertson*, 262 Cal.Rptr. 173 (Cal.App.5th Dist.1989).

An off-duty police officer observed a suspicious-looking driver sitting in a car with the motor running. The police officer approached the car with his off-duty revolver and ordered the driver to get out. The driver made what the police officer took to be a move for a weapon, and the police officer shot the driver in the face. After the driver and his wife filed a lawsuit against the police officer, the officer's homeowner's insurer filed a lawsuit in federal court seeking a ruling that it was not liable for defense or indemnity because a provision in the police officer's policy excluded coverage when liability arises out of "business pursuits of the insured." The U.S. Court of Appeals, Eighth Circuit, ruled that the police officer's conduct was related to his employment because as a policeman he had an obligation to respond to suspected criminal activity, and because he invoked his official authority by displaying his badge and ordering the driver out of the car. Coverage under the police officer's homeowner's policy was precluded by the "business pursuits" exclusion. *American Family Mut. Ins. Co. v. Nickerson*, 813 F.2d 135 (8th Cir.1987).

A Minnesota man, a full-time laborer and machine operator, repaired bicycles in the garage of his residence as a hobby. He maintained no business records and frequently fixed bikes for no charge at all. He did not advertise and people brought bicycles in to be repaired as a result of word of mouth. For several years, the man also repaired bicycles for a local hardware store when its customers would bring them in to be fixed. In 1979, a person was injured on a bike that the man had worked on and sued him on the grounds that the injuries were a direct result of negligent repairs. The man's personal liability carrier denied coverage because of the business pursuits exclusion in the policy. The Minnesota Court of Appeals stated that general principles of insurance policy interpretation require that an insurer who denies coverage because of a policy exclusion must bear the burden of proof and that all exclusion clauses would be strictly interpreted against the insurer. The court explained that the exclusion would normally apply to activities which persons would carry out for the purpose of earning a livelihood such as a trade, profession, or occupation. In this case, stated the court, the man was unaware of whether he generated any income from his activities and he neither advertised nor kept any business records. In strictly construing the policy exclusion, the court determined

Sec. III   POLICY EXCLUSIONS 289

that the man's activities did not comprise a business pursuit. The court ruled that the policy provided coverage for the alleged negligent bicycle repair. *Reinsurance Ass'n of Minnesota v. Patch*, 383 N.W.2d 708 (Minn.App.1986).

D. Earth Movement Exclusions

In several cases coverage depended on whether damage resulted from "earth movement." Damage due to earth movement is often excluded from coverage.

Washington homeowners purchased a homeowner's policy which excluded coverage for earth movement or foundation cracking where negligent construction or defective materials directly or indirectly caused the loss. Two years later, heavy rains caused a hillside to slide away and the foundation of the house to crack. The homeowners reported a claim to the insurer's adjuster within the one-year reporting period, but the claim was rejected as one resulting from earth movement. After spending $27,000 for repairs, another heavy rain resulted in a second slide and similar damage to the foundation. When the insurer again denied the homeowners' claim, they filed a lawsuit in Washington Superior Court. The court ruled for the insurer and the homeowners appealed to the Washington Court of Appeals, which reversed, noting that the undisputed cause of the loss was poor construction of the filled area adjacent to the foundation. The court of appeals applied the "efficient proximate cause rule" which states that a covered peril which sets into motion a chain of causation leading to uncovered losses will result in coverage of uncovered losses. However, the court of appeals ruled that the trial court had properly rejected the homeowners' motion to amend their complaint to include damages from the first slide.

On appeal to the Supreme Court of Washington, the court accepted the insurer's argument that the efficient proximate cause rule did not control this matter. The policy unambiguously excluded coverage for earth movement or foundation cracking where negligent construction or defective materials directly or indirectly caused the loss. The court of appeals had incorrectly interpreted the ensuing loss clause of the negligent construction/defective material exclusion as a grant of coverage for negligent construction. The court reversed the court of appeals and noted that the intent of the ensuing loss clause was not to enlarge the list of items covered under the policy, but to cover losses which ensued from the uncovered loss and which were otherwise covered. *McDonald v. State Farm Fire and Casualty Co.*, 837 P.2d 1000 (Wash.1992).

A couple purchased a home in Malibu, California, which they insured with an all risk homeowner's policy. The policy excluded coverage for loss caused by settling and cracking of foundations, walls and ceilings. It also excluded loss resulting from earth movement water damage where natural water exerted pressure on the foundation. The insureds then received a letter from Los Angeles County informing them that it believed an incipient landslide might be developing on the mesa where their home was located. The couple subsequently noticed cracking in various walls. They submitted a claim to their insurer. It inspected their house and paid them over $14,000 to cover physical damage to the building. However, it neither admitted nor denied liability. The insureds asserted that they were entitled to $231,000 to stabilize the ground under their home. The insurer, though, filed a declaratory relief action seeking a ruling that its policy did not extend to the cost of such action. After a jury trial, the insureds were awarded $55,000 for bad faith and unfair claims practices damages; however, the jury determined that the insurer was not responsible for the land stabilization costs. Both parties appealed to the California Court of Appeal, Second District.

On appeal, the insurer argued that the judgment for the insureds had been erroneously determined because the predominating cause of the loss was earth movement, an excluded peril. The court of appeal agreed. It noted that although some evidence existed to indicate that negligent acts might have been a contributing factor, they were not the predominant cause of the loss. Further, any failure to prevent the earth movement due to negligence could not make earth movement into a covered loss. Earth movement was still excluded by the policy. Thus, the court reversed the jury's holding and ruled for the insurer. The damage was not covered by the policy. *State Farm Fire & Cas. Co. v. Von Der Lieth*, 275 Cal.Rptr. 590 (Cal.App. 2d Dist.1990).

Pennsylvania homeowners purchased an all-risk insurance policy which contained an earth movement exclusion. The clause provided that there would be no coverage for losses resulting directly or indirectly from earth movement. Causes of the loss included earthquakes, landslides, mud flows, and earth sinking, rising or shifting. Subsequently, the insureds sustained damage to their home when the hillside in their backyard collapsed. This occurred because the hillside they shared with their neighbor had been overburdened by construction on their neighbor's property. The insureds sought coverage which their insurer refused. The trial and appellate courts ruled in favor of the insurer in the lawsuit which followed, so the insureds appealed to the Supreme Court of Pennsylvania. The supreme court held that the earth movement exclusion in the policy was ambiguous and that a reasonable insured could conclude that it was applicable only to earth movement which was caused by natural events. Since the movement here had been caused by man-made events, the policy would be construed so as to provide coverage. The court reversed the lower courts' decisions, and held in favor of the insureds. *Steele v. Statesman Ins. Co.*, 607 A.2d 742 (Pa.1992).

An Arizona insured's home was damaged by soil collapse due to water which had escaped from a broken automatic sprinkler system. An inspection revealed that the collapse of soil had caused substantial cracking and sloping of the walls and floor slabs of the house. The insured informed its insurer of the loss. After investigating the claim, the insurer agreed to pay up to $10,000 and to replace, rebuild, stabilize and otherwise restore the land but refused to pay for the damage to the house because it was excluded by the provisions of the policy. The insured then filed suit in an Arizona trial court which entered judgment for the insured. The insurer appealed to the Arizona Court of Appeals.

The insured contended that the earth movement exclusion was ambiguous or in the alternative that it only applied to widespread natural disasters. The "earth movement" exclusion stated that earth movement meant the sinking, rising, shifting, expanding or contracting of the earth, all whether combined with water or not. The policy further stated that the company did not insure for loss regardless of the cause of the event. The insured contended that another part of the insurance policy provided coverage for water loss damage. Therefore, the insured stated that it was covered by one part of the policy. The court did not agree, stating that the policy specifically stated that no coverage would be provided for loss due to the combined effects of

Sec. III   POLICY EXCLUSIONS   291

accidental discharge of water and earth movement. Therefore, the court reversed the decision of the trial court and held for the insurer. *Millar v. State Farm Fire & Cas. Co.*, 804 P.2d 822 (Ariz.App.1990).

The owners of a Utah apartment complex sought coverage under their insurance policy after an underground water pipe ruptured on the premises. The owners claimed the water damage resulted in the apartments settling eight inches. The insurer denied coverage and the insureds filed suit. The trial court found that the property damage was caused by earth movement and, therefore, was excluded from coverage under the policy. The insureds appealed to the Court of Appeals of Utah.

On appeal, the insureds asserted that the earth movement provision did not exclude their loss, but referred only to natural phenomena. They asserted that the exclusion should not be construed to include the effects of a water pipe rupture. The appellate court, however held that the clear language of the policy excluded coverage of any loss from earth movement and affirmed the judgment of the lower court. *Village Inn Apartments v. State Farm Fire & Cas. Co.*, 790 P.2d 581 (Utah App.1990).

Insured Oregon homeowners noticed a crack in their basement wall. During the next week, other cracks appeared upstairs. The cracks enlarged and doors became misaligned with their frames, failing to close properly. A city water department employee discovered that water was running from a broken pipe in a house adjacent to the insured's. The water had been running under the earth below the insured's foundation for about two months. When the employee shut the water off, the insureds noticed no further damage or movement of their house. The insurer sent an engineer to investigate the loss. He concluded that the structural damage to the foundation was a result of the flowing water which led to erosion, sinking, or contraction of the soil around the foundation. The insurer denied coverage because the policy excluded losses from the foundation's settling. The insureds then sued the insurer in an Oregon trial court, which ruled for the insurer. The insureds appealed to the Court of Appeals of Oregon.

The insurer contended that the insureds were not covered because the loss consisted entirely of settlement of the foundation. The insureds asserted that the exclusion in the policy covered only normal or gradual settling, rather than damage caused by an external force. The insureds also argued that the loss consisted of more than just settling. The court ruled that the cause of the losses was not important. If the losses consisted of settling only, the policy excluded them. The court further held that the insureds' loss here was only settling, even though it was severe. Had the loss "ensued from" the settling, the court would have granted coverage. The court affirmed the trial court's decision, denying coverage. *Montee v. State Farm Ins. Co.*, 782 P.2d 435 (Or.App.1989).

An explosion occurred in a Louisiana restaurant. One month later, an insured who lived two miles away from the restaurant filed a claim with his homeowner's insurer, alleging that the explosion had damaged his fireplace by causing it to crack and pull apart from the frame of the house. The insurer denied coverage, pointing to a clause which excluded coverage for damages caused by earth movement or shifting of the earth unless due to an explosion. The insurer's agent inspected the fireplace and determined that the cracking of the fireplace was the result of ground settlement and was unrelated to the explosion. The insured then sued the insurer in a Louisiana trial court. At trial the insured presented evidence that the fireplace had not been cracked prior to the explosion. The court held that the insurer was required to pay for the damaged fireplace. The insurer then appealed to the Louisiana Court of Appeal.

The court of appeal stated that the insured's evidence was too weak to prove that the damages were caused by the explosion. Even if the trial court had believed the insured's evidence that the damage was not caused by ground settlement, the evidence did not prove that the damages were caused by the explosion. The court ruled that the trial court had erroneously shifted the burden of proof to the insurer by finding that the insurer had failed to show other causes of the damage. It reversed the judgment for the insured and held that the fireplace damage was excluded under the policy. *Thibodeaux v. Audubon Ins. Co.*, 539 So.2d 689 (La.App.3d Cir.1989).

A Washington insured's home was destroyed in a landslide after an unusually severe wind and rain storm. The insurer sought an order to determine its obligation to provide coverage. It contended that under the insured's "all risk" homeowner's policy the loss was not covered. Under the policy, earth movement was an excluded peril, whereas wind and rain were both insured perils. The insurer denied coverage based on an exclusion in the homeowner's policy which stated that losses caused by landslides, "whether occurring alone or in any sequence with a covered peril" would be excluded from coverage. After examining the landslide area, an engineer found that the landslide might have been precipitated by unstable soil conditions created by the storm. He also found that the primary cause of the landslide was the record rainfall that saturated the ground. The trial court granted the insurer's order denying coverage. The insured appealed to the Washington Court of Appeals.

On appeal, the insured argued that the trial court had failed to utilize proximate cause analysis in the interpretation of his homeowner's policy. The insured argued that a combination of wind and rain, rather than earth movement, was the proximate cause of the insured's loss. The court concluded that it must look beyond the occurrence of a loss in which an excluded peril was one of the events in the sequence of events precipitating the loss. In this case, the proximate cause of the landslide was the severe wind and rain storm that preceded the slide, both of which were insured perils under the policy. The home which was destroyed in the landslide was covered under the "all risk" homeowner's policy. The trial court's decision was reversed. *Safeco Ins. Co. of Amer. v. Hirschmann*, 760 P.2d 969 (Wash.App.1988).

IV. MISREPRESENTATION

Coverage under a homeowner's insurance policy may be denied if the insured made material misrepresentations on the policy's application.

A Georgia couple applied for homeowner's insurance, denying that any of their policies had been canceled in the last five years. In fact, their previous homeowner's policy had been canceled for delinquent premium payments. When their house was destroyed by fire, the insurer contended that the policy was void from the outset due to the misrepresented material facts. A federal district court granted summary judgment to the insurer, and the U.S. Court of Appeals, Eleventh Circuit, affirmed. Regardless of the homeowners' good faith in filling out the application, the material misrepresentations barred recovery. *Nappier v. Allstate Ins. Co.*, 961 F.2d 168 (11th Cir.1992).

An insured homeowner in California had a policy which did not cover any claims when the insured had concealed or misrepresented any material fact. Under the policy, "insured" was defined to include permanent members of the insured's household. Damage resulting from the insured's intentional acts were not covered. The homeowner filed a claim for vandalism and the insurer paid nearly $19,000. The insurer received a call from a neighbor who stated that on the date of the alleged vandalism he had heard shouting and things being broken inside the insured's home. He also knew that the insured's son was home at the time of the disturbance. An oral examination was conducted where the homeowner was required to testify under oath. She admitted that she had falsified the claim and the insurer denied further payment. She then sued the insurer for failure to pay all property damage arising from the claim. A Los Angeles County Superior Court judge granted the insurer's dismissal motion and the homeowner appealed to the California Court of Appeal, Second District, Division 3.

The court upheld the superior court decision noting that "if the misrepresentation concerns a subject reasonably relevant to the insured's investigation, and if a reasonable insurer would attach importance to the fact misrepresented, then it is material." The homeowner's concealment of the fact that her son lived at home and caused the damage were sufficient to establish materiality. Because the homeowner misrepresented these facts, the insurer was not required to pay for the damages. *Cummings v. Farmers Ins. Exchange*, 249 Cal.Rptr. 559 (App.2d Dist.1988).

Georgia insureds sought recovery under their homeowner's policy for loss of personal property. The insurer denied their claim and voided their policy because they had materially misrepresented the circumstances of their alleged loss. The policy provided that a lawsuit could not be brought against the insurer unless it was started within twelve months after the loss. The insureds filed suit against the insurer in a Georgia trial court twenty-one months after the loss occurred. The court held for the insurer and the insureds appealed to the Court of Appeals of Georgia. The court ruled that the voiding of the policy did not preclude the insurer from relying on the insureds' failure to file suit within the policy's twelve month limitation period. The insureds were denied coverage. *Jones v. Valley Forge Ins. Co.*, 382 S.E.2d 404 (Ga.App.1989).

A Tennessee homeowner obtained homeowners insurance. He stated on his application that he had not made any homeowner's claims in the previous three years. Three and one-half months after he purchased the insurance a fire destroyed his home. He notified the insurer but the insurer refused to cover the claim. An investigation showed that the homeowner had made a claim under his previous homeowner's policy within three years of his application. He sued the insurer in a Tennessee federal district court. It granted the insurer's motion to dismiss the claim and the homeowner appealed to the U.S. Court of Appeals, Sixth Circuit.

The court of appeals affirmed the district court's holding. It noted that Tennessee Code § 56-7-103 provided that a policy could be canceled if misrepresentations increased the risk of loss. It also provided that if a misrepresentation increased the risk of loss, the policy was voidable even if the misrepresentation was innocent. The court observed that previous Tennessee cases held that any misrepresentations which influenced whether an application was accepted were automatically considered misrepresentations that increased the risk of loss. Information regarding prior losses was of the utmost importance to insurers. *Howell v. Colonial Penn Ins. Co.*, 842 F.2d 821 (6th Cir.1987).

A Missouri couple sought recovery under their homeowner's policy after their home was destroyed by fire. Their insurer declined coverage claiming that they made material misrepresentations in their application. The Missouri Court of Appeals upheld the insurer's decision to decline coverage. It observed that a representation made when applying for insurance which is not incorporated into the policy must be both false and material if the insurer is to avoid payment. The test of materiality, held the court, was whether, if stated truthfully, the answer might influence an insurer to reject a risk. The court noted that the insurer offered evidence showing that it insured low risk property and declined high risks. The insurer's broker also testified that at the time of application, the wife falsely answered "no" when asked whether her husband had ever been incarcerated. The wife also failed to disclose that another home owned by them had been destroyed by fire less than three years before their application for the policy. The court concluded that the materiality test had been met by the insurer when it demonstrated that it would not have issued a homeowner's policy to the couple had it known the truth about the husband's incarceration and the previous fire loss. The couple could not recover under their homeowner's policy. *Galvan v. Cameron Mut.Ins.*, 733 S.W.2d 771 (Mo.App.1987).

After a homeowner filed a claim with his insurer for losses incurred in a home burglary, the insurer asked a U.S. district court to relieve it of its obligation to pay the claim. The insurer argued that the homeowner breached his contractual duty to submit to questioning by refusing to answer questions that were material to the homeowner's claim and the insurer's obligations under the policy. The court observed that the policy provided that homeowners who claimed a loss had to submit to questioning and that the insurer was not obligated to provide coverage for any insured who had intentionally concealed facts relative to the claim. The homeowner argued that he refused to answer the questions because the insurer either failed or refused to explain their relevancy. Noting that the explanation of the relevancy of questions was consistent with insurance law and local court rules, the court concluded that since the insurer had not explained the relevancy of its questions, it would deny the insurer's request for relief from its obligations. The court ordered the insurer to explain the relevancy of the questions. Once this was done, the court held that the homeowner was required to answer. *Twin City Fire Ins. Co. v. Harvey*, 662 F.Supp. 216 (D.Ariz.1987).

CHAPTER SEVEN

LIABILITY AND CASUALTY INSURANCE

		Page
I.	SCOPE OF COVERAGE	296
	A. Liability and Casualty Insurance Distinguished	297
	B. Policy Terms	298
	C. "Accidents" and "Occurrences"	302
	D. Primary/Excess Insurance	306
	E. Cancellation	308
	F. Exclusions	310
	G. Joint and Several Liability	318
II.	PREMIUMS	319
	A. Coverage Disputes	319
	B. Liability for Payment of Premiums	321
III.	NOTICE/PROOF OF LOSS REQUIREMENTS	322
IV.	BURGLARY AND THEFT INSURANCE	325
	A. Preconditions for Coverage	325
	B. "Visible Force and Violence" Requirements	327
	C. Exclusions	328
V.	FIRE INSURANCE	330
	A. Arson Investigations	330
	B. Coverage Disputes Involving Arson	332
	1. Arson Allegations—Generally	332
	2. Joint Ownership	334
	C. Insureds' Misconduct	337
	D. Buildings Covered	340
	E. Insurers' Right to Repair or Rebuild	341
	F. Mortgagees vs. Mortgagors	343
	G. Technical Problems with Policies	345
VI.	BUSINESS AND INDUSTRIAL INSURANCE	346
	A. Business Risks	346
	B. "All Risk" Policies	352
	C. "Occurrences"	354
	D. Exclusions	355
	1. Exclusions Generally	355
	2. Polluter's Exclusions	360
	E. Products Liability	367
VII.	AIRCRAFT INSURANCE	369
	A. Pilot Qualifications	369

           1. Coverage Awarded 369
           2. Coverage Denied 370
       B. Airworthiness Certification 372
       C. Conversions to Criminal Use 373
       D. Exclusions Generally 374

VIII. FEDERAL FLOOD INSURANCE 376

IX. MARINE INSURANCE 378
       A. Coverage Allowed 378
       B. Coverage Denied 381

X. "DRAM SHOP" LIABILITY 382

XI. TITLE INSURANCE 386

XII. STATE AND LOCAL GOVERNMENT LIABILITY 391

XIII. FARMOWNER'S INSURANCE 395
       A. Exclusions 396
       B. Theft Loss Coverage 399

XIV. FIDELITY BONDS 400

XV. CONSTRUCTION INSURANCE 403

I. SCOPE OF COVERAGE

Disputes have arisen between insurers and insureds concerning the scope of coverage under liability and/or casualty insurance policies.

    A homosexual couple who had lived together for 18 years applied for a joint umbrella liability policy in the amount of $ 1 million. The insurer refused to issue the applicants a joint policy for a single premium because such policies are only issued to married couples. Instead, the insurer offered the applicants separate umbrella policies, each with its own premiums. The applicants refused and requested a ruling from the Department of Insurance whether the insurer's refusal discriminated against them in violation of the Insurance Code. After the department decided to take no action, the applicants sued the insurer claiming they had been discriminated against on the basis of sexual orientation in violation of the Unruh Civil Rights Act, Insurance Code § 679.71, which bars discrimination in the issuance of policies, and Insurance Code § 1861.05, which bars discrimination in the setting of rates for insurance policies. The insurer demurred and the court issued a judgment dismissing the action in its entirety. The applicants appealed to the Court of Appeal, Third District.
    On appeal, the applicants only argued that the refusal to issue the policy was discriminatory under the Unruh Act. The court stated that there was no discrimination on the basis of sexual orientation. The applicants were denied the joint policy because they were not married, and in that respect they were treated the same as all

Sec. I   SCOPE OF COVERAGE   297

other unmarried persons, heterosexual or otherwise. No other unmarried persons were treated any differently than the applicants. Discrimination on the basis of marital status simply was not covered under the Unruh Act. The court noted that the applicants' true quarrel was with the Civil Code § 4100 which does not allow homosexual partners to marry. *Beaty v. Truck Insurance Exchange*, 8 Cal.Rptr.2d 593 (Cal.App.3d Dist.1992).

A. Liability and Casualty Insurance Distinguished

Generally, liability insurance covers amounts that an insured becomes legally responsible to pay to other parties. Casualty insurance provides protection to the insured for losses where other parties are not involved.

In a Mississippi case, a bank sought to recover on a "stop payment or dishonor liability insurance" endorsement to its comprehensive general liability insurance policy. The bank paid $36,064.30 to one of its depositors when it received checks totaling that amount which had been routinely processed through the federal reserve system. The bank president approved payment even though there were insufficient funds in the depositor's account to cover the checks. Two days after the receipt of the checks the bank, in an attempt to improve its legal position, sent notice of dishonor to the depositor. However, under state and federal law, checks received through the federal reserve system are considered honored unless notice of dishonor is filed by midnight of the day after receipt. The bank was therefore obligated to pay the amount, and it sought to recover that amount from its insurer.

The endorsement in question provided that the insurer agreed to "pay on behalf of named insured all sums which named insured shall become legally obligated to pay as damages" in some instances involving the stop payment or dishonoring of checks. The issue before the U.S. Court of Appeals, Fifth Circuit, was whether the money paid by the bank constituted "damages" within the meaning of the endorsement. The court ruled that a distinction existed between "indemnity against liability to third persons" and "indemnity against loss by the insured." The court concluded that the insurance policy provided only for losses sustained by a third party for which the bank was ultimately held liable (liability insurance); it did not provide first party protection for the bank (casualty insurance). Thus the bank was denied recovery under the policy endorsement. *Alcorn Bank & Trust Co. v. United States Fidelity & Guar. Co.*, 705 F.2d 128 (5th Cir.1983).

A Texas case further illustrates the meaning of the term "liability insurance." Here, an oil company engaged in an offshore drilling operation chartered a vessel that, due to the negligence of its owner, sank beneath a temporary drilling rig. Demands made by the oil company for the removal of the vessel were ignored by the vessel's owner. Because the oil company wanted to install a permanent rig at the site it was finally forced to pay for the vessel's removal itself. The oil company then filed suit against the vessel's owner and its own insurer in an attempt to recover the expense incurred in raising the boat.

After a lower court held in favor of the oil company the defendants appealed to the U.S. Court of Appeals, Fifth Circuit. The policy on the boat required the insurer to cover only those expenses that the insured "shall have become legally liable to pay and shall have paid." Thus, the issue before the court of appeals was whether the oil company was legally liable for the removal of the vessel. The court of appeals held that the oil company was not legally liable to remove the boat because it was not its owner and it did not sink as a result of the oil company's negligence. Because of the absence of any legal obligation to remove the boat, its removal was not covered by the liability policy. The lower court's holding in favor of the oil company was reversed. *Continental Oil Co. v. Bonanza Corp.*, 706 F.2d 1365 (5th Cir.1983).

B. Policy Terms

The following cases involve judicial interpretation of basic policy terms. Courts will not extend coverage to incidents which do not reasonably fall under an insurance policy's terms.

Two school districts in Wisconsin purchased liability insurance which would indemnify them for losses they became obligated to pay as damages because of personal injury. Personal injury included discrimination injury so long as it was not expected or intended by the insureds, or committed at their direction or with their consent. The two school districts were then named as defendants, along with 22 other school districts and the state of Wisconsin, in federal racial discrimination litigation. The complaint sought declaratory, injunctive, and remedial relief, asserting that the school districts had participated in and been affected by segregation activities by the state. The insurers for the school districts refused to provide a defense, and the school districts eventually entered into a settlement agreement, denying that they had violated the law, but agreeing to such remedial measures as minority recruitment programs. The school districts then sued their insurers for reimbursement of attorney's fees and for the expenses associated with their compliance with the settlement. The trial court granted summary judgment to the insurers, and the school districts' appeal was heard by the Supreme Court of Wisconsin.

The supreme court reversed the trial court's decision. It noted that the definition of "damages" was the lynch pin on which the case turned. The insurers maintained that the cost of complying with an injunctive decree did not satisfy the definition of "damages" in the policies. However, the court looked at the term "damages" as an ordinary lay insured would, and found that it included the costs of complying with injunctive or equitable relief. Further, the term "damages" was not limited to compensation for past wrongs, but also included reimbursement for monies spent in funding programs designed to remedy alleged discrimination. The court held for the school districts. *School District of Shorewood v. Wausau Ins. Co.*, 484 N.W.2d 314 (Wis.1992).

A Missouri school district purchased a liability insurance policy which covered claims made against it for wrongful acts. The policy did not exclude claims for intentional wrongful acts by district employees. Two years later, the district was sued by ten teachers under 42 U.S.C. § 1983, who claimed the district involuntarily reassigned them and denied contractual benefits in retaliation for their joining an educational association. The insurer argued that the policy excluded the district's actions because they were not "wrongful acts." The U.S. Court of Appeals rejected the insurer's arguments. The term "wrongful acts" included affirmative and wilful behavior such as had occurred by the district. However, the insurer prevailed on the issues of vexatious refusal to pay and attorney's fees. The insurer had made a good faith argument that coverage did not exist, and the policy should not require the

Sec. I   SCOPE OF COVERAGE   299

insurer to pay the insured's attorney's fees where it was seeking coverage. *New Madrid School Dist. v. Continental Cas. Co.*, 904 F.2d 1236 (8th Cir.1990).

A private country club allowed a local high school to use its tennis courts for matches. However, when a visiting team showed up with a member who was black, the country club refused to let her play. She sued the country club for discriminating against her, and it brought suit against its insurer, seeking a declaration that the insurer was required to defend it. The trial court ruled for the insured country club, and the liability insurer appealed to the Court of Appeals of Arkansas. On appeal, the insurer argued that it could not be liable because its policy did not provide coverage for the insured's actions. The country club maintained that its act could be construed to be an eviction of the girl, and that the policy provided coverage for wrongful eviction. The court agreed with the insured, and found that the term "eviction" was ambiguous. Thus, the country club's actions could be construed as an eviction of the girl, and the insurer was required to defend. The underlying lawsuit resulted in a verdict for the country club, so the issue of indemnification was rendered moot. The lower court's decision was affirmed. *Ins. Co. of North America v. Forrest City Country Club*, 819 S.W.2d 296 (Ark.App.1991).

The owner and the managing agent of a brownstone in Manhattan purchased a comprehensive general liability policy from an insurer which defined "bodily injury" as "bodily injury, sickness or disease." Sometime later, during renovation of the premises, part of a ceiling collapsed. The tenants of the apartment where it occurred brought a lawsuit against the insureds for negligence and infliction of emotional distress. The complaint did not allege any physical injury or contact. A jury awarded the tenants over $400,000 for their personal injuries. The insureds then sued their insurer for indemnification. The trial court and appellate court ruled for the insureds, and the insurer appealed to the New York Court of Appeals. On appeal, the insurer argued that there was no coverage available for emotional distress in the absence of physical injury or contact. The court, however, disagreed. It found the term "bodily injury" to be ambiguous. Further, the inclusion of the categories "sickness" and "disease" enlarged the term "bodily injury." Since sickness and disease could include mental as well as physical ailments, the policy had to be interpreted in favor of the insureds. The court of appeals held that purely emotional injury was covered by the policy and accordingly it affirmed the lower courts' decisions. *Lavanant v. General Accident Ins. Co.*, 584 N.Y.S.2d 744 (Ct.App.1992).

An Illinois state fairground association leased the fairgrounds to an organization which sponsored a motorcycle race. The sponsored race was cancelled due to inclement weather but many patrons remained and either watched or participated in an unsponsored, unauthorized motorcycle race. A motorcycle accident killed one spectator and injured another. At the time of the accident, the association maintained insurance with a limit of liability of $3 million. The policy provided that the coverage did not apply to automobile or motorcycle racing or stunting. The injured spectator and the deceased's estate filed suit against a number of defendants including the association. The actions were consolidated and jury verdicts were returned in favor of the plaintiffs. The insurer then filed the present declaratory judgment action to determine its liability. The district court awarded judgment for the insurer and the plaintiffs appealed to the U.S. Court of Appeals, Seventh Circuit. The court determined that the association may very well have intended the policy language to include unsponsored events but such an intention was unreasonable in light of the unambiguous language. Therefore, the court of appeals upheld the decision of the trial court. *Granite State Ins. Co. v. Degerlia*, 925 F.2d 189 (7th Cir.1991).

In a rare case, the U.S. Court of Appeals, Eighth Circuit, reversed one of its own decisions. Previously it had ruled that cleanup costs incurred by the federal government and the state of Missouri could be recovered from a chemical company's liability insurer because cleanup costs were considered "damages" under the policy. The original case was returned to a U.S. district court which held that the liability insurer must defend and indemnify the chemical company. The liability insurer once again appealed to the U.S. Court of Appeals, Eighth Circuit. The language of the policy provided that the liability insurer would "pay on behalf of the insured all the sums which the insured shall become legally obligated to pay as damages because of ... property damage." The issue before the court of appeals was whether the term "damages" in the policy included cleanup costs. The court observed that the term "damages", as used in the insurance field was not ambiguous. "Damages" would have covered the destruction or injury to the property itself but did not include the cost of cleaning up the property which was what the federal and state government were seeking. The court determined that it would be unfair to require the liability insurer to pay for something that it did not intend to cover. The court also pointed out that the Resource Conservation and Recovery Act (RCRA) and the Comprehensive Environmental Response and Compensation Liability Act (CERCLA) differentiate between cleanup costs and damages. The court concluded that claims under the acts should only be for damage to the property itself and that claims for cleanup costs under CERCLA and RCRA were not claims for "damages" under general liability policies. *Continental Ins. Cos. v. Northeastern Pharmaceutical & Chemical Co.*, 842 F.2d 977 (8th Cir.1988).

An action was brought in an Arkansas federal district court to determine whether the phrase "as damages" in the insuring clause of a standard form comprehensive general liability (CGL) policy covers clean-up costs incurred under a consent decree between the insured and the U.S. Environmental Protection Agency. The cases on this issue are sharply divided. Applying Arkansas law, the court found that no cases existed which addressed the issue. It then used Missouri law to hold that no coverage existed. The U.S. Court of Appeals, Eighth Circuit, affirmed. The U.S. Supreme Court remanded. Before the court of appeals again, the court reviewed the district court's decision *de novo* (as though the case were before it for the first time). Since there were no Arkansas cases on point, and since Missouri law followed the same general principles of insurance law as Arkansas, the court of appeals agreed that no coverage had to be provided for clean-up costs under such a CGL policy. It affirmed the district court's decision. *Parker Solvents Co. v. Royal Ins. Companies*, 950 F.2d 571 (8th Cir.1991).

An insured was accidentally thrown from a horse and suffered severe injuries. Her spinal cord was severed and she became permanently paralyzed, losing the use of her legs. One year before the accident she obtained an accident policy. The policy stated "... loss means actual severance through or above the wrist or ankle joints...." The insurer denied coverage and the insured sued it in a Montana district court. The court held for the insured, stating that the spinal cord severance caused the complete loss of use of her legs. This was what the policy intended to cover. The insurer appealed to the Montana Supreme Court. The supreme court held for the insured, reasoning that the policy language did not require actual amputation. The insured's interpretation was reasonable and entirely consistent with the language of the policy. The policy did not require "amputation" or "dismemberment." The district court's decision was upheld. *Bauer v. Kar Products, Inc.*, 749 P.2d 1385 (Mont.1988).

A boat owned by a Florida boat builder collided with a seawall, damaging its hull. The boat builder's insurer offered to pay for the repair of the damages. However, rather than repairing the boat, the boat builder returned the boat's reusable machinery (valued at $50,324.19) to inventory and sold the damaged hull for $40,000. Unable to reach a settlement, the boat builder sued its insurer. A U.S. district court awarded the boat builder damages of $125,268.67 (value of the boat minus the salvage amount). The insurer appealed to the U.S. Court of Appeals, Eleventh Circuit.

At issue was the method of arriving at the damage amount. The policy stated in part that "There shall be no recovery for a constructive Total Loss under this policy unless the expense of ... restoring the Vessel ... to the stage of her construction at the time of loss would exceed her value at such stage of construction...." The boat builder's expert witness testified that repairs would have cost $150,000; the insurer's expert witness testified that repairs would have cost between $13,000 and $20,000. The boat builder contended that repairs would not have restored the boat to the stage of her construction at the time of loss. Therefore, it was entitled to a new boat. The insurer argued that the boat builder was only entitled to a boat in seaworthy condition. The court of appeals agreed with neither party, holding that the term "stage of her construction at the time of loss" meant that the boat, once repaired, had to be capable of being sold for a price at least equal to the boat's value at the time of the accident. The boat had to be seaworthy *and* capable of being sold since the boat builder's primary concern was the saleability of its boat. The court of appeals remanded the case to the district court to determine actual damages pursuant to the policy's valuation clause. *Magnum Marine Corp., N.V. v. Great American Ins. Co.*, 835 F.2d 265 (11th.Cir.1988).

Several youths broke into an elementary school and engaged in acts of random destruction and arson. The fires were reported at 4:10 p.m. The group left the elementary school and traveled to a nearby junior high school where they continued their destruction by "trashing" two classrooms. After leaving the junior high school, the vandals parted company. One of the original vandals, joined by two new participants, returned to the junior high several hours later to start several fires in the previously ransacked classrooms. This second round of fires was reported about 8:07 p.m. The group then left and was joined by one of the original participants. This new, larger group attempted to reenter the junior high, but police turned them away. Instead, they traveled to the elementary school, ransacked the staff lounge and set more fires. This third alarm was reported at 9:18 p.m. The school was insured against such losses by a school liability package. Each school location was insured to $300,000,000 per location, per loss occurrence, subject to a self-insured retention of $100,000 per each occurrence. The insurer agreed to cover the claim, subject to the $300,000 self-insured retention, claiming three separate incidents. The school district claimed that the vandalism was only one incident, noting that the policy stated that all incidents of riot during a consecutive 72-hour period are considered one loss. The insurer argued that the vandalism was not a riot and a California trial court agreed. The school appealed.

The Court of Appeal, First District, held that the term "riot" did not apply to the acts of the vandals in this case. Vandalism, arson, or other such acts, do not constitute a riot if they are conducted away from public view with the intent that they remain unobserved. Hidden, destructive acts are also not deemed a riot merely because, upon discovery, the authorities' responsive or remedial efforts disturb the peace and quiet of the community. The loss was the result of not one but three separate occurrences. Thus, the school district was responsible for the $300,000 retention amount. *North Bay Schools Ins. Auth. v. Industrial Indem. Co.*, 10 Cal.Rptr.2d 88 (Cal.App.1st Dist.1992).

A private college contracted with an ice show to allow performances in the college's ice arena. The college obtained a general liability policy to cover events at the performance, and also added an endorsement which named it as an additional insured. A patron was injured in a fall on a walkway adjacent to a field house following a performance. A lawsuit was brought by the injured party, and the school and insurer disputed whether the policy afforded coverage. A trial court ruled in favor of the insurer, and the college appealed to the Supreme Court, Appellate Division, of New York. The endorsement naming the college as an additional insured provided coverage only for liability "arising out of the ownership, maintenance or use of that part of the premises ... leased to the named insured." The court rejected the school's argument that the lease extended to external walkways. Similarly, the court refused to rule that coverage should be provided because the accident "arose out of use" of the leased facility. The trial court's order in favor of the insurer was affirmed. *Rensselaer Polytechic Institute v. Zurich American Ins. Co.*, 575 N.Y.S.2d 598 (A.D.3 Dept.1991).

C. "Accidents" and "Occurrences"

Some of the following cases illustrate the rule that intentional harm is usually outside the scope of policies covering "accidents" and/or "occurrences." Others illustrate the rule that there will be coverage only when "occurrences" fall within the policy period.

Between June and October of 1984, a minor child resided at an apartment building and allegedly ingested lead-based paint chips, causing himself personal injury. The child's mother filed a negligence action against the apartment building's owners. The apartment building's insurance policy, however, expired November 1, 1983. The apartment building's insurer brought a declaratory judgment action to determine whether it had to indemnify the apartment owners. A district court held that the insurer was obligated to defend and indemnify the owners, and the insurer appealed that decision to the Ohio Court of Appeals. On appeal, the insurer argued that its duty to provide defense and indemnification attached at the time the damage to the child occurred, not when the negligence was allegedly committed. The appellate court agreed, noting that the plain intent of the policy was to provide coverage when an "occurrence" causes "bodily injury" and when that "injury occurs during the policy period." Because the child's injury occurred well outside the policy period, and because the child's injury was the "occurrence" under the policy, the court reversed the lower court's decision and held in favor of the insurer. *Ruffin v. Sawchyn*, 599 N.E.2d 852 (Ohio App.8th Dist.1991).

Sec. I				SCOPE OF COVERAGE	303

A motor company purchased a comprehensive liability insurance policy. Subsequently, a former company employee filed suit against the employer for wrongful discharge. The employer commenced a declaratory judgment action seeking to require the insurer to defend it in the suit. A lower court granted summary judgment to the insurer, and the court of appeals affirmed. The employer appealed to the Supreme Court of Iowa. On appeal, the employer argued that the employee's claim of wrongful discharge was a tort and was therefore the type of conduct which constituted an occurrence under the policy, requiring coverage. However, after examining common law precedent, the court held that an intentional termination did not constitute an "occurrence" within the policy's language. One could not unintentionally fire an employee. Secondly, the employer argued that the damages sought by the employee for a wrongful discharge were the type covered under a bodily injury and property damage provision of the policy. However, the court also rejected this argument, holding that the employee's petition for damages sought loss of wages and fringe benefits rather than damages for bodily injury which the policy would cover. Accordingly, the court denied coverage to the employer and affirmed the court of appeals' decision. *Smithway Motor Xpress v. Liberty Mut.*, 484 N.W.2d 192 (Iowa 1992).

Several gunshot victims filed suit against an Arkansas sporting goods store. The victims alleged that the store had negligently sold a pistol and a shotgun to a man who later used the guns in a shooting spree. The store sought a declaratory judgment to determine the amount of coverage that would exist under its liability insurance policy. A trial court held that the $300,000 policy limit applied to each victim. This meant that the insurer would be liable for up to the policy limit for each victim's injuries. On appeal, the Arkansas Court of Appeals dismissed the trial court's decision, holding that there was no justiciable controversy and the action was premature, since the victims had not yet obtained a judgment against the store. The insurer appealed to the Arkansas Supreme Court which found that there was a justiciable controversy. It then reversed the trial court's decision and held that although several people were injured by the man in the same shooting spree, there was only one occurrence within the policy meaning. Therefore, the insurer would only be liable up to $300,000 for all of the victims in the event of a judgment against the store. The court reversed the trial court's decision. *Travelers Indem. Co. v. Olive's Sporting Goods, Inc.*, 764 S.W.2d 596 (Ark.1989).

A New York manufacturer owned and operated a plant in Puerto Rico. Several residents of a nearby community sued the plant for personal injuries suffered from exposure to toxic chemicals which had been intentionally discharged by the plant. The manufacturer conceded that it had intentionally, although lawfully, discharged waste from the plant. The manufacturer notified its general liability insurers of the personal injury lawsuit and demanded that they undertake its defense. The insurers denied coverage claiming that the policies excluded coverage for any loss resulting from the discharge of toxic chemicals or pollutants. The only exception to that exclusion was for sudden and accidental discharge. A New York trial court ordered the insurers to defend the insured and the insurers appealed. The Supreme Court, Appellate Division, reversed, and the insured appealed to the Court of Appeals of New York. The court of appeals held that the insured's intentional discharge of toxic waste chemicals was not an accidental occurrence. The court noted that the insured had knowingly discharged the pollutants. This discharge resulted in harm to the environment. Because the discharge was intentional, it could not be considered accidental and was not qualified as an exception to the pollution exclusion clause. The court of appeals affirmed the appellate division court's decision denying coverage. *Technicon Electronics v. American Home*, 544 N.Y.S.2d 531 (Ct.App.1989).

The owner of a shopping center in Kansas City, Missouri, rented part of it to a styling salon. The premises leased by the salon were damaged as a result of a flood. The center owner entered into an oral agreement whereby the salon owner agreed to repair the premises and the center owner agreed to abate her rent. After encountering difficulties with the center owner, the salon owner filed an action in a Missouri trial court alleging that the center owner breached their oral contract. After commencement of the action by the salon owner, the center owner filed a third party petition against his insurer through which he sought indemnification. The trial judge granted summary judgment to the insurer. The insured appealed to the Missouri Court of Appeals. The liability portion of the policy was activated in the event of an occurrence which was defined by the policy as "an accident including continuous or repeated exposure to conditions which results in bodily injury or property damage neither expected nor intended from the standpoint of the insured." The court determined that breach of contract to abate rent or breach of the lease agreement in no way falls under the definition of occurrence. Thus there was no coverage afforded under the liability portion of the policy. The insured then argued that he was afforded coverage under the comprehensive general liability portion of the policy which covered incidental contracts. The court, however, noted that if the incidental contract did not include an assumption of liability by the insured, no coverage was provided under the policy. Since an agreement to abate rent is not an assumption of liability, the insurer was not liable under the incidental contract part of its policy. The court of appeals affirmed the trial court's decision. *West v. Jacobs*, 790 S.W.2d 475 (Mo.App.1990).

A Colorado insured operated a garage and truck rental business which was insured under a liability policy. One of the rental trucks was transferred to the garage because it needed maintenance. Two young boys, while trespassing on the insured's property, started the truck and moved it, injuring one of the boys. The insured sought coverage under his policy. The insurer denied coverage and brought an action for declaratory judgment, to determine whether the trespasser's injuries were covered by the policy. On cross motions for summary judgment, a Colorado trial court found that the policy covered the accident and summary judgment was entered for the insured. The insurer appealed to the Colorado Court of Appeals.

The court of appeals held that the events leading up to the injury constituted an accident within the meaning of the policy. Under the policy the insured was covered for bodily injury or property damage caused by an accident resulting from garage operations. The court noted that the insured's rental vehicle which was involved in the accident was a covered automobile under the policy. Garage operations included all operations necessary or incidental to a garage business. The insured owned, maintained and used the premises on which the injury occurred for a garage business. The presence of the rental truck at the garage for maintenance was necessary or incidental to the garage's operation. Thus the accident resulted from garage operations. The court of appeals affirmed the trial court's decision. *Farmers Alliance Mut. Ins. v. Reeves*, 775 P.2d 84 (Colo.App.1989).

A Louisiana psychiatrist allegedly contracted to build a retail store with one of his patients who owned a construction company. After the store was near completion, the psychiatrist allegedly told the patient that he was not personally bound under the agreement, but had been acting as an officer of a new company which was insolvent. The patient sued the psychiatrist on several theories, including negligent misrepresentation. The psychiatrist sued his liability insurer in a Louisiana trial court for a declaratory judgment that it had to defend him in the lawsuit. After the trial court held that the insurer had to defend, it appealed to the Louisiana Court of Appeal.

On appeal, the insurer argued that it had no duty to defend because the occurrence necessary to trigger coverage occurred before its policy went into effect. The court of appeal disregarded this argument and affirmed the trial court's order. It held that although there was some doubt about whether the oral misrepresentation took place during policy coverage, it appeared that the insurer was potentially liable. The court noted that Louisiana law allows for a liberal interpretation for determining when an occurrence may have happened. The court ordered the insurer to defend the psychiatrist. *Colomb v. U.S. Fidelity and Guar. Co.*, 539 So.2d 940 (La.App.4th Cir.1989).

The Environmental Protection Agency (EPA) notified a Pennsylvania publisher that it might be responsible under federal law for a toxic waste site in New Jersey. The publisher had sold ink roller waste to a company which had dumped the waste at the site. After negotiations with the EPA, the publisher voluntarily agreed to clean up the site. It then demanded that its previous liability insurer indemnify it under an expired policy for the costs of defending itself and for the site cleanup costs. The expired policy contained a clause which provided coverage for property damage. The publisher sought a declaratory judgment in a federal district court that the insurer was liable. The insurer moved for a dismissal of the action, claiming that there had been no occurrence to trigger coverage under the policy. It also contended that the publisher had not been damaged within the policy's meaning, since cleanup costs are equitable. Finally it argued, that even if the policy applied, coverage was voided because the publisher had failed to provide timely notice. The district court denied the insurer's dismissal motion and concluded that actual conflicts existed, requiring a trial. First, it adopted the injury-in-fact analysis, holding that "occurrence" required the publisher to prove that actual damage had occurred during the time the insurer's policy was effective. It noted that a dispute existed regarding the date of actual injury. The court also rejected the insurer's second argument, stating that the term "damages" has been held to include certain equitable relief under Pennsylvania law. Finally, the court stated that the insurer must show that it was prejudiced by the publisher's late notification of the occurrence in order to avoid its policy obligations. The court denied the insurer's dismissal motions and the publisher's declaratory judgment action resumed. *Triangle Publications v. Liberty Mut. Ins. Co.*, 703 F.Supp. 367 (E.D.Pa.1989).

A sixty-five-year-old female employee was injured when her employer grabbed her by the arm and neck and escorted her out the back door of his cafe. The incident aggravated her pre-existing degenerative arthritis condition. The woman settled her claim for personal injuries with her employer on the basis that any judgment would be collectable only from his liability insurance company. The insurance company brought an action seeking a court ruling relieving it of liability. A U.S. district court in South Dakota granted the ruling and the woman appealed.

The employer's liability policy covered claims arising from "accidental events," and went on to say that these events "must be something you did not expect or intend to happen." The woman argued that her injuries were "accidental" and therefore covered under the policy. However, the U.S. Court of Appeals, Eighth Circuit, drew a distinction between accidental conduct and accidental results. The court ruled that the language of the policy was meant to cover accidental conduct, but not the accidental results of intentional conduct. The court focused on the term "event" as defined in the insurance policy. It noted that intentional events were expressly excluded from coverage. The fact that the employer did not intend to inflict injury was not important. All results of his intentional action were excluded from coverage. The district court's ruling in favor of the insurance company was affirmed. *St. Paul Fire & Marine Ins. Co. v. McBrayer*, 801 F.2d 1012 (8th Cir.1986).

D. Primary/Excess Insurance

A Texas construction company purchased primary insurance and excess liability coverage. A crane subsequently collapsed killing two men, injuring another, and causing substantial property damage. The company was named as a defendant in three lawsuits. During the pendency of the suits, the primary insurer was placed in receivership. The construction company had submitted bills to its excess insurer in connection with the wrongful death action. The excess insurer moved for summary judgment claiming it did not have a duty to defend until the primary insurer's policy limits were exhausted. The trial court granted summary judgment to the excess insurer and the construction company appealed to the Court of Appeals of Texas.

The construction company contended that since the primary insurer was insolvent, there was not valid and collectible insurance available and therefore the excess policy applied. The court disagreed, determining that if excess liability carriers are required to defend in cases where the primary carrier would defend except for insolvency, a heavy burden would be placed on the excess carrier. Such a rule would require insurers to scrutinize one another's financial well-being before issuing secondary policies. Therefore, the court affirmed the decision of the trial court in favor of the excess insurer. *Emscor, Inc. v. Alliance Ins. Group*, 804 S.W.2d 195 (Tex.App.1991).

A student of a private high school was severely injured in a football game. He brought suit against the school for his injuries, and settled with the school and its primary liability carrier. The settlement granted $640,834.75 to the student in exchange for a release of his claims against the school, except those claims that he may have against the school's excess insurer. The policy providing excess coverage allowed $5 million in liability coverage to the school, or alternatively, upon waiver of any claims against the school, it provided lifetime medical and rehabilitative expenses directly to the injured person. The football player brought a claim against the excess insurer, and the school brought a separate action seeking a determination of coverage. A referee recommended dismissal of the school's suit, a trial court refused to confirm, and appeal was taken to the Supreme Court, Appellate Division of New York. The referee had found that the school lacked standing and that the coverage issue was nonjusticiable. The appellate court agreed; because the claims against the school had been released it was no longer legally concerned. Further, the school held no legally protectable interest. The school's suit was dismissed and all issues of coverage would be determined by the student's action. *Matter of Ideal Mutual Ins. Co.*, 571 N.Y.S.2d 18 (A.D.1 Dept.1991).

An Alabama waterskier was severely injured in a boating accident. She sued both the operator of the boat, who was covered under a homeowner's policy, and the owner of the boat, who was covered under a personal umbrella liability policy. Both insurers claimed they were liable only for excess coverage and the case went before a state trial court. The court held that the homeowner's policy insurer was the primary insurer and appeal was taken to the Supreme Court of Alabama. While primary coverage ordinarily follows ownership, the owner's umbrella policy in this case was designed to be a "true excess" policy. The umbrella carrier was not attempting to limit its risk nor was it trying to escape responsibility. The court affirmed the trial court's decision. *Independent Fire Ins. Co. v. Mutual Assurance, Inc.*, 553 So.2d 115 (Ala.1989).

A marine corporation purchased two insurance policies on vessels that it owned: one from a primary insurer, and the other from an excess insurer. The policies provided coverage for personal injuries arising out of the ownership of the vessels. The primary policy's limit was $500,000 and the excess insurer's policy provided indemnity for personal injury claims from $500,000 up to $20,000,000. Subsequent to the insured's procurance of the policies, a worker was injured while working on one of the insured's vessels. He sued the insured in a Texas trial court, seeking damages for his injuries. The primary insurer initially provided a defense for the insured, but it later became insolvent and the insured hired a private law firm to defend it. Eventually, with the excess insurer playing a major role in the negotiations, the suit was settled. The insurer then sought contribution from the insured for $500,000, the amount the primary insurer should have paid. Upon the insured's refusal to contribute more than $25,000, the insurer sued it in the U.S. District Court, S.D. Texas. The insurer asserted that because the insured had refused to contribute its "deductible" amount, the insurer was entitled to sue it for reimbursement. The court, however, noted that the insurer had essentially assumed the insured's defense by its prominent role in settling the underlying claim. Further, the court stated that the insurer did not effectively establish a reservation of rights at the time of the settlement. Thus, the insurer was precluded from seeking reimbursement from the insured because it had settled the claim and the insured had relied on the settlement. The court dismissed the insurer's claim. *Arkwright-Boston Manufacturers Mut. Ins. Co. v. Aries Marine Corp.*, 736 F.Supp. 1447 (S.D.Tex.1990).

A restaurant chain corporation purchased liability coverage with three layers of insurance policies. The primary policy provided coverage to $500,000; the first excess policy provided coverage from $500,000 to $10,000,000; and the second excess policy (provided jointly by two insurers) provided coverage in excess of $10,000,000. While the three policies were in effect, a customer was injured "at or near" a restaurant owned by the corporation. In the subsequent personal injury action, a settlement was agreed to for $687,500. The primary insurer paid its policy limits, but the first excess insurer became insolvent. A question then arose as to who would have to pay the remaining $187,500. The insured filed a declaratory relief action in a California trial court against the second excess insurers and against the California Insurance Guarantee Association (CIGA) seeking to determine who must pay. The court entered summary judgment in favor of the second excess insurers, and the insured appealed to the Court of Appeal, Second District. An examination of the second excess insurers' policies showed that the insurers' liability would attach "only after the underlying insurer has paid or has been held liable to pay the full amount of the underlying coverage, ... and that [the second excess insurers] will then be liable to pay only the excess of the underlying policy limit." The insured contended that the language "held liable to pay" could be interpreted to require the insurers to drop down to the first excess insurer's position on its insolvency. The court disagreed because the policies further qualified that language by stating that the insurers' liability would attach only to sums in excess of the full amount of the underlying coverage. Since the language was clear and unambiguous, the court held that the second excess insurers did not have to drop down and provide coverage. It affirmed the trial court's decision. *Denny's Inc. v. Chicago Ins. Co.*, 286 Cal.Rptr. 507 (Cal.App.2d Dist.1991).

E. Cancellation

An Arizona man was severely injured in a motorcycle accident. He then instituted a suit against several defendants based on various negligence theories; all defendants prevailed except the owners of a motorcycle repair garage who were allegedly negligent in repairing the motorcycle which caused his accident. The garage owners had obtained a liability policy, but it was cancelled in November for nonpayment of premiums. In January of the next year they turned the garage over to another person who obtained another liability policy. The insurer for the original garage owners refused to defend or indemnify them against the claims because the accident occurred outside the coverage period. After a default judgment was entered, the garage owners executed an assignment to the motorcycle victim of any potential claims against the insurer in exchange for a promise not to execute against them personally. The victim then filed a lawsuit against the insurer in an Arizona trial court. The trial court granted summary judgment in favor of the insurer. The victim then appealed to the Court of Appeals of Arizona.

The victim contended that the garage owners had a reasonable expectation of coverage during the time that the alleged negligence occurred even if the policy had expired before the actual accident. The court determined that there was no reasonable expectation of coverage since the bodily injury occurred after the policy expired. The evidence showed that the garage owners received accurate information from the agent whenever they inquired about their coverage. Moreover, the court noted that there was no evidence showing that their belief regarding coverage was any different from the stated terms found in the policy. The court affirmed the trial court's decision. *Shade v. U.S. Fidelity Guar. Co.*, 801 P.2d 441 (Ariz. App.1990).

An insurer terminated the authority of an insurance agency to represent it. The insurance agency was later purchased by an agent who then issued a homeowner's policy on the insurer's form without the insurer's knowledge. After the homeowner's property was destroyed by fire the insurer denied coverage. A Mississippi circuit court, without a jury, upheld the insurer's decision to deny coverage and the homeowner appealed to the Mississippi Supreme Court.

On appeal, the homeowner contended that a "special notice" of policy termination, which he received from the insurer eleven months after the fire, indicated that the insurer was liable for coverage. The supreme court held for the insurer. The "special notice" did not indicate coverage. The insurer had testified that, when loss

Sec. I   SCOPE OF COVERAGE   309

claims were filed pursuant to genuine or alleged policies, the information was routinely entered into a computer. The computer automatically prepared and mailed notices of expiration to the named insured, in this case the homeowner. Nothing in the record indicated that the "special notice" was anything more than the insurer said it was. The supreme court also observed that the agent knew that the insurer had no contract with the homeowner since she had attempted to secure coverage for the homeowner with another insurer on the day of the fire. The insurer was not liable. *Nunley v. Merrill*, 513 So.2d 582 (Miss.1987).

A township mutual insurance company issued a fire insurance policy to a farm partnership. The insurer sent the partnership four premium notices and on October 22, 1984, it sent a notice to the partnership by certified mail that the policy would terminate on November 1, 1984, for nonpayment of premium. The cancellation date passed and on November 3, the partnership's combine was destroyed by fire. The partnership filed a claim but it was denied due to the cancellation. The Minnesota Court of Appeals held that the partnership had not received notice of final cancellation. The mutual insurance company appealed to the Minnesota Supreme Court. The supreme court noted that Minnesota law provided that a mutual insurer "may ... cancel any policy after giving not less than 10 days written notice to the insured by ... certified mail to the last known address of the insured...." The mutual insurance company contended that it fully complied with the law when it sent the notice by certified mail. The partnership asserted that the insurer had to prove that the partnership actually received notice of cancellation in order for the insurer to escape liability. The supreme court observed that under state no-fault legislation, proof of mailing of notice is sufficient to show that proper notice has been given. By analogy it held that the use of certified mail in this case provided the partnership with "constructive receipt of the cancellation notice," thus satisfying the statutorily prescribed cancellation procedure. The lower court's decision was reversed. *Schneider v. Plainview Farmers Mut. Fire Ins. Co.*, 407 N.W.2d 673 (Minn.1987).

A Florida couple purchased a fire insurance policy on their house on December 8, 1983. On February 8, 1984, the couple's house was destroyed by fire. When they notified their insurer of the fire, the insurer told them their coverage had been canceled effective January 25, 1984, and that a cancellation notice had been mailed to them on January 13, 1984. The insurer told the couple that their coverage had been canceled because their house did not meet underwriting guidelines. The couple filed suit against their insurer and the agent seeking the face amount of the policy. A circuit court held that because the insurer had mailed the cancellation notice to the couple almost four weeks prior to the fire, the insurer had a complete defense against the couple's claim. It ruled that no trial was necessary and it absolved the insurer from any liability under the fire insurance policy. The couple appealed.

The Florida District Court of Appeal reversed the circuit court's ruling on the ground that the crucial inquiry was whether the policy provided for written notice of cancellation. The couple's policy stated: "This policy may be cancelled at any time by this company by giving to the insured a ten-days written notice of cancellation with or without tender of the excess of said premium above the pro rata premium for the expired time...." Because the policy provided for written notice of cancellation and did not specify the method of giving notice, the appeals court held that "the effective date of cancellation is to be determined based upon the date of *receipt* of the notice by the insured." Since the circuit court had improperly ruled that the mailing of the cancellation notice was sufficient to cancel the policy, the appeals court reversed and remanded the case for a determination of whether the couple had received the notice prior to the date of the fire. *Nunley v. Florida Farm Bureau Mut. Ins. Co.*, 494 So.2d 306 (Fla.App.1st Dist.1986).

F. Exclusions

As with other types of insurance, exclusions from coverage in liability and casualty insurance policies are strictly construed by the courts, and any ambiguities are usually resolved against the insurer.

A man pled guilty to the murders of his wife and son, and to the attempted murder of his daughter. He was sentenced to concurrent terms of fifty-five years for the murders and twenty years for the attempted murder. The personal representative of the deceased, and best friend of the daughter, brought suit against the man and his insurer. She alleged that the man had negligently caused the death and injuries. The insurer then filed suit seeking a declaration that the acts were excluded from coverage under an intentional acts clause and that it had no duty to defend. The trial court entered judgment in favor of the insurer, and the representative appealed to the Supreme Judicial Court of Maine.

An insurer ordinarily has a duty to defend the insured if the complaint against the insured provides a legal or factual basis under which the insurer may be required to indemnify. However, the doctrine of collateral estoppel provides that an issue which is determined against a party at one proceeding may bar that party from relitigating the same issue in a later proceeding. The man was, therefore, barred from contesting his intent to cause injury. Further, other parties may be barred from relitigating that issue in certain instances. The court ruled that in the interest of judicial economy the representative must be barred from relitigating the man's intent. The representative argued that a guilty plea, as opposed to a jury verdict, should not bar relitigation. The court felt that this bar would not offend the principles of due process; the man had a full and fair opportunity to litigate his intent, and in light of the sentences had ample incentive to do so. These facts were compounded by a lack of evidence to support an allegation of only negligence. The judgment was affirmed. *State Mutual Ins. Co. v. Bragg*, 589 A.2d 35 (Me.1991).

An insured business owner experienced three burglary attempts. Her son then decided to stay overnight to guard the store. He fell asleep and was awakened by someone attempting to enter the building. He fired one shot eighteen inches from the bottom of the door, and called the sheriff. When the sheriff arrived, he discovered an eleven-year-old boy shot in the knee. The parents sued the owner for gross negligence in injuring their son. The insurer then filed a declaratory judgment action seeking to determine that it was not required to defend or indemnify due to the intentional act exclusion in the policy. The trial court found for the insured and the insurer appealed to the Court of Appeals of Indiana. The court noted that intent may be established by showing an actual intent to injure or by showing that the insured acted while he was consciously aware that harm caused by his actions was practically certain to occur. The facts indicated that the son was awakened and shot at the lower portion of the door hoping to scare the intruder away. Therefore, the court found that no intent to harm could be inferred from these actions as a matter of law. The appellate court upheld the decision of the trial court. *Auto-Owners (Mutual) Ins. Co. v. Stroud*, 565 N.E.2d 1093 (Ind.App.1st Dist.1991).

A marine salvage business sold a crane mounted on a barge to a marine salvage operation. The crane was designed to be mounted on a truck, tracks, or a barge. The barge was not self-propelled. While recovering a sunken boat, the owner of the salvage operation lost an arm in part of the crane mechanism. He sued the marine salvage business, which was insured under a comprehensive liability policy with limits of $500,000. The insurer undertook defense of the business without any reservation of right to later contest coverage. Later, the insurer withdrew its defense claiming that a "watercraft exclusion clause" precluded coverage. The business and owner stipulated a $1 million default judgment. In exchange for a covenant not to execute on the judgment, the salvage business assigned all rights and interest against its insurer to the owner. The owner then tendered a $500,000 settlement offer to the insurer. The insurer never responded. The insurer brought a declaratory relief action in federal court, but the court granted summary judgment to the owner, awarding $1 million in coverage and $123,000 in post-judgment interest. The insurer appealed to the U.S. Court of Appeals, Ninth Circuit.

On appeal, the insurer argued that the policy precluded coverage. It also argued that it should not be liable for more than its policy limits, nor for the interest. The court disagreed. First, it held that the watercraft exclusion was ambiguous because the term "watercraft" was not defined in the policy and may or may not have included the unpowered barge. Moreover, the operation of the crane, which could be assembled not only on a barge, but elsewhere, would arguably require a separate analysis from that of the barge for purposes of the exclusion. Construing the ambiguity against the insurer, the claim did not fall within the exclusion. Second, the court stated that an insurer who fails to accept a reasonable settlement offer assumes the risk that it will be held liable for all damages resulting from such refusal. The insurer's duty to the insured in this regard was not changed because of the covenant not to execute. The failure to settle still left a $1 million judgment against the insured, since a covenant not to sue is not a release. Finally, the court held that interest was due because a stipulated judgment has the same effect as a case tried on the merits. *Consolidated American Ins. Co. v. Mike Soper Marine*, 951 F.2d 186 (9th Cir.1991).

An insured under a commercial umbrella policy obtained a bulldozer for a demonstration from a company which sold and leased construction equipment. The insured apparently drove the bulldozer out onto ice, where it fell through, sustaining damage. The company sued the insured for negligence, and the insured sued its insurer to determine if coverage was available. An exclusion in the policy provided that the policy would not apply where another's personal property was damaged while "in the insured's care, custody, or control." A trial court granted summary judgment to the insurer, and appeal was taken to the Supreme Court of New Hampshire. On appeal, the insured asserted that the company had arranged for the bulldozer demonstration, and had supervised and directed the actual demonstration, retaining care, custody, and control of the bulldozer at all times. It charged that, at the very least, there was an issue of fact to be ascertained. The supreme court agreed. Merely by driving the bulldozer, the insured could not necessarily be said to have been in control of it. If the company was directing the operation of the bulldozer, then the insured was simply an instrumentality of the company, and not in control.

The court reversed and remanded the case. *Happy House Amusement, Inc. v. New Hampshire Ins. Co.*, 609 A.2d 1231 (N.H.1992).

A New Hampshire contractor purchased a comprehensive general liability insurance policy for his construction contracting business. The contractor hired an inexperienced laborer. The contractor told the laborer that he would pay him per hour as a subcontractor, responsible for his own taxes, social security payments and health insurance. The laborer was employed exclusively and continuously by the contractor and worked under his close supervision. While roofing a building, the laborer fell onto the frozen ground and suffered serious injuries. The laborer brought a claim against the contractor for bodily injuries. The contractor's insurer sought a declaration in a New Hampshire trial court that coverage was not provided for the claim. The trial court held for the insurer and the contractor appealed to the Supreme Court of New Hampshire. The supreme court held that the laborer was an employee, within the meaning of an exclusion in the insured's comprehensive liability policy, rather than a subcontractor. The court noted that he was subject to the contractor's immediate control, was not engaged in a distinct business, and was an unskilled laborer rather than a specialist. The contractor supplied the location and special tools, employed the laborer exclusively and paid him by the hour, not the job. All of these factors indicated that the man was an employee. Because he was an employee, the policy did not provide coverage for claims due to bodily injury. The supreme court affirmed the trial court's decision. *Merchants Ins. Group v. Warchol*, 560 A.2d 1162 (N.H.1989).

A New York tenant fell down a flight of steps in a building owned by an insured landlord. The tenant was one of three tenants renting from the insured. The insurer denied coverage because the insured had breached an exclusionary clause in the policy which disallowed coverage if the premises were rented for use as a residence by more than two tenants. The insured unsuccessfully sued her insurer in a New York trial court and appealed to the Supreme Court, Appellate Division. The appellate court held that the policy clearly excluded coverage because the landlord had admitted renting to more than two tenants. The court affirmed the trial court's decision, and disallowed coverage. *Bates v. Cole*, 550 N.Y.S.2d 721 (A.D.2d Dep't 1990).

Six months after a moveable irrigation system was installed, the system was repaired and modified. It was then moved to another location. A Georgia man was electrocuted while operating the system. The general liability insurer for the repair company brought a declaratory judgment action claiming that there was no coverage afforded under the policy. The trial judge awarded coverage, and the insurer appealed to the Court of Appeals of Georgia. The appellate court reversed stating that the completed operations hazard exclusion in the policy was applicable because it was unambiguous. The exclusion stated that there would be no coverage for bodily injury or property damage arising out of a representation or warranty made if the bodily injury or property damage occurred after the repair and modification operations had been completed. *Travelers Ins. Co. v. Ty Co. Services, Inc.*, 399 S.E.2d 562 (Ga.App.1990).

An insurer issued a liability policy to an insured which covered "injury or damage for which [the insured became] legally liable." It included coverage for

Sec. I	SCOPE OF COVERAGE	313

wrongful eviction, but excluded coverage where an injury was expected or intended by the insured. Subsequently, a lawsuit was brought against the insured by the holder of an easement who claimed that the insured had interfered with his use of the easement by placing a locked gate across the road which was being used as the easement. When the insurer declined to defend the suit, the insured sued to recover defense costs. The trial court granted summary judgment to the insurer, and the insured appealed to the Supreme Court of New Mexico. On appeal, the court noted that the broad coverage provisions of the policy insured against wrongful eviction, and that the exclusion for intentional acts was repugnant to the insuring clause. Thus, it was ineffective to preclude coverage in this case. The insured reasonably expected to be covered for wrongful evictions by the main section of the policy. Accordingly, the court reversed the trial court's decision and held that the insurer had a duty to defend its insured. *Knowles v. United Services Automobile Association*, 832 P.2d 394 (N.M.1992).

A couple purchased a nine-unit apartment building in California. They obtained an insurance policy which covered all risks of direct physical loss which were not specifically excluded. The policy excluded losses for any earth movement, inherent defects, and faulty workmanship or materials. A series of cracks developed in the drive wall, driveway, and each slab of the building. The couple filed a claim with their insurer. The insurer refused coverage citing the policy exclusions. The couple, however, stated that the damage was the result of improper soil testing by the city of San Diego and improper construction by the contractor. A federal district court dismissed the case and the couple appealed to the U.S. Court of Appeals, Ninth Circuit. The couple argued on appeal that the faulty workmanship exclusion was ambiguous and should not preclude recovery. The court of appeals stated that only a strained construction of the exclusion for faulty workmanship would permit recovery for losses caused by negligent design and construction. It also stated that since the nature of the expansive soil was not readily discoverable, the exclusion for inherent defects also provided a basis for exclusion. The court of appeals affirmed the district court's decision. *Tzung v. State Farm Fire & Cas. Co.*, 873 F.2d 1338 (9th Cir.1989).

A Louisiana school official asked a student to run an errand for a school event. The student asked a fellow student to drive him. The two students ran the errand, but on the way back to the school they caused a car accident which resulted in severe injuries to the owner of the other car. She sued the driver of the car, his father, his father's insurer, and her own insurers. Eventually, she recovered a judgment of $1.6 million. The driver's father then sued the school and its insurers, asserting that the school was vicariously liable for his son's tortious acts, and that the school's liability policy provided coverage. The trial court found that the school's insurer was liable for coverage, and it appealed to the court of appeals, which affirmed. The insurer sought further review from the Supreme Court of Louisiana. The supreme court stated that the insurer's policy was clear and unambiguous. It stated that, "[a]nyone else is an insured while using with your permission a covered auto you own, hire or borrow..." Here, the automobile involved in the accident had not been "borrowed" by the school. The school did not acquire temporary possession, dominion or control over the car; it merely received a benefit from the car's use by another person. Accordingly, the school did not sufficiently possess, dominate or control the vehicle so as to make it a "borrowed" vehicle under the policy. The court reversed the decision of the lower courts, and held for the insurer. *Schroeder v. Board of Supervisors of Louisiana State Univ.*, 591 So.2d 342 (La.1991).

A volunteer church bus driver molested and sexually assaulted two girls and subsequently pled guilty to the molestation. The girls' parents sued, and the church's insurer made a summary judgment motion claiming it owed no duty to defend or indemnify the church. A federal district court granted the insurer summary judgment, and the church appealed. On appeal to the U.S. Court of Appeals, Tenth Circuit, the church argued that the insurer had to indemnify it since the girls' parents were suing it for negligently failing to investigate the driver's background and negligently failing to discharge the volunteer; therefore, the policy exclusion for wilful violation of a penal statute was not applicable. However, the court disagreed, noting that although the church had only negligence claims asserted against it, the girls' personal injuries for which their claims were asserted arose out of the volunteer's wilful violation of the penal statute. Accordingly, the exclusionary clause applied and the summary judgment was affirmed in favor of the insurer. *All American Ins. Co. v. Burns*, 971 F.2d 438 (10th Cir.1992).

An Alabama school employee was killed when the mini-van he was driving suddenly started on fire. The mini-van was owned and maintained by the school district. His survivors sued the board of education and four individual supervisors employed by the school district. The survivors claimed that the employees had a duty to make working conditions safe and had failed to do so. The employees sought a declaratory judgment that the school's general liability insurer had an obligation to defend them in the lawsuit. An Alabama trial court held for the employees. The insurer appealed to the Supreme Court of Alabama. On appeal, the insurer argued that it was free from defending the employees under two policy exclusions. First, that a clause excluding coverage for liability arising out of operation of the school's vehicles precluded coverage. A second clause excluded coverage for the death of any of the insured's employees. The supreme court rejected the insurer's interpretations of the exclusions. It concluded that the first exclusion did not apply because the employees' liability did not arise from the mini-van's operation. The second exclusion also did not apply, since the van driver was not employed by the supervisory employees, who were also named insureds under the school district's policy. The court ordered the insurer to defend the employees in the lawsuit. *Guaranty Nat. Ins. Co. v. Bd. of Educ.*, 540 So.2d 745 (Ala.1989).

The supreme court also heard another case arising out of the same accident. The school district's fleet automobile insurer sought a declaratory judgment that it would not be responsible for the driver's death. An Alabama trial court granted the insurer's declaratory judgment. The employees and the board appealed to the Supreme Court of Alabama. On appeal, the insurer contended that an exclusion for bodily injury to an insured's employee excluded coverage because the driver was the board's employee. However, the supreme court rejected the insurer's interpretations and reversed the lower court's decision. It held that the exclusion was ambiguous, in that it was not clear if "insured" referred to the supervisory employees or to the board. The court remanded the case for further proceedings. *Wilson v. State Farm Mut. Auto. Ins.*, 540 So.2d 749 (Ala.1989).

Sec. I SCOPE OF COVERAGE 315

A Texas woman and her husband were patrons of an insured restaurant. As they were returning to their car in the restaurant's parking lot, they were assaulted by an unknown man who shot the husband. The wife then sued the restaurant for wrongful death, alleging that the restaurant had been negligent in failing to provide adequate security and in failing to warn them of the danger of criminal attack. The restaurant's general liability insurer brought a declaratory judgment action in a Texas trial court to determine whether its policy required it to defend or indemnify the restaurant. The insurer argued that the policy excluded claims arising out of assault and battery. After the trial court found that the insurer's policy did not cover the restaurant's lawsuit, the restaurant appealed to the Court of Appeals of Texas.

On appeal, the restaurant asserted that the lawsuit was not a claim arising out of assault and battery because it was based on negligence. The court of appeals affirmed the trial court's decision, ruling that the lawsuit arose out of an assault and battery and was therefore excluded by the policy. It reasoned that the lawsuit would not have been brought in absence of the assault and battery committed against the husband. The court also stated that the policy unambiguously excluded claims arising out of assault and battery regardless of the case. The insurer was not liable. *Garrison v. Fielding Reinsurance, Inc.*, 765 S.W.2d 536 (Tex.App.1989).

An insurer extended a general liability policy to a dance club and its landlord. The policy excluded coverage for acts amounting to "assault and/or battery." While the policy was in force, a patron of the dance club was apparently raped and sodomized in the women's bathroom. She sued both the insureds. When they sought defense and indemnification, the insurer sued for declaratory relief in a federal district court. The court found that the exclusion was ambiguous, and was not so broad as to include rape and sodomy. It ordered the insurer to provide a defense to its insureds, with indemnity to follow if liability was found. *United National Ins. Co. v. Waterfront Realty Corp.*, 777 F.Supp. 254 (S.D.N.Y.1991).

A Wisconsin mother sued a facility on behalf of her severely mentally retarded daughter who was sexually molested and became pregnant while in the insured facility's custody. The insured diagnosed the daughter's pregnancy during the fifteenth or sixteenth week of gestation. The insurer brought a declaratory judgment action to determine its obligations under the policy. The policy contained a sexual abuse exclusion which stated that the coverage would not apply to any claim, demand, or causes of action arising out of or resulting from sexual abuse.

The complaint filed by the mother in the underlying lawsuit alleged failure to supervise and untimely detection of pregnancy. The insured argued that it might be found solely liable under the ultimate detection of pregnancy claim. However, the court found that the language "arise out of or relate to" sexual abuse included all claims brought by the mother. Therefore, the court held that the exclusion applied to deny coverage. *IPCI Ltd. v. Old Republic Ins. Co.*, 758 F.Supp. 478 (E.D.Wis.1991).

A Louisiana woman attended an after-hours party at a lounge owned by an insured. During the party, another guest threw a drink in the woman's face and then apparently attacked her. The incident occurred in full sight of a lounge employee. Subsequently, the injured woman filed suit against the lounge owner and its insurer, asserting negligence as the basis for her recovery. The insurer charged that it had excluded coverage for any claims based on assault and battery. The trial court agreed with the insurer's interpretation, and the injured woman appealed to the Court of

Appeal of Louisiana. On appeal, the court noted that the policy had unambiguously excluded coverage in this case. Even though the woman's claim alleged negligence, her injuries stemmed from an alleged assault and battery. She could not avoid this result by pleading negligence on the part of the insured. The court refused to find an ambiguity in the policy, and affirmed the trial court's grant of summary judgment to the insurer. *Wallace v. Huber,* 597 So.2d 1247 (La.App.3d Cir.1992).

An employee of an entity which provided acrobatic watershows at Sea World was killed while performing in a jet ski show. The employer was insured under a policy which named Sea World as an additional insured. The deceased's estate received workers' compensation death benefits from the employer, but later brought suit against Sea World. The insurer intervened in the suit and sought a declaration of its obligations under the policy. It contended that an "exhibition participants" exclusionary clause precluded coverage. A state court held that the exclusion was inapplicable, and the insurer appealed to the Florida District Court of Appeal.

A primary issue on appeal was the construction and applicability of the "exhibition participants" exclusionary clause. Because the policy did not further define "exhibition," the trial court had found the term to be ambiguous and accordingly construed it against the insurer. The appellate court noted that the lack of a definition does not always create an ambiguity, and that other courts have ruled such an exclusion to be unambiguous. A four part test was adopted for determining the applicability of the "exhibition participants" exclusion clause: 1) that the event in which the person was injured was a contest or exhibition; 2) that the contest or exhibition was of an athletic or sports nature; 3) that the contest or exhibition was sponsored by the named insured; 4) that the injured person was practicing for or participating in the contest or exhibition at the time of the injury. After application of this test, the court held that the exclusion applied and therefore precluded coverage. *Jefferson Insurance Co. of New York v. Sea World of Florida, Inc.,* 586 So.2d 95 (Fla.App.5 Dist.1991).

A developer contracted to build a golf course and hired a contractor to construct the project. Substantial parts of the golf course were built on federally protected wetlands, and the contractor failed to obtain the necessary permits for construction in such areas because it did not realize the land was protected. When the developer was notified of its obligation to create other wetland areas as a means of mitigating damages, it sued the contractor. The contractor then sought defense and indemnification from its general liability insurer, and the trial court held that the policy provided coverage. The insurer appealed to the Georgia Court of Appeals. On appeal, the court noted that the intent of the contractor to build the golf course where it did was not sufficient to invoke an intentional acts exclusion in the policy. The mere appreciation of the risk that the wetlands might be federally protected did not amount to intent to destroy the wetlands. Further, the business risk exclusion did not apply because there was no allegation that the contractor had failed to build the golf course in a workmanlike manner. The court affirmed the decision of the trial court and held that insurance coverage existed. *Glens Falls Ins. Co. v. Donmac Golf Shaping Co.,* 417 S.E.2d 197 (Ga.App.1992).

An Ohio man purchased a motorcycle liability insurance policy which provided coverage for personal injuries and property damage caused by his operation of the motorcycle. Both the insured and his wife were deemed to be covered persons under

Sec. I   SCOPE OF COVERAGE   317

the policy such that bodily injury or property damage suffered by them would be excluded from coverage. However, the policy also had a guest passenger clause which provided coverage for a passenger. Subsequently, the insured's wife was killed while riding as a passenger on the motorcycle. The insurer denied coverage. A state trial court found in the insurer's favor, and appeal was taken to the Ohio Court of Appeals. On appeal, the insured argued that the guest passenger clause created an ambiguity sufficient to provide coverage. However, the court disagreed. It stated that where the policy had clearly excluded coverage for the wife, the addition of the guest passenger clause could not void that exclusion unless it did so expressly. Since the clause did not expressly void the exclusion, the trial court's ruling for the insurer was affirmed. No coverage was found. *Progressive Specialty Ins. Co. v. Easton*, 583 N.E.2d 1064 (Ohio App.2nd Dist.1990).

A garbage truck operator was killed while unloading his truck. Another truck backed into him, pinning him between the two vehicles. His widow brought a wrongful death action against the garbage company and its liability insurer. She asserted that the garbage truck was "mobile equipment" which was excluded from the definition of "automobile." Automobiles were excluded from coverage under the liability policy. The trial court disagreed, granting summary judgment to the insurer. The Court of Appeal of Louisiana affirmed. Here, the truck was being used as a vehicle at the time of the accident. Thus, coverage was barred by the terms of the policy. *Williams v. Galliano*, 601 So.2d 769 (La.App.1992).

A Wisconsin boy dropped off his parents' car at a repair garage. While returning in a loaner car to pick up the repaired car, he struck a little girl. The girl sued the driver and various insurers in a Wisconsin district court. The district court determined that the repair garage's liability insurer had primary coverage, and this insurer appealed. The Court of Appeals of Wisconsin, however, held that the son was a garage "customer" within the meaning of the liability policy exclusion, even though it was his parents who owned the car being repaired by the garage and who were financially obligated to the garage. Accordingly, the decision was reversed and the garage's insurer was not required to provide coverage. *Mattheis by Vowinkel v. Heritage Mut. Ins.*, 487 N.W.2d 52 (Wisc.App.1992).

An insurer issued an office building package policy to a corporation and its president which provided liability coverage for personal injury, including libel and slander. However, the policy excluded coverage for publishing done by or for the insureds. The president wrote an article which was published in a magazine, and which resulted in a libel suit against him. He brought suit against his insurer in a federal district court, seeking a declaration that it must defend and indemnify him. The court, however, found that the exclusion was unambiguous, clearly denying coverage for such activity. The court granted summary judgment to the insurer. *Schiff v. Federal Ins. Co.*, 779 F.Supp. 17 (S.D.N.Y.1991).

A bank purchased a directors' and officers' liability insurance policy which excluded claims made by one director or officer against another. Subsequently, the bank was placed in receivership, and the FDIC stepped in. It intended to recover from certain directors and officers. Their insurer sued to enforce the exclusion, but the Oklahoma federal district court stated that the reason for the exclusion was to prevent collusion and the FDIC's involvement was clearly not collusive. The exclusion did not apply to bar recovery by the FDIC. *American Casualty Co. v. Federal Deposit Insurance Corp.*, 791 F.Supp. 276 (W.D.Okl.1992).

G. Joint and Several Liability

A Louisiana man who worked for a cotton gin company received a massive injury to his right hand when it got caught in the lint cleaner rollers of a gin machine. The employee brought in a federal district court a products liability suit for defective design against the company which designed the gin. The employee's workers' compensation insurer also wished to intervene to obtain reimbursement for injury compensation paid to the employee as a result of the accident. The district court apportioned sixty percent of the fault to the employee for failure to follow established procedures, thirty percent fault to his company, and ten percent to the gin manufacturer under a strict liability theory. The worker and the workers' compensation insurer appealed to the U.S. Court of Appeals, Fifth Circuit.

The appellate court, after reviewing the trial court's findings, affirmed the employee's and manufacturer's percent of damages but held that a consideration of the fault of the workers' compensation insurer through the employer was in error. The court based its reasoning on the fact that since the employer had paid the workers' compensation benefits to the employee it was immune from further liability and the employer's fault in the incident was irrelevant. Consequently, the court reapportioned the thirty percent fault assigned to the insurer so that 85.71% was assigned to the employee and 14.29% to the gin manufacturer, with attorney's fees to be paid in like proportion. *Davis v. Commercial Union Ins. Co. v. Continental Commercial Union Ins. Co. v. Continental Gin Co.*, 892 F.2d 378 (5th Cir.1990).

A Louisiana yacht owner entrusted the nighttime operation of his yacht to one of his companions. The companion caused the yacht to collide with a bridge, sinking the vessel. Seven of eight passengers survived. The victim's father brought a wrongful death action against the yacht owner, his yacht insurer, the companion who was driving, and his two insurers. During trial in a federal district court, the defendants settled with the victim's father, but the trial went on to determine liability between the yacht owner and the driver. The district court found the yacht operator seventy-five percent at fault for negligently operating the yacht, and the yacht owner twenty-five percent at fault for negligently entrusting the vessel to an inexperienced person at night. The settlement failed to exhaust any single policy. However, the district court treated the operator's umbrella insurer as a primary insurer. It ordered the owner's yacht insurer to pay 3/14 liability and the operator's insurers to pay the remaining 11/14. The operator's insurers then appealed to the U.S. Court of Appeals, Fifth Circuit. The court of appeals disagreed with the district court's formulation of liability. Because the operator's homeowner's policy was listed as an underlying insurer in the umbrella policy, the umbrella insurer was a true excess insurer and was only liable when the homeowner's policy had been exhausted. Because the owner's yacht policy and the homeowner's policy provided sufficient coverage, the operator's umbrella policy was not exposed to liability. *Truehart v. Blandon*, 884 F.2d 223 (5th Cir.1989).

An Ohio bar patron challenged a man to drink ten drinks in rapid succession. The man did and immediately proceeded to drive home. He was killed in a traffic accident and his widow sued the bar. Its insurer settled the claim and sued the patron who bought the drinks, seeking contribution. The patron's dismissal motion was granted by the trial court and the insurer appealed to the Ohio Court of Appeals which overturned the dismissal. It held that a patron who purchases liquor for an intoxicated person, knowing such service is wrong, may be jointly liable. The patron appealed to the Ohio Supreme Court. The court noted that liability for consumption of drinks lay with the actual consumer, except where the seller knew that the consumer's will was so impaired that it was impossible for him to refrain from drinking. However, this exception was inapplicable in this case. The insurer's argument of joint liability was invalid because the tavern had not been found liable. Thus, the insurer could not seek compensation for joint liability. The duty imposed on taverns to exercise reasonable care did not extend to patrons who purchased alcohol from the tavern for fellow patrons. The insurer was not entitled to contribution from the patron and the case was dismissed. *Great Cent. Ins. Co. v. Tobias*, 524 N.E.2d 168 (Ohio 1988).

A woman was injured at Disney World when the bumper car she was driving collided with another bumper car driven by her fiance. She brought suit against Disney World and its insurer, the Insurance Company of North America. The jury returned a verdict finding the woman 14% at fault, her fiance 85% at fault and Disney World 1% at fault. The trial judge entered judgment against Disney World and its insurer for 86% of the damages. Disney World appealed.

The Florida District Court of Appeal observed that according to Florida law, the doctrine of joint and several liability is applicable and binding on the courts. Under this doctrine, a codefendant (the woman's fiance in this case) must resort to contribution among joint tortfeasors (Disney World) in order to obtain relief. If the codefendant is "judgment proof," then the solvent defendant (Disney World) must pay it all. Since the woman's fiance was unable to pay the judgment against him, the burden fell on Disney World to pay both defendants' portion of the judgment.

Although the appeals court affirmed the trial court's decision, it certified the question of whether joint and several liability was applicable to this case to the state supreme court. The decision that Disney World and its insurer were 86% liable for the woman's damages was upheld. *Walt Disney World Co. v. Wood*, 489 So.2d 61 (Fla.App.4th Dist.1986).

II. PREMIUMS

The cases in this section illustrate the judicial concern for fair, even-handed treatment of disputes involving insurance premiums. In these cases the courts balance insurers' rights to collect premiums where coverage has been extended with insureds' expectations regarding coverage.

A. Coverage Disputes

A California savings and loan association sued its directors' and officers' liability insurer to establish the limits of its policy. By establishing these limits, the association hoped to facilitate settlement of an underlying lawsuit in which the association claimed damages from five former officers for breach of fiduciary duty, negligence, mismanagement and waste in over 200 loan transactions. The policy stated that the liability limits were $20 million for each loss with a $20 million annual aggregate limit for each director and officer. The insurer argued that the maximum liability was $20 million because the claim constituted a single loss. The association argued that there were numerous losses and that the liability for the five officers should be $100 million. A federal district court ruled that the claims constituted more than one loss and the insurer appealed to the U.S. Court of Appeals, Ninth Circuit.

On appeal, the insurer argued that the district court had improperly asserted jurisdiction over the matter and that a "no-action" clause in the policy barred declaratory judgment actions prior to the settlement of the claim. The insurer also argued that the district court's holding was inconsistent with the policy. The court of appeals stated that the district court had properly asserted jurisdiction over the actions since there was a real dispute which made settlement improbable. The court also noted that the "no-action" clause did not apply to a case adjudicating issues of coverage and defense. The court also concluded that the fact that the loan losses had originated from an aggressive loan policy did not require single loss treatment. Numerous business decisions had taken place after the loan policy was in effect which required the exercise of business judgment. The court of appeals affirmed the district court's judgment. *Eureka Federal S&L v. Amer. Cas. Co. of Reading*, 873 F.2d 229 (9th Cir.1989).

In 1974, an Arkansas company purchased a life insurance policy for one of its employees. The company then assigned its interest in the policy to a bank. The bank utilized the automatic premium loan provision of the policy to make premium payments. In June 1980, the bank defaulted on its premium payments when the cash value of the policy could no longer be used to pay premiums. The insured employee became disabled in May 1980, due to a heart attack. The insurance company notified the bank in January 1981, that the policy had lapsed. In June 1981, the bank discovered that the employee was disabled. It contacted the insurance company in July, demanding reinstatement of the policy based on the man's total disability and the premium waiver disability benefit provision in the policy. The insurance company refused to reinstate the policy because the bank had not provided "written notice and proof of total disability within one year of the due date of the first premium in default," as the policy required. The bank sued, arguing that the man's disability, not notice of that disability, created the insurer's duty to waive premiums. It also pointed out that notice and proof of disability were given as soon as reasonably possible. A trial court ruled in favor of the bank and the insurer appealed.

The Court of Appeals of Arkansas agreed with the trial court that the insurance company's duty to waive premiums was triggered by the disability, not notice of the disability. The court disagreed, however, with the trial court's finding that notice and proof of disability were given as soon as reasonably possible. The court said failure to give timely notice and proof of disability "has been excused only in those cases where there were grave and extenuating circumstances prohibiting timely notification." No evidence was presented proving that the man was unable to notify the insurance company of his disability. The appellate court reversed the lower court's decision and entered a judgment for the insurance company. *American General Life Ins. Co. v. First American Nat'l Bank*, 716 S.W.2d 205 (Ark.App.1986).

At issue before the New Jersey Superior Court was whether an insurer is obligated to advise an insured of the expiration of a fire insurance policy. In 1979, a car wash owner purchased a fire insurance policy from an agent who was employed by the insurer. Upon expiration of the initial policy's one-year term, the insurer forwarded a new policy and an invoice for the premium due to the agent who then forwarded a premium bill to the car wash owner. The car wash owner paid the premium, thereby renewing the policy for an additional year. At the end of the second year, however, no demand for premium or notice that the policy would expire was forwarded to the car wash owner. A $95,000 fire loss occurred at the car wash. The car wash owner requested payment under the policy and the insurer denied coverage, contending that the policy had expired prior to the loss. The car wash owner sued the insurer in a New Jersey trial court which held in his favor. The insurer appealed.

The New Jersey Superior Court affirmed the trial court's ruling. The court held that state law required insurers to give notice of the intention not to renew based on premiums not paid on or before the expiration date. Here, the fire insurer failed (in violation of state law) to give notice to the car wash owner of the expiration date of the fire policy. The court therefore ruled that the insurer was liable to the car wash owner for his fire loss. The court also held that the insurance agent could not be held liable to the insurer for contribution for damages since the notice obligation was placed solely on the insurer, not on the agent. *Barbara Corp. v. Maneely Ins. Agency*, 484 A.2d 1292 (N.J.Super.A.D.1984).

B. Liability for Payment of Premiums

A North Dakota trucker purchased a business liability policy from an insurance agency. The following year, he placed his vehicles in his sons' names because he was unable to secure financing in his own name. The sons occasionally worked for the trucking business. The named insureds in the policy were changed from the trucker to his sons, his wife and the business itself. The following year, the trucker requested renewal and the agency paid his premiums to the insurer. The trucker then defaulted on his premium payments. The agency canceled the policy and sued the trucker, his wife, sons and business for unpaid premiums and late charges. The trucker then filed for bankruptcy, listing the agency as a creditor. The bankruptcy court discharged this debt. However, the court found that the agency's insurance services covered vehicles used by the trucking business, the family farm and personal vehicles. The court ruled that the sons commonly owned the vehicles and used the trucking business as a means to insure them. Because they had benefitted from the insurance services, the sons were liable for unpaid premiums for vehicles held in their names. The sons appealed to the North Dakota Supreme Court.

On appeal, the sons argued that they should not be liable for the payments because they had not contracted with the insurance agency. The supreme court agreed, citing a number of cases which held that named insureds were not liable for premium payments unless they had actually contracted to pay the premiums. There was no evidence that the father was acting as the sons' agent or that the business was operated as a partnership. Therefore, the sons were not liable for the unpaid premiums. *Home Ins. of Dickinson v. Speldrich*, 436 N.W.2d 1 (N.D.1989).

In a case of first impression in Mississippi, that state's supreme court has held that an "additional insured" under an insurance policy is not liable for the payment of premiums. The additional insured in this case was a franchisor who required that its franchisee obtain certain insurance coverage with the franchisor named as an additional insured. When the franchisee failed to make premium payments, the insurer brought suit against both the franchisee and the franchisor. The insurer obtained default judgments against the franchisee, but the franchisor contended it could not be held liable for the premium payments. The supreme court agreed, citing an Alaska case which was decided on similar facts. The court said that absent a contract to pay premiums there is no liability for such payment. Here, the additional insured made neither an express nor an implied agreement to pay any premiums, and, thus, there was no duty to do so. *A. Copeland Enterprises v. Pickett & Meador*, 422 So.2d 752 (Miss.1982).

A different result was reached in an Alabama case in which an insurance agency sued a real estate developer to recover unpaid premiums. The premiums were owed on a policy written at the request of the developer to cover a real estate development he was promoting. Listed as insureds on the policy were the developer, his wife and the corporate name of the property under development. Since the property was not actually incorporated, the developer paid the premiums himself for three years. When the property became incorporated, however, the developer informed the insurer of the changes and asked that the listed corporate name be changed to reflect the newly created company. The developer did not ask the insurer to remove his or his wife's name from the policy. At trial, the developer claimed that he should not be held personally responsible for the corporation's premium payments. The Alabama Supreme Court affirmed the trial court's ruling that the developer's failure to have his name removed from the policy made him liable for the premium payments. The supreme court, however, reversed the trial court's ruling that the developer was solely liable for the payments; the corporation was also liable. *Smith v. Thompson Agency*, 430 So.2d 859 (Ala.1983).

III. NOTICE/PROOF OF LOSS REQUIREMENTS

Insureds are required to comply with reasonable notice and proof of loss requirements.

A truck driver worked for an insured as an interstate hauler. During a trip from Kentucky to Pennsylvania, he deviated from his route, stopping at his girlfriend's place of work. While there, he got into an argument and eventually drove his semi-tractor into the building where his girlfriend worked. One person died, eighteen were injured. The truck driver was convicted of murder, attempted murder and battery, among other things. Two of the injured people then sued the truck driver, alleging that he had *negligently* caused their injuries. A default judgment was entered against the truck driver, and the two injured persons sought to recover their damages from the insurer. The trial court granted their motion for summary judgment, and the insurer appealed to the Court of Appeals of Indiana, Fifth District. On appeal, the court noted that the insurer had had notice of the underlying tort claim against the driver. Rather than undertake his defense, however, it had determined that there was no coverage available under the policy and chosen not to intervene in the underlying lawsuit. Because of that decision, it was precluded from asserting that coverage was unavailable. An insurer who refuses to defend its insured does so at its own peril. Nevertheless, the court remanded the case for a determination as to whether the driver was driving the truck as an employee (so as to be an insured) because he had been outside his specific, scheduled route at the time of the incident. The court reversed the summary judgment award. *Liberty Mutual Ins. Co. v. Metzler*, 586 N.E.2d 897 (Ind.App.5th Dist.1992).

A private North Carolina university became involved in a lawsuit when it tried to sell a psychiatric hospital it owned. The university was sued by two doctors and then counterclaimed against them for intentional torts including defamation, interference with contract and unfair trade practices. The university incurred legal fees of about $29,000 before notifying its general liability insurer. The underlying suit was favorably settled and the university sought reimbursement for legal expenses from two insurers. The university's errors and omissions insurer agreed to pay $20,000 of the $51,000 in legal fees which the university had paid. However, the university's general liability insurer refused to pay anything because it had not been immediately notified of the underlying action. The university sued the general liability insurer in a North Carolina trial court which denied the insurer's motion to dismiss the lawsuit. The action was not barred by a three-year statute of limitations. The university had not acted in bad faith by failing to notify the insurer immediately, as it had believed it should make its claim at the conclusion of the underlying lawsuit. The court found the university entitled to almost $23,000 plus interest, but amended its ruling so that the $20,000 received by the university from its errors and omissions carrier was credited against the judgment. Both parties appealed to the North Carolina Court of Appeals.

The court ruled that the statute of limitations commenced on the date the contractual promise was broken and not when the insurer refused to defend. Thus, the university was entitled to recover attorney fees for only the three years previous to its filing of the lawsuit. The court reversed and remanded the case for a redetermination of the legal fees. On remand, the court was to take into consideration the university's good faith delay in requesting defense, and the fact that the insurer was not materially prejudiced by the delay. The general liability insurer was entitled to a $20,000 credit for the settlement payment made by the errors and omissions carrier. *Duke Univ. v. St. Paul Mercury Ins. Co.*, 384 S.E.2d 36 (N.C.App.1989).

An insured developer purchased four adjacent lots in West Palm Beach, Florida. The developer began construction on the properties, committing substantial sums of money. When it applied for a building permit, the city inspected the property and found a sewer line directly under one of the proposed building sites. The city refused to grant a permit until the developer relocated the sewer line, which it did. The developer then demanded reimbursement of the sewer line relocation costs from its insurer, which denied coverage. The insured successfully sued the insurer in a Florida trial court, and the insurer appealed to the District Court of Appeal of Florida, Fourth District. The insurer argued that the insured failed to give notice of the claim, which the policy required. The insurer also contended that there had been more feasible alternative remedies available than that which the insured had chosen. The court disagreed, ruling that because the failure to notify did not prejudice the rights of the insurer, the insurer could not deny coverage for that reason. The court further ruled that the insured effected a commercially reasonable solution to the problem, and therefore did not increase the insurer's liability under its policy. The court affirmed the trial court's decision, granting coverage. *Attorneys' Title Ins. Fund, Inc. v. Rogers*, 552 So.2d 329 (Fla.App.4th Dist.1989).

A Kentucky insured owned a drapery shop which was partially destroyed by fire. She retained an attorney to handle her insurance claim. The policy clearly stated that any suit on the policy must be brought within one year after the loss. After preliminary negotiations, the attorney and insurer were unable to reach an agreement. Approximately six months after the loss, the insurer finally made an offer to settle all claims. Eleven months after that, the attorney wrote a letter to the insurer accepting the settlement offer. However, because the anniversary date of the loss had passed without a settlement or a lawsuit, the insurer claimed it was no longer obligated to pay anything. The insured sued her attorney, who paid her the amount of the settlement. The attorney then sued the insurer in a Kentucky trial court and won a judgment for that same amount. The court of appeals reversed the decision and appeal was taken to the Supreme Court of Kentucky.

The supreme court held that the insurer was no longer liable to pay on the policy. Even though the insurer had admitted coverage under the policy, it had reserved all the policy conditions and defenses, including the one year limitation on settlement or suit. Because the attorney had not been misled or induced by the insurer to wait beyond the one year period, the insurer was no longer required to pay on the policy. The court agreed with the court of appeals, and held that the insurer was not liable to the attorney for the settlement amount. *Edmondson v. Pennsylvania National Mutual Casualty Ins. Co.*, 781 S.W.2d 753 (Ky.1989).

The granddaughter of a New York couple fell down a flight of stairs in premises owned by them. The girl sustained a serious injury to her eye. Under the terms of the couple's liability policy, they were to notify the insurer as soon as practicable of any accidents for which they might be liable. However, they did not notify their insurer until over nine years later, when they were sued by their granddaughter. The trial court excused the delay in notification because there had been no indication that anyone would pursue a claim against the couple. The insurer appealed to the Supreme Court, Appellate Division, which held that the nine year delay in notification was not reasonable even though the couple was unaware that an interfamilial lawsuit could be commenced against them. The court reversed the trial court's decision and held that the insurer was not liable. *Greater New York Mutual Ins. Co. v. Farrauto*, 551 N.Y.S.2d 277 (A.D.2d Dept.1990).

A business obtained liability policies from two different insurers. Five years after an adjoining landowner obtained a $29,000 judgment against the business for damages to the adjoining landowner's property, the business sued the insurers in a Utah district court seeking indemnification for the judgment. Both insurers asked the court for a declaration that they had no duty to indemnify on the ground that the business gave them untimely notice of the lawsuit. The court granted the insurers' requests and the business appealed to the Utah Supreme Court.

The business contended that the district court should not have ruled for the insurers because they had failed to show that the delay in notice resulted in the judgment against it. The supreme court held for the insurers, observing that there were several indicators in the record that the delay resulted in the judgment against the business. The delay gave the insurers no opportunity to investigate, attempt to settle or employ their own counsel to defend the business. The business violated the terms of the policies which stated that, in the event of a claim, written notice to the insurers had to be given as soon as practicable. Five years was deemed impracticable. The insurers were not liable to indemnify the business for the $29,000 judgment. *Busch Corp. v. State Farm Fire & Cas. Co.*, 743 P.2d 1217 (Utah 1987).

After a New York business which manufactured sun care products was sued for products liability, it notified its insurer of the lawsuit. The insurer notified the business that there was no coverage due to late notice by the business. After the original products liability lawsuit was settled, the business sued the insurer seeking defense and settlement costs. A U.S. district court held for the business and the insurer appealed. Before the U.S. Court of Appeals, Second Circuit, the insurer contended that the business's breach of the policy's notice requirement to give written notice "as soon as practicable" concerning any occurrence relevant to coverage relieved it of any duty to defend or indemnify the business.

The court of appeals held for the insurer, observing that a primary purpose of a notice-of-occurrence requirement is to enable insurers to reduce future risks to the public by preventing the continued manufacturing of known harmful products by their insureds. Here, the business knew of product complaints almost three years before it notified the insurer of the formal lawsuit against it. Because compliance with a notice-of-occurrence provision is a condition precedent to an insurer's liability under New York law, the court of appeals held that the insurer had no duty to defend or indemnify the business. *Commercial Union Ins. Co. v. Int'l Flavors & Fragrances*, 822 F.2d 267 (2d Cir.1987).

IV. BURGLARY AND THEFT INSURANCE

Disputes have arisen under burglary and theft insurance policies involving proofs of loss, what property is covered, the "visible force and violence" requirement, employee dishonesty and other exclusions from coverage.

A. <u>Preconditions for Coverage</u>

A breast clinic purchased medical equipment by making a down payment with the balance due upon delivery of all equipment. The clinic executed a certificate of acceptance when nearly all the equipment had been delivered. When a dispute arose over the equipment's installation, the clinic declined final payment until it could be satisfied that the equipment was properly installed. Representatives of the seller entered the clinic "under the guise of performing corrective installation work" and removed several components of the purchased equipment. The clinic filed a claim under its insurance policy for a loss due to theft. The Florida District Court of Appeal ruled that title to the equipment passed to the clinic upon delivery. The removal of previously delivered equipment was therefore theft which was covered under the clinic's policy. *St. Paul Fire & Marine Ins. Co. v. Pensacola Diagnostic Center & Breast Clinic*, 505 So.2d 513 (Fla.App.1st Dist.1987).

In a California case a manufacturer of stereo components based in Los Angeles was the victim of complex fraud perpetrated by two of its employees. A sales representative submitted fictitious purchase orders for equipment from dishonest northern California dealers. An accountant received these fictitious orders and issued shipping documents for the equipment to be shipped to San Francisco. Instead, the components were sent to another Los Angeles firm which shipped them to Japan for sale through unauthorized dealers. The trucking outfit that delivered the goods to the other Los Angeles firm charged for the fictitious shipments to San Francisco. The accountant issued invoices applying lower than normal sales prices on the fraudulently sold equipment, and extended the terms of the company's ten percent discount for prompt payment from thirty days to ninety days. Once the products were sold in Japan, the sales representative paid the company the lowered invoice prices less the ten percent discount.

The company sued to recover from its insurer under a comprehensive employee dishonesty policy. A U.S. district court entered a judgment finding 1) the proper measure of the value of lost equipment was the cost to the company to produce replacement components, reduced by the total amount of payments made by the sales representative on the fraudulently sold components; 2) fraudulent freight payments and commissions paid on the fraudulent sales could not be recovered under the policy; and 3) payments received from another insurance policy should be subtracted from the amount of damage awarded under the policy. The payments made by the sales representative were found to exceed the company's replacement cost for the components; therefore no damages were awarded. The company appealed.

The U.S. Court of Appeals, Ninth Circuit, modified the district court's ruling. The court of appeals agreed that payment received by the company from its other insurance policy should be subtracted from the present damage award. It ruled, however, that the proper measure of lost equipment should be the equipment's fair market value rather than the cost of replacement to the company, because the insurance company, not the insured, was responsible for replacement. The court held that using the fair market value as the measure of damages also automatically incorporated the fraudulent shipping charges into the recovery. The court calculated a total award to the insured company of $295,636. The case, thus modified, was remanded for further proceedings. *James B. Lansing Sound v. Nat'l Union Fire Ins. Co. of Pittsburgh, Pa.*, 801 F.2d 1560 (9th Cir.1986).

After a woman lost her $40,000 ring she filed a claim with her insurer. In the course of the insurer's investigation it requested tax returns from the woman and her husband for specified years. The woman refused to produce the tax returns and sued the insurer seeking a declaration from a New York state court that she was not obligated to supply the returns. The woman's lawsuit was dismissed on the ground that the insurer had not yet denied the claim; thus there was no legal controversy between them.

Approximately one month after the dismissal she and her husband produced the requested tax returns and sought recovery for the ring. However, the insurer denied coverage because her claim had not been brought within one year of the discovery of the loss of the ring, a condition for recovery stated in the policy. The woman again sued the insurer in a U.S. district court, which dismissed her claim. The woman appealed to the U.S. Court of Appeals, Second Circuit, which reversed the district court ruling. Under a New York statute, the woman's second lawsuit was not time-barred where the first lawsuit was dismissed for a technical defect. The court of appeals remanded the case to the district court to allow the woman to proceed with her claim. *Harris v. United States Liability Ins. Co.*, 746 F.2d 152 (2d Cir.1984).

Theft insurance was denied in an Arizona case due to the insured's noncooperation. A man submitted an insurance claim for stolen firearms covered under a "Voluntary Excess Firearms Protection" policy. Attached to the claim was a list of sixty items allegedly stolen. The insurer informed the insured that 1) there was no documentation verifying his ownership of the firearms, 2) there was no documentation verifying the values of the firearms and 3) the value stated on the insured's proof of loss did not correspond with the amount of the claim presented. The insurer requested that, pursuant to a policy requirement, the insured submit to an examination under oath. During this examination the insured refused to answer several questions relating to the number of guns he owned, whether he had sold any of the guns and the source of his income. The insurer then denied the claim on the ground of noncooperation of the insured. The insured sued the insurer to recover for the allegedly stolen guns in an Arizona trial court, which denied the insurer's motion for summary judgment. The insurer appealed to the Arizona Court of Appeals, which reversed the trial court's ruling, holding that the insured had no Fifth Amendment right to refuse to answer questions posed by the insurer during the sworn examination. Thus, the insured's refusal to answer the questions constituted a breach of the terms of the policy which barred him from recovery on his claim. *Warrilow v. Superior Court*, 689 P.2d 193 (Ariz.App.1984).

B. "Visible Force and Violence" Requirements

An insured had in place a policy which covered "safe burglaries." While the policy was in effect, the insured was burglarized. A large safe showed signs of being tampered with, but nothing was taken from it. However, a large sum of money was taken from a small safe which showed no signs of forced entry. Based on the lack of visible marks, the insurer denied coverage. In the lawsuit which followed, the trial court granted summary judgment to the insurer, and the insured appealed to the New York Supreme Court, Appellate Division. That court upheld the ruling for the insurer because the policy clearly and unambiguously required evidence of physical force as a condition for payment. *Prince Check Cashing Corp. v. Federal Ins. Co.*, 582 N.Y.S.2d 751 (A.D.2d Dept.1992).

At the close of a business day in January 1981, a Nebraska merchant fastened shut his business's door with two bars in such a manner that it was impossible to open the door from the outside. The next morning numerous pieces of stereo equipment were missing from the building. Although there were no signs of forcible entry, the door bars were found lying on the ground. The merchant attempted to collect under his burglary insurance policy, but his insurer denied coverage. It cited the policy requirement that burglary be evidenced by visible marks of forcible entry. The merchant sued the insurer and a county court held that this definition of burglary violated public policy. The Nebraska Supreme Court reversed the decision, holding that the visible force requirement was valid as a means of preventing coverage for "inside jobs." Here there were no visible marks indicating forcible entry. *Lumbard v. Western Fire Ins. Co.*, 381 N.W.2d 117 (Neb.1986).

A Louisiana employee arrived at work and discovered a door of his employer's office building was open. He also noticed that a fence had been cut open. There was no sign of forced entry into the building. It was later discovered that items valued in excess of $5,000 were stolen. The employer's insurer denied coverage under a burglary policy on the ground that the policy expressly provided that signs of forced entry into a building must be present as a condition to recovery. The employer then sued the insurer in a Louisiana trial court which held in favor of the insurer. He appealed to the Louisiana Court of Appeal, which held that limiting liability for burglary to situations where there was proof of forced entry was not against public policy. Further, the fence surrounding the office building was not part of the "premises" within the meaning of the insurance policy. Since there was no sign of forced entry into the office building itself, the court found no basis upon which the employer could recover his loss. *Delta Decks v. United States Fire Ins. Co.*, 463 So.2d 653 (La.App.4th Cir.1985).

A Massachusetts jewelry store owner brought an action to recover insurance proceeds for losses suffered by the store in a burglary. The insurer claimed that the burglary was staged by the owner and refused to settle the claim. At the trial, considerable evidence was presented which lent credence to this theory. In fact, the burglary occurred before a big sale, in anticipation of which the owner had greatly increased the store's insurance coverage. The jury returned a verdict for the insurer on the contract claim but dismissed both parties' claims for damages pursuant to the state's consumer protection statute. Both parties appealed.

The Massachusetts Appellate Court affirmed the jury's verdict as to the contract issue and went on to discuss the trial court's dismissal of the insurer's consumer protection claim. The insurer argued that dismissal of its claim was erroneous and that it should be reimbursed for the investigation and for legal expenses incurred because of the allegedly staged burglary. Agreeing that the insurer was not precluded from pursuing consumer protection remedies for unfair and deceptive practices, the appeals court remanded the issue to the trial court for further proceedings. *Sidney Binder v. Jewelers Mutual Ins., Inc.*, 552 N.E.2d 568 (Mass.App.Ct.1990).

C. Exclusions

A North Carolina bank purchased a bankers blanket bond indemnifying it for property losses resulting from theft, false pretenses and larceny committed by persons present on the bank's premises. A stockbroker swindled the bank for $2.765 million by arranging a fraudulent purchase of nonexistent securities. The broker arranged the swindle over the telephone from his offices in New York. The bank unsuccessfully attempted to obtain coverage from its insurer and sued it in a federal district court. It argued that money deposited in its bank was constructively on the premises. The court disagreed, ruling in favor of the insurer and its decision was affirmed by the U.S. Court of Appeals, Fourth Circuit. The policy specifically limited coverage to losses from fraud by persons located on the bank's premises. *Southern Nat'l Bank of North Carolina v. United Pacific Ins.*, 864 F.2d 329 (4th Cir.1989).

A New York bank made loans for over $3 million and accepted bills of lading as security. When the loans were in default, the bank presented the bills of lading at which time they were determined to be invalid, because they were signed in illegible script by an unknown person and described shipments for coffee which had never taken place. At all times the bank was covered by a bankers blanket bond that covered forgeries. The insurer denied coverage and the insured brought this action in a federal district court. The district court granted summary judgment to the insurer and the insured appealed to the U.S. Court of Appeals, Second Circuit. The appellate court stated that the bills of lading were not forgeries within the meaning of the bankers blanket bond because forgery is defined as "signing the name of another with the intent to deceive." Since the bank offered no proof that the signer of the document wrote someone else's name, the appellate court affirmed the decision of the trial court. *French American Banking v. Flota Mercante Grancolombia NA, S.A.*, 925 F.2d 603 (2d Cir.1991).

A Pennsylvania sweater manufacturer began to suspect that an employee was stealing its goods. Empty sweater boxes were found in an abandoned stairwell, wire

Sec. V   BURGLARY AND THEFT INSURANCE   329

which sectioned off an area in which finished sweaters were stored was found to have been cut, and significant quantities of sweaters and yarn were missing. After an investigation, the sweater manufacturer found that one of its employees had been stealing sweaters and yarn having a value of more than $200,000. The sweater manufacturer sought reimbursement for the loss from its "all risks" insurer. The insurer refused, contending that a policy exclusion precluded coverage for loss caused by any dishonest act on the part of the insured or its employees. The sweater manufacturer then sued its insurer in a Pennsylvania trial court to obtain reimbursement. The trial court dismissed the claim and the manufacturer appealed to the Supreme Court of Pennsylvania.

On appeal, the manufacturer argued that the exclusion language was ambiguous and did not clearly preclude coverage for losses sustained by employee theft. The superior court, however, affirmed the trial court's decision, holding that the policy exclusion clearly provided in unambiguous terms that there was no coverage for losses caused by employee theft. The court also rejected the manufacturer's argument that the exclusion only excluded coverage for losses occurring to property specifically entrusted to an employee. It concluded that the exclusion was clearly intended to apply to all employee thefts. The court held that the insurer had no duty to reimburse the manufacturer for the stolen yarn and sweaters. *Wexler Knitting Mills v. Atlantic Mut. Ins.*, 555 A.2d 903 (Pa.Super.1989).

A manufacturer was covered by a comprehensive crime insurance policy which specifically excluded coverage for loss of potential income. The manufacturer had a complete monopoly on the sale of a sealant used in nuclear power facilities because it was the sole possessor of the sealant's formula. One of the manufacturer's employees leaked the formula (a trade secret) to another company, which used the formula to make a sealant which it sold to one of the manufacturer's customers. The company which received the formula made $139,298 in gross revenues from the sale of sealant. The manufacturer claimed a loss from its crime insurer in the amount of the other company's gross revenue made from the sealant. The insurer refused to pay on the ground that the loss was a loss of potential income. When the manufacturer sought a ruling in U.S. district court saying that it was entitled to payment, the court instead ruled for the insurer. The manufacturer appealed.

The U.S. Court of Appeals, Seventh Circuit, noted that the manufacturer had not been deprived of the formula, but only of profits it would have made if not for the other company's use of the formula. It was as if the employee had stolen a machine from the manufacturer, and then the machine had been returned in perfect condition at a later date, said the court. In that case no covered loss would have occurred even though the manufacturer would have lost potential profits from the machine's use. Because the leak of the formula was not an actual loss, it was not covered by the comprehensive crime insurance policy. The district court's ruling in favor of the insurer was affirmed. *U.S. Gypsum Co. v. Ins. Co. of North America*, 813 F.2d 856 (7th Cir.1987).

V. FIRE INSURANCE

The cases in this section involve both home and business fire insurance policies.

A. Arson Investigations

After a Texas couple's home was destroyed by fire, the fire insurer concluded that the fire was set intentionally and thus refused to make any payment on the policy. The couple then brought suit in a federal court to recover under the policy. At trial, the insurer introduced evidence showing that the couple's house was unoccupied for several weeks prior to the fire but that a neighbor had seen a light in the home a few hours before the fire. The insurer also introduced a witness who saw a pickup truck leaving the road accessing the residence right before the fire started. Only the couple had a key to the house and they also owned a pickup truck. The insurer also showed that the couple was in financial trouble. The trial court entered judgment for the insurer finding that the fire was intentionally set. The insureds appealed to the U.S. Court of Appeals, Fifth Circuit.

The couple contended that the district court erred by not granting their motion for judgment notwithstanding the verdict. The couple contended that because the insurer introduced only evidence pertaining to motive and no evidence that would show that the couple intentionally burned the home, the district court erred as a matter of law in submitting the case to the jury. The court noted that under Texas law there is a presumption against arson by an insured; however, an insurer is entitled to overcome this presumption by circumstantial evidence. The court noted that although there was no direct evidence indicating that the couple had set the fire, there was ample evidence that they had a financial motivation to commit arson. Therefore, taking all the facts and inferences in the light most favorable to the jury verdict the evidence was sufficient to uphold that verdict. *First State Bank of Denton v. Maryland Cas. Co.*, 918 F.2d 38 (5th Cir.1990).

An Iowa insured's beauty college building and its contents were severely damaged by fire. The fire was found to be caused by arson. The insured made a claim for benefits under the policy but the insurer denied the claim. The insurer then instituted this action in a federal district court alleging that the insured caused the fire and asking that the policy be declared null and void. At trial the insurer produced evidence of financial hardship on the part of the insured. Also, the insured had no alibi. The jury returned a verdict for the insurer and the insured applied for a judgment notwithstanding the verdict. The court noted that a judgment notwithstanding the verdict may be granted only when there is no reasonable inference to sustain the jury's verdict. The court determined that it was undisputed that the fire was caused by arson and that the insured had a motive. There was, however, no other circumstantial evidence to point to the insured. There are currently two rules governing this issue: 1) the jury may be permitted to determine the guilt of the insured and 2) the jury will not be allowed to determine the guilt of the insured in the absence of any surrounding circumstantial evidence. Since the Iowa Supreme Court had not ruled on this issue the court drew an inference as to what that court would probably rule. The court noted that in a 1935 Iowa Supreme Court case where the insured was over-insured and the fire was caused by arson, the court determined that this was not sufficient evidence to prove the guilt of the insured. Similarly, the court here determined that the fact of arson and a motive was not enough to determine the guilt of the insured. The court, therefore, granted judgment for the insured. *St. Paul Fire and Marine Ins. Co. v. Salvador Beauty College*, 731 F.Supp. 348 (S.D.Iowa 1990).

A Minnesota restaurant was destroyed by a gas explosion. An investigation resulted in charging a restaurant employee with arson. The insured submitted a proof of loss to his insurer. It then demanded that the insured submit to an examination under oath. Because his attorney was unavailable on the requested date, he informed the insurer that he would not be available that day. The examination was not rescheduled and the owner sued the insurer in a Minnesota trial court, seeking coverage. The trial court granted the insurer's dismissal motion and the owner appealed to the court of appeals which affirmed the dismissal. The owner then appealed to the Minnesota Supreme Court. The supreme court reversed the lower court decisions. It noted that in similar cases in other states, courts have held that initiating the suit prior to examination did not constitute a forfeiture of benefits. A single examination postponement due to the unavailability of one's attorney did not constitute noncooperation. Therefore, the case was remanded to the trial court for a new trial. *McCollough v. Travelers Cos.*, 424 N.W.2d 542 (Minn.1988).

In May 1983, a small shopping center in Georgia was substantially damaged by fire. The owner of the shopping center filed a claim with his insurer. The insurer denied his claim after finding evidence suggesting that the owner had set the fire. The insurer sought a declaratory judgment that it had no duty to indemnify the owner. The owner filed a counterclaim alleging bad faith. At trial the insurer presented evidence that the owner had set the fire and evidence defending against the owner's as yet unpresented bad faith claim. The district court found for the insurer, and the owner appealed. The U.S. Court of Appeals, Eleventh Circuit, faced the issue of whether evidence of the owner's prior criminal charges and his currently pending burglary charge should have been admitted. It noted that the owner and his attorney originally introduced the pending burglary charge as evidence that he was upset and distracted by the burglary charge when he made misstatements in his depositions. The court ruled that having introduced the burglary charge evidence in the first place, the owner could not seek reversal based on that evidence's admissibility. The court found that evidence of the prior pimping, pandering and drug charges against the owner had no bearing on his motive, opportunity, or other factors relating to the charge that he committed arson. It held that "[b]ecause of the nature of the charges and their lack of relevance to the facts at issue in the case, it was error to admit the testimony about them." The judgment of the district court was vacated and the case was remanded for a new trial. *Aetna Cas. & Sur. Co. v. Gosdin*, 803 F.2d 1153 (11th Cir.1986).

The U.S. Supreme Court has held that arson investigators are required to obtain search warrants before conducting inspections of burned premises. The only exception to this requirement is where circumstances exist that will not "tolerate the delay necessary to obtain a warrant or to secure the owner's consent to inspect the fire-damaged premises." Such circumstances might be an immediate threat that the blaze will rekindle or where an investigation is necessary to preserve evidence from intentional or accidental destruction.

This case arose after a couple's home was damaged by a fire while they were out of town. Firefighters extinguished the blaze and five hours later a team of arson investigators arrived at the home to investigate the cause of the blaze. When they arrived, they encountered a crew which had received instructions from the owners, through their insurance agent, to secure the house. Nevertheless, the investigators entered the residence and conducted an extensive search without obtaining a search warrant. In the basement they found two fuel cans and a crock pot attached to an electrical timer. The investigators concluded that the fire had been deliberately set. The couple was subsequently charged with arson.

At trial, the couple moved to suppress all the evidence seized in the warrantless search. A Michigan trial court held that circumstances existed to justify the warrantless search, a decision which the Michigan Court of Appeals reversed. The U.S. Supreme Court agreed and stated that the couple retained a "reasonable expectation of privacy" in their home. All of the evidence was properly suppressed except for two fuel cans which had been removed from the home by the firefighters and placed in plain view of the arson investigators in the owners' driveway. *Michigan v. Clifford*, 464 U.S. 287, 104 S.Ct. 641, 78 L.Ed.2d 477 (1984).

B. Coverage Disputes Involving Arson

In most states insurers must prove by a "preponderance of the evidence" that an insured committed arson in order for the insurer to avoid liability. Stated another way, it must appear more likely than not that arson occurred. Additionally, arson committed by a spouse or other family member usually will not preclude recovery by other named insureds.

1. Arson Allegations—Generally

Three New York residents purchased a motel for investment purposes. The motel consisted of two main buildings, six cottages and a couple of smaller buildings. The investors purchased fire insurance policies for $50,000 on each of the two main buildings. Over the next three years, the motel lost money. Also, the department of health inspected the motel and determined that it was unsatisfactory. Eventually, the investors raised the coverage on the two main buildings to $80,000 each. A fire subsequently broke out in the two main buildings, which were heavily damaged. Evidence showed that the two fires had been separate and distinct, and a gasoline can had been found in the debris of each building. The investors submitted a claim, which their insurer denied. Their insurer then sued in a New York trial court seeking a declaration that it was not liable to pay under the policy. The jury determined that the investors had been guilty of misrepresenting their losses and of increasing the hazard of loss by fire, and ruled for the insurer. The insureds then appealed to the Supreme Court, Appellate Division.

On appeal, the investors argued that they had contracted for and completed renovation work prior to the fire and that they therefore had no motive to set or increase the risk of a fire. The appellate court rejected their argument, noting that they had also increased their insurance coverage. The court recognized that evidence of an insured's desperate financial condition is a motive for arson and the motel had been a losing proposition from the start. The court found the evidence sufficient to establish motive, material misrepresentations and an increase in risk of loss by fire. The court affirmed the jury's verdict, and disallowed coverage. *Home Ins. Co. of Indiana v. Karantonis*, 550 N.Y.S.2d 77 (A.D.3d Dep't 1989).

A Montana family's residence was destroyed by fire and allegedly burglarized one evening. The insureds sought coverage under their fire insurance policy, but believing the insureds deliberately set the fire, the insurer refused to pay. Additionally, the insurer alleged that the insureds misrepresented certain facts when applying for the policy. The trial court heard extensive evidence on cash flow problems the family was having and it also heard testimony from the insurance agent who issued the policy to the insureds. On the latter issue, the agent testified that the insureds had represented to him that they had incurred no previous fire losses, when in fact the insureds had had two prior fire losses within the last ten years. The insurer claimed it would never have issued the policy if it had known of the prior losses. The trial court held for the insurer and relieved the insurer from its obligation to pay under the policy. The decision was appealed to the Supreme Court of Montana which stated that the policy issued specifically excluded coverage to insureds who deliberately set fire to their property with intent to destroy it. Because sufficient evidence was presented to establish this, the trial court's ruling was upheld. *Emasco Ins. Co. v. Waymire*, 788 P.2d 1357 (Mont.1990).

An Alaska Dairy Queen was destroyed by an explosion and fire. Its insurer denied coverage under a fire insurance policy due to arson. The insurer then asked a superior court for a declaration that it had no duty to provide coverage. The declaration was granted and the owner of the Dairy Queen appealed to the Alaska Supreme Court. The question before the supreme court was whether the superior court correctly decided that the insurer had to meet a lesser standard of proof (preponderance of the evidence) than that argued for by the Dairy Queen's owner (clear and convincing evidence). The owner argued that the higher standard of proof should have been met by the insurer since it was applied by other states in fraud cases. The owner claimed that fraud cases were similar to arson cases. The supreme court upheld the superior court decision in favor of the insurer. Alaska had not recognized the higher standard of proof in fraud cases. Furthermore, public policy denied the owner the right to recover when he intentionally set fire to property covered by an insurance contract. This public policy would be hindered if proof by a higher standard was required. *Dairy Queen of Fairbanks v. Travelers Indem. Co. of America*, 748 P.2d 1169 (Alaska 1988).

An insured sought coverage for damage to his property under his fire insurance policy in a Mississippi trial court. The insurer moved for a decision in its favor based on some evidence that the insured may have set the fire. The trial court denied the request and the insurer appealed to the Mississippi Supreme Court. The supreme court noted that under state law, wilful arson on the part of an insured is a defense to an insurer's liability. The insurer was required to prove that the fire was intentionally set by the insured by clear and convincing evidence. To do this the insurer had to prove the insured had a motive and opportunity to destroy the property.

The supreme court, not presented with this issue previously, had to decide whether the insurer had to prove arson by a "preponderance of the evidence" or by the more stringent standard of "clear and convincing evidence." The supreme court noted that arson was similar to fraud. The nature of the insurer's defense was that the insured had attempted to defraud the insurer. State law required a party charging fraud to prove fraud by clear and convincing evidence. The supreme court upheld the trial court's decision. No reason had been suggested why fraud by arson should be established by the lower standard of proof. On remand to the trial court the insurer would have to prove arson on the part of the insured by "clear and convincing evidence." *McGory v. Allstate Ins. Co.*, 527 So.2d 632 (Miss.1988).

2. Joint Ownership

A man who was separated from his wife confessed to setting fire to their Mississippi home. The wife made a claim for the proceeds of a fire insurance policy. The insurer claimed that the wife was guilty of complicity, made false representations on her claims, and was not entitled to coverage even if innocent of complicity. The Mississippi Supreme Court then ruled in another case that an innocent wife may recover the benefits of a fire insurance policy if she was innocent of complicity in the fire. After settling her contractual claim, the wife sued the insurer in a federal district court for noncontractual claims which included punitive damages. The court entered judgment on all remaining disputes in favor of the insurer. The wife appealed the decision to the U.S. Court of Appeals, Fifth Circuit.

The important issue in this case was the claim for punitive damages. Under Mississippi law, punitive damages may be awarded when a plaintiff shows that an insurer has denied a claim without an arguable basis for doing so, and with gross malice or gross negligence toward the insured's rights. The court ruled that the woman failed to prove either element. The court found a reasonably arguable basis for denying the claim under three theories. First, the Mississippi Supreme Court had not decided, at the time of the denial, whether an innocent wife could recover the benefits of a policy when her husband had committed arson. Second, the insurer showed that it had a reasonable belief that the wife was guilty of complicity based on the wife's own statements and actions. Third, the insurer showed that the wife had made false and overvalued claims; this can lead to denial of coverage in some instances. The wife had also failed to prove malice or gross negligence. Judgment for the insurer on all claims was affirmed. *Dunn v. State Farm Fire and Casualty Co.*, 927 F.2d 869 (5th Cir.1991).

A Texas couple purchased a house and insured it against fire damage. In 1986, the couple separated. The husband remained in the home, and the wife left the state. In 1987, the house was destroyed by fire. The couple jointly filed a claim with their insurer; the husband then filed for divorce. The insurer denied the couple's claim, asserting that the husband had committed arson. After the divorce became final, the couple sued the insurer for breach of contract. The court granted summary judgment to the insurer, and the wife appealed to the U.S. Court of Appeals, Fifth Circuit. On appeal, she argued that she was entitled to half of the proceeds even if her ex-husband had committed arson because the wrongdoer would not be receiving any benefit as a result of the insurer's payment. The court, however, while acknowledging that the wife's share of the property was now separate because of the divorce, noted that the couple was still married at the time the insurer rejected the claim. Thus, if the insurer had paid the claim, the husband would have benefitted by virtue of the fact that all their property was community at that time. The insurer did not have to indemnify the innocent co-insured, and the district court's decision was affirmed. *Webster v. State Farm Fire & Casualty Co.*, 953 F.2d 222 (5th Cir.1992).

A couple in Iowa had a fire in their home. Later the husband was convicted of arson. The husband and wife brought suit in an Iowa trial court to recover under their homeowner's policy. The husband later dismissed himself from the lawsuit leaving his co-insured wife as the sole plaintiff. There was no evidence that the wife was implicated in the arson. The trial court certified the question of coverage to the Supreme Court of Iowa. The main question addressed in this lawsuit was whether an innocent co-insured could recover under the policy when it clearly excluded recovery on a loss caused by an intentional act of "an insured." This was the first time a court in Iowa had addressed this issue. Under a contract analysis, any ambiguous language in a policy is to be construed against the insurer. The word to be examined is the "an" before insured in the exclusionary clause. The supreme court ruled that this word was not ambiguous. It also noted precedent in other jurisdictions finding the word "an" to be unambiguous. It therefore reasoned that the innocent co-insured should have been able to read it without assuming coverage for herself in this situation. The court further suggested that insurers choose another word in the future and that a more clearly worded phrase would discourage fraud. The court found that a co-insured was not eligible to recover for the intentional act of an insured. *Vance v. Pekin Ins. Co.*, 457 N.W.2d 589 (Iowa 1990).

While a New Jersey couple's home was engulfed in a blaze, the husband was seen running from the house. The couple initiated a loss claim with their insurer. Because of the abrupt onset of the fire and its quick spread throughout the residence, arson was immediately suspected. The husband went to trial for arson but was acquitted. The husband and wife then instituted an action against the insurer, after the insurer agreed to pay the wife her property loss but would not pay damages to the husband. At trial, the jury determined that the actual cash value of the premises jointly owned was $46,000. It also determined that the husband committed arson, thus barring any claim by him. The insureds then appealed to the Superior Court of New Jersey, Law Division. The couple contended that they had a tenancy by the entirety and this allowed full recovery by the innocent spouse regardless of the fact that she resided with the guilty spouse. The court noted that New Jersey had adopted the rule that an innocent spouse may not be barred from recovery under a fire insurance policy claim when the other spouse had committed arson. However, the court determined that this rule of law should not be applied to an innocent spouse cohabiting with the guilty spouse. Thus, the court held that the fire loss claim of an innocent spouse may be no more than one half of the value of the property, when continuing to remain married and cohabit with the guilty spouse. *Jonax v. Allstate Ins. Co.*, 582 A.2d 1050 (N.J.Super.L.1990).

An insurer issued a fire insurance policy to a landlord who rented out the property to a couple. When a fire destroyed the kitchen and caused smoke damage to the rest of the house, the insurer paid over $38,000 to the landlord. It then brought a subrogation action against the tenants, asserting that they had negligently caused the fire. A trial court determined that the tenants were coinsureds under the policy, barring a subrogation action. On appeal to the Supreme Court of North Dakota the judgment was affirmed. Since there was no express agreement to the contrary, the tenants had to be considered coinsureds with the landlord. *Community Credit Union of New Rockford v. Homelvig*, 487 N.W.2d 602 (N.D.1992).

An Illinois couple entered into a contract for deed to purchase a house. They then purchased a fire insurance policy on the residence which covered loss to real property, personal property and living expenses. Less than a year later the house was severely damaged by a fire. After an investigation the insurer denied the claim, asserting that the wife had been responsible for the fire. The couple sued their insurer in an Illinois trial court which held that there was enough evidence to deny the wife's claim, but determined that the husband was an innocent insured and granted him coverage for half the loss. However, it then awarded a setoff of that entire amount to the insurer for the sum it had paid to the mortgagees. The couple appealed to the Appellate Court of Illinois. On appeal, the court first noted that since there was substantial evidence of arson, it had been proper to exclude the wife from coverage under the policy. It then noted that although the husband was entitled to half the amount of the loss as an innocent insured, the insurer could set off what it owed him against what it had paid out; however, the insurer could only deduct that portion of the award which represented the loss of real property. No setoff was allowable against the husband's personal property losses and living expenses. As modified, the appellate court affirmed the trial court's decision. *Fittje v. Calhoun County Mutual County Fire Ins. Co.*, 552 N.E.2d 353 (Ill.App.4th Dist.1990).

A West Virginia woman instituted a lawsuit to recover a portion of the fire insurance proceeds paid to her ex-husband after their former marital home burned down. She alleged that the insurer was obligated to pay her one half of the insurance proceeds because at the time of the fire she owned and retained a one-half interest in the property. Her ex-husband, however, was the sole insured on the policy, and so the insurer paid the full amount of the claim to him. The insurer argued that it should be discharged from all claims under the policy, having already paid the insured. The trial court granted summary judgment to the woman for half of the proceeds. The West Virginia Supreme Court reversed. Finding the statutory language to be unambiguous, the court held that the insurer was fully discharged from liability once the proceeds were paid. *Mazon v. Camden Fire Ins. Ass'n*, 389 S.E.2d 743 (W.Va.1990).

A Montana couple divorced. The husband was awarded their trailer house and the wife left many items of personal property there. Subsequently, her ex-husband intentionally set fire to the trailer house and committed suicide within it. The wife submitted a claim to her insurer for the value of her personal goods lost in the fire, which the insurer denied. The wife then successfully sued in a Montana trial court and the insurer appealed to the Supreme Court of Montana. The supreme court held that the policy clearly stated that a loss caused by an intentional act of an insured barred coverage. Here, the husband had been an insured and his act was clearly intentional. The court reversed the trial court's decision, and denied coverage. *Woodhouse v. Farmers Union Mut. Ins. Co.*, 785 P.2d 192 (Mont.1990).

In Pennsylvania, a fire damaged the home and possessions of a plant safety foreman and his family. Earlier that night, he had taken his wife and two children to his mother-in-law's home because of threats he claimed were made by disgruntled steelworkers angered by his enforcement of safety regulations. After returning home and falling asleep, he said he was awakened by two men who tied him up and set fire to the house. He testified that after the two men left, he was able to free himself and flee the burning building. When he and his wife sued to recover on their fire policy, the court found sufficient evidence to show that he had in fact set the fire himself, intending to use the insurance money to pay off gambling debts. His wife had no knowledge of these actions. The Pennsylvania Superior Court reasoned that it would follow the common law principle that one should not be permitted to profit from his or her own wrongdoing. On the other hand, the wife should not be denied recovery because of a "mere family relationship" with the arsonist. The court allowed the wife to recover one-half of the insurance proceeds but denied any recovery to her husband. *Maravich v. Aetna Life & Cas. Co.*, 504 A.2d 896 (Pa.Super.1986).

C. Insureds' Misconduct

A Louisiana insured sustained a loss when a fire occurred at his warehouse facility. The loss was investigated by the insurer which concluded that the fire damage totaled close to $100,000. The insurer paid $30,000 less than the estimated loss because of a dispute regarding inventory reports. The insured then filed a suit seeking an award for the difference between the amount of his loss and the amount paid. The insurance contract provided that the insured was required to report in writing each month the value of the estimated property. If the inventory was not properly reported and a loss occurred, the insured would be penalized. The purpose of the penalty provision was designed to make certain that the insured did not fail to properly report his end of the month inventory in an effort to reduce his premium. The trial court found that the insured filed a value report in January of 1982 and then in February telephoned an additional inventory report which related back to that value report. Essentially, the court found that the phone conversation acted as an amendment to the written report. It ruled for the insured. The insurer appealed to the Court of Appeal of Louisiana. The court of appeal had to determine whether the trial court erred in determining that the telephone conversation related back to the value report for the prior month. It stated that the trial court was not clearly in error to find that any report of additional inventory after the written report would have to relate back to the prior written report. The court affirmed the trial court's decision. *Ducote v. Audubon Ins. Co.*, 566 So.2d 1029 (La.App.3d Cir.1990).

A Michigan couple owned property for which they purchased fire insurance. Both the husband and wife were listed as insureds on the policy. Subsequently, the wife moved out of the home with the children, intending to file for divorce. The house then burned down, while the husband was the only resident. The wife then sued the insurer in a federal district court, seeking to recover benefits under the policy. The insurer defended by stating that the husband had set fire to the home in violation of an exclusionary clause in the policy. The policy excluded coverage if "any insured" intentionally concealed or misrepresented any material fact or circumstance, before or after the loss. It asserted that if either insured made a misrepresentation, then no recovery could be had by either insured under the policy.

The court disagreed, holding that the policy did not conform with the Michigan standard fire policy. The standard policy provided that coverage would be excluded if "the insured" willfully concealed or misrepresented any material fact or circumstance. Michigan courts had interpreted that policy to void only the fraudulent insured's claims, and to allow innocent insureds to recover. Even though the insurer's exclusionary clause was clear and unambiguous, the court determined that it must be reformed to comply with the Michigan standard fire policy. Since only policies which conform with the standard fire policy may be issued, and since the policies had been interpreted to protect an innocent insured, the court read the insurer's policy as protecting the innocent insured. The court held for the insured. *Ponder v. Allstate Ins. Co.*, 729 F.Supp. 60 (E.D.Mich.1990).

An insured filed a claim for fire damage to his home. During the investigation of the fire, the insurer found 32 containers filled with gasoline at the opposite end of the premises from where the fire started and therefore did not think that the containers were involved in the fire. When the insured was questioned about the containers, he claimed he used them for his and his neighbor's snowmobiles. Subsequently, the insured made an unsworn statement to the insurer affirming this assertion. Later on, the insured stated under oath that his earlier statement was inaccurate. He confessed that he had brought the gasoline containers to his yard, intending to throw the gasoline on his neighbor's lawn in retaliation for several bad business deals. Consequently, the insurer denied the insured's claim on the grounds of concealment and material misrepresentation. The insurer brought a declaratory judgment action in federal district court, claiming that it had no liability for the fire loss. The insurer moved for summary judgment. The insured argued that summary judgment should be denied because he retracted his material misrepresentations at the subsequent interview. Regardless of whether the insured's earlier statements were made under oath, the court determined that his statements constituted material misrepresentations. Accordingly, the court held that the insured's false statements rendered the policy void and it granted the insurer summary judgment. *Pacific Indem. Co. v. Golden*, 791 F.Supp. 935 (D.Conn.1991).

An Alabama insured's leased property was destroyed by fire. The renter claimed he came home, put a pot with grease in it on the stove and turned it on low. When he returned to the kitchen, the smoke was so thick he fled the house. After the insured filed a claim, the insurance inspector took photographs of the kitchen stove which indicated that the stove was on high. The insurer paid the insured the value of the claim and then instituted this action in an Alabama trial court against the renter. The trial court determined that the fire was the result of the renter's negligence and entered judgment in the amount of the claim for the insurer. The renter appealed to the Supreme Court of Alabama.

To reverse the trial court's findings of negligence on the part of the renter, the supreme court would have to find the trial court's holding to be plainly erroneous; however, here there was sufficient evidence of negligence on the part of the renter. The supreme court thus determined that the conclusions that the trial court derived from the facts were not clearly erroneous and it affirmed the trial court's decision. *Paige v. State Farm Fire and Casualty Co.*, 562 So.2d 241 (Ala.1990).

The Massachusetts Supreme Judicial Court has held that an insurer cannot escape liability to a lending company when collateral for a loan was intentionally destroyed by its owner. The case involved a lending company which loaned money to an automobile owner. The automobile was identified as collateral for the loan. The automobile owner obtained a liability and physical damage policy in which the lender was named as the loss payee. It also contained a "standard mortgage clause" which provided that the lender's coverage could not be forfeited by the act of any other person. After the automobile owner destroyed the automobile by arson, the lending company sued the insurer to recover under the liability and physical damage policy. The insurer contended before the supreme judicial court that the policy defined "loss" as "direct and accidental loss" and, because the automobile owner intentionally burned the automobile, no covered loss occurred regardless of who presented the claim. In effect, it contended that the definition of loss should be applied despite the presence of the standard mortgage clause.

Sec. V   FIRE INSURANCE   339

The supreme judicial court rejected the insurer's argument for two reasons. First, such a broad reading of the policy would allow the insurer to escape its basic promise to hold the lending company harmless from the acts of the automobile owner. Second, if the argument that the lending company could only recover for accidental loss was correct, the inclusion of specific prohibitions on recovery elsewhere in the policy were meaningless. The supreme judicial court concluded therefore, that "loss" included losses caused by the automobile owner except where explicitly prohibited in the policy. The insurer was liable to the lending company. *Gibraltar Financial Corp. v. Lumbermens Mut. Cas. Co.*, 513 N.E.2d 681 (Mass.1987).

In a New York case, the Home Insurance Company issued a fire insurance policy which imposed certain duties of cooperation upon the insured. The policy provided that in case of loss, the insured "shall see that the following duties are performed ... as often as we reasonably require: (1) exhibit the damaged property; (2) provide us with records and documents we request and permit us to make copies; and (3) submit to examination under oath and subscribe the same." After a fire destroyed the insured's premises, Home's preliminary investigation disclosed that the fire had been incendiary in nature. The insured was then summoned for an examination under oath. However, he refused to answer several material questions concerning his financial status and the condition of the premises at the time of the fire. He persisted in his refusal despite being warned by Home that noncooperation would result in a disclaimer of coverage. Two warning letters were also sent to the insured, but he continued to refuse to supply answers and, contrary to his assurances at the under-oath examination, he refused to supply an itemized list of expenditures relating to the destroyed premises.

Due to the insured's breach of his contractual duty to cooperate, Home disclaimed coverage, and the insured brought suit in state court. The court granted summary judgment in favor of Home (and dismissed the lawsuit), but ordered that if the insured would supply answers to Home's inquiries, then the judgment would be rescinded and the suit against Home could proceed. Home appealed to the New York Supreme Court, Appellate Division, and won a reversal. The appellate court ruled that the insured's complaint should have been dismissed and summary judgment granted unconditionally in favor of Home. The insured's continued failure to supply the requested information constituted a breach of the policy conditions and the lower court should have granted unconditional summary judgment in Home's favor. *Averbuch v. Home Ins. Co.*, 494 N.Y.S.2d 738 (A.D.2d Dept.1985).

A building owner in New York who wanted to convert his property from commercial to residential tenancy began a "freeze-out" campaign designed to force his commercial tenants out of his buildings. He instructed the superintendent of maintenance to turn the nighttime heat down to twenty-five degrees in the coldest winter months and to turn the heat off completely between the hours of 11:00 a.m. and 2:00 p.m. In addition, he installed a furnace designed to start up only when the outside temperature reached below freezing. After a fire started in one of the owner's three adjoining buildings, firemen attempted to extinguish the flames by attaching a fire hose to a device outside the buildings which was connected to the sprinkler system. This effort failed because water contained in the pipes of the sprinkler system was frozen. Consequently, the three buildings were nearly totally destroyed by the fire. The building owner sought coverage for his losses under his fire insurance policy. The insurer denied coverage on the ground that the owner violated the "false swearing" clause of the insurance policy covering the buildings. During the investigation of the fire, the building owner had stated that he kept the buildings heated at forty degrees during the night and that the superintendent of maintenance was exclusively responsible for maintaining the heating and sprinkler systems. The owner brought suit against his insurer. The U.S. Court of Appeals, Second Circuit, reversed a U.S. district court ruling in favor of the insured, saying that the false statements were relevant and germane to the insurer's investigation of the fire and that violation of the false swearing clause voided coverage. *Fine v. Bellefonte Underwriters Ins. Co.*, 725 F.2d 179 (2d Cir.1984).

D. Buildings Covered

A married couple owned a house in Texas. However, in November 1985, they decided to move to Utah for employment reasons; but they retained ownership of their Texas house. In April 1986, they returned to Texas and discovered that their house had been vandalized. They submitted a theft claim and were reimbursed by their insurer. They then returned to Utah. Six months later the couple's parents visited the Texas property and discovered that the house had been destroyed by fire. After the insurer investigated, it denied the fire claim because a policy exclusion clause stated that the insurer would not be liable if the house was vacant for more than 90 days. The policy also provided that a "building in the course of construction shall not be deemed to be vacant." The insureds sued the insurer, maintaining that the house was insured because it was under construction. A Texas district court held that the insurer had properly denied coverage. The insureds appealed to the Texas Court of Appeals. On appeal, the insureds first argued that the vacancy clause should not bar their claim since they had relatives occasionally visit their property to do yardwork and to keep up the premises. The appellate court disagreed because an insurance adjuster of 40 years found that the home contained no refrigerator, living room or bathroom furniture, and that unburned mattresses were left in the yard. The insureds further argued that the vacancy clause was suspended by the fact that they contacted a man to perform general repairs to their home. The couple contended that his work constituted construction upon their home. Therefore, even if their house was vacant, they were insured since the house was in the process of construction. The court, however, noted that the term "construction" means creation of a new structure, not mere repairs. Accordingly, the court affirmed the lower court's decision in favor of the insurer. *Jerry v. Kentucky Cent. Ins. Co.*, 836 S.W.2d 812, (Tex.App.1st Dist.1992).

A Georgia man purchased a mobile home owner's insurance policy. At that time, his mobile home was situated within fifty feet of a fire hydrant. Five years later, the man had the mobile home moved to a new location without notifying his insurer. Subsequently, the mobile home was destroyed by a fire. The man filed a claim with his insurer which was denied. The man sued unsuccessfully in a trial court and appealed to the Court of Appeals of Georgia. The appellate court found the policy to be ambiguous because it covered "the mobile home on the resident's premises," then defined "resident's premises" as the mobile home. The court ruled that a reasonable layman policyholder could easily believe that coverage was provided without reference to the mobile home's location. The court reversed the trial court's decision, and granted coverage. *Cantrell v. Nationwide Mutual Fire Ins. Co.*, 387 S.E.2d 42 (Ga.App.1989).

A manufacturing company insured its business property at four different locations with St. Paul Surplus Lines Insurance Co. The insurance covered the buildings and their contents for a single premium of $7,392. Attached to the policy was a "schedule of locations" which set forth the valuation of each building and its contents. The combined figure from all four locations was $528,000. When the building and its contents at the Marshall, Arkansas, location were destroyed by fire, the manufacturer recovered $220,000 under the policy. Although the schedule of locations valued the building and contents at $220,000, the manufacturer contended that it should recover the entire $528,000 that the policy covered at all its locations. It argued that since it made a single premium payment, it should be entitled to recover its actual loss at any location up to the total policy amount of $528,000. The Arkansas Court of Appeals ruled that the amount for which an insurance contract is issued may be apportioned to different items. The court was unable to detect any ambiguity in the contract. The court affirmed the decision of the circuit court and dismissed the case. *Bratton v. St. Paul Surplus Lines Ins. Co.*, 706 S.W.2d 189 (Ark.App.1986).

Two buildings in Louisiana were purchased simultaneously by an insured. Although the buildings were adjacent to one another, they had different addresses. When fire insurance was procured, the address of only one of the buildings was given to the insurance broker. The insured thought that by insuring one of the buildings he was also insuring the other. The insurance coverage was for $75,000 with a $1,000 deductible, more than enough to cover both buildings. The building not listed on the policy suffered fire damage of $13,466 and the adjacent building listed on the policy suffered $490 in damage as a result of the same fire. A U.S. district court held that since the insured provided the description of the property to be covered and since the insurer at no time contemplated coverage on the nonlisted building, there was no ambiguity in the insurance contract absent a finding of mutual mistake by the parties or mistake on one side and fraud on the other. *Halpern v. Lexington Ins. Co.*, 558 F.Supp. 1280 (E.D.La.1983).

After a Michigan insured's auto business was damaged by a fire, his insurer denied his insurance claim. The insured sued. A Michigan district court denied the insurer's motion for summary judgment. The Michigan Court of Appeals affirmed, and the insurer appealed to the Michigan Supreme Court. On appeal, the insured argued that the insurer violated the Civil Rights Act by denying his claim on the basis of national origin. The supreme court, however, held that the insurer did not violate the insured's civil rights because the insurer did not deny the insured's access to insurance coverage but rather denied his claim under an issued policy. The rights and obligations of the insured and insurer were of a private nature, removed from the reach of the Civil Rights Act. The court reversed the judgment on the civil rights claim and remanded the case. *Kassab v. Michigan Basic Property Ins.*, 491 N.W.2d 545 (Mich.1992).

E. Insurers' Right to Repair or Rebuild

A Georgia insured owned rental property which was damaged by fire. The insured hired a construction company to repair the damage. The insured authorized his fire insurer to pay the construction company directly for the repairs. The construction company was acting for the insured and not for the insurer or the adjuster. The insured signed a sworn proof of loss statement against the insurer for $19,869.88 as full compensation for the property damage. The insurer paid the construction company this amount; however it failed to obtain the insured's approval of the work. The insured then sued the insurer in a Georgia trial court alleging breach of policy. The trial court granted summary judgment for the insurer and the insured appealed to the Court of Appeals of Georgia. On appeal, the insured argued that the insurer had breached the policy by paying the contractor directly and by failing to obtain the insured's approval of the repair work before payment was made. The court of appeals disregarded this argument and affirmed the trial court's order. It held that the authorization executed by the insured did not impose an obligation on the insurer to supervise, certify or inspect the contractor's work. The court of appeals affirmed the trial court's decision and granted summary judgment for the insurer. *Antonone v. Atlantic Mut. Fire Ins. Co.*, 382 S.E.2d 126 (Ga.App.1989).

A Michigan insured's home was damaged by fire in January 1984. She filed a claim with her fire insurer who refused to honor the claim or have the property appraised. By city order the house was demolished in January 1986. One month later the insurer presented $30,000 to the insured for structure damage. After an appraisal in August 1986, the insurer notified the insured that it still owed her approximately $55,000. The insured claimed that the balance was over $63,000. The insurer unsuccessfully sought to enforce the appraisal award in a Michigan trial court. It then appealed to the Michigan Court of Appeals.

On appeal, the insurer argued that the trial court wrongly awarded the replacement cost ($63,000) of the insured's home because she failed to repair or rebuild the home. It pointed to a provision in the policy which stated that "we shall pay no more than the actual cash value of the damage until repair or replacement is completed." The court of appeals determined that the insured was entitled to the full replacement value even though she had not done what the policy required. It observed that the insurer impeded resolution by refusing to deal with the insured and by delaying appointment of an appraiser. Failure to make substantial payment to the insured for over two years showed a lack of good faith in processing the claim. Failure to pay the claim prevented the insured from complying with the obligation to repair or rebuild. *Pollock v. Fire Ins. Exchange*, 423 N.W.2d 234 (Mich.App.1988).

A Maine homeowner possessed a homeowner's policy with $50,000 coverage for total loss and replacement. Immediately after a fire destroyed his home he notified his insurance agent of the loss and a week later he met with a claims adjuster. The claims adjuster told the homeowner that under the terms of the policy the homeowner could receive an amount representing either the actual cash value of the house or the repair or replacement value up to $50,000. The adjuster added that in order to recover the repair or replacement value, the policy required the homeowner to completely replace or repair the house within 180 days. After the insurer paid the homeowner $24,000 ($16,000 of which was for the actual cash value of the home) it asked a superior court for a declaration that the homeowner was only entitled to that amount. The superior court held for the homeowner and the insurer appealed to the Maine Supreme Judicial Court. The supreme judicial court held for the homeowner, observing that he was entitled to the replacement cost of the home due to a blatant misrepresentation by the insurer's adjuster. The policy, contrary to what the adjuster told the homeowner, did not require the homeowner to replace or repair the home within 180 days in order to receive the replacement value. Although the insurer was aware of the misrepresentation made by its adjuster, it did not take any affirmative steps to correct the error. The adjuster's misrepresentation caused the homeowner to delay the construction of a new home because he couldn't be certain that such construction would be covered. Since it would be wrong to allow the insurer to avoid liability based on uncertainty it helped create, the homeowner was entitled to the replacement cost of his home. *Maine Mut. Fire Ins. Co. v. Watson,* 532 A.2d 686 (Me.1987).

A man's home was destroyed by fire. His homeowner's insurance provided replacement cost coverage for both real and personal property. However, the policy paid actual cash value unless the property had actually been replaced. The insurer litigated its liability and argued that the fire was intentionally set. A jury in a federal district court disagreed and found that the insurer was liable. The man then alleged that, because of the delay caused by the litigation, the condition in the policy requiring actual replacement should not be enforced. The measure of damages issue came before the U.S. Court of Appeals, which certified a question to the Supreme Court of Virginia: Is the measure of damages in this case the replacement cost of the dwelling and personal property lost in the fire, or is it the actual cash value thereof? The policy stated that "covered property losses will be *settled*" by paying only actual cash value unless replacement has occurred within a specified time period. The insured contended that because the insurer contested its liability instead of settling, it had waived its right to require replacement. The court disagreed; the term *settled* in this context was construed to include a determination of value whether by settlement, arbitration, or judgment. The insured's next contention was that the policy's terms were less favorable to an insured than were the terms of the standard policy which were mandated by law. The court held that the standard policy was inapplicable to the replacement cost provisions as they were not required by statute. Lastly, the insured argued that he was prevented from satisfying the policy's specified time limit for replacement as a result of the insurer's refusal to pay an initial amount representing the actual cash value. The contention that the insured was so obligated was not supported by policy language, and the argument failed. The insured was limited to recovering actual cash value. *Whitmer v. Graphic Arts Mutual Ins. Co.,* 410 S.E.2d 642 (Va.1991).

F. Mortgagees vs. Mortgagors

Disputes have arisen between mortgagees and mortgagors over who is entitled to the proceeds of a fire insurance policy. In resolving such disputes the courts will attempt to determine whose interests the procurement of the fire insurance policy was designed to safeguard.

An insured bank held a mortgage of $1.4 million on real property. When a fire damaged the property, appraisers determined the cash value of the loss to be $730,000. The mortgagor's insurer paid the bank that amount. The bank then sued its own insurer to recover for loss to its mortgage interest. It claimed that it was entitled to the amount by which the loan exceeded its recovery. The trial court granted summary judgment to the insurer, holding that the bank had recovered all that it was entitled to. The bank appealed to the Appeals Court of Massachusetts. On appeal, the bank argued that it was entitled to recover the replacement cost (rather than the actual cash value) of the property. However, since the mortgage interest was the amount of the debt, not exceeding the value of the property, the bank was not entitled to more than it had already received. Since the bank had already received the full amount of the loss, it could not use its own policy to recover for the nonappreciation of the property in the real estate market. The trial court's decision was affirmed. *Abington Savings Bank v. Rock*, 584 N.E.2d 640 (Mass.App.Ct.1992).

The New Jersey Superior Court, Chancery Division, decided a case involving a dispute between mortgagees and mortgagors as to payment of insurance proceeds from a fire policy on mortgaged property. The issue in the case was whether the mortgagors were entitled to the proceeds of the policy (which insured the interest of both the mortgagors and the mortgagees) to rebuild the property, or whether the proceeds should be applied in reduction of the mortgage where the value of the vacant land exceeded the balance due on the mortgage. The court held in favor of the mortgagors. It looked at the policy language itself, which gave an option to the insurer/mortgagor to repair, rebuild or replace destroyed or damaged property within a reasonable time. It said that this policy provision, coupled with a covenant in the mortgage to repair, established that the purpose of the policy was to protect the mortgagee's interest in the property in the event the security was impaired. This interest was in fact protected by the policy. The court noted that the mortgagees had suffered no damage as a result of the fire (which destroyed the premises) since the vacant land remained as full security for the mortgage debt. In addition, the mortgagors would be placed at a distinct disadvantage if the proceeds were paid directly to the mortgagees, given the currently prevailing high interest rates and the general scarcity of mortgage money. *Starkman v. Sigmond*, 446 A.2d 1249 (N.J.Super.Ch.Div.1982).

A Tennessee businessman of Greek heritage owned a restaurant and hired a fellow countryman to work in the place. Eventually, the employee became the manager of the restaurant and acquired a half-interest in it. He then purchased the business in its entirety (including the building and land) from the co-owner. A bank lent $100,000 to the buyer, secured by a first mortgage, and the seller agreed to carry a $90,000 second mortgage. The buyer procured fire insurance, naming the bank as first mortgagee and the seller as second mortgagee. The property then burned. The insurer paid its liability for loss to the real property, but refused to pay the seller for the loss of the personal property. The seller successfully sued the insurer in a Tennessee trial court, gaining recovery as a third party beneficiary under the policy, and the insurer appealed to the Court of Appeals of Tennessee.

On appeal, the court held that although both the buyer and seller had intended the seller's interest in both the real and personal property to be protected under the policy, such was not made clear to the insurer. Only the real property was protected under the policy with respect to the seller. However, if the buyer were entitled to recovery under the policy for the loss to the personal property, the seller might be able to recover on equitable principles. The court reversed the lower court's decision in favor of the seller and remanded the case to the trial court because there remained some question as to whether the buyer had committed arson. If so, no recovery would be available. *Zaharias v. Vassis*, 789 S.W.2d 906 (Tenn.App.1989).

G. Technical Problems with Policies

A Montana couple purchased a fire insurance policy on a house they owned. The value of coverage was agreed to be $66,000. Subsequently, the couple sold the house on a contract for deed in the amount of $50,000. The buyer also insured the house. Shortly thereafter, a fire destroyed the house. The buyer's insurer paid its limits to the sellers as loss payees, and the sellers then sought to collect from their own insurer. It remitted payment of $50,000, claiming that the couple's insurable interest could be no greater than the sale price. The sellers filed suit in a state trial court, seeking to recover the remaining balance under the policy ($16,000). The court granted their motion for summary judgment, and the insurer appealed. On appeal to the Supreme Court of Montana, the court noted that the sellers had an interest in the property which was insurable. Under the doctrine of equitable conversion, they had retained legal title to the property as security for the purchase price. The buyer, meanwhile, had a beneficial interest in the property. The court then looked at the insurer's *pro rata* clause (limiting the insurer's liability where the insureds carried other insurance on the property) and determined that it should not be enforced in this case because the buyer and the sellers both carried insurance covering different interests. The court affirmed the trial court's order against the insurer. *Musselman v. Mountain West Farm Bureau Mutual Ins. Co.*, 824 P.2d 271 (Mont.1992).

A New York insured suffered fire loss and sought coverage from his fire insurer. The insurer denied coverage stating that the policy was effectively cancelled two weeks prior to the fire loss. The insurer brought a motion to dismiss which the insured opposed by asserting that his name had been misspelled on the cancellation, thus making it ineffective. The motion was denied. The insurer appealed to the appellate division. The appellate court reversed and granted the motion to dismiss stating that even though the insured's name was misspelled on the cancellation it did not rebut the presumption that the insured had received valid notice of cancellation of the policy. *Abuhamra v. New York Mutual Underwriters*, 566 N.Y.S.2d 156 (A.D.4th Dep't 1991).

An insured couple suffered the loss of a garage and a storage shed due to fire. The couple notified their fire insurer and hired legal counsel which attempted to negotiate a settlement. Proof of loss problems developed, and the insureds rejected a settlement offer and threatened to sue. The insurer then denied the claim. Thirteen months later the insureds brought suit, but it was dismissed by a state court. The policy provided that an "action" must be brought within twelve months of the loss. The dismissal was appealed, and was heard by the Court of Appeals of Georgia.

The couple contended that the term "action" was ambiguous. The court stated that the term was to be read in conjunction with the clause entitled "suit against us," and that it was then unambiguous and enforceable. The insureds next argued that the insurer's act of negotiation effectively waived the insurer's right to insist on the twelve month limitation. The court noted, however, that insureds are required to show that they were made to believe that they would be paid without litigation or treated unfairly. The record held no evidence that either condition was satisfied. The limitation was not waived, and the dismissal was affirmed. *Giles v. Nationwide Mutual Fire Ins. Co.*, 405 S.E.2d 112 (Ga.App.1991).

VI. BUSINESS AND INDUSTRIAL INSURANCE

When interpreting business risk and industrial operations insurance policies, the courts apply traditional insurance law principles. However, because the insureds in such cases are not consumers but are instead businessmen and businesswomen, the courts are often less likely to find that such insureds are deserving of judicial protection. Awards of punitive damages are, for the same reasons, also less likely.

A. Business Risks

A Minnesota manufacturer obtained a comprehensive general liability insurance policy for its business which included business interruption coverage. A two inch overhead pipe carrying water for cooling and air conditioning then ruptured and water flooded the insured's place of business. The water damage forced the insured to shut down production for nine weeks. However, the insured was able to fill its orders with salvaged products and met all of its orders during the business interruption. The insured then sought to recover under the business interruption policy. The insurer denied coverage and the insured instituted an action in a Minnesota trial court. The trial court denied the insured's recovery for business interruption loss. The insured appealed to the Court of Appeals of Minnesota.

The court noted that the issue was whether the insured was entitled to recover under its business interruption policy when it suffered no loss of sales and also whether it was entitled to recover for the additional expenses to correct a rust problem resulting after the rupture of the water pipe. The court noted that the evidence presented at trial supported the fact that the insured incurred no loss from the business interruption. The court did, however, determine that the business interruption coverage extended to the additional rust prevention expenses as a result of an actual loss. The court of appeals affirmed in part and reversed in part. *Metalmasters of Minneapolis v. Liberty Mut. Ins.*, 461 N.W.2d 496 (Minn.App.1990).

The owners of a motel in Washington purchased an insurance policy which provided coverage for business interruption. On May 18, 1980, Mount Saint Helens erupted, dumping six inches of ash on the motel. Yet, it remained open. However, the cleanup and repair expenses totaled more than $7,000. Further, the physical attractiveness of the motel was damaged, resulting in fewer motel guests. The owners sought to recover both their costs of repair and business interruption losses. The insurer only paid the repair costs. The owners then filed suit in a state trial court which held in their favor, and the insurer appealed to the Court of Appeals of Washington. On appeal, the insurer contended that because the motel was not required to suspend operations following the volcanic eruption, the policy did not provide coverage. The court looked to the purpose of business interruption insurance and found that it was to indemnify for loss due to inability to continue to use the business premises. Here, the owners were able to continue with motel operations. None of the rooms were unavailable because of ash damage. Since the policy implied that loss had to force the insureds to cease business operations, and since they had not been forced to stop running the motel, the court reversed the lower court's holding and ruled for the insurer. *Keetch v. Mutual Of Enumclaw Ins. Co.*, 831 P.2d 784 (Wash.App.1992).

Sec. VI   BUSINESS AND INDUSTRIAL INSURANCE   347

A violent snowstorm in Virginia caused a great deal of snow to accumulate on the sides of eight greenhouses. The greenhouses' metal ribs sagged and caved in, but the plastic covering did not break, and the plants were not damaged. Long after the storm, the greenhouse operator decided to move some of the hanging plants from the damaged sides of the greenhouses to the undamaged sides. Because he relocated the plants, the plants began to receive less air and light. This overcrowding damaged the plants, and as a result the plants had to be sold for a lower price. The greenhouse operator sued his insurer for the loss in revenue. A federal magistrate found in favor of the operator, and the jury awarded him $165,000 in damages. The insurer appealed to a federal district court. On appeal, the insurer argued that the policy only covered direct loss caused by perils to the greenhouse. The insurer further argued that the plant damage did not result from the snow's weight or from any immediate force generated by the storm. Instead, the damage had stemmed from the greenhouse operator's decision to move the plants. Thus, it was overcrowding and not the storm itself which caused the loss. The district court agreed. It reversed and vacated the damage award, finding in favor of the insurer. *Florists' Mut. Ins. Co. v. Tatterson*, 802 F.Supp. 1426 (E.D.Va.1992).

A New York company purchased a comprehensive business policy listing the corporation as a named insured. While the corporation was closed for a two week summer vacation, its president worked on a personal project on the premises. A fire occurred during this period, and the insurer paid the corporation over $200,000 under the policy for fire damage. The insurer then sued the president in a state court, seeking reimbursement for its paid claim.

The president asked the court to dismiss the case, arguing that the law does not allow an insured to be sued by his own insurer for a loss which was covered under a policy. The president also asserted that the decision to let employees use the premises for personal projects was a business decision that protected him from liability. The court ruled that the policy covered only the corporation as a named insured. Even though the president was an officer of the corporation, the court held that it existed as a separate entity apart from him. The court denied the president's motion to dismiss, and allowed the insurer to sue him for its loss. *Fireman's Ins. Co. v. Wheeler*, 548 N.Y.S.2d 870 (Sup.Ct.1989).

In the three "jewelers block" insurance cases which follow, policy language is extremely important because this is an area which lends itself easily to fraud.

An insured jewelry company's president lost a bag of jewelry during a business trip. He stated that he did not know how or where the loss occurred. The "jewelers block" insurers denied coverage based on an exclusion for "unexplained loss, mysterious disappearance or loss or shortage disclosed on taking inventory." The New York Supreme Court granted summary judgment to the insurers, and the insured appealed to the Appellate Division. Although the Second Circuit Court of Appeals had held this exclusion to be ambiguous (excluding only losses discovered on taking inventory), the appellate court stated that it was not. Clearly, the loss was *unexplained* and fell within the boundaries of the exclusion. *Maurice Goldman & Sons v. Hanover Ins. Co.*, 578 N.Y.S.2d 551 (A.D.1st Dept.1992).

An insured New York gem trader went out to eat dinner. While dining, he placed a camera bag filled with diamonds valued at $267,514.30 on an adjacent empty chair.

As he left the restaurant, the insured unknowingly left the diamonds behind. While in transit he realized that he left the diamonds at the restaurant. He returned to the restaurant and discovered the diamonds were gone. After the insurer investigated, it refused to cover the lost diamonds. It contended that the insured had not complied with the policy's personal conveyance clause which required that the diamonds be in the "close personal custody and control" of the insured. The insured sued and a federal district court granted him summary judgment. The insurer appealed to the U.S. Court of Appeals, Second Circuit. On appeal, the appellate court focused on the distinction between "mislaid" and "lost" property. Only if the diamonds were considered "lost," would coverage be available under the "close personal custody and control" clause. The court determined that the insured's diamonds constituted mislaid property because the insured purposefully put his camera bag on an adjacent chair and then forgot to pick it up as he left the restaurant; the diamonds could only be classified as "lost" property if the insured had unintentionally put the diamonds on the chair and then left. Because the diamonds were mislaid property, the insured had not maintained "close personal custody and control" over them. Therefore, the court reversed the lower court's decision and held in favor of the insurer. *Saritenjdiam, Inc. v. Excess Ins. Co., Ltd.*, 971 F.2d 910 (2d Cir.1992).

A man had procured a jeweler's block policy and occasionally increased the policy limits in order to cover associates' jewels on consignment, then also naming the associates as loss payees. The jeweler later appeared in soiled pants and alleged that he had been robbed, and the associates eventually brought third party claims against the insurer. Through depositions and the use of full body photographs supplied by Interpol, it was established that the jeweler had operated with an alias and had in fact been imprisoned in Switzerland, Germany and Belgium for jewel theft. The insurer contended that this misrepresentation allowed it to cancel the policy *ab initio* — as if it had never been issued. A declaratory judgment action was brought by the insurer in a federal district court. The insurer contended that a jeweler's block policy is like a marine policy and that the doctrine of *Uberrimae Fidei* was applicable. This doctrine requires the highest degree of good faith in a contract, and requires an applicant for such insurance to voluntarily disclose all known circumstances which may have a bearing on the risk assumed. The insurer provided testimony that had the truth been known the policy would not have been issued. The issue then became whether the doctrine was applicable. Florida law defines marine insurance as: "insurance against any kind of loss or damages to precious stones, jewels, jewelry, gold, silver, and other precious metals, whether used in business or trade or otherwise and whether the same be in courts [sic] of transportation or otherwise." The court ruled that the doctrine was applicable to jeweler's block policies, and that the duty had been breached. The veracity of the theft would remain unknown due to the jeweler's fleeing of the country and escaping knowledge of his whereabouts, but the insurance policy was nonetheless void due to a failure to disclose pertinent facts. *Jackson v. Leads Diamond Corp.*, 767 F.Supp. 268 (S.D.Fla.1991).

A Washington company, insured by a business liability policy, sold leases of master audio recordings to a group of investors, representing that the recordings were of unreleased works by popular artists and that they could be used to produce marketable reel-to-reel tapes and cassettes. The representations turned out to be false. Title to the recordings was not clear, so it was unlikely that reproductions could be marketed. Also, the master tapes were of poor quality. The investors sued the company, among others, alleging violations of the Washington Securities Act and Consumer Protection Act, and misrepresentation. The business policy which the company had purchased provided coverage for bodily injury or property damage related to the business' operation, and for damages based on advertising offenses. The trial court granted summary judgment for the investors, and the insurer appealed to the Court of Appeals of Washington.

On appeal, the court noted that the investors' injuries were clearly not personal injuries or injuries to tangible property, so there could be no coverage under those provisions of the policy. It then noted that advertising offenses were essentially acts that involved unfair competition against competitors. Here, the complaints alleged only unfair and deceptive practices to consumers. Accordingly, the court reversed the trial court's decision and held that the insurer was not liable. *Boggs v. Whittaker, Lipp & Helea, Inc.*, 784 P.2d 1273 (Wash.App.1990).

An Israeli immigrant, who was an artist, purchased casualty insurance for his paintings. He stated in his application form that he had not had any prior insurance cancelled, and that his paintings would not regularly be left unattended day or night. In fact, his previous insurer had cancelled his policy two months prior for "excess concentration of values at one location." Further, the insured left his premises unattended during an eighteen day trip to California shortly after coverage was obtained. The insured then suffered loss and damage to some of his paintings. When he filed a claim with the insurer, it denied coverage due to his misrepresentations on the application. A trial court granted summary judgment to the insurer in the lawsuit which followed, but refused to grant summary judgment to the broker who sold the policy. The broker appealed to the New York Supreme Court, Appellate Division. On appeal, the broker asserted that since the policy application had been delivered to the insured as a blank form, and since the insured had completed the application by himself, the broker could not have issued any warranties or made any misrepresentations to the insured regarding coverage. The court agreed. Here, the insured had admitted that he had no contact with any of the broker's representatives when filling out the application. Thus, the answers which were deemed to be material misrepresentations could only have been provided by the insured, and the policy could be voided. The appellate court reversed that part of the trial court decision which denied summary judgment to the broker. *Shteiman v. Underwriters at Lloyds of London*, 579 N.Y.S.2d 402 (A.D.1st Dept.1992).

A Virginia realty company owned a warehouse located at the base of a hill. The warehouse consisted of a group of interconnected single-story warehouse units constructed of cinderblock and reinforced concrete. The realty company extended the rear wall above the roof line off the warehouse buildings. It poured fill material and concrete behind the rear cinderblock wall of the warehouses on the hillside. On top of it, it placed five house trailers. The realty company then discovered some cracks in the warehouse walls and city building officials inspected them and condemned the property. During this time the realty company had been covered by a special multiperil insurance policy. After it fixed the damage, the realty company sought coverage from its insurer. After the insurer denied coverage, the realty company filed suit in a Virginia trial court. A trial was held in which the realty company presented expert testimony that excessive earth pressure was the sole cause of structural damage. After the jury found in favor of the realty company the insurer appealed to the Supreme Court of Virginia.

The insurer contended that the loss due to the warehouses' structural failure was not a fortuitous loss and therefore not a peril insured under the policy. In addition, the insurer argued that the realty company's claim fell within several policy exclusions. The supreme court rejected these arguments, upholding the jury verdict in favor of the realty company. The court noted that multiperil policies only cover risks and afford no coverage for a loss that is known or inevitable. A fortuitous loss may include a loss resulting in part from the insured's negligence. Neither party knew that the retaining wall would fail to support the fill. Both parties had presented adequate evidence for the jury to determine that the structural damage was caused by earth pressure and therefore covered as a risk under the policy. The insurer was ordered to pay the realty company. *Fidelity & Guar. Ins. Co. v. Allied Realty Co.*, 384 S.E.2d 613 (Va.1989).

A pro-am golf tournament was sponsored at a golf course in Santa Fe. An automobile dealership agreed to provide a new vehicle to anyone who scored a hole-in-one on a certain hole. It obtained insurance in the event it would have to pay off. The application stated that the number of shots in the tournament would be 65. Because the course was a nine hole course and the tournament was 18 holes, the target hole was played twice, and a hole-in-one was scored on the second time through. The insurer refused to reimburse the car dealer, and a lawsuit ensued. The trial court granted summary judgment to the car dealer, and the insurer appealed to the Supreme Court of New Mexico. The supreme court affirmed the trial court's ruling because it determined that the parties had intended the word "shots" to mean the number of participating players and not the number of attempts to score a hole-in-one on the target hole. The ambiguity presented by the word "shots" enabled the court to construe the provision in favor of the insured. Here, the application should have informed the insured that on a nine-hole course, where eighteen holes were played, the number of shots is twice the number of players. This it did not do. The insurer was ordered to indemnify the car dealer. *Crawford Chevrolet v. National Hole-In-One Ass'n*, 828 P.2d 952 (N.M.1992).

A Nevada couple bought a thoroughbred horse. Because the horse was valued at $75,000, they decided to procure equine life insurance. The couple asked one of their employees to procure the insurance. Their employee contacted a customer service representative for the insurance company, who requested that a veterinarian's certificate verifying that the horse was in good health and a bill of sale be sent before the insurance could be procured. On July 1, 1989, the employee faxed these documents to the representative who then sent the documents via regular mail to the insurance agent. Two days later, the horse became quite ill. It died on July 4, 1989. When the couple contacted the insurer, it denied them coverage, maintaining that a policy had not yet been procured. The couple sued the insurer, and a trial court entered judgment in favor of the couple. The insurer appealed to the Supreme Court of Nevada. On appeal, the insurer claimed that the couple was not affected by its failure to produce insurance since the couple would not have been covered by the insurance even if the insurer had assented to coverage. Before the couple could be properly insured, they had to prove that the horse was free of any illness. Since the couple could not establish that the horse was in sound health on July 2, 1989, the insurer claimed it was not liable. The supreme court disagreed, noting that the couple complied with the representative's request for the veterinarian's certificate and bill of sale. Since the insurer considered the health condition satisfied when these documents were sent and since no one knew of the horse's illness at the inception of the policy, the supreme court affirmed the trial court's decision in favor of the couple. *Lucini-Parish Ins. v. Buck*, 836 P.2d 627 (Nev.1992).

A co-operative association in Washington which grew, stored and sold apples purchased an insurance policy to insure against damage to stored apples for the upcoming year. The association's storage area was a controlled atmosphere warehouse which was divided into large rooms where temperature, oxygen content, carbon dioxide content, and humidity could be controlled. Essentially, each storage area had its own artificial environment. During the insured year, the association discovered that some of its apples were damaged and it filed a claim with its insurer. The insurer determined that the loss was not compensable and refused to pay the claim. A lawsuit followed. Before the U.S. District Court for the Eastern District of Washington, the insurer contended that the loss was not "fortuitous." In other words, it was not dependent on chance. The court, however, determined that the association's choice of atmospheric conditions for the storage of apples was a calculated business decision based upon a foreseeable risk. The association had no reason to believe that the temperature at which it was storing apples would lead to damage. Accordingly, the damage had to be considered fortuitous. The court ruled in favor of the association and ordered the insurer to pay the claim. *Underwriters Subscribing to Lloyd's Ins. v. Magi*, 790 F.Supp. 1043 (E.D.Wash.1991).

The owners of an Illinois apple orchard purchased a policy of crop hail insurance. After a hail storm, they sought damages for the yield reduction to their apple crop. The adjuster sent by the insurer picked only apples that could be reached from the ground in his assessment of the loss. The insureds felt that he should also have obtained sample apples from the tops of trees where damage would likely be heavier. They obtained another appraisal from an independent adjuster, but the insurer refused to negotiate with them regarding the loss. The insureds sued for coverage, and also asserted that the insurer had acted in bad faith. A jury found for the insureds on both counts, and the insurer appealed to the Appellate Court of Illinois. The appellate court held that the evidence supported the jury's verdict. There was no showing that the finding had been erroneous, unsubstantiated or the result of prejudice. Further, the insurer's continued refusal to negotiate with the insureds could be considered vexatious and unreasonable under the circumstances. The court affirmed the jury's verdict in favor of the insureds, and held that they were entitled to attorney's fees, costs and prejudgment interest pursuant to the Illinois Insurance Code. *Boyd v. United Farm Mutual Reinsurance Co.*, 596 N.E.2d 1344 (Ill.App.5th Dist.1992).

A Wisconsin man and his wife formed a partnership which operated an eight-unit apartment building. They purchased a comprehensive general liability policy which covered business liability, loss to property, and bodily injury. The policy extended coverage to the man as the named insured, his spouse, employees of the business and the partnership. The man maintained his home, the apartment building and a shed located on a separate lot where he stored a tractor mower used to cut the lawn at all three properties. One day, the insured brought his four-year-old granddaughter along while he worked. The child wandered away and was struck when her grandfather backed up the trailer. Because she was severely and permanently injured, her parents sued the grandfather, his partnership and his homeowner's insurer. A Wisconsin court dismissed the complaint against the homeowner's insurer and determined that the partnership carrier should cover the loss. The partnership insurer appealed to the Wisconsin Court of Appeals, which reversed the trial court. The parents appealed to the Supreme Court of Wisconsin. The court determined that the circuit court had correctly found that the partnership insurer was required to provide coverage. The accident took place at the shed lot, which was used for both personal and partnership activities. The policy covered both the partnership and its partners as individuals. The policy also listed the grandfather's home address rather than the address of the apartment as the address of the named insured. The policy failed to limit liability to business-related liability, covering the partnership without restriction. The supreme court reversed the decision of the court of appeals. *Grotelueschen v. American Family Mutual*, 492 N.W.2d 131 (Wis.1992).

B. "All Risk" Policies

The owners of a mall in Colorado initiated a renovation of the facility. During the renovation, some ceilings were torn, scattering asbestos particles into various parts of the mall. The State Health Department then issued an order which effectively closed the mall and the businesses in it. The owners of a retail store, insured by a business policy, sought coverage for loss of property and income. The policy provided "property and income coverage against loss from all hazards of accidental direct physical loss subject to" other provisions contained in the policy. The policy also stated that contamination was a peril which was not insured. The owners brought suit to recover benefits under the policy. Summary judgment was granted to the insurer, and the owners appealed to the Colorado Court of Appeals. The appellate court determined that the insurer had clearly made the general coverage provision subject to certain named perils which were not insured. This specific contamination exclusion operated to limit coverage which would otherwise have to be provided because the asbestos was a substantial contributory cause of the loss. The court thus affirmed the grant of summary judgment to the insurer. *J & S Enterprises v. Continental Casualty Co.*, 825 P.2d 1020 (Colo.App.1991).

A Kansas automobile dealer's new-car inventory was severely damaged by hail. The dealer's floor-plan financier was covered under a commercial inland marine insurance policy. The policy covered all risks of direct physical loss or damage to the insured's automobiles except for loss or damage caused directly or indirectly by loss of market. The insurer paid the financier to cover the cost of repairing the damaged vehicles. The dealer sought additional sums claiming the vehicles were worth less after the damage and repairs than they were before the damage. The insurer refused to pay the additional amount and the dealer sued the insurer in a federal district court. The court granted the insurer's motion for summary judgment and the dealer then appealed to the U.S. Court of Appeals, Tenth Circuit.

The court of appeals held that the policy covered post-repair diminution in value of the dealer's damaged inventory. The coverage was not defeated by the loss of market exclusion. The court noted that there was a difference between the terms market and market value. A market is the geographical or economic extent of commercial demand for a particular product. Market value is the price that a product can command in a given market. A market is lost when a product is no longer demanded by its intended purchasers. In this case, however, the vehicles in the dealer's inventory had suffered depreciation due to physical alteration which was a loss of market value. The court of appeals reversed the district court's decision and remanded the case for further proceedings. *Boyd Motors, Inc. v. Employers Ins. of Wausau*, 880 F.2d 270 (10th Cir.1989).

A Texas energy corporation purchased an all-risk or builder's risk policy to insure against physical loss or damage to property in an oil refinery expansion project. One part of the project required the construction of a citrate scrubber which converts the gas into an acid. The citrate scrubber was put into operation but it was damaged as a result of faulty design and inadequate materials. The company had to shut down the refinery several times for repairs. It then sought compensation for the repairs and replacement parts from its builder's risk insurer. The insurer denied coverage and the corporation sued it in a Texas trial court. A jury determined that the insurer had a duty to indemnify the corporation and that it had breached its duty of good faith and fair dealing in denying coverage. The insurer appealed to the Texas Court of Appeals.

The court of appeals held that although the damage was directly caused by rust, the rust was caused by faulty design. Because faulty design was insured, this clause did not exclude coverage. A second clause excluded coverage for the cost of making good on faulty design except if the faulty design causes physical damage. Although the damage had been caused by faulty design, there had also been physical damage. The court of appeals held that the exclusion should be construed in favor of the insured. The loss caused by faulty design was not excluded. The court sustained the jury verdict against the insurer for bad faith, but reduced the damages awarded. The lower court's actual damage award of $10 million was unsupported because the company had not provided evidence of business interruption loss. The court of appeals remanded the case to determine damages. *National Fire Ins. v. Valero Energy Corp.*, 777 S.W.2d 501 (Tex.App.-Corpus Christi 1989).

Property owned by Colorado insureds was destroyed when a dam broke and water swept over it. They sought benefits under their "all-risk" business insurance policies. However, the policies excluded coverage for flood damage. The insureds filed a complaint for a determination of coverage under the policy. A district court held for the insurer. The insureds appealed the case to the Colorado Supreme Court, arguing that the term "flood" was not defined in the policy and was therefore ambiguous. The large-scale inundation of water upon the insureds' property was a "flood" within the word's common usage. The court affirmed the district court's decision holding that the dam breakage was a flood and therefore excluded under the policy. *Kane v. Royal Ins. Co. of America*, 768 P.2d 678 (Colo.1989).

A Pennsylvania employee used his employer's van to commute between home and work. The employer instructed the employee not to drink and drive or use the van for personal reasons. After attending a wedding reception where he consumed several drinks, the employee drove the van to his girlfriend's house. On the way there he struck and killed a pedestrian. The pedestrian's estate sued the employee who sought coverage from the employer's insurer. The insurer denied coverage because of the employee's violation of his employer's instructions. The employee sued the insurer in a Pennsylvania trial court which held that the insurer had to provide coverage. The insurer appealed to the Pennsylvania Superior Court.

The superior court held that the employee's deviation from his employer's express permission was sufficient to deny coverage. Although the employer authorized the employee to use the van to attend the reception, he had repeated the no drinking and driving instruction. Because the employee violated the vehicle use restriction, the insurer was not required to provide coverage to the employee. *Gen. Acc. Ins. Co. of America v. Margerum*, 544 A.2d 512 (Pa.Super.1988).

C. Occurrences

A North Dakota fireplace and chimney installation business purchased liability insurance from an insurer. During the time the company was covered, it negligently installed a fireplace in a home. As a result of this negligent installation, a fire occurred in the home two years after the policy had expired. The policy was an occurrence type liability policy which provided coverage if the event insured against took place within the policy period. Coverage was denied. The insured sued the insurer unsuccessfully in a North Dakota trial court and then appealed to the Supreme Court of North Dakota. The supreme court noted that the occurrence insured against happened more than two years after the policy had been cancelled. The court affirmed the trial court's decision. *Friendship Homes, Inc. v. American States Ins. Co.*, 450 N.W.2d 778 (N.D.1990).

A California company's ex-employee brought suit against the company for wrongful termination of employment, including claims for bodily injury arising from emotional distress caused by the termination. The company tendered defense in the suit to its general liability insurer, which refused to defend the insured. The insurer's refusal caused the company to be financially unable to defend the civil action against it, requiring it to settle the case and to stipulate a judgment. As part of the settlement, the company assigned its rights to sue the insurer for violating California Insurance Code § 790.03 to the ex-employee. The employee then brought suit claiming that the insurer's actions were wilful, malicious, oppressive, and fraudulent. A California trial court dismissed the case and the employee appealed to the Court of Appeal, Second District. On appeal, the employee argued that the insurer had a duty to defend because there was the potential of bodily injury liability. The employee also argued that the company and its agents had a reasonable expectation of defense in the case. The court of appeal disagreed and affirmed the dismissal. The court stated that bodily injury arising from termination of employment is not covered by a general liability policy, because termination of employment is not an occurrence within the policy. The court also stated that it was not reasonable for the insured to expect its insurance policy to cover the employer's liability for an employee's emotional distress arising from termination of employment. *Dyer v. Northbrook Property and Cas. Ins. Co.*, 259 Cal.Rptr. 298 (App.2d Dist.1989).

An Ohio savings and loan association suffered substantial losses because of dishonest and fraudulent acts of employees. The association filed a proof of loss with its fidelity insurer which paid the claims. The association also subrogated its right to recover against the employees to the insurer. The insurer then sued the individual directors and officers of the association in a federal district court, charging negligence in violation of their fiduciary duties and improper supervision of the dishonest employees. The directors' and officers' request for a summary judgment in their favor was granted. The insurer then appealed to the U.S. Court of Appeals, Sixth Circuit.

Noting that this was a case of first impression in the Sixth Circuit, the appellate court agreed with the district court decision. It said that a fidelity insurer cannot be subrogated to the rights of its insured unless the equities in favor of the fidelity insurer are greater than those of the person against whom subrogation is invoked. The balance of equities in this case would not permit the fidelity insurer to be subrogated to the insured's claim of negligence against its own officers and directors. The rationale for this decision was that the insurer accepts not only the risk that some third party may cause the casualty but also that its own insured may negligently cause the loss. The insurer, however, has consented to the latter risk in exchange for the premiums received for the insurance issued. Allowing the insurer to recover against the savings and loan directors and officers would allow the insurer to avoid a risk it assumed and bargained for in issuing the fidelity insurance and in accepting the premium. *Home Indem. Co. v. Shaffer*, 860 F.2d 186 (6th Cir.1988).

A hang glider manufacturer discontinued its general liability policy in 1975. The policy was issued by Hallmark Insurance Company. In 1978, a hang glider operator was killed while using one of the manufacturer's hang gliders. The hang glider had been manufactured while the manufacturer was covered by the Hallmark policy. The operator's estate filed a wrongful death action against the manufacturer who sought defense and indemnification from Hallmark. Hallmark refused coverage. Both the estate and the manufacturer filed a bad faith claim against Hallmark in a Los Angeles County Superior Court. Hallmark moved for dismissal stating that the policy only covered accidents which occurred during the policy period. The superior court denied the motion and ordered a trial on the merits of the claim. Hallmark appealed to the California Court of Appeal, Second District, Division 3.

The manufacturer argued that the policy was ambiguous and that a policy exclusion failed to expressly limit coverage to an occurrence during the policy period. Hallmark argued that previous California cases held that an "occurrence" was when the accident occurred, not when the act leading to the accident was committed. Hallmark then pointed to the policy language which stated that bodily injury for which there was coverage meant " ... sickness or disease sustained by any person which occurs during the policy period, including death...." The court held for Hallmark stating that the manufacturer's position was out of line with the prevailing rule in California and other jurisdictions. It also determined that because the policy language was not ambiguous, the manufacturer could not have reasonably expected coverage. Therefore, the court held that the insurance policy did not cover accidents occurring outside the policy period. The case was dismissed. *Hallmark Ins. Co. v. Superior Court*, 247 Cal.Rptr. 638 (App.2d Dist.1988).

D. Exclusions

1. Exclusions Generally

A Massachusetts insured owned a parking ramp that was insured against damage but had a corrosion exclusion. Over the years, the salt from the roads would enter on the tires of vehicles and eventually chloride ions leaked through the concrete and attacked the steel reinforcing bars causing structural damage. The insurer denied coverage and the insured brought this action in a Massachusetts trial court which granted summary judgment to the insurer. The insured appealed to the Appeals Court of Massachusetts. The insured contended that the corrosion exclusion was only for wearing away by natural means of weather. The court, however, disagreed and stated that corrosion was due to some chemical reaction. Therefore, corrosion by chloride ion leakage would fall within the exclusion. *Bettigole v. American Employers Ins. Co.*, 567 N.E.2d 1259 (Mass.App.Ct.1991).

A New York insured sustained water damage to his property after a windstorm blew open a roof door. Subzero air entered the building, causing a pipe to freeze and burst, resulting in water damage. The policy insured against direct loss by windstorm or hail but it had an exclusion for water damage due to a ruptured pipe. The insurer refused to pay the claim and the insured brought an action in a New York trial court. The court granted summary judgment for the insurer and the insured appealed to the Supreme Court, Appellate Division. The appellate court reversed, stating that the term direct loss was equivalent to proximate cause and the court found that the damage was proximately caused by the windstorm. *E.A. Granchelli v. Travelers Ins. Co.*, 561 N.Y.S.2d 945 (A.D.4th Dep't 1990).

A Minnesota corporation, engaged in the business of packaging and distributing soil additive products, purchased a comprehensive general liability insurance policy which provided advertising injury liability coverage. Subsequently, the company was sued for allegedly mislabeling its composted cow and sheep manure products. The corporation entered into a settlement agreement and assigned it rights and claims under its policy. In the lawsuit which followed, a federal district court ruled for the insurer and appeal was taken to the U.S. Court of Appeals, Eighth Circuit.

On appeal, the insurer contended that no coverage existed under its policy because the corporation's actions were excluded. It argued that the exclusion covered both the incorrect description of goods and mistakes in the advertised prices. The court of appeals agreed. It noted that the clause which excepted injury arising out of "incorrect description or mistake in advertised price" clearly defined the exclusions. It thus affirmed the district court's decision. *New Hampshire Ins. Co. v. Power-O-Peat, Inc.*, 907 F.2d 58 (8th Cir.1990).

A carrier contracted with a corporation to transport fresh pork products from Iowa to New York by October 15. The truck driver picked up the pork on October 13 and called to check in with his supervisor on October 14. By October 16, the corporation notified the carrier that the pork had not arrived. Subsequently, the highway patrol found the pork in the truck, which had been abandoned. The refrigeration unit had stopped because it had run out of fuel. As a result, most of the pork was not salvageable. The carrier sought a declaratory judgment that its cargo insurer was liable. A district court held for the insurer, and the carrier appealed to the Iowa Court of Appeals. On appeal, the carrier argued that it was entitled to coverage since the pork spoilage was caused by a mechanical failure or breakdown of the refrigeration unit. The court, however, held that the evidence established that the truck driver had abandoned the pork products at the truck stop and neglected to make arrangements for the continued refrigeration of the pork. This was not a mechanical failure or breakdown but a negligent act by the driver. Thus, the driver's negligence precluded coverage for the carrier, and the court affirmed the district court's judgment. *Thorco Leasing v. Lumbermens Mut.*, 489 N.W.2d 31 (Iowa App.1992).

Sec. VI   BUSINESS AND INDUSTRIAL INSURANCE   357

The operator of a retail store in Florida was insured under a policy which excluded loss caused or contributed to by water backing up from a sewer or drain. A blockage in a main drain pipe that serviced the entire mall (before the point where sewage entered the city's sewage system) caused flooding in the insured's store. In the dispute regarding coverage, a trial court held for the insured, finding that the blockage occurred in a plumbing system before the water reached a sewer or drain. The District Court of Appeal reversed because sewers and drains are devices which carry water and sewage away from property, and here, even though the blockage wasn't in the city's system, it was still in a sewer or drain. *Old Dominion Ins. Co. v. Elysee, Inc.*, 601 So.2d 1243 (Fla.App.1st Dist.1992).

An Oregon sawmill hired an insured contractor to install a fire sprinkling system. The contractor hired subcontractors to install a water reservoir tank. A landslide totally destroyed the tank and other parts of the project. The sawmill sued the contractor and two subcontractors for negligence and breach of contract for causing the landslide. The contractor tendered defense of the lawsuit to its insurer under its comprehensive general liability policy. The policy insured general contractors against risks occurring after completion of construction projects. The insurer accepted defense with a full reservation of its rights to deny coverage. It then contended that the policy did not cover losses which arose from subcontractor work. The contractor sued the insurer in a federal district court, which granted the insurer's motion for summary judgment. The insured appealed to the U.S. Court of Appeals, Ninth Circuit. The appeals court considered the policy's completed operations hazard exclusion. In this case, the policy covered all damages arising from bodily injury and property damage caused by an occurrence. "Completed operations hazard" implied only bodily injury and property damage arising out of operations after completion of operations by the named insured. The exclusion at issue extended only to property damage and work performed by the named insured. The court concluded that the parties intended the exclusion to apply only to work performed by the named insured and not its subcontractors. The appeals court reversed the district court's decision and held for the insured. *Fireguard Sprinkler Systems v. Scottsdale Ins.*, 864 F.2d 648 (9th Cir.1988).

A contractor built a grain storage facility in Illinois. Insurance covered the construction of the storage tank, and upon its completion, a new policy excluded claims for property damage arising out of completed tank erection operations. Subsequently, the storage tank collapsed, and its owner sued the contractor, obtaining a judgment of $2.2 million. In the lawsuit concerning coverage, the trial court held for the insurer. The Appellate Court of Illinois affirmed, finding that the first policy had expired by its terms and the second policy clearly excluded coverage for such an event. *Seegers Grain Co. v. Kansas City Millwright Co.*, 595 N.E.2d 113 (Ill.App.1st Dist.1992).

A worn out cable snapped on a shiploader at a Louisiana bulk terminal. Extensive damage was done to the insured's loader. The insured filed claims with several of its insurers, but the insurers all refused to pay. The policies covered risk of direct physical loss or damage. The insurers contended that the accident fell within the "mechanical breakdown" exclusions in their policies. Under the exclusions, the insured was not covered for losses caused by mechanical breakdown unless an "insured peril ensued." The insured sued the insurers in a federal district court to recover damages. The district court ruled that the usual purpose of mechanical breakdown exclusions was to exclude routine and minor maintenance from coverage. Such an exclusion was not designed to insulate an insurance company from liability for "catastrophic" losses. The court ruled that the catastrophic consequences of the shiploader accident were covered. The insurers appealed to the U.S. Court of Appeals, Fifth Circuit. On appeal, the insured contended that the damage to the shiploader was a separate ensuing peril, which was an insured risk of physical loss. The insurers argued that the mechanical breakdown was the cause of the accident and since the shiploader itself sustained all of the damage, no insured peril ensued. The insurance policy did not state that catastrophic damage to a machine caused by its own mechanical breakdown could not be included within the term "ensuing peril." The court of appeals held that the policies covered all risks except those explicitly excluded from coverage. Thus the insurers were required to provide coverage to the insured for the damage. *Lake Charles Harbor & Term. D. v. Imperial Cas.*, 857 F.2d 286 (5th Cir.1988).

A Wisconsin insured owned and operated a bowling alley which was covered under an owners', landlords' and tenants' liability policy. The insured commenced a sexual relationship with a sixteen-year-old girl. The majority, if not all, of their contacts took place after business hours on the premises of the bowling alley in a back room. The girl was diagnosed as having genital herpes and she sued the insured and his insurer alleging intentional and/or negligent transmission of a sexually transmitted disease. A Wisconsin trial court granted summary judgment for the insurer finding that the girl's claim was not covered under the policy. The girl then appealed to the Court of Appeals of Wisconsin. The court of appeals noted that under the insured's policy, coverage existed for bodily injury caused by an occurrence arising out of the ownership, maintenance or use of the insured's premises. The court held that the liability policy did not provide coverage for the negligent or intentional transmission of a sexually transmitted disease. The sexual contacts between the insured and the girl took place after business hours and were not incidental to the ownership, maintenance or use of the premises. The court of appeals affirmed the trial court's decision. *Reznichek v. Grall*, 442 N.W.2d 545 (Wis.App.1989).

An Arizona housemover purchased a $500,000 liability insurance policy. The policy excluded coverage for bodily injury arising from the use of an automobile. An employee of the insured was killed when standing on top of a house being moved. While the house was in transit, it came in contact with a power line over the street and the employee was electrocuted. The building was towed by a tractor owned by the insured. The employee's surviving spouse sued the tractor driver and the insured for wrongful death in an Arizona trial court. The evidence at trial indicated negligent instruction and supervision of employees involved in the move, negligent operation of the vehicle, and negligent preparation of the building.

The trial court granted the insured's summary judgment motion for coverage. The insurer appealed to the Arizona Court of Appeal. The appeals court noted the evidence showing concurrent negligence in preparing and moving the building. The accident was the result of both nonauto and auto-related causes. Because concurrent negligence had been established the policy exclusion did not preclude coverage. Coverage could not be denied because a separate excluded risk contributed to the death. The court noted that the policy was issued to a business in which use of motor

Sec. VI   BUSINESS AND INDUSTRIAL INSURANCE   359

vehicles was understood. The court affirmed the trial court's decision in favor of the insured. *Scottsdale Ins. Co. v. Van Nguyen*, 763 P.2d 540 (Ariz.App.1988).

A Louisiana landlord leased a building to an insured to be used as a grocery store. During remodeling by the insured, part of the roof collapsed, resulting in damage to the building. The landlord paid for the initial repair work but refused to pay for the complete costs. The insured then withheld rent payments until the repair costs were recouped from the landlord. The landlord sued the insured for damages and back rent and the tenant's insurance company for the money paid for the initial repair work. The trial court held the tenant liable for damages and back rent and his insurer liable for the initial repair work. The insurer appealed to the Court of Appeal of Louisiana.

The issue on appeal was whether the business insurance policy covered damage to leased property. The insurance policy generally excluded coverage of leased premises but the policy also had a section which covered damages that arose out of an insured peril. Because the peril which caused the damage was not specifically excluded from coverage in the policy, the court of appeal determined that the loss resulted from an insured peril, and affirmed the trial court's decision. *Fanara v. Big Star of Many, Inc.*, 558 So.2d 316 (La.App.3d Cir.1990).

A Wisconsin sign business was insured under a comprehensive general liability policy. The insured removed a restaurant's existing outdoor sign and furnished a new neon sign. The sign did not function properly and the restaurant sued the insured and its insurer. The insured's policy excluded coverage for "property damage to the insured's products arising out of such products." The trial court dismissed the insurer from the lawsuit and the insured appealed to the Court of Appeals of Wisconsin. The court held that the policy excluded coverage for the restaurant's alleged loss of revenues. The loss of the sign's use was property damage to the insured's product. The insurer was properly dismissed from the case. *Trio's, Inc. v. Jones Sign Co., Inc.*, 444 N.W.2d 443 (Wis.App.1989).

A New York company stored 430 bags of black pepper in a warehouse. The company sold the pepper to a spice dealer. When the dealer sent a truck to claim the pepper, 298 bags could not be located. The dealer sued the warehouse's insurer to recover the loss under its liability policy. The policy contained a clause which excluded coverage of unexplained loss, mysterious disappearance and loss or shortages disclosed upon taking inventory. A New York federal district court held that the exclusionary clause was ambiguous and did not preclude coverage. This was a kind of loss that the warehouse had intended to insure against. The pepper could not be considered a loss of "inventory;" thus the insurer was required to provide coverage. *McCormick & Co. Inc. v. Empire Ins. Group*, 690 F.Supp. 1212 (S.D.N.Y.1989). The insurer appealed to the U.S. Court of Appeals, Second Circuit.

On appeal, the insurer claimed that the exclusionary clause was not ambiguous. The only reasonable interpretation was that the clause excluded from coverage any loss that was unexplained or mysterious, regardless of whether the loss was discovered upon taking inventory. The court of appeals held that the policy's exclusionary clause was ambiguous. Although the insurer's interpretation of the clause was reasonable, the clause could also be read to apply only to losses, disappearances, or shortages disclosed upon taking inventory. The court of appeals affirmed the district court's decision. *McCormick & Co. Inc. v. Empire Ins. Group*, 878 F.2d 27 (2d Cir.1989).

A communications company obtained an insurance policy which provided replacement cost coverage for its radio and television equipment and provided coverage against certain business income losses. The policy listed four premises that were covered by the policy: Jefferson City, Montana; Centertown, Montana; Des Moines, Iowa; and "various unscheduled locations." After obtaining this policy, the company decided to move its offices and equipment from Centertown, Montana, to a new location in Jefferson City. In order to transfer its large satellite dish to Jefferson City, the company used a helicopter with cables attached to the dish. As the helicopter was flying over a wheat field adjacent to the Jefferson City site (a covered premise) the bolts broke and the dish fell, damaged beyond repair. The insurer refused to pay the replacement cost of the dish, so the company brought an action against the insurer. A circuit court ruled in favor of the insurer, and the company appealed to the Missouri Court of Appeals.

On appeal, the company contended that its insurance policy was ambiguous as to whether the equipment was covered "while in transit," and therefore the ambiguity must be resolved in its favor. The appellate court disagreed. Because the policy did not address coverage of property in transit, the coverage hinged on finding an ambiguity in the locations listed in the policy. The equipment schedule clearly described four different "covered premises" in the policy. The one which applied to the dish was the "various unscheduled locations" since the wheat field was not within the boundary of any of the three listed cities. However, the maximum liability for such losses was $15,000, which the insurer had already paid. No further coverage was required. The company also argued that the insurer had to cover the costs of a small satellite dish as a "business income loss." The company bought the small dish after the helicopter crash so it would not have to suspend its communication operations. The court also rejected this claim since the small dish was never needed and never used by the company. Thus, the court ruled in favor of the insurer and affirmed the trial court's verdict. *Learfield Comm. v. Hartford Acc. & Indem.*, 837 S.W.2d 299 (Mo.App.W.D.1992).

2. Polluter's Exclusions

An insured under a general liability policy leased a private residence to a tenant whose children were apparently poisoned by lead in paint, putty or plaster. A lawsuit was brought against the insured. The insurer claimed that the lead in the house was a pollutant and thus triggered the pollution exclusion clause in the policy. The trial court ruled for the insured, and direct appellate review was granted by the Supreme Judicial Court of Massachusetts. The appellate court agreed with the trial court that coverage had to be provided. The exclusion did not clearly limit liability for leaded materials in a private residence. *Atlantic Mutual Ins. Co. v. McFadden*, 595 N.E.2d 762 (Mass.1992).

A limited partnership in Utah owned a self-service gasoline station which began recording huge gasoline shortfalls in November 1985. A company was hired to check the system for a gasoline leak. It discovered a broken pipe which connected the storage tanks to the dispensers and repaired the leak. Subsequently, the neighboring property was found to be contaminated and the government ordered the partnership to clean up the soil. The partnership sought to recover cleanup costs from its liability insurer, which began to pay under the policy but then claimed that coverage was unavailable. The partnership sued seeking coverage. The policy contained a pollution exclusion clause which defeated coverage for damages caused by the discharge of contaminants or pollutants, but the exclusion did not apply if the discharge was sudden and accidental. The trial court found the discharge to be sudden and accidental, and the insurer appealed to the Court of Appeals of Utah. On appeal, the court noted that the evidence had clearly shown that the break was a "clean break." In other words, it happened quickly and unexpectedly. The insurer's argument that the leak was not sudden because three months had gone by before it was discovered was also rejected by the court. Here, damage to the line caused an immediate spill which merely remained undiscovered for a few months. Thus, it was still a sudden spill. The court affirmed the lower court's ruling and held the insurer liable for the cleanup costs. *Gridley Associates v. Transamerica Ins. Co.*, 828 P.2d 524 (Utah App.1992).

A corporation held over sixty comprehensive general liability insurance policies issued by various insurers. The policies contained several common elements: they provided that the insurers would cover only sums which the corporation was legally obligated to pay; they required that the money paid be a result of the corporation's liability for property damage; and they limited coverage to amounts paid for "damages" or "damages and expenses." Subsequently, the United States and various local administrative agencies filed suits against the corporation for alleged violations of CERCLA (the Comprehensive Environmental Response, Compensation and Liability Act) and other environmental acts. The government sought to compel the corporation to cease disposing of hazardous waste and to remove contaminants already present. It further sought reimbursement for the investigatory and monitoring costs it had incurred. The corporation brought a declaratory relief action seeking to determine whether the policies it owned would cover the costs it might have to pay. The insurers sought summary judgment which the trial court denied. The court of appeal reversed, and the Supreme Court of California granted review.

The supreme court first noted that nearly every state appellate court has determined that coverage is available for cleanup costs under identical policies. It then noted that reimbursement costs were sums which the corporation could become legally obligated to pay. Further, the court determined that environmental contamination constituted property damage. Finally, it stated that reimbursement and cleanup costs were "damages" so as to preclude the insurers from denying coverage under their policies. It thus reversed the court of appeal's decision and remanded the case for further discovery. *AIU Ins. Co. v. FMC Corp.*, 274 Cal.Rptr. 820 (Cal.1990).

An Oregon paint processing company dissolved and its assets were sold to another corporation which continued to operate the business, leasing the property. The previous paint company had dug an unlined pit holding used solvent, waste water, and paint sludge. The Department of Environmental Quality sent the lessor (also the widow of the previous paint company owner) a notice of an environmental violation. The lessor then submitted claims under the two insurance policies that had been purchased for the paint company and the lessor. The previous insurer had named the paint company as the named insured under its policy. The present insurer had issued policies in which the named insureds included both the paint company and the lessor. Both insurers denied the claims. The lessor then brought this action in an Oregon trial court. The trial court granted summary judgment to the insurers and the lessor appealed to the Court of Appeals of Oregon.

The previous insurer contended that the lessor was not covered because her obligation for cleanup was based on her status as property owner, not as a paint company shareholder, for which she had owned one share. The lessor argued that she had exercised a degree of control as a shareholder that caused her to be liable along with the paint company. The court, however, disagreed and concluded that the lessor had not shown any shareholder duty that would give rise to liability and, therefore she would not be covered by the policy. The court next turned to the lessor's argument concerning the present insurer. The policy issued by the present insurer stated: "the company will pay damages because of bodily injury or property damage to which this insurance applies caused by an occurrence." An occurrence means an accident, "including continuous and repeated exposure to conditions, which results in property damage neither expected nor intended from the standpoint of the insured." The court noted that the evidence was clear that the paint company intended to release the pollutants into the waste pit as a regular part of its business operations and would not be covered under the policy. The court of appeals affirmed the trial court's decision. *Mays v. Transamerica Ins. Co.*, 799 P.2d 653 (Or.App.1990).

A manufacturer of electrical capacitors was sued by government agencies for the cleanup costs of a local river. The river had been contaminated by the manufacturer's continuous release of liquid PCBs. The manufacturer's liability insurer denied a duty to defend or indemnify because the policy excluded damage resulting from pollution. An exception to the pollution exclusion was possible, however, if the pollution was sudden and accidental. The manufacturer asserted that, by a small percentage, the continuous release had been increased by a 1973 flood and a 1975 fire, and that the entire release was therefore sudden and accidental. The insured sued in a federal district court. The court found that some of the damage caused by the flood was covered, but the damage from the fire was not; it then provided a formula to determine possible damages. The insurer appealed to the U.S. Court of Appeals, First Circuit.

The record of the earlier opinion was used to illustrate the multitude of problems which may arise when a court examines a sudden and accidental exception and attempts to "distinguish virtually indistinguishable events." Specifically, a difficulty springs from determining what sort of event may be sufficiently unexpected, and another from attempting to determine damages. The court then refocused the analysis on the purpose for the exception. It distinguished between "clean" businesses with a little chance of pollution, and businesses which, by their ordinary operation, create a risk of pollution; the distinction is to be made in view of a business's nature and history. The latter were ruled to be excluded from coverage even in consideration of the sudden and accidental exception. The court explained that the exception "should not be construed to provide coverage in these circumstances — in other words, when the discharge is ... caused by events not clearly beyond the long-range expectations of the insured." The insurer was ruled not to have a duty to defend or indemnify. *Lumbermans Mutual Casualty Co. v. Belleville Industries*, 938 F.2d 1423 (1st Cir.1991).

The state of Colorado sued local mining companies for clean-up costs brought about by the flow of acid-mine water into nearby streams. A landowner, although not engaged in mining, owned land containing unused mines and shafts. The mining companies notified the landowner that they would sue for contribution if the state was successful in its suit. The landowner sought a defense from his liability insurer, which denied a duty to defend or indemnify because of a "pollution exclusion" clause. The landowner argued that the policy was ambiguous, and that the pollution exclusion clause was inapplicable to him. His insurer received a declaration in state court that it had no duty to defend or indemnify, and the landowner appealed to the Colorado Court of Appeals.

The pollution exclusion clause excluded coverage for damage caused by pollution. An exception to the pollution exclusion was allowed when the pollution was sudden and accidental. The landowner contended that this "exception to the exception" was ambiguous. The court disagreed. The landowner then argued that the pollution exclusion clause eliminates coverage only for those who actively pollute, and was inapplicable to nonindustrial landowners. Again the court disagreed, despite a dissent. It found that the pollution exclusion applied to what had caused the damage — not to who caused it. Finally, it was argued that the flow of acid-mine water fit within the sudden and accidental exception. A showing of only accidental discharge was ruled to be insufficient to bring damage within this exception; the insured must also show that the damage was sudden. The insurer showed that the flow had occurred over many years, and also that the insured possessed the knowledge of how the pollutant was created and what effect mine-shafts had on its flow. The pollution was found not to fit in either of the unexpectedness or temporal dimensions of "sudden." The insurer was held to have no duty to defend or indemnify the landowner. *West American Ins. Co. v. Baumgartner*, 812 P.2d 696 (Colo.App.1990).

After a Connecticut fuel oil salesman's insurance was cancelled, he directed an agent to procure new coverage for him. The agent procured coverage from an insurer and apparently indicated to the insured that the policy contained no pollution coverage. Inadvertently, the certificate of insurance did not contain this exclusion. When the insurer learned of this, it reissued the certificate of insurance containing the pollution exclusion. The new endorsement was dated the very day of an oil spill. The insurer commenced this action for declaratory relief to determine its liability under the policy. The trial court held for the insurer and the insured appealed to the U.S. Court of Appeals, Second Circuit.

On appeal, the insured contended that he was entitled to the certificate as it was issued to him originally. The court, however, rejected this contention and determined that the agent's knowledge of the exclusion would be imputed to the insured because he was acting on the insured's behalf, and because he had testified that he told the insured of the exclusion. The appellate court affirmed the decision of the trial court. *Western World Ins. Co. v. Stack Oil, Inc.*, 922 F.2d 118 (2d Cir.1990).

A metallurgical company leased a piece of property in New York where it manufactured foil elements for use in smoke detectors. Thereafter, the state brought an action against it and against the owner of the land it occupied, asserting violations of the Comprehensive Environmental Response, Compensation and Liability Act (CERCLA). The state contended that, throughout its operation, the company had disposed of a radioactive substance into a town's sewer system, sewage treatment plant and landfill. The company sought to be indemnified and defended by its general liability insurers. It brought a declaratory action in a federal district court, but the judge granted summary judgment to the insurers. It then appealed to the U.S. Court of Appeals, Second Circuit.

The insurers, in the appeal, argued that their policies only applied if the pollutants were released or escaped suddenly and accidentally. The court examined the exclusionary clauses of their policies, and agreed that the insurers were not liable. Here, the pollution damage seemed to have resulted from purposeful conduct, the state having alleged that the company continuously and intentionally polluted. Since this discharge could not be considered accidental, the court affirmed the district court's decision, and held that the insurers need not defend or indemnify the company. *EAD Metallurgical, Inc. v. Aetna Casualty and Surety Co.*, 905 F.2d 8 (2d Cir.1990).

A company which was insured under a comprehensive general liability policy was notified by the Environmental Protection Agency that it might be responsible for cleanup costs under the Comprehensive Environmental Response, Compensation, and Liability Act of 1980. In a lawsuit which was brought to determine if coverage had to be provided for "damages" under the policy, the Missouri federal district court held that Missouri precedent required a ruling in favor of the insurer. No coverage had to be provided. *U.S. Fidelity and Guarantee Co. v. Citizens Electric Co.*, 791 F.Supp. 231 (E.D.Mo.1991).

Michigan residents sued a manufacturer for its contribution to a hazardous waste site that had contaminated the earth. The company was assessed cleanup and settlement costs. It then requested reimbursement for the costs from its insurance company and, after receiving no response, filed an action against the insurance company. The policy excluded coverage for damage caused by pollution unless the damage was caused by a "sudden and accidental" discharge, dispersal, release, or escape of the pollutant. A federal district court found for the insurer, and the company appealed to the U.S. Court of Appeals, Sixth Circuit.

The court of appeals determined that the term "sudden" was to be given its plain meaning of quick and without warning. The insurance company contended that because the waste was accumulated at the site for a period of years, there was no "sudden" discharge. The court of appeals determined that mere delivery of waste for storage at a facility was not a discharge of pollutants into the environment. The "sudden" release of the waste, once it was stored at the waste site, would fall within the policy. However, here there was no evidence that any pollution damage had been caused by a "sudden" discharge of the insured's pollutant from the facility. The court of appeals affirmed the district court's decision. *Fl Aerospace v. Aetna Cas. and Sur. Co.*, 897 F.2d 214 (6th Cir.1990).

A Georgia insured owned fifty-two acres of land which he allowed the city of Jacksonville, Florida, to use as a landfill. The city dumped industrial and chemical waste at the site for several years and then returned the land to the insured completely filled, graded and seeded. The insured had no knowledge that the site was used for dumping hazardous waste. Seven years later the Environmental Protection Agency (EPA) determined that the groundwater beneath the site had been contaminated by the release of hazardous substances. The EPA informed the insured and the city that they were required to take corrective action. The insured filed a declaratory judgment action in a Georgia trial court to determine whether his comprehensive general liability policy covered the cleanup costs. Under the policy, hazardous waste cleanup was excluded unless the waste discharge was sudden. The case was removed to the U.S. District Court for the Southern District of Georgia which granted summary judgment for the insurer. The court found the policy's exclusion clause clear and unambiguous. The dumping of toxic waste occurring over several years was not sudden and coverage was denied. The insured appealed to the U.S. Court of Appeals, Eleventh Circuit, which certified the question to the Supreme Court of Georgia.

On appeal, the insured argued that "sudden" as used in the policy meant unexpected. The insurer contended that the only possible meaning for sudden was "abrupt." The court found that "sudden" was capable of more than one reasonable interpretation and construed it in favor of the insured to mean "unexpected." The court ruled that the pollution exclusion clause did not preclude coverage for the discharge of pollutants over an extended period of time. *Claussen v. Aetna Cas. & Sur. Co.*, 380 S.E.2d 686 (Ga.1989).

A corporation purchased various comprehensive general liability policies from several insurers. The policies contained a pollution exclusion clause which stated that no coverage would be provided for personal injury or property damage arising out of the discharge or escape of toxic chemicals or other waste materials. The exclusion did not apply if the discharge or escape was sudden and accidental. After the discovery of environmental pollution at sites where the corporation disposed of industrial waste, the corporation was targeted for cleanup costs associated with its actions. It sought a declaratory judgment that the insurers had to defend and indemnify it. A New York trial court ruled for the insurers, and the corporation appealed to the Supreme Court, Appellate Division. On appeal, the court noted that the corporation's long-term, intentional disposal of industrial waste was not covered under the "sudden and accidental" exception to the pollution exclusion clause. Only sudden discharges, which occurred at a fixed time, were meant to fall within the "accident-based" policies' coverage. The appellate court then looked at the various administrative proceedings the corporation was involved in, and determined that since they sought only voluntary participation in the clean up, no defense had to be provided there. The court modified and affirmed the trial court's ruling in favor of the insurers. *Borg-Warner Corp. v. Ins. Co. of North America*, 577 N.Y.S.2d 953 (A.D.3rd Dept.1992).

A company engaged in the business of hauling industrial waste from production sites to disposal sites. The Environmental Protection Agency (EPA) notified the company of potential liability due to pollution at the disposal sites. The company accordingly notified its liability insurers. The insurers noted that the pollution had allegedly occurred over a considerable amount of time, and brought a separate suit seeking a declaration that it had no duty to defend or indemnify. A federal district court granted summary judgment to the insurers on all issues, and its decision was appealed to the U.S. Court of Appeals, Third Circuit. Applying Pennsylvania law, the court first held that a "sudden and accidental" exception to a pollution exclusion clause required that both elements be satisfied. The insured argued that the exception required only that the pollution be unintended. Though many courts have accepted that argument, Pennsylvania courts have not. An attempt by the insured to construe the exclusionary clause to apply only to "active" polluters, as opposed to "passive" polluters, was also rejected. The insured then urged that the policy excluded coverage only for the insured's acts which cause pollution — not for liability arising from other pollution. Again the court held for the insurer. The policy excluded coverage for "the" discharge of pollutants and made no mention of any party. The EPA's allegations were clearly outside the scope of the policy. The insurer therefore had no duty to defend the insured. The decision of the district court was affirmed. *Northern Ins. Co. v. Aardvark Assoc.*, 942 F.2d 189 (3d Cir.1991).

An Alabama insured conducted strip mining on leased land. After the operations had ceased, a pit that had been dug filled with water and contaminated the landowners' water supply because of toxic chemical runoff. The landowners sued the insured in an Alabama circuit court. The court ruled that a clause in the insured's liability policy excluded coverage for contamination of the owners' water supply. The owners appealed to the Supreme Court of Alabama which held that the policy expressly excluded coverage for pollution damage. The insurer would not be required to indemnify the insured if it was held liable to the owners. The court affirmed the judgment of the circuit court. *Hicks v. American Resources Ins. Co.*, 544 So.2d 952 (Ala.1989).

A Texas insured was to provide labor and equipment for the construction of an underground, concrete water storage tank. In addition to constructing the tank, the insured was to prevent water damage to the tank during its construction. Although precautionary measures were taken, surface runoff entered the tank excavation site which resulted in structural damage. Prior to making repairs to the tank, the insured notified its insurer of the damage. The insurer inspected the damaged tank and found that the loss was not covered because the damage was due to faulty workmanship, which was excluded under the policy. The insured then sued the insurer in a Texas trial court for recovery under the policy. The trial court granted the insurer's summary judgment motion and the insured appealed to the Court of Appeals of Texas.

The court of appeals held that the policy did not cover the water damage to the tank. Property which must be repaired or replaced because of faulty workmanship was not covered under the policy. The court noted that the insured was contractually obligated to keep the excavation site dry until the tank was completed. Its failure to do so constituted faulty workmanship which was not covered by the policy. The court of appeals affirmed the trial court's decision. *Gar-Tex Const. v. Employers Cas. Co.*, 771 S.W.2d 639 (Tex.App.1989).

A Pennsylvania manufacturer deposited a large amount of hazardous waste on its property. The manufacturer sold the property to another party who in turn sold it to a developer. Pursuant to a federal directive, the developer was forced to clean up the hazardous waste. It incurred nearly $220,000 in expenses. It sought indemnification from the manufacturer. When the manufacturer refused the developer sued it in a Pennsylvania federal district court. The district court ruled that the price the developer paid for the property "reflected the possibility of environmental risk" and it accepted that risk when it purchased the property. The developer appealed to the U.S. Court of Appeals, Third Circuit.

The developer argued that under the Comprehensive Environmental Response, Compensation and Liability Act (CERCLA), the manufacturer was not allowed to assert the 'buyer beware' defense. The appeals court noted that both the current property owner as well as the owner of the property at the time the hazardous substance was deposited were liable for rectifying the condition. Although the CERCLA statute did not list the buyer beware doctrine as a defense, the appeals court determined that the statutory language did not explicitly prohibit it. However, in keeping with the congressional intent of encouraging responsible parties to clean up property, the buyer beware doctrine could not be a defense to liability for contribution. The developer was entitled to seek contribution from the manufacturer. *Smith Land & Improvement Corp. v. Celotex Corp.*, 851 F.2d 86 (3rd Cir.1988).

E. Products Liability

An insurer issued a products liability policy to a boat parts manufacturer. The coverage included bodily injury and death which occurred during the policy period, and which was caused by an accidental occurrence. The manufacturer sold a stick steering mechanism to a boating company. The mechanism was incorporated into its boats. The manufacturer then ceased doing business. Shortly thereafter, a couple purchased a boat containing the mechanism. A boating accident resulted in the death of their son, and the couple sustained bodily injuries also. The products liability insurer denied coverage because the accident had occurred after the policy had lapsed. In the lawsuit which followed, the trial court ruled for the insurer. The couple appealed to the Missouri Court of Appeals. They asserted that the insurer did not unambiguously limit coverage to injuries occurring during the policy period. The appellate court, however, found that the policy was clear in limiting coverage, and accordingly it affirmed the trial court's decision. *Universal Reinsurance Corp. v. Greenleaf*, 824 S.W.2d 80 (Mo.App.1992).

A recently-hired employee in Louisiana asked his supervisor to teach him how to operate a mobile crane. The supervisor stood on the crane's ladder while the employee sat inside the crane's cab. The supervisor reviewed the controls with the employee and instructed him how to extend, raise, lower, and rotate the boom. As the employee began to rotate the boom slightly, the crane began to tip. The supervisor told him to retract the boom, but the employee couldn't. After the supervisor jumped from the crane, the employee also attempted to jump but was crushed beneath the crane. The employee died two hours later. The employee's widow sued the crane's manufacturer and its products liability insurer. A district court found in favor of the widow and the insurer, and the manufacturer appealed to the Court of Appeals of Louisiana. On appeal, the manufacturer argued that it adequately warned the employee because it provided an operations manual containing adequate safety instructions. The manufacturer also argued that its failure to give a clear warning was not the cause of the accident. Rather, the decedent failed to read the manual and failed to attend the training class. The appellate court held that the risk of a tipover posed such a serious harm that the manufacturer had an elevated duty to warn of this danger inside the cab of the crane. Because the cab did not contain any safety instructions on tipovers and the operator's manual failed to give any instruction on what an operator should do in the event of a tipover, the court held that the manufacturer breached its duty to warn. Accordingly, the court held that the manufacturer's insurer was not required to provide coverage and defense to the crane manufacturer (because its coverage was for products liability and not for negligence). Thus, the court affirmed the verdict of the district court. *Easton v. Chevron Industries, Inc.*, 602 So.2d 1032 (La.App.4th Cir.1992).

An insured manufacturer produced a brand of tampons which were implicated in several cases of toxic shock syndrome. The expenditures of legal fees and settlement costs arose from more than 1,000 injury and death claims. The dispute involved the insured manufacturer and several insurers who had issued liability policies to the manufacturer to cover the period when the injuries were allegedly sustained. The policies included coverage for product liability claims. A particular insurer which provided liability insurance for a period of one year provided $25 million dollars in coverage in excess of primary insurance. The policy contained a $1 million deductible subject to an aggregate annual deductible of $10 million. Approximately seventy-five to eighty claims against the manufacturer fell within the insurer's umbrella policy. However, only one of these cases exceeded $1 million. The manufacturer and the insurer disagreed about the proper deductible amount. The manufacturer claimed that there was a $1 million deductible but the insurer maintained that the applicable deductible was $10 million dollars per year and $1 million per occurrence. The central disagreement concerned the proper definition of occurrence. The jury found that under the policy the lawsuits and claims involved multiple occurrences. Consequently, the insured manufacturer's deductible was $10 million dollars per policy year. The insurer was ordered to reimburse the manufacturer only $5,500. The insured then appealed to the Seventh Circuit Court of Appeals.

The insured contended that the court committed reversible error when it refused to instruct the jury that the manufacturer was entitled to have the policy construed in any reasonable manner that afforded coverage. The appellate court disagreed stating that under Ohio law it is clear that the rule is grounded in the need to protect an insured from an insurer who had exclusive control of the drafting process. That concern was not implicated here. The record clearly established that the manufacturer was a co-drafter of the policy and not simply a party given a take it or leave it option. Therefore, the insured was not entitled to an instruction requiring the jury to interpret ambiguity in the policy in favor of the insured. The court of appeals affirmed the trial court's decision. *Northbrook Excess and Surplus v. Proctor & Gamble, Co.*, 924 F.2d 633 (7th Cir.1991).

A Texas corporation held both a primary and an excess liability insurance policy. When the company was sued in a products liability suit, the primary insurer undertook the corporation's defense. However, the primary insurer was soon declared insolvent and placed in receivership. The attorney hired to defend the case withdrew, and the corporation demanded that the excess insurer assume the duty to defend and indemnify. The excess insurer refused. The corporation hired its own attorney who reached a settlement in the case. The corporation agreed to the entry of an $800,000 judgment against it and relinquished its claims against the excess insurer to the injured party. In return, the injured party agreed not to take any action against the corporation. The corporation and the injured party then sued the excess insurer to recover for bad faith and the proceeds of the policy. A federal district court dismissed the case and the matter was appealed to the U.S. Court of Appeals, Fifth Circuit. The Fifth Circuit noted that the excess insurance policy provided a defense only if no primary insurer was obligated to defend the corporation. The court held that the placement of the primary carrier into receivership did not extinguish its obligation to defend. Therefore, the excess insurer had no duty to defend. The court also noted that the policy forbade any actions against the excess insurer until the amount of the insured's obligation had been determined by an actual trial. Since the parties had agreed to a verdict, there was no actual trial, and the action could not be sustained. The court of appeals affirmed the district court's dismissal. *Harville v. Twin City Fire Ins. Co.*, 885 F.2d 276 (5th Cir.1989).

Pursuant to a state program, an Oregon girl was given a DPT vaccination. The vaccination caused her severe mental and physical handicaps. She sued two manufacturers who could not prove that they did not produce the vaccine that actually caused the injury. An Oregon federal district court granted the manufacturers' dismissal motion. The girl appealed to the U.S. Ninth Circuit Court of Appeals. She argued that the manufacturers should be required to prove that they did not produce the vaccine. If either one or both failed they should be held liable. The appeals court held that the girl must prove which manufacturer produced the vaccine. It then sent the case back to the federal district court to determine if she could prove such facts. *Senn v. Merrill-Dow Pharmaceuticals*, 850 F.2d 611 (9th Cir.1988).

A veterinarian drove an insured automobile to the New Orleans fairgrounds where she was treating sick and injured horses. She parked the car near a barn. A thoroughbred racehorse being exercised by its trainer then became spooked, threw its rider, and ran toward the barn, trampling the car on its way to the stable. The insurer paid for the damage to the car, and then sought subrogation from the owner and trainer of the horse. The trial court ruled in favor of the insurer. On appeal to the Louisiana Court of Appeal, the court found that the defendants were strictly liable for the damage caused by the runaway horse. The court affirmed the judgment for the insurer. *State Farm Mutual Automobile Ins. Co. v. Simon*, 598 So.2d 1255 (La.App.1992).

VII. AIRCRAFT INSURANCE

As long as pilot qualification requirements and aircraft airworthiness certification requirements are clearly and unambiguously set forth in an aircraft insurance policy, the courts will require that insureds comply with such requirements as a prerequisite to coverage.

A. Pilot Qualifications

1. Coverage Awarded

A Texas man sought insurance coverage for his airplane even though he was not yet a pilot. The policy provided coverage only if the plane was piloted by a properly certificated pilot. The insured indicated that he was already certificated on his application to the insurer, and received a policy. The insured took flying lessons from a qualified instructor. During one lesson, the plane was damaged while landing with both the instructor and the insured on the controls. The plane was damaged in the amount of $111,440. The insured then filed a claim which the insurer denied. The insured sued the insurer in a Texas trial court, seeking compensation for his damages and punitive damages from the insurer for its bad faith in refusing to pay on the claim. The insured won and the insurer appealed to the Court of Appeals of Texas.

The insurer argued that, because both the insured and his instructor were on the controls, it was not required to pay on the policy. The insurer also argued that because the insured had misrepresented his statement to the insurer, it was not bound by the policy. The court ruled that simultaneous piloting, with one of the pilots a qualified instructor, fell within the conditions of the policy. The court further held that, under Texas law, the insurer was required to give notice of its refusal to be bound. Since a good faith legal controversy had existed between the insurer and the insured, the court denied the application of punitive damages, awarding only actual damages.

National Union Fire Ins. Co. v. Hudson Energy Co. Inc., 780 S.W.2d 417 (Tex.App.-Texarkana 1989).

A pilot with a visual flight rating (VFR) crashed under weather conditions which required an instrument flight rating (IFR). The pilot had taken off under VFR conditions and filed an approved VFR flight plan. Shortly after takeoff, the plane crashed, killing all five people on board. The pilot's liability insurer refused coverage because the plane crashed under conditions that required the pilot to have an IFR. His wife sued the insurer in a Washington trial court. The insurer argued that the pilot had violated regulations for VFR flights by entering airspace which required an IFR. This excluded him from coverage under the terms of a policy clause. The terminology of the clause was not defined in the policy. The insurer also argued that the clause was unambiguous regarding coverage. The trial court held for the insurer and the wife appealed to the Washington Court of Appeals which upheld the decision. The wife then appealed to the Washington Supreme Court.

The supreme court held that the clause was ambiguous and construed it in the wife's favor. It held that the clause applied to the flight as a whole which meant that if the pilot filed an approved VFR plan and took off under VFR conditions, coverage would be provided for the whole flight. The supreme court reasoned that if the flight was viewed as a whole, the pilot would know from the moment he took off that he was covered. Following the reasoning of the insurer, the coverage would come and go whenever the flight conditions changed from VFR to IFR. Because the weather conditions at the time and place of departure were controlling, the insurer had to provide coverage. *Nat'l Union Flyer Ins. Co. v. Zuver*, 750 P.2d 1247 (Wash.1988).

Two men died in the crash of a new airplane that one of them was piloting. They had purchased the airplane earlier that day. At the time of the crash, the pilot was insured for personal injury and property damage by a policy issued to cover another airplane he owned. A clause in that policy provided that a "newly acquired aircraft" would be covered under the policy if the insurer was notified of its purchase within thirty days. The clause limited coverage "to those aircraft which [the pilot] acquired by himself." After the insurer was ordered to pay the policy limits by a Texas trial court, it appealed to the Texas Court of Appeals.

The insurer argued on appeal that since the pilot did not own the aircraft outright, it was not covered by the policy. The Texas Court of Appeals noted that the clause would be satisfied if 1) the pilot acquired ownership, and 2) the insurance company was notified within thirty days following the purchase. There was no doubt that the pilot was an owner of the aircraft. Because the policy did not expressly require the pilot to be its "sole and unconditional owner" it could not be interpreted to require such ownership. Furthermore, since the notice requirement had been satisfied by the pilot's estate, the policy covered the new aircraft upon purchase. The intervention of the accident after the purchase but before notice was given did not invalidate the policy's coverage. The district court's judgment requiring the insurer to pay $100,000 to the passenger's estate was affirmed. *American Eagle Ins. Co. v. Lemons*, 722 S.W.2d 229 (Tex.App.1986).

2. Coverage Denied

The owner of a Cessna multiengine aircraft contacted an independent insurance agency, seeking liability coverage for his plane. He informed the agent that his pilot was a twin-engine rated pilot with 400 hours of flight time. The agent located an insurer who agreed to provide coverage. On the application, the pilot stated that he was a single and multiengine rated pilot. After the policy was in effect, the plane crashed while the pilot was at the controls. The pilot and three passengers were killed. The insurer then discovered that the pilot was not a multiengine rated pilot but rather a student pilot. It brought a declaratory relief action against the owner and others, seeking a declaration that coverage was not available. The court ruled for the owner, and the insurer appealed to the Court of Appeals of Ohio. The appellate court noted that the evidence was sufficient to support the trial court's holding that there was no causal connection between the pilot's lack of certification and the accident. The court went on to say, however, that since the qualifications of the pilot were relevant and material to the issuance of coverage, the policy was void due to the misrepresentations of the pilot. The insurer did not have to show that the breach of the policy terms was the cause of the accident. The trial court's decision was reversed. *American Continental Ins. Co. v. Estate of Gerkens*, 591 N.E.2d 774 (Ohio App.3d Dist.1990).

An insured Arizona pilot and two others were killed in a small aircraft crash. Survivors filed a claim for coverage against the pilot's insurer. The insurer then discovered that the pilot had no medical certificate at the time of the accident. According to federal regulations, pilots must have an appropriate medical certificate. The insured's policy required valid medical certification to qualify for coverage. The insurer filed a lawsuit in an Arizona trial court for a declaration that its policy did not cover the accident. The trial court ruled in the insurer's favor and the insured's estate appealed to the Arizona Court of Appeals. The appeals court ruled that aviation insurance coverage should not be denied unless the excluded risk had a causal connection to the loss. The appeals court reversed the trial court's decision, and the insurer appealed to the Arizona Supreme Court.

The supreme court noted that the exclusion pertained to any accident occurring while the aircraft was flown by a pilot who was not properly certified. The exclusion was not limited to accidents caused by pilot failure. Public policy favored a rule encouraging safe aircraft operation and the exclusion encouraged compliance with safety regulations. The insurer was not required to demonstrate a causal relation between the crash and the pilot's lack of certification. The court overruled the appeals court decision, and reinstated the trial court's decision for the insurer. *Security Ins. Co. v. Anderson*, 763 P.2d 246 (Ariz.1988).

An airplane owner had liability insurance covering deaths of passengers carried in his airplane. The policy contained a pilot warranty which provided that coverage was effective only when the airplane's pilot possessed a valid pilot certificate and a current medical certificate. When the airplane crashed into a mountain, its pilot and two passengers were killed. The pilot held a valid certificate but his medical certificate was not current. The crash was caused by pilot error, not the pilot's medical condition. Heirs of the passengers who died sued the pilot's estate and the airplane's owner, seeking wrongful death damages. The insurer then requested a court declaration that the pilot's failure to possess a current medical certificate precluded coverage under the policy. The insurer admitted in a stipulation that the policy "was in full force and effect" on the date of the crash. The Superior Court, San Diego County, concluded that this admission waived the insurer's contention that a current medical certificate was required to trigger the policy's coverage. The court ruled in favor of the passengers' heirs because the pilot's failure to possess a current certificate did not cause the accident. The insurer appealed.

The California Court of Appeal, Fourth District, noted that despite admitting that the policy was in full force and effect, the insurer had retained defenses "relating to the failure of the pilot to have in his possession a current medical certificate at the time of the accident." The insurer's admission simply meant that "the policy was issued, premiums were paid and the contract for insurance had not been terminated." The court ruled that the insurance contract was clear in requiring that the pilot possess a current medical certificate without regard for a causal connection between the pilot's medical condition and an accident. The contract was valid as written and no coverage existed at the time of the accident. The Superior Court's decision in favor of the passengers' heirs was reversed. *Natl. Union Fire Ins. Co. of Pittsburg v. Estate of Meyer*, 237 Cal.Rptr. 632 (App.4th Dist.1987).

B. Airworthiness Certification

A Vermont man completed an application for aviation liability insurance in which he stated that the airplane involved had passed an annual inspection within the last twelve months. In fact, it had not. After the airplane crashed, causing extensive property damage and injuries, the insured sued his insurer because of its refusal to pay. The insured contended before the Vermont Supreme Court that the insurer had to establish a causal connection between the misrepresentation and the loss before it could deny coverage. Conversely, the insurer claimed that the statement by the insured that the airplane had been inspected materially affected its acceptance of the risk and, therefore, it should not be held liable. The supreme court noted that Vermont law did not require the insurer to show that the misrepresentation was causally related to the loss. The burden upon the insurer was met when it established that there was a causal connection between the misrepresentation and its decision to issue the policy. The insurer had no duty to pay the claim. *McAllister v. Avemco Ins. Co.*, 528 A.2d 758 (Vt.1987).

The co-owners of a Piper Twin Commanche aircraft sued their aircraft insurer after it refused to pay a claim. While one of the owners, a business associate and a pilot were flying through cloud cover in California, the pilot attempted to find a way through mountains and clouds. Unfortunately, through a combination of "downdraft" conditions and the plane's inability to climb at a normal rate, they were forced down onto a mountain. Although no one was seriously injured, the plane was nearly a total loss. The plane's owners made a claim for hull damage and their insurer refused indemnification, stating that an exclusion barring coverage unless the plane's airworthiness certificate was "in full force and effect" applied to preclude coverage. The insurer contended that the airplane owner's failure to get an annual inspection suspended the airworthiness certificate, excluding coverage. The owners argued that the exclusion's language was ambiguous and thus invalid. The Court of Appeal of California affirmed a trial court ruling in the insurer's favor. The court found the exclusion to be clear and unambiguous and coverage was denied. *Threlkeld v. Ranger Ins. Co.*, 202 Cal.Rptr. 529 (App.5th Dist.1984).

C. Conversions to Criminal Use

The following two cases involve exclusions from coverage in the event an aircraft is converted to a criminal use, such as drug smuggling or theft.

A California couple purchased a new twin-engine airplane and leased it to an airline which they partly owned. The airline decided to sublease the airplane, and the couple obtained aviation insurance for the aircraft in anticipation of the sublease. The airline delivered possession of the airplane to the sublessee on August 1, 1980. The policy named the couple and the sublessee as insureds and provided that it covered any "physical damage loss" to the airplane, including disappearance. "Disappearance" was defined in the policy as "missing and not reported for sixty days after commencing a flight." The policy provided that the plane was covered only when used for "pleasure and business" by the sublessee. The airplane was last seen on August 5, 1980. Information accumulated by the insurer indicated that the sublessee had leased another airplane under similar circumstances which had been seized in Columbia, South America, for illegal entry. The sublessee's agent, who negotiated both leases, was implicated in a ring of international drug smugglers who stole twin-engine airplanes for use in drug smuggling. The agent was linked to the disappearance of several airplanes, including two owned by the airline and insured by the insurer.

The couple submitted a claim in the amount of $240,000 under the aviation policy for the missing airplane. The insurer denied the claim, alleging that the couple had failed to establish "physical damage loss" to or "disappearance" of the airplane within the meaning of the policy. The couple filed a lawsuit against the insurer in the Superior Court, Los Angeles County, claiming that the insurer had breached the implied covenant of good faith and fair dealing. The Superior Court awarded judgment to the insurer and the couple appealed. The California Court of Appeal, Second District, noted that several facts supported the insurer's denial of the claim. First, the airplane was reported missing shortly after the policy was obtained. Second, there was no evidence that the couple had made any efforts on their own to investigate the airplane's mysterious disappearance. Third, the couple had purchased the airplane and immediately leased and then subleased to people already under investigation for both drug smuggling and similar mysterious disappearances of other airplanes, including at least two owned by the airline and leased to the sublessee. The court ruled that the couple had failed to establish physical damage or disappearance within the meaning of the policy. Moreover, a mere inability to locate the airplane did not prove that a covered "disappearance" had occurred because it had not disappeared "after commencing a flight." The insurer's denial of the couple's claim was warranted, and the decision of the Superior Court was affirmed. *Congleton v. National Union Fire Ins. Co.*, 234 Cal.Rptr. 218 (App.2d Dist.1987).

The Court of Appeal of New Mexico held that an insurer was not liable for damages to a plane which crashed after unloading 300 pounds of smuggled marijuana. A lessee of the plane unloaded the marijuana at a New Mexico ranch and crashed at takeoff. The insurer argued that a clause excluding coverage if the airplane was converted to a criminal use precluded recovery. The lessor/insured responded that the plane was not being "converted" at the time it crashed because the marijuana had already been unloaded. Further, the crash was not attributable to the plane's criminal use. The Court of Appeal affirmed a trial court's ruling that the lease agreement made it clear that the plane was not to be used for any violation of federal or state controlled substances laws. Thus, the plane had been converted to a criminal use and the exclusion applied. *Gelder v. Puritan Ins. Co.*, 668 P.2d 1117 (N.M.App.1983).

D. Exclusions Generally

Two co-owners of a Piper airplane purchased an aviation insurance policy which provided them with liability protection up to a limit of $100,000 for each passenger. The policy did not provide bodily injury protection for either insured or for a spouse who resided in the same household as an insured. Subsequently, the aircraft was involved in an accident in Kansas, while being operated by one of the owners. His wife, a passenger at the time, was injured in the accident. She sued the co-owner of the plane, hoping to obtain benefits under the policy. The insurer brought suit in a federal district court, seeking a declaration that it need not defend or indemnify its insureds due to the spousal exclusion in the policy. Cross motions were brought for summary judgment. The insurer asserted that the passenger was the spouse of an insured and that she resided with him at the time of the accident; thus, she was barred from recovery under the policy. The court agreed. It found that the policy unambiguously excluded coverage. Even though the policy "lumped" both insureds together, and the passenger could not be the spouse of both of them, there was no inherent ambiguity about the exclusion. Accordingly, the insurer had no duty to defend or indemnify the owners. However, the court noted that the wife was not barred from maintaining her suit against them for negligence in maintaining and flying the plane. *RLI Ins. Co. v. Kary*, 779 F.Supp. 1300 (D.Kan.1991).

A Japan Air Lines (JAL) 747 was damaged when it slid off an icy taxiway at the Anchorage International Airport. JAL was insured under a policy issued by Lloyd's of London in which the state was an additional insured because it owned the airport. An airport lease contained a clause requiring JAL to hold the state harmless for claims arising out of JAL's use of the tarmac's loading area. Lloyd's sued the state, claiming that the accident resulted from the faulty design and maintenance of the taxiway. An Alaska trial court jury held the state eighty percent liable and JAL twenty percent liable for the accident. The state appealed to the Alaska Supreme Court.

The state argued that the hold-harmless clause precluded recovery because the taxiway was a necessary and incidental use of the loading area. Lloyds argued that the policy only covered risks which arose out of JAL's operations or activities on the loading area. It also claimed that coverage for taxiway operations was not within the parties' expectations. The supreme court noted that previous cases held that premises operations coverage included liability for all operations necessary or incidental to the use of the loading area. Thus, taxiing the aircraft was an operation necessary to JAL's use of the loading area. Policy language indicated that the state could reasonably expect coverage. The trial court decision was reversed and Lloyds was obligated to provide coverage. *State of Alaska v. Underwriters at Lloyds, London*, 755 P.2d 396 (Alaska 1988).

An Alaskan aircraft struck and killed a man as he drove his snowmobile across a closed portion of an airport runway. The snowmobile driver's estate brought a wrongful death action against the airport owner. The owner's insurer then obtained a release by settling with the estate for $800,000, three quarters of which was termed a loan. The settlement obligated the estate to file a wrongful death action against the State Department of Transportation and Public Facilities (DOT). The estate then filed suit alleging that the state had been negligent in design and maintenance of the airstrip. The DOT filed a third-party complaint against the insurer claiming to be an additional insured under an agreement between the airport owner and the insurer. The court granted summary judgment to the insurer. The DOT appealed to the Supreme Court of Alaska. The certificate of insurance promised coverage both to the DOT as an additional insured and to the owner for all airport premises and operations within the state of Alaska. The court, however, found that the premises clause excluded coverage on behalf of either insured for injuries caused by an aircraft. The court remanded the case for further proceedings to determine if the insurer had violated its agreement to waive subrogation against the state. *State Dep't of Transportation v. Houston Cas.*, 797 P.2d 1200 (Alaska 1990).

A Pennsylvania man was piloting a leased plane when he had to make an emergency landing. A passenger and the pilot were killed. The pilot's wife sued the leasing company and obtained a writ of execution against the company. She joined the insurer as garnishee. Under the aircraft policy, each passenger was insured to $50,000; however, the maximum coverage for nonpassengers was $100,000. The Pennsylvania Court of Common Pleas found that the insured was both a pilot and a passenger since he was riding in the plane and thus could only recover up to $50,000. The insured's wife appealed to the Superior Court of Pennsylvania.

The superior court held that the pilot was a nonpassenger, entitling his wife to the larger insurance coverage. The court noted that the contract defined passenger as a person who was in, on or boarding an aircraft for a flight or attempted flight. It said that the word passenger did not include pilot. The insurer did not interchange the words pilot and passenger in the policy and intended to differentiate between them. To find that a pilot, while in the process of flying a plane, is a passenger would have twisted ordinary word meanings. The superior court reversed the trial court's decision. *Loomer v. M.R.T. Flying Serv., Inc.*, 558 A.2d 103 (Pa.Super.1989).

Two insurers, New Hampshire Insurance Company (NHI) and United States Aviation Underwriters (USAU), sued each other for contribution in a personal injury action against a Puerto Rican insured. The insured operated a helipad. A man was severely injured when struck by a helicopter which was landing on the insured's premises. The insured had three insurance policies at the time of the accident. NHI had issued a comprehensive general liability policy for the insured's premises. USAU had issued an aircraft operations liability policy and an airport liability policy to a company which provided transportation for the insured's employees. The company had listed the insured as an additional named insured on both policies. A settlement was negotiated between the injured man and the two insurers. Each insurer reserved the right to sue the other for contribution. NHI denied coverage stating that its policy did not apply to bodily injury arising out of the use of any aircraft rented or loaned to any insured. The U.S. District Court for the District of Puerto Rico held that the contract between the insured and the company was a lease and, accordingly, that the exclusion in the policy effectively precluded coverage under the NHI policy. However, USAU was found liable under the airport policy. USAU appealed the decision to the U.S. Court of Appeals, First Circuit.

The court ruled that NHI's general liability policy plainly excluded coverage of the risks from aircraft that the insured or its employees owned, rented, borrowed or operated. The company had included the insured as an additional named insured on USAU's policies. This suggested that the insured and the company understood that NHI's policy did not cover risks arising out of the operation of the helipad. Because the helicopter was provided for the insured's exclusive use as part of that lease, the court held that the helicopter was "rented or loaned" to the insured within the meaning of the exclusion in NHI's policy. The decision of the U.S. district court finding USAU liable under the airport policy was affirmed. *Reyes-Lopez v. Misener Marine Const. Co.*, 854 F.2d 529 (1st Cir.1988).

An architectural firm in Georgia owned an airplane which was covered under a policy of aviation insurance for "personal and pleasure use and use in direct connection with the insured's business, excluding any operation for which a charge is made." The firm used a pilot who flew for the firm as an independent contractor and also flew the airplane with the firm's permission for his own business purposes. During a return flight from Kentucky to Georgia, the plane crashed, killing the pilot and the plane's passengers. The insurer sought a ruling from the Georgia Court of Appeals that it was not liable to pay claims filed under the policy because the fatal flight was one for which a charge had been made. The insurer presented evidence that the pilot had charged some passengers in the past, including passengers to and from Kentucky. The president of the architectural firm, however, testified that the fatal flight was flown on behalf of his firm and that to his knowledge no charges were to be made to the passengers. Because the insurer presented no concrete evidence that the flight was not undertaken for free to the passengers, the court ruled that the flight was covered by the policy. *U.S. Fire Ins. Co. v. Cowley & Assocs.*, 359 S.E.2d 160 (Ga.App.1987).

VIII. FEDERAL FLOOD INSURANCE

The cases in this section arose under the Federal Emergency Management Agency's (FEMA) National Flood Insurance Program.

An Oklahoma man was required to purchase flood insurance to obtain a house loan through the Veterans Administration. An agent authorized to provide insurance under the National Flood Insurance Program (NFIP) prepared a flood insurance policy describing the home as "inside the city limits of Norman." The house was actually located outside the city limits of Norman and did not qualify for the NFIP. The Federal Emergency Management Agency (FEMA) issued a flood insurance policy. In May, 1982, the home was flooded and the homeowner reported the loss. The NFIP administrator denied the claim because the home was not located in a community participating in the NFIP. The homeowner sued the agent in a federal district court for his negligence in issuing the flood insurance policy. The homeowner also brought suit against the FEMA for equitable estoppel. The district court found for the homeowner against the defendants and stated that the FEMA was equitably estopped from denying liability and was jointly and severally liable. The FEMA appealed to the U.S. Court of Appeals, Tenth Circuit. The issue on appeal was whether equitable estoppel can be maintained against the government for the unauthorized acts of its agents. The court of appeals ruled that equitable estoppel against the government may apply in some cases where there is "affirmative

Sec. VIII FEDERAL FLOOD INSURANCE 377

conduct." However, mere negligence, as in this case, on the part of a government agent does not rise to the level of affirmative conduct. The court of appeals reversed the judgment against the FEMA. *Penny v. Giuffrida*, 897 F.2d 1543 (10th Cir.1990).

This action was comprised of various claims by homeowners whose homes were extensively damaged when a creek flooded following a downpour. Each of the insureds held a flood insurance policy issued by a governmental agency. The agency determined that certain losses of the insureds were not covered by the policies. Specifically, at issue was an exclusion in the policy regarding basement coverage. In the policy, "basement" is defined as the level "which has its floor subgraded (below ground level) on all sides." The insureds contended that this language was ambiguous and asserted that because their lower levels exited to their backyards with only a few upward steps the exclusion should not apply to them. The federal district court, although sympathetic to the insureds' plight, held that the clear language of the policy excluded the losses at issue. Subgrade means below ground level and since none of the insureds' homes were true walkouts the case had to be dismissed. *Nelson v. Becton*, 732 F.Supp. 996 (D.Minn.1990).

In December 1981, the National Flood Insurance Program (NFIP) notified a Georgia man that his flood insurance policy would expire on January 30, 1982, unless the NFIP received a premium payment before that date. On February 3, 1982, the man tendered his premium payment to the insurance agency through which he had originally purchased his NFIP policy. The agency promised to forward the premium to the NFIP and, aware of an imminent danger of flooding, it telephoned the NFIP and requested instructions. The agency was told to send the premium and the NFIP said it would decide what to do about coverage if the man filed a claim. On February 3 and 4, 1982, the man's house was damaged by flooding. The NFIP denied his claim on the ground that his policy had expired on January 30. He sued his insurance agency, alleging breach of contract, negligence and misrepresentation. A state superior court ruled against the man and he appealed.

The Georgia Court of Appeals upheld the lower court's ruling. First, the agency had not breached any contractual duty owed to the man because its only duty was to mail the premium to the NFIP. The agency fulfilled that duty by mailing the premium the same day. Second, the agency could not be held liable for negligence in preventing the man's flood insurance policy from lapsing because the policy had already lapsed when the man sought assistance in renewing it. The only negligent party was the insured himself. Third, the man argued that the insurance agency was liable for misrepresentation because on February 3, 1982, it told him his coverage was still "good." This misrepresentation provided no grounds for relief for the man because it caused him no actual damages, due to his failure to prove that without the misrepresentation he would have immediately gone out and purchased coverage elsewhere. The superior court's ruling against the man was upheld. *Parris v. Pledger Ins. Agency*, 348 S.E.2d 924 (Ga.App.1986).

Homeowners in Florida sought to recover under both their homeowner's and flood insurance policies after Hurricane Dennis struck Florida and damaged their home. After coverage was denied under both policies the homeowners brought suit to recover in a U.S. district court. The court found that the damage to the home was caused by flooding, a peril specifically excluded from the couple's homeowner's insurance policy. It found, however, that the policy issued to the couple by FEMA would cover their losses despite the FEMA's argument that the damage resulted not from flood *per se*, but from extremely quick or rapid ground settlement, a hazard excluded by FEMA's policy. The court noted that no evidence was offered by any party suggesting that the couple's house would have "rapidly settled" absent the flooding. In addition, there was no activity of any person that had any effect on the house above or beyond the flood itself. Thus, FEMA was liable for the losses. *Quesada v. Director, Federal Emergency Management Agency*, 577 F.Supp. 695 (S.D.Fla.1983).

IX. MARINE INSURANCE

The standard marine insurance policy is designed to afford coverage for losses caused by "perils of the sea" which are beyond the control of the insured.

A. Coverage Allowed

A Mexican company owned a diving support vessel, insured under a marine insurance policy, which sank during a violent storm in the Bay of Campeche, approximately fifty miles off the coast of Mexico. The wreck came to rest near an oil exploratory zone. The insurers' adjuster concluded that the sunken vessel would definitely have to be removed. The insurers, however, notified the company that if the removal of the wreck was to be covered under the policy, it would have to be "compulsory by law." The Mexican port captain for the area issued an order requiring the company to post a bond to guarantee the salvaging of the vessel. The company interpreted this to mean that immediate removal of the wreck was necessary. It began salvaging operations, then sought to recover its costs from the insurers. Two insurers refused to pay, and in the lawsuit which followed, a federal district court ruled for the insurers. The company appealed to the U.S. Court of Appeals, Third Circuit, which held that a remand was necessary to determine whether the port captain's order was a removal order which was "compulsory by law." Here, the district court had applied the law incorrectly. The court stated that removal would be deemed compulsory where either a statute, regulation or governmental order directed it or where removal would be reasonable under a cost benefit analysis (cost of removal versus amount of liability which could be imposed for failing to remove the wreck). *Grupo Protexa, S.A. v. All American Marine Slip*, 954 F.2d 130 (3rd Cir.1992).

An importer of fruit obtained a marine insurance policy which covered property loss caused by "vandalism, sabotage, or malicious act[s]" and included acts "carried out for political, technical, terroristic or ideological purposes. The policy did not cover loss resulting from delay or loss of market. Subsequently, the U.S. Embassy in Santiago, Chile, received two anonymous phone calls regarding poisoned fruit. The caller said the fruit had been poisoned to protest the plight of the Chilean poor. Due to increased inspection levels, FDA and customs officials found two grapes which had been contaminated with cyanide. Consumer confidence plummeted, and the importer lost millions of dollars. It sought to recover from its insurer. Before the U.S. District Court for the Eastern District of Pennsylvania, the insurer asserted that the Chilean government had reimbursed the importer for nearly the full amount of its loss. Further, the insurer claimed that the loss arose from loss of market and that, if it incurred any liability at all it was only responsible for the damage to the two grapes which had been poisoned. The court determined that physical damage was not a prerequisite to liability, and the jury then found for the importer in the amount of $217,000, determining that terroristic acts had caused the losses. Both parties filed post trial motions, but the court denied them. It upheld the ruling in all respects. *New Market Investment Corp. v. Fireman's Fund Ins. Co.*, 774 F.Supp. 909 (E.D.Pa.1991).

A captain was operating his boat near Grand Bahama when his crew spotted an abandoned yacht. The yacht was completely submerged with only the tip of her bow above water. The captain towed the abandoned yacht to Grand Bahama where the Bahamian customs police took possession. The captain's salvage efforts were successful. An insurer had issued a policy covering the yacht's owner against loss of the vessel. The insurer retrieved the vessel and returned it to the insured. The captain sued the yacht owner and its insurer in a federal district court. The captain argued that the insurer had received a direct benefit from his salvage efforts and was liable to him for the benefit it received. The insurer filed a motion to dismiss the lawsuit, stating that under Florida law a claim could not be brought against the insurer until the injured party had first received a judgment. The district court granted the insurer's motion. The captain then appealed to the U.S. Court of Appeals, Eleventh Circuit.

The court of appeals held that the captain could sue the insurer for salvage compensation without first obtaining judgment against the owner. The captain's claim was not a claim under the insurance policy, but was rather an independent claim based upon the benefit accrued directly to the insurer because of his salvage efforts. The captain's claim against the insurer was not barred under Florida law. The district court's order dismissing the captain's claim was vacated and remanded. *Cresci v. The Yacht, "Billfisher", Official No. 517-614*, 874 F.2d 1550 (11th Cir.1989).

An insured sued its insurer after the insurer refused to pay on a claim regarding goods damaged during customs inspections. The insured was in the business of exporting agricultural and related products to the Middle East. The shipment in dispute contained frozen meat and seafood products being shipped to Saudi Arabia which were crushed and torn open during customs inspections. The insurer sent an agent of an international loss adjusting company to assess the damage. The insured was informed by the agent that the damage would be covered under the insured's "all risk" marine insurance policy. The foreign company which received the shipment in the end never paid for the undamaged portion of the shipment and the insurer never paid for the damaged portion. In fact, the insurer cancelled the insured's policy after the damage claim was submitted. Further, the insurer telexed the international loss adjusting company and told it to refrain from giving information to claimants concerning whether or not there would be coverage on a certain claim.

The insured corporation sued in a federal district court which ruled in the insurer's favor on the bad faith claim. The jury then found for the insurer on the breach of contract claim. However, it found the insurer liable on a promissory estoppel theory and awarded damages of $290,810.60. The judge reduced the damage award to $35,000. Both sides appealed to the U.S. Court of Appeals, Eighth Circuit. The appellate court partially reversed the trial court's damage award. The court held that the trial court's award of $35,000, for the damaged portion of the shipment, along with the jury's award of $55,810.60 for the third parties' refusal to pay for the undamaged portion of the shipment (since recovery from a foreign company was remote) was the correct amount of damages. With this change, the trial court's judgment was affirmed. *Midamar Corp. v. Nat'l Ben Franklin Ins. Co. of Ill.*, 898 F.2d 1333 (8th Cir.1990).

In 1984, a forty-foot aluminum cargo container packed with Sony stereo equipment was loaded aboard a ship in Japan. The ship encountered a storm on its way to Long Beach, California, which destroyed the storage container and stereo equipment. After the shipper's insurer paid it for the cargo lost, the insurer filed a lawsuit against the ship's owner for damages alleging that the loss had been caused by negligence. The ship's owner asserted the peril of the sea defense under the Carriage of Goods by the Sea Act (COGSA). When a U.S. district court ruled in favor of the ship's owner, the insurer appealed.

The U.S. Court of Appeals, Ninth Circuit, considered the insurer's argument that the ship's owner had not proven that the cargo's loss was caused by perils of the sea. The court noted that "perils of the sea" is generally defined as "a fortuitous action of elements at sea, of such force as to overcome the strength of a well-found ship or the usual precautions of good seamanship." The court cited previous federal decisions which have established that "the central inquiry is into the measure of the violence of the winds and the tempestuousness of the sea." The facts of the case established that the ship "encountered at least four waves in excess of 60 feet which rolled the vessel more than 40 degrees. A substantial number of waves between 40 and 60 feet in height battered the [ship]." The sustained winds encountered by the ship were the highest ever recorded in the area "with gusts in excess of 95 knots." Because the ship's owner had established the severe conditions necessary to establish the perils of the sea defense and the insurer had not proven any negligence on the part of the ship's owner or crew, the decision of the district court excusing the ship's owner from liability was affirmed. *Taisho Marine & Fire Ins. Co. v. M/V Sea-Land Endurance*, 815 F.2d 1270 (9th Cir.1987).

An insurer issued a liability policy on a fishing vessel. The vessel was mortgaged in the amount of $214,000. The mortgagee was named as the payee of the policy. The policy covered "perils ... of the seas" except those excluded elsewhere in the policy. A hull mortgage endorsement attached to the policy stated that "... the interest of the mortgagee shall not be impaired ... by any act [or] neglect of the mortgagor, owner, master, agent, or crew of the vessel insured by this policy, or by any failure to comply with any warranty or condition over which the mortgagee has no control or over which [it has] control but [has] not exercised such control, provided that the loss in the absence of such act or neglect or breach of warranty or condition would have been a loss recoverable under the policy." The owner of the vessel intentionally scuttled it. He then submitted a claim to the insurer seeking the full amount of coverage. The mortgagee also made a claim for the loss under the policy. The insurer refused to pay, instead seeking a court declaration that it had no liability because the sinking of the vessel was caused by an uninsured peril. A U.S. district court held for the insurer and the mortgagee appealed to the U.S. Court of Appeals, Ninth Circuit.

On appeal, the mortgagee contended that it was entitled to coverage for the vessel even though the owner intentionally sank it. The insurer contended that the "provided" clause in the hull mortgage endorsement precluded coverage for scuttling. The court of appeals reversed the district court decision, holding that the "loss" in the hull mortgage endorsement was loss or damage, not risk. Here, the loss was destruction of the ship by water. If the sinking had not been caused by the owner's act it would have been a peril of the sea which the policy covered. Without owner misconduct, the loss would have been recoverable. The "provided" clause did not take back what the main clause gave — protection to the mortgagee against scuttling. The insurer was liable to the mortgagee for the loss of the vessel. *Zurich Ins. Co. v. Wheeler*, 838 F.2d 338 (9th Cir.1988).

B. Coverage Denied

A commercial fisherman purchased a marine insurance policy with a machinery endorsement which provided that no loss to machinery would be covered unless caused by stranding, sinking, fire, or collision with another vessel. Subsequently, the vessel sprang a leak in its forward compartments. It took on water about mid-way up the engine block. However, the aft compartments remained intact, and the vessel stayed afloat. When the fisherman sought coverage for the damage, a lawsuit ensued. The case came before a New Jersey federal district court. The fisherman acknowledged that the vessel had not sunk, but he claimed that it was sinking when the damage occurred. The court disagreed. It stated that the vessel was merely "taking on water" or flooding, and that it was not even in the process of sinking. Further, "sunk" was generally understood to mean that the object had gone to the bottom or that it had sunk as far as possible. The court granted summary judgment to the insurer, and held that no coverage existed. *DeRose v. Albany Ins. Co.*, 792 F.Supp. 973 (D.N.J.1992).

A boat company owned two vessels which were out of service and moored at a dock in Louisiana. The boats were insured under a policy with a "named perils" clause, which provided coverage for, among other things, perils of the seas and assailing thieves. The boats vanished one evening without a trace of force or thievery. The water in the canal was only about four feet deep, so it was determined the vessels could not have sunk. The boat company sought coverage from its insurer, and when relief was denied, it sued in a federal district court. The court ruled for the insurer, and the boat company appealed to the U.S. Court of Appeals, Fifth Circuit.

The appellate court first stated that when insurance is provided by a named-perils clause, the initial burden is on the insured to prove that the loss occurred by the named peril. Since the boats were out of service, no presumption of seaworthiness could be extended to them. The court further held that theft from a dock was not covered under either the "perils of the sea" clause, or the "assailing thieves" clause. Not only had the boat company not shown that the vessels had been stolen, but even if they had been, the "assailing thieves" clause extended only to theft of personal property on vessels and not theft of the vessels themselves. The court affirmed the trial court's decision, denying coverage. *Opera Boats, Inc. v. La Reunion Francaise*, 893 F.2d 103 (5th Cir.1990).

An insured, who was an importer of women's apparel, obtained a marine cargo insurance policy, effective May 16, 1985. The policy contained a warehouse coverage endorsement which extended coverage to goods temporarily detained in stores and warehouses within the U.S. On August 3, 1985, the insured sustained water damage to goods being stored at its premises and sought reimbursement from its insurer. The insurer denied coverage, arguing that because the crates had been shipped to the insured prior to May 16, 1985, the policy did not afford coverage. The trial court held for the insurer. The insured appealed. The New York Supreme Court, Appellate Division, stated that the warehouse endorsement only extended to the goods insured by the policy and because these goods were originally shipped before the policy went into effect they were not insured. It thus affirmed the trial court's decision. *Pali Fashions, Inc. v. New Hampshire Ins. Co.*, 551 N.Y.S.2d 215 (A.D.1st Dep't 1990).

The owners of a yacht purchased an insurance policy on it which contained navigational limits as to where the yacht could be used, and a chartering endorsement which allowed the insureds to day-charter the yacht for not more than five days per year. There was also a trip endorsement which extended the navigational limits for a five-month period. The insureds chartered the yacht to a sailing school for five months, during which time the yacht was apparently lost at sea. When the insureds sought coverage, the insurer sued to obtain a declaration that the policy was void. A New York federal district court noted that the marine policy clearly and unambiguously prohibited charters of longer than a day. Thus, the five-month charter breached the policy conditions. Even though the insureds argued that the insurer knew of the charter and even though the trip endorsement covered the same dates as the charter agreement, such was not enough to create an ambiguity in the policy. The policy stated that only by obtaining written permission could the insureds charter the yacht for more than a day and still remain covered for loss. The court granted the insurer's motion on the pleadings. *Commercial Union Ins. Co. v. Horne*, 787 F.Supp. 337 (S.D.N.Y.1992).

X. "DRAM SHOP" LIABILITY

At least one state supreme court has ruled that under compulsory "dramshop" insurance systems, coverage must be provided only to innocent third-party victims of the negligence of intoxicated tavern patrons. Other courts have found coverage for other reasons.

A Texas man owned a corporation where he employed himself as general manager and was responsible for the employment, training and termination of employees at a local bar. He obtained an insurance policy which excluded liability for the sale of liquor to a minor or anyone who is under the influence. The corporation, the corporate owner, and the bar were sued alleging negligent sale of liquor to a minor under the influence of alcohol by an employee who was under age and improperly trained. The insurer instituted the present action seeking a determination of its liability to defend. The trial court granted summary judgment to the insurer and the insured appealed to the Court of Appeals of Texas.

On appeal, the court noted that every allegation in the complaint contained the selling or serving of alcoholic beverages to a minor or person under the influence of alcohol. The insured asserted that the insurer was obligated to defend because of the potential for his personal liability under the policy terms due to employment matters. The court, however, found that there were no alternative grounds of negligence upon which the trial court could possibly have found negligence. Therefore, since the policy excluded coverage for selling or serving of alcoholic beverages to minors and those under the influence of alcohol, the insurer was entitled to judgment as a matter of law. The appellate court affirmed the decision of the trial court. *Thornhill v. Houston General Lloyds*, 802 S.W.2d 127 (Tex.App. 1991).

An uninsured South Dakota man became intoxicated and caused a car accident in which a girl was injured. The girl sued the fraternal lodge which had allegedly served alcohol to the man. The parties came to a settlement which called for payment of $359,000 by the lodge's liability insurer and two auto liability insurers. The two insurers that had paid out uninsured motorist benefits kept their subrogation rights. These insurers then sought a declaratory judgment in a South Dakota trial court that the lodge's comprehensive general liability insurer indemnify them. After the trial court dismissed the subrogated insurers' claim, they appealed to the Supreme Court of South Dakota. On appeal, the lodge's liability insurer maintained that its policy did not apply because it excluded coverage for bodily injury or property damage by organizations engaged in the business of selling or serving alcohol. The other insurers argued that the liability policy did apply, because the lodge was a nonprofit corporation, and therefore could not be "engaged in the business" of selling or serving alcohol. The supreme court held that the exclusionary clause in the policy was unambiguous and precluded coverage for the underlying lawsuit. The court noted that most of the lodge's income was generated by its alcohol sales, that it paid state sales tax on its bar operations and had state and city liquor licenses. The supreme court affirmed the trial court's decision that the lodge's liability insurer had no duty to indemnify the other insurers. *McGriff v. U.S. Fire Ins. Co.*, 436 N.W.2d 859 (S.D.1989).

After drinking at a bar, a Montana man was involved in a car accident, suffered a broken neck and became quadriplegic. He sued the bar owner in a Montana trial court for his injuries, alleging negligence in selling him alcohol. The bar owner was insured under a policy which excluded coverage for selling alcoholic beverages. The court ruled in favor of the insurer and the injured party appealed to the Montana Supreme Court. The supreme court rejected the injured party's argument that the bar owner's liability was based on negligence as distinguished from serving alcohol. Coverage was specifically excluded under the policy. The supreme court upheld the trial court's decision for the insurer. *Sheffield Ins. v. Lighthouse Properties*, 763 P.2d 669 (Mont.1988).

An Oregon grocery store owner requested full coverage. The policy accepted excluded coverage for the sale of alcohol. A minor purchased alcohol from the store and was later involved in an accident in which another person was killed. The decedent's estate filed a wrongful death action against the insured and won a judgment of $675,000. The insured instituted a separate action to estop the insurer from denying coverage. After a jury found for the insured, the trial court granted the insurer's motion for judgment notwithstanding the verdict. The insured appealed to the Court of Appeals of Oregon. The appellate court affirmed the decision of the trial court, noting that the insurer had no duty to ensure that the owner was covered for the negligent sale of alcohol. *DeJong v. Mutual of Enumclaw*, 800 P.2d 313 (Or.App.1990).

A tavern in West Virginia was sued by a man who was injured in an automobile accident with an intoxicated patron of the tavern. The tavern filed suit in a U.S. district court seeking a declaration of coverage from its business insurer. The insurer moved for summary judgment because of an exclusionary clause which precluded coverage for third party injuries when the insured was in the business of selling alcohol. The tavern and its insurer disagreed over whether the policy was ambiguous and therefore needing a construction from the court. The insurer argued that while one clause might have been difficult, the meaning could be found elsewhere in the contract. The general rule is that insurers must make exclusionary clauses plain, clear and conspicuous. The court found the clause headed "Host Liquor Liability Coverage" to be very difficult but not ambiguous. The clear meaning of this clause could also easily be found in several other places. Further, even a very liberal court construction of ambiguous clauses will not allow the distortion of plain contract language. The insurer's motion for summary judgment was granted. *Zurich Ins. Co. v. Uptowner Inns, Inc.*, 740 F.Supp. 404 (S.D.W.Va.1990).

A Hawaii bar had a policy which covered injuries arising out of the "selling, serving or giving of alcoholic beverages." An intoxicated patron was asked to leave the bar after he became obnoxious. He refused to leave and started a fight with a bar employee. The patron was allegedly injured and sued both the bar and the employee. The bar sought defense for itself and the employee from its insurer which refused coverage. The insurer sought a declaration from a Hawaii federal district court that it was not obligated to defend and/or indemnify the bar or its employee.

The insurer asserted that it did not have to defend the bar because the patron's injuries did not arise out of the bar's selling, serving or giving of any alcoholic beverages. It also asserted that it had no duty to defend the employee. The court accepted the second argument stating that the policy did not cover employees. However, the court rejected the insurer's first argument because state law did not permit a bar to knowingly allow an intoxicated patron to remain in the bar. State law also required insurers to defend insureds against covered claims as well as noncovered claims. Lastly, the court stated that if the employee was acting within the scope of his employment, he would be able to recover his defense costs from the bar. The bar in turn would be able to recover from the insurer. Therefore, the insurer was required to defend the bar in the patron's lawsuit but not required to defend the employee. *CIE Serv. Corp. v. W.T.P.*, 690 F.Supp. 910 (D.Hawaii 1988).

A nineteen-year-old man became intoxicated at a bar and was injured when his truck left the road. He sued the bar in a state trial court, alleging that the bar coerced him into drinking several alcoholic beverages while he was under the influence of alcohol. The man asserted that the drinks arrived at his table even though he had not ordered them. The trial court held for the bar and the man appealed to the Hawaii Supreme Court. At issue was whether the bar owed a duty to the man under the state dramshop law. The man argued that the bar was liable because he was unsophisticated and because he was intimidated and coerced into drinking too much by the bar's employees. He asserted that the intimidation and manipulation were affirmative acts which increased his peril. The bar argued that it should have no duty to determine the sophistication of its customers. The supreme court held that the bar owed a duty to avoid affirmative acts which increased the peril to an intoxicated customer. However, in the absence of harm to an innocent third party, serving liquor to an intoxicated customer was not actionable. State dramshop laws did not require bars to determine their customers' sophistication. The trial court decision was upheld and the bar was not liable for the injuries to the man. *Feliciano v. Waikiki Deep Water Inc.*, 752 P.2d 1076 (Hawaii 1988).

A Connecticut boy was killed when he left a friend's graduation party. He was struck by a car driven by a minor driver who had also attended the party. The driver was seen drunk and staggering into his car. The boy's father sued, in a Connecticut trial court, the friend's parents who hosted the party. He alleged the hosts were guilty of violating the state dramshop act. He also sued under common law negligence and reckless and wanton misconduct theories. The host asked the trial court to strike the portion of the complaint that alleged negligent serving of alcohol. The motion was granted and the case was submitted to the jury which held for the host. The father appealed to the Connecticut Supreme Court.

At issue on appeal was whether the trial court should have stricken the allegation of negligent serving of alcohol to minors who were known to be intoxicated. Previous Connecticut cases held that no cause of action existed against one who furnished liquor to a person who voluntarily became intoxicated and injured another person. These holdings were due to the fact that the cause of the intoxication was not the furnishing of the liquor but the consumption of it. However, the supreme court noted that recent legislative acts provide that those who serve liquor to minors are criminally liable. It held that minors should not be held to assume the same responsibility as adults. It overruled the previous decisions which granted immunity to social hosts. The trial court's striking of the negligent serving of alcohol to minors was inappropriate and warranted a new trial. *Ely v. Murphy*, 540 A.2d 54 (Conn.1988).

A motorcyclist was killed after leaving a party at a friend's house. The motorcyclist's wife sued the friend in a Washington trial court for wrongful death. She alleged that the friend negligently furnished alcohol to her husband while he was intoxicated. The court held that there was no social host liability in Washington. The wife appealed to the Washington Court of Appeals which also held for the friend. The wife then appealed to the Washington Supreme Court. She argued for the need to compensate victims injured by drunk drivers. Imposing social host liability would reduce drunk driving by requiring hosts to use greater care in serving alcohol. The friend argued that such a duty would impose substantial financial liability on social hosts. The supreme court upheld the lower court decisions. It noted that the implications required a balancing of costs and benefits to the public. This balancing should be done by the state legislature. The supreme court also observed that the legislature had previously enacted a dramshop act which imposed civil liability on social hosts but later repealed the act. This indicated a legislative disapproval of social host liability. The friend was not liable. *Burkhart v. Harrod*, 755 P.2d 759 (Wash.1988).

A bouncer for a drinking and eating establishment in Massachusetts used force in ejecting a forty-five-year-old customer because the customer had failed to produce identification which proved his age. The ejection resulted in injuries and a subsequent lawsuit against the business. The business brought a separate action against its liquor liability insurer and sought a declaration that its insurer had a duty to defend the business in the lawsuit and indemnify it for any loss. A state court granted summary judgment to the insurer, and the business appealed to the Supreme Judicial Court of Massachusetts.

The policy provided coverage for the negligent sale, distribution, or serving of alcohol. The complaint did not state that the patron had been drinking; thus, the insurer asserted that the injuries were not covered under the policy. It also asserted that the injuries were excluded because they were intentional. The business argued that reasonable force was allowed due to the nature of the business, and that the use of excessive force was negligent, not intentional. The court stated that even if it assumed that force could be used negligently, the complaint at most concerned "collateral activities" to the sale of alcohol. The complaint's allegations were ruled to be insufficient to state a claim which could be insured. Further, the language of this policy was created by the legislature in an act which mandated liquor liability coverage. Therefore, the language was to be construed more narrowly. The court held that this incident was not the type intended by the legislature to be insured. Judgment for the insurer was affirmed. *Jimmy's Diner, Inc. v. Liquor Liability Joint Underwriting Ass'n of Massachusetts*, 571 N.E.2d 4 (Mass.1991).

XI. TITLE INSURANCE

Most title insurers provide policies covering the risk that a title may be found to contain defects. Coverage is often provided up to the appraised value of the property.

Various corporations operated chemical processing plants on a thirty acre stretch of property in Santa Clara County for a number of years. Underground tanks, pumps and pipelines were used to store, handle and dispose of certain hazardous substances. Eventually, the soil and groundwater became contaminated. The property was purchased by an investment company which subsequently sold several lots to an apartment development company. The company purchased title insurance for the lots, but apparently did not learn that the property was contaminated. When the company discovered the hazardous substances, it incurred costs for the removal of the environmental contamination. It then sought reimbursement from its title insurer. The insurer denied coverage. The insured sued its insurer, but the state trial court dismissed the complaint. The insured appealed to the California Court of Appeal, Sixth District. On appeal, the court noted that title insurance was designed to cover only matters which affected an insured's title. Where the state of the title was other than represented by the policy so as to cause a loss to the insured, the policy would reimburse for that loss. Here, however, the court stated that the presence of hazardous substances on the property did not constitute an encumbrance on the title. The contamination, while it may have had an effect on the marketability of the land, did not affect the title to the property. As such, the policy did not cover the costs of the environmental cleanup and the trial court had correctly dismissed the action against the insurer. *Lick Mill Creek Apartments v. Chicago Title Ins. Co.*, 283 Cal.Rptr. 231 (Cal.App.6th Dist. 1991).

An insurer examined the title to property located in Manhattan and certified it as marketable. The insurer then issued title insurance to the buyer. At the closing, the deed was given to an agent of the insurer for recording. The agent failed to record the deed for four months. One month after closing, the insured contracted to sell the property. Later, the contract was cancelled when the parties learned that the original seller had reconveyed the property by deed to another party. This second deed was recorded prior to that of the insured. The insurer brought an action on behalf of the insured to set aside the second deed. The court upheld the second deed. The insured then brought suit against the insurer for negligence in failing to properly perform its obligations and breach of contract for failing to record the deed timely. An arbitrator dismissed the contract cause of action beyond the point where it exceeded the face value of the policy, since the insurer's liability could not be enlarged beyond the terms of the contract. The arbitrator also dismissed the negligence cause of action.

On appeal to the New York Supreme Court, Appellate Division, the insured argued that the insurer's failure to properly record the deed was a service outside the scope of the policy and therefore damages arising out of the insurer's negligence would not be limited to the face value of the policy. The insurer argued that its policy contained a merger clause which restricted any other services rendered in connection with the policy to the terms and conditions of the policy. Because recording the title was connected to the issuance of the policy, the insurer claimed its liability was limited to the value of the policy. The supreme court disagreed, finding the policy's reference to "other services" vague. Since clauses purporting to limit liability are strictly construed against the insurer, the court held that the policy's merger clause did not bar a claim for negligent performance of services outside the scope of the policy. It also held that the contract had been breached. *Cruz v. Commonwealth Land Title Ins. Co.*, 556 N.Y.S.2d 270 (A.D. 1st Dep't 1990).

A Georgia landowner purchased two tracts of land. A title insurance policy was issued covering the tracts. The policy insured the landowner against loss or damage if the title proved to be unmarketable. The policy excluded coverage for defects in the survey. When the landowner began to develop the tracts, he discovered that the eastern and western boundaries of the property were twenty feet shorter than described in the deed. These boundaries, however, were fixed by an ascertained boundary, a public alley. The landowner sued the insurer in a Georgia trial court to recover under the policy for loss of acreage. After the trial court entered summary judgment for the insurer, the landowner appealed to the Court of Appeals of Georgia.

On appeal, the landowner argued that the insurer had agreed to insure the length of the boundary lines from the legal description. The court of appeals held that the title insurance policy insured against loss or damage from unmarketable title. The policy, however, did not cover losses resulting from shorter call lines than the legal description. The ascertained boundaries in the legal description controlled over the courses and distances. The policy did not cover surveying defects. The court of appeals affirmed the lower court's decision. *Lynburn Enterprises, Inc. v. Lawyers Title Ins. Corp.*, 382 S.E.2d 599 (Ga.App.1989).

A Connecticut company agreed to sell seventy-eight dwelling units at two locations. The property was insured under a title policy. The policy excluded coverage for defects, liens, encumbrances, adverse claims and other matters resulting in no loss or damage or which were agreed to or assumed by the insured. The day before the closing, the buyers discovered that the legal description contained in the sales contract and the proposed deed included more property than the buyers had intended to purchase and the sellers had intended to sell. At the closing, neither the buyers nor their attorneys mentioned the discovery of the extra property. The sellers provided the buyers with a warranty deed that contained the same property description as the sales contract. The buyers then notified the title insurer that title to a portion of the property that it had insured was held by another person. The buyers demanded reimbursement for the loss of the property. The insurer denied the claim. The buyers sued the insurer in a Connecticut trial court which found for the insurer. The buyers appealed and the case was transferred to the Supreme Court of Connecticut.

The supreme court held that the buyers did not suffer compensable loss under the policy. The sales contract and warranty deed included more property than the buyers had intended to buy. There was no evidence to suggest that the property actually sold to the buyers had a value less than the purchase price. The court also noted that the buyers had discovered the discrepancy prior to closing, yet they agreed to receive the defective deed. The buyers were precluded from recovering damages. *Cohen v. Security Title and Guar. Co.*, 562 A.2d 510 (Conn.1989).

A Texas real estate partnership purchased an apartment building and secured a title insurance policy on the property. Almost four years later the partnership obtained a purchase offer, but the prospective buyer discovered an easement and canceled the deal. The title insurer acknowledged its liability to the partnership for loss caused by the title defect, which their appraiser valued at $26,000. The partnership then reduced its sales price by that amount but secured no further offers. The title insurer refused to pay damages in excess of their $26,000 appraised value of the easement. Claiming that the easement made the property unmarketable, the partnership sued the insurer in a Texas trial court under the Texas Deceptive Trade Practices, Consumer Protection Act (DTPA). The partnership claimed that the insurer failed to inform it about the easement and that the insurer had a duty to disclose title defects. The trial court ruled for the partnership, stating that the insurer's failure to disclose the easement was false, misleading and deceptive under the DTPA. Under the statute, the court awarded damages of $80,000, the decline in fair market value of the property, plus $24,000 for other costs and trebled the damages for a total recovery of $312,000 plus interest and attorney's fees. The insurer appealed to the Texas Court of Appeals, Texarkana. The court noted that title insurers had a duty to indemnify insureds against title defect losses, but had no duty to examine or disclose title defects. Title insurers had a duty distinct from that of title abstractors and recovery against title insurers was limited to the actual amount of loss proven by the title defect. In this case, the title insurer had no knowledge of the easement and could not be liable for false, misleading or deceptive trade practices. There was no evidence that the title insurer had made any special representation to the partnership leading to any reliance apart from the title policy. The court reversed the trial court's decision and remanded the case for consideration of the proper damages. *Stewart Title Guar. Co. v. Cheatham*, 764 S.W.2d 315 (Tex.App.1988).

The federal government discovered that a person recently convicted of drug conspiracy and money laundering still retained a substantial equitable interest in a piece of property. As a result, it sought to claim the property. Before it could do so, the property and its mortgage were transferred to another person insured by a title insurer. A federal trial court set aside the mortgage in favor of the government, holding that the insured knew that the transfer was fraudulent. The insured then instituted this title insurance action, seeking recovery on the basis that the insurer breached its mortgage guarantee on the property. The trial court dismissed the complaint and the insured appealed. The New York Supreme Court, Appellate Division, affirmed the dismissal stating that because the insured knew and suppressed the fact that the transfer of the property was done fraudulently, the contract with the title insurer was void and no recovery under the contract could be had as a result. *Schultz Management v. Title Guaranty Co.*, 551 N.Y.S.2d 527 (A.D.1st Dep't 1990).

In December 1979, a New Jersey developer contracted to purchase property. The price was to be determined on a per acre basis. The contract provided that the developer would obtain roughly nineteen acres at $16,000 per acre. The final price would be adjusted for any deviation in the acreage. Even though a surveyor had surveyed the property in 1975, the developer requested an updated survey. The developer then purchased a title insurance policy which guaranteed a good and marketable title to the property. On the closing date the developer called the surveyor and received oral confirmation that the 1979 update survey supported the results of the 1975 survey. The closing agreement was based on the sale of eighteen acres of land. The seller's attorney used the description in the 1975 survey in preparing the deed. The 1975 survey had a different description and total acreage than that contained in the deed granted to the seller.

In 1985, the developer sought to purchase lots adjacent to the property acquired in 1979. He hired a surveyor to survey the new property and the property acquired in 1979. The new survey revealed that the developer only owned 12.4 acres, not eighteen acres. The developer then sued the title insurer in a New Jersey trial court for failing to convey a clear and marketable title. The developer sought to recover the difference between the price paid and the actual value of the property. The trial judge determined that the loss of acreage was within the coverage of the title policy and awarded the developer $88,000. The title insurer appealed to the New Jersey Superior Court, Appellate Division. The appellate court observed that the purpose of title insurance is to indemnify the insured against loss or defects in the title. It affirmed the trial court's decision that the title insurer guaranteed the developer a good and marketable title to the property. Because the developer had demonstrated that the title was defective and unmarketable, the title insurer was liable for the difference. *Walker Rogge v. Chelsea Title & Guar.*, 536 A.2d 1309 (N.J.Super.A.D.1988).

A title insurer issued a "preliminary report" erroneously stating that certain property was encumbered by only one deed of trust. The property was in fact encumbered by two such deeds. Although they never saw this preliminary report, a group of creditors advanced a $72,000 loan secured by what was allegedly a second deed of trust on the property. After this loan transaction was completed, the title insurer issued a standard policy to the creditors, insuring the property as being subject to only one prior deed of trust. Shortly thereafter, the borrower defaulted on the $72,000 loan. When the creditors attempted to foreclose, it was discovered that their interest was third in priority rather than second. The title insurer promptly took action to prevent the creditors' interest from becoming impaired. Although the creditors recovered their full principal balance, interest and expenses on the $72,000 loan, they sued the title insurer, claiming it had breached its duty to diligently search the title records. The Superior Court, Marin County, ruled against the creditors. On appeal by the creditors, the California Court of Appeal, First District, rejected the argument that liability could be based upon the title insurer's preliminary report, pointing out that none of the creditors had seen or relied upon the preliminary report before making the loan. It therefore upheld the ruling absolving the title insurer from liability. *Lawrence v. Chicago Title Ins. Co.*, 237 Cal.Rptr. 264 (App.1st Dist.1987).

The purchaser of a condominium sought to obtain title insurance to protect his interests. His attorney applied for a title commitment which was issued by the insurer. The letter from the insurer stated that the previous mortgage would have to be paid off and canceled before full coverage would be available. The purchaser gave an endorsed check to his attorney so that the mortgage could be paid. However, the attorney never paid the mortgage. After misappropriating the funds, he was convicted and disbarred. Meanwhile, the mortgagee sought to foreclose because no one was paying the debt. In the lawsuit which followed, the trial court held that the title insurer had to pay the outstanding mortgage. The insurer appealed to the Superior Court of New Jersey, Appellate Division. On appeal, it contended that the trial court had erred in considering the purchaser's attorney to be its agent. The court agreed. The attorney was only the purchaser's agent. Accordingly, any loss had to be imposed on the purchaser because he was the one who dealt with the wrongdoer. The court held that the title insurer was not liable for the amount owed on the mortgage and reversed the trial court's decision. *Sears Mortgage Co. v. Rose*, 607 A.2d 1327 (N.J.Super.A.D.1992).

A corporation loaned $15,000 to the purchaser of a home. It took back a first lien, and then purchased a mortgagee's title insurance policy from an insurer. The sellers of the house received a second lien on the property. When the buyer defaulted on both liens, the sellers sued the president of the corporation for fraud involving title to real property. The corporation was neither sued nor served. This lawsuit was settled. Subsequently, the corporation filed suit against its insurer, seeking to recover the attorney's fees it had expended in the underlying suit. After a bench trial, the court ruled for the insurer; the corporation appealed to the Court of Appeals of Texas. On appeal, the corporation asserted that because it had answered the complaint, and because the $15,000 loan it had made had been challenged, it was the true defendant in the underlying suit, and thus entitled to attorney's fees. The court, however, disagreed. First, the corporation was not a named party in the settled suit. Second, the cause of action against the president was for fraud, which was excluded under the policy. Finally, the fact that the insurer had filed an answer in the prior lawsuit to avoid any possible default judgment did not amount to a waiver of its assertions of noncoverage. The court affirmed the trial court's ruling in favor of the insurer. *Daca, Inc. v. Commonwealth Land Title Ins. Co.*, 822 S.W.2d 360 (Tex.App.1992).

A couple was considering the purchase of real property and obtained a title insurance binder. The binder contained two exclusions: for claims based on possession and not shown by the public records, and for boundary line disputes which could be revealed by an accurate survey. The couple then paid for a survey which was to be done by an outside company which was to have reported any defects to the insurer. The insurer, however, failed to report any defects to the couple. After they purchased the property, an adjoining land owner asserted a claim to a portion of the property. The couple brought suit seeking to quiet title, and faced an identical counterclaim brought by the adjoining landowner. The insurer refused to defend the counterclaim. A separate claim was then brought by the couple against the insurer asserting breach of contract and negligent misrepresentation. A trial court dismissed the claims, and the couple appealed to the District Court of Appeal of Florida. The breach of contract claim was based on the insurer's failure to defend. Even though the action was initially brought by the insureds, the addition of the counterclaim was held by the court to give rise to a duty to defend. On the negligent misrepresentation claim, the insurer argued that a tort claim may not be founded on a faulty search of records. The court agreed, but held that the insurer and the surveyor were in contractual privity; tort liability may therefore be based on fraud, because a title insurer has a duty to disclose all known defects. The dismissal was reversed, and the claims were scheduled for trial. *Crawford v. Safeco Title Ins. Co.*, 585 So.2d 952 (Fla.App.1 Dist.1991).

XII. STATE AND LOCAL GOVERNMENT LIABILITY

Although state and local governments are often immune from lawsuits under the doctrine of sovereign immunity, in the majority of states a governmental unit is deemed to have waived its immunity to the extent of any insurance it may have purchased.

A man filed a civil rights complaint in a federal district court against an Illinois city and the police officers who arrested him. He alleged that the officers had used excessive force during the arrest and that the city had allowed the violations. When the city sought defense from its primary general liability insurer, the general insurer refused to defend either the officers or the city. The city then procured defense from its excess insurer which settled the lawsuit. The excess insurer then sought a declaration in a federal district court that the city's general liability insurer had to reimburse it for defending the police officers and the city. The district court found that the general liability insurer was not obligated to defend. The excess insurer appealed to the U.S. Court of Appeals, Seventh Circuit.

On appeal, the excess insurer pointed to an endorsement in the general liability insurance policy which covered employees acting within the scope of their employment. The general liability insurer maintained that the policy endorsement excluded any claim arising out of the wilful misconduct of a policeman. The court of appeals affirmed the district court's decision, concluding that the man's injuries were expected or intended by the officers. The officers should have reasonably anticipated his injuries, and coverage under the general insurer's policy was therefore excluded. The court held that the general liability insurer also had no duty to reimburse the excess insurer for the city's defense. Since the arrested man's complaint alleged that the city had been reckless, his injuries were expected and therefore excluded by the policy. The court upheld the district court's decision, finding that the general insurer was under no duty to defend the police officers or the city. *Calvert Ins. Co. v. Western Ins. Co.*, 874 F.2d 396 (7th Cir.1989).

An Indiana city's newly elected mayor discharged several employees based upon their political affiliation. The discharged employees filed a complaint in a federal district court alleging violations of their constitutional rights. The court granted summary judgment in favor of the employees concluding that they had been deprived of their constitutional rights under the First and Fourteenth Amendments. The city sought indemnification from its insurer. The insurer denied coverage and the city filed a complaint in an Indiana trial court. The trial court granted summary judgment to the insurer and the city appealed to the Court of Appeals of Indiana.

On appeal, the city contended that the mayor's actions were not intended to deprive the employees of their constitutional rights and, therefore, the policy exclusion did not apply. The court, however, noted that the federal district court had granted summary judgment in favor of the discharged employees. In order to grant summary judgment the federal court must have found the mayor's acts to be intentional acts. Therefore, the court found that the policy exclusion for intentional acts should be upheld and it denied coverage to the city. *City of Muncie v. United Nat'l Ins. Co.*, 564 N.E.2d 979 (Ind.App.4th Dist.1991).

The city of Laguna Beach purchased two comprehensive general liability policies from an insurer. The policies stated that coverage would be provided for property damage liability imposed by law. The policies stated that they did not provide coverage for inverse condemnation (a form of eminent domain). Subsequently, heavy rains started a landslide which caused heavy damage to two residences. The owners brought suit against the city. Meanwhile, the city retained various expert geotechnicians to stabilize and reconstruct the slide area. The cost was $830,000. The jury returned a verdict against the city on the liability issue of inverse condemnation. The city then appealed and entered into settlement negotiations with the residence owners. It managed to settle with both owners. It then sued the insurer, seeking coverage under its contract and seeking reimbursement for the "mitigation expenses" it incurred in fixing the slide area. The trial court held that the city was entitled to coverage under the policy, but could not recover its "mitigation expenses." Both parties appealed to the Court of Appeal, Fourth District.

On appeal, the court noted that the policies clearly and unambiguously excluded coverage for inverse condemnation. Further, although the city had settled its claim with the residence owners, a trial had occurred and judgment had been rendered under an inverse condemnation theory. The court then noted that the "mitigation expenses" were also not recoverable because there had been no damage since the original slide had occurred; thus, there was not any damage to mitigate. The court affirmed in part and reversed in part, ruling for the insurer in all respects. *City of Laguna Beach v. Mead Reinsurance Corp.*, 276 Cal.Rptr. 438 (Cal.App.4th Dist.1990).

A former town clerk sued a Louisiana town for wrongful discharge. The town asked the clerk to resign upon recommendation of the district attorney. After she refused to resign, she was indicted on theft and malfeasance counts relating to her co-signing checks on town accounts during her employment. The clerk was found not guilty on all counts. She then sued the town and its general liability insurer in a Louisiana trial court, alleging that her dismissal had been arbitrary and capricious. She sought reimbursement of attorney's fees, back wages and damages for mental anguish, as well as reinstatement with full benefits. The trial court granted the insurer's summary judgment motion. The clerk appealed to the Louisiana Court of Appeal. On appeal, the insurer maintained that two policy exclusions precluded coverage for the clerk's injuries. The court of appeal agreed, and affirmed the lower court's decision. It held that because both exclusions excluded coverage for employee injuries arising out of their employment, the insurer was not liable. The court concluded that since the clerk's allegations originated from her employment and not from subsequent actions as a city employee, her injuries also arose from her employment. The insurer was dismissed from the lawsuit. *Watson v. Town of Arcadia*, 542 So.2d 1168 (La.App.2d Cir.1989).

A county sheriff's office purchased an insurance policy for comprehensive liability. The policy contained an exclusion which provided that the insurance did not apply to "any claims made by anyone related to their employment ... by [the sheriff's office]." Subsequently, a sheriff's deputy was accidentally shot by a fellow officer during a detectives meeting. The injured deputy sought coverage under the policy, which the insurer denied. A Florida trial court granted summary judgment to the deputy, and the insurer appealed to the District Court of Appeal. On appeal, the insurer contended that the language of the exclusion was clear and unambiguous. Since the deputy was "anyone" and since he admitted that he had been shot by a fellow officer during the course of his employment, the policy did not provide coverage. The appellate court agreed with the insurer that the exclusion applied. The use of "anyone" rather than "any employee" in the exclusion suggested that the insurer wanted to exclude more than just employer-employee claims; it also wanted to exclude employee-employee claims like the one present in this case. The court reversed the decision of the trial court and held for the insurer. *Great Global Assurance Co. v. Shoemaker*, 599 So.2d 1036 (Fla.App.4th Dist.1992).

The city of Louisville maintained a health benefits plan for its employees and their family members. Ten insureds were involved in separate accidents, unrelated to their work for the city. Their medical expenses were paid by their no-fault insurers. They then sought coverage from the city. The city's plan had a coordination of benefits clause which made payment by the city contingent upon an absence of other medical benefits, except those from an individual policy. Further, a subrogation clause allowed the city to recover amounts paid to the insureds by the parties responsible for the injuries. When the city denied coverage, the insureds sued. The trial court ruled in their favor, and the city appealed. On appeal to the Kentucky Court of Appeals, the court noted that since the plan excepted from contingency payments insurance which was owned individually, and since the no-fault policies which had provided coverage were individually owned, the city could not avoid making payments under its plan. Further, since the subrogation clause only allowed recovery from the parties who caused the injuries, the city could not attempt to recover its payments from the no-fault insurers. The trial court's decision was affirmed. *City of Louisville v. McDonald*, 819 S.W.2d 319 (Ky.App.1991).

A Washington City purchased an errors and omissions policy from an insurer which provided coverage for all loss from any claim or suit for wrongful acts made against the city during the life of the policy. Loss was defined as any amount the city was obligated to pay a claimant. While the policy was in effect, a firefighter died while fighting a fire. His wife sued the city for negligence. The insurer denied coverage, asserting, among other exclusions, one which excluded liability for payment of damages arising from, or caused by, death. The trial court granted summary judgment to the insurer, and the city appealed. On appeal to the Court of Appeals of Washington, the city argued that by so limiting the coverage, the insurer was really providing no coverage at all. The insurer explained that, unlike a general liability policy, an errors and omissions policy is intended to insure against third party claims for misfeasance and malfeasance of public officers which result in financial loss. The court sided with the insurer. Here, the damage claim against the city clearly arose out of the death of the firefighter. Thus, the insurer was held not liable. *City of Everett v. American Empire Surplus Lines Ins. Co.*, 823 P.2d 1112 (Wash.App.1991).

A Minnesota boy tunneled into a snow drift in the back of a parking lot. The boy was struck and seriously injured by a county snowplow which was clearing the lot. He sought to recover basic economic loss benefits from the county's insurer. The insurer denied coverage and the boy sued it in a Minnesota trial court. The trial court held that the boy's injuries arose out of the use of the snowplow; thus the county's insurer would have to provide coverage. The insurer appealed but the appeals court affirmed the trial court decision. It held that basic economic loss benefits should be provided because the boy suffered a loss through injury arising out of the use of a motor vehicle. Thus, the county's insurer was required to provide basic economic loss benefits to the boy. *Anderson v. St. Paul Fire & Marine Ins.*, 427 N.W.2d 749 (Minn.App.1988).

A New York county sought indemnification from its liability insurer for a negligence suit brought as a result of a slip and fall on a sidewalk adjacent to the county library. The library's policy insured its premises, but specifically excluded liability relating to maintenance and operation of public streets and sidewalks. The New York Supreme Court, Appellate Division, dismissed the claim, stating that sidewalks had to be specifically included in the meaning of premises. *Estate of Belmar v. County of Onondaga*, 537 N.Y.S.2d 353 (A.D.4th Dep't 1989).

A Michigan city had a program to help control insects and pests, which included periodic spraying of chemicals. During one session of spraying, the chemical entered a man's window and injured him. The man brought suit against the city, which tendered its defense to its liability insurer. The insurer cited a pollution exclusion clause and sought a declaration that it had no duty to defend the city. A trial court agreed with the insurer, but was reversed on appeal. The case was then consolidated with similar cases and heard by the Supreme Court of Michigan. The exclusionary clause disclaimed liability arising from pollution, unless the pollution was sudden and accidental. The city argued that although the release of the chemical into the atmosphere was deliberate, its release into an area where it could cause harm was accidental. The court held that the exclusionary clause and exception thereto addressed the release into the atmosphere, and that the pollutant's migration after its release was irrelevant. Despite a dissent which argued that the chemicals did not constitute a pollutant, the decision of the court of appeals was reversed. The insurer was held to have no duty to defend or indemnify the city. *Protective National Ins. Co. of Omaha v. City of Woodhaven*, 476 N.W.2d 374 (Mich.1991).

An insurer issued a commercial general liability policy to a city, which contained a pollution exclusion clause, denying coverage for bodily injury arising out of the discharge of pollutants. The city then sprayed a malathion mixture from a vehicle as an insecticide. Malathion is widely used throughout the United States and has been approved by the EPA as an insecticide of low mammalian toxicity which does not pollute the environment. Two city residents claimed that they suffered personal injuries as a result of breathing and ingesting the malathion mixture, and they sued the city. The city's insurer denied that it had to provide coverage, claiming that its pollution exclusion clause applied. The case came before a federal district court which held in favor of the city. The malathion mixture was not a "pollutant" under the terms of the insurance policy. Even though malathion could pose a danger to humans or the environment, the normal use of the chemical was not harmful. Accordingly, the pollution exclusion clause did not apply, and the claims against the city were covered by the policy. *Westchester Fire Ins. Co. v. City of Pittsburg, Kansas*, 791 F.Supp. 836 (D.Kan.1992).

A New York village issued a building permit for the construction of a house. Relying on this permit, the builder substantially completed the house, but had to end construction when the city notified him that he was building within a flood zone. The builder sued the village and settled for $16,250 in damages with the agreement that he would demolish the house. The village sued its liability insurer for indemnification for the $16,250. Both the insurer and the village moved for summary judgment.

The insurer argued to the New York Supreme Court that it did not have to indemnify the village since the issuing of the permit was not a sudden and unexpected event, accident or "occurrence" as required by the liability policy. The court, however, noted that whether the mistaken issuance of the building permit was an "accident" depended upon the village's point of view as to whether the event was unexpected or unforeseen. When the village issued the building permit, it never intended that the builder would be permitted to build his home only to be forced to demolish it. The damage was clearly unintended. Accordingly, the court ordered that the insurer had to indemnify the village for the damages incurred in the suit. *Village of Camden v. National Fire Ins. Co.*, 589 N.Y.S.2d 293 (Sup.1992).

A municipality in Illinois participated in the Intergovernmental Risk Management Agency (IRMA). Part of IRMA's function was to provide risk management services, including the defense and settlement of claims. The municipality then hired a contractor to work on a sewer project. It required the contractor to name it as an additional insured under a commercial general liability insurance policy. When an employee of the contractor was killed while working on the project, his estate filed suit against the municipality. The insurer paid $1.4 million to settle the litigation, then brought suit against IRMA seeking contribution. The trial court granted summary judgment to IRMA, and the insurer appealed to the Appellate Court of Illinois. On appeal, the insurer contended that IRMA's contract with the municipality amounted to primary insurance coverage, obligating it to reimburse the insurer for half the settlement. The court, however, found that IRMA's protection was similar to self-insurance and that IRMA ought not to be treated as a private insurance carrier. Accordingly, the court found that the insurer had no right of equitable contribution from IRMA, and the trial court decision was affirmed. *Aetna Casualty Assurity Co. v. James J. Benes and Associates,* 593 N.E.2d 1087 (Ill.App.2d Dist.1992).

XIII. FARMOWNER'S INSURANCE

The cases in this section deal with insurance policies issued to farmers, which typically attempt to exclude liability for automobile accidents.

The owner of farmland in Illinois had a fifty percent interest in the crops located on it. He obtained crop insurance for his interest. He paid two separate premiums for two different fields — one reflected a higher risk because of a later planting. Subsequently, the crops in the later-planted field were destroyed by hail damage. However, the crops in the other field produced better than the bushel guarantees in the policy. When the insured sought to recover on his loss, the insurer offset the surplus from the field which had produced a surplus. The insured sued to recover the full amount of the loss from the hail-damaged field. The trial court granted summary judgment to the insured, and the insurer appealed to the Appellate Court of Illinois. On appeal, the insurer contended that the crop damage should be determined by considering the overall production of both fields. The court, however, disagreed. Since a separate premium was applied to each field, each crop was considered a separate crop under the policy. As a result, the insured was entitled to his full fifty percent interest in the loss without any offset from the surplus from the producing field. The court affirmed the trial court's decision for the insured. *Miller v. American National Fire Ins. Co.,* 582 N.E.2d 212 (Ill.App. 3rd Dist.1991).

A. Exclusions

The owners of a Montana farm purchased insurance to protect themselves from liability. Subsequently, while one of the owners was piloting an airplane, a crash ensued and a passenger was injured. The passenger claimed coverage. The insurer brought a declaratory relief action charging that no coverage existed, and was granted summary judgment. The passenger appealed to the Supreme Court of Montana which upheld the trial court's decision. The policy clearly excluded coverage for injuries arising from the use of an airplane and, further, the passenger was unable to show that the insurer had misrepresented the scope of coverage to the insureds such that they detrimentally relied on it. The insurer was not liable for coverage. *Truck Ins. Exchange v. Waller*, 828 P.2d 1384 (Mont.1992).

An Arkansas farmer obtained crop damage insurance which covered 900 acres of wheat. Apparently, 675 were actually planted with wheat and the rest were purportedly planted with soybeans. The insured sustained hail damage and sought 100% recovery under his policy. The insurer denied the claim and the insured instituted this action in a federal trial court. The insurer contended that there was material misrepresentation and that the insurer would only pay for the acreage actually planted in wheat as determined after the loss. The jury found that there was crop damage, but that the damage was much less than claimed. The jury granted 5% crop damage coverage to the insured. The insured then appealed to the U.S. Court of Appeals, Eighth Circuit.

On appeal, the insured contended that the trial court erred in submitting the material misrepresentation issue to the jury. The jury had found material misrepresentation by the insured in applying for coverage on behalf of his family. The appellate court determined that the materiality of the applicant's misrepresentation as to acreage planted in wheat was properly sent to the jury. Therefore, the court upheld the trial court's decision. *Reeves Trucking v. Farmers Mutual Hail Ins. Co.*, 926 F.2d 749 (8th Cir.1991).

A North Carolina farmer agreed to allow two neighboring farmers to harvest his hay. The two harvesters were responsible for providing all equipment, hiring the help and transporting the hay to the barns. One of the harvester's relatives volunteered his services and the use of his pick-up truck to assist in the harvesting. A son of one of the harvesters and the grandson of the other were also helping out in hopes of earning some extra money, although they had not been promised any compensation. The harvesters loaded the pick-up truck with hay and the two boys were riding on top of this load when the vehicle struck a mud hole. One boy was thrown from the vehicle and struck his head on the highway. That evening, one of the harvesters paid the youths ten dollars each upon the advice of his insurance agent, who told them it was important to demonstrate that the boys were working for the harvesters. However, the harvester's insurer denied coverage citing an exclusion for farm employees, and also an exclusion for injuries resulting from the use of a loaned vehicle. The injured youth sued the insurer and the trial court ruled in his favor. The insurer then appealed to the Supreme Court of Virginia.

The supreme court noted that the terms "employee" and "loaned" in the respective policy exclusions were not defined. The court stated that employee could mean either a regular continuous worker, in which case the exclusion would not apply, or it could mean one who does incidental work. Similarly, the court stated that a "loan" could be either a formal bailment, or a loose formal arrangement. Since the policy exclusions were ambiguous, the court construed the policy so as to grant coverage. *American Reliance Ins. Co. v. Mitchell*, 385 S.E.2d 583 (Va.1989).

A Missouri farmer procured a farm operations insurance policy and an automobile insurance policy from two separate insurers. The farmer and his son, who was also a farmer, then attempted to move a 1,500 gallon water barrel to another location by loading it onto the back of the insured's pickup truck. The insured attached a chain and a hook to the water barrel and to a tractor, which hoisted the barrel into the air. The chain and hook gave way, and the water barrel fell on the insured's son. The farm operations insurer contended that it was not liable for coverage because the injury had resulted from "the ownership, maintenance, use, loading or unloading of a motor vehicle." The automobile insurer asserted that because the tractor had been used to load the water barrel, and because the tractor was farm equipment, it was not liable for coverage. The son sued in a Missouri trial court, which held both insurers liable, and they appealed to the Missouri Court of Appeals.

The court of appeals held that the phrase "farm machinery" did not include either a log chain, or a tractor used to load the truck. Accordingly, the automobile insurer was liable for coverage. The injury had occurred while the vehicle was being loaded, and the "farm equipment" exclusion did not apply to bar coverage. The court further held that the farm operations insurer could properly deny coverage because the injury fell within its exclusion for the loading of a vehicle. The court reversed the trial court's decision as it related to the farm operations insurer, and held the automobile insurer solely liable to defend and indemnify the insured. *Continental Ins. Co. v. Jaecques*, 782 S.W.2d 819 (Mo.App.1990).

An Iowa farmer's tractor was damaged when the farmer's son drove it into a culvert. The tractor was towed into town for repairs. After repairs, the farmer noticed that the transmission had been damaged as a result of the tow. The farmer then sought damages for repair of the transmission from a policy which provided coverage for loss resulting from the tractor's overturn or a collision. After an Iowa trial court held that the policy did not cover the transmission damage, the farmer appealed to the Iowa Court of Appeals. The court of appeals reversed, ruling that the parties could have reasonably foreseen that a collision would result in the need for towing. Because the towing damage was proximately caused by the collision, the insurer was required to pay. *Bettis v. Wayne County Mut. Ins. Ass'n*, 447 N.W.2d 569 (Iowa App.1989).

A Missouri farmer had an insurance policy covering a truck and flatbed trailer which he used for farm purposes. The policy stated that "... it is understood and agreed that the insured vehicle is to be used exclusively for the farm use of the named insured only." In order to give himself more pasture area the farmer began removing approximately forty-five to fifty old cars from his farm property. He then began hauling the cars to Kansas City. On one of his trips he was involved in an accident in which a woman was injured. He sought coverage which the insurer denied. The insurer then sued the farmer in a Missouri trial court seeking an order that the insurance policy provided no coverage because the truck was not being used for farm purposes. The court held in favor of the farmer. The insurance company appealed to the Missouri Court of Appeals. The court of appeals concluded that the activities in question were part of a farming operation even though the farmer was paid for the scrap metal involved and earned a substantial part of his income by hauling the scrap metal. Because the removal of the cars was part of the farming operation and would allow the farmer to expand his land area available for pasture, trips to the scrapyard were part of the general farming operation. *Farm Bur. Town & Country Ins. v. Franklin*, 759 S.W.2d 361 (Mo.App.1988).

A farmer was driving his truck on an Iowa highway. As the truck rounded a curve, an auger attached to the truck's left side came loose at one end and extended across the center line of the road. A motorcyclist traveling in the other direction was injured when he swerved to avoid being hit by the auger. The farmer's truck was equipped with a gravity box for hauling fertilizer and shelled corn. The auger was permanently affixed to the gravity box to aid in unloading its contents.

At the time of the accident the truck was neither registered as a motor vehicle nor insured under an automobile liability policy. The farmer's farm liability policy excluded coverage for bodily injury or property damage arising out of the use of a motor vehicle. The policy defined a motor vehicle as "a land motor vehicle, trailer, or semi-trailer designed for travel on public roads (including any machinery or apparatus attached thereto)...." When the motorcyclist sued the farmer for damages the farmer made a demand on his farm liability insurer to defend the suit. The insurer sought a ruling that coverage was excluded under the policy and that it had no duty to defend. An Iowa district court denied the insurer's request, and when this decision was affirmed by the state court of appeals, the insurer appealed to the Iowa Supreme Court.

The supreme court addressed the issue of whether the accident caused by the auger was "vehicle-related." It ruled that the policy's definition of motor vehicle was not ambiguous. The auger was an apparatus attached to the truck and therefore was part of a motor vehicle under the policy. Because the motorcyclist's injuries resulted from the farmer's use of a motor vehicle, coverage under the farmer's liability policy was excluded, and the insurer had no duty to defend the farmer. *North Star Mut. Ins. Co. v. Holty*, 402 N.W.2d 452 (Iowa 1987).

Insured Arkansas farmowners purchased a farmowner's insurance policy. The policy excluded business pursuits from coverage. The insureds' farm included 160 acres of land on which they maintained several thoroughbred race horses. The insureds entered a race horse in an event at a county fair. The horse left the track and injured a spectator, who then submitted a claim to the insureds. They sought defense under the farmowner's policy, but the insurer refused coverage and filed a declaratory judgment action in an Arkansas trial court. The court ruled for the insureds and awarded them attorney's fees, but refused to enhance the judgment with a penalty which the insureds had requested. Both parties appealed to the Arkansas Supreme Court. The supreme court reviewed conflicting trial evidence about whether the horses were maintained as a business or hobby. The insureds' income tax returns showed that the venture was operated as a business, but only because their tax preparers had refused to prepare their returns as a nonbusiness venture. It was legitimate to infer that the horse racing was a pastime conducted primarily for the insureds' enjoyment rather than for business reasons. Because the insurer bore the burden of proving that the policy excluded coverage for the spectator's injury, the trial court could appropriately resolve doubt against the insurer. The supreme court also affirmed the trial court's award of attorney's fees, and refused to impose a twelve percent penalty which the insureds had requested. The twelve percent penalty claim had been based upon an Arkansas statute which involved cases seeking a money judgment. The statute was inapplicable to cases such as this in which a declaratory judgment was sought. *Shelter Mut. Ins. Co. v. Smith*, 779 S.W.2d 149 (Ark.1989).

B. Theft Loss Coverage

Two South Dakota insureds operated a hog farm. They kept detailed records and conducted year-end inventories. After conducting an inventory, the insureds determined that 917 market-weight hogs had been stolen. However, the insureds had not noticed a dwindling number of hogs. They were not selling fewer hogs or bringing in less income. The insureds filed a claim under the theft clause of their commercial farm policy. The insurer sought a declaratory judgment in a South Dakota circuit court to determine coverage under the policy. The insureds' answered and counterclaimed against the insurer, claiming that the theft was covered. The circuit court denied the claim, finding that the insureds had failed to produce sufficient evidence of theft. The insureds then appealed to the Supreme Court of South Dakota.

The court noted that the policy's theft clause excluded loss by theft where it involved escape, mysterious disappearance or unaccountable shortage. The insureds had the burden of proving theft, including the amount and value of the stolen property. Once this was established, the insurer had the burden of proving the mysterious disappearance exclusion. The court found that the circumstantial evidence presented did not establish a prima facie case of loss by theft. Thus the insurer was not required to prove the policy exclusion of mysterious disappearance. The supreme court affirmed the circuit court's decision for the insurer. *Ins. Co. of N. America v. Schultz*, 441 N.W.2d 686 (S.D.1989).

A farmer in Illinois undergoing bankruptcy proceedings brought suit against his insurer claiming that 2,500 hogs had been stolen from him sometime between September 1975, and August 1977. Suit was brought after the insurer refused to pay the claim because of the failure to comply with reporting terms under the policy. The insurer also denied that the loss was due to theft. The Appellate Court of Illinois affirmed a trial court ruling in favor of the insurer, saying that the farmer had failed to prove that the hogs were actually stolen. The farmer had reported nothing unusual at his farm from where the majority of the pigs were taken. Further, there was no evidence that his German shepherd watchdog warned of intruders on any occasion. The farmer testified that he found gates to his pens open on several occasions but he could not remember the particular times. There was no testimony which related to the circumstances surrounding the loss of his pigs. In addition, the farmer took no monthly counts, reported no feed consumption drop and reported no approximate dates when he discovered losses. Further, he could not prove any real relationship between the unlocked gates or unusual truck noises and specific losses, and a hired hand testified that many pigs had died from overcrowding or exposure. A professional hog buyer testified that it would have taken twelve semitrailers or 240 pickup trucks to haul away 2,500 pigs and each loading process would be noisy and would take at least twenty minutes to an hour. Thus, the court was not persuaded that the farmer's losses were attributable to theft and held that the insurer was not liable. *Benson v. Bradford Mut. Fire Ins. Corp.*, 459 N.E.2d 689 (Ill.App.2d Dist.1984).

XIV. FIDELITY BONDS

Fidelity bonds insure against fraudulent and dishonest acts of employees of the insured. The following cases involve disputes which have arisen over the scope of such coverage.

A bank president who was also a majority shareholder used bank funds to pay off outstanding loans from the bank to himself, his sons, and his former business partner. The FDIC discovered the misapplication of funds and immediately ordered the bank's capital account to be encumbered to cover the liability. The board of directors then sought insurance coverage. The bank's insurer brought a declaratory judgment action for nonliability on the bank's fidelity bond. A Minnesota district court and the court of appeals held the insurer liable for the entire amount. The insurer appealed to the Supreme Court of Minnesota. On appeal, the insurer argued that it was not liable to the bank because the president was not a bank employee within the terms of the policy. It said that, pursuant to the "alter ego defense," the president (as a controlling stockholder) could not be an employee because he was so closely identified with the bank that he ceased to be an employee. The appellate court disagreed, finding that the insurer failed to prove that any member of the board other than the president knew or participated in his scheme. The insurer nevertheless contended that the alter ego doctrine did not depend on the board's ratification of the president's misconduct but merely on his status as a majority and controlling shareholder. The court rejected the insurer's argument and affirmed the lower court's decision that the insurer was liable on the bond. *Transamerica Ins. Co. v. F.D.I.C.*, 489 N.W.2d 224 (Minn.1992).

An Oregon credit union treasurer loaned $62,000 of credit union funds to another employee without prior approval from the credit committee. This was a violation of credit union policies and state law. The loan was secured by property for which an inaccurately high appraisal had been made. The employee defaulted, and the sale of collateral failed to bring the loan balance. The treasurer also executed a consultant agreement regarding the construction of a new building without showing the agreement to the credit union board. He entered into contracts for interior and general work without board knowledge or approval. Because of the improper contracts, the credit union acquired a building which it did not need and which was worth less than it paid. The credit union sued its fidelity bond insurer in a federal district court, seeking payment on its loan and building losses. The court ruled for the insurer and the credit union appealed to the U.S. Court of Appeals, Ninth Circuit.

On appeal, the insurer conceded that the claims resulted from "fraud, dishonesty or failure of an employee to perform his duties well and faithfully," but asserted that the type of loss suffered by the credit union was not covered. The court of appeals disagreed, finding that although the credit union's loss on the loan was not a loss of money, it was a loss of a security, and thus qualified for coverage. Further, the court held that the credit union suffered a loss on its building at the moment when its treasurer extended the loan with insufficient collateral. Thus, the building loss was also covered as a security loss under the fidelity bond. The court reversed the district court's decision, and held the fidelity bond insurer liable. *Portland Federal Employees Credit Union v. Cumis Ins. Soc., Inc.*, 894 F.2d 1101 (9th Cir.1990).

Sec. XIV　　　　　　　　　　　　　　　　　　　FIDELITY BONDS　401

An Iowa loan officer operated a fraudulent loan scheme, asking two bank customers to borrow money from the bank and then in turn lend part of the money back to the loan officer. When the customers demanded payment from the bank officer and did not receive it, they indicated their intention to sue the bank. The bank entered into settlement negotiations with the bank customers which resulted in settlement agreements and mutual releases. After the bank filed proof of loss and was denied coverage under the bankers blanket bond, the bank filed a breach of contract claim against the insurer in a federal district court. The court entered judgment in favor of the bank for the losses sustained and for attorney's fees, but ruled against the bank on its potential income losses from the loans. The insurer appealed and the bank cross-appealed to the U.S. Court of Appeals, Eighth Circuit.

The appellate court noted that the bond specifically provided coverage for loss resulting from fraudulent acts of an employee, and reasonable attorney's fees if expended in defense of "any suit or legal proceeding." The court found that the bank sustained a direct loss from the fraudulent acts of its loan officer, and that the bond did not limit the scope of a "legal proceeding" to formally commenced lawsuits. The bond also provided that the underwriter would not be liable for potential income, including interest not realized by the insured, because of a loss covered under the bond. The court of appeals affirmed the decision of the district court. *First American State Bank v. Continental Ins. Co.*, 897 F.2d 319 (8th Cir.1990).

A fidelity bond insurer sold a bond to a brokerage firm in Arkansas. The bond covered losses due to the fraudulent or dishonest acts of an employee. Three people then invested approximately $700,000 in securities with the brokerage firm. The investments were then lost due to the allegedly fraudulent and dishonest acts of the president and owner of the firm. The three investors sued the fidelity bond insurer in Arkansas trial courts, but the cases were removed to federal district court and consolidated for trial. The jury ruled for the investors, and the insurer appealed to the U.S. Court of Appeals, Eighth Circuit.

On appeal, the insurer argued that the fidelity bond had expressly not provided coverage to third parties, but only to the brokerage firm. Thus, the investors should not have been able to sue it under the fidelity bonds. The appellate court, however, noted that as a matter of public policy expressed by Arkansas law, the investors had standing to sue despite the bond's contrary language. The court further noted that Ark. Code Ann. § 23-42-305(a)(4) stated: every bond shall provide for suit thereon by any person who has a cause of action under this chapter. This gave the investors a statutory right to sue despite the bond's exclusion. The court of appeals affirmed the district court's decision. *Foster v. National Union Fire Ins. Co.*, 902 F.2d 1316 (8th Cir.1990).

The manager of a title insurance company engaged in a real estate fraud scheme with an investor. He issued fraudulent and deceptive title insurance policies which intentionally omitted disclosure of prior mortgages and other encumbrances on properties. Eventually, the fraud was exposed and the manager was sentenced to prison. The title company was deluged by claims from customers whose titles were not as represented in their policies. The title company settled the claims, then turned to its fidelity bond insurer for indemnification of the loss. The fidelity bond provided that the insurer would indemnify for loss resulting from dishonest or fraudulent acts of an employee, but limited the types of dishonesty for which it provided coverage. One of the exclusions was for liability of the insured arising out of title searches and reports. The insured sued the insurer in a federal district court, and when coverage was awarded, the insurer appealed to the U.S. Court of Appeals, Seventh Circuit.

The appellate court held that the policy excluded losses arising from both honestly issued and fraudulent title reports and searches. The insurance contract did not differentiate between honest and dishonest trading. The court noted that coverage for fraud could have been obtained for a higher premium, and the insured had not chosen that route. Because the losses resulted from fraudulent title policies and improper title reports, the court ruled that the losses were excluded. The court reversed the district court's decision and denied coverage to the insured. *Continental Corp. v. Aetna Casualty and Surety Co.*, 892 F.2d 540 (7th Cir.1989).

A Kentucky man sued a city and one of its police officers under 42 U.S.C. § 1983 for violation of his civil rights. The trial court directed a verdict in favor of the city only, but the jury returned a verdict for the plaintiff against the police officer. Subsequently, the man filed an amended complaint against a fidelity bond insurer which named the officer as principal and the city as obligee. The matter came before the U.S. District Court, E.D. Kentucky, where a motion was made for judgment on the pleadings.

The court noted that the issue was whether the fidelity bond existed to indemnify those citizens who had incurred damages because of the improper acts of officers during the performance of their duties, or whether the bond served to indemnify liabilities suffered by the city, as obligee, because of the acts of its officers. The court then noted that, although the bond was not an official bond, it was nevertheless valid as a common law obligation. Thus, since the obligee was the city and the city had not suffered any losses or damage because of the prior lawsuit, the fidelity bond insurer was not liable to the plaintiff. The insurer could only be liable if actual losses had been sustained by the city. The court thus granted the insurer's motion for a judgment on the pleadings. *Thornsberry v. Western Surety Co.*, 738 F.Supp. 209 (E.D.Ky.1990).

An officer of a Georgia insured's business misappropriated funds. The insured was covered under two fidelity bonds which provided coverage against losses caused by fraudulent or dishonest acts committed by employees. The bonds required the insured to file suit within one year after discovery of a loss and to provide detailed proof of loss. In May 1985, an investigation was made into the possible misappropriation, which led to an indictment and trial of the officer. During the investigation, records were seized and audits conducted. The officer was acquitted at trial in February 1986. The insured then hired the same accounting firm which had completed earlier audits to perform another audit. The insured received the results of the audit in February 1987. It then submitted a notice and proof of loss to the insurer which the insurer denied, claiming that the insured had failed to file suit within one year from the date of the loss. The insured sued the insurer in a Georgia trial court to collect on the fidelity bonds. The trial court denied the insurer's motion for summary judgment and the insurer appealed to the Court of Appeals of Georgia.

On appeal, the insurer argued that the insured had discovered the loss by the date of the trial, but had failed to give timely notice. The court of appeals held that the insured had "discovered" the misappropriation of funds when it received the auditor's report in 1987. The fidelity bonds required the insured to file suit within one year of the date the insured discovered the loss. Until receipt of the auditor's report, the insureds did not have detailed proof of the loss. Thus the loss was not discovered until 1987 rather than 1986. The court of appeals affirmed the trial court's denial of summary judgment. *U.S. Fidelity & Guar. v. Macon-Bibb*, 381 S.E.2d 539 (Ga.App.1989).

XV. CONSTRUCTION INSURANCE

A builder obtained a builder's risk policy for a commercial project, and added the mortgagee to the policy. The policy excluded liability for damage caused by extremes of temperature and freezing. During construction a sprinkler head froze and broke, thereby releasing water and causing substantial damage through flooding. The insureds brought suit against the insurer to recover for flood damage. The insurer contended that the damage was caused by freezing and was thus excluded from coverage. A New York court granted judgment for the insureds, and the insurer appealed to the Supreme Court, Appellate Division of New York. The court explained that a causation analysis in insurance litigation differs from a causation analysis in tort litigation. The court explained that causation in insurance litigation depends on the nature of what has been contracted for between the parties. Here, though the damage actually resulted from flooding, the court held that it was caused by the freezing temperature. The earlier decision was reversed, and judgment was entered for the insurer. *Album Realty v. American Home Assurance Co.*, 574 N.Y.S.2d 704 (A.D.1 Dept.1991).

A builders group purchased builders risk insurance from an insurer for a commercial structure which it was constructing. The policy provided coverage both for the building itself and for loss of rents, but did not cover the cost of "making good faulty or defective workmanship, material, construction or design." However, the exclusion did not apply to damage resulting from any of the above defects. The building was not completed as scheduled because of various defects in first floor and parking level slabs. Yet, when the builders group sought compensation for loss of rents, the insurer refused to pay. The insured sued for breach of contract. The insurer moved for summary judgment, asserting that the insured had been unable to obtain a certificate of occupancy because of an excluded defect (without resulting physical damage) and thus no coverage was available. The trial court granted summary judgment to the insurer.

On appeal to the California Court of Appeal, Second District, the court noted that the building had suffered physical damage within the meaning of the insuring clause. The court rejected the insurer's argument that faulty workmanship was not a covered peril so as to provide coverage for loss of rents. It stated that since damage resulting from faulty workmanship was covered, so also economic loss resulting from faulty workmanship must be covered. The court then held that the damage referred to in the policy included economic damages such as loss of rents. Accordingly, the court of appeal reversed the trial court's decision and held for the insured. *Rosenberg v. First State Ins. Co.*, 280 Cal.Rptr. 388 (Cal.App.2d Dist.1991).

A contractor purchased a liability policy which contained a work product exclusion, stating that the insurer would not protect against claims for property damage to completed work that the contractor performed where the damage arose out of the work itself. A couple then hired the contractor to build a house on their property. The house was built too close to the property line in violation of zoning requirements, and the couple sued the contractor, alleging that it had negligently sited the house too close to the property line. The contractor brought suit against its insurer, seeking defense and indemnification. When the trial court denied the insurer's motion for summary judgment, appeal was taken to the Supreme Court of Vermont. On appeal, the court noted that the type of loss for which coverage was being sought was exactly the type excluded by the work product clause. The policy here was intended to cover tort liability for physical damage to others, not liability for economic loss due to the product being less than what was bargained for. Since there was no possibility of coverage in this situation, the insurer had no duty to defend and its motion for summary judgment should have been granted. *Garneau v. Curtis & Bedell, Inc.*, 610 A.2d 132 (Vt.1992).

A general contractor hired a subcontractor to move a state historical monument. The monument was damaged during excavation by the subcontractor, and the contractor incurred expenses to rebuild it. The subcontractor notified its insurer of the damage and the insurer denied liability, citing a clause which denies coverage for damaged property over which the insured exercised physical control. The general contractor disagreed with the subcontractor's insurer's interpretation and later furnished the insurer with a copy of the costs and a notification of its intent to sue. It also obtained a default judgment against the subcontractor, and accepted as satisfaction of the judgment an assignment of the subcontractor's rights against its insurer. More than four years after the damage, the contractor brought an action against the insurer. Summary judgment was granted against the insurer, and it appealed to the Colorado Court of Appeals.

The first issue concerned the selection of the correct statute of limitations. The court ruled that the claim was not barred even when applying the shorter time period as urged by the insurer. The contractor's claim against the insurer was ruled not to have accrued until it obtained a judgment and subsequent assignment of rights. The second issue involved the insurer's assertion that it did not receive timely notice of the claim against the subcontractor in the earlier action. It claimed that this made the assigned subcontractor's rights invalid. It was ruled that when the insurer denied coverage it had also waived its right to receive notice of suit or to later assert a notice defense; the insurer could not contest the subcontractor's liability. The issue finally became whether the damage was covered under the policy. The court stated that the exclusion of liability for property damage was in conflict with a later clause which eliminated the exclusion if the work was warranted to be done in a workmanlike manner. The judgment against the insurer was affirmed. *Flatiron Paving Co. of Boulder v. Great Southwest Fire Ins. Co.*, 812 P.2d 668 (Colo.App.1990).

A contractor began building a house for a man in Maryland. The contractor agreed to maintain $750,000 worth of builder's risk insurance on the house during the construction. However, it only obtained a $250,000 policy. A fire occurred during construction which caused extensive damage. The homeowner sued the contractor for negligence and breach of contract for its failure to obtain the proper insurance. The contractor's business liability insurer refused to defend the suit. After settling the case and receiving an assignment of rights, the homeowner sued the insurer, seeking the difference between the damage suffered and the insurance proceeds already received. The trial court granted summary judgment to the insurer, and the homeowner appealed to the Court of Special Appeals of Maryland. On appeal, the homeowner contended that because he suffered *property damage* which was caused by an *occurrence*, the insurer was bound to provide coverage for his loss.

The court, however, stated that the insurer's policies required a direct causal link between the insured's liability and the property damage. Here, the contractor's liability to the homeowner was not a result of the fire damage. Rather, its liability arose from its negligence and breach of contract with respect to obtaining the proper amount of insurance during construction. The court also stated that the insurer was not liable for defense costs because the underlying suit was not for damages on account of property damage. The trial court's decision was affirmed. *Pyles v. Pennsylvania Manufacturers' Ass'n Ins. Co.*, 600 A.2d 1174 (Md.App.1992).

A general contractor responsible for building a water treatment plant in Montana procured a surety bond. A subcontractor agreed with the general contractor to provide supplies. When the general contractor allegedly refused to pay for some of the materials the subcontractor sought payment from the surety. It also refused and the subcontractor sued the surety in a Montana federal court seeking compensation. It alleged that the surety's bad faith prior to and during litigation constituted an unfair settlement practice. It sought compensatory and punitive damages under state law. The federal district court dismissed the claim and the subcontractor appealed to the U.S. Court of Appeals, Ninth Circuit. Because Montana law did not provide a precedent, the circuit court certified a question to the Montana Supreme Court.

At issue was whether a "surety" is an insurer within the meaning of Montana law and is subject to suit for bad faith insurance practices. The supreme court noted that Montana law defined an insurer as including "every person engaged as indemnitor, surety, or contractor in the business of entering into insurance contracts." The plain language of the statute makes suretyship a regulated insurance class. Under the statute, one who issues surety bonds is in the "business of insurance." The case was returned to the court of appeals with the understanding that the surety was obligated to act in good faith. *K-W Industries v. National Sur. Corp.*, 754 P.2d 502 (Mont.1988).

A Kansas utility contracted with a construction company to build a dam. The utility furnished the soil for the dam, which was tested and approved by a third party. The tests and soil were faulty, and the dam was defective. The dam was then demolished and reconstructed. The original contractor sued the utility for the unpaid balance on their contract, and faced a counterclaim for breach of contract. The construction company then filed a separate suit against its general liability insurer seeking a declaration that the insurer was required to provide a defense in the suit brought by the utility. Cross motions for summary judgment were submitted to a federal district court which applied Kansas law. The insurer argued that it was not required to provide a defense because the policy was inapplicable due to several exclusionary clauses. The first exclusion relied on by the insurer was a "sistership exclusion." This exclusion was held by the court only to exclude coverage for damage to others' work — not to an insured's own work. The insurer then claimed that an "injury to *product*" exclusion applied. The term *product* was construed to be consistent with its use in product liability cases. Because the dam could not be the subject of such a suit, the exclusion was held to not apply. An "injury to work" clause was the next exclusion asserted by the insurer. The dam was undisputedly work. The policy, however, was a broad form policy instead of a standard form policy. A broad form policy exclusion was found to be inapplicable to work performed by subcontractors such as the soil testers in this case. The insurer lastly asserted that coverage was excluded by a "faulty workmanship" exclusion. However, the faulty workmanship exclusion was inapplicable to completed operations. In arriving at the holding, the court relied both on ambiguities in the policy and the insurance industry's later modification which clarified the exclusion. The insurer was ordered to defend the contractor. *Green Construction Co. v. National Union Fire Ins. Co.*, 771 F.Supp. 1000 (W.D.Mo.1991).

A construction company entered into a contract with a Virginia county to build a pumping station. The company then subcontracted out the excavation work. The subcontractor agreed to indemnify and hold harmless both the contractor and the county, and it purchased a contractor's general liability policy in furtherance of its obligations. The contractor was named as the certificate holder. Shortly after the excavation began, a total collapse of an earthen cofferdam appeared imminent, and an emergency backfilling operation was undertaken to avoid this result. The contractor then notified the insurer and filed a claim for property damage coverage. The insurer denied liability. In the lawsuit which followed, a federal district court granted summary judgment to the insurer. After an appeal to the U.S. Court of Appeals, Fourth Circuit, a question regarding the coverage was certified to the Court of Appeals of Maryland. The question before the court was whether the certificate holder could recover under the policy for the costs associated with its efforts to prevent further property damage by backfilling the excavation. The court noted that the insurance contract only provided coverage when the insured had a legal responsibility to pay a property damage claim caused by an occurrence. Here, there was no *occurrence* under the policy, nor was there a claim made by a third party for property damage. The claim, instead, was for reimbursement by an insured for preventive costs it had incurred. The court thus answered the certified question in favor of the insurer. *Schlosser v. Ins. Co. of North America*, 600 A.2d 836 (Md.1992).

A Missouri construction company owned a crane which was insured under a liability policy. The crane overturned and was damaged while carrying an 800-pound steel cage column. The insurer's claims examiner investigated the accident and relied on representations made by the insured's vice president who said that there had been no load on the crane, that the ground beneath it was muddy, and that the crane had a thirty-five ton capacity. The claims examiner recommended that the claim be paid. Meanwhile, she contacted the crane operator who stated that the crane overturned because he had not used outriggers and had misjudged the boom's angle and length. Because of the conflicting stories the insurer continued to investigate and ultimately denied the claim based on a policy provision which excluded coverage for loss or damage due to the weight of a load exceeding the crane's registered lifting or supporting capacity. The insured sued the insurer for repair costs in a federal district court contending that the clause "registered lifting or supporting capacity" was ambiguous. The district court found for the insurer and the insured appealed to the U.S. Court of Appeals, Eighth Circuit.

The court of appeals noted that the crane operator's testimony indicated that the crane was overloaded, even though the load was less than the maximum the crane could lift under other circumstances. The court ruled that the insured's claim was barred by the policy exclusion which denied coverage for loss or damage due to the weight of the load exceeding the registered lifting or supporting capacity. The court of appeals affirmed the district court's decision. *Kloster Co., Inc. v. Michigan Mut. Ins. Co.*, 882 F.2d 1308 (8th Cir.1989).

A corporation which owned and rented out cranes purchased an all-risk policy from an insurer to protect itself from property damage while its cranes were being used by other businesses. One of its rented cranes was subsequently buried by sulphur. Apparently, the addition of some polluted water created sulphuric acid and the crane was irreparably damaged by the corrosive effects of the acid. The insured filed a claim with its insurer, and it was denied. Several requests for reconsideration were also denied over the next 109 days, and, over a year after the claim was filed, the insured brought suit against the insurer. The insurer moved for summary judgment, asserting that the suit had been brought over a year after the damage had occurred and was thus barred by the limitations clause of the policy. The trial court granted the motion, and the insured appealed to the California Court of Appeal, Sixth District. On appeal, the court referred to *Prudential-LMI Commercial Ins. v. Superior Court* and decided that the rule announced in that case ought to apply to commercial all-risk policies as well as to homeowner's policies. The court stated that the limitations period would be tolled from the time the insured reported the claim until the time the insurer rejected it. Because of this analysis, the lawsuit fell within the one-year limitations period and was not time barred. The court further noted that this rule applied retrospectively because it was not a change in the law, but a declaration of existing law. The court of appeal reversed the trial court's decision. *San Jose Crane & Rigging, Inc. v. Lexington Ins. Co.*, 278 Cal.Rptr. 301 (Cal.App.6th Dist.1991).

A California construction company agreed to perform structural repairs to a hotel. It contracted with a subcontractor to restore the hotel's exterior facade. Unbeknownst to all concerned, the subcontractor used a patching material which had been designed for use only on horizontal surfaces. As a result, the plaster began deteriorating. The hotel's management notified the construction company of the damage, but as of this time the reason for the deterioration was unclear. Also at this time, the construction company was insured by a comprehensive general liability insurer. Subsequently, the insured switched insurers; it also discovered the reason for the plaster's deterioration. When the hotel recovered an arbitration award from the construction company for $354,000, the first liability insurer paid that amount. It then brought suit against the second insurer for equitable subrogation, contribution and declaratory relief. The trial court granted the second insurer's motion for summary judgment and the first insurer appealed to the California Court of Appeal, Fourth District.

On appeal, the court adopted the line of reasoning it had used in a similar case, *Home Ins. Co. v. Landmark Ins. Co.*, where it held the first insurer liable. In *Home*, a building's exterior began spalling (cracking and chipping) and continued to deteriorate into a second insurer's policy period. The court found that the date of manifestation determined which insurer must indemnify a loss. Here, as in *Home*, the loss first manifested itself during the first policy period. Even though the reason for the loss was not known until the second insurer's policy took effect, the damage first occurred during the first insurer's policy period. The court thus affirmed the trial court's decision and held the first insurer liable for the whole loss. *Fireman's Fund Ins. Co. v. Aetna Cas. & Surety Co.*, 273 Cal.Rptr. 431 (Cal.App.4th Dist.1990).

CHAPTER EIGHT

PROFESSIONAL MALPRACTICE INSURANCE

                                                                                             Page

I.   COVERAGE FOR ACTIVITIES WITHIN THE SCOPE OF PROFESSIONAL SERVICES 409

II.   POLICY COVERAGE DATES 415

III.   FRAUD BY PROFESSIONALS 420

IV.   SUITS BASED ON ERROR OR MISTAKE 422

V.   LIABILITY OF A PROFESSIONAL'S EMPLOYER 423

VI.   OTHER MALPRACTICE CASES 425
      A. Liability Limits and Subrogation Rights 425
      B. Bad-Faith Claims 428

I. COVERAGE FOR ACTIVITIES WITHIN THE SCOPE OF PROFESSIONAL SERVICES

In general, malpractice insurance policies do not protect against all forms of a professional's conduct. Conduct must be within the scope of professional services, or necessary to the professional's work, in order to be covered under most malpractice insurance policies.

An architectural firm submitted a bid to design three schools for an Alaska school district. Another firm sued it for misrepresenting to the school district that it had certain employees and experience, when it did not. One of the firm's two insurers successfully defended the suit, then sought a *pro rata* share from the other insurer. The court granted summary judgment to the nonpaying insurer, and the first insurer appealed to the Supreme Court of Alaska, which reversed. The providing of a bid was held to be a professional service for which the nonpaying insurer had to provide a defense. It consisted of more than just a price quote. The nonpaying insurer was liable for its share of defense costs. *American Motorists Ins. Co. v. Republic Ins. Co.*, 830 P.2d 785 (Alaska 1992).

A woman visited her gynecologist and was sexually assaulted following the examination. Following the gynecologist's conviction for forcible rape, the victim brought a malpractice action. She then brought a separate declaratory judgment action against the gynecologist's malpractice insurer seeking coverage for her injuries. A state court granted summary judgment to the insurer, and the victim appealed to the Supreme Court of Nevada. The malpractice policy provided coverage for injuries which "arose out of" professional services. This coverage was contended by the victim to be broader than coverage from policies which covered injuries "caused by" professional services. She argued that an "arose out of" policy should provide coverage for a rape which arose from rendering professional services, and should only exclude a rape which was separate and distinct from those services, such as a rape occurring outside the office. The insurer argued that the policy excluded coverage for any rape. The court agreed that the policy precluded coverage for a sexual assault. It also held that coverage was precluded by the intentional acts exclusion; a forcible rape would be known by a gynecologist to be an act with substantial certainty to cause harm to the victim. The victim alternatively argued that enforcing the policy, thereby denying her recovery, was against public policy. The court disagreed and noted that an insurance policy is a contract, and that if an insurer is not paid to assume a risk then it has no obligation to pay. The judgment was affirmed. *Rivera v. Nevada Medical Liability Ins. Co.*, 814 P.2d 71 (Nev.1991).

A Massachusetts man was treated by a physician and later sued him for negligence. The man's wife and daughter also sued for loss of consortium. The malpractice insurance policy limit was $100,000 for each claim, or all claims, because of injury or death to any one person. The insurer sought a judicial determination of its liability and the case was brought before the Supreme Judicial Court of Massachusetts. The insurer argued that the policy only covered one claim because the wife's claim was essentially derivative of the husband's injury. The insurer also argued that all suits brought against it as a result of a single instance of malpractice constituted only one claim for policy purposes. The court ruled that the language, "injury to any one person," is broad enough to include consortium injuries. Further, the court held that there were two possible interpretations of the policy. Because the policy could be read two ways, the court ruled that it must be construed for the insured. The court held the insurer liable for loss of consortium damages. *Pinheiro v. Medical Malpractice Joint Underwriting Ass'n of Mass.*, 547 N.E.2d 49 (Mass.1989).

An Arkansas patient obtained a medical malpractice judgment against her psychologist, who had engaged her in sexual activity. The psychologist's insurer defended him under a reservation of rights, contending that its professional liability policy excluded sexual acts claims. The patient brought a declaratory action against the insurer, seeking an order requiring the insurer to pay the psychologist's judgment. A federal district court found for the insurer and the patient appealed to the U.S. Court of Appeals, Eighth Circuit. The court held that the malpractice policy contained an exclusion for sexual acts claims. Sex was an essential element of the patient's cause of action. The sexual relationship between the psychologist and the patient was so intertwined with the psychologist's malpractice that it was inseparable. The patient was denied coverage. *Govar v. Chicago Ins. Co.*, 879 F.2d 1581 (8th Cir.1989).

A California doctor was subpoenaed to testify before a federal grand jury concerning his alleged dispensation of steroids and other drugs in violation of law. He was subsequently indicted in federal court on these same charges. After a criminal complaint was brought against him, the doctor tendered the defense of both the grand jury investigation and the criminal charges to his professional liability insurer. The insurer refused to accept his defense. He then filed a declaratory relief action, seeking a determination that the insurer had a duty to defend and indemnify him. The trial court granted the insurer's summary judgment motion, and the doctor appealed to the

California Court of Appeal, First District. The court of appeal noted that the policy had been set up to provide protection against professional liability claims which might be brought against the doctor in his practice as a physician or surgeon. Further, the policy was to cover the doctor for damages resulting from the provision or withholding of professional services. In this case, the only court case at issue was a criminal suit brought against the doctor. The court thus determined that there was no possibility of coverage arising from the policy. It held that the insurer had no duty to defend or indemnify the doctor. The court refused to let the doctor convert his malpractice policy into a comprehensive legal services policy, and affirmed the trial court's decision. *Perzik v. St. Paul Fire & Marine Ins. Co.*, 279 Cal.Rptr. 498 (Cal.App.1st Dist.1991)

An Arizona attorney orchestrated the formation of a limited partnership. The partnership had serious financial difficulties and the attorney left the country. The other partners filed a complaint against the attorney individually and against his firm. His firm had previously represented the partners of the limited partnership in connection with various legal matters. The partners alleged attorney malpractice, breach of fiduciary duty, fraud, fraudulent sale of unregistered securities, breach of contract, and negligence. The attorney's professional liability insurer accepted his defense under a reservation of rights. The insurer then filed for declaratory relief against the attorney and his firm seeking a declaration that no coverage existed under his malpractice policy. The trial court found in favor of the insurer. The limited partners appealed to the Court of Appeals of Arizona. The attorney had convinced his associates to invest as limited partners and to borrow money. The ultimate liability on one loan had been personally guaranteed by the partners and that was where the money was primarily lost. The court determined that the attorney's negligent acts were indirectly the cause of the loss. The proximate cause was the limited partnership's present inability to pay the loans that it had personally guaranteed. Therefore, the loss was directly attributable to the business failure and not to the attorney's action as an attorney. The court upheld the judgment of the trial court and found for the insurer. *Potomac Ins. Co. v. McIntosh*, 804 P.2d 759 (Ariz.App.1990).

Two attorneys worked together in a law firm for thirteen years. After one of them became dissatisfied with the other's management of the firm, he left the firm and terminated their business relationship. The remaining attorney (the insured), who had coverage under three malpractice insurance policies, allegedly refused to pay his former associate's remaining salary and sent defamatory letters to his former clients. The attorney responded by suing the insured. The insured tendered defense of the lawsuit to his malpractice insurers. One insurer agreed to provide coverage but the other two refused. The insurer providing coverage sought a judicial declaration that the other two insurers were also obligated to provide coverage. Citing *Blumberg v. Guar. Ins. Co.*, 238 Cal.Rptr. 36 (App.2d Dist.1987), the California Court of Appeal, Second District, refused to order coverage. The other insurers' policies provided coverage for damages arising out of "any act, error or omission in professional services rendered or that should have been rendered...." Professional services were defined as "all services rendered or which should have been rendered for others...." There had to be professional malpractice in order for liability to arise under the policies, and the court held that the mere business conflict which existed in the present case did not amount to professional malpractice. The two insurers were declared free from liability under the malpractice insurance policies. *Transamerica Ins. Co. v. Sayble*, 239 Cal.Rptr. 201 (App.2d Dist.1987).

A North Dakota medical provider was one of eleven defendants in a suit brought by a local doctor. The doctor alleged harm due to the loss of an exclusive contract. Three allegations applied to the provider: restraint of trade in violation of federal antitrust laws, tortious interference with the doctor's contract, and intentional infliction of emotional distress. The provider had both primary and excess malpractice insurance policies, and the defense of the suit was tendered to the insurers. The insurers, however, denied a duty to defend. The medical provider brought a separate suit in a federal district court, settled with one insurer, and brought a summary judgment motion against the other. The insurer countered with its own summary judgment motion. The policy's coverage agreement specified that the insurer would indemnify the insured for liability arising from "rendering or failure to render professional services." The provider argued that the harm allegedly arose because it had provided professional services thereby causing harm to another doctor. It contended that the policy was not limited to patient treatment. The insurer did not contest that the provider provided medical services, but argued that the doctor's harm was not proximately caused by those services. The court ruled the policy to be unambiguous and inapplicable to the claims alleged. The insurer had no duty to defend and was granted summary judgment. *Central Dakota Radiologists v. Continental Casualty Co.*, 769 F.Supp. 323 (D.N.D.1991).

After an emergency center was sued for negligence, its malpractice insurer asked a Georgia superior court for a declaration that it had no duty to defend in the negligence case. The superior court ruled against the insurer and it appealed to the Georgia Court of Appeals. The insurer argued that it had no duty to defend the emergency center since a doctor, employed by the emergency center, failed to cooperate in the insurer's investigation of the incident. The court of appeals observed that the policy issued by the insurer contained a clause requiring the cooperation of the insured in defending a suit. It noted that such clauses were valid in Georgia and required the cooperation of anyone who reaped the benefit from the shouldering of the defense by the insurer, that is, one named as a defendant in the lawsuit. Here, the doctor who failed to cooperate had not been named by the alleged injured parties in their complaint against the emergency center. Thus, although the doctor was an insured under the malpractice insurance policy, he did not stand to reap any benefit from the assumption of the defense by the insurer and therefore, had no duty to cooperate with the insurer's investigation. The cooperation clause did not apply and the insurer had a duty to defend the emergency center. *St. Paul Fire & Marine Ins. Co. v. Albany Emergency Center*, 361 S.E.2d 687 (Ga.App.1987).

An Arizona gynecologist was sued on account of his alleged improper and intentional clitoral manipulations during gynecological examinations. He sought coverage under a professional liability policy issued by St. Paul Fire & Marine Insurance Company, which denied coverage on the ground that his alleged conduct was outside the scope of his professional duties. The Arizona Court of Appeals ruled that the alleged conduct occurred "in the course of and as an inseparable part of the providing of professional services" and afforded coverage. The court disagreed with St. Paul's argument that "indemnification of a physician for performing antisocial, illegal, immoral and unprofessional acts" was contrary to public policy. Arizona's public policy, stated the court, "favors protecting the interests of injured parties." *St. Paul Fire & Marine Ins. Co. v. Asbury*, 720 P.2d 540 (Ariz.App.1986).

A dentist sexually assaulted a patient after he administered excessive amounts of nitrous oxide to her. She brought suit against the dentist who sought coverage from his malpractice insurer. A district court dismissed the insurer's declaratory relief action. The insurer appealed, and the appellate court reversed and remanded. Subsequently, the Connecticut Supreme Court transferred the appeal to itself. The insurer argued to the court that the dentist's act did not constitute a "professional act" because the administration of nitrous oxide did not require the use of any intellectual skill or specialized knowledge. The court disagreed, finding that the gas's administration was inseparable from the dentist's conduct. Therefore, the court held that the malpractice policy had to extend coverage for the dentist's assault. *St. Paul Fire and Marine Ins. Co. v. Shernow*, 610 A.2d 1281 (Conn.1992).

Three women filed lawsuits against a dentist alleging that he had sexually molested them. The dentist's malpractice insurance covered him for damages arising from the performance of "professional services rendered." The women amended their lawsuits to include allegations of negligence and recklessness in relation to the dentist's performance of professional services. The dentist's insurer undertook the dentist's defense under a reservation of rights and sought a determination of its obligations under the policy. The South Carolina Supreme Court ruled that although the insurer was not obligated to indemnify the dentist for damages arising from his alleged intentional sexual misconduct, it was obligated to defend him since the lawsuit alleged negligence and recklessness arising from his work as a dentist. *S.C. Medical Malpractice Liability Ins. Joint Underwriting Ass'n v. Ferry*, 354 S.E.2d 378 (S.C.1987).

From June 1979, through May 1981, a woman received psychiatric treatment from a California psychiatrist. She suffered from a psychosis that stemmed in part from childhood sexual molestation. In about May 1981, the psychiatrist entered into a sexual relationship with the woman which lasted until October 1981. The woman filed a lawsuit against the psychiatrist in 1982 alleging medical malpractice and infliction of emotional distress. His malpractice insurer undertook defense of the lawsuit. The malpractice insurer tendered the defense to the psychiatrist's personal liability insurer and his excess (umbrella) insurer. Both of the latter refused to contribute. A settlement was reached which paid the woman $77,000. The malpractice insurer contributed $29,999 and the personal liability insurer contributed $45,001. The malpractice insurer filed a lawsuit in U.S. district court seeking contribution from the personal liability and excess insurers which sought a ruling that they were not bound to defend or indemnify the doctor for the settlement.

In determining coverage, the district court noted that expert testimony indicated that the psychiatrist had committed malpractice both by entering into a sexual relationship with the patient and by terminating her treatment without taking steps to see that her psychiatric treatment continued. The psychiatrist's malpractice insurance policy covered professional malpractice but excluded harm arising from "sexual intimacy." The court, however, ruled that the policy covered the woman's claim because the termination of treatment was one of the proximate causes of her injuries.

The court observed that the psychiatrist's personal liability policy expressly excluded coverage for "bodily injury ... arising out of the rendering or failure to render professional services." Since the claims arose out of the rendering of professional services the personal liability policy did not apply. The personal liability insurer was therefore entitled to recover from the malpractice insurer its contribution to the woman's settlement. The psychiatrist's excess insurance policy also provided limited primary coverage. The policy indicated that it would supply primary coverage in situations where the psychiatrist's basic policies did not apply. The district court decided that although the excess insurer and the personal liability insurer were not liable for any amount of the settlement, the woman's suit had constituted a potentially valid claim under both when filed. The court therefore held that the malpractice insurer was entitled to a *pro rata* reimbursement for defense costs. *Cranford Ins. Co. v. Allwest Ins. Co.*, 645 F.Supp. 1440 (N.D.Cal.1986).

An attorney purchased a comprehensive professional liability insurance policy which provided that the insurer would pay money that the attorney became legally obligated to pay as a result of claims "arising out of the rendering or failure to render professional services for others in [his] capacity as a lawyer." He was later sued for malpractice and breach of duty because he had allegedly sold trust property belonging to his client to a company which he owned and controlled. He notified his insurer, but it denied coverage. He then sued his insurer in a federal district court. The insurer moved for summary judgment. He asserted that the insurer had wrongfully refused coverage, and that it had breached a duty of good faith owed to him. The district court examined the policy and found that it potentially provided coverage. The exclusion in the policy for work performed by an attorney with respect to a trust did not bar coverage here because the complaint stated that the attorney had breached a duty to his client. Thus, the claims did not necessarily relate to the trust. The court denied the insurer's motion for summary judgment and held that the insurer had to provide a defense to the attorney. *Clauder v. Home Ins. Co.*, 790 F.Supp. 162 (S.D.Ohio 1992).

An attorney in Arizona was sued by two of his clients after they had allegedly lost "millions of dollars" in investments that the attorney had recommended to them. The investments were corporations and partnerships which the attorney formed or operated. While some of the loss was due to bona fide market losses, the clients alleged that fraudulent actions accounted for a portion of it. In addition to acting as an investment counselor, the attorney (who was also a CPA) performed legal work for the clients in the areas of taxation and accounting. Although he charged the clients for his legal services, he never billed them for any work performed in the ventures in dispute. The attorney's malpractice insurer, General Accident Insurance Company, sought a ruling from a U.S. district court on whether it was required to defend the attorney in a legal malpractice suit. The insurer argued that the attorney had not been acting in a legal capacity when managing the investments; thus, the losses were not covered by his malpractice policy. The court agreed with the insurer, holding that the attorney had been acting as a business agent rather than as an attorney. The clients appealed. The U.S. Court of Appeals, Ninth Circuit, noted that the policy provided coverage only for "professional services" and specifically excluded dishonest or fraudulent acts. The court determined that the attorney had been acting as the client's "coventurer" but had not rendered professional services. Hence, the attorney's actions were not covered under his malpractice policy and the decision of the district court was affirmed. *General Accident Ins. Co. v. Namesnik*, 790 F.2d 1397 (9th Cir.1986).

After a physician testified that he suspected a child of having been abused by the child's father, the father sued him (and the others who had testified against him) alleging a conspiracy to defame him and deprive him of his visitation rights with his son. The doctor sought coverage from his medical malpractice insurer, which denied that it had a duty to defend or indemnify. The trial court held for the insurer. The Louisiana Court of Appeal found that the malpractice insurance policy did not unambiguously exclude coverage for the alleged conspiracy. It therefore reversed, holding that the insurer had to defend the doctor in the underlying suit. *St. Amant v. Mack*, 590 So.2d 1283 (La.App.1st Cir.1991).

II. POLICY COVERAGE DATES

Since malpractice suits might not be filed for months or even years after the professional's contact with the aggrieved client, disputes have arisen over liability coverage. Policy dates can be critical in ascertaining the extent of coverage.

A hospital was in the process of changing malpractice insurers, and notified its present insurer of all potential claims before the expiration of its policy. These potential claims did materialize into actual claims after the expiration of the policy, and the hospital and the insurer disagreed as to whether the insurer was required to defend or indemnify the hospital. The insurer contended that the notification received did not constitute "claims." The dispute eventually went to trial in a state court, and the insurer added a counterclaim against the hospital for a failure to repay a $10,000 settlement which was paid by the insurer, as the hospital had a $50,000 deductible. On the counterclaim, the hospital argued that it was not asked to consent to the judgment and was thus not responsible to repay the insurer. Both disputes were resolved in favor of the hospital and were eventually appealed to the Supreme Court of Alabama.

First addressed was what constituted a "claim." The insurer's policy provided a definition, but the court noted that the term "claim" had been used several times throughout the policy, and in different contexts had different meanings. The policy was held to be ambiguous. Upon finding an ambiguity, the court applied three requirements: 1) the incident must occur within the policies' dates, 2) it must be reported to the insurer within those dates, and 3) the report must contain particular information so as to distinguish it from an incident report. The reports in this case were held to constitute a claim. On the counterclaim, the policy had provided a clause which granted the insurer discretion to settle suits. However, the law provides that when a settlement will actually be paid entirely by the insured as part of a deductible, the insured possesses a direct financial stake in the settlement; it thus must be granted a chance to reject or accept offers. Both judgments in favor of the hospital were affirmed. *St. Paul Fire & Marine Ins. Co. v. Edge Memorial Hospital*, 584 So.2d 1316 (Ala.1991).

A hospital obtained a claims-made liability policy to replace its previous insurance. The hospital subsequently received notice of a lawsuit arising from a complicated birth occurring prior to the effective date of the replacement policy. The insurer denied coverage because it felt that the hospital should have been placed on notice of the potential for a suit and accordingly made a claim against its prior insurer. The hospital contended that it had not been put on notice, and alternatively that the insurer was estopped from denying coverage because it knew that the hospital's risk management procedures were subpar when it accepted the risk. The insurer sought a declaration of its rights in a federal district court. The replacement policy provided that coverage was inapplicable to harm which occurred prior to the effectiveness of the policy "if the insured could have reasonably foreseen that such harm might result in a claim." The court then focused on the facts which could have put the hospital on notice. The complications of the birth and later physical condition were found to not necessarily put the hospital on notice. Later requests for medical records by government agencies and university services for crippled children were viewed similarly, but numerous and increasingly specific requests for records by a known personal injury lawyer were not. The facts were ruled to be of such a nature that they should have put the hospital on notice. The court further ruled that the insurer was not estopped from denying coverage — even the subpar risk management procedures should have detected the potential for a claim. The policy was held to be inapplicable. *American Continental Ins. Co. v. Marion Memorial Hospital*, 773 F.Supp. 1148 (S.D.Ill.1991).

A North Carolina couple sued the wife's psychiatrist for initiating a sexual relationship with her while she was a patient. They asserted that in doing so he had breached his duty to ensure that she received adequate medical care. The psychiatrist was insured by two insurers during the time the wife was a patient. After the predecessor insurer was sent a copy of the complaint, it responded by denying coverage, stating that the alleged acts did not occur during its policy term. The present insurer settled both claims for approximately $500,000, and filed a complaint in a federal trial court seeking a contribution from the predecessor insurer. The trial court granted summary judgment in favor of the present insurer and the predecessor insurer appealed to the U.S. Court of Appeals, Fourth Circuit. The predecessor insurer contended that the allegations of the underlying complaint demonstrated that the injuries took place after its policy had expired. The court determined that once the predecessor insurer breached its duty to defend the insured psychiatrist against malpractice actions, the predecessor insurer waived any opportunity to litigate whether the underlying offense occurred within its policy period. Therefore, the court found for the present insurer, and the predecessor insurer was liable for one-half of the costs and the settlement. *St. Paul Fire and Marine Ins. Co. v. Vigilant Ins. Co.*, 919 F.2d 235 (4th Cir.1990).

A Wisconsin woman was negligently injured by a podiatrist in 1983 and 1984. On August 26, 1986, she sued the podiatrist and his insurer in a Wisconsin trial court. The insurer moved to dismiss the complaint against it and the woman sought summary judgment on the issue of policy coverage. The trial court found that coverage existed and the trial on the issue of the doctor's negligence proceeded. Eventually, the doctor was found negligent and the insurer was required to pay the $200,000 policy limit. The insurer appealed to the Court of Appeals of Wisconsin. On appeal, the insurer contended that the policy was no longer an "occurrence" policy but a "claims-made" policy. The policy stated that if claims were filed against the insured a surcharge would be charged and if the insured failed to pay the surcharge within ninety days then the insurer could "deny liability on any claim against the insured irrespective of the policy year in which the incident occurred." The podiatrist did not pay the surcharge within the ninety days. Therefore, the trial court determined that, based on this clause, the insurer was not liable and the claim against it should have been dismissed. The injured woman, however, contended that the insurance laws of Wisconsin required the insurer to inform the insureds ten days prior to a policy termination. Since the insurer was from the Cayman Islands and was not licensed in the state of Wisconsin, the court determined that the insurance laws did not apply to it and reversed the trial court's decision. *Stone v. Seeber*, 455 N.W.2d 627 (Wis.App.1990).

An attorney drafted a land contract which became the subject of a dispute and eventually led to a lawsuit and an adverse decision for his clients. The attorney who represented the clients in the action informed the drafting attorney that the clients wished him to notify his professional liability insurer in case the appeal of the decision failed. The drafting attorney responded that he would forward the potential claim to his insurer, but he did not. A malpractice action was eventually brought, and the insurer denied the duty to defend or indemnify because it contended that a claim had not occurred during the policy, and because it did not receive timely notice. A state circuit court ruled against the insurer, which then appealed to the Court of Appeals of Wisconsin.

The first issue was whether the letter which was sent to the drafting attorney constituted a claim as defined in the policy. The insurer contended that the letter made no demand for money and thus did not constitute a claim. While many inquiries do not constitute a claim, the court held that the letter in this context could only be reasonably construed to be a notification that the clients intended to hold the attorney financially responsible if the appeal was unsuccessful; it thus constituted a claim. The next issue concerned the effect of untimely notice. The policy provided that untimely notice would not invalidate a claim unless the insurer was prejudiced thereby. The insurer contended that lack of notice precluded it from intervening in the land contract action against the clients. The court questioned whether intervention would have been allowed, and ruled that the outcome of such intervention was purely speculative. The insurer's ability to conduct discovery and prepare a malpractice defense was unaffected, and the court held that no prejudice had occurred. The judgment was affirmed. *Rentmeester v. Wisconsin Lawyers Mutual Ins. Co.*, 473 N.W.2d 160 (Wis.App.1991).

A California attorney purchased a claims-made professional liability insurance policy. He renewed the policy once, but was notified by the insurer that the policy would not be renewed again. He was, however, given the opportunity to obtain an "extended reporting period endorsement" for an additional premium. He refused, and the policy expired. Prior to its expiration, a complaint was filed against the attorney for legal malpractice. He was unaware of the complaint, however, until after the reporting period of the policy had passed. When he requested a defense, the insurer refused. The attorney sued his insurer for breach of contract and breach of the implied covenant of good faith and fair dealing. The court granted the insurer's motion for summary judgment, and the attorney appealed to the California Court of Appeal, Second District.

On appeal, the attorney asserted that the "notice prejudice" rule barred the insurer from denying coverage because it was not substantially prejudiced by the late notice given. He also asserted that public policy should prevail over a strict reading of the policy, and further contended that the policy was ambiguous. The court of appeal first noted that the reporting and notice provisions were not ambiguous. The policy merely required claims to be made and reported to the insurer while the policy was in force. The court then stated that the notice prejudice rule was developed for occurrence policies (as opposed to claims-made policies), and that to allow an extension because of lack of prejudice would extend policy coverage beyond the date bargained for by the insurer. Finally, the court held that the attorney had been offered the opportunity to extend the reporting period and had rejected it; thus, he could make no public policy claims of unfairness. The court affirmed the trial court's decision in favor of the insurer. *Slater v. Lawyers' Mutual Ins. Co.*, 278 Cal.Rptr. 479 (Cal.App.2d Dist.1991).

In January 1981, a New York doctor applied for professional liability coverage. Through an error on the part of the insurer, a policy was not issued until June 1982. At that time the insurer issued two policies, one effective for 1981 and the other for 1982. The doctor requested that his 1981 policy be cancelled. The insurer agreed to cancel the policy retroactively. Subsequently, the estate of a former patient sued the doctor for malpractice committed during 1981. The doctor then sued the insurer claiming it had a duty to defend him. The insurer claimed that since the decision to cancel the policy was mutual, the policy was not in effect in 1981. The trial court entered judgment on behalf of the doctor, and the insurer appealed. The appeals court affirmed the trial court's decision and held that the cancellation of the insurance policy was invalid. The court noted that the strong public interest in having insured doctors exceeded the interests of the parties to the contract. *Van Amerogen v. Donnini*, 555 N.Y.S.2d 877 (A.D.3d Dep't 1990)

A New York law firm took on a case involving a breach of contract. The firm failed to timely reactivate the case after it had been delayed in the courts. As a result, the clients' case was dismissed. The clients commenced a malpractice action against the firm which was settled for $300,000. The settlement was paid in equal shares by the law firm and two of its insurers. A third insurer refused to indemnify the firm under a policy containing a $250,000 limitation. The law firm sought a declaration that the third insurer was required to pay its policy limit of $250,000 or that it should bear a *pro rata* share of the settlement. A trial court dismissed the law firm's complaint. The firm appealed to the New York Supreme Court, Appellate Division.

On appeal, the insurer argued that since its policy had been effective four years after the firm took the case, the acts of malpractice were not committed and did not take place during the policy period. In addition, it was only after the policy period expired that the complaint against the law firm was filed. The court disagreed, ordering the third insurer to pay its *pro rata* share of the malpractice settlement. It said that the malpractice in question consisted of a continuous error and omission of the law firm to prosecute the clients' action from the time that it took the case until the action was dismissed. Within that time period, the third insurer's policy had been effective for two years. The court found that the major portion of the law firm's malpractice had been committed during the period when it neglected to protect the interests of its clients. This neglect was still occurring while the third insurer's policy was in effect. It was sufficient by the terms of the policy that at least some of the malpractice be committed in the operative time period. The court also noted that nothing in the third insurer's policy mandated that any act, error or omission by the insured be reduced to a single occurrence or that it take place in its entirety during the effective date of the policy. The lower court's decision was reversed and the third insurer was ordered to indemnify the insured. *Levine v. Lumbermans Mut. Cas. Co.*, 538 N.Y.S.2d 263 (A.D.1st Dept.1989).

An insured attorney's legal malpractice insurance was cancelled upon his death. The insured's estate brought suit against the insurer for the unauthorized cancellation of the insurance. The trial court granted summary judgment in favor of the insurer, which had a letter from the insured's agent requesting cancellation. The estate then moved to join the agent as a party in the matter because he had cancelled the coverage without the personal representative's permission while a claim was pending. The court resolved the claim against the agent in the estate's favor, stating that the agent should have waited for instructions from the estate before cancelling the policy. The agent appealed to the District Court of Appeal of Florida, Third District, which affirmed the lower court's ruling. *Poe & Assoc., Inc. v. Estate of Vogler*, 559 So.2d 1235 (Fla.App.3d Dist.1990).

An insured Illinois doctor owned a professional liability policy which provided him with coverage and defense for malpractice claims. A client filed a complaint against him in an Illinois circuit court alleging negligent diagnosis and treatment causing permanent injuries. The alleged negligence occurred during the policy period. However, the complaint was not served on the insured until after his liability policy had terminated. He wrote to his insurance agent about the pending lawsuit stating that the complaint was filed during the coverage period. The insurer notified the insured that it would not provide coverage or defense and also asked an Illinois trial court to determine the rights and liabilities of the parties. The court found that the insurer had no duty to defend or indemnify the insured. The insured appealed to the Illinois Appellate Court. On appeal, the insured argued that the policy and cancellation form language created an ambiguity about when a claim was made under the policy. Under the policy language, a claim was to be made when the insured suffered a loss. Loss was not defined in the policy. The policy itself implied that loss could mean "accident or incident" or an "injury" which could result in a claim. Loss could also be interpreted as the filing of a formal complaint against the insured. The appellate court construed the ambiguity against the insurer. It reversed the trial court's decision and remanded the case for further consideration. *St. Paul Ins. Co. of Illinois v. Armas*, 527 N.E.2d 921 (Ill.App.1st Dist.1988).

The U.S. Court of Appeals, Ninth Circuit, reversed a U.S. district court's ruling that reporting requirements in policies for claims are valid and fall outside the scope of California's substantial prejudice rule. In this case, National Union Fire Insurance Company provided legal malpractice insurance to members of the Los Angeles County Bar Association. The policy limited National Union's liability to malpractice claims "first made against the insured and reported to the [insurer] during the policy period." Upon the policy's expiration in 1983, several insureds had claims against them which had not yet been reported to National Union. When National Union refused to provide coverage citing the policy's reporting requirement, the bar association's new insurer asked the district court for a declaration that National Union was liable. The district court held that National Union's reporting requirement was valid and denied coverage. The court of appeals disagreed. It noted that in California, insurers must "show material and substantial prejudice from an insured's failure to timely report a claim before they may deny liability on that basis." The mere fact that the insureds in this case did not notify National Union of claims against them until after the policy expired did not defeat coverage, held the court of appeals, despite the policy language requiring claims to be "made and reported" within the policy's term. The district court's ruling was reversed and the case was remanded for further proceedings. *New England Reinsurance Corp. v. Nat'l Union Fire Ins. Co. of Pittsburg*, 822 F.2d 887 (9th Cir.1987).

III. FRAUD BY PROFESSIONALS

Malpractice insurance policies generally do not provide coverage for a professional's fraudulent acts.

An energy cooperative agreed to hold an investment interest in a nuclear powered generating plant. A public utility also held an interest, and was given sole responsibility for its production. The utility contracted with an engineering firm whose work was faulty, and eventually the Nuclear Regulatory Commission temporarily stopped work. The costs of the project greatly increased, the engineering firm avoided disclosure and misstated cost estimate increases to the energy cooperative, and eventually the utility abandoned the project. The abandonment caused the cooperative to lose its $466,000,000 investment. The cooperative brought suit against the firm and alleged both fraud and negligence. The firm's professional liability insurer brought a separate action against the firm in state court, and sought to avoid providing a defense to the firm. The insurer argued that a conflict of interest precluded defense, and that coverage was excluded. It was unsuccessful and appealed to the Appellate Court of Illinois.

The insurer argued that the policy's definition of damages did not include economic loss. The court held that the policy could cover a loss caused by faulty construction which leads to an inability to use property. The next issue was whether the insurer was required to provide a defense due to its claim of untimely notice, and the eventual conflict of interest that might arise because of it. The insured was ruled to have a right to be reimbursed for the expenses of an attorney of its choice in such instances; the insurer might later raise the notice defense in a supplemental suit. Another argument was that wrongful concealment was the true basis of the complaint, and that this was not an occurrence as defined in the policy. However, the court held that a lone count of negligence in the complaint would create a duty to defend. The insurer finally claimed that coverage was excluded. It noted that the complaint alleged fraud, conspiracy, and other charges which were not the customary or usual professional services of an engineering firm. Again the insurer was unsuccessful; an allegation of negligence, which could be covered under the policy, was found to be connected to all claims. The decision of the lower court was affirmed. *Gibralter Casualty Co. v. Sargent & Lundy*, 574 N.E.2d 664 (Ill. App.1st Dist.1990).

An accountant conducted his practice through a sole proprietorship, then formed a corporation. The corporation purchased a claims-made liability policy which provided coverage for services rendered prior to the inception of coverage if a claim was made during the policy period, and if "no insured had any knowledge of any circumstances which might have resulted in a claim at the effective date of the policy." While the policy was in force, the accountant and his corporation were sued for fraud committed by the accountant prior to the policy's inception. The insurer brought suit, seeking a declaration that it need not cover the insured. A federal district court granted summary judgment to the insurer. On appeal to the U.S. Court of Appeals, Seventh Circuit, the argument was made that the policy's protection was merely illusory if the above-quoted language was not held to be against public policy. However, the court analogized the policy in this case to a health insurance policy which prohibits coverage for a preexisting known condition. Such limitations are clearly permissible. Since the accountant in this case almost certainly knew that he was likely to be charged with fraud when his corporation bought the policy, no coverage had to be provided. The court affirmed the summary judgment in favor of the insurer. *Truck Ins. Exchange v. Ashland Oil Inc.*, 951 F.2d 787 (7th Cir.1992).

A group of physicians formed a self-insurance fund to provide occurrence coverage malpractice insurance. The fund in turn hired an outside service to provide management. The service procured an actuarial study which suggested the necessity of a large assessment. The service did not disclose this information to the fund's trustees. The trustees accordingly reported as an inducement that the fund did not anticipate charging an assessment. The service was eventually replaced for unrelated reasons. After an assessment, the physicians became aware that previous management had known of the need for an assessment but had failed to disclose the information. Numerous physicians refused to pay the assessment, then sued the fund for fraud and breach of contract. A trial court ruled for the fund because it found that the misrepresentations had not been relied upon. Three doctors appealed that ruling to the District Court of Appeal of Florida. The appellate court reversed the factual findings concerning reliance, and found that the fund had breached its contract. The issue then became the measure of damages. The appropriate remedy for fraud is rescission: the parties should be restored to their original positions while not allowing the wrongdoer to profit from fraud. The physicians sought a return of premiums, but the fund argued that they had already received the benefit of coverage and that the return of premiums would thus not return the doctors to their original position. The court agreed with the fund that the premiums should not be returned; the doctors had received the benefit of their bargain without paying the assessment, and the fund would not profit from the fraud by its management. *Arad v. Caduceus Self Ins. Fund*, 585 So.2d 1000 (Fla.App. 4 Dist.1991).

A client sued a Texas law firm alleging that a deed obtained by the law firm in payment for its services was procured "under fraud, duress, undue influence, and involved the breach of an attorney-client privilege...." When the law firm's malpractice insurer refused to defend it against the client's claims, the law firm sued the insurer for breach of contract. The U.S. Court of Appeals, Fifth Circuit, observed that an exclusion in the law firm's policy provided that defense coverage did not apply "to any dishonest, fraudulent, criminal or malicious act or omission of the Insured...." The question before it was whether the common meaning of "fraud," as it appeared in the exclusion, included both actual fraud (intentional deceit) and constructive fraud (a breach of duty which has a tendency to deceive). The insurer argued that the law firm's alleged breach of its ethical duties constituted a form of fraud and that, since the exclusion for fraudulent actions was express, it had no duty to defend the law firm. However, the court of appeals held that the exclusion only applied to actual fraud and that therefore, the insurer had a duty to defend. This was due to the fact that the client's complaint included allegations (duress and undue influence) that the law firm was liable for constructive fraud. The insurer was liable for breach of contract. *Brooks, Tarlton, Gilbert, Douglas & Kressler v. United States Fire Ins. Co.*, 832 F.2d 1358 (5th Cir.1987).

An insurance adjuster in Oklahoma settled an automobile accident claim with certain injured parties. He told the parties that the policy limits covering the claim were $10,000 per person and $20,000 per occurrence. Later it was discovered that the policy limits were in fact $25,000/$50,000. The injured parties brought suit against the adjuster alleging fraud by misrepresentation and bad faith and sought $235,000 in actual damages and $6,765,000 in punitive damages. The adjuster then notified his professional liability insurer of the claim. The insurer agreed to defend. A settlement was reached in which the professional liability insurer and the insurer of the automobile claim would each pay $150,000. At this point the professional liability insurer refused to contribute to any settlement fund on the ground that the policy excluded coverage for fraud on the part of the insured. A federal district court in Oklahoma held that the professional liability insurer was barred from claiming the fraud exclusion in the policy because the injured parties were prejudiced by the delay in raising such a defense until the eve of trial. The court noted that the insurer at all pertinent times had knowledge of its policy exclusions and was in charge of the defense in the lawsuit. Thus, stated the court, the insurer had waived its defense by waiting until settlement was reached before claiming the fraud exclusion. The court further found that the settlement was reasonable under the circumstances and apportioned the settlement as one-half actual damages and one-half punitive damages. *Gay & Taylor, Inc. v. St. Paul Fire & Marine Ins. Co.*, 550 F.Supp. 710 (W.D.Okla.1981).

IV. SUITS BASED ON ERROR OR MISTAKE

Some policies obligate the insurer to defend the professional even if the lawsuit was based on an error or mistake.

A legal malpractice case involved a Pennsylvania lawyer who owned all of the shares in a tire business. The tire business agreed to purchase another business and, pursuant to the agreement, obtained fire insurance for the to-be-purchased business. After a fire destroyed the to-be-purchased business its owners hired the lawyer's law firm to handle its claim against the insurer. A settlement offer by the insurer was rejected by the law firm, which then sued the insurer, mistakenly naming the lawyer's tire business as the plaintiff. The trial court held for the insurer. The owners of the to-be-purchased business then sued the law firm for malpractice. They alleged that the law firm negligently failed to name the to-be-purchased business as a plaintiff in the lawsuit against the insurer, and also that it submitted erroneous proof of the fire loss and failed to notify them in a timely fashion that fraud had been raised as a defense by the insurer. Holding for the law firm, the U.S. Court of Appeals, Third Circuit, observed that the malpractice policy provided coverage. The negligence and breach of contract allegations concerned the failure to render competent professional services. These allegations clearly fell within the terms of the malpractice policy. The court of appeals held that the law firm's insurer had to defend the law firm against the owners of the to-be-purchased business. *Niagara Fire Ins. Co. v. Pepicelli, Pepicelli & Youngs, P.C*, 821 F.2d 216 (3d Cir.1987).

A child psychiatrist in California carried a policy which provided standard malpractice insurance coverage, including "any claims or suits based upon ... error ... or mistake." There was an exclusion for suits "arising out of the performance of criminal acts." When the child psychiatrist was prosecuted for Medi-Cal fraud and theft, he requested that his insurer defend him in the criminal proceedings. The insurer refused. The psychiatrist was found innocent of all charges when the court determined that the alleged criminal conduct was the result of mistakes and errors in billing. The psychiatrist then filed suit in California Superior Court to recover the costs of his defense from his insurer, but the court dismissed his suit. He appealed.

The California Court of Appeal affirmed the decision against the psychiatrist. A duty to defend arises only when the insured might be held liable for damages. A criminal case, on the other hand, can result only in fines or imprisonment which are not considered to be "damages" for insurance purposes. The appeals court therefore affirmed the ruling that the psychiatrist had to bear the costs of his own defense to the criminal charges. *Jaffe v. Cranford Ins. Co.*, 214 Cal.Rptr. 567 (App.4th Dist.1985).

V. LIABILITY OF A PROFESSIONAL'S EMPLOYER

In most employee-employer relationships, the employee is an agent of the employer. For this reason the employer is usually held liable for the acts of the employees, providing the acts arise out of and are within the scope of employment. Professionals, on the other hand, are often treated by the courts as independent contractors and must generally provide for their own liability insurance.

A twenty-year-old woman with a history of asthma suffered an acute asthma attack and died one day after an examination at a West Virginia medical center. The woman's doctor was a full-time state employee for the state-run center, who maintained a separate malpractice policy for his part-time private medical practice. The woman's estate filed a wrongful death action against the State of West Virginia, Board of Vocational Rehabilitation and against the treating physicians on the basis of negligent care and treatment. The state's malpractice policy provided coverage for liability for claims arising from acts occurring within the scope of the doctor's duties as a state employee. However, the state's insurer denied coverage and filed a declaratory judgment action in a West Virginia circuit court to determine whether it or the doctor's private carrier owed coverage. The state's insurer argued that its policy precluded coverage because the doctor maintained a private policy and because the doctor personally acted negligently. It also argued that the other insurance clause contained in its policy obligated it to provide only excess coverage.

The doctor's private carrier argued that its policy could not be construed as a primary policy because the two policies did not insure the same risk. It also argued that the personal acts exclusion in the state's policy was ambiguous because of the phrase "personal acts or omissions of a professional nature." The private carrier argued that this language excluded only the doctor's private practice from coverage. The circuit court agreed with the private carrier, and the state's insurer appealed to the Supreme Court of Appeals of West Virginia which affirmed the circuit court's decision. It stated that the policies did not insure the same risks and that the state's policy was ambiguous because it had at least two possible interpretations. Where ambiguities exist in insurance policies, they are to be strictly construed against the insurer. *State of West Virginia v. Janicki*, 422 S.E.2d 822 (W.Va.1992).

An Ohio hospital entered into a one-year employment contract with a resident internist. The hospital agreed to provide the internist with professional liability coverage through a blanket insurance policy. After the employment contract had been printed and before the internist became a resident, the hospital elected to become self-insured. The resident was sued for medical malpractice. He was covered by an individual professional policy issued by the hospital's insurer. The policy limited liability to $200,000 for each medical incident. It also contained an "other insurance" provision which reduced the insurer's liability by requiring contribution if there was "other insurance" covering the same loss. The medical malpractice case was settled for $300,000. The insurer contributed its policy limit of $200,000 and the hospital contributed $100,000. The insurer then brought a declaratory judgment action to determine whether the hospital's contractual obligation to provide liability coverage for its residents was "other insurance" under the policy. An Ohio trial court held that the resident-hospital contract was not other insurance. The insurer appealed to the Court of Appeals of Ohio.

The court of appeals held that self-insurance was not insurance. The court noted that insurance shifts the risk of loss from an insured to an insurer. Self-insurance was the retention of risk of loss by the one upon whom it was directly imposed by law or contract. The hospital had agreed to assume a risk of loss which as an employer it already had by law. The employment agreement merely shifted the entire risk of loss as between the parties to the hospital. The court of appeals affirmed the trial court's decision. *Physicians Ins. Co. of Ohio v. Grandview Hospital & Medical Center*, 542 N.E.2d 706 (Ohio App.1988).

A company in the business of collecting and distributing human plasma agreed to sell its entire production of plasma to a corporation which manufactured human plasma derivatives. The collecting company was required to test for the presence of hepatitis B surface antigen (HBsAg) for each unit of blood it sold by conducting two separate tests. Initial tests on four units of plasma indicated that HBsAg was present in each of them. However, due to a medical technician's error, the follow-up tests were performed on four other units of plasma, which did not show the presence of HBsAg. As a result, the purchasing corporation's supply was contaminated and a portion had to be destroyed. The purchaser sued the seller for breach of contract. The seller made a claim for indemnity from its liability insurer and also demanded that its insurer defend it in the lawsuit. The insurer refused, stating that it was not required to indemnify the seller for damage caused in the course of providing a professional service. The seller sued the insurer in a federal district court. The court held for the insurer and the seller appealed to the U.S. Court of Appeals, Eleventh Circuit. On appeal, the seller argued that a medical technician did not have the requisite training to qualify as a professional and that the technician's job of transposing test results was not a professional service. The court of appeals disagreed. The court agreed with the district court's assertion that while a medical technician is not a "professional," if delegated certain professional duties, he or she can be considered a professional for insurance purposes. The court of appeals affirmed the district court's decision. *Alpha Therapeutic Corp. v. St. Paul Fire and Marine Ins. Co.*, 890 F.2d 368 (11th Cir.1989).

A woman in California and her minor children brought suit against a malpractice insurer alleging that a doctor's medical malpractice resulted in the death of the woman's husband. The doctor had performed gastric surgery upon the patient. Following the surgery the patient developed symptoms of peritonitis, a condition which can lead to death if not promptly and properly treated. A hospital employee reported this condition to the doctor, who allegedly gave no instructions or orders with respect to the patient's treatment. The patient died that same day.

In the widow's wrongful death action against the doctor, the hospital's insurer refused to defend him on the ground that the medical malpractice insurance policy issued to the hospital in which the doctor performed the surgery did not cover the doctor. The doctor carried no private medical malpractice insurance. When the widow and her children obtained a judgment against the doctor and sought to recover on the hospital's insurance policy, the insurer refused payment.

The Supreme Court of California held that the doctor was not an "insured" under the policy issued to the hospital. The policy exclusion for an "individual hired or employed by or on behalf of a patient at the hospital" was interpreted by the court to mean that the doctor, who was in private practice and was hired by the deceased patient, was not included in the hospital's coverage because he was not an "employee" of the hospital. Thus, the widow and children were not entitled to recover on the hospital's insurance policy. *Garcia v. Truck Ins. Exchange*, 682 P.2d 1100 (Cal.1984).

VI. OTHER MALPRACTICE CASES

A. Liability Limits and Subrogation Rights

A paving and grading company retained a lawyer to render legal services in connection with a construction project in which it was involved. Apparently, the lawyer failed to serve a stop notice on the construction lenders within the statutory time, and also failed to file a complaint to foreclose a mechanic's lien within the statutory period (both are procedures aimed at recovering the client's funds). The company sued the lawyer for legal malpractice, and the lawyer's insurer was substituted as the defendant in the suit. The attorney's malpractice policy had a limit of $250,000 per claim and an annual limit of $750,000. The policy stated: two or more claims arising out of a single act, error or omission or a series of related acts, errors or omissions shall be treated as a single claim. The company asserted that it had two separate claims against the lawyer, while the insurer contended that only one claim had been advanced. The trial court held for the company, and the insurer appealed.

On appeal to the California Court of Appeal, First District, the insurer maintained that the company had merely presented two theories of liability for the lawyer's failure to collect a single construction bill. The court of appeal disagreed and held that each error by the lawyer created a separate claim. Since each error was independent of the other, rather than causally connected, the two errors by the lawyer did not constitute a series of related acts or omissions under the policy. The fact that both errors occurred with respect to the same project was not enough to turn them into a liability covered by a single claim. The court thus affirmed the trial court's decision and held that the company had presented two separate claims against the lawyer. *Bay Cities Paving & Grading, Inc. v. Lawyers' Mutual Ins. Co.*, 285 Cal.Rptr. 174 (Cal.App.1st Dist.1991).

A Florida physician who was found liable in a medical malpractice suit sought contribution from the Florida Patient's Compensation Fund. After his request for contribution was dismissed he appealed to the Florida District Court of Appeal which reversed and remanded the case to a Florida circuit court. The court ruled for the physician, stating that the fund did not have a valid third-party claim against the physician's insurer. The fund appealed to the District Court of Appeal of Florida. The court found that the physician's insurer owed a fiduciary duty to protect the interests of the fund in the medical malpractice action. The fund had stated a valid third-party cause of action against the insurer for breach of that duty. Because the insurer had failed to file appropriate pleadings in defense of the physician in the original action it exposed the fund to contribution claims by the physician. The appeals court reversed and remanded the circuit court's decision. *Florida Patient's Comp. Fund v. Caduceus Ins.*, 546 So.2d 13 (Fla.App.3d Dist.1989).

In 1984, the Minnesota Supreme Court held that a malpractice insurer had no duty to provide coverage for attorney's fees which were forfeited in a client's malpractice suit. The attorney had breached his duty to represent his client with undivided loyalty. The insurer, which served as the liability insurer for the attorney's law firm, then sued the attorney. It sought subrogation of amounts it had already paid on behalf of the law firm due to the attorney's alleged misconduct. A district court asked the Minnesota Supreme Court to rule on the question of whether an agreement entered into between the attorney and his law firm extinguished the subrogation rights of the law firm's insurer for claims paid due to the attorney's misconduct.

The supreme court observed that under the law firm's by-laws, the firm agreed to indemnify the attorney and hold him harmless for all costs and expenses arising out of its business if he acted in good faith. The law firm had paid all costs and expenses in lawsuits against the attorney thus indicating its belief in his good faith. Both the unambiguous language of the by-laws and the past actions of the law firm indicated that the subrogation rights of the law firm's insurer had been extinguished. The supreme court rejected the insurer's argument that such indemnification agreements were violative of public policy due to the legislature's consistent approval of corporate indemnification agreements. Also, such agreements only violated public policy when parties were guilty of illegal or intentional conduct. Here, there was no such activity. The supreme court observed that the insurer could have expressly forbidden such agreements in its insurance policy with the law firm but had failed to do so. The supreme court remanded the case to a district court with instructions to enter judgment for the attorney. *St. Paul Fire & Marine Ins. Co. v. Perl*, 415 N.W.2d 663 (Minn.1987).

An eleven-month-old infant suffered permanent injuries when he received a drug overdose during a hospital stay. The infant's parents filed a lawsuit against the doctors who prescribed the drug, the hospital and the drug company. The suit alleged 1) that the doctors were negligent in prescribing an inappropriate dosage, 2) that the hospital was negligent in filling the prescription without recognizing that the dosage was inappropriate for the infant, and 3) that the drug company used a misleading label on the drug that "failed to alert users to the difference in potency between two similarly named pharmaceuticals." The drug company was covered by an excess products liability policy with a $1 million retention. The drug company itself was liable for the first $1 million of any judgment against it. The policy included a vendor's endorsement which extended protection to those who distributed or sold the drug company's products in the course of their business. Under the policy's terms, the insurance company "had the right and duty to defend in suits against the insured." In January 1983, the drug company notified the insurance company that it would be held liable for the costs of defending the lawsuit and that the doctors and the hospital were covered by the policy's vendor endorsement. The suit was settled out of court for $1.9 million, apportioned as follows: Drug company: $950,000; Hospital: $300,000; Doctors: $650,000. When the insurance company refused to pay any part of the settlement the drug company filed a lawsuit against it claiming its refusal to pay was unjustifiable.

The drug company argued that because the doctors and hospital were additional insureds under the policy, their contributions amounting to $950,000 should be credited toward the $1 million retention. The insurance company claimed that the doctors and hospital were not covered by the vendor's endorsement, and that it was not responsible for paying any part of the settlement because the drug company's $1 million retention had not been exceeded. The federal court agreed with the insurance company and ruled in its favor. The drug company appealed.

The main issue on appeal was whether the doctors and hospital were covered by the vendor's endorsement to the drug company's insurance policy. The U.S. Court of Appeals, Third Circuit, noted that the doctors did not "sell or distribute" the drug using the normal meanings of these terms. They therefore did not qualify as "vendors" under the policy endorsement. However, the hospital did sell the drug, the court decided, and it was therefore covered by the policy. Any part of the settlement arising from the hospital's function as a seller of the drug was therefore covered by the policy. The court of appeals observed that a question of fact remained as to how much of the hospital's settlement apportionment arose from its actions as a seller of the drug. The court remanded the case for clarification of this remaining question of fact. It overturned the trial court's grant of summary judgment in favor of the insurance company. *Cooper Laboratories v. Int'l Surplus Lines Ins. Co.*, 802 F.2d 667 (3d Cir.1986).

An Arizona motorist died following an automobile accident in 1975. The motorist's family filed a wrongful death lawsuit against a doctor and his professional corporation alleging that the named doctor and another doctor working for the professional corporation both failed to examine the motorist's spinal x-rays which showed a fracture dislocation of his cervical vertebra, a condition which was left untreated and caused his death. The professional corporation was covered under a professional liability policy which provided each employed doctor coverage of up to $3 million per occurrence. When the insurer became insolvent, the Arizona Property and Casualty Insurance Guarantee Fund (APCIGF) assumed its obligations under the policy. APCIGF, however, provides coverage of no more than $99,900 for each covered claim. APCIGF sought a ruling from an Arizona superior court that the failure of both doctors to review the motorist's x-rays constituted only one occurrence under the policy. This ruling was granted but then reversed by the Arizona Court of Appeals. The doctor and the professional corporation appealed to the Arizona Supreme Court.

The policy defined "occurrence" as "any incident, act or omission, or series of related incidents, acts or omissions resulting in injury...." The supreme court decided that in order for omissions to be "related" and therefore constitute one occurrence under the policy, they had to be causally related to each other. Because the doctors each failed to examine the x-rays on separate days, and because there was no causal relationship between each doctor's failure to examine the x-rays, two covered occurrences existed for which APCIGF was liable. The decision of the court of appeals that the doctors' omissions were not sufficiently related to constitute only one occurrence was affirmed. *APCIGF v. Helme*, 735 P.2d 451 (Ariz.1987).

B. Bad-Faith Claims

The litigation preceding this bad faith claim arose when a Montana man died. Upon his death his wife hired an attorney to handle the estate, including preparation of their tax return. The attorney made an error in the computations which resulted in the woman having to pay $5,000 she should not have paid. Although she did not technically file a malpractice suit within the policy period, she did file a complaint with the Commission on Practice and the court concluded that there was coverage as a matter of law. A subsequent verdict was returned against the attorney and the judgment was satisfied by the attorney's insurer shortly thereafter. The woman's allegations of bad faith remained to be resolved, however. The matter was again brought before the trial court to determine the merit of the woman's allegation of a lack of good faith in the insurance company's negotiation settlement of the malpractice claim. The trial court granted summary judgment in favor of the insurer, reasoning that the company had reasonable grounds to deny coverage on the claim. The woman appealed, contending that the insurance company had a duty to conduct a reasonable investigation before refusing to pay the claim and breached this duty by not doing so. The Montana Supreme Court agreed. Holding that there were genuine issues of material fact which precluded summary judgment the court reversed and remanded for further proceedings. *Walker v. St. Paul Fire and Marine Ins. Co.*, 786 P.2d 1157 (Mont.1990).

An oral surgeon performed an operation on a patient during which the patient's heart temporarily stopped, causing permanent brain damage. The patient's wife sued the surgeon for her husband's injuries. The surgeon's insurer defended the surgeon based on his liability policy. The policy stated that "[t]he Company may make such investigation and settlement of any claim or suit as it deems expedient." The surgeon notified the insurer's attorney that he had not been negligent and that he wished to participate in an active defense. One month before the patient's wife filed the suit, the surgeon was charged with conspiracy to murder his business partner. In early 1983, the patient's wife notified the surgeon's attorney that she was willing to settle the case for $300,000. The insurer agreed despite the surgeon's reluctance. Three years later the surgeon sued his insurer in a Virginia federal district court alleging bad faith settlement. The district court held for the insurer and the surgeon appealed to the U.S. Court of Appeals, Fourth Circuit.

The insurer argued that the policy gave the insurer the absolute right to settle any claim within the policy limits. The surgeon asserted that the policy required the insurer to deal fairly with him in the claim handling and disposition. He also asserted that had the insurer thoroughly investigated the claim, it would have discovered evidence to vindicate him. The court noted that great deference was given to insurers who elect to settle a claim within policy limits. The court was fully satisfied that the settlement was reasonable. The fact that the patient had suffered horrible and permanent injury showed the potential for a significant damage award. It also noted that the unfavorable publicity surrounding the surgeon's criminal difficulties

Sec. VI   OTHER MALPRACTICE CASES   429

probably would have affected the case. The surgeon also failed to show how an investigation would have vindicated him. The insurer was not liable for bad faith. *Gardner v. Aetna Cas. & Sur. Co.*, 841 F.2d 82 (4th Cir.1988).

A doctor purchased a Defendant's Reimbursement Policy in 1968. The policy provided that it would pay the doctor $200 for each day he was required to attend "the trial of a civil suit for damages against [him]." The policy provided coverage for the doctor if he was named as a defendant in either a malpractice or an automobile accident lawsuit. Coverage was limited to $5,000 "Per Trial." Coverage for hearings before administrative agencies with the power to discipline physicians was not mentioned in the policy.

In 1976, the California attorney general filed an accusation against the doctor alleging that he falsified Medicare statements and falsified hospital charts and records. The Attorney General requested that the Board of Medical Quality Assurance (BMQA) revoke the doctor's license to practice medicine in California. No damages were requested in the accusation. Administrative hearings were held on the accusation over a period of thirty-nine days. The doctor submitted a claim to the insurer for the time he was required to spend at the administrative hearings. The insurer denied the claim, stating that the administrative hearings were not covered by the policy. The doctor sued the insurer for bad faith refusal to pay benefits due under the policy. The Superior Court, Los Angeles County, ruled in favor of the doctor and the insurer appealed.

The California Court of Appeal, Second District, noted that "courts may not rewrite the insurance contract or force a conclusion to exact liability where none was contemplated." The court ruled that the unambiguous language of the policy stated that coverage was triggered when the doctor was required to attend "the trial of a civil suit for damages." The court ruled that this policy language was "clear and unambiguous with respect to its non-inclusion of coverage for administrative hearings like those before the BMQA." The hearings were not a "trial", nor did the attorney general's accusation request "damages" against the doctor. The court decided that no coverage existed for the doctor's attendance at the administrative hearings. The Superior Court's decision was reversed. *Hackethal v. National Casualty Co.*, 234 Cal. Rptr. 853 (App.2d Dist.1987).

CHAPTER NINE

WORKERS' COMPENSATION

                                                                                Page

I. "ARISING OUT OF" AND "IN THE COURSE OF" EMPLOYMENT 432
   A. The Coming and Going Rule 432
   B. Personal Accidents in the Course of Employment 435
      1. Injuries Occurring While Engaged in Conduct Not Approved by Management 435
      2. Injuries Occurring Due to Intentional Acts of Third Parties 436
      3. Injuries Occurring While Engaged in Conduct Intended for Personal Comfort 436
      4. Injuries Occurring While Engaged in Company Activities Having a Dual Purpose of Business and Pleasure 438
   C. Accidents "in the Course of" but not "Arising out of" Employment 439
   D. Injuries Arising out of Accidents in Which the Employee-Employer Relationship was Disputed 440
   E. Chain of Causation: Chronic Conditions Initially Arising out of Work-Related Injuries 442
   F. Preexisting Conditions 444

II. MULTIPLE EMPLOYERS 446

III. THE EMPLOYEE'S EXCLUSIVE REMEDY 448
   A. Statutory Employment 448
   B. Tort Actions Based on Alleged Intentional Harm 450

IV. DISABILITY PAYMENTS UNDER WORKERS' COMPENSATION 451
   A. Temporary Total Disability 452
   B. Permanent Partial Disability 453
   C. Permanent Total Disability 454

V. DEATH BENEFITS 457

VI. SETOFF OF BENEFITS 459

VII. STATUTE OF LIMITATIONS 461

VIII. MISCELLANEOUS WORKERS' COMPENSATION CASES 463
   A. Employee Incarceration While Receiving Benefits 463
   B. Violation of Safety Laws by Employer 464
   C. Other Employer Misconduct 466

IX. THE LONGSHORE AND HARBOR WORKERS'
COMPENSATION ACT (LHWCA) 467

I. "ARISING OUT OF" AND "IN THE COURSE OF" EMPLOYMENT

Workers' compensation is a system of industrial insurance with its emphasis on the injuries of the worker. It is based on the principle that the inherent risks of performing a job should be placed upon the employer who can then obtain insurance coverage for protection against losses.

The workers' compensation system is based on "liability without fault" and is more closely associated with the law of contract than with tort. In exchange for relieving the employer of responsibility for damages measured by common-law standards and payable when its conduct is found to be at fault, the employer contributes reasonable amounts for workers' compensation insurance which becomes payable in the event of workers' injuries according to a schedule established by state law. The employee, on the other hand, gives up his or her right to sue the employer for damages in tort in the event of injuries. In return the employee no longer bears the economic risk of being injured on the job and is compensated for injuries "arising out of and in the course of employment."

The scope of coverage of workers' compensation is of vital importance to the employee, the employer and the employer's insurer. The mass of litigation which has arisen in this area over the years attests to its significance.

A. The Coming and Going Rule

A California man worked for a company that bought and remodeled old homes for rental purposes. Employees arrived at the company warehouse on weekday mornings and then drove to various work sites throughout the city. They were paid from the time they left the warehouse for a job site to the time they terminated work at the job site. On June 5, 1984, the man in this case commuted to work with a coworker. He then traveled to the job site, and returned to the warehouse at day's end between 5:30 and 6:00 p.m. When he returned, several employees and an employing partner were drinking beer in the company parking lot. The man and his coworker voluntarily joined the group to drink beer. Such drinking had occurred occasionally in the past with at least one of the employing partners participating. Both partners "passively permitted and consented" to the drinking. Company funds were not used to purchase the beer and employees were prohibited from storing beer in the company refrigerator. The drinking continued for several hours. The man then began his usual commute home with his coworker. Neither of them could remember much about the drive home. An accident occurred in which the man was rendered a paraplegic. He filed a claim for workers' compensation benefits which was denied. The Workers' Compensation Appeals Board affirmed the denial, and the employee petitioned for judicial review.

The Court of Appeal, Fifth District, noted that injuries occurring when an employee is engaged in off duty travel, off of the employer's premises, are not compensable under the Workers' Compensation Act unless the travel is "undertaken for the employer for his benefit at his direct or implied request" (the "going and coming" rule). In this case, the going and coming rule barred the man's claim unless

Sec. I	ARISING OUT OF EMPLOYMENT	433

his intoxication resulted from "[e]mployee social and recreational activity on the company premises, endorsed with the expressed or implied permission of the employer," that was "conceivably of some benefit to the employer...." Here the drinking after work was not an established company activity. The man participated in the drinking voluntarily and did not feel that it was "mandated by the employment relationship." The drinking, therefore, was not done in the course of the man's employment and his claim for workers' compensation was barred. *Aetna Casualty & Surety Co. v. Workers' Compensation Appeals Board,* 232 Cal.Rptr. 257 (App.5th Dist.1986).

A Washington man, while serving as a county juror, was seriously injured in an automobile accident as he was driving home from jury duty. The county had been paying a mileage rate for his transportation to and from the courthouse. He sought workers' compensation benefits, asserting that he had been injured in the course of his employment. The workers' compensation board determined that benefits were not available and he appealed to a Washington trial court which affirmed the board's decision. He further appealed to the Supreme Court of Washington. On appeal, the court first recognized that many states do not consider jurors to be employees of the counties where they serve. Those states list or define employment which is included for workers' compensation purposes. However, Washington's workers' compensation law is much broader, and lists only employment that is excluded from workers' compensation benefits. Since jury service is not within the list of excluded employment, the court found that the juror was an employee of the county. Also, because the county had an obligation to compensate the juror for his transportation expenses, his commuting to and from the courthouse constituted an act in the course of his employment. Finally, the court noted that it was better for the county to treat the juror as an employee because this would preclude holding the county liable in negligence by a judge or other county employee. The court reversed the trial court's decision, and granted benefits to the juror. *Bolin v. Kitsap County,* 785 P.2d 805 (Wash.1990).

A Florida man suffered a compensable injury for which his orthopedic surgeon prescribed swimming as a part of his recovery. While on the way home from swimming, the man was involved in an automobile accident. He sought workers' compensation benefits and the judge of compensation claims determined that the accident was compensable. The employer appealed to the Court of Appeal of Florida. The appellate court upheld the award of benefits stating that a claimant injured while reasonably pursuing prescribed medical treatment should be compensated because the injuries remained within the chain of industrial causation. *Little Caesar's Pizza v. Ingersoll,* 572 So.2d 8 (Fla.App.2d Dist.1990).

An Oregon woman worked for a company as a fabricator. She claimed she suffered a disability due to her occupation, which was caused by repetitive pivoting from side to side as required by her job. After her shift ended one day, the woman injured herself while she was getting into her car. She had parked in the employee parking lot. Her knee twisted, made a popping noise and she experienced immediate pain. Thereafter, she underwent surgery. The employee filed a workers' compensation claim for permanent impairment, alleging that her knee injury was the product of an occupational disease, and that the twisting of her knee in the parking lot was an injury that occurred in the course and scope of her employment. The board denied her benefits, and the employee appealed to the Court of Appeals of Oregon. The court of appeals affirmed in part the decision of the board, determining that the knee injury was not the product of an occupational disease. It found conflicting medical evidence concerning the origin of the employee's disability. However, the court held that the knee injury was compensable under the parking lot exception to the "going and coming rule." This rule provides that injuries sustained while going to and from work are not compensable. An exception to the rule exists, however, when the injury occurs on the employer's premises, including an employee parking lot. Since the injury occurred on employer-controlled premises while the employee was traveling from work, it made the incident sufficiently work-connected. The court reversed the board's decision in part and held that the employee's injury was within the course and scope of her employment. *Boyd v. SAIF Corp.*, 837 P.2d 556 (Or.App.1992).

A church custodian was killed in an automobile accident in Greensboro, N.C. while on his way to church. On the day before his death, a church volunteer told him that she wanted to come to the church at 8:00 a.m. the next day. He told her that since a snow storm was predicted, he would spend the night at the church and unlock it the following morning. Later that night, after leaving his parents' house to return to the church for the night, he was involved in a fatal accident. His heirs filed a workers' compensation claim against his employer and its insurer. They argued that the custodian was either on a "special errand" for his employer or that he was, at least, on a "dual purpose" trip for the benefit of his employer. The North Carolina Court of Appeals stated that, as a general rule, injuries occurring while a worker is commuting to and from work do not arise "out of and in the course of" employment and are thus not compensable. On the other hand, a special errand for the employer's benefit is an exception to the rule. After reviewing the evidence, the court held that the employee's going to the church several hours prior to his actual starting time was not a special errand. The court ruled that the employee's heirs were not entitled to receive workers' compensation benefits. *Schmoyer v. Church of Jesus Christ of Latter Day Saints*, 343 S.E.2d 551 (N.C.App.1986).

The Supreme Court of California ruled that a teacher was entitled to workers' compensation benefits for injuries sustained when she was assaulted in her car immediately after leaving a school parking lot to go home from work. The teacher's car had been immobilized by departing school children who blocked traffic. Ordinarily, the operating of the going and coming rule would not permit compensation because the injury occurred during the teacher's commute. However, where the employment creates a special risk which extends beyond the boundaries of the employment premises, compensation will be allowed if injury occurs within the zone of that risk. Here a special risk had been created by the flow of children from the school grounds into the street. Accordingly, the court held that the coming and going rule did not bar compensation. The teacher was allowed to collect workers' compensation benefits. *Parks v. Workers' Compensation Appeals Board*, 660 P.2d 382 (Cal.1983).

Sec. I　　　　　　　　　ARISING OUT OF EMPLOYMENT　　435

B. Personal Accidents in the Course of Employment

1. Injuries Occurring While Engaged in Conduct Not Approved by Management

In Virginia, a warehouseman who had a drinking problem was injured on the job when he fractured both of his heels in a fall. A sample of his blood was drawn at a hospital. A doctor testified that the blood alcohol content revealed that the warehouseman was intoxicated at the time of the accident. Relying on the doctor's testimony, the employer argued that by reporting to work intoxicated, the warehouseman had removed himself from the scope of his employment and that he was therefore barred from workers' compensation. The Virginia Court of Appeals acknowledged that an employee may abandon his employment by reaching an advanced stage of intoxication so that he is no longer able to perform his job. Any injuries suffered thereafter are not in the course of employment. The rule did not apply here, however, because the warehouseman was not too drunk to perform his job. Since the employer failed to prove that the intoxication had proximately caused the warehouseman's injuries, workers' compensation benefits were awarded. *American Safety Razor Co. v. Hunter*, 343 S.E.2d 461 (Va.App.1986).

The father of a janitorial company employee was denied workers' compensation death benefits when his son was killed while engaging in horseplay at his workplace. The accident occurred when a janitorial crew, having finished its duties for the day, became involved in a game of hide and seek. When a piece of heavy equipment being used as a hiding place was inadvertently turned on, the employee was killed. In rendering its opinion, the Utah Supreme Court stated that its inability to grant compensation was based on the fact that the employee was not engaged in those things which it should reasonably be expected an employee would do in connection with his or her duties. The court acknowledged that there are certain circumstances when horseplay may be reasonably expected of an employee in connection with his duties. It stated, however, that the hide and seek game presented too serious a deviation from the normal work duties to be considered acceptable. *J & W Janitorial Co. v. Industrial Comm'n of Utah*, 661 P.2d 949 (Utah 1983).

An employer appealed from an order of the New York Workers' Compensation Board awarding benefits to an injured employee. The employer and its insurance carrier argued that the injuries were a result of "horseplay" by the employee, thus arising outside the course of his employment. The evidence established that the employees had regularly exercised while on break, performing pushups and chinups. The employer was aware of and permitted such activities. The injury occurred when the employee attempted to perform a handstand on a swivel chair. The New York Supreme Court, Appellate Division, agreed with the determination of the Workers' Compensation Board that, in these circumstances, the injury arose in the course of employment and was therefore compensable. *Aucompaugh v. General Electric*, 490 N.Y.S.2d 647 (A.D.3d Dept.1985).

After a mechanic was injured in a fight with a janitor, the mechanic sought workers' compensation benefits. The fight occurred at work and arose during a dispute concerning some hand cleaner owned by the mechanic. The Supreme Court of Tennessee declared that injuries resulting from fights "purely personal in nature" do not arise out of the course of employment and are not compensable. Because the dispute between the mechanic and the janitor arose out of the mechanic's personal property, benefits were denied. *Brimhall v. Home Ins. Co.*, 694 S.W.2d 931 (Tenn.1985).

2. Injuries Occurring Due to Intentional Acts of Third Parties

In Lufkin, Texas, an employee of a chicken processing plant was working on some equipment inside a chain link fence which surrounded the plant while two city policemen were on the street investigating a chicken truck for a traffic violation. The two policemen apparently became enraged at the employee and drove their squad car through the company gate and up to the employee. They beat him to the ground with a flashlight and then shot him four times. The employee claimed that his injuries were work-related and sued his employer's workers' compensation carrier for benefits. The employee was awarded partial and temporary disability payments by the trial court and the insurer appealed. The Texas Court of Appeals noted that according to the Texas Workers' Compensation Act, an employee does not cease to be in the course of his employment when he is not actually performing his job duties because an emergency requires him to do what seems "necessary and understandable." For this reason, the court affirmed the decision of the trial court and ordered the employer's insurer to pay workers' compensation benefits to the injured employee. *Traders & General Ins. Co. v. Allen*, 705 S.W.2d 374 (Tex.App.9th Dist.1986).

In another Texas case, an assistant manager of a hamburger shop was stabbed by a former mental patient because the patient had seen the assistant manager talking with the patient's former girlfriend at the hamburger shop. The Texas Workers' Compensation Act does not cover injuries sustained in the course of employment caused by the acts of third persons, which are intended to injure the employee for personal reasons. The Texas Supreme Court noted that it was the assistant manager's job to deal with customers and keep them satisfied. The assistant manager met the patient's former girlfriend when she visited as a customer. Because the stabbing was incidental to the assistant manager's duties, it arose out of his employment. The supreme court ruled that the assistant manager was entitled to workers' compensation benefits. *Nasser v. Security Ins. Co.*, 724 S.W.2d 17 (Tex.1987).

3. Injuries Occurring While Engaged in Conduct Intended for Personal Comfort

A Texas worker became covered by paint while at work. He used gasoline to remove some of the paint and then decided to go home to finish getting cleaned up. As he entered his bathroom a water heater pilot light ignited the gasoline fumes and triggered a flash fire. Because of the paint that still remained on his body the worker suffered fatal burns. His estate sought compensation from his employer's workers' compensation carrier. It denied coverage stating that the death did not occur in the course of employment. The estate then sued the carrier in a Texas trial court which held for the estate. The carrier appealed to the Texas Court of Appeals which overturned the trial court decision. The estate then appealed to the Texas Supreme Court. The supreme court noted that under the Texas Workers' Compensation Act, coverage was provided for all injuries incurred while the employee was furthering the employer's business, regardless of whether the injury occurred on the employer's

Sec. I　　　　　　　ARISING OUT OF EMPLOYMENT　　437

premises. The supreme court noted that previous cases had highlighted the importance of the origin of the injury because the real question was whether the event was an industrial accident. It rejected the carrier's assertion that the fire did not occur while the man was working. It overturned the lower court's decision because the worker became covered with paint while he was furthering the business of his employer. The fact that the fumes ignited at home did not preclude the injury from being one sustained in the course of employment. The estate could recover from the workers' compensation carrier. *Lujan v. Houston Gen. Ins. Co.*, 756 S.W.2d 295 (Tex.1988).

The South Carolina Court of Appeals has ruled that the death of a worker while engaging in sexual intercourse was not caused by an accident arising out of his employment. His estate contended that the worker's fatal stroke was directly related to stress caused by his job. An expert witness for the man's employer and its workers' compensation insurer testified that the stroke was caused by the rupture of a berry aneurysm. Such strokes, he said, are commonly associated with sexual intercourse. The court denied workers' compensation benefits to the claimants. *Nawa v. Wackenhut Corp.*, 341 S.E.2d 800 (S.C.App.1986).

In June 1983, a New York secretary lit a cigarette during her lunch break in an employee lunchroom. "Within seconds thereafter, [her] dress became a sheet of fire." As a result of the fire she suffered first, second and third degree burns over fifty to sixty percent of her body and missed work until December 1983. The secretary filed a claim for workers' compensation, which was awarded by the workers' compensation board. The employer appealed. On appeal, the employer argued that the board's factual finding that the cause of the intense fire was unknown was not supported by the record. It pointed to the testimony of the employer's nurse, who testified that the woman had said a cigarette ash had fallen onto her dress just before the fire started. The court ruled that the board was within its discretion in rejecting the nurse's account as inaccurate. It also held that even if a cigarette ash had fallen on the woman's dress, the "swiftness and intensity of the fire was unexplained." The Supreme Court, Appellate Division, ruled that the woman's injuries occurred during the course of employment because she was having lunch in an area designated by the employer and the act of smoking a cigarette was a reasonable and expected activity and thus she was entitled to workers' compensation. *Iacovelli v. New York Times Co.*, 507 N.Y.S.2d 922 (A.D.3d Dept.1986).

A man employed by a Florida fruit company was struck by an automobile while he was walking across the street to purchase cigarettes at a nearby convenience store. He was on duty at the time of his injury. He testified that he had no regularly scheduled breaks, but was allowed to attend to his personal comfort during lulls in employment. He purchased his cigarettes at the convenience store because they were cheaper than those offered in the fruit company's cigarette machine. The plant superintendent testified that employees frequented the convenience store during working hours and that they were encouraged, but not required, to punch out before leaving the premises. In light of these facts the workers' compensation commissioner found that the employee had been in "the scope and course of his employment" at the time of the injury and awarded medical and temporary disability benefits. The Florida Court of Appeal upheld the award, holding that the employee's trip across the street to buy cigarettes "was a foreseeable and non-prohibited refreshment break activity, ... [which] did not remove him from the scope and course of his employment." The employee was thus entitled to benefits. *Holly Hill Fruit Products v. Krider*, 473 So.2d 829 (Fla.App.1st Dist.1985).

4. Injuries Occurring While Engaged in Company Activities Having a Dual Purpose of Business and Pleasure

An employee was involved in an out-of-town project on behalf of his employer which involved his staying in a motel. Following completion of the project, he entertained his employer's clients at a local restaurant, partially to obtain further business from them. During the course of a dinner, they were waited on by a waitress who, later in the evening, accompanied the entire party to the motel. Upon leaving the motel, she was assaulted by someone unconnected with the party. Attempting to assist the waitress, the employee was himself assaulted and injured. He then sought compensation for the injuries resulting from this incident. The Maine Workers' Compensation Commission denied his claim, a decision upheld by both the Superior Court and the Supreme Judicial Court of Maine. The issue presented to the appellate court was whether the injuries sustained by the employee arose out of and in the course of his employment. The court held that there was no causal connection between the conditions under which the employee worked and the injury which arose. The employee's voluntary acts were held to be the main cause of his injury. His claim for workers' compensation benefits was denied. *Comeau v. Maine Coastal Services*, 449 A.2d 362 (Me.1982).

Injuries suffered while participating in athletic contests formed the basis for workers' compensation cases in Oregon and Massachusetts. In both instances benefits were denied. The Oregon case involved a police officer who suffered a knee injury while playing in a benefit basketball game between his department and his city's fire department. The Oregon Court of Appeals stated that the injury occurred during receational activity rather than while the officer was on duty; the game was not played on police department premises; the city did not require or endorse participation in the game; and the city obtained no tangible benefit so as to establish the necessary relationship between the officer's actions and benefit to the city. The claim was therefore denied. *Matter of Compensation of Richmond*, 648 P.2d 370 (Or.App.1984).

In the Massachusetts case an employee was injured while playing on a company softball team. He sought workers' compensation benefits which were denied by the Supreme Judicial Court of Massachusetts. The court decided that the injury was not one "arising out of and in the course of the employee's employment" since the operation of the team did not have a sufficient connection with the employee's employment to warrant an award. Any benefit to the employer was at best inferential and insignificant. Coverage was denied. *Kemp's Case*, 437 N.E.2d 526 (Mass.1982).

A New York man was injured while participating in a basketball game during a picnic. The picnic had been organized by a coffee club made up of his coworkers. He filed a claim for workers' compensation benefits, and the Workers' Compensation Board ruled that he had sustained a compensable injury under the workers' compensation law. The New York Supreme Court, Appellate Division, reversed the decision of the board. It held that the evidence was insufficient to establish employer sponsorship of the activity so as to render the employer liable to the man for the injuries sustained at the picnic. There was no overt encouragement of participation in the picnic by the employer. The court found that the use of employer stationery and telephone lines to organize the picnic was insufficient to establish employer sponsorship under the workers' compensation law. Notwithstanding that the employer assented to the existence of the coffee club on the business premises and derived a general benefit from the picnic in the form of increased morale and efficiency, the court found that the evidence did not provide a basis for a finding of compensability. Therefore, it dismissed the claim for workers' compensation benefits. *Farnan v. NYS Dept. of Social Services,* 589 N.Y.S.2d 713 (A.D.3d Dept.1992).

An employee of a manufacturing company, on medical leave because of a nonwork-related hand injury, was invited to a company Christmas party and also to the company's plant to pick up a Christmas turkey. While in the company parking lot, she slipped and fell, injuring herself. She then sought workers' compensation. The Minnesota Supreme Court concluded that the employee's injury arose out of and in the course of her employment. This conclusion was based upon the rationale that the Christmas party and the turkey were actually a part of the employee's compensation and that the employer had directed its employees to come to the company premises if they wished to receive this compensation. Workers' compensation benefits were paid to the employee. *Johnson v. Toro Co.*, 331 N.W.2d 243 (Minn.1983).

C. Accidents "in the Course of" but not "Arising out of" Employment

A Florida man arrived at work one day and sat down, crossing his left leg underneath him. Five minutes later he decided to change positions and when he did so, his knee popped and locked. The worker was diagnosed as having a torn meniscus of the left knee. Four months later, the man sustained a temporary re-injury of the same knee at work. He sought workers' compensation benefits which were denied. The worker took his claim to a Florida trial court which found in his favor. The employer and the workers' compensation carrier appealed. The District Court of Appeal of Florida held that the mere occurrence of an injury at work, without more, was not enough to establish compensability. The worker's injury here did not arise in the course of his employment. Accordingly, the appellate court reversed the trial court's ruling and held the injury noncompensable. *Strategic Marketing Systems v. Soranno*, 559 So.2d 353 (Fla.App.1st Dist.1990).

A Louisiana man slipped and fell from a ladder, injuring his knee, while in the course and scope of his employment. The employer's insurer concluded that the injury was covered and paid the man's medical expenses and disability benefits. Four years later, the man began experiencing back pain which grew progressively worse and eventually resulted in his hospitalization. He claimed that the back injury was work related, arising from the limp he had developed. The insurer denied coverage and the man sued in a Louisiana trial court. The jury ruled for the insurer, and the insured appealed to the Court of Appeal of Louisiana, Third Circuit. The insurer argued that because the back injury did not arise until four years after the work related incident, it was not covered. Also, the insurer contended that the insured was not totally disabled within the policy. The court stated that there was insufficient evidence to link the two injuries, so it ruled that the back injury was not work related. However, the court held that the insured's knee injury did totally disable him under the policy because he could not return to work. The court affirmed the trial court's decision in part, disallowing disability benefits for the back injury, but reversed in part by allowing full benefits for the knee injury. *Rodriguez v. American Standard Life and Accident Ins. Co.*, 553 So.2d 479 (La.App.3d Cir.1989).

Some courts have denied workers' compensation benefits when an employee's injuries have occurred due to risks faced by the general public which are not increased or otherwise affected by the employment duties.

The North Carolina Court of Appeals ruled that although an employee may die within the "course and scope" of his employment, this does not necessarily indicate that the employee died from an injury "arising out of" his employment. The case involved a truck driver who was found lying face down on the ground at the rear of a new van he was to have loaded onto a transport trailer. The court held that the plaintiff failed to show that the death occurred in the course of employment. His widow, therefore, was denied workers' compensation benefits. *Pickrell v. Motor Convoy*, 346 S.E.2d 164 (N.C.App.1986).

A Nebraska social worker on his way to make a professional call encountered a violent and unusual rainstorm with winds up to 100 miles per hour which caused a tree to fall on his car. His neck was broken, totally disabling him. Benefits were awarded him by the Nebraska Workmen's Compensation Court. The social work agency/employer appealed, asserting the evidence was insufficient to support a finding that the workers' injury resulted from an accident which arose either out of or in the course of his employment. The Supreme Court of Nebraska agreed with the appellant saying that it is only when an accident arises both out of and in the course of employment that an employee is entitled to benefits under the provisions of the Nebraska Workmen's Compensation Act. The term "arising out of" describes the accident and its origin, cause and character; the term "in the course of" refers to the time, place and circumstances surrounding the accident. A claimant must establish both. Here, the worker suffered an injury and it was *in the course of* his employment. However, the accident did not *arise out of* his employment. The risks the worker took were not inherent in his job but were risks to which the general public was exposed. *McGinn v. Douglas County Social Servs. Admin.*, 317 N.W.2d 764 (Neb.1982).

D. Injuries Arising out of Accidents in Which the Employee-Employer Relationship was Disputed

Generally, an employee-employer relationship must have been established prior to the injury in order for an injured worker to be eligible for workers' compensation benefits.

A sole proprietor was injured on the job. When he reported his injury, his insurance agent told him that he was not covered. The insured disregarded his agent's information and filed a claim for medical and disability benefits. The insurer erroneously paid this claim for over two years. When the insurer finally realized its mistake, it denied any further coverage. A compensation judge awarded the insured benefits because he had come to rely on the payments. The insurer appealed to the

Sec. I   ARISING OUT OF EMPLOYMENT   441

District Court of Appeal of Florida. The court held that no coverage could be permitted despite the insured's contention that he relied upon the benefits for health care. The court reversed and remanded the administrative decision and held in favor of the insurer. *Tradewinds Construction v. Newsbaum*, 606 So.2d 708 (Fla.App.1st Dist.1992).

A Virginia woman helped care for a friend's horses. They were kept at a horse boarding and training farm and, as a favor to the friend, the farm owner permitted the woman's horse to be lodged at the farm without charge. However, it was understood that from time to time the woman would help out with chores around the farm if she saw something that needed to be done. Otherwise, she was to receive no compensation other than the boarding of her horse. She was later injured and sought workers' compensation benefits, but the industrial commission denied them. She appealed to the Virginia Court of Appeals, which affirmed the commission's decision. It stated that the woman had not been in the farm owner's control as an employee, but rather the relationship was one of reciprocal gratuity. Thus, workers' compensation benefits were not available. *Behrensen v. Whitaker*, 392 S.E.2d 508 (Va.App.1990).

A California man worked for a company that supplied maintenance workers for eight to ten oil companies in the Ventura County Area. The man was so experienced that he needed no supervision on the job. When he reported for work at an oil company, he would be given a task and left to complete it as he saw fit. When the man was injured in a fire at a USA Petroleum Corporation (USA) facility, he filed a lawsuit against USA seeking personal injury damages. The Superior Court, Ventura County, found for the injured man and awarded him $377,673. USA appealed this award. Before the Court of Appeal, Second District, USA argued that the man was its "special employee" and that his recovery should therefore be limited to workers' compensation. This argument was based on the fact that USA had a right to exercise control over the details of the man's work. The court, citing previous decisions of the California Supreme Court, noted that the paramount consideration in deciding the question of special employment is the exercise of control rather than the right to control. In this case, USA had the right to control the man's work but did not exercise that right. The court noted that many other factors are also taken into account when the existence of special employment is considered. The court could not, therefore, rule as a matter of law that the man was a special employee simply because USA had the right to control his work. The Court of Appeal affirmed the Superior Court's negligence award against USA. *Barajas v. USA Petroleum Corp.*, 229 Cal.Rptr. 513 (App.2d Dist.1986).

An Ohio gasoline service station employee was injured and hospitalized when she inhaled carbon monoxide fumes. Her employer had started the engine of his recreational vehicle to charge the battery in anticipation of an upcoming vacation. He neglected to turn off the engine before departing for the day. The employee asked for and received workers' compensation damages for her injuries. She then filed suit against the employer (who was also the owner of the station) for negligence. The employer/owner moved for summary judgment on the basis that the workers' compensation remedy received by the woman was her exclusive remedy. The trial court overruled this motion and the jury granted $35,000 in damages. The employer/owner appealed to the Court of Appeals of Ohio.

On appeal, the employee argued that the employer/owner was acting in a dual capacity and had independent obligations arising out of his conduct which arose separately from those arising out of the workers' compensation act. The employee argued that as a sole proprietorship the employer acted in the capacity of co-employee. The decisive dual capacity test asks whether the second function generates obligations unrelated to those flowing out of those of an employer. Within the boundaries of safety, a sole proprietor may do what he or she likes while on the business premises. To hold that the employer would be an employer while repairing customer automobiles but an employee while he charges his own car battery would not be supported by the law. Therefore, her sole remedy was workers' compensation. *Hillman v. McCaughtrey*, 564 N.E.2d 1123 (Ohio App.1989).

In North Carolina, an eight-year-old boy was awarded workers' compensation benefits. The boy's mother was working for a convenience store and service station as a part-time cashier. She took the job on the condition that her son be permitted to stay there with her when he got out of school. On some afternoons, the boy helped out around the station at the request and under the supervision of the manager. He performed such tasks as taking out the garbage and restocking the vending machines. Each afternoon the boy did this work, the manager paid him "a dollar or so." One afternoon, while helping the manager, the boy slipped and fell on a place that was always greasy and slick.

The North Carolina Court of Appeals held that the boy was a "casual employee" and was entitled to workers' compensation benefits. In applying North Carolina law, the court looked to G.S. 97-2(2) which defines the word *employee*: "Every person engaged in an employment under any appointment or contract of hire or apprenticeship, express or implied, oral or written, including aliens, and also minors, whether lawfully or unlawfully employed." The fact that the boy was too young to be lawfully employed was irrelevant. Workers' compensation benefits were awarded. *Lemmerman v. A.T. Williams Oil Co.*, 339 S.E.2d 820 (N.C.App.1986).

E. Chain of Causation: Chronic Conditions Initially Arising out of Work-Related Injuries

A Utah man was employed in late August, 1987. His responsibilities included cleaning food processing equipment by using large high-pressure hoses. They worked with hand grips that required continuous pressure throughout his eight hour work shift. After one month, he experienced pain in his hands several times and eventually reported to a doctor who instituted a medical release. Shortly thereafter, he was terminated by the company. It was determined that surgery was required on both his wrists. He then filed for workers' compensation benefits with the industrial commission. The administrative law judge found that his work activities were not what an average person normally would encounter and his injury was thus compensable. The company sought review from the industrial commission which upheld the administrative law judge's award. The company then appealed to the Court of Appeals of Utah. The appellate court noted that the issue was whether the employment activities of the worker were sufficient to satisfy the legal standard of unusual or extraordinary efforts so as to constitute a compensable industrial accident. The court noted that the worker's eight to ten hour shifts operating high-pressure hoses that required continual pressure using both hands constituted extraordinary efforts. Therefore, it upheld the industrial commission's award of medical benefits and temporary total disability benefits. *Stouffer Foods v. Industrial Comm'n of Utah*, 801 P.2d 179 (Utah App.1990).

An Illinois man was injured while working. He continued working and two months later he was diagnosed as having a back condition for which he claimed workers' compensation benefits. The arbitrator found that his back condition was causally connected with his work and awarded benefits. However, on review, the industrial commission found that various subsequent activities had broken the causal chain between the claimant's injury and the diagnosis. On appeal, the Appellate Court of Illinois noted that after the injury the claimant hunted ducks, chopped wood, pulled tires off a pickup truck and moved a large safe using a dolly. The doctor who diagnosed the claimant testified that it would be impossible to differentiate between activities which caused the original injury and these activities. Therefore, the court determined that these activities broke the causal connection between the injury and the back condition and that no benefits would be awarded. *Hebeler v. Holland Co.*, 565 N.E.2d 1035 (Ill.App.2d Dist.1991).

A ditch digger received a tick bite and showed both the tick and the bite to his supervisor. The man later developed symptoms consistent with Lyme's disease and was unable to work. A workers' compensation claim was denied by the employer because of a negative serological test. A judge of compensation claims heard conflicting testimony from doctors concerning the presence of Lyme's disease, and chose to award benefits. The employer then appealed to a Florida appellate court. The first issue on appeal was whether the finding of Lyme's disease was supported by the evidence. Because of the difficulty in diagnosing the disease, the court felt that the finding was based on competent evidence. The second issue concerned the connection between the disease and employment. The employer contended that, because the claim involved a disease instead of an accident, the connection to employment required a demonstration of causal connection by clear evidence rather than a logical connection as was required by the trial court. The alternative standard applies, however, only when the disease is not the result of an accident. A disease is deemed to be an accident when it is caused by an unusual event or exposure. The court ruled that the insect bite was an accident, and affirmed the award. *Foxbilt Electric v. Stanton*, 583 So.2d 720 (Fla.App.1 Dist. 1991).

A Montana man worked at an auto body shop for nine years. During this time he was exposed to various chemical compounds that he used in the course of his work as a "body man." In February 1983, he developed a rash which spread from one shoulder over his back and to his hands and fingers. The rash was an allergic reaction to the chemicals he used in his work. It forced him to quit his job in March 1984. At the time of injury, the man's employer was insured against workers' compensation claims by the Intermountain Insurance Co. When he finally quit, however, the employer was enrolled with the State Compensation Fund. Intermountain denied coverage under the Workers' Compensation Act. The state fund paid benefits to the man under the Occupation Disease Act. The man filed a suit in the workers' compensation court seeking a determination that his allergy was an injury compensable under the Workers' Compensation Act. The court declared that the allergy was both an injury and a disease and the worker could therefore elect a remedy under either the Workers' Compensation Act or the Occupational Disease Act. Intermountain appealed. The Montana Supreme Court observed that the allergic reaction occurred unexpectedly and that its onset was time-definite. These facts supported its classification as an injury. The court found that the allergy could also be considered an *occupational disease*, defined as a "disease arising out of or contracted from and in the course of employment." The supreme court affirmed the workers' compensation court's decision finding the allergy to be both an injury and a disease and allowing the worker to elect a remedy either under the Workers' Compensation Act or the Occupational Disease Act. *Bremer v. Buerkle*, 727 P.2d 529 (Mont.1986).

In the course of his employment with a painting contractor, a Colorado man's face was splattered with a caustic solution used to remove paint. He suffered severe burns and disfigurement and subsequently became severely self-conscious, depressed and prone to fits of rage. His wife and children were forced to flee to a shelter for battered women and he committed suicide when his wife failed to contact him as he demanded. The man's widow then filed for workers' compensation death benefits. The Colorado Court of Appeals held that a chain-of-causation test should be applied: "If a work connected injury causes a deranged mental condition which in turn is a proximate cause of the injured workers' suicide, then the decedent workers' dependents are entitled to compensation." The court reasoned that the man's disfigurement had induced depression, instability and a general personality change. Because these factors were deemed to have been the proximate cause of his suicide, death benefits were awarded. *Jakco Painting Contractors v. Industrial Comm'n of Colorado*, 702 P.2d 755 (Colo.App.1985).

F. Preexisting Conditions

An Alaska man suffered a work-related back injury. Shortly thereafter, he began exhibiting symptoms of chronic hypertension. He began to receive workers' compensation benefits to pay for his medical expenses in connection with his hypertension. Before the Alaska Workers' Compensation Board, his employer and its carrier rebutted the presumption that his hypertension was job-related. His claim for continuing compensation was denied. A trial court reversed the board's decision, holding that it was not supported by substantial evidence. Appeal was then taken to the Supreme Court of Alaska. On appeal, the court noted that the board had reasonably relied on the testimony of a doctor who stated that the employee had been on the way to developing chronic hypertension well before he slipped and injured his back. The doctor concluded that neither the injury nor its pain was a substantial or contributing factor to the development of the employee's hypertension. The employee's high blood pressure following the injury was simply "part of a natural progression of his condition." The supreme court reversed the trial court's decision and held for the employer and its carrier. *W. R. Grasle Co. v. Mumby*, 833 P.2d 10 (Alaska 1992).

An Illinois woman worked in a manufacturing plant for twenty-six years. Her job required that she move moderately heavy weights. In 1984, she began experiencing pain in her shoulder, forearm and hand. She received minor treatment once a week until June of 1985 when she felt a sharp pain in her shoulder which went into her neck. She took three weeks' vacation in July, and noticed that when she was off work, she experienced no pain. In August, she visited a doctor, who kept her from working and eventually operated on her shoulder. Later, it was discovered that she had been previously treated for bursitis. She applied for workers' compensation benefits, received them, and her employer appealed. The state industrial commission found that although the worker had failed to show when she had sustained her injuries, they arose out of her employment. The employer sought review in an Illinois trial court, which held that she sustained her injuries in June. The employer appealed to the Appellate Court of Illinois, Fourth District.

The appellate court ruled that even if an employee had suffered a preexisting condition, she would not be denied an award if the condition was aggravated or accelerated by her employment. Further, the court stated that denying an employee benefits for a work-related injury which was not the result of a sudden accident penalized her for faithfully performing her duties despite injury. The court also noted that the date on which the injury occurred was the date when a reasonable person would have noticed that the injury was related to the job. The court affirmed the trial court's decision, granting benefits from June of 1985. *General Electric Co. v. Industrial Comm'n*, 546 N.E.2d 987 (Ill.App.4th Dist.1989).

A construction company hired a worker to perform heavy construction work, relying on the worker's assertion that he had no previous back injuries. However, the employee had previously suffered back fractures and had undergone treatment for ruptured disks. Within three months of employment, the employee was injured while operating a jackhammer on a scaffold. The following work day, he could not walk and sought medical attention. When the employee submitted a workers' compensation claim, the employer's workers' compensation carrier sued the employee in a Tennessee trial court, stating that he should not recover any workers' compensation benefits. The court ruled for the insurance company, finding that the employee had misrepresented his physical condition when he was hired, that the employer had relied on this misrepresentation and that medical evidence indicated a causal connection between the previous back injuries and the employee's present injury. The employee appealed to the Tennessee Supreme Court, which held that the employer's reliance on the misrepresentation and the causal connection between the previous back injury and the present injury prevented recovery. The trial court's decision was affirmed. *U.S. Fidelity and Guar. Co. v. Edwards*, 764 S.W.2d 533 (Tenn.1989).

A Tennessee employer hired a mildly retarded worker to do labor. The worker was injured while shoveling woodchips and was taken to a hospital and treated by a doctor selected by his employer. However, the employee was dissatisfied and consulted a different doctor on the advice of his attorney. He did not notify his employer that he was dissatisfied with the company's recommended doctor. In the litigation which followed, the employer contended that the employee had misrepresented his physical condition in applying for employment. Therefore, he should not receive workers' compensation benefits. The trial court determined that the worker was fifty-five percent disabled as a result of the job injury, and that the employer's insurance carrier was liable for the unauthorized medical expenses. The employer's insurer appealed to the Tennessee Supreme Court. Evidence indicated that the employee's mild retardation, which had required the employer's secretary to help him fill out the employment application, was a factor indicating that he had not wilfully misrepresented his physical condition upon hire. However, the court ruled that the employee had no reasonable excuse for seeking additional medical service without consulting his employer. His limited mental capacity had no bearing on that issue. The court reversed the trial court's decision and ruled that the insurer was not liable for the employee's unapproved medical expenses. *Dorris v. INA Ins. Co.*, 764 S.W.2d 538 (Tenn.1989).

A South Carolina man worked as a masseur for thirty-three years. His job required him to stand about seven hours a day. After approximately twenty-eight years, he began experiencing painful swelling in his feet and legs, a result of varicose veins. He received surgery on his legs, but was forced to retire after thirty-three years because of the continuing pain and swelling in his legs. He filed a claim for total and permanent disability benefits for accidental injury. The workers' compensation commission denied recovery, and a trial court affirmed. The masseur appealed to the South Carolina Court of Appeals. On appeal, the issue was whether the employee had sustained an injury by accident. The court concluded that the employee had not suffered an injury by accident. The long periods of standing had the natural and expected result of worsening the masseur's varicose veins. However, since the employment was not the cause of the varicose veins, the masseur was not entitled to recovery for his health problems. The court affirmed the denial of benefits. *Havird v. Columbia YMCA*, 418 S.E.2d 329 (S.C.App.1992).

II. MULTIPLE EMPLOYERS

Cases have arisen where the employee is working for two or more employers when he or she is injured. The courts must then decide which employer is responsible for workers' compensation benefits.

A man accidently injured his thumb while operating a nail gun. The whereabouts of his employer or the subcontractor above his employer were unknown at the time, and the employee received medical attention from a supervisor for the general contractor before returning to work. Two months later the employee was diagnosed as suffering from arthritis caused by infection of his thumb. The employee then made a claim for workers' compensation benefits from his employer, the subcontractor above his employer, and the general contractor. A commission found that neither the employer nor the subcontractor had received timely notice of the injury, and accordingly awarded benefits against the general contractor. The dispute eventually reached the Virginia Court of Appeals.

Virginia Worker's Compensation Code § 65.1-30 provides that a contractor may be liable to any worker on a project notwithstanding the worker's direct employment by another direct entity. Virginia law also requires that each entity in the employment hierarchy receive timely notice of a claim. Credible evidence was found to support the findings that the direct employer and subcontractor had not received notice of the injury. Also affirmed was that the employee had no reasonable excuse for failing to give notice; the direct employer and subcontractor were thus excused of any liability. Despite the language of the law, the general contractor argued that the employee could only bring a claim against the first insured subcontractor in the employment hierarchy. It also contended that the minor medical service performed did not alert it to a possible claim, especially in light of the hierarchy. The court noted that the purpose of § 65.1-30 was to "make liable to every employee engaged in that work, every such owner, or contractor, or subcontractor, above such employee." The award of benefits against the general contractor was affirmed. *Wagner Enterprises, Inc. v. Brooks*, 407 S.E.2d 32 (Va.App.1991).

Sec. III   MULTIPLE EMPLOYERS   447

An Alaska man operated a labor dispatch service which supplied workers to oil companies. In order to determine the proper workers' compensation premium for the operator's workforce, the insurer applied the "payroll limitation rule." Under this rule, the insurer had to determine an employee's "total time employed" during the policy. The total time employed was defined as "the sum of the portions of all contracts of employment" within the policy period. The operator's employees worked regular, seven-day, twelve-hour shifts, one week on and one week off. The insurer figured that such employees were employed by the operator under a single employment contract. Thus the insurer computed the "total time employed" for these employees at fifty-two weeks per year for purposes of the payroll limitation rule.

The operator sued the insurer in an Alaska trial court claiming that each one-week stint on the oil platform constituted a separate "contract of employment." Thus, the insurer should have considered only twenty-six weeks of employment per year per employee in calculating the operator's workers' compensation premium. The trial court determined that no overcharge had occurred, and the operator appealed to the Supreme Court of Alaska. The court held that, based on the insurance company's application of the payroll limitation rule, the operator was not overcharged. The court examined the nature and terms of the employment contract existing between the operator and his employees. The workers were intended to be employed under a single contract for continuous week-on/week-off employment. The insurer had correctly applied the payroll limitation rule. The supreme court affirmed the lower court's decision. *Wade Oilfield v. Providence Wash. Ins.*, 759 P.2d 1302 (Alaska 1988).

An insurance company appealed a decision of the Arkansas Workers' Compensation Commission which held it liable for the payment of benefits to an employee for an admittedly compensable injury received while working for an employer who ran several businesses from one location. The employee had worked off and on for the employer in several capacities during a period of 14 years. His last employment was primarily as a truck driver for the trucking company but he, as well as other employees, was guaranteed a 40 hour week and was expected to work at a gas station during his off time. He received an injury on a long-haul mission for the trucking company while unloading a grain truck belonging to the employer. The employer contended that the policy covered only the employees who worked at the gas station, that there was no coverage for an employee while working for the trucking company, and that there was no substantial evidence to support the commission's decision that the two businesses were not separate and distinct. The question for the Court of Appeals of Arkansas was whether the enterprises carried on by the employer were so interrelated and connected as to constitute one sole proprietorship rather than a dual employment situation. The court noted that the employer was assigned only one identification number for withholding of taxes, social security and unemployment insurance. Moreover, all employee contributions were paid to one fund. Based on this evidence the court affirmed the Commission's finding that the policy covered all employees of this employer. *Great Cent. Ins. Co. v. Mel's Texaco*, 651 S.W.2d 101 (Ark.App.1983).

III. THE EMPLOYEE'S EXCLUSIVE REMEDY

Direct lawsuits for damages against employers are usually barred by the express language of the workers' compensation statutes, thus making workers' compensation the employee's exclusive remedy for work-related injuries. In other words, an employee cannot sue his or her employer for damages contending that the employer's negligence caused the employee's injuries. On the other hand, some courts have allowed recovery in lawsuits for intentional harms inflicted on employees by the employer or a co-worker.

A. Statutory Employment

A man was hired by a Georgia city as a police officer in 1985. In 1986, the city lent his services to an adjacent city as part of the Locals to Help Locals program. This program, administered by the Georgia Crime Prevention Council, was to provide agents who were unknown locally to law enforcement agencies conducting short term undercover investigations. The lending cities were still to provide pay and workers' compensation benefits. While on loan for an undercover drug investigation, the police officer was shot and killed. The officer's mother sued the lending city and the police chief in a Georgia trial court which granted summary judgment in favor of the city and the chief. The mother appealed to the Court of Appeals of Georgia.

The court noted that under the lending program the lending city would continue to be responsible under workers' compensation for injuries sustained while the officer was on loan to the receiving city. Under the workers' compensation act, the decedent's dependents would receive benefits. Because the police officer left no dependents within the meaning of the act the benefits were paid to the Georgia Subsequent Injury Trust Fund. The mother contended, however, that the lending city was not the police officer's employer within the meaning of the act. The court determined that regardless of whether the lending city was the employer within the meaning of the act, the police officer and the lending city had a contract which stated that workers' compensation would be the exclusive remedy if the police officer were injured. Therefore, the appellate court affirmed the trial court's decision. *Adams v. Collins*, 392 S.E.2d 549 (Ga.App.1990).

An employee of a contractor engaged in cleaning up a mining site sued the mine operator to recover for injuries sustained as a result of alleged hazards on the premises. Under the Louisiana workers' compensation statute, when a principal contracts to have work performed that is part "of his trade, business or occupation" the principal (here the mine operator) becomes the statutory employer of the contractor's employees and is therefore liable for workers' compensation benefits to them. An injured employee's exclusive remedy against his statutory employer is for workers' compensation, thus barring the employee from suing his employer for damages. The U.S. Court of Appeals, Fifth Circuit, stated that since the clean up work was customarily contracted out rather than performed by the mine operator's own employees, it was not part of the "trade, business, or occupation" of the mine operator. The court therefore ruled that the operator was not a statutory employer and remanded the case for further proceedings. *LeBlanc v. Goldking Production Co.*, 706 F.2d 149 (5th Cir.1983).

A Louisiana carpenter employed by a contractor doing work for Shell Oil Company was injured when a pressurized line burst, spraying him with acid and causing chemical burns. He sued Shell for damages. The applicable statute states that when a principal has contracted to have work performed "which is part of his trade, business or occupation" he shall be liable for workers' compensation benefits to the contractor's employees. A statutory employer subject to paying compensation benefits cannot be held liable for damages by an injured employee of the contractor. The U.S. Court of Appeals, Fifth Circuit, held that there existed a genuine issue of fact as to whether the work the carpenter was doing was an integral part of Shell's own trade, business or occupation. In reviewing the evidence, the court noted that both Shell's statement of uncontested facts and the affidavit of its maintenance manager stated that, while Shell uses its own employees to perform small and medium scale maintenance, it customarily contracts with outside concerns to perform large scale repairs, such as the job in question. Under these facts, the work being done by the contractor was not part of Shell's trade, business or occupation. Because the carpenter, therefore, was not a statutory employee, he could sue Shell for damages. *Williams v. Shell Oil Co.*, 677 F.2d 506 (5th Cir.1982).

An underaged Louisiana employee brought a tort action against his employer after he was injured in a work-related accident. Before the Louisiana Supreme Court, the employee maintained that since the duties he was performing at the time the accident occurred were in violation of the Child Labor Law, he was exempt from the exclusivity of workers' compensation and, therefore, entitled to sue for damages. The Louisiana Supreme Court, while acknowledging that the employee was, in fact, engaged in activities that violated the Child Labor Law, nevertheless affirmed the trial court's decision that he had failed to state a cause of action. The Workers' Compensation Act provides that it applies to "every person" performing services in the course of his employment. Whether the employee is performing duties in violation of the Child Labor Law does not alter the exclusivity of workers' compensation coverage. The case was remanded to the trial court for further proceedings. *Mott v. River Parish Maintenance, Inc.*, 432 So.2d 827 (La.1983).

A tragic school bus accident in Arkansas in which many students and faculty members were either killed or injured resulted in a lawsuit to determine which victims were entitled to the proceeds of the liability insurance policy covering the bus. The students claimed that because of the exclusivity of workers' compensation, the teachers were not entitled to any part of the policy's proceeds. The teachers argued that it was against public policy to foreclose their right to the insurance policy proceeds in light of state law giving school districts tort immunity but requiring them to carry liability insurance on their motor vehicles. The Arkansas Supreme Court agreed with the students that workers' compensation was the exclusive remedy between an employer and an employee. It further stated that public policy interests dictate that other statutes must yield to the Workers' Compensation Act. The teachers' exclusive remedy for their injuries was through workers' compensation. *Helms v. Southern Farm Bureau Cas. Ins. Co.*, 664 S.W.2d 870 (Ark.1984).

B. Tort Actions Based on Alleged Intentional Harm

A thirty-year-old Louisiana man who was foreman of a mustard mill unit for a food company looked down into a mustard tank and saw a fellow employee lying unconscious at the bottom. He immediately summoned the seventy-six-year-old plant superintendent who started to descend the rope ladder inside the tank to rescue the employee. The foreman persuaded the older man to let him go instead. While the foreman descended the superintendent went to find other employees to assist in the rescue. When they returned they found the foreman unconscious at the bottom of the tank. They then phoned the fire department which forced an opening in the tank wall and removed the two men. The first employee died and the foreman suffered severe brain damage. The executrix of the deceased employee's estate and the wife and son of the foreman brought actions against the superintendent and the food company. The defendants moved for summary judgment on the grounds that the tort actions were barred by the exclusive remedy rule of the workers' compensation statute. The trial court granted summary judgment to the defendants and the plaintiffs appealed to the Court of Appeal. The court of appeal reversed and the defendants appealed to the Supreme Court of Louisiana.

On appeal, the plaintiffs contended that the superintendent's act was an intentional tort and therefore summary judgment was improper. The court noted, however, that when there was consent, there could be no recovery for an intentional act. The foreman consented to whatever harmful act the superintendent desired or believed to be certain would befall the foreman when he descended to rescue the other employee. Therefore, the court reinstated the summary judgment motion. *Fricke v. Owens-Corning Fiberglas Corp.*, 571 So.2d 130 (La.1990)

A Florida man sustained a back injury in the course and scope of his employment. His employer and its workers' compensation carrier accepted it as compensable and made a lump-sum settlement of his claim. A few months later, the claimant shot himself in the shoulder in a botched suicide attempt. He claimed that this injury was causally related to the back injury and that he was entitled to medical benefits. Before the judge of compensation claims, the employer and the carrier argued that the shoulder injury was the result of psychiatric problems, or alternatively, that it was the result of an accident unrelated to either the back injury or employment. However, they did not assert that the injury was caused by the claimant's wilful intention to injure or kill himself. After a ruling in favor of the claimant, the employer and the carrier appealed to the District Court of Appeal of Florida. On appeal, they charged that the judge had erred by granting compensation where the claimant had intended to kill himself. However, since this was a question of fact, and since the employer and the carrier had failed to raise this issue in the proceedings below, they were deemed to have waived it, and were required to pay the claimant's medical expenses for the shoulder injury. The trial court's decision was affirmed. *Bay Automotive and U.S.F.& G. v. Allaire*, 593 So.2d 589 (Fla.App.1st Dist.1992).

An Illinois carpenter was rendered a paraplegic when he fell from a scaffold. At the time of the accident his employer was insured for $100,000 for workers' compensation and $300,000 for manufacturer and contractor coverage. The employer's insurer paid all the carpenter's medical bills up to the maximum amount available under the Illinois Workers' Compensation Act. A claims adjuster befriended the carpenter until the state Structural Work Act statute of limitations had expired. The Act allows an injured worker to recover for disability, pain and suffering, lost wages and earnings and reasonable medical expenses. The claims adjuster convinced the carpenter that the insurer would protect his legal rights. Upon learning that the adjuster was misleading him, he sued the insurer for fraud in an Illinois federal district court. It awarded him $3 million in compensatory damages and $2 million in punitive damages. The insurer appealed to the U.S. Court of Appeals, Seventh Circuit.

In upholding the $5 million award, the appeals court held that the carpenter's recovery was not limited to workers' compensation. His injury from the alleged fraud arose from his relationship with the insurer, not out of the course of his employment. The insurer made false statements which the carpenter detrimentally relied on. Because of the insurer's wilful and wanton conduct, the appeals court determined that the imposition of punitive damages was proper. It also determined that the punitive damage award was not excessive. The carpenter was entitled to the $5 million award. *West v. Western Cas. & Sur. Co.*, 846 F.2d 387 (7th Cir.1988).

A Utah restaurant supervisor was escorting a waitress home when they were accosted by two men. The men forced them back to the restaurant so they could get into a safe. Even though the supervisor knew the combination, he refused to open the safe. The men then repeatedly raped the waitress before the supervisor finally agreed to open the safe. The waitress sued the restaurant owner in a Utah federal district court for negligently failing to instruct the supervisor how to handle a robbery. The owner argued that the rape occurred during the course of employment; thus the waitress's only remedy against him was workers' compensation. The district court jury held for the waitress and the owner appealed to the U.S. Court of Appeals, Tenth Circuit. The court of appeals upheld the district court decision. There were genuine issues of whether the rape occurred during the course of employment, thus justifying a jury decision. The district court correctly decided that the owner was negligent in not instructing the supervisor of restaurant policy concerning robberies. Lastly, the district court properly held that because the owner had clocked out the waitress forty-five minutes before she ended her shift, the rape did not occur during the course of employment. The jury decision in favor of the waitress was upheld. *Massie v. Godfather's Pizza*, 844 F.2d 1414 (10th Cir.1988).

IV. DISABILITY PAYMENTS UNDER WORKERS' COMPENSATION

A common set of distinctions applied to work-related injuries consists of four categories: temporary partial, temporary total, permanent partial and permanent total. Disability is considered temporary where it is presumed that the employee, within some period set by state law, will be able to return to work with his abilities to perform the job undiminished. In these cases, the employee is generally entitled to receive workers' compensation benefits based on a percentage of his actual wage loss. On the other hand, disability is rated permanent when the employee's working abilities are expected to remain impaired beyond the recuperation period. The benefits paid for permanent injuries are not tied to actual wage losses but are generally determined according to scheduled benefits established by the state's workers' compensation laws.

A. Temporary Total Disability

A California man worked as a truck driver for a Los Angeles school district. In 1976, and again in 1979, he suffered industrial injuries to his back and legs which resulted in temporary disability for two-and-a-half years, and permanent disability of 66%. In 1983, a workers' compensation judge awarded him temporary and permanent disability benefits, and indemnity for further medical treatment. In 1987, the driver underwent back surgery and the school district paid for the treatment. He was again temporarily totally disabled. Nine years after his 1979 injury, the driver petitioned to reopen his original award. He claimed that he had suffered a "new and further disability" under § 5410 of the California Labor Code and that because the new disability was caused by medical treatment provided according to his existing award, he was entitled to further recover temporary total disability (TTD) benefits under § 545 of the Code. The workers' compensation judge granted him relief, but the appeals board rescinded the award. The court of appeals affirmed the decision, and the driver appealed to the Supreme Court of California.

On appeal, the driver argued that an award of future medical treatment such as he had received implicitly included an award of future TTD benefits as a secondary consequence. The court disagreed. It noted that medical treatment and TTD benefits were two different classes of benefits. Section 4656 was intended to remove the cap on TTD payments, but it was not meant to permit an applicant to receive TTD benefits whenever the applicant needed medical treatment for a previous injury and had also been awarded future medical benefits. Although it was possible the driver had suffered a new and further disability under § 5410, this section required him to bring his petition within 5 years from the date of the original injury. He had waited 9 years in this case. The court thus rejected the driver's arguments, holding that his interpretation of California law would lead to unlimited TTD benefits when awards for future medical treatment were made. The court affirmed the court of appeal's decision. *Nickelberg v. W.C.A.B.*, 285 Cal.Rptr. 86 (Cal.1991).

After a sales clerk at a Washington, D.C., fashion store suffered a back injury, the fashion store's workers' compensation insurer, Hartford Accident and Indemnity Company, began paying workers' compensation benefits. The woman moved five times in the next two years, including moves to Montana, Virginia and California. While she resided in California, Hartford's vocational rehabilitation consultant notified the woman of three job opportunities in Washington. She failed to respond to any of these job notices. Because her doctor had reported that she was once again able to work an eight hour day with some limitations, her employer and Hartford sought and received a Department of Employment Services ruling that she was ineligible for benefits. The woman appealed. The District of Columbia Court of Appeals agreed with the department's ruling and held that the woman had "failed to accept employment commensurate with her abilities" [D.C.Code § 36-308(c)]. It made no difference that she was in California and the job opportunities were in Washington. Hartford was therefore relieved of its duty to pay workers' compensation benefits to the injured employee. *Joyner v. D.C. Dep't of Employment Services*, 502 A.2d 1027 (D.C.App.1986).

B. Permanent Partial Disability

An Iowa woman worked in a factory on a machine which melted paraffin in a vat. When she placed a solid sheet of paraffin into the vat, some of the hot wax splashed onto her face, burning her severely. She received permanent scarring above her lip and was paid temporary total disability benefits for nine months. She later requested permanent disability benefits, but the industrial commissioner rejected her claim. She appealed unsuccessfully to an Iowa trial court and further appealed to the Supreme Court of Iowa. The supreme court held that the employee had failed to show any impairment of future usefulness and earnings in any job as a factory worker, and thus she was not entitled to permanent disability benefits. The court affirmed the trial court's decision. *Byrnes v. Donaldson's, Inc.*, 451 N.W.2d 810 (Iowa 1990).

A Tennessee man suffered a work-related injury to his lower back and was assessed a fifteen percent permanent partial anatomical disability to the body as a whole. Five years later, the claimant again injured his back due to another work-related injury. His anatomical disability was assessed at ten to fifteen percent of the body as a whole. The trial court, however, found that the claimant had suffered a forty-five percent permanent vocational disability to the body as a whole as a result of the second back injury. The insurer appealed to the Supreme Court of Tennessee. The insurer contended that the evidence did not support an award of permanent partial disability because the anatomical disability and restrictions did not change after the second injury. From the doctor's testimony the court concluded that the claimant's impairment was permanent and resulted from the second injury. The court noted that there was undisputed proof that the claimant was fifty-one-years-old and had an eighth grade education and no vocational training. His primary work experience was limited to jobs requiring heavy physical exertion and he was disqualified from sixty-seven percent of the jobs in the local area which he had been capable of performing before his second injury. The supreme court upheld the trial court's decision. *Worthington v. Modine Mfg. Co.*, 798 S.W.2d 232 (Tenn.1990)

A forty-year-old Louisiana woman worked in a school lunchroom. One day the worker slipped on a wet floor in the cafeteria and twisted her back. She reported the incident and began receiving workers' compensation benefits. After those benefits were reduced because the worker was able to perform most of her previous duties, she sued her employer and its insurer to have the benefits restored. A Louisiana trial court decided that medical testimony indicated that there was no physical reason for the worker's pain and it declared her not disabled. The worker appealed to the Louisiana Court of Appeal. The court affirmed the trial court's finding. It held that the worker was not disabled under state law, which required a worker to be unable to perform his or her previous duties in order to be declared disabled. Since the worker was able to perform most of her previous duties, she was not disabled. *Dailey v. Royal Ins. Co.*, 551 So.2d 55 (La.App.1st Cir.1989).

Prior to becoming a firefighter, a man underwent two preemployment physical exams. His first exam resulted in a determination that he was not qualified for the duties of a firefighter. The results of the second exam were that he was qualified. Both examinations revealed that he suffered from hypertension, but neither exam found evidence of heart disease. After he was employed as a firefighter, he became disabled with heart disease. The firefighter sought workers' compensation benefits, and the Connecticut Workers' Compensation Commissioner denied the benefits. An appeal followed. On appeal to the Connecticut Court of Appeals, the firefighter argued that a state statute entitled him to benefits. He contended that his preemployment physical revealed only evidence of hypertension and not heart disease, and that he was entitled to benefits for his disability stemming from the subsequently discovered heart disease. The court, however, held that the statute plainly required a denial of benefits for not only the hypertension but also the heart disease. The court held that the statute required that the physical exam on entry into service must fail to reveal evidence of both hypertension and heart disease before the claimant can be eligible for any disability benefits. Accordingly, the decision was affirmed. *Suprenant v. City of New Britain*, 611 A.2d 941 (Conn.App.1992).

C. Permanent Total Disability

A Colorado firefighter was injured in a car accident and forced to exhaust his accrued sick leave and vacation pay. After taking a ninety-day temporary disability leave, the firefighter was placed on leave without pay for one year. On learning that the firefighter was permanently disabled, the city terminated his employment. The city offered the firefighter the right to maintain group health coverage for ninety days. It sent him a notice of his right to elect coverage under 42 U.S.C. § 300bb-1, a federal statute providing for continuation coverage of group health plans for state and local employees. The firefighter never returned the required forms for continued coverage and became covered under his wife's separately-maintained group health plan. The firefighter remained under his wife's plan and the city did not extend continuation coverage. The firefighter sued the city in a federal district court, claiming that his status as a covered dependent under another health plan did not terminate his continued coverage rights. The court ruled that group health coverage could be terminated on the day on which the beneficiary became covered under any other group health plan or became entitled to Medicare benefits. The court granted the city's motion for summary judgment.

The firefighter then appealed to the U.S. Court of Appeals, Tenth Circuit. The court of appeals held that the district court's interpretation of § 300bb-1 did not reflect Congress' true intent. It stated that § 300bb-1 was the result of congressional concern with the growing number of Americans without any health insurance coverage. The court considered congressional debates over the continuation coverage rules and concluded that the purpose of § 300bb-1 was to reduce the extent to which certain events could create a significant gap in health coverage. The court stated that the firefighter's case presented the precise gap in coverage which troubled Congress, since he was terminated because of the catastrophic car accident which otherwise would have put his family at risk. The court held that the city could not terminate continuation coverage on the basis that he was covered under his wife's policy. It reversed and remanded the case to the district court. *Oakley v. City of Longmont*, 887 F.2d 249 (10th Cir.1989).

An insurance claims adjuster fell out of his car and injured his elbow while in the course of his work. The elbow damage was severe, and the employee filed a workers' compensation claim. A Tennessee trial court determined that the employee had a vocational disability of eleven percent, but denied future medical benefits. The employee appealed to the Supreme Court of Tennessee. The supreme court ruled that there was no vocational disability. The employee had five years of college education and extensive special insurance training. He had returned to work only a few days after the injury and had worked regularly in the meantime. Ninety-five percent of his work was in the office, and because he was continuing to do satisfactory work, there was no evidence of vocational disability. However, there was no justification for the trial court's denial of future medical expenses. The insurer would be required to pay future medical expenses if the employee could prove they were related to his injury. *Shadle v. Amerisure Co.*, 764 S.W.2d 542 (Tenn.1989).

A Florida man fell from a theatre marquee and suffered a depressed skull fracture. After examination by several physicians he was found to be permanently and totally disabled, with severe neurological and psychiatric impairments, as well as a sixty-two percent loss of vision. As a result of the above information a compensation claims court issued an order finding the man permanently totally disabled. After the order was issued the man moved to Nevada and shortly thereafter, with the full knowledge of his carrier, he began working for minimum-wage as a theatre usher at a theatre where his father worked. The carrier viewed the income from this job as being sheltered and it did not affect his disability benefits. Several years later the carrier discovered that the man had also obtained a job as a changemaker at a casino. The carrier decided the income the man received from that job was not sheltered and terminated the man's benefits. At a subsequent hearing a compensation claims judge ruled in favor of the carrier. The worker appealed.

On appeal, the District Court of Appeal of Florida found the ruling at the hearing was not supported by the evidence. In finding in favor of the worker, the court made reference to the "odd lot employment" doctrine, which states that total disability may be found where workers, while not incapacitated, are not employable in any well-known branch of the labor market. Because the carrier had not presented any evidence about whether the job was created especially for the injured worker or whether the tasks he performed were identical to those which others in similar positions performed, the court reinstated the disability benefits and remanded for further findings. *Malm v. Holiday Theatres*, 560 So.2d 270 (Fla.App.1st Dist.1990).

A North Dakota man worked as a ranch foreman. While managing the ranch, he was thrown from his horse, and injured his left hip and pelvis. He did not fully recover, and was prevented from performing any physical labor which precluded his return to ranch manager. He received workers' compensation benefits, including medical, disability, and partial permanent impairment for his injury. The workers' compensation bureau indicated that the man was not employable without retraining, but that he possessed strong academic and mental abilities. A vocational rehabilitation plan was recommended for education that would enable him to return to employment. He resisted retraining and demanded a lump sum equal to the present value of all future disability payments on the grounds that he was totally and permanently disabled. The bureau offered him a lump sum equal to the cost of retraining. The district court found that the employee failed to provide any evidence that a lump sum payment was in his best interest in any way other than economically, and denied his request for payment. He appealed to the Supreme Court of North Dakota. On appeal, the employee relied on medical testimony which indicated that he was permanently disabled and the pain of his physical limitations was all that he could handle. The court, however, saw no medical opinion in the record that said the employee's physical condition and chronic pain precluded his education and retraining. The employee tested very high cognitively, but was simply unwilling to consider a retraining program. Therefore, the court found that since the employee was a candidate for rehabilitation, the workers' compensation bureau did not abuse its discretion in denying a lump sum payment. *Schiff v. N.D. Workers Comp. Bureau*, 480 N.W.2d 732 (N.D.1992).

An Oregon man was injured in an industrial accident at a time when he was unmarried and had two children. He then married and had a third child. Following that, he was awarded workers' compensation benefits for permanent total disability. The hearing referee determined that his wife and three children should be taken into account for purposes of calculating his benefits. The workers' compensation board reversed that decision, finding that only his prior two children could be counted in the calculation. The worker appealed to the Court of Appeals of Oregon. On appeal, the claimant argued that only the rate of compensation should be determined as of the date of the injury, not the number of members of his family. Oregon law states that, for adopted children, the child must be part of the worker's family before the injury in order to be included in the benefits calculation. Further, under Oregon law, adopted children are treated the same as biological children. Therefore, even though the law was silent on natural children, the court found that, unless born prior to the injury, they could not be included in the calculation. The same reasoning applied to the worker's wife. The court affirmed the board's decision. *Jackson v. Bogart Const.*, 821 P.2d 420 (Or.App.1991).

A Minnesota employee, while working for a lumber company, sustained back injuries. On the advice of his doctor, he sought lighter, more sedentary work. The employer complied with this request. Subsequently, the employee and his doctor informed the employer that the employee was incapable of any employment. A dispute then arose over the employee's functional capacities. Frustrated over the dispute, the employee threatened to kill himself and other company employees. Consequently, the company fired the employee for his misconduct. The employee filed for workers' compensation benefits. A compensation judge awarded him benefits, and the employer appealed. The Workers' Compensation Court of Appeals reversed; the employee appealed to the Supreme Court of Minnesota. On appeal, the court held that the Workers' Compensation Act should not deprive an employee of permanent compensation even when the employee is fired for misconduct. Although the worker threatened to kill other employees, he was otherwise eligible for benefits. Furthermore, the court rejected the employer's argument that the employee should be denied benefits because the employee could not produce evidence of a diligent job search. Because of the employee's poor health, age, and inability to train for another job, he did not need to present further evidence that he looked for work. Accordingly, the court reinstated the decision of the compensation judge which held in favor of the employee. *Boryca v. Marvin Lumber & Cedar*, 487 N.W.2d 876 (Minn.1992).

V. DEATH BENEFITS

State laws governing death benefits to survivors of workers sustaining fatal work-related injuries have been the subject of an abundance of litigation in recent years.

A New Mexico man worked as a lopper, which required him to clean cutting sites of leftover debris after the trees were removed. He and his crew worked at various job sites throughout the state. Because the sites were in remote areas, the crew camped on the job sites. The worker died from carbon monoxide released by smoldering charcoal from a hibachi grill as he slept in his van. His widow applied for and was denied death benefits by the New Mexico Worker's Compensation Administration. She appealed the decision to the Court of Appeals of New Mexico. The court of appeals held that the "bunkhouse rule" applied in determining that the worker's death was compensable as arising out of the course of his employment. This was because his nightly presence was reasonably necessary at the logging site to perform his job. There were no other reasonable accommodations. The court held that even though the injury occurred during off time, the injury was considered as occurring in the course of employment because the worker was reasonably using the employer's premises. Additional findings were required to determine whether the worker was an independent contractor with regard to reimbursement of equipment rental fees and whether this should have been included in the calculation of his average weekly wage for determining his benefits. The court remanded the issue to the district court. It reversed the decision of the Workers' Compensation Administration, and found that the worker died in an accident arising out of and in the course of his employment. *Lujan v. Payroll Express, Inc.*, 837 P.2d 451 (N.M.App.1992).

A Pennsylvania woman died in the course of her employment with a coal mining company. Subsequently, the decedent's widower received compensation benefits in accordance with the Pennsylvania Workmen's Compensation Act. After a period of eight years, the employer filed a petition for termination of benefits, and asserted that the claimant had violated the Act by engaging in a meretricious relationship. At a hearing, the claimant admitted to living with a woman and having sexual relations with her for three and one-half years. As a result of this testimony, the employer's termination petition was granted, and the Workers' Compensation Appeal Board affirmed. The claimant appealed to the Supreme Court of Pennsylvania. On appeal, the court upheld the termination of benefits. The claimant contended, among other things, that certain provisions of the Act violated his constitutional rights to privacy, due process, and equal protection. The court noted, however, that when the Pennsylvania legislature promulgated the Act, it was properly concerned with fostering good morals; and encouraged legally recognized and responsible family relationships while discouraging the formation of illicit relationships. For this reason, among others, the court affirmed the decision of the Workers' Compensation Appeal Board for the termination of benefits. *McCusker v. W.C.A.B. (Rushton Mining Co.)*, 603 A.2d 238 (Pa.Cmwlth.1992).

An Alabama man, while working for a grain company, became trapped in a grain bin and died. The employer's workers' compensation (WC) carrier paid death benefits to the widow. She then brought a wrongful death action against the manufacturer and the assembler of the bin. She sued as the administratrix of the estate rather than as a dependent. When the WC carrier sought to intervene in the lawsuit the trial court refused to allow it. The carrier appealed to the Supreme Court of Alabama. The supreme court noted that the carrier should have been permitted to intervene in the case. Alabama law provides that a WC carrier is entitled to full reimbursement for death benefits where the family of the deceased recovers damages from a third party tortfeasor which exceed the carrier's liability. Even though the widow in this case had sued as the administratrix rather than as a dependent, the carrier could still intervene in the action. Otherwise, an insurer's right to reimbursement could be circumvented by a dependent's filing of an action as an administrator of an estate. *Miller's Mutual Ins. Ass'n v. Young*, 601 So.2d 962 (Ala.1992).

An Alabama employee died while at work. His wife sought workers' compensation death benefits in an Alabama trial court. She alleged that she was the dependent of the deceased employee and entitled to recover benefits. She testified, however, that she had not lived in the same household as the deceased for the past five years. She further testified that the deceased employee did not give her any money during this time. Their daughter indicated that her father had left because he had a drinking problem, and was seeing another woman. The employer filed a motion for summary judgment contending that the woman was not a dependent of the decedent and therefore not entitled to benefits. The trial court granted the summary judgment motion and the wife appealed to the Court of Civil Appeals of Alabama.

Alabama law provides that the wife of a deceased employee is presumed to be wholly dependent upon the deceased employee unless it is shown that 1) she was living voluntarily apart from her husband or 2) that the husband had not contributed to her support for more than twelve months prior to his death. The appellate court affirmed the decision of the trial court, noting the testimony of the wife indicating that she was living apart from the deceased voluntarily. The court found the daughter's testimony to be insufficient to overcome the defendant's motion for summary judgment. *McCain v. Capital Veneer Works, Inc.*, 571 So.2d 1215 (Ala.Civ.App.1990).

A Massachusetts man committed suicide by hanging himself in his own home. During the evening, prior to the suicide, he conducted himself in a routine manner. He left a note which indicated that his employer had harassed him for four years. His widow brought a claim for workers' compensation benefits, which was denied. She appealed that decision to the Appeals Court of Massachusetts. The appellate court held that she had to show her husband had suffered a personal injury arising out of and in the course of his employment, a causal connection between the injury and her husband's suicide, and that, due to the injury, he was of unsound mind, enough to make him irresponsible for his act. The court noted first that she had not shown a causal connection between any injury the man may have suffered and his suicide. It also stated that she had not shown her husband to be of unsound mind because, prior to the suicide, he had exhibited no signs of any psychological problems. The court ruled that there must be an unsoundness of mind apart from the suicide itself. The court affirmed the denial of benefits to the woman. *McCarthy's (Dependent's) Case*, 548 N.E.2d 888 (Mass.App.Ct.1990).

In a California case, a man was hired by Boeing Services International (BSI) as a range inspector. His job duties included locating and identifying unexploded ordnance on U.S. army firing ranges. The man was assigned to a group helping to

Sec. VI   SETOFF OF BENEFITS   459

clear unexploded ordnance from a former hand grenade range on a California military installation. A member of the team stepped on an unexploded hand grenade lying beneath the surface of the ground, causing it to explode. The man died from injuries caused by this explosion. The Workers' Compensation Appeals Board approved an agreement settling in full all workers' compensation benefits BSI owed to the man's wife and children. They received $76,500. The man's family subsequently filed a claim under California Labor Code § 4553 for additional compensation. When the case was dismissed by a superior court, the man's family appealed.

The California Court of Appeal noted that § 4553 of the California Labor Code provides for a one-half increase in the amount of compensation otherwise recoverable when an employee is injured by reason of "serious and willful misconduct" on the part of his employer. The court also observed that the workers' compensation system "balances the advantage to the employer of immunity from liability at law against the detriment of relatively swift and certain compensation payments." This balance would be disturbed, said the court, if it accepted the idea that any misconduct of an employer that could be characterized as intentional warranted a lawsuit for damages. The court ruled that the family had failed to present facts which indicated that BSI intended that the man be injured. For this reason the Court of Appeal upheld the lower court's dismissal of the family's case. Because the family failed to allege that BSI "acted deliberately with the specific intent to injure," their recovery was limited to applicable workers' compensation limits. *Stalnaker v. Boeing Co.*, 231 Cal.Rptr. 323 (App.4th Dist.1986).

In Mississippi, a female news reporter was killed in an automobile accident en route to the television station where she worked. Her survivors appealed this case to the Mississippi Supreme Court, contending that the Workers' Compensation Commission erred in requiring that the survivors prove that they were dependents of the reporter and by denying them funeral and death benefits. In applying the law to the facts of the case, the court found the applicable Mississippi statute unconstitutional. Under the statute, a widow was presumed to be wholly dependent on her deceased husband but a widower was required to prove his dependency. The court noted that the United States Supreme Court in *Wengler v. Druggist Mutual Ins. Co.*, 446 U.S. 142 (1980), had declared a very similar statute in Missouri unconstitutional. The Mississippi Supreme Court decided to follow *Wengler* and hold the statute unconstitutional. The survivors were allowed to collect death and funeral benefits under workers' compensation. *Wilson v. Service Broadcasters*, 483 So.2d 1339 (Miss.1986).

VI. SETOFF OF BENEFITS

A number of cases have arisen over the question of whether an insurer may reduce the amounts payable on a separate policy by the amount of workers' compensation a worker is receiving where the worker is receiving benefits from both sources simultaneously. Courts have been split over the issue.

A New Jersey woman worked for a major department store as a salesperson when she was injured in an automobile accident. She lost ten weeks of work; however, she was reimbursed by her employer's state-approved private disability income plan. The insured had personal injury protection benefits with her automobile insurance company which covered lost income due to an automobile accident. She sought to collect from her insurer for her lost income. It refused and she sued in a New Jersey trial court. The trial court found for the insurer, stating that since the insured had already collected her lost income from her employer she was not entitled to more. The insured appealed to the Superior Court of New Jersey, Appellate Division. The insured claimed that since her insurance coverage was for lost income up to $400 per week and the state-approved plan had a limit of $236 per week, she was entitled to the $164 difference. The appellate court agreed, stating that the additional benefits that the department store provided were not subject to collateral source deduction and the insured was entitled to the $164 per week from her automobile insurer. The appellate court reversed the trial court's decision. *O'Boyle v. Prudential*, 575 A.2d 515 (N.J.Super.A.D.1990).

A Michigan insured was employed at a carwash when she was pinned between two automobiles and injured. The insured was covered under a no-fault automobile liability policy that specifically provided for noncoordinated personal protection insurance (PIP) benefits. The insured received workers' compensation benefits and also filed a claim with the insurer for PIP benefits. The insurer paid the claim, but deducted a setoff equal to the amount of workers' compensation benefits. The insured sued the insurer in a Michigan circuit court to recover the setoff. The circuit court found for the insured, and the insurer appealed to the Court of Appeals of Michigan. The court of appeals noted that the insured's policy provided that the insurer could subtract benefits provided under the laws of any state or federal government from benefits otherwise payable under the policy. The court found that this provision clearly and unambiguously authorized the insurer to deduct workers' compensation benefits, which were required under Michigan law, from PIP benefits. Nothing in the policy indicated that this provision only applied where the insured had elected to coordinate benefits. Under Michigan's no-fault automobile insurance act, workers' compensation benefits must be subtracted from PIP benefits in order to eliminate double recovery. The court of appeals reversed the circuit court's decision. The insurer was entitled to deduct the insured's workers' compensation benefits from PIP benefits. *Conrad v. Auto Club Ins. Ass'n*, 442 N.W.2d 762 (Mich.App.1989).

A Colorado employee was injured in an automobile accident while in the scope of employment, and received temporary disability benefits from his employer's workers' compensation insurance carrier. A suit was then brought by the employee against the third party tortfeasor. A settlement was reached, the workers' compensation carrier was repaid, and the remainder of the settlement went to the employee. The employee was then awarded $14,982 in workers' compensation permanent partial disability benefits, but the ALJ again allowed a setoff and no payment was made. The employee disagreed, and filed suit seeking to invalidate both the order and the earlier setoff. Colorado's system for allocation of liability for personal injury protection (PIP) benefits was argued by the worker to preclude the setoff. The case reached the Supreme Court of Colorado. Colorado's no-fault act requires insurers to absorb the PIP expenses for their own insured, and precludes any claim for PIP benefits against a tortfeasor. The state's workers' compensation system requires an employer's carrier to pay PIP benefits. In order to remove the possibility that an injured party will recover duplicate PIP benefits, a "primacy rule" specifies that the loss be borne by the workers' compensation carrier. Therefore, the settlement received from the tortfeasor could not have legally included PIP benefits, and the

Sec. VII   STATUTE OF LIMITATIONS   461

workers' compensation carrier had no right to a setoff in either dispute. *Tate v. Industrial Claim Appeals Office*, 815 P.2d 15 (Colo.1991).

An Alabama man was employed by a garage as a wrecker operator at the Mobile International Speedway. When he was not operating the wrecker, the employee drove the garage's race car on the speedway for advertising purposes. He was not permitted to race the car unless there was no wrecker service to perform. Unfortunately, while racing the car one day, he collided with another car and sustained serious, permanent injuries. His group life and health insurer paid him $282,000 in reasonable and necessary medical expenses. The employee then filed suit against the garage, seeking workers' compensation benefits. The Alabama Court of Civil Appeals awarded permanent disability benefits and medical expenses, finding that a release executed by the employee on behalf of the garage was void as against public policy. The release had purported to free the garage of workers' compensation liability for any work-related injuries sustained by the employee. The court further allowed the employee's group life and health insurer to intervene in the lawsuit, on the grounds that the policy it had issued to the employee contained an exclusion for injuries compensable by workers' compensation. Because the court determined that the garage was liable for workers' compensation benefits, it ordered the garage to reimburse the employee's group life and health insurer for the $282,000 medical expenses payment it had made to the employee. *Kennedy v. Cochran*, 475 So.2d 872 (Ala.Civ.App.1985).

VII. STATUTE OF LIMITATIONS

The state laws generally provide time limits for filing claims for injuries under workers' compensation.

An Oregon man worked for a small amusement park and go-cart rental business. Eventually he became a part owner, as well as the manager of the business. He suffered several back injuries over the years, and after the last one, he filed a claim for workers' compensation benefits. However, the claim was made more than two years after the injury. The insurer denied the claim because it had not been timely filed. Following administrative hearings in which the employee was awarded benefits, the insurer appealed to the Oregon Court of Appeals. On appeal, the insurer asserted that Oregon law required notice of an injury to be given to the employer within thirty-days. Further, the law required the employer to notify the insurer within five days of its receiving notice. The court found that the employer had been given notice in a timely manner, thus entitling the employee to benefits. Even though the insurer had not been timely notified, it could not deny benefits to the employee on that basis. It could only seek reimbursement for any penalties assessed for late processing. Although part of the employee's duty as manager was to notify the insurer of injuries, and although he failed to do so, he was still entitled to benefits. The award was affirmed. *Barney's Karts, Inc. v. Vance*, 821 P.2d 422 (Or.App.1991).

After an industrial accident, an Arizona claimant entered into a written agreement with his employer, whereby his hospital bills were to be paid by his employer in exchange for the claimant agreeing not to institute any action. One year later, the employer ceased paying the medical bills and the claimant sought legal advice. The attorney sent a letter to the Industrial Commission in which was provided information regarding the claimant's injury, the agreement, and his desire to file a workers' compensation claim for benefits. After eight months, the special fund, a division of the Industrial Commission, sent a workers' injury claim report. The report was completed and returned. The special fund denied the claim as untimely and, on administrative review, the denial was affirmed. The claimant appealed to the Court of Appeals of Arizona.

On appeal, the claimant contended that his workers' compensation claim was timely because it was tolled during the time that the parties were acting in conformity with the written settlement agreement. The court held that since he acted with diligence in seeking legal advice and having his attorney send a notice of claim letter to the Industrial Commission the employee's claim was not untimely. The court also held that the workers' compensation statutes did not contain form requirements and that a written manifestation of an intent to claim benefits under the compensation act was enough. The court of appeals reversed the decision of the administrative review board. *Allen v. Ind. Comm'n of Arizona*, 787 P.2d 1107 (Ariz.App.1990).

An employee, driving a company vehicle in the course of his employment, was injured when a Southern California Rapid Transit District (RTD) bus entered an intersection on a red light and struck his vehicle. On April 25, 1985, his employer's workers' compensation insurer presented a claim for damages to the RTD which it never acted on. On May 16, 1985, he presented a claim for damages to the RTD which was rejected on June 4, 1985. On February 14, 1986, the employer's insurer filed its complaint for damages resulting from the accident. Subsequently, the employee filed a complaint in intervention in March 1986, more than six months after the RTD rejected his claim. The RTD asked the Superior Court, Los Angeles County, for a ruling in its favor on the ground that the employee's action was barred by a six-month statute of limitations. The superior court held for the RTD despite the fact that the statute of limitations does not apply when an employee intervenes in a workers' compensation case against a private party. The employer's insurer appealed.

The issue before the California Court of Appeal, Second District, was whether the statute of limitations should apply in a suit of this type where the tortfeasor (wrongdoer) is a government entity, in this case the RTD. The court of appeal observed that the law was clear that when an employer or its insurer filed a timely lawsuit against a tortfeasor to recover workers' compensation paid to an injured employee, the employee may intervene to recover damages for personal injury even if the complaint of intervention is not filed within the time period allowed by the statute of limitations. The RTD claimed that lawsuits against government entities should be treated differently. However, it suggested no reason why California Labor Code § 3853 (which states that either an employer or employee may at any time before trial join with the other in a lawsuit) should not apply to timely lawsuits against government agencies. The dismissal of the employee's complaint was reversed. *Home Ins. Co. v. Southern California Rapid Transit Dist.*, 241 Cal.Rptr. 858 (App.2d Dist.1987).

The application of the appropriate statute of limitations for filing a workers' compensation claim for additional benefits was at issue before the Illinois Supreme Court. At the time the claimant was injured the Illinois Workmen's Compensation Act required that injured employees must file their claims within one year of the last payment date if compensation was paid. While the present claim was still pending, the statute was amended to allow claims to be filed within three years of the last

Sec. VIII   MISCELLANEOUS CASES   463

payment date. One year later the statute was amended, providing that a claim could be filed within two years of the last payment of benefits. At the time this last amendment was passed, one year had expired since the claimant had received his last payment. However, the claim for additional compensation was not made until two years and eight months after the final payment. The issue was whether the prior three-year statute of limitations applied which would permit the claim or whether the more recent two year limitation applied barring the claim.

The supreme court held that the two-year statute of limitations applied, and that the claim was barred. The court stated that an amendment shortening a statute of limitations is to be applied retroactively if application of the amendment leaves the claimant with a reasonable amount of time after the amendment's effective date to file his claim. Here the change from a three-year to a two-year limitations period was made one year after final benefit payments were made. Thus, one year remained under the new two-year limitations period in which to file the claim. The court stated that this was a reasonable length of time. *Phillips Products Co. v. Industrial Comm'n*, 446 N.E.2d 234 (Ill.1983).

VIII. MISCELLANEOUS WORKERS' COMPENSATION CASES

As illustrated by the following cases, workers' compensation litigation may involve peripheral issues.

A. Employee Incarceration While Receiving Benefits

The Wyoming Supreme Court has decided that a worker's imprisonment does not require a suspension of temporary total disability payments. The worker fractured his right ankle in an industrial accident on October 26, 1984, and was expected to return to work the following February. Payments were made from the time of the injury but were suspended on January 21, 1985, when the district court discovered that the worker had been in jail since December 20, 1984. Reversing, the supreme court stated that workers' compensation law is governed by contract principles rather than tort law. In other words, the system is not based on the fault of either the worker or the employer but instead provides benefits whenever a work-related injury arises. For this reason, the court held that the worker was entitled to benefits despite his imprisonment. *In the Matter of Injury to Spera*, 713 P.2d 1155 (Wyo.1986).

An employee of a logging company injured his back in the course of his employment. The man began receiving temporary total disability benefits a week later. A year later the man was incarcerated in a correctional facility. He continued to receive disability benefits. After his release he was declared medically stationary and was awarded fifteen percent permanent partial disability. However, the order allowed the employer to offset the benefits paid during the time he was incarcerated. The worker requested a hearing. The Workers' Compensation Board held that the worker was entitled to temporary disability benefits during his incarceration. The employer then appealed to the Court of Appeals of Oregon. The appellate court held that because the man was a "worker" when he filed his suit and his departure from the workforce was a direct result of his injury, he was entitled to collect disability benefits throughout the time he was incarcerated. *Forshee & Langley Logging v. Peckhan*, 788 P.2d 487 (Or.App.1990).

The Court of Appeals of New York has dealt with the issue of whether a claimant, suffering from a prior work-related permanent partial disability, is entitled to continue receiving workers' compensation benefits during the period he is confined to a hospital for the criminally insane. The claimant was awarded benefits after becoming disabled while working in New York State. Several years later he returned to his native Italy and was arrested for fatally shooting two persons and wounding a third. After undergoing psychiatric examinations, the Italian court acquitted him of the crime due to "total insanity." He was then ordered committed to a hospital for the criminally insane for a minimum of ten years.

The workers' compensation board declared, at the request of the claimant's former employer, that the compensation payments should be halted during the time of the claimant's confinement. This decision was reversed by a lower court, and the employer appealed. The Court of Appeals acknowledged that under state law a claimant is not entitled to compensation benefits while incarcerated after conviction of a crime. However, it rejected the employer's claim that the man's commitment to a hospital for the criminally insane was the equivalent of a criminal conviction. As the Italian court had acquitted him of the charges, there was no basis for suspension of payments. *Klonowski v. Dep't of Fire*, 448 N.E.2d 423 (N.Y.1983).

B. Violation of Safety Laws by Employer

An Ohio employee was injured when he fell off a ladder at a federally owned nuclear energy plant operated by a private corporation. He received a basic workers' compensation award. The employee then filed for an additional workers' compensation award, alleging that his injury resulted from the violation of a state safety code. The Ohio Constitution provides for an additional award of fifteen to fifty percent of the original award when a private employer violates the state safety code. When the Ohio Industrial Commission refused to hear the claim the employee appealed to the Ohio Court of Appeals. It ordered the commission to hear the claim. The commission appealed to the Ohio Supreme Court which upheld the decision. The commission then appealed to the U.S. Supreme Court.

The issue on appeal was whether the Ohio law could be applied against a federally owned plant. The commission argued that imposing the Ohio law on the federally owned plant was a violation of the Supremacy Clause. The Supremacy Clause states that where federal and state laws conflict, the federal law prevails. The commission then argued that Congress did not intend to authorize the supplemental award permitted by Ohio law. The employee argued that Congress would have expressly rejected authorization for an additional award had it intended to do so. The Supreme Court held for the employee. It stated that Congress knew different state workers' compensation laws existed when it authorized federally owned plants to be subject to state workers' compensation laws. The case was remanded to the commission in order to hear the employee's claim for an additional award. *Goodyear Atomic Corp. v. Miller*, 486 U.S. 174, 108 S.Ct. 1704, 100 L.Ed.2d 158 (1988).

An employee at a lumber company in Vermont worked at a job which required her to repeatedly lift lumber from a pallet and load it onto a conveyor belt. She sustained a back injury while engaged in this activity, and brought suit against the company's workers' compensation insurer. She alleged that the insurer had negligently inspected the insured's premises and failed to assist the insured in creating a safe work place. A federal district court granted a directed verdict for the insurer; the U.S. Court of Appeals, Second Circuit, vacated and remanded the case, and the district court reinstated its decision. The injured worker again appealed. On appeal, the court noted that the Vermont Supreme Court had explicitly adopted § 324A of the Restatement of Torts (Second). Thus, a jury issue existed as to whether the insurer, by its advertisements, had undertaken to perform a duty owed by the employer to its employee. A jury could have found that the insurer undertook to conduct an active loss prevention program at the lumber company. If so, and if the insurer did not perform its duty with reasonable care, then that failure could have resulted in the employee's injury. The court reversed and remanded the case for a new trial. *Pratt v. Liberty Mutual Ins. Co.*, 952 F.2d 667 (2d Cir.1992).

A New York employee was working inside a digester tank at a treatment facility plant. While he was disassembling scaffolding, he fell 17 feet from the tank and sustained personal injuries. At the time of the accident, he was not wearing either a safety belt or a lanyard, which he knew were available on the project work site. The employee sued the owner and general contractor. The Supreme Court granted summary judgment to the owner and general contractor, and the employee appealed to the Supreme Court, Appellate Division. On appeal, the court found that the owner and contractor were absolutely liable for the employee's injuries. The court stated that the owner and general contractor had a nondelegable duty to provide, to furnish, to place, and to operate safety devices to protect their employees from falling. It was not enough to relieve them of liability because they had made safety devices available to the employee while he was working. Furthermore, the general contractor and owner failed to prove that the employee refused to use the safety devices. Therefore, the court reversed the trial court and held in favor of the employee. *Donovan v. City of Buffalo*, 586 N.Y.S.2d 843 (A.D.4th Dept.1992).

Two Alabama women were injured at work when a cart used to load lumber broke, causing a pile of lumber to fall on them. The women sued their employer's workers' compensation insurer in an Alabama trial court, alleging that their injuries had been caused by the insurer's negligent inspection of the employer's premises. The insurer contended that it had no duty to inspect for the employees' benefit, but rather had inspected for its own purposes. After the trial court dismissed the suit in the insurer's favor, the women appealed to the Alabama Supreme Court. On appeal, the women alleged that the insurer had assumed the duty of inspection and had failed to notice that lumber carts used on the premises posed serious hazards. They also presented testimony from a safety consultant who stated that the insurer's inspection had been improperly performed.

The supreme court reversed the trial court's dismissal, concluding that under Alabama law, a workers' compensation carrier may be liable when it voluntarily undertakes to inspect an employer's premises for safety. It stated that the women had to prove that the insurer had assumed a duty by voluntarily undertaking the inspection and had breached that duty, proximately causing their injuries. After an examination of the evidence, the court concluded there was evidence that the insurer's inspection was a safety inspection. It remanded the case for trial. *Hodge v. U.S. Fidelity and Guar. Co.*, 539 So.2d 229 (Ala.1989).

C. Other Employer Misconduct

Claimants were independent contractors who installed carpets for a Florida carpet company and were injured on the job. At the time they were injured, the carpet company was withholding money from their paychecks for workers' compensation coverage. After worker's compensation claims were filed, the insurer determined that there was no coverage provided by the carpet company because these installers were not covered employees under the terms and conditions of the policy issued to the carpet company. Prior to entering into its insurance contract, and in order to protect itself from liability, the carpet company routinely withheld a percentage of an installer's pay to cover any workers' compensation. The carpet company understood that under its contract with the insurer, its practice of sometimes covering the installers would continue. While the carpet company generally required the independent installers to obtain their own workers' compensation coverage, the owner testified that sometimes when his company was trying out installers or had part-time crews, the carpet company would deduct money for workers' compensation to ensure that these installers would be covered. The claimants filed suit with the Workers' Compensation Board. The judge determined that the insurer was estopped from denying coverage. The insurer appealed to a federal district court.

On appeal, the court noted that the insurer was aware of the deductions made from carpet installers' wages for premiums and the insurer's failure to advise the carpet company to discontinue the policy after coverage was issued by it estopped the insurer from denying coverage to the carpet company. The court affirmed the Workers' Compensation Board's decision, stating that promissory estoppel may be used to create insurance coverage where to refuse to do so would sanction fraud or other injustice. *United Self Insured Services v. Faber*, 561 So.2d 1358 (Fla.App.1st Dist.1990).

A famous rock star contracted with a company to set up her shows during her Pennsylvania tour. She also hired a second company to provide lighting and sound systems. The first company then hired a subcontractor to provide equipment loaders. One of the loaders was injured when he fell from a ramp placed on the door jamb of a trailer. The loader sued all three companies in a Pennsylvania trial court and obtained a verdict for negligence against the subcontractor and the second company. The trial court also found that the state's no-fault act precluded evidence of the loader's past medical expenses and lost wages. The subcontractor and second company then appealed to the Superior Court of Pennsylvania.

On appeal, the subcontractor argued that the loader had assumed the risk of working on the ramp. The court held that since the subcontractor had failed to obtain workers' compensation insurance, the assumption of risk defense was banned by statute. It held that the second company was also precluded from using the assumption of risk defense because the loader did not perceive the dangerousness of the ramp. Even though it was not the loader's employer, it still could be liable for negligence. The court also rejected the argument that the loader was precluded from introducing evidence of past wage loss and medical expenses. It held that the loader was not entitled to no-fault vehicle benefits since he was not occupying, entering into or alighting from a vehicle; thus, he was not a victim as required under the no-fault act. However, the court ordered a new trial to determine the loader's damages. *Martin v. Recker*, 552 A.2d 668 (Pa.Super.1988).

An injured employee sued his employer's workers' compensation insurer for bad faith refusal to pay benefits. The insurer asked a New Mexico trial court to dismiss the employee's claim. The trial court refused and the insurer appealed to the New Mexico Court of Appeals. The court of appeals granted the insurer's dismissal motion and the employee appealed to the New Mexico Supreme Court. The issue on appeal was how the New Mexico Insurance Code affected the Workers' Compensation Act. The employee argued that the insurance code amended the Workers' Compensation Act by allowing a separate claim for bad faith refusal to pay benefits. The insurer argued that the workers' compensation insurance policy was a contract between the insurer and the employer. Therefore, workers were not actually insureds and could not sue independently for bad faith. The insurer also argued that the policy specifically precluded third party claims against the insurer. The supreme court held that the legislature intended to provide workers with a separate right to sue insurers for bad faith. This right to sue only applied to intentional, wilful refusal to pay benefits. The insurance code expanded the definition of "insured" to include "claimants." The court reasoned that intended beneficiaries have a right to recover even though they are not parties to the policy itself. The supreme court reinstated the employee's claim against the insurer. *Russell v. Protective Ins. Co.*, 751 P.2d 693 (N.M.1988).

IX. THE LONGSHORE AND HARBOR WORKERS' COMPENSATION ACT (LHWCA)

The LHWCA is a federal law intended to protect workers engaged in maritime employment on or near navigable waters.

A Georgia mechanic employed by a maritime business which maintained and repaired equipment used to transport goods traveling from sea to land and back again was injured while working. The mechanic sought workers' compensation benefits under the Longshoremen's and Harbor Workers' Compensation Act (LHWCA). The maritime business and its insurer denied coverage and the mechanic sought review from an administrative law judge who found for the mechanic and awarded him benefits. The employer and carrier appealed to the Benefits Review Board which upheld the judge's findings. They then appealed to the U.S. Court of Appeals, Eleventh Circuit. The appellate court noted that the U.S. Supreme Court has extended the longshore status to those workers who indirectly work with cargo. Since the mechanic worked on the containers in which the cargo was shipped and was thus an integral part of the cargo process, the court determined that the mechanic would be considered a maritime employee under the LHWCA. Therefore, the court of appeals affirmed the board's decision to award workers' compensation benefits to the mechanic. *Atlantic Container Service, Inc. v. Coleman*, 904 F.2d 611 (11th Cir.1990).

In December 1978, the Superior Court, Los Angeles County, ordered an insurer liquidated and appointed a liquidator. The insurer had written workers' compensation policies which resulted in claims for benefits under the federal Longshoremen's and Harbor Workers' Compensation Act. The insurer's liquidator alleged that these federal claims were covered claims and were the responsibility of the California Insurance Guarantee Association (CIGA). CIGA paid the claims "under protest," asserting that they were not covered claims under the California Insurance Code.

CIGA alleged that the claims were the liquidator's sole responsibility. It sought a determination in Superior Court that the federal claims were the responsibility of the liquidator and that CIGA was entitled to reimbursement of the amounts it had paid in settlement and adjustment of the claims. The Superior Court ruled against CIGA which then appealed.

The California Court of Appeal, Second District, noted that workers' compensation insurers are required to participate in CIGA. The California Insurance Code defines workers' compensation as "insurance against loss from liability imposed by law upon employers to compensate employees and their dependents for injuries sustained by the employees arising out of and in the course of employment...." The court noted that this definition was broad enough to encompass claims for benefits under the LHWCA. The Insurance Code's definition of "covered claims" obligates CIGA, "in the case of a policy of workers' compensation insurance, to provide workers' compensation benefits under the Workers' Compensation Law of this state...." The court refused to accept CIGA's contention that this language was intended to limit CIGA's responsibility to claims for state workers' compensation benefits only. It declared that "[t]he inclusion of coverage for federal claims is consistent with the general purpose of CIGA to protect California from the insolvency of insurers and the resulting adverse effects on employers and workers." The decision of the Superior Court that CIGA was responsible for the claims was affirmed. *CIGA v. El Dorado Ins. Co.*, 234 Cal.Rptr. 734 (App.2d Dist.1987).

A Texas grain inspector was injured when he slipped and fell on wet grain dust in a commercial shipping vessel. Two years later, the inspector required back surgery. He also suffered from spondylolisthesis, a defect in the back where the neural arch is not fully joined together. Although the defect can be aggravated by trauma, medical testimony established that this would manifest itself in a reasonably short period of time, three or four weeks from the trauma at the most. The man sought recovery from the stevedore and the vessel operator for his injuries in a federal trial court. The court noted that since the injury occurred on a commercial shipping vessel over navigable waters, the general maritime law controlled this case. Therefore, the inspector had to prove the fault of the defendants in not adhering to the standards of reasonableness. The court noted that neither the stevedore nor the ship's crew could wash the grain dust off the deck with a hose because of the federal prohibition of harbor pollution. The court also noted that the grain inspector knew of the hazard and had to exercise some responsibility for his own safety. Therefore, he could not recover for his injuries. *Alphin v. Marquesa Maritime, Inc.*, 747 F.Supp. 1223 (E.D.Tex.1990).

A worker fell from a ladder and injured himself while repairing a barge floating on the Elizabeth River, a navigable waterway of the United States. The employer maintained that the employee was not entitled to workers' compensation. However, the Virginia Worker's Compensation Commissioner awarded the employee benefits. The employer appealed, claiming that the U.S. Constitution prohibited a state's workers' compensation commission from exercising jurisdiction over a maritime injury. The Virginia Court of Appeals, however, disagreed and held that the board had authority to award benefits since the employee was in a "maritime but local job." Accordingly, the commissioner's decision was affirmed. *Norfolk Shipbuilding & Drydock v. Duke*, 420 S.E.2d 528 (Va.App.1992).

A cook for a catering company that served an oil rig in the Gulf of Mexico became ill. As he was being lowered into a boat to be taken to land, a crane operator dropped the transport basket he was in, injuring him. He sued his employer for negligence under maritime and federal law. His employer was insured by a workers' compensation and liability policy. The policy excluded coverage for ocean and marine injuries. However, it also noted that the employer catered to off-shore oil rigs and agreed to cover the employer's liability for employee sickness. After the cook's suit had been filed, the employer's insurer was declared insolvent. The employer then settled the case and sought reimbursement from the Louisiana Insurance Guaranty Association (LIGA), a state organization designed to pay the coverage of insolvent member insurers. LIGA denied coverage, contending that the cook's claim involved ocean marine insurance because he sought recovery under maritime laws and such coverage was specifically excluded by the association. A federal district court held that the employee's policy had not been an ocean marine insurance policy and ordered LIGA to pay. The U.S. Court of Appeals, Fifth Circuit, certified a question to the Louisiana Supreme Court.

After noting that ocean marine insurance was not defined by the state's insurance code, the supreme court concluded that the phrase referred to traditional marine insurance, or property insurance on hulls, freights and cargoes. It ruled that the exclusion for ocean marine insurance does not apply to employers' liability policies which incidentally cover risks associated with maritime activities. Since the cook's injuries had nothing to do with ocean marine insurance, LIGA had to reimburse the employer. *Deshotels v. SHRM Catering Services*, 538 So.2d 988 (La.1989).

A California shipyard worker injured his back while working as a stage rigger, a moderately heavy job. He returned to work two months later, but reinjured his back seven months after returning to work. Shortly before his second injury, he was examined by a specialist who estimated that the man had suffered an eight percent overall impairment. One year after he suffered his second injury, he was rated at twenty percent overall disability and was restricted to light work. When the man sued, an administrative law judge and the benefits review board held that the employer was liable under the Longshoremen's and Harbor Workers' Compensation Act. The employer appealed. Before the U.S. Court of Appeals, Ninth Circuit, the employer argued that it should not be liable for the second injury because the employee had actually suffered permanent impairment in the first injury. Substantial evidence supported the decision of the administrative law judge that the first injury resulted in no permanent disability. The employee had resumed his regular job including overtime without any restrictions or pay reduction, stated the court. In addition, his medical record indicated no objective evidence of permanent disability. The decisions of the administrative law judge and the benefits review board were affirmed. *Todd Shipyards Corp. v. Director, Office of Workers' Compensation Programs*, 793 F.2d 1012 (9th Cir.1986).

CHAPTER TEN

STATE AND FEDERAL LAW

    Page

I. FEDERAL REGULATION 471
   A. ERISA Cases 471
   B. Other Federal Cases 478

II. STATE LAW REQUIREMENTS 480
   A. State Regulatory Authority 480
   B. Arbitration 487
   C. Subrogation 489

I. FEDERAL REGULATION

Insurers must comply with a growing number of state and federal laws in order to do business. The most important federal statute regulating insurers is the McCarran-Ferguson Insurance Regulation Act, 15 U.S.C. §§ 1011-1012, which is reproduced in Appendix A of this volume. A growing area of federal law is pension benefit regulation, which is covered under the Employee Retirement Income Security Act, (ERISA), found at 29 U.S.C. § 1001(a), *et. seq.*

A. <u>ERISA Cases</u>

A District of Columbia workers' compensation act required employers who provide health insurance for their employees to provide equivalent health insurance coverage for injured employees eligible for workers' compensation benefits. An employer filed an action in the U.S. District Court for the District of Columbia against the District and its mayor, claiming that the act was preempted by the Employee Retirement Income Security Act (ERISA), which superseded state laws that related to any employee benefit plan covered by ERISA. The court granted the District's motion to dismiss. On appeal, the U.S. Court of Appeals reversed, holding that preemption was within ERISA's structure and plain meaning. The District appealed.

The U.S. Supreme Court affirmed the judgment of the court of appeals. It stated that a law "relates to" a covered employee benefit plan if it has a connection with or reference to such a plan. ERISA preempts any state law that refers to or has a connection with covered benefit plans that do not fall within its exceptions — even if 1) the law is not specifically designed to affect such plans, 2) the effect is only indirect, and 3) the law is consistent with ERISA's substantive requirements. The Court held that any employer-sponsored health insurance programs are subject to ERISA regulation, and any state law imposing requirements by reference to such covered programs must yield to ERISA. Even though the act's requirements "related to" an ERISA-exempt workers' compensation plan, ERISA's exemptions do not limit its preemptive sweep once it is determined that a law "relates to" a covered plan. The Court held that ERISA's coverage is broad and that it superseded the workers' compensation act because the act related to a covered plan. The District could not require employers to provide equivalent health insurance coverage for injured employees who were eligible for workers' compensation. *District of Columbia v. Greater Washington Board of Trade*, 113 S.Ct. 580 (1992).

The U.S. Supreme Court has ruled that the Employee Retirement Income Security Act of 1974 (ERISA) preempts lawsuits based on state common law for alleged improper processing of benefit claims. In this case an employee filed a lawsuit in federal court seeking damages under Mississippi law for wrongful failure to pay insurance benefits and fraud. The Supreme Court ruled that the employee's lawsuit alleging improper processing of a benefit claim under an employee benefit plan fell under ERISA's preemption clause. *Pilot Life Ins. Co. v. Dedeaux*, 481 U.S. 41, 107 S.Ct. 1549, 95 L.Ed.2d 39 (1987).

In a companion case, the Supreme Court ruled that such lawsuits filed in state court that are preempted by ERISA may be removed to federal court. The employee in this case filed a lawsuit in a Michigan trial court for wrongful discontinuation of disability benefits. The employee's benefits were terminated when the employee refused to return to work after an insurer determined that he was no longer disabled. The Supreme Court ruled that the lawsuit was preempted by ERISA, which provides an exclusive federal court forum for resolving lawsuits by beneficiaries to recover benefits from a covered plan. The lawsuit was therefore properly removed from state to federal court. *Metropolitan Life Ins. Co. v. Taylor*, 481 U.S. 58, 107 S.Ct. 1542, 95 L.Ed.2d 55 (1987).

In a more recent Supreme Court case a Pennsylvania corporation operated a self-funded healthcare plan (plan), an employee welfare benefit plan within the meaning of ERISA which provided health benefits to employees and their dependents. Among the provisions was a subrogation clause which stated that a plan member agreed to reimburse the plan for benefits paid if the member recovered on a claim in a liability action against a third party. An employee's daughter was involved in an automobile accident. The plan paid a portion of her medical expenses. The employee brought a negligence action on his daughter's behalf in a Pennsylvania trial court against the driver. The parties settled the claim. While the action was pending, the employer notified the employee that it would seek reimbursement for the amounts it had paid for the medical expenses. The employee replied that he would not reimburse the plan asserting that Pennsylvania's Motor Vehicle Financial Responsibility Law precluded subrogation by the employer. A federal district court ruled that the employer could not subrogate. The U.S. Court of Appeals, Third Circuit, affirmed. The employer then appealed to the U.S. Supreme Court. ERISA's preemption clause broadly established an area of exclusive federal concern: any state law that relates to a covered benefit plan. Since the Pennsylvania statute related to a covered employee benefit plan, the statute was preempted by ERISA. The Court vacated the decision of the appellate court and remanded the case. *FMC Corp. v. Holiday*, 111 S.Ct. 403, 112 L.Ed.2d 356 (1990).

The U.S. Court of Appeals, Ninth Circuit, has held that the above U.S. Supreme Court decisions addressing ERISA preemption required that a lower federal court's damage award against an insurer be reversed. The case arose when a California couple's son was born two months prematurely while they were on vacation in

Holland. The couple was insured by the husband's employer under a group medical insurance policy. The insurer refused to forward any medical expenses to the couple while they were in Holland and later delayed payment of the son's other medical expenses. Claiming bad faith, the couple sued the insurer and a U.S. district court awarded them $252,234 in compensatory damages and $500,000 in punitive damages due to the insurer's inexplicable delays and its failure to investigate their claims. The court of appeals observed that the Supreme Court's decision in *Pilot Life Ins. Co. v. Dedeaux*, and *Metropolitan Life Ins. Co. v. Taylor*, made clear that where an insurance lawsuit relates to an employee benefit plan, the lawsuit is preempted by the federal Employee Retirement Income Security Act. Similarly, lawsuits alleging improper claims processing which are based upon state common law (rather than state statutory law) are also preempted by ERISA. Because in the present case the claims against the insurer arose under an employer's group medical insurance policy, the couple's state common law "bad faith" claims were preempted. The appeals court therefore reversed the damage awards levied against the insurer. *Kanne v. Connecticut General Life Ins. Co.*, 819 F.2d 204 (9th Cir.1987).

A woman who suffered from advanced breast cancer was insured under an employee benefits plan which was governed by the Employee Retirement Income Security Act of 1974 (ERISA). She applied to the insurer for coverage for a necessary chemotherapy-bone marrow transplant, but the insurer denied coverage, claiming that it had amended the benefits contract to exclude such treatment. Because the hospital would not treat the insured without a certification of payment, she obtained a temporary restraining order to receive the treatment. She then sought a preliminary injunction to prevent the insurer from refusing to pay for the treatment. The U.S. District Court for the District of Columbia looked at the amendment to determine whether it complied with the requirements of ERISA. It found that the insurer failed to give thirty days' notice of the amendment and that, as a result, the amendment was not effective. Further, the content of the notice was unsatisfactory because it did not clearly exclude the treatment at issue. Finally, since a balancing of harms showed that death could result to the insured if the injunction was not granted, and that only monetary damage would be suffered by the insurer, the court ruled in the insured's favor, granting her motion for a preliminary injunction. *Wilson v. Group Hospitalization and Medical Services, Inc.*, 791 F.Supp. 309 (D.D.C.1992).

A corporation purchased a group health insurance plan from an insurer, which plan qualified as an ERISA plan under the Employee Retirement Income Security Act. The corporation failed to remit the premium that was due in November 1987. Subsequently, the insurer informed the corporation that it was cancelling the health insurance plan. The corporation failed to inform its employees that their health coverage had been canceled. The employees were not notified of the loss of insurance until March 1988. Meanwhile, certain employees incurred medical expenses which would have been covered under the plan. They brought suit against the insurer in an Alabama trial court, but the action was removed to a federal district court. The court granted summary judgment to the beneficiaries, and the insurer appealed to the U.S. Court of Appeals, Eleventh Circuit. On appeal, the court noted that even though the primary responsibility for notifying the beneficiaries of coverage suspension and cancellation belonged to the corporation, the insurer might also be liable if it had knowledge that the corporation had breached its duty. Further, if the insurer misrepresented to the employees that they were still covered after the corporation had stopped making premium payments, it would be liable. Since questions of fact existed, summary judgment was improper. The court reversed and remanded the case for a determination as to whether the insurer knew of the corporation's breach of its fiduciary duty under ERISA. *Willett v. Blue Cross and Blue Shield of Alabama*, 953 F.2d 1335 (11th Cir.1992).

An employer purchased a group health insurance plan which qualified under the Employee Retirement Income Security Act of 1974 (ERISA). The employer, however, failed to pay the first premium due in November 1988. Subsequently, the employer went out of business and asked the insurer to cancel the health insurance policy. The employer, however, failed to inform its employees that their health coverage had been canceled. Meanwhile, an employee's wife became pregnant, and she claimed that in December 1988, one of the insurer's employees advised her that she was covered for her childbirth expenses. After the birth, the insurer partially paid for the childbirth expenses and refused to pay any more because the policy was canceled as of November 1, 1988. When the couple contacted the employer to find out why the policy had been canceled the employer professed ignorance despite the fact that he had signed a letter requesting cancellation of the coverage. The employee's wife filed a suit against the insurer in federal district court which entered judgment in her favor. The insurer appealed to the U.S. Court of Appeals, Fourth Circuit.

On appeal, the wife contended that the insurer's representations that she was covered prevented it from terminating coverage under equitable estoppel principles. The wife did concede that ERISA preempted her state common law cause of action for equitable estoppel. However, she argued that estoppel principles may be imported into ERISA in the name of federal common law. The court, however, disagreed and stated that equitable estoppel could not be permitted to vary the written terms of this insurance plan. More importantly, the court believed that the use of estoppel principles to modify the insurance plan would conflict with ERISA's emphatic preference for written agreements. The court held that due to a written provision contained in the policy, the policy was void for nonpayment of premiums. Accordingly, the court reversed the district court's decision and held in favor of the insurer. *Coleman v. Nationwide Life Ins. Co.*, 969 F.2d 54 (4th Cir.1992).

A Virginia foundry company offered its employees a retirement plan providing normal benefits at age 65. In addition, early retirement benefits were payable at age 55 but reduced for each year by which retirement preceded age 65, and unreduced early retirement benefits were available to those who had at least 30 years of service and were at least age 62. After the foundry was sold, the benefit plan was terminated. Five employees who participated in the plan received the normal retirement benefit which they would have received had they retired at age 65. They sued the company in a Virginia trial court, claiming they should have received unreduced early retirement payments, a sum greater than that which they did receive. The employees argued that the failure to pay the unreduced early retirement benefits violated § 4044(a) of the Employee Retirement Income Security Act (ERISA), the federal act governing employee retirement benefits. The company removed the case to a federal district court, which granted summary judgment for it. The employees appealed to the U.S. Court of Appeals, Fourth Circuit, which reversed the summary judgment, holding that before residual funds from the plan could revert to the employer, it would have to pay early retirement benefits to plan participants even if those benefits were not accrued at the time of plan termination. The U.S. Supreme Court granted certiorari.

Before the Supreme Court, the company contended that unreduced early retirement benefits are not "accrued benefits" under ERISA and the employees were therefore not entitled to additional benefits. The residual funds should revert back to the company, it argued. The Court reversed the Court of Appeals' decision and held that § 4044(a) does not create benefit entitlements but simply provides for the orderly distribution of plan assets required by ERISA's provisions. The Court concluded that neither ERISA's language nor its legislative history indicated a Congressional intent to confer a right to benefits that are not provided for within the employer's benefit plan. ERISA is not a source of new entitlements but rather is a distribution mechanism for plan assets created by a benefit plan. Although the Supreme Court reversed in regard to the employees' § 4044(a) argument, it also remanded the case to determine whether the employees could receive damages on two alternate theories. *Mead Corp. v. Tilley*, 490 U.S. 714, 109 S.Ct. 2156, 104 L.Ed.2d 796 (1989).

A tire company provided employee benefit plans which were governed by ERISA. When the company sold its plastics division its employees in the division were rehired by the new company. The company denied the employees' requests for severance benefits and for information about their benefits. The employees sued the company in a federal district court, alleging, among other things, that § 1024 of ERISA had been violated when the company refused disclosure. The district court granted summary judgment for the company, concluding that the employees were not plan "participants" within the section's meaning. On appeal to the U.S. Court of Appeals, Third Circuit, the court reversed, holding that the right to disclosure extends to people who are entitled to plan benefits and to those who claim to be, but are not so entitled. The U.S. Supreme Court granted certiorari.

The Supreme Court rejected the Court of Appeals' interpretation of "participant," stating that its definition strayed from the statutory definition language in § 1002 of ERISA. It held that "participant" should mean either employees in, or reasonably expected to be in, currently covered employment, or former employees who have a reasonable expectation of returning to covered employment or who have a colorable claim to vested benefits. In order to establish a colorable claim, an employee must show that he or she will prevail in a suit for benefits or that he or she will fulfill eligibility requirements in the future. The Court concluded that companies will likely disclose information if there is any doubt the employee is a "participant." The Supreme Court then remanded the case to determine whether the employees were "participants" within the new definition. *Firestone Tire and Rubber Co. v. Bruch*, 489 U.S. 101, 109 S.Ct. 948, 103 L.Ed.2d 80 (1989).

An Alabama newspaper provided its employees with medical insurance coverage. One of its editors had a son whose premature birth necessitated a series of surgical operations and physical therapy. While the son's second operation was imminent, the newspaper offered alternate coverage from two health maintenance organizations to its employees. At an informational meeting for one of the HMOs, the editor was told that his son's medical expenses would be completely covered. In reliance on this information, the editor dropped his old coverage, which had provided eighty percent coverage, and enrolled in the HMO plan. He then learned that the HMO would only cover his son's expenses for sixty days. He asked the HMO to provide at least the eighty percent coverage he had been receiving, but the HMO refused. Instead, it offered to extend the coverage for sixty more days. The editor sued the HMO for fraud in an Alabama trial court. The HMO moved for a directed verdict, claiming that the claim was preempted by the Employee Retirement and Income Security Act of 1974 (ERISA). The court refused the motion and the jury returned a verdict for the editor. The HMO appealed to the Supreme Court of Alabama. The supreme court noted that ERISA, the federal legislation which comprehensively regulates employee benefit plans, only preempts state laws which relate to employee benefit plans. The court stated that the fraud action was not a law "relating to" employee benefit plans. The editor had not claimed any improper processing of a claim, nor any benefits under the terms of the plan. Rather, he claimed he was fraudulently induced to drop his existing coverage. Therefore, the court upheld the trial court's decision. *HealthAmerica v. Menton*, 551 So.2d 235 (Ala.1989).

An insured applied for health insurance coverage through her employer's group health insurance plan, which covered chiropractic services. After obtaining coverage, the insured was diagnosed and treated by a chiropractic physician for "severe biochemical imbalance compounded with possible neurological damage." The doctor prescribed laboratory testing, massage therapy and vitamin supplements. The group carrier denied the insured's claims, and the insured sued it in a Florida state court alleging that the insurer had breached its insurance contract. The insurer removed the action to a federal district court, asserting that the case arose under the federal Employee Retirement Income Security Act of 1974 (ERISA). The court denied the insured's motion to remand the case to the state court and ruled that ERISA preempted the breach of contract claim. After a voluntary dismissal of the case, the insured later resubmitted claims for services by a chiropractic physician in Florida who treated her after she had been diagnosed and treated in Illinois. After the insurer learned that the insured had been diagnosed as having multiple sclerosis, it paid nearly all of the insured's previously submitted claims but denied payment for the vitamin supplements. The insured again filed a complaint in a Florida state court, and again the case was removed to federal district court. The district court granted the insurer's motion to dismiss the case and the insured appealed to the U.S. Court of Appeals, Eleventh Circuit.

The court of appeals stated that ERISA was a comprehensive statute which subjected employee benefit plans to federal regulation and preempted and superseded all state laws relating to employment benefit plans covered under ERISA. Noting that the U.S. Supreme Court has construed ERISA's preemption clause as expansive, the court affirmed the district court's order dismissing the case. ERISA preempted state statutes and common law causes of action such as bad faith, refusal to pay and breach of contract. *Swerhun v. Guardian Life Ins. Co. of America*, 979 F.2d 195 (11th Cir.1992).

A Virginia woman, through her employer, participated in its qualified self-funded employee benefit plan, which was administered by an insurer. The plan fell within the province of the Employee Retirement Income Security Act of 1974 (ERISA). It also provided that medical and disability benefits would not be payable to a person covered under the plan when an injury was caused by another person. However, the plan did allow for monies to be advanced so long as the covered person signed an agreement to repay any payments advanced. Subsequently, the woman was involved in a car accident which was not her fault. On her written request, the insurer advanced her almost $6,000 in medical expenses without first obtaining a signed repayment agreement. When the insured recovered damages from the party who hit her, she refused to reimburse the insurer and it brought an action under ERISA for recovery of the advanced monies in a federal district court. The court ruled for the insured, finding that the insurer's failure to obtain a signed repayment provision constituted noncompliance with the plan and barred its recovery of advanced expenses. The insurer appealed to the U.S. Court of Appeals, Fourth Circuit.

On appeal, the court first noted that it had jurisdiction because a federal question was involved even though there was no federal statutory provision which granted such jurisdiction. The court then determined that because the plan contractually provided for the repayment of advanced monies, and because the insured was aware of the plan's reimbursement provision, it was appropriate in the circumstances of this case to require the insured to reimburse the insurer. The court thus fashioned a federal, common law rule of unjust enrichment to prevent the insured from obtaining a double recovery, and reversed the district court's decision. *Provident Life and Accident Ins. Co. v. Waller*, 906 F.2d 985 (4th Cir.1990).

A Florida man and his wife received health and medical benefits under an insurance policy issued by the husband's employer's insurer. Thereafter, the wife gave birth to a healthy girl but began to develop ill feelings toward the baby and herself. She was subsequently readmitted and treated for postpartum depression. After the wife was released from the hospital, the couple was denied hospitalization benefits so they sued the insurer in a federal district court for additional compensation of over $33,000. They brought the action under the Employee Retirement Income Security Act of 1974 (ERISA). The district court held that the wife's medical bills fell within the mental illness provision of the policy rather than the sickness section, and thus were limited. The couple appealed to the U.S. Court of Appeals, Eleventh Circuit. On appeal, the couple asserted that the postpartum depression was caused by the pregnancy and that it was thus included in the sickness section of the policy. The court, however, stated that the couple had failed to demonstrate that the wife suffered an organic mental illness such as to constitute a sickness. The court also noted that the wife had not received treatment different than that rendered to other patients suffering from other forms of mental disorder. Finally, the court held that the couple had not been entitled to a jury trial because their claim under ERISA was equitable in nature. The court thus affirmed the district court's decision in favor of the insurer. *Blake v. Union Mutual Stock Life Ins. Co. of America*, 906 F.2d 1525 (11th Cir.1990).

An insurer issued a group insurance policy to an employer as part of an employee benefit plan. The plan qualified as an ERISA plan under the Employee Retirement Income Security Act of 1974. Subsequently, an employee of the insured was injured in an automobile accident and was unable to return to work. He filed a claim for long-term disability benefits with the insurer, which was promptly approved. The benefits were scheduled to last only 24 months unless, after that period, the employee was "unable to engage in any and every gainful occupation for which he was reasonably [qualified]." At the end of two years, the insurer notified the employee that he would not be eligible for continuing benefits. Yet it continued to make payments to him while he challenged its decision. A federal district court denied him continuing benefits, and he appealed to the U.S. Court of Appeals, Eighth Circuit. On appeal, the court noted that the administrative record was full of medical reports and assessments which indicated that the employee was able to work. Further, the insurer had given the employee multiple opportunities to submit evidence of his inability to return to work, and the employee had failed to do so. Finally, the employee had turned down an opportunity to work in an electronics repair business, confirming that he was suited for a number of jobs. Because the insurer had given adequate notice of the claim denial, and because the employee had been given a "full and fair review" under ERISA, the district court's denial of benefits was affirmed. *Davidson v. Prudential Ins. Co. of America*, 953 F.2d 1093 (8th Cir.1992).

B. Other Federal Cases

An Alabama insurance agent solicited Roosevelt City, Alabama, for health and life insurance for its employees. The agent prepared applications for the city and its employees for group health and life policies. The initial premium payments were taken by the agent and submitted to the insurers with the applications. An arrangement was made for the health insurer to send its premium billings to the agent at his office. The premium payments were then to be effected through payroll deductions and the city clerk would issue a check to the agent. The agent did not remit the premium payments but instead misappropriated most of the funds. However, the insurer did not send notices of lapsed coverage to the employees. Instead, these notices were sent to the agent. One of the employees was hospitalized and upon her discharge was required to make payment on her bill because the hospital could not confirm her health coverage. Her physician, when he was not paid, placed her account with a collection agency. The agency obtained a judgment against the woman and her credit was adversely affected. The city workers then filed this suit naming the insurer and the agent, asking for damages for fraud. The case was submitted to the jury and the jury returned a verdict against the insurer and the agent for over $1,000,000 which included a large sum for punitive damages. The Alabama Supreme Court affirmed this decision and the insurer appealed to the U.S. Supreme Court.

The issue, on appeal, was the constitutionality of certain punitive damage awards. The insurer contended that the award violated due process as the product of unbridled jury discretion. The court noted that the punitive damage award did not violate due process. First, the trial court's instructions placed reasonable constraints on the exercise of the jury's discretion by expressly describing the purposes of punitive damages to be retribution and deterrence, by requiring the jury to consider the character and degree of the particular wrong, and by explaining that the imposition of punitive damages was not compulsory. Second, the trial court conducted a postverdict hearing which set forth standards to ensure the meaningful and adequate review of the punitive damages award. Third, the petitioner received the benefit of the appropriate review by the state supreme court which approved the verdict and brought in all relevant factors for ensuring that the punitive damages were reasonable. The Alabama Supreme Court's decision upholding the punitive damage award was affirmed. *Pacific Mut. Life Ins. Co. v. Haslip*, 111 S.Ct. 1032, 113 L.Ed.2d 1 (1991).

A tort judgment of $1.15 million was returned against an insured Michigan business. $950,000 was to be covered by its insurer. The insurer, however, was declared insolvent. The insurer was a member of the Michigan Property and Casualty

Guaranty Association (association), which was a group of insurers created to produce a common fund that would be used to pay covered claims of an insolvent member. The insured filed a claim for the $950,000 but the association rejected the claim because the insured's net worth exceeded the statutory limit. The insured then brought this suit in a federal trial court challenging the constitutionality of the net worth statutory limit. The trial court held for the insured and the association appealed to the U.S. Court of Appeals, Sixth Circuit. The court noted that the level of scrutiny required to overturn a legislative enactment for irrationally discriminating between groups under the Equal Protection Clause is a rational basis review. Under the rational basis test a statutory discrimination will not be set aside if any set of facts reasonably may be conceived to justify it. Therefore, the court had to decide whether the Michigan legislature's determination that net worth was an appropriate means of predicting the ability of a company to absorb unexpected loss was so irrational that no set of facts reasonably could be conceived to justify it. The court noted that testimony suggested that net worth was an unreliable and imperfect measure of ability to absorb loss. However, the test for constitutional purposes is not whether the legislative scheme is imperfect, but whether or not it is wholly irrational. While the association did not by any means prove that net worth was the best mechanism for determining ability to absorb loss, it did provide sufficient evidence to suggest that factual circumstances were conceivable which could justify the legislature's use of net worth. The district court erred in determining that the Michigan law was not rationally related to a legitimate state purpose under current constitutional standards. Therefore, the appellate court reversed the decision of the trial court. *Borman's v. Michigan Property & Casualty Guaranty Ass'n*, 925 F.2d 160 (6th Cir.1991).

A reinsurance company entered into four indemnity reinsurance contracts with a life insurance company. The reinsurer agreed to indemnify the life insurer for any claims it paid out, in return for a certain percentage of the insurer's premiums. The reinsurer also agreed to pay the insurer ceding commissions — an upfront fee. The reinsurer then deducted the full amount of the ceding commission from its income tax return. The Commissioner of Internal Revenue did not allow the deduction, concluding that the ceding commission had to be capitalized and amortized over the life of the insurance agreement. The reinsurer then appealed to the Tax Court, which reversed and allowed the deduction. The U.S. Court of Appeals, Fifth Circuit, reversed the Tax Court's decision, holding that ceding commissions represent payments to acquire an asset with an income producing life that lasts substantially longer than one year. The U.S. Supreme Court granted certiorari.

Before the Supreme Court, the reinsurer argued that since the Internal Revenue Code did not specifically address the issue, an analogy should be made to agent commissions paid by a life insurance company, which are fully deductible. The Court, however, rejected this analysis, concluding that an agent's commission is an administrative expense for services rendered, whereas a ceding commission is given for the company's assets, rather than for services. It held that ceding commissions paid under an indemnity reinsurance agreement must be amortized over the anticipated life of the agreement. Ceding commissions in indemnity reinsurance are similar to those in assumption reinsurance, which currently must be capitalized and amortized. The Supreme Court reinstated the Commissioner's decision disallowing the reinsurer's full deduction. *Colonial Amer. Life Ins. Co. v. Comm'r of Internal Revenue*, 109 S.Ct. 2408 (1989).

A three-year-old Pennsylvania child suffered severe head injuries in a traffic accident. As a result, she required special education services for which her parents sued their insurer. After making initial payments for educational services, the insurer refused to provide further benefits. The parents then sued their insurer in a federal district court. The insurer then filed a third-party complaint against the student's school district under the Education for All Handicapped Children Act (EHA). The insurer alleged that the school district was primarily responsible for providing special education services. The district court ruled that the EHA did not provide general jurisdiction for special education issues in federal courts. Only students seeking special education services could invoke the EHA. Federal regulations under the statute stated that insurers were not relieved from paying for services to handicapped students. Accordingly, the insurer had no standing to bring an EHA lawsuit against the school district. There was no connection between the insurance company's obligation to satisfy its claim and an appropriate education for the student. The court dismissed the insurer's third-party complaint. *Gehman v. Prudential Property and Cas. Ins. Co.*, 702 F.Supp. 1192 (E.D.Pa.1989).

II. STATE LAW REQUIREMENTS

This section deals with cases involving state regulatory agencies and particular statutes. For specific requirements of state law, please refer to the specific subject area of insurance in this volume.

A. State Regulatory Authority

A Minnesota man was seriously injured in an accident involving a tire rim manufactured by a tire company. In the lawsuit that followed, the man was awarded compensatory damages of $3 million dollars and punitive damages which were reduced by the Minnesota Supreme Court to $4 million dollars. After the case became final, the tire company requested that its insurers reimburse it for the punitive damage awards. The insurers filed a declaratory judgment action in a Minnesota state court. The tire company removed the action to a federal district court seeking resolution of the punitive damages issue. The federal district court granted summary judgment to the insurer and the insured appealed to the U.S. Court of Appeals, Eighth Circuit.

On appeal, the tire company raised two issues. The tire company felt the trial court erred in ruling that punitive damages were not insurable under Minnesota law and also erred in applying Minnesota's standard of law instead of Georgia law to the question concerning insurability of punitive damages. The appellate court found that Minnesota does not normally allow coverage as a rule for punitive damages because it is against Minnesota public policy. The court then moved on to the conflict between Minnesota and Georgia law. In making its decision the court looked to the choice of law standard approved by the Minnesota Supreme Court. One of the things the court considered was the advancement of the forum state's governmental interest. The Minnesota general rule against insurability of punitive damages is related to its interest in preventing injury to its citizens by allowing punitive damages as punishment to wrongdoers. The state's interest in protecting its citizens and punishing wrongdoers could be furthered only if the responsible parties felt the effects of the punitive damage awards. Therefore, the Eighth Circuit Court of Appeals affirmed the decision of the trial court in applying Minnesota's standard of law in this case. *U.S. Fire Ins. Co. v. Goodyear Tire & Rubber Co.*, 920 F.2d 487 (8th Cir.1990).

An employee was injured in an accident while in the course of employment and driving her personally owned vehicle. The accident was caused by another driver, and the employee collected benefits from that driver's insurer. She then exhausted the limit of underinsured coverage from her personal policy. Her employer carried a general liability policy, which contained an endorsement providing an employee with excess liability coverage for nonowned vehicles driven by employees, but it did not purport to include underinsured coverage. The employee argued that the purchasing of such insurance required, under Arizona law, an accompanying offer of underinsured coverage. An Arizona trial court agreed, and held that an absence of such an offer leads to an imputation of coverage. The decision was reversed on appeal, and the case reached the Supreme Court of Arizona.

The first issue was whether the policy was in fact an excess policy. There was no evidence that the insurer had calculated a premium on the basis that coverage would apply only after primary coverage limits were exhausted. Also important was that, had the employee been uninsured, the coverage would have become primary. The policy was ruled not to be solely an excess policy. The issue then became whether the requirements of the Arizona Uninsured Motorist Act applied even though the insurance was provided as part of a general liability policy. The act expressly applied to any automobile liability policy, and required a written offer of underinsured coverage. The insurer argued that "any automobile liability policy" meant only policies which an automobile owner was required to purchase under the mandatory insurance law. The court rejected this argument on several grounds, and noted that the mandatory insurance statutes and the Uninsured Motorist Act were completely separate. Even their scopes were different; mandatory insurance protects the public, and underinsured coverage protects the purchaser of insurance against the public. The requirement of an offer of underinsured protection was ruled applicable to the policy at issue, and the absence of the offer resulted in an imputation of coverage for the employee. The court limited its holding by hinting at a possible exception for true excess policies. The trial court's judgment was affirmed. *St. Paul Fire & Marine Ins. Co. v. Gilmore*, 812 P.2d 977 (Ariz.1991).

An Iowa woman was injured in a motorcycle accident and her injuries exceeded $75,000. At the time of the accident, she had uninsured and underinsured motorist coverages of $25,000 each. The owner of the motorcycle was insured for $50,000 personal injury liability under his policy. However, his insurer became insolvent and was placed in liquidation after the accident. As a result of its insolvency, the insurer for the woman paid her $25,000 and considered this the full limits of its liability. She then filed a claim with the Iowa Insurance Guarantee Association (IGA) asserting that she had a right to recover from IGA the $50,000 liability limits she would have received under the motorcycle owner's policy. IGA responded that under the nonduplication of recovery provisions of the Iowa law it was entitled to an offset of $25,000 for the uninsured motorist benefits previously paid by her insurer. The woman resisted the offset on the ground that no duplication of recovery existed. She claimed that the offset amounted to a windfall for IGA which deprived her of the benefit of premiums paid for uninsured and underinsured coverage. IGA brought this petition for a declaratory judgment action. The court ruled that although IGA stands in the shoes of the insolvent insurer, it is entitled to credit for payments made by the injured party's own insurer. The woman then appealed to the Supreme Court of Iowa. The court noted that accident victims must exhaust their uninsured/underinsured motorist coverages before filing a claim with the state's insurance guarantee association. Upon payment of the claim, IGA is entitled to a credit for the uninsured/ underinsured motorist coverage already collected by the victim. The court recognized that such an interpretation may result in unfairness but upheld the decision of the trial court. *Stecher v. Iowa Ins. Guarantee Ass'n*, 465 N.W.2d 887 (Iowa 1991).

The Massachusetts Commissioner of Insurance issued regulations restricting certain insurance underwriting practices with respect to testing prospective insureds for life, accident or health insurance for exposure to AIDS. Shortly thereafter, a number of insurers and insurance trade associations sued the commissioner challenging the regulations and the commissioner's authority to promulgate such regulations. The purpose of the regulations was to eliminate unfair discrimination in underwriting decisions and to protect the privacy rights of insurance applicants. The commissioner moved for summary judgment which was granted by the court. The insurers appealed to the Supreme Judicial Court of Massachusetts. On appeal, the commissioner argued that Massachusetts law implicitly authorized him to promulgate any regulation that was reasonably necessary to enable him to carry out his duties. The court disagreed and held that the commissioner did not have implied authority to promulgate regulations prohibiting or restricting insurance underwriting practices. The court noted that the commissioner was seeking in good faith to deal with one aspect of an important public health problem and it said it was up to the legislature to decide what, if any, authority it would give to the commissioner to regulate the underwriting practices of insurers. *Life Ins. Ass'n of Mass. v. Com'r of Ins.*, 530 N.E.2d 168 (Mass.1988).

Partners in a Louisiana limited partnership sued a bank and its officers' and directors' insurer in a Louisiana district court. The insurer argued that the investors had no right of action against it under the Louisiana Direct Action Statute. The trial court dismissed the investors' direct action against the insurer. The investors appealed to the Court of Appeal of Louisiana, Fourth Circuit, which held that the policy covering the officers and directors was an indemnity policy, and thus the investors had no direct right of action against the insurer. The court noted that the policy required a discharge of liability as a condition precedent to recovery under the policy. This clearly indicated that the policy was an indemnity policy and not a general liability policy. Thus the policy was not within the scope of the Louisiana Direct Action Statute and the investors were precluded from a direct right of action against the insurer. The court of appeal affirmed the district court's decision. *Quinlan v. Liberty Bank & Trust Co.*, 545 So.2d 1140 (La.App.4th Cir.1989).

A federal district court in Minnesota certified questions of law to the Minnesota Supreme Court in three cases involving hazardous chemical waste cleanup lawsuits filed against Minnesota corporations by environmental agencies. In each case, the insurers denied coverage to their insureds under comprehensive general liability policies; and the insureds complied with state directives to clean up soil and groundwater contamination, and to reimburse state agencies for cleanup costs. The insurers argued that the policies indemnified their insureds only when they were legally obligated to pay damages to third parties. The insurers claimed that "damages" only meant legal damages and not restitution paid in compliance with injunctive orders, which they claimed was equitable relief. The insureds argued that under Minnesota law, there was no longer a distinction between legal damages and equitable relief. The Minnesota Supreme Court ruled that the amounts the insurers had paid out were "damages" within the meaning of the policies. Although some federal courts applying state law in districts such as South Carolina, Illinois and Florida had held that damages did not cover cleanup costs, Minnesota used the rule applied in most states, including New York, California, Michigan and Pennsylvania, which interpreted "damages" to include sums paid for claims brought under environmental statutes. *Minnesota Mining and Mfg. v. Travelers Indem. Co.*, 457 N.W.2d 175 (Minn.1990).

A California woman worked as a waitress for approximately two years. During that time, she was diagnosed with breast cancer, underwent a mastectomy and had reconstructive surgery performed. On the date she was scheduled to return to work she was terminated. She sued her employer for, among other claims, wrongful discharge and unlawful discrimination. The employer tendered the defense of this action to its general liability insurer which undertook the defense under a reservation of rights. However, it was then declared insolvent and the California Insurance Guarantee Association (CIGA) became responsible for all "covered claims" against the insurer. CIGA brought a declaratory relief action, seeking a determination that the underlying claim was outside the scope of coverage of the liability policy and that it need not provide a defense. The trial court granted a stay of further proceedings in the declaratory relief action pending the trial in the underlying action. CIGA petitioned for a writ of mandate from the California Court of Appeal, Second District.

The court of appeal noted that CIGA's first duty was to determine if the claims against it (through the insolvent insurer) were covered. The court then stated, however, that in spite of its statutory limitations, CIGA still had substantial obligations to the insolvent insurer's insureds. The court of appeal pointed out the approaching trial date in the underlying action and stated that CIGA did not have the right to seek a delay of that trial to get a resolution of the declaratory relief action. It ordered CIGA to defend the underlying action and denied the petition for the writ. *California Insurance Guarantee Ass'n v. Superior Court*, 283 Cal.Rptr. 104 (Cal.App.2d Dist.1991).

In a case involving the mailing of nonrenewal notices, two insurers mailed notices to all their holders of private passenger automobile insurance policies in September and October of 1988. Both insurers had ceased marketing all property and casualty personal lines policies at the time the notices were mailed. However, neither insurer had submitted a formal application to the Commissioner of Insurance to withdraw from the California insurance market. After the commissioner determined that the insurers had violated the nonrenewal provisions of Proposition 103, the insurers brought suit in a trial court, seeking to set aside her decision. When the court ruled against them, they appealed to the Court of Appeal, Second District.

The court of appeal first noted that its decision in *AIU Ins. Co. v. Gillespie* applied to nonrenewal notices mailed prior to November 8, so long as the policies were still in effect at that time. The court then looked to the insurers' supplementary argument that they were exempt from the mandatory renewal provisions because they had mailed their notices in anticipation of withdrawal from the California automobile insurance market. The court determined, however, that until an insurer surrenders its certificate of authority, it is required to follow the mandate of

Proposition 103's requirements. Only when an insurer surrenders its certificate is it precluded from writing new business. Thus, because the insurers had not formally applied to withdraw, their nonrenewal notices were not valid. The appellate court affirmed the trial court's decision. *Gillespie v. Dairyland Ins. Co.*, 273 Cal.Rptr. 80 (Cal. App.2d Dist.1990).

The California Automobile Assigned Risk Plan (CAARP) was created to provide insurance to high risk drivers who would otherwise not be able to afford insurance. The Insurance Commissioner, by virtue of Insurance Code § 11620, had the authority to design and implement a "reasonable plan for the equitable apportionment" of assigned risks among the state's insurers. Due to the continuing increase of assigned risks in southern California, the commissioner instituted a new method of statewide, random risk assignment. One particular insurer had routinely declined to accept assigned risks from southern California, since it did most of its business in northern and central California. After the change, the insurer was forced to accept a larger share of assigned risk business.

In addition, the commissioner began the Urban Credit Program, which gave insurers credit for policies written in certain high risk areas in southern California against the total number of assigned risks they would have to accept. Because of the way the program was structured, however, insurers already doing business in those areas had their assigned risk quotas reduced to nothing, without assuming any new risks. This meant a heavier burden for other insurers, including the northern insurer at issue. The insurance commissioner eventually suspended the program, but granted only prospective relief to the insurer, refusing to adjust for risks assigned during the term of the program's operation. The insurer sought a writ of mandamus to stop the statewide risk assignment plan and compel retroactive relief from the Urban Credit Program.

The Court of Appeal, First District, refused to issue the writ. The court stated that the statewide, random assignment of automobile insurance risks was consistent with the commissioner's statutory mandate. The statute only required the assignment to be consistent with the scope of an insurer's territorial operations insofar as was possible. Since a territorial policy of assignments had proven to be unfeasible, the commissioner had met her obligations. In addition, while the Urban Credit Program may have been a bad idea, it was not outside the commissioner's authority and a retroactive order of relief would be inappropriate. *California State Auto. Assoc. Inter-Ins. Bur. v. Garamendi*, 8 Cal.Rptr.2d 366 (Cal.App.1st Dist.1992).

Pennsylvania amended its Motor Vehicle Financial Responsibility Law in February 1990 to roll back rates on private passenger automobile insurance. The rollback was anywhere from 10 to 22%. Any insurer aggrieved by the rollbacks could seek relief from the Insurance Commissioner. The commissioner could grant relief when she deemed it necessary in extraordinary circumstances. Various insurers then sought such relief and further sought rate increases for several programs. The insurance department denied the request for relief, and after a hearing the insurance commissioner upheld the denial of relief. The insurers appealed to the Commonwealth Court of Pennsylvania. They argued on appeal that the rollback rates were confiscatory in violation of the U.S. Constitution. The court disagreed. It found the department's methodology for establishing a target rate of return to be reasonable. The court then noted that there was substantial evidence to support the commissioner's decision. The court affirmed the order and adjudication of the insurance commissioner, and held that the insurers were not entitled to extraordinary circumstances relief. *Boston Old Colony Ins. Co. v. Insurance Dep't.*, 604 A.2d 1191 (Pa.Cmwlth.1992).

The Pennsylvania Motor Vehicle Financial Responsibility Law (PMVFRL) requires an insurer to provide uninsured motorist coverage equal to the policy's bodily injury liability coverage unless the insured waives the requirement. The law provides that a named insured may request in writing coverage in amounts less than the limits of liability for bodily injury but not less than the amount required by statute. The law also requires that insurers provide notice to insureds concerning the availability of coverages and the insureds' right to select coverage amounts. It also creates a presumption that an insured's signature on a certain portion of the form evidences "actual knowledge and understanding of the availability of these benefits and limits as well as the benefits and limits ... [the insured has] selected."

An insured was riding as a passenger in a car driven by his fiancee. An accident occurred where the fiancee was killed and the insured was injured. Both the insured and the deceased fiancee's estate sought coverage under a policy issued by an insurer. When the policy was purchased the insured checked a box indicating he wished to have minimal uninsured motorist coverage. However, because of some misaligned carbon copies there was a dispute about which box was actually checked. The insured asked a federal district court to settle the dispute. The court reformed the policy to increase the insured's uninsured motorist coverage. It determined that the presumed waiver under the PMVFRL was rebuttable and not conclusive. The PMVFRL placed the burden of proof on the insurer to establish that the insured knowingly and intelligently waived the statutory requirement that uninsured motorist coverage equal bodily injury coverage. The insurer appealed to the U.S. Court of Appeals, Third Circuit. That court reversed the district court's decision stating that the enactment of the PMVFRL and its elaborate waiver provision was an attempt by the Pennsylvania General Assembly to eliminate confusion about the waiver sufficiency. Once it was proven that an insured voluntarily signed the waiver, he could not rebut it. As long as the policy limitations are clearly worded and conspicuously displayed, then absent proof of fraud, the insured may not assert that he failed to read the limitation or that he did not understand it. The appellate court reversed the district court's decision and remanded the case for further action. *Prudential Property & Cas. Ins. v. Pendleton*, 858 F.2d 930 (3d Cir.1988).

A Michigan insured was severely injured in an automobile accident while operating a federal government motor vehicle. The insured was an active member of the armed forces who was qualified for federal military medical benefits. He was also the owner of an automobile which was insured by a no-fault policy. The military paid for the insured's hospital expenses. The insured then sued his insurer in a Michigan trial court seeking additional benefits. The trial court ruled that the medical benefits provided by the military were required to be set off under the no-fault act. However, because the insured was not offered the option of coordination of benefits, the insurer had forfeited the right to a setoff. The insurer appealed to the Michigan Court of Appeals, which reversed the trial court's order. The insured appealed to the Supreme Court of Michigan. The supreme court held that Michigan law required that the medical benefits be set off from no-fault insurance benefits. However, since the insurer failed to offer the insured a coordinated no-fault automobile policy as required under the no-fault act, the insurer was precluded from setting off the military medical benefits received by the insured from the no-fault insurance benefits. The court held in favor of the insured. The supreme court reversed the appeals court decision and reinstated the trial court order. *Tatum v. Government Employees Ins. Co.*, 431 N.W.2d 391 (Mich.1988).

A Colorado woman was injured in an automobile mishap with another driver whose insurer later became insolvent. Colorado law has provided for an insurance guarantee association in order to protect the claimants of insolvent insurers. A claimant, however, must first "exhaust" any coverage that it may have against its own insurer. The woman brought a $25,000 lawsuit against her insurer for uninsured motorist benefits, and settled the claim for $22,500. She then sought the remainder of her damages from the association. A state court ruled that the association must assume its role of insurer, and thus defend the tortfeasor and assume liability up to the statutory limit. Specifically, the association was ruled liable for $100,000, to be reduced by the woman's policy limit of $25,000. The association appealed to the Colorado Court of Appeals. The initial issue questioned whether a settlement for less than the policy limit constituted "exhaustion" as required by the statute. The question was one of first impression. Colorado public policy favors settlement of lawsuits, and the court accordingly agreed with the trial court that settlement should constitute exhaustion. It also agreed that the liability should be the difference between the available policy limit and the statutory limit, as this would encourage good faith negotiations. The final issue questioned the applicability of the remainder of the insolvent insurer's duties to the association. The court ruled that the association "stepped into the shoes" of the insurer, and assumed all duties and obligations. The decision of the trial court was affirmed. *Colorado Ins. Guarantee Ass'n v. Harris*, 815 P.2d 983 (Colo.App.1991).

A New Jersey stock insurance company which issued various types of insurance policies and surety bonds was declared insolvent by an order of liquidation. A question then arose as to whether the surety bond claimants were entitled to fourth or fifth priority with respect to the estate's assets. New Jersey law puts "claims by policyholders, beneficiaries and insurers" under the fourth priority, and all other claims under the fifth priority. The question of whether surety was insurance thus came before the New Jersey Superior Court, Chancery Division. The estate's liquidator noted that Pennsylvania had determined that surety bond holders were not holders of claims against insurance policies. However, the court found that New Jersey's law used different language to govern liquidation priorities. It also stated that there was no reported case in New Jersey which held that surety was not insurance. Accordingly, the court determined that the law clearly made surety the same as insurance. The surety bond holders were therefore entitled to fourth priority status the same as other insurance policy claimants. *In Re Integrity Ins. Co.*, 598 A.2d 940 (N.J.Super.Ch.1991).

A woman had her home damaged by fire. Her homeowner's insurer denied benefits because it alleged that the fire had been intentionally set. The insured contended that the insurer acted in bad faith when it refused to pay, and brought suit against it for punitive damages in a federal district court. The insurer countered by arguing that New Jersey law does not recognize such an action, and accordingly moved for a dismissal. The New Jersey Supreme Court had not addressed the issue involved in this case, and a federal court had to decide whether to create a new state-law cause of action. The court stated that it generally would not create new state law, and was even more reluctant to do so in this case because the New Jersey legislature had recently addressed the issue. The court ruled that no such cause of action exists in New Jersey. *Carfagno v. Aetna Casualty and Surety Co.*, 770 F.Supp. 245 (D.N.J.1991).

A man obtained a judgment against an insured tortfeasor, which was later appealed by the insured's automobile insurer. During the appeal's pendency, the insurer made several attempts at a settlement for less than the judgment amount. The offers were refused, the judgment was affirmed, and a claim for bad faith refusal to pay was eventually brought against the insurer based on delayed payment. A state court granted summary judgment dismissing the suit because the man had alleged only a single occurrence of unfair practices — not a general business practice. An allegation of a single occurrence was held to be insufficient to state a claim, regardless of the claim's merits. The Court of Appeals of Kentucky reversed the dismissal. It noted that the bad faith statute had been amended to allow an action based on a single occurrence. The case was remanded to determine whether the insurer had a reasonable basis to delay payment. *Simpson v. Travelers Ins. Co.*, 812 S.W.2d 510 (Ky.App.1991).

B. Arbitration

An Ohio couple purchased an insurance policy which provided for arbitration with respect to the determination of liability or damages in any uninsured motorists claim. The policy further stated that any judgment obtained against an uninsured would be binding on the insurer only if the judgment was obtained with the insurer's written consent. The insureds were then injured when an uninsured motorist drove through a stop sign. Their insurer's attorney sent them a letter authorizing them to take a default judgment against the uninsured. They did so. The attorney then accompanied them to the damages hearing. When the insureds finally sought payment from their insurer, it requested arbitration. The insureds sued. After losing at the trial and appellate levels, the insurer appealed to the Supreme Court of Ohio. The question before the court was whether the letter sent by the insurer amounted to consent so as to preclude arbitration. The court found that it was a consent. By consenting to the default judgment and not requesting arbitration until after the judgment had been entered, the insurer had waived its right to submit either liability or damages to arbitration. The court affirmed the lower courts' decisions. *Bryant v. Clark*, 584 N.E.2d 687 (Ohio 1992).

Three Minnesota women driving in a car did not see a stop sign and their failure to stop caused a collision between their car and a school bus. The driver of the car and the bus driver sustained injuries. When their respective insurers were unable to agree on apportionment of fault, they submitted to arbitration. The driver of the auto was declared one hundred percent at fault. The auto driver then brought suit for personal injuries against her two passengers in a Minnesota court. The passengers' insurers moved for, and were granted, summary judgment due to the arbitration ruling. The driver then appealed to the Court of Appeals of Minnesota. The appeals court noted that an arbitration hearing can bar a party from later litigation, but not in all cases. In examining this case, the court questioned if the driver was actually a party in the arbitration hearing. If so, was she given a fair and full opportunity to be heard? The driver was a named party in the hearing. However, she had not been required to attend. Though the driver retained separate counsel, her attorney was not invited to the hearing. The driver did not ask for or acquiesce to an arbitration hearing. It was also clear that the driver did not understand that the hearing could be a final judgment. Without input from the separate counsel, the court found the driver to be a party in name only. To be barred from further litigation requires a party to be "more than merely a name on the documents." The appeals court reversed the summary judgment and remanded the case for trial. *Houlihan v. Fimon*, 454 N.W.2d 633 (Minn.App.1990).

A Massachusetts woman was injured in an automobile accident and made an initial settlement of $50,000 with the other parties' insurers. She then sought arbitration for underinsured benefits from her and her husband's insurers. The arbitrator determined her damages to be $65,000, and the two insurers paid the additional $15,000. Subsequently, she remembered that her son had underinsured coverage of $100,000. She brought suit against his insurer, seeking to recover monies from it as well. The trial court granted summary judgment to the insurer, and she appealed to the Supreme Judicial Court of Massachusetts. The appellate court found that she was barred from her suit against her son's insurer by the doctrine of collateral estoppel, or issue preclusion. She had been given a full and fair opportunity to arbitrate the amount of damages she incurred, and she could not now try to relitigate this question. The court affirmed the trial court's decision for the insurer. *Miles v. Aetna Casualty and Surety Co.*, 589 N.E.2d 314 (Mass.1992).

A Pennsylvania insured was severely injured when he was struck by a motor vehicle while he was a pedestrian. At the time, he was covered by a motor vehicle policy which included underinsured motorist coverage. The man's injuries resulted in over $75,000 in medical expenses. His insurer paid $15,000 in underinsured motorist benefits pursuant to the specific limit set forth in the policy. The insured sought to have the insurer arbitrate the limits of his underinsured coverage, which he believed should have been $100,000 instead of $15,000. He claimed that the insurer did not provide sufficient information to permit him an informed choice as to available coverage. The arbitration provision of the policy stated that if the insured and the insurer did not agree as to the amount of damages, either party could make a written demand for arbitration. The trial court refused to require the insurer to arbitrate the claim, and the insured appealed to the Superior Court of Pennsylvania.

The court reviewed the language of the arbitration clause and determined that arbitration is mandated whenever the insured and insurer disagree as to when a party is legally entitled to recover damages. The dispute, in its broadest sense, involved a disagreement as to the amount of damages which the insured would and could possibly receive under the policy. Therefore, the order of the trial court was reversed and the insurer was required to arbitrate. *Lamar v. Colonial Penn Ins. Co.*, 578 A.2d 1337 (Pa.Super.1990).

A Delaware insured was involved in an automobile accident with an uninsured motorist, and sustained permanent injuries. She made a written demand for arbitration, and was awarded $90,000. The insurer then demanded a trial *de novo* (as if the arbitration had never occurred) by virtue of a policy provision. The policy stated that either party could demand a trial *de novo* if the arbitration award exceeded state financial responsibility limits. The trial court ruled for the insured, and the

Supreme Court of Delaware affirmed. It held that the provision violated public policy because it provided an escape device in favor of the insurer. *Worldwide Ins. Group v. Klopp*, 603 A.2d 788 (Del.Supr.1992).

A New York insured was injured when the vehicle he was driving was struck in the rear by another vehicle. The unidentified vehicle fled from the scene of the accident. The insured then made a claim under his policy for uninsured motorist coverage. The insurer refused to pay the medical claims and the matter ultimately proceeded to an arbitration hearing. The arbitrator awarded $85,000 to the insured. The insurer moved to vacate the award in a New York trial court. The trial court granted the motion and the insured appealed to the Supreme Court, Appellate Division. On appeal, the insurer contended that the arbitrator exceeded his power and that the award lacked a rational basis. The insurer based this contention on the fact that the vehicle had been pushed only a few feet and the insured received no immediate medical treatment and never missed a day of work due to his injuries. In fact he did not seek medical attention until two weeks after the accident. The insurer also contended that the arbitrator did not make a finding of serious injury. However, the court noted that an arbitrator need not justify his award by setting forth the reasons for his determination. All that was required was that the record contain a rational basis for the award. The court found that there was rational basis based on the doctor's reports. Accordingly, the arbitrator's award was affirmed and the trial court's decision reversed. *Commercial Union Ins. Co. v. Ewall*, 562 N.Y.S.2d 484 (A.D.1st Dep't 1990).

Three separate lawsuits in Florida concerned the appropriateness of awarding attorney's fees which were incurred during arbitration proceedings. All three actions arose in the construction industry and were brought by owners or subcontractors against the general contractor or surety bond issuer. All three disputes were referred to arbitration as per the parties' contracts. The suits then went to court, and on appeal each plaintiff sought attorney's fees. One court awarded the fee, another refused to award fees, and another refused to confirm an award. The Supreme Court of Florida certified the suits for review and consolidated the actions into one hearing.

Florida Statutes § 682.11 (1987) provides that an arbitrator or umpire may stipulate that one party pay fees and expenses "not including counsel fees." Another statute, however, allows recovery of attorney's fees for parties to a bond "in case of suit." The supreme court agreed that this conflict allowed an award: "attorney's fees ... are not barred merely because the amount due the insured was established pursuant to arbitration rather than through a judicial determination." The court held that the effect of § 682.11 was merely to prohibit an arbitrator from awarding attorney's fees; it was ruled inapplicable to a court. *Ins. Co. of North America v. Acousti Engineering*, 579 So.2d 77 (Fla.1991).

C. Subrogation

A freight company chose to be a self-insured employer for purposes of Ohio's workers' compensation laws. It obtained a surety bond, and then procured excess indemnity insurance for payments in excess of $50,000. The freight company later filed a petition in bankruptcy, and the Ohio Industrial Commission demanded payment on a debt from the surety bond insurer. That insurer then brought an action against the excess insurer, seeking contribution of the amount it owed in excess of

$50,000 — under principles of subrogation. The trial court ruled in its favor, and the excess insurer appealed to the Ohio Court of Appeals. On appeal, the excess insurer argued that the surety was subrogated only to the rights of an obligee, and not to the rights of its principal. The court, however, disagreed. It stated that where the rights of the principal are closely related to the debt the surety must pay, equity is served by allowing subrogation to the rights of the principal. Since the freight company could have required indemnification from the excess insurer, the surety could also do so. The trial court's ruling was affirmed. *American Ins. Co. v. Ohio Bureau of Workers' Compensation*, 577 N.E.2d 756 (Ohio App.1991).

A New York attorney rented space from a partnership, in which he was a partner, and maintained his law office at the insured premises. The insurer issued a separate fire policy to him, insuring his personal property in his law office on the premises. A fire occurred at the insured premises which substantially damaged the structure and its contents. The partnership submitted a claim to the insurer and stated that the cause and origin of the fire were unknown to it. The insurer investigated and paid the partnership in full satisfaction of its claim. The law partner also submitted a claim under his separate policy for property damage sustained to his law office as a result of the fire. However, the insurer rejected the claim on the ground that there was evidence to show that the lawyer had deliberately caused the fire. The insurer then commenced an action in a New York trial court alleging that the fire was intentionally and deliberately set by the lawyer and that the insurer was subrogated to the rights of the partnership against the lawyer. The trial court awarded summary judgment in favor of the insurer and the lawyer appealed to the Supreme Court, Appellate Division.

The lawyer contended that the insurer was not obligated to pay the partnership claim since the fire insurance policy contained a specific exclusion of liability where any insured set the fire. Since the insurer had a clear and valid defense to the claim by the partnership under the express provisions of the policy, the lawyer argued that it was not entitled to be subrogated to the rights of the partnership. The lawyer also asserted that the insurer had no right of subrogation against him, since he was a general unlimited partner and was an insured himself. The court noted that where the interests of the co-insured are considered joint and nonseparable, it has been held in New York that an innocent co-insured may not recover on a fire insurance policy following the act of arson by another insured. In the instant case, the interests of the innocent partnership and the lawyer were not joint because the lawyer did not act within the scope of partnership business when he set the fire. The court affirmed the trial court's decision. *Hartford Fire Ins. Co. v. Advocate*, 560 N.Y.S.2d 331 (A.D.2d Dep't 1990).

A Tennessee couple purchased a new vehicle, executing a retail installment contract at the same time. They then obtained an insurance policy which also named the lienholder as a loss payee. When the policy period ended, the couple did not pay the premium, causing the insurance to lapse. The insurer then notified the lienholder that the cancellation would occur in ten days. Four days later, the vehicle was totaled in an automobile accident. The insurer paid the lienholder, and then sought subrogation from the couple as was provided for in the policy. The trial court held for the insureds, and the insurer appealed to the Court of Appeals of Tennessee. On appeal, the insurer asserted that since the insureds had let the policy lapse, the insurer had no liability to them, and thus was authorized to be subrogated to the lienholder's rights. The court agreed, noting that insurers, generally, are allowed to be subrogated to a mortgagee's rights upon payment of a loss to the mortgagee. Here, the insureds had been given a reasonable opportunity to insure themselves against loss, and had chosen not to do so. The court reversed the lower court's decision and allowed the insurer the right to subrogate. *Chrysler Credit Corp. v. Noles*, 813 S.W.2d 437 (Tenn.App.1990).

A medical insurer paid medical costs on behalf of an insured who was injured in an automobile accident caused by a third person. The payment was made in reliance on a subrogation provision. The insured and his wife later filed claims against the third person for bodily injury, pain and suffering, loss of employment, loss of future wages, and loss of consortium — they did not include a claim for medical expenses. The medical insurer sought to intervene and asserted a right of subrogation. The trial court had ruled against a conventional right of subrogation because the employee had not sought medical expenses, but, notwithstanding that, held that the insurer had a right to "legal subrogation." Many Alabama cases involving subrogation were currently pending, and the Supreme Court of Alabama granted appeal. The court cited the underlying principles of subrogation, and declared that a right to subrogation will arise when an insured is made whole. It further held that the policy was sufficient to induce subrogation: "it is irrelevant as to how the indemnitee may allocate the amounts recovered from the tortfeasor." The factors in determining the presence of the right to subrogation were cited to be: 1) the total dollar amount recovered by the injured party, and 2) the total loss suffered. Because the total loss suffered in this case had not been determined by a court, it was impossible to decide whether the right of subrogation had arisen. The finding that a legal right of subrogation had arisen was reversed, but the allowance of the insurer's intervention in order to protect its interests was affirmed. *McKleroy v. Wilson*, 581 So.2d 796 (Ala.1990).

A family had homesteaded an area on Lake McDonald before the establishment of Glacier National Park, and the area had been left for the use of the entire family up to the present time. The agent who sold an insurance policy on the cabin to the legal owner knew that the cabin was used by various members of an extended family. The legal owner's brother and nephew were vacationing at the cabin when an electric blanket started a fire which destroyed the entire structure. The insurer paid benefits to the owner, but later sought subrogation against the brother and nephew. A Montana court granted the insurer summary judgment on that issue, and the decision was appealed to the Supreme Court of Montana. The issue was which persons could be considered insureds for the purposes of subrogation. With respect to a seasonal cabin used by an extended family, the issue had not been previously litigated. The right of subrogation arises in other contexts only against third persons to whom an insurer owes no duty. The court held that to allow the insurer to recover against the guest of the named insured would have the effect of transferring the risk back to the insured himself. The holding was supported in this case by the fact that the agent knew of the entire family's use of the cabin. The summary judgment granted to the insurer was reversed. *Continental Ins. Co. v. Bottomly*, 817 P.2d 1162 (Mont.1991).

A man was covered by medical insurance while involved in an automobile accident caused by a third person. He received a $25,000 settlement from the third person's insurer, but did not pay his medical bills. Upon the man's signing a subrogation agreement, the man's insurer later paid over $15,000 in medical expenses. The agreement provided that he would repay any benefits paid by his insurer "from the judgment I or my dependent receives" from the tortfeasor. The insurer subsequently learned of the previous settlement and demanded repayment. The man refused to repay because he felt that the agreement's language did not mandate a repayment if the settlement was received before the agreement was signed. The insurer successfully sued in a state court, and the man appealed to the Supreme Court of Alabama. The court looked beyond the language of the subrogation agreement to the "equitable considerations that are the underpinnings of subrogation." Those considerations greatly favored the insurer: "1) the insured should not recover twice for a single injury and 2) the insurer should be reimbursed for payments it made that in fairness should be borne by the wrongdoer." Further, the agreement in this case was ruled to encompass payment received before the agreement was signed. The court did not, however, merely affirm the judgment which had been awarded to the insurer. It noted that a right of subrogation does not arise until the insured has been made whole. The case was remanded for the trial court to first determine the insured's damages, and secondly to enter judgment consistent with the appellate court's holdings. *Sharpley v. Sonoco Products Co.*, 581 So.2d 792 (Ala.1990).

A truck driver was injured when his truck was struck by another truck. The injured truck driver collected personal injury benefits from his own insurer, and later filed a tort suit against the other driver's insurer for the same benefits. The injured party's insurer notified the tortfeasor of a separate subrogation claim, but the tortfeasor's insurer did not receive notice of the subrogated claim until five months later — after it had entered into a settlement with the injured party. After learning of the subrogated claim, the tortfeasor's insurer refused to pay the settlement. A lawsuit developed, and a federal district court ruled that the settlement must be honored, but that the injured party's insurer must be paid by the injured party. Appeal was taken to the U.S. Court of Appeals, Eleventh Circuit.

The first issue involved the enforcement of the settlement. The tortfeasor's insurer argued that it was unenforceable due to a lack of notice of the subrogated claim. The injured party was ruled to have no duty to inform the tortfeasor's insurer of the subrogation claim because he did not know that it existed. Further, an insurer is charged with the knowledge of its insured. The tortfeasor's insurer then claimed that the subrogated claim was waived due to the injured party's insurer's failing to intervene in the tort action. The court disagreed; the insurer seeking subrogation had no notice of the tort action, and under those circumstances did not waive its rights. The court ruled that the injured party was entitled to the settlement without any liability to his insurer, and that his insurer could recover from the tortfeasor's insurer via subrogation. *Martin v. Commercial Union Ins. Co.*, 935 F.2d 235 (11th Cir. 1991).

A Michigan man was insured by a no-fault automobile policy and by a group major medical policy. He was then seriously injured in an automobile accident. His medical expenses were covered by both policies, and he elected to coordinate medical expense coverage as he was permitted to do by Michigan law. The no-fault insurer notified the health insurer that the latter's coverage was primary, but it paid almost all the insured's medical bills. Four years later, it sued the health insurer to recover reimbursement. The health insurer asserted that the one-year limitation period had passed, and moved for summary judgment. The trial court denied the motion, but the court of appeals reversed. Further appeal was taken to the Supreme Court of Michigan. The supreme court noted that even though the no-fault insurer had paid benefits under a no-fault policy, its lawsuit for reimbursement was not an action based on the no-fault act (and thus governed by the one-year statute of limitations). Rather, its suit was in the nature of a common law contract action for which a six-year statute of limitations applied. The no-fault insurer was merely subrogating itself to the position of the insured who would have had six years in which to bring the suit. Accordingly, the court ruled in favor of the no-fault insurer, and reversed the court of appeals' decision. *Auto Club Ins. Ass'n v. New York Life Ins. Co.*, 485 N.W.2d 695 (Mich.1992).

A woman was injured in an automobile accident which involved another insured auto and a phantom truck. Her theory was that both the drivers of the auto and the truck were negligent and responsible for her injuries. She settled the claim with her insurer for uninsured motorist benefits. Under the settlement she received the policy limits of $150,000 on behalf of the phantom truck in exchange for a release and grant of subrogation rights. The settlement provided that she would bring an action against the other insured driver on behalf of her insurer, and that she would receive any money awarded in excess of $150,000. The driver of the other auto claimed that the insurer could not be subrogated to the woman's rights because it had not fully compensated her for her injuries, and because the woman was left open to pursue claims against the negligent parties. The state court found that subrogation rights could not be enforced, and the insurer appealed. This exact issue had not been decided by a Florida court. Ordinarily, subrogation rights do not exist until a party has completely compensated the injured party and thereby extinguished the party's claims against other tortfeasors. This had not occurred in this case. However, the party seeking rights of subrogation in this case was not a joint tortfeasor, as in earlier subrogation cases. It was the plaintiff's insurer. The court ruled that the cooperative effort was allowable, and recognized an exception to general subrogation principles when an insurer and insured have entered a settlement clearly specifying a grant of subrogation rights. The judgment of the trial court was reversed, and a trial was ordered to determine damages. *Collins v. Wilcott*, 578 So.2d 742 (Fla.App.5th Dist.1991).

A county hospital error caused a man to fall into a persistent vegetative state. It faced a $175,000 claim for loss of consortium from the man's wife, and a $316,000 claim for medical expenses by an insurer that was subrogated to the man's interests. Under Minnesota law, the county had its liability for an accident limited to $200,000. The county contended that both claims should be subject to a single cap, and the wife argued that each claim was legally separate and should be subject to its own limit. A trial court held that all claims were subject to a single cap, an appellate court reversed, and the Supreme Court of Minnesota granted review. The scope of the liability limitation statute is written toward several claims being brought by an individual claimant, but expressly includes claims for loss of services or support arising from the same tort. The wife claimed that this inclusion was intended to prevent manipulation of claims that could lead to double recovery and that her claim should not be barred as it was not double recovery. The court examined the history of the section, and disagreed. The purpose of the law was to limit claims arising from an accident, not claims from a single claimant; the wife's claim was thus merged with her husband's. The court held that both claims were subject to a single cap. *Rowe v. St. Paul Ramsey Medical Center*, 472 N.W.2d 640 (Minn.1991).

An insured woman was seriously injured in an automobile collision which was the result of another driver's negligence. The other driver's insurance policy contained a $10,000 limit for personal injury. The woman's injuries exceeded that amount. Without the insurer's knowledge, she settled with and released the other driver and his insurer and then collected from her insurer under an underinsured motorist clause. Her insurer later claimed subrogation rights and sued the other driver and his insurer. The negligent driver's insurer successfully pled payment and release in a Mississippi trial court, and the woman's insurer appealed to the Mississippi Supreme Court.

The trial court had held that the woman's insurer, through statutory subrogation, assumed the woman's rights, and was barred from recovery due to the release. On appeal, her insurer argued that the subrogation rights arose nonstatutorily from the contract. Mississippi law, however, provides that the uninsured motorist clause be part of all automobile insurance contracts sold within the state, whether written therein or not. The uninsured motorist clause addresses subrogation rights, and the court ruled that it would bar the woman's insurer from recovery as the legislature intended its use of "subrogated" to have the meaning of its ordinary use. Nothing in the woman's policy enlarged these rights. The woman's insurer then argued that subrogation rights differ when concerning underinsured motorists as opposed to uninsured motorists. The court again disagreed and ruled that underinsured motorists are included in the uninsured motorist clause even though the exact word "underinsured" had never been used. The trial court's judgment was affirmed. *St. Paul Property and Liability Ins. Co. v. Nance*, 577 So.2d 1238 (Miss.1991).

During a repair, a farmer had two vehicles parked along the shoulder of a road. An uninsured motorist struck the vehicles, and the farmer made a claim against the insurer of each vehicle. He settled a claim for no-fault benefits against one insurer, and a subsequent settlement with the other insurer included a release of all claims. The insurer that paid no-fault benefits (secondary insurer) sought to recover them from the other insurer (primary insurer) through a subrogated claim. The primary insurer argued that it did not have notice of the subrogation, and that the release thus precluded all claims — including subrogation. A trial court disagreed, and the primary insurer appealed to the Court of Appeals of Minnesota. In order to encourage payment of benefits, Minnesota law provides that a lower priority insurer which pays no-fault benefits is granted subrogation rights against the higher priority insurer. The subrogation claim may be asserted only when recovery absent subrogation would allow duplicate benefits. Other equitable concerns of subrogation do not apply in a no-fault context. Therefore, the claim in this case could be asserted only against the insured. Importantly, the court distinguished cases involving primary insurers which had received notice of a subrogated claim prior to settlement. The decision of the trial court was reversed. *Farm Bureau Mutual Ins. Co. v. National Family Ins. Co.*, 474 N.W.2d 424 (Minn.App.1991).

APPENDIX A

McCARRAN-FERGUSON
INSURANCE REGULATION ACT

Historically, the U.S. Supreme Court consistently held that the business of insurance was not "commerce" within the meaning of the U.S. Constitution's Commerce Clause, and thus insurance was beyond the scope of federal control. This view changed with the Supreme Court's decision in *United States v. South-Eastern Underwriters Ass'n,* 322 U.S. 533, 64 S.Ct. 1162, 88 L.Ed. 1440 (1944), which declared that the business of insurance was interstate commerce subject to the Sherman Antitrust Act. Congress responded quickly by enacting the McCarran-Ferguson Insurance Regulation Act, 15 U.S.C. § § 1011-1012 (1945). This Act, reproduced below, reserved to the states the right to regulate the business of insurance.

§ 1011. Declaration of policy

Congress declares that the continued regulation and taxation by the several States of the business of insurance is in the public interest, and that silence on the part of the Congress shall not be construed to impose any barrier to the regulation or taxation of such business by the several States.

§ 1012. Regulation by State law; Federal law relating specifically to insurance; applicability of certain Federal laws after June 30, 1948

(a) The business of insurance, and every person engaged therein, shall be subject to the laws of the several States which relate to the regulation or taxation of such business.

(b) No Act of Congress shall be construed to invalidate, impair, or supersede any law enacted by any State for the purpose of regulating the business of insurance, or which imposes a fee or tax upon such business, unless such Act specifically relates to the business of insurance: Provided, That after June 30, 1948, the Act of July 2, 1890, as amended, known as the Sherman Act, and the Act of October 15, 1914, as amended, known as the Clayton Act, and the Act of September 26, 1914, known as the Federal Trade Commission Act, as amended, shall be applicable to the business of insurance to the extent that such business is not regulated by State law.

APPENDIX B

SUBJECT MATTER TABLE
OF RECENT LAW REVIEW ARTICLES

AIDS
Clifford, Karen A. and Russel P. Inculano. *AIDS and insurance: the rationale for AIDS-related testing.* 100 Harv.L.Rev. 1806 (1987).

Group health benefits discrimination against AIDS victims: falling through the gaps of federal law — ERISA, the Rehabilitation Act and the Americans with Disabilities Act. 24 Loy.L.A.L.Rev. 861 (1991).

Hermann, Donald H. J. *AIDS: malpractice transmission liability.* 58 U.Colo.L.Rev. 63 (1986-87).

Left of center and right in front of us: AIDS testing in insurance underwriting— the social and economic implications of this practice on individuals and society. 17 Cap.U.L.Rev. 273 (1988).

Padgug, Robert A. and Gerald Oppenheimer. *AIDS, health insurance and the crisis of community.* 5 Notre Dame J.L.Ethics & Pub.Pol'y 35 (1990).

Papa, Nicholas A. Comment. *Testimony and the health industry's response to the AIDS epidemic.* 18 Ohio N.U.L.Rev. 687 (1992).

Schatz, Benjamin. *The AIDS insurance crisis: underwriting or overreaching?* 100 Harv.L.Rev. 1782 (1987).

Stone, Deborah A. *The rhetoric of insurance law: the debate over AIDS testing.* 15 Law & Soc.Inquiry 385 (1990).

Stone, Sandra Elizabeth. Note. *HIV testing and insurance applicants: exploring constitutional alternatives to statutory protections.* 19 Hastings Const.L.Q. 1163 (1992).

Tort liability for AIDS? 24 Hous.L.Rev. 957 (1987).

Twenty-Third Annual Symposium. AIDS: At the Limits of the Law. 34 Vill.L.Rev. 755 (1989).

Automobile Insurance
Buckle up Ohio — Wood v. Shepard is on some rough road. [Hill v. Allstate Ins. Co., 50 Ohio St.3d 243, 553 N.E.2d 658 (1990)] 17 Ohio N.U.L.Rev. 201 (1990).

Buckling up: how the mandatory seatbelt law affects the seatbelt defense. 17 SW.U.L.Rev. 597 (1988).

The continuing controversy of the seatbelt defense. 27 Hous.L.Rev. 179 (1990).

Dvorak, Lori A. Note. *No-fault automobile insurance law: speaking out on New Jersey's verbal threshold.* 16 Seton Hall Legis.J. 716 (1992).

Insurance—Parents of an unborn but viable fetus can maintain an action for loss of consortium under the uninsured motorist provision of their automobile insurance policy upon the death of their child. [Craig v. IMT Insurance Co., 407 N.W.2d 584 (Iowa 1987)] 37 Drake L.Rev. 731 (1987-88).

Automobile Insurance (Continued)

Interpretation and application of the "arising out of the use" clause in an automobile liability insurance policy. [Kohl v. Union Ins. Co.,731 P.2d 134 (1986)] 65 Denver U.L.Rev. 77 (1988).

Knoll, John J. *Kansas automobile insurance: current issues and problems.* 29 Washburn L.J. 600 (1990).

Krening, Eric. *Recognizing a reality: the tort fault liability concept at the foundation of Idaho's motor vehicle insurance law.* 26 Idaho L.Rev. 309 (1989-1990).

Lingle, T. Andrew. *The Pennsylvania Motor Vehicle Financial Responsibility Law of 1990: constitutionality of achieving affordable insurance rates through freeze and rollback measures.* 96 Dick.L.Rev. 303 (1992).

Little, John S. Comment. *Recent developments in the Tennessee law of uninsured motorist coverage.* 58 Tenn.L.Rev. 413 (1991).

Missouri's stance on household exclusion clauses in automobile insurance contracts: consistent with public policy? [American Family Mutual Ins. Co. v. Ward, 789 S.W.2d 791 (Mo.1991, en banc.)] 56 Mo.L.Rev. 443 (1991).

No-fault personal injury automobile insurance: the Quebec and New York experiences and a proposal for California. 14 Hastings Int'l & Comp.L.Rev. 505 (1991).

O'Connell, Jeffrey. *A model bill (and commentary thereon) allowing choice of coverage under Michigan's no-fault auto insurance law.* 17 J.Legis. 155 (1991).

Proposition 103: too good to be true. [Calfarm Ins. Co. v. Deukmejian, 48 Cal.3d 805, 71 P.2d 1247, 258 Cal.Rptr. 161 (1989, en banc)] 12 Whittier L.Rev. 403 (1991).

Shelley, Scott C. Note. *Constitutional law — Fifth Amendment — surtaxes and assessments imposed by New Jersey's Fair Automobile Insurance Reform Act do not violate due process or constitute a taking without just compensation.* [State Farm v. State of New Jersey, 124 N.J. 32, 590 A.2d 191 (1991)] 22 Seton Hall L.Rev. 1529 (1992).

Stewart, Martha Eugenia. Note. *An insured's right to recover attorney's fees under Florida's uninsured motorist statute.* [Moore v. Allstate Insurance, 553 So.2d 1368 (Fla.1st DCA 1989)] 20 Stetson L.Rev. 363 (1990).

Sugarman, Stephen D. *California's insurance regulation revolution: the first two years of Proposition 103.* 27 San Diego L.Rev. 683 (1990).

The 1990 Pennsylvania auto insurance law: an analysis of "bad faith" and the "limited tort option." 29 Duq.L.Rev. 619 (1991).

Tort Law—No Fault Insurance Symposium. 26 San Diego L.Rev. 977 (1989).

Uninsured motorist insurance, the commercial fleet policy, and Harris v. Magee: a modest proposal for change. [Harris v. Magee, 573 So.2d 646, (Miss.1990)] 61 Miss.L.J. 171 (1991).

Aviation Insurance

Insurance—requirement that insured's breach of aircraft insurance policy contribute to loss for insurance company to avoid liability — under Texas law, when an insurance company pleads an exclusion, an insured party seeking to recover under the policy has the burden of proving that its breach of the insurance policy did not contribute to the loss. [Ideal Mut. Ins. Co. v. Last Days Evangelical Ass'n, 783 F.2d 1234 (5th Cir.1986)] 53 J.Air.L. & Com. 581 (1987).

Aviation Insurance (Continued)

Sugarman, Stephen P. *Right and wrong ways of doing away with commercial air crash litigation: Professor Chalk's "market insurance plan" and other no-fault follies.* 52 J.Air.L. & Com. 681 (1987).

Bad Faith

Bad-faith denial of insurance claims: whose faith, whose punishment? An examination of punitive damages and vicarious liability. 65 Tul.L.Rev. 395 (1990).

Breach of an insurer's good faith duty to its insured: tort or contract? 1988 Utah L.Rev. 135.

Common-law bad faith in White v. Western Title Insurance Co.: the duty continues. [White v. Western Title Insurance Co., 710 P.2d 309 (1985)] 21 Loy.L.A.L.Rev. 399 (1987).

First party bad faith in Kentucky: What remains after Federal Kemper Insurance v. Hornback? 75 Ky.L.J. 939 (1986-87).

Lass, Christina M.L. Note. *The injured third party in California: extending bad faith for full compensation.* 26 Val.U.L.Rev. 843 (1992).

Living on the edge of bad faith: have we accidentally allowed self-insureds to escape liability? 19 U.West.L.A.L.Rev. 89 (1987).

No faith in bad faith. 41 Hastings L.J. 201 (1989).

Payne, Donna Gooden. Note. *Insurer bad faith: the need for and exception to the attorney-client privilege.* 11 Rev.Litig. 111 (1991).

Porter, J. Benson, Jr. Note. *The need for revisiting the imposition of bad faith liability.* [Industrial Indemnity Co. v. Kallevig, 114 Wash.2d 520 (1990)] 15 U.Puget Sound L.Rev. 203 (1991).

Rice, Willy E. *Judicial bias, the insurance industry and consumer protection: an empirical analysis of state Supreme Courts' bad-faith, breach-of-contract, breach-of-covenant-of-good-faith and excess-judgment decisions, 1990-1991.* 41 Cath.U.L.Rev. 325 (1992).

Smith, Glenn E. *Understanding the new tort of first party bad faith in Wyoming: McCullough v. Golden Rule Ins. Co.* 26 Land and Water L.Rev. 225 (1991).

Standards of liability for bad faith refusal to pay benefits in first party insurance. 29 Ariz.L.Rev. 115 (1987).

Texas Supreme Court characterizes duty of good faith and fair dealing and insurers' standard for meeting it ... or does it? [Viles v. Security National Ins. Co., 788 S.W.2d 566 (Tex.1990)] 22 Tex.Tech.L.Rev. 257 (1991).

Volk, Peter A. Comment. *Bad faith breach of insurance contract: Idaho's misapplication of tort law.* 28 Idaho L.Rev. 457 (1991-92).

Woodham, Barry D. Student Comment. *"Constructive denial," "debatable reasons," and bad faith refusal to pay an insurance claim — the evolution of a monster.* 22 Cumb.L.Rev. 349 (1991-1992).

Director and Officer Liability

Anbari, M. Mazen. Comment. *Banking on a bailout: directors' and officers' liability insurance policy exclusions in the context of the savings and loan crisis.* 141 U.Pa.L.Rev. 547 (1992).

Bean, Russell K. *Corporate director liability.* 65 Denver U.L.Rev. 59 (1988).

Elam, Linda C. Comment. *Financial institution deposit insurance — directors' and officers' liability insurance policies — public policy regarding regulatory exclusions.* 59 Tenn.L.Rev. 305 (1992).

Director and Officer Liability (Continued)

Kanzler, Jay L., Jr. *A look at the director and officer liability insurance crisis: insuring a balance of interests.* 19 N.Ky.L.Rev. 489 (1992).

Palmore, Melanie K. Comment. *"Insured v. insured" exclusions in director and officer liability insurance policies: is coverage available when Chapter 11 trustees and debtors-in-possession sue former directors and officers?* 9 Bankr.Dev.J. 101 (1992).

Romano, Roberta. *What went wrong with directors' and officers' liability insurance?* 14 Delaware J.Corp.L. 1 (1989).

Statutory and non-statutory responses to the director and officer liability crisis. 63 Ind.L.J. 181 (1987-88).

Wallace, Perry E. Jr. *Liability of corporations and corporate officers, directors, and shareholders under Superfund: Should corporate and agency law concepts apply?* 14 J.Corp.L. 839 (1989).

Walter, Paula. *Statutory indemnification and insurance provisions for corporate directors—to what end?* 38 Drake L.Rev. 229 (1989).

Where have all the directors gone: corporate director and officer liability and coping with the insurance crisis. 36 Clev.St.L.Rev. 575 (1988).

Dram Shop Insurance/Liquor Liability

Alcohol and hazing risks in college fraternities: reevaluating vicarious and custodial liability of national fraternities. 7 Rev.Litigation 191 (1988).

Am I my brother's keeper? Social host liability under dram shop acts and common law negligence. 32 Wash.U.J.Urb. & Contemp.L. 149 (1987).

Comparative negligence and dram shop laws: does Buckley v. Perolo *sound last call for holding New Jersey liquor venders liable for the torts of intoxicated persons?* 62 Notre Dame L.Rev. 238 (1987).

Dram shop liability: should the intoxicated person recover for his own injuries? 48 Ohio St.L.J. 227 (1987).

Tort law—limits on dram shop liability; barring recovery of bar patrons, their estates and survivors. [Bertelmann v. Taas Associates, 69 Haw., 735 P.2d 930 (1987)] 11 U.Hawaii L.Rev. 277 (1989).

Employment

Herman, Anthony. *Wrongful discharge actions after* Lueck *and* Metropolitan Life Insurance*: the erosion of individual rights and collective strength?* 9 Indus.Rel.L.J. 596 (1987).

Holmes, Roxanne L. *Insurance for claims of wrongful employment termination.* 91 Dick.L.Rev. 895 (1987).

Excess Insurance

Drop down liability of excess insurers for insolvent primary carriers: the search for uniformity in judicial interpretation of excess insurance policies. 33 Ariz.L.Rev. 239 (1991).

Insolvency in the insurance industry and "drop down" coverage: a realistic solution. 8 J.L.& Com. 423 (1988).

Sledge, Margaret M. and Gerald M. Baca. *Rights and duties of primary and excess insurance carriers.* 15 Tul.Mar.L.J. 59 (1990).

Group Insurance
Blackwell, Debbie L. and Michael H. Taggart. *More rules for Section 125 Cafeteria plans: Some help and some hurt.* 25 Tulsa L.J. 261 (1989).

Cabrera, Anthony Sebastian. Comment. *The Medigap Reforms of the Omnibus Budget Reconciliation Act of 1990: are the protections adequate?* 6 Admin.L.J.Am.U. 321 (1992).

The COBRA strikes at group health insurance plans: divorced women's rights to continue coverage. 92 Dick.L.Rev. 253 (1987).

Peterson, Jurt and Gordon Bosserman. *Administration of insurance benefits: what's new?* 13 Whittier L.Rev. 429 (1992).

Healthcare Liability Insurance
Baron, Roger M. *The retention of insurance overpayments by healthcare providers.* 30 S.Tex.L.Rev. 387 (1989).

Belk, Jennifer. Comment. *Undefined experimental treatment exclusions in health insurance contracts: a proposal for judicial response.* 66 Wash.L.Rev. 809 (1991).

Curran, Angela S. *Long-term health care insurance challenges: meeting the needs of an aging population.* 21 Loy.U.Chi.L.J. 1075 (1990).

Flynn, Michael. *Private medical insurance and the collateral source rule: a good bet?* 22 U.Tol.L.Rev. 39 (1990).

Greaney, Thomas L. *Competitive reform in health care: the vulnerable revolution.* 5 Yale J.on Reg. 179 (1988).

Infertility: a survey of the law and analysis of the need for legislation mandating insurance coverage. 27 San Diego L.Rev. 715 (1990).

Kaplan, Susan B. Comment. *A legal perspective on national health insurance: current issues in Canada's program.* 9 Wis.Int'l L.J. 515 (1991).

Kaplow, Louis. *The income tax as insurance: the casualty loss and medical expense deductions and the exclusion of medical insurance premiums.* 79 Cal.L.Rev. 1485 (1991).

Mehlman, Maxwell J. *Fiduciary contracting: limitations on bargaining between patients and health care providers.* 51 U.Pitt.L.Rev. 365 (1990).

Mihaly, Peter H. Note. *Health care utilization review: potential exposures to negligence liability.* 52 Ohio St.L.J. 1289 (1991).

O'Connell, Jeffrey. *Must health and disability insurance subsidize wasteful injury suits?* 41 Rutgers L.Rev. 1055 (1989).

O'Rourke, Melissa R. Comment. *The status of infertility treatments and insurance coverage: some hopes and frustrations.* 37 S.D.L.Rev. 343 (1992).

Paying the piper: third-party payor liability for medical treatment decisions. 25 Ga.L.Rev. 861 (1991).

Pauly, Mark V. *Competition in health insurance markets.* 51 Law & Contemp.Probs. 237 (1988).

The emerging liability of third party health care payors. [Wickline v. State, 228 Cal.Rptr. 661 (1986)] 24 San Diego L.Rev. 1023 (1987).

Tichon, Michael J., Lloyd Bookman and Jeremy N. Miller. *When health care doesn't pay: reimbursements, fraud and abuse.* 13 Whittier L.Rev. 413 (1992).

Homeowner's Insurance

Alvey, Constance M. Note. *Intentional injury exclusion.* [American Family Mutual Insurance Co. v. Pacchetti, 808 S.W.2d 369 (Mo.1991, en banc)] 60 UMKC L.Rev. 559 (1992).

Exclusion of automobile related liability under a homeowner's insurance policy. [Fortune v. Wong, 702 P.2d 299 (1985), and Hawaiian Ins. & Guar. Co. v. Chief Clerk, 713 P.2d 427 (1986)] 9 U.Haw.L.Rev. 345 (1987).

Frey, Daniel K. Comment. *Application of intentional acts exclusion under homeowner's insurance policies to acts of child molestation.* [Allstate Insurance Company v. Troelstrup, 789 P.2d 415 (Colo.1990)] 68 Denv.U.L.Rev. 429 (1991).

Homeowner's insurance coverage of negligent transmission of sexually transmitted disease. 31 B.C.L.Rev. 1209 (1990).

Silverman, Tracy E. Note. *Voluntary intoxication: a defense to intentional injury exclusion clauses in homeowner's policies?* 90 Mich.L.Rev. 2113 (1992).

Insurance—Generally

Afanasyeva, Larisa. *Insurance and risk management of joint ventures in the USSR.* 22 N.Y.U.J.Int'l L.& Pol. 447 (1990).

Anderson, Mercelita C. Comment. *Genetic testing in insurance underwriting: a blessing or a curse? An examination of the tension between economics and equity in using genetic testing in risk classification.* 25 Creighton L.Rev. 1499 (1992).

Antognini, Richard L. *When will my troubles end? The loss in progress defense in progressive loss insurance cases.* 25 Loy.L.A.L.Rev. 419 (1992).

Berch, Rebecca White. *Insurer-insured conflicts: can insurer-retained counsel be true to the insured?* 23 Land & Water L.Rev. 185 (1988).

Bowdre, Karon O. *Guaranty association law in Alabama.* 20 Cumb.L.Rev. 321 (1989-1990).

Calnan, Alan. *The admissibility of insurance questions during voir dire: a critical survey of federal approaches and proposals for change.* 44 Rutgers L.Rev. 241 (1992).

Captive insurance companies and section 162 of the Internal Revenue Code. [Mobil Oil Corp. v. United States, 8 Cl.Ct. 555 (1985)] 2 Am.U.J.Int'l L. & Pol'y 303 (1987).

Concurrent proximate causes in insurance disputes: after Garvey, what will policyholders expect? 29 Santa Clara L.Rev. 423 (1989).

Conflict of interest: attorney as title insurance agent. 4 Geo.J.Legal Ethics 687 (1991).

Cooney, J. Mark. Comment. *The extension of Michigan's "innocent co-insured" doctrine from marriage to business partnerships?* 8 Thomas M. Cooley L.Rev. 637 (1991).

Cooper, R. Brent and Michael W. Huddleston. *Insurance law.* 43 Sw.L.J. 343 (1989).

Craig, Deborah Tharnish and Kimberly K. Mauer. *Chapter 507C—the supervision, rehabilitation and liquidation of insurance companies in Iowa: where no person has gone before.* 36 Drake L.Rev. 317 (1986-87).

Deere, Donald R. *On the potential for private insurers to reduce the inefficiencies of moral hazard.* 9 Int'l Rev.L.& Econ. 219 (1989).

Insurance—Generally (Continued)
    De Smedt, Philippe. *EEC competition rules apply to the insurance sector:* VDS v. Comm'n, 11 B.C.Int'l & Comp.L.Rev. 75 (1988).
    Dewey, Robert V., Jr. and Stephen J. Heine. *Survey of Illinois law — insurance.* 14 S.Ill.U.L.J. 1057 (1990).
    Dobbs, Dan B. *Accountability and comparative fault.* 47 La.L.Rev. 939 (1987).
    Doctors, insurers, and the antitrust laws. 37 Buffalo L.Rev. 789 (1988/89).
    Expanding the insurer's duty to defend in Iowa. [First Newton Nat'l Bank v. General Cas. Co. of Wisconsin, 426 N.W.2d 618 (Iowa 1988)] 74 Iowa L.Rev. 965 (1989).
    Genetic testing and insurance classification: national action can prevent discrimination based on the "luck of the genetic draw." 93 Dick.L.Rev. 729 (1989).
    Giblin, Joseph J. *Captive insurance companies: Valid insurance?* 7 B.U.J.Tax L. 61 (1989).
    Goodwin, David B. *Disputing insurance coverage disputes. [Book review/essay of]* Handbook on Insurance Coverage Disputes, by Barry R. Ostrager and Thomas R. Newman. 43 Stan.L.Rev. 779 (1991).
    Gravelle, Hugh. *Insurance law and adverse selection.* 11 Int'l Rev.L.& Econ. 23 (1991).
    Hanson, John. D. and Kyle D. Logue. *The first-party insurance externality: an economic justification for enterprise liability.* 76 Cornell L.Rev. 129 (1990).
    Holmes, Eric Mills. *A conflicts-of-interest roadmap for insurance defense counsel: Walking an ethical tightrope without a net.* 26 Willamette L.Rev. 1 (1989).
    Incorporation of nonfiduciary liability under ERISA. [Nieto v.Ecker, 845 F.2d 868 (9th Cir.1988)] 73 Minn.L.Rev. 1303 (1989).
    Insurance company insolvencies and insurance guaranty funds: a look at the nonduplication of recovery clause. 74 Iowa L.Rev. 927 (1989).
    Insurance insolvency: Who protects the policyholder? [Nasello v.Transit Casualty Co., 530 So.2d 1114 (La.1988)] 64 Tul.L.Rev. 259 (1989).
    Insurance representation: insurance litigation and the unauthorized practice of law. [In re Allstate Ins. Co., 722 S.W.2d 947 (Mo.1987)] 56 UMKC L.Rev. 167 (1987).
    Insurers and genetic testing: shopping for that perfect pair of genes. 40 Drake L.Rev. 121 (1991).
    Jerry, Robert H., II. *New developments in Kansas insurance law.* 37 Kan.L.Rev. 841 (1989).
    Kerns, Christopher and Gretchen Sievers. *Insurance law.* 21 Loy.U.Chi.L.J. 445 (1990).
    Kohane, Dan D. *Insurance law.* 41 Syracuse L.Rev. 433 (1990).
    Kohane, Dan D. *Insurance law.* 40 Syracuse L.Rev. 433 (1989).
    Kroll, Barry L. and John M. Edwards. *Insurance law (Survey).* 19 Loy.U.Chi.L.J. 525 (1988).
    Lopez-Aguado, Sondra M. Note. *The Americans with Disabilities Act: the undue hardship defense and insurance costs.* 12 Rev.Litig. 249 (1992).
    Lowe, Robert. *Genetic testing and insurance: Apocalypse now?* 40 Drake L.Rev. 507 (1991).

Insurance—Generally (Continued)

Mattis, Brian. *Earthquake and earth movement claims under all-risk insurance policies in the New Madrid Fault Zone.* 21 Mem.St.U.L.Rev. 59 (1991).

McDowell, Banks. *Causation in contracts and insurance.* 20 Conn.L.Rev. 569 (1988).

McDowell, Banks. *Choice of law in insurance: using conflicts methodology to minimize discrimination among policyholders.* 23 Conn.L.Rev. 117 (1990).

McKenzie, W. Shelby and H. Alston Johnson. *Insurance.* 51 La.L.Rev. 249 (1990).

Obinata, Naomi. Comment. *Genetic screening and insurance: too valuable an underwriting tool to be banned from the system.* 8 Santa Clara Computer & High Tech.L.J. 145 (1992).

Palomar, Joyce D. *Bank control of title insurance companies: perils to the public that bank regulators have ignored.* 44 Sw.L.J. 905 (1990).

Perspectives on the Insurance Crisis. 5 Yale J.on Reg. 367 (1988).

Pock, Maximilian A. *Insurance (Survey).* 39 Mercer L.Rev. 241 (1987).

Pock, Maximilian A. *Insurance.* 42 Mercer L.Rev. 259 (1990).

Roth, Suzan E. Comment. *Defining "duty" in the duty-to-settle doctrine as applied to third-party insurance claims in Georgia.* [Southern General Ins. Co. v. Holt, 409 S.E.2d 852 (Ga.Ct.App.1991)] 8 Ga.St.U.L.Rev. 809 (1992).

Setoff — setoff of judgments not to be used to create windfall or reduce contractual obligations of insurance companies. [Pham v. Welter, 542 So.2d 884 (Miss.1989)] 61 Miss.L.J. 193 (1991).

Stueber, Thomas J. *Insurance coverage for patent infringement.* 17 Wm. Mitchell L.Rev. 1055 (1990).

Supreme Court disregards congressional intent that indemnity reinsurance ceding commissions be deductible. [Colonial American Life Ins. Co. v. Commissioner, 109 S.Ct. 2408 (1989)] 39 Am.U.L.Rev. 1267 (1990).

Symposium: Current Issues in Insurance Law. 51 Ohio St.L.J. 773 (1990).

The duty to defend. [Brown v. Lumbermens Mutual Cas. Co., 326 N.C. 387, 390 S.E.2d 150 (1990)] 13 Campbell L.Rev. 141 (1990).

The end of private party enforcement of the Unfair Practices Act against insurance companies. [Moradi-Shalal v. Fireman's Fund Ins.Cos., 758 P.2d 58 (1988)] 20 Pac.L.J. 1373 (1989).

The extraterritorial reach of state insurance holding company statutes and the case for restraint. 24 Cornell Int'l L.J. 165 (1991).

Trimble, John C. *Survey of recent developments in insurance law.* 23 Ind.L.Rev. 431 (1990).

Wagar, Nelson W., III. *Insurance law.* 36 Loy.L.Rev. 867 (1990).

Whether insurers must defend PRP notifications: an expensive issue complicated by conflicting court decisions. 10 N.Ill.U.L.Rev. 579 (1990).

Williams, Cherry D. *A new twist in insurance litigation:* Stowers *suits by excess carriers against primary carriers.* 33 S.Tex.L.Rev. 1 (1992).

Winslow, Donald Arthur. *A note on retrospectively rated insurance and federal income taxation.* 79 Ky.L.J. 195 (1990-91).

Works, Robert. *Back to the future of postloss insurance conditions in Nebraska:* German Insurance Co. v. Fairbank, 32 Neb. 750, 49 N.W. 711 (1891). 70 Neb.L.Rev. 229 (1991).

Liability Insurance
Abraham, Kenneth S. *Making sense of the liability insurance crisis.* 48 Ohio St.L.J. 399 (1987).
Achampong, Francis. *The liability insurance capacity crunch and tort liability reform.* 16 Cap.U.L.Rev. 621 (1987).
A negligent party is underinsured whenever available proceeds from his liability insurance are insufficient to compensate the injured party's actual damages; statutorily provided set-off is to be subtracted from amount of actual damages incurred. [Stracener v. United Services Automobile Ass'n, 777 S.W.2d 378 (Tex.1989)] 32 S.Tex.L.Rev. 153 (1990).
Cleanup costs are not "damages" under a standard liability policy. [Continental Insurance Companies v. Northeastern Pharmaceutical & Chemical Company, 842 F.2d 977 (8th Cir.1988)] 22 J.Marshall L.Rev. 703 (1989).
Comprehensive general liability insurance coverage for CERCLA liabilities: a recommendation for judicial adherence to state canons of insurance contract construction. 61 U.Colo.L.Rev. 407 (1990).
The Court of Appeals brings ambiguity to the interpretation of "professional services." [Duke University v. St. Paul Fire & Marine Insurance Co., 96 N.C.App. 635, 386 S.E.2d 762, disc. rev. denied, 326 N.C. 595, 393 S.E.2d 876 (1990)] 69 N.C.L.Rev. 1644 (1991).
Defending sexual molestation claims under a Comprehensive General Liability policy: issues of scope, occurrence, and expert witness testimony. 39 Drake L.Rev. 477 (1989-1990).
Goundry, Frederick W., III. Casenote. *Insurance — professional liability — insurer must prove actual prejudice to escape liability because of late notice by insured where claims-made policy is ambiguous as to coverage.* [St. Paul Fire & Marine Ins. Co. v. House, 315 Md. 328, 554 A.2d 404 (1989)] 19 U.Balt.L.Rev. 582 (1990).
Incorporation of nonfiduciary liability under ERISA. [Nieto v.Ecker, 845 F.2d 868 (9th Cir.1988)] 73 Minn.L.Rev. 1303 (1989).
Ingram, John Dwight. *The "expected or intended" exclusion clause in liability insurance policies: what should it exclude?* 13 Whittier L.Rev. 713 (1992).
Insurance coverage of CERCLA response costs: the limits of "damages" in comprehensive general liability policies. 16 Ecology L.Q. 755 (1989).
Insurance law: The doctrine of reasonable expectations — "Each person" liability limit of insurance policies encompasses recovery for all claims which arise from one bodily injury including claim for parents' loss of consortium. [Lepic v. Iowa Mutual Insurance Company, 402 N.W.2d 759 (Iowa 1987)] 37 Drake L.Rev. 741 (1987-88).
Insurance law: hazardous waste and the Comprehensive General Liability Insurance policy. 1988 Ann.Surv.Am.L. 461.
James, C.M., III. Student article. *Delaware versus the Federal Reserve Board: differing views on bank holding company involvement in insurance.* 34 How.L.J. 453 (1991).
Mack, Nina Reid and Francis M. Mack. *Constructive claims under the comprehensive general liability policy.* 40 S.C.L.Rev. 1003 (1989).
Mental incapacity and liability insurance exclusionary clauses: the effect of insanity upon intent. 78 Calif.L.Rev. 1027 (1990).
O'Brien, John E. *Panel II: liability and insurance: introduction.* 4 J.L.& Tech. 19 (1989).

Liability Insurance (Continued)

O'Connell, Jeffrey. *A correct diagnosis of the ills of liability insurance — and a false cure: a comment on the reports of the Federal Tort Policy Working Group.* 63 Notre Dame L.Rev. 161 (1988).

Reese-Aldana, Gina. Comment. *The drama of third-party payer tort liability for cost containment decisions: a critical review.* 12 Whittier L.Rev. 591 (1991).

The duty to defend in liability insurance policies: has it gone too far? [Redgrave v. Boston Symphony Orchestra, Inc., 855 F.2d 888 (1st Cir. 1988)] 11 Loy.Ent.L.J. 205 (1991).

The intentional act exclusion clause in the general liability policy — what did you intend? [Breland v. Schilling, 550 So.2d 609 (La.1989)] 65 Tul.L.Rev. 443 (1990).

The liability insurance intentional injury exclusion in cases of child sexual abuse. [N.N. v. Moraine Mutual Ins. Co., 153 Wis.2d 84, 450 N.W.2d 445 (1990)] 1991 Wis.L.Rev. 139.

Wans, Lawrence Alan. Comment. *Washington's judicial invalidation of unambiguous exclusion clauses in multiple causation insurance cases.* 67 Wash.L.Rev. 215 (1992).

When does exhaustion of policy limits terminate an insurer's duty to defend? [Brown v. Lumbermens Mutual Casualty Co., 326 N.C. 387, 390 S.E.2d 150 (1990)] 69 N.C.L.Rev. 1660 (1991).

Life Insurance

Achampong, Francis. *Death from autoerotic asphyxiation and the double indemnity clause in life insurance policies: the latest round in accidental death litigation.* 21 Akron L.Rev. 191 (1987).

Bennett, Kathryn R. Case note. *Distribution of life insurance proceeds when the primary beneficiary is disqualified.* [Spencer v. Floyd, 30 Ark.App. 230, 785 S.W.2d 60 (1990)] 45 Ark.L.Rev. 213 (1992).

Kuzemczak, Jerry. *Legislative survey. New Jersey Assembly Bill 5051 — a bill to establish New Jersey Life and Health Insurance Guaranty Association Fund; a fund to protect policyholders in the event that the insurance company becomes impaired or insolvent; and to provide for related matters — N.J.Stat.Ann.§§ 17B: 32A-1 to -19 (West 1991)* 16 Seton Hall Legis.J. 849 (1992).

The Louisiana abuse of rights doctrine. [Massachusetts Mutual Life Insurance Co. v. Nails, 549 So.2d 826 (La.1989)] 64 Tul.L.Rev. 1295 (1990).

Rice, Ann E. Recent decision. *Insurance — the U.S. Court of Appeals for the Third Circuit held that, under Pennsylvania law, the phrase "on authorized business" in a life insurance policy was ambiguous and could reasonably be interpreted to apply to an employee who was murdered by her estranged husband after she had completed her work shift but before she had left her employer's premises.* [McMillan v. State Mutual Life Assurance Co. of Am., 992 F.2d 1073 (3d Cir.1990)] 30 Duq.L.Rev. 427 (1991).

Uniform Probate Code Section 2-202: A proposal to include life insurance assets within the augmented estate. 74 Cornell L.Rev. 511 (1989).

Malpractice Insurance

Caps, "crisis," and constitutionality—evaluating the 1986 Kansas medical malpractice legislation. 35 Kan.L.Rev. 763 (1987).

Challenging medical malpractice damage award caps on Seventh Amendment grounds: attacks in search of a rationale. 59 U.Cin.L.Rev. 213 (1990).

Chapman, Hon. Charles and Robert Robertson. *To boldly go where no one has gone before: the final frontier of Illinois expert witness testimony in medical malpractice cases.* 21 Loy.U.Chi.L.J. 757 (1990).

Educational malpractice: a cause of action that failed to pass the test. 90 W.Va.L.Rev. 499 (1988).

Following the doctor's orders — caps on noneconomic damages in medical malpractice cases. 22 Rutgers L.J. 173 (1990).

Griffith, Richard L. and Jordan M. Parker. *With malice toward none: the metamorphosis of statutory and common law protections for physicians and hospitals in negligent credentialing litigation.* 22 Tex.Tech.L.Rev. 157 (1991).

Hammarlund, John T. Note. *Community health centers and rising malpractice premiums: an overview of the community health center program and proposed solutions to the malpractice insurance rate crisis.* 1 Cornell J.L.Pub.Pol'y 135 (1992).

Kinney, Eleanor D. and William P. Grofein. *Indiana's malpractice system: no-fault by accident?* 54 Law & Contemp.Probs. 169 (Winter 1991).

Koffler, Joseph H. *Legal malpractice damages in a trial within a trial—a critical analysis of unique concepts: areas of unconscionability.* 73 Marq.L.Rev. 40 (1989).

Lawyers beware: Texas adopts the discovery rule for legal malpractice. [Willis v. Maverick, 760 S.W.2d 642 (Tex.1988)] 20 Tex.Tech.L.Rev. 1279 (1989).

Louisiana Supreme Court avoids deciding constitutionality of malpractice recovery limit. [Williams v. Kushner, 549 So.2d 294 (La.1989, per curiam)] 64 Tul.L.Rev. 1329 (1990).

Luft, Harold S., Patricia P. Katz, and Douglas G. Pinney. *Risk factors for hospital malpractice exposure: implications for managers and insurers.* 54 Law & Contemp.Probs. 43 (Spring 1991).

Medical malpractice—the constitutionality of statutory caps on noneconomic damages. [Fein v. Permanente Medical Group, 38 Cal.3d 137, 695 P.2d 665, 211 Cal. Rptr. 368 (1985)] 11 S.Ill.U.L.J. 1269 (1987).

Minto, Robert W. Jr. and Marcia D. Morton. *The anatomy of legal malpractice insurance: a comparative view.* 64 N.D.L.Rev. 547 (1988).

Nye, David J., Donald G. Gifford, Bernard L. Webb, and Marvin A. Dewar. *The causes of the medical malpractice crisis: an analysis of claims data and insurance company finances.* 76 Geo.L.J. 1495 (1988).

Rolph, John E. *Merit ratings for physicians' malpractice premiums: only a modest deterrent.* 54 Law & Contemp.Probs. 65 (Spring 1991).

Southwick, Lawrence, Jr. and Gary J. Young. *Doctors, lawyers, and malpractice insurance: is physician discipline or legal restrictions the answer?* 12 Law & Pol'y 155 (1990).

Malpractice Insurance (Continued)

Stilling, William J. Comment. *Who's in charge: the doctor or the dollar? Assessing the relative liability of third party payors and doctors after Wickline and Wilson.* 18 J.Contemp.L. 285 (1992).

The medical malpractice crisis: will no-fault cure the disease? 9 U.Haw.L.Rev. 241 (1987).

Marine Insurance

Admiralty law: Carriage of Goods by the Sea Act—Quasi-deviation. [Sedco, Inc. v. M/V Strathewe, 800 F.2d 27 (2d.Cir.1986)] 9 N.Y.L.Sch.J.Int'l & Comp.L. 435 (1988).

Admiralty law — the Federal Maritime Lien Act — extending maritime lien to insurance creditors. [Equilease Corp. v. M/V Sampson, 793 F.2d 598 (5th Cir.1986)] 11 Suffolk Transnat'l L.J. 127 (1987).

Admiralty Law Institute Symposium: Marine Insurance. 66 Tul.L.Rev. 257 (1991).

Brice, Geoffrey. Q.C. *Unexplained losses in marine insurance.* 16 Tul.Mar.L.J. 105 (1991).

Milikan, Jess B. *Selected coverage problems in marine liability insurance.* 3 U.S.F.Mar.L.J. 173 (1990/91).

Reeder, Chris. *Maritime lien status for unpaid hull or liability insurance premiums: whether the nonpayment of hull and protection and indemnity insurance premiums should create a United States maritime lien against the insured vessel in favor of the insurer.* 15 Tul.Mar.L.J. 285 (1991).

Ronneberg, Norman J., Jr. *An introduction to the protection and indemnity clubs and the marine insurance they provide.* 3 U.S.F.Mar.L.J. 1 (1990/91).

Wilson, Cheryl L. Comment. *The direct action statute and ocean marine insurance: can protection and indemnity insurers convince the courts "to manacle an old and beaten enemy?"* 37 Loy.L.Rev. 121 (1991).

Municipal Liability

Barger, Richards D. and Eugene E. Mueller. *"Speaking with one voice": constitutional failure of state insurance government ownership statutes.* 26 U.S.F.L.Rev. 657 (1992).

Coffey, Tamura D. Comment. *Waiving local government immunity in North Carolina: risk management programs are insurance.* 27 Wake Forest L.Rev. 709 (1992).

A foreseeability-based standard for the determination of municipal liability under section 1983. 28 B.C.L.Rev. 937 (1987).

Rynard, Thomas W. *The local government as insured or insurer: some new risk management alternatives.* 20 Urb.Law. 103 (1988).

Pollution Liability

Abraham, Kenneth S. *Environmental liability and the limits of insurance.* 88 Colum.L.Rev. 942 (1988).

Anderson, Eugene R., Sharon A. Merkle, and Natalia Kisseleff. *Liability insurance coverage for pollution claims.* 12 U.Haw.L.Rev. 83 (1990).

Pollution Liability (Continued)

Are costs to clean up — cleanup costs? Federal Courts refuse to agree on whether toxic waste cleanup costs are "damages" under Missouri law. [Jones Truck Lines v. Transport Ins. Co., No. 88-5723 (E.D.Pa.May 10, 1989)] 55 Mo.L.Rev. 591 (1990).

Avery, Daniel R. *Massachusetts follows the judicial trend: a reasoned and proper approach to determine recovery for environmental cleanup costs under comprehensive general liability insurance policies.* 24 Suffolk U.L.Rev. 891 (1990).

Ballard, Nancer and Peter M. Manus. *Clearing muddy waters:anatomy of the Comprehensive General Liability pollution exclusion.* 75 Cornell L.Rev. 619 (1990).

Barnhill, Kathryn E. *Trustees' reasonable expectations of coverage for environmental liability: old insurance for new problems.* 39 Drake L.Rev. 843 (1989-1990).

Calnan, Alan. *The insurance exclusionary rule revisited: are reports of its demise exaggerated?* 52 Ohio St.L.J. 1177 (1991).

Cleanup costs are not "damages" under a standard liability policy. [Continental Insurance Companies v. Northeastern Pharmaceutical & Chemical Company, 842 F.2d 977 (8th Cir.1988)] 22 J.Marshall L.Rev. 703 (1989).

Closing Pandora's box: environmental-quality insurance as an alternative to broadening CERCLA liability. 16 Wm.Mitchell L.Rev. 1041 (1990).

Coverage for gradual pollution under the comprehensive general liability policy in Georgia. [Clausen v. Aetna Casualty & Surety Co., 259 Ga. 333, 380 S.E.2d 686 (1989)] 41 Mercer L.Rev. 1041 (1990).

Environmental cleanup costs and insurance: seeking a solution. 24 Ga.L.Rev. 705 (1990).

Environmental law: environmental cleanup costs are "damages" under Oklahoma insurance law. [Nat'l Indem. Co. v. U.S. Pollution Control, Inc., 717 F.Supp. 765 (W.D.Okla.1989)] 43 Okla.L.Rev. 705 (1990).

Excluding the pollution exclusion. [City of Johnstown, New York v. Bankers Standard Ins. Co., 877 F.2d 1146 (2d Cir.1989)] 38 Wash.U.J.Urb.& Contemp.L. 287 (1990).

Insurance coverage for hazardous waste cleanup: the Comprehensive General Liability Insurance policy defined. 39 Cath.U.L.Rev. 195 (1989).

Insurance coverage for pollution liability in the United States and the United Kingdom: covering troubled waters. 23 Case W.Res.J.Int'l L. 109 (1991).

Insurance coverage of CERCLA response costs: the limits of "damages" in comprehensive general liability policies. 16 Ecology L.Q. 755 (1989).

Jackson, Brooke. *Liability insurance for pollution claims: avoiding a litigation wasteland.* 26 Tulsa L.J. 209 (1990).

Kalis, Peter J. and Thomas M. Reiter. *Forum non conveniens: a case management tool for comprehensive environmental insurance coverage actions?* 92 W.Va.L.Rev. 391 (1989-90).

Mielenhausen, Thomas C. *Insurance coverage for environmental and toxic tort claims.* 17 Wm.Mitchell L.Rev. 945 (1991).

Miller, David W. *Whether governmentally compelled cleanup costs constitute "damages" under CGL policies: the nationwide environmental liability dilemma and a California model for its resolution.* 16 Colum.J.Envtl.L. 73 (1991).

Pollution Liability (Continued)

Mosher, Joel R. *Insurance issues in hazardous waste cases.* 39 Drake L.Rev. 881 (1989-1990).

Murphy, Sharon M. Note. *The "sudden and accidental" exception to the pollution exclusion clause in comprehensive general liability insurance policies: the Gordian Knot of environmental liability.* 45 Vand.L.Rev. 161 (1992).

Myers, Timothy J. Case note. *Insurance coverage for CERCLA cleanup costs: resolving the intercircuit conflict.* 45 Ark.L.Rev. 747 (1992).

Pasich, Kirk A. *The breadth of insurance coverage for environmental claims.* 52 Ohio St.L.J. 1131 (1991).

Passing the big bucks: contractual transfers of liability between potentially responsible parties under CERCLA. 75 Minn.L.Rev. 1571 (1991).

Paying the costs of hazardous waste pollution: why is the insurance industry raising such a stink? 1991 U.Ill.L.Rev. 173.

Raskoff, Mark C. *Arguments advanced by insureds for coverage of environmental claims.* 22 Pac.L.J. 771 (1991).

Ribner, Seth A. *Modern environmental insurance law: "sudden and accidental."* 63 St.John's L.Rev. 755 (1989).

Ritchie, Steven L. Case note. *Do Comprehensive General Liability Insurance policies cover bodily injury and property damage caused by hazardous waste disposal?* [Montrose Chemical Corp. of California v. Admiral Ins. Co., 3 Cal.App.4th 1511, 5 Cal.Rptr.2d 358, Cal.Ct.App., 2d Dist., (Feb. 27, 1992)] 8 Santa Clara Computer & High Tech.L.J. 507 (1992).

Shokes, Deane S. Note. *Insurers liable for environmental response costs.* [AIU Ins. Co. v. Supreior Court, 51 Cal.3d 807, 799 P.2d 1253, 274 Cal.Rptr. 820 (1990)] 28 San Diego L.Rev. 711 (1991).

Stanzler, Jordan S. and Charles A. Yuen. *Coverage for environmental cleanup costs: history of the word "damages" in the standard form Comprehensive General Liability Policy.* 1990 Colum.Bus.L.Rev. 449.

The pollution exclusion clause: in favor of the insurer or the insured? [Just v. Land Reclamation, Ltd., 155 Wis.2d 737, 456 N.W.2d 570 (1990)] 40 Wash.U.J.Urb.& Contemp.L. 209 (1991).

Zurzolo, Tracy L. Recent decision. *Environmental law — insurers obligated to provide coverage for gradual, unintentional pollution discharge.* [New Castle County v. Hartford Accident & Indemnity Co., 933 F.2d 1162, 3d Cir. (1991)] 65 Temp.L.Rev. 1081 (1992).

Products Liability

Abraham, Kenneth S. *Products liability law and insurance profitability.* 19 J.Legal Stud. 837 (1989).

Attanasio, John B. *The principle of aggregate autonomy and the Calabresian approach to products liability.* 74 Va.L.Rev. 677 (1988).

Babcock, Charles W. *Could we alone have this? Comparative legal analysis of product liability law and the case for modest reform.* 10 Loy.L.A. Int'l & Comp.L.J. 321 (1988).

Campbell, Richard P. *The protective order in products liability litigation: safeguard or misnomer?* 31 B.C.L.Rev. 771 (1990).

Custom's proper role in strict products liability actions based on design defect. 38 UCLA L.Rev. 439 (1990).

Products Liability (Continued)

Cortese, Alfred W., Jr. and Kathleen L. Blaner. *The anti-competitive impact of U.S. product liability laws: are foreign businesses beating us at our own game?* 9 J.L.& Com. 167 (1989).

Drug product liability and health care delivery systems. 40 Stan.L.Rev. 989 (1988).

The evolution of useful life statutes in the products liability reform effort. 1989 Duke L.J. 1689.

Jones, William K. *Strict liability for hazardous enterprise.* 92 Colum.L.Rev. 1705 (1992).

Liability of alcoholic beverage manufacturers: no longer a pink elephant. 31 Wm.& Mary L.Rev. 157 (1989).

Priest, George L. *Can absolute manufacturer liability be defended?* 9 Yale J. on Reg. 237 (1992).

Viscusi, W. Kip. *The performance of liability insurance in states with different products-liability statutes.* 19 J.Legal Stud. 809 (1990).

When the smoke clears, where will Louisiana stand? An analysis of Louisiana products liability doctrine in tobacco litigation. 65 Tul.L.Rev. 417 (1990).

Punitive Damages

Are excessive punitive damages unconstitutional in Georgia?: This question and more in ... [Colonial Pipeline Co. v. Brown, 258 Ga.115, 365 S.E.2d 827 (1988)] 6 Ga.St.U.L.Rev. 85 (1989).

Boyle, John D. and Michael R. O'Malley. *Insurance coverage for punitive damages and intentional conduct in Massachusetts.* 25 New Eng.L.Rev. 827 (1991).

Current constitutional challenges to the administration of punitive damages. 14 Okla.City U.L.Rev. 421 (1989).

Durrant, Sean Peterson. Case note. *Constitutional law — The Color of Money: does the excessive fines clause impose a limit of proportionality on the amount of punitive damages assessed in a civil action between private parties?* [Browning-Ferris Indus. of Vermont, Inc. v. Kelco Disposal, Inc., 109 S.Ct. 2902 (1989)] 26 Land & Water L.Rev. 803 (1991).

Giesel, Grace M. *The knowledge of insurers and the posture of the parties in the determination of the insurability of punitive damages.* 39 U.Kan.L.Rev. 355 (1991).

Hart J. Mark. *The constitutionality of punitive damages:* Pacific Mutual Life Ins. Co. v. Haslip. 21 Cumb.L.Rev. 585 (1990-1991).

Imposition of punitive damages for an insurer's tortious breach of contract. 19 Conn.L.Rev. 329 (1987).

Maya, John A. Note. *Punitive damages and the mass tort: an insurance alternative to the consequences of multiple liability.* 42 Syracuse L.Rev. 1241 (1992).

Statutory interpretation: should Oklahoma's new limits on punitive damages operate retrospectively? 40 Okla.L.Rev. 455 (1987).

Williams, David H. Response. *What Dan Quayle doesn't know about punitive damages.* 14 U.Ark.Little Rock L.J. 725 (1992).

Settlement

Good faith settlements: the inequitable result of the evolving definition of "equity." 22 Cal.W.L.Rev. 362 (1986).

Hoyt, Hon. Kenneth M. *How settlements affect nonsettling tortfeasors' liability: from no contribution to equitable apportionment.* 17 Tex.Tech.L.Rev. 775 (1986).

Negligent failure of an insurer to settle a claim — New Mexico does not recognize this cause of action. [Ambassador Ins. Co. v. St. Paul Fire & Marine Ins. Co., 690 P.2d 1022 (1984)] 17 N.M.L.Rev. 197 (1987).

Personal injury settlement releases are avoidable on grounds of mutual mistake. [Williams v. Glash, 789 S.W.2d 261 (Tex.1990)] 22 Tex.Tech.L.Rev. 309 (1990).

Stacking

The death of basic no-fault stacking in Hawaii. [Rana v. Bishop Ins. of Hawaii, 713 P.2d 1363 (1985)] 9 U.Haw.L.Rev. 321 (1987).

Stacking up to full recovery. 35 Loy.L.Rev. 409 (1989).

Subrogation

Entman, June F. *More reasons for abolishing Federal Rule of Civil Procedure 17(a): the problem of the proper plaintiff and insurance subrogation.* 68 N.C.L.Rev. 893 (1990).

"In good hands" or "bad faith?" An insurer's failure to waive subrogation rights in Pennsylvania underinsured motorist cases. 91 Dick.L.Rev. 981 (1987).

Insurance law — underinsurance claims — subrogation and consent to settle clauses in underinsured motorist endorsement are invalid as written. [Longworth v. Van Houten, 223 N.J.Super. 174, 538 A.2d 414 (App.Div.1988)] 21 Rutgers L.J. 213 (1989).

Kircher, John J. *Insurer subrogation in Wisconsin: the good hands (of a neighbor) in another's shoes.* 71 Marq.L.Rev. 33 (1987).

Roessler, Norma. Recent decision. *Gilding the lily in insurance subrogation cases?* [Powell v. Blue Cross & Blue Shield, 581 So.2d 772 (Ala.1990)] 43 Ala.L.Rev. 169 (1991).

The real party under Rule 17(a): the loan receipt and insurers' subrogation revisited. 74 Minn.L.Rev. 1107 (1990).

Tort Law

A gap in the North Carolina motor vehicle liability policy statute: Joint tortfeasors — When and how does underinsured motorist coverage apply? 12 Campbell L.Rev. 99 (1989).

Barrett, Sidney R., Jr. *Recovery of economic loss in tort for construction defects: a critical analysis.* 40 S.C.L.Rev. 891 (1989).

Compensation, fairness, and the costs of accidents — should Pennsylvania's Legislature modify or abrogate the rule of joint and several liability among concurrently negligent tortfeasors? 91 Dick.L.Rev. 947 (1987).

Crowe, William L., Sr. *The anatomy of a tort — part 5 — apportionment, contribution, and indemnity among multiple parties in the area of damages — a second reader.* 35 Loy.L.Rev. 351 (1989).

Giesel, Grace M. *A proposal for a tort remedy for insureds against brokers, excess insurers, reinsurers, and the state.* 52 Ohio St.L.J. 1075 (1991).

Tort Law (Continued)

Greer, Edward. *Insurance coverage and alternative funds in toxic tort litigation.* 2 J.Envtl.L.& Litigation 107 (1987).

Insurance law: The doctrine of reasonable expectations — "Each person" liability limits of insurance policies encompasses recovery for all claims which arise from one bodily injury including claim for parents' loss of consortium. [Lepic v. Iowa Mutual Insurance Company, 402 N.W. 2d 759 (Iowa 1987)] 37 Drake L.Rev. 741 (1987-88).

Little, Joseph W. *Eliminating the fallacies of comparative negligence and proportional liability.* 41 Ala.L.Rev. 13 (1989).

Miller, Richard S. and Geoffrey K. S. Komeya. *Tort and insurance "reform" in common law court.* 14 U.Haw.L.Rev. 55 (1992).

Miraballes, Susana B. Note. *The environment tort victim: will Connecticut pave the road to recovery?* 12 Bridgeport L.Rev. 759 (1992).

O'Connor, Daniel S. Note. *Torts — wrongful discharge — Maryland limits the scope of the wrongful discharge tort where statutory civil remedies are available.* [Makovi v. Sherwin-Williams Co., 316 Ms. 603, 561 A.2d 179 (1989)] 20 U.Balt.L.Rev. 290 (1990).

Priest, George L. *The current insurance crisis and modern tort law.* 96 Yale L.J. 1521 (1987).

Priest, George L. *The Monsanto Lectures: modern tort law and its reform.* 22 Val.U.L.Rev. 1 (1987).

Rudolph, Wallace M. *The tort crisis: causes, solutions and the Constitution.* 11 U.Puget Sound L.Rev. 659 (1988).

Rumors of crisis: considering the insurance crisis and tort reform in an information vacuum. 37 Emory L.J. 401 (1988).

Schwartz, Gary T. *The ethics and the economics of tort liability insurance.* 75 Cornell L.Rev. 313 (1990).

Schwartz, Gary T. *A proposal for tort reform: reformulating uninsured motorist plans.* 48 Ohio St.L.J. 419 (1987).

Thompson, Melissa Moore. Comment. *Causal inference in epidemiology: implications for toxic tort litigation.* 71 N.C.L.Rev. 247 (1992).

Tort liability of third party payors. [Wilson v. Blue Cross of Southern California, 222 Cal.App.3d 660, 271 Cal.Rptr. 876 (1990)] 24 Creighton L.Rev. 1399 (1991).

Torts — contract — joint tortfeasor pursues a breach of warranty cross-claim: what is the proper measure of damages? [Centric Corp. v. Drake Building Corp., 726 P.2d 1047 (1986)] 23 Land & Water L.Rev. 629 (1988).

Vetri, Dominick. *The integration of tort law reforms and liability insurance ratemaking in the New Age.* 66 Or.L.Rev. 277 (1987).

Zillman, Donald N. *Congress, courts and government tort liability: Reflections on the discretionary function exception to the Federal Tort Claims Act.* 1989 Utah L.Rev. 687 (1989).

Underinsured/Uninsured Motorist Coverage

Arbitration awards in uninsured and underinsured motorist insurance provisions: which public policy to apply? [Mendes v. Automobile Ins. Co. of Hartford, 212 Conn. 652, 563 A.2d 695 (1989)] 1990 J.Dispute Resolution 431.

Underinsured/Uninsured Motorist Coverage (Continued)
California's collateral source rule and plaintiff's receipt of uninsured motorist benefits. 37 Hastings L.J. 667 (1986).
Douglass, John G. and Francis E. Telegadas. *Stacking of uninsured and underinsured motor vehicle coverages.* 24 U.Rich.L.Rev. 87 (1989).
"In good hands" or "bad faith?" An insurer's failure to waive subrogation rights in Pennsylvania underinsured motorist cases. 91 Dick.L.Rev. 981 (1987).
A gap in the North Carolina motor vehicle liability policy statute: Joint tortfeasors — When and how does underinsured motorist coverage apply? 12 Campbell L.Rev. 99 (1989).
Huelsmann, Martin J. and William G. Knoebel. *Underinsured motorists: an evolving insurance concern.* 17 N.Ky.L.Rev. 417 (1990).
Insurance — has the Tennessee Supreme Court misinterpreted the legislative intent of the uninsured motorist statutes? [Dockins v. Balboa Ins. Co., 764 S.W.2d 529 (Tenn.1989)] 20 Mem.St.U.L.Rev. 683 (1990).
Interpreting the recently enacted California underinsurance provisions of the Uninsured Motorist Statute. 14 Pepperdine L.Rev. 691 (1987).
Lamson, Stephen. *The impact of the Federal Arbitration Act and the McCarran-Ferguson Act on uninsured motorist arbitration.* 19 Conn.L.Rev. 241 (1987).
Plunkett, Gary D. *Unknown effects of Wood v. Shepard on uninsured and underinsured motorist coverage in Ohio.* 39 Clev.St.L.Rev. 49 (1991).
Unraveling the underinsured motorist web: Ohio underinsured motorist coverage. 20 Akron L.Rev. 749 (1987).
Watts, William W. *Uninsured motorist coverage exclusions: a chronicle of the Alabama decisions.* 20 Cumb.L.Rev. 267 (1989-1990).

Workers' Compensation
Altman, Leslie. Jay Benanav, Steve Keefe and Joan Volz. *Minnesota's workers' compensation scheme: the effects and effectiveness of the 1983 amendments.* 13 Wm. Mitchell L.Rev. 843 (1987).
Ashcraft, William O. and Anita M. Alessandra. *A review of the new Texas workers' compensation system.* 21 Tex.Tech L.Rev. 609 (1990).
Bagley, H. Michael, Daniel C. Kniffen and John G. Blackmon, Jr. *Workers' compensation.* 41 Mercer L.Rev. 429 (1989).
Byrne, D. Andrew and Ted C. Raynor. *Tennessee workers' compensation — where is the proper venue?* 20 Mem.St.U.L.Rev. 189 (1990).
Campbell, Elizabeth. *Waiver of rights and release from liability in worker's compensation redemption proceedings under § 686 of the Michigan Act.* 1990 Det.C.L.Rev. 1.
Eligibility for workers' compensation in cases of nontraumatic mental injury: the development of the unusual stress test in Wisconsin. 1987 Wis.L.Rev. 363.
An expansive interpretation of Louisiana worker's compensation law. [Sparks v. Tulane Medical Center Hosp. & Clinic, 546 So.2d 138 (La.1989)] 64 Tul.L.Rev. 970 (1990).
Houses and wages: an increase in workers' compensation recovery (Survey). [Derebery v. Pitt County Fire Marshall, 347 S.E.2d 814 (1986)] 65 N.C.L.Rev. 1499 (1987).

Workers' Compensation (Continued)
Mental/mental claims under the Louisiana Worker's Compensation Act after Sparks v. Tulane Medical Center Hospital and Clinic: a legislative death knell? [Sparks v. Tulane Medical Center Hospital and Clinic, 546 So.2d 138 (La.1989)] 50 La.L.Rev. 609 (1990).

Potter, Robert R., and Mark J. Goodman. *Workers' compensation (Survey).* 39 Mercer L.Rev. 377 (1987).

Sanders, Michael D. and Jeffrey Nyquist. *Workers' compensation.* 37 Wayne L.Rev. 1227 (1991).

Sullivan, J. Thomas. *Retaliatory firings: the remedy under the Texas Workers' Compensation Act.* 19 Tex.Tech.L.Rev. 85 (1988).

The first step toward limiting worker's compensation liens on third-party tort recoveries. [Dietrick v. Kemper Ins. Co., 76 N.Y.2d 248, 556 N.E.2d 1108, 557 N.Y.S.2d 301 (1990)] 6 St.John's J.Legal Comment. 201 (1990).

Vance, Ruth C. *Recent developments in workers' compensation.* 24 Ind.L.Rev. 975 (1991).

Vance, Ruth C. *Vocational rehabilitation benefits under Indiana's workers' compensation law.* 24 Val.U.L.Rev. 255 (1990).

Workers' compensation — employee compensated for injuries sustained while en route to treatment for work-related injury. [McElory's Case, 494 N.E.2d 1 (1986)] 21 Suffolk U.L.Rev. 344 (1987).

Workers' compensation reform in Oklahoma: exclusion of injuries sustained at recreational or social events. 26 Tulsa L.J. 405 (1991).

APPENDIX C

SUBJECT MATTER TABLE OF INSURANCE CASES DECIDED BY THE UNITED STATES SUPREME COURT

Agents
Osborn v. Ozlin, 310 U.S. 53, 60 S.Ct. 758, 84 L.Ed. 1074 (1940).

Antitrust
McLain v. Real Estate Board of New Orleans, 444 U.S. 232, 100 S.Ct. 502, 62 L.Ed.2d 441 (1980).

Arson Investigation
Michigan v. Clifford, 464 U.S. 287, 104 S.Ct. 641, 78 L.Ed.2d 477 (1984).
Russello v. U.S., 464 U.S. 16, 104 S.Ct. 296, 78 L.Ed.2d 17 (1983).

Automobile Insurance
Allstate Ins. Co. v. Hague, 449 U.S. 302, 101 S.Ct. 633, 66 L.Ed.2d 521 (1981).
California State Automobile Ass'n Inter-Insurance Bureau v. Maloney, 341 U.S. 105, 71 S.Ct. 601, 95 L.Ed. 788 (1951).
State Farm Mut. Auto. Ins. Co. v. Coughran, 303 U.S. 485, 58 S.Ct. 670, 82 L.Ed. 970 (1938).

Carriers
Aschenbrenner v. U.S. Fidelity & Guar. Co., 292 U.S. 80, 54 S.Ct. 590, 78 L.Ed. 1137 (1934).

Conflict of Laws
Boseman v. Connecticut General Life Ins. Co., 301 U.S. 196, 57 S.Ct. 686, 81 L.Ed. 1036 (1937).

Due Process of Law
Iowa Mut. Ins. Co. v. LaPlante, 480 U.S. 9, 107 S.Ct. 971, 94 L.Ed.2d 10 (1987).
State Board of Ins. v. Todd Shipyards Corp., 370 U.S. 451, 82 S.Ct. 1380, 8 L.Ed.2d 620 (1962).
McGee v. International Life Ins. Co., 355 U.S. 220, 78 S.Ct. 199, 2 L.Ed.2d 223 (1958).
State Farm Mut. Auto. Ins. Co. v. Duel, 324 U.S. 154, 65 S.Ct. 573, 89 L.Ed. 812 (1945).

ERISA
FMC Corp. v. Holliday, 111 S.Ct. 403, 112 L.Ed.2d 356 (1990).
Firestone Tire and Rubber Co. v. Bruch, 489 U.S. 101, 109 S.Ct. 948, 103 L.Ed.2d 80 (1989).
Mead Corp. v. Tilley, 490 U.S. 714, 109 S.Ct. 2156, 104 L.Ed.2d 796 (1989).

Metropolitan Life Ins. Co. v. Taylor, 481 U.S. 58, 107 S.Ct. 1542, 95 L.Ed.2d 55 (1987).

Pilot Life Ins. Co. v. Dedeaux, 481 U.S. 41, 107 S.Ct. 1549, 95 L.Ed.2d 39 (1987).

Massachusetts Mut. Life Ins. Co. v. Russell, 473 U.S. 134, 105 S.Ct. 3085, 87 L.Ed.2d 96 (1985).

Nachman Corp. v. Pension Benefit Guar. Corp., 446 U.S. 359, 100 S.Ct. 1723, 64 L.Ed.2d 354 (1980).

Equal Protection

Metropolitan Life Ins. Co. v. Ward, 470 U.S. 869, 105 S.Ct. 1676, 84 L.Ed.2d 751 (1985).

Watson v. Employers Liability Assur. Corp., 348 U.S. 66, 75 S.Ct. 166, 99 L.Ed. 74 (1954).

Lincoln Nat'l Life Ins. Co. v. Read, 325 U.S. 673, 65 S.Ct. 1220, 89 L.Ed. 1861 (1945).

Exclusions

Travelers' Protective Ass'n of America v. Prinsen, 291 U.S. 576, 54 S.Ct. 502, 78 L.Ed 999 (1934).

St. Paul Fire & Marine Ins. Co. v. Bachman, 285 U.S. 112, 52 S.Ct. 270, 76 L.Ed 648 (1932).

Federal Regulation

District of Columbia v. Greater Washington Board of Trade, 113 S.Ct. 580 (1992).

U.S. v. South-Eastern Underwriters Ass'n, 322 U.S. 533, 64 S.Ct. 1162, 88 L.Ed. 1440 (1944).

Fire Insurance

Central Tablet Mfg. Co. v. U.S., 417 U.S. 673, 94 S.Ct. 2516, 41 L.Ed.2d 398 (1974).

Group Health Plans

Metropolitan Life Ins. Co. v. Massachusetts, 471 U.S. 724, 105 S.Ct. 2380, 85 L.Ed.2d 728 (1985).

Allis-Chalmers Corp. v. Lueck, 471 U.S. 202, 105 S.Ct. 1904, 85 L.Ed.2d 206 (1985).

Haynes v. U.S., 353 U.S. 81, 77 S.Ct. 649, 1 L.Ed.2d 671 (1957).

Insurable Interests

U.S. v. Supplee-Biddle Hardware Co., 265 U.S. 189, 44 S.Ct. 546, 68 L.Ed. 970 (1924).

"Insurance" Defined

Union Labor Life Ins. Co. v. Pireno, 458 U.S. 119, 102 S.Ct. 3002, 73 L.Ed.2d 647 (1982).

Group Life & Health Ins. Co. v. Royal Drug Co., 440 U.S. 205, 99 S.Ct. 1067, 59 L.Ed.2d 261 (1979).

S.E.C. v. Variable Annuity Life Ins. Co., 359 U.S. 65, 79 S.Ct. 618, 3 L.Ed.2d 640 (1959).

Judicial Misconduct
Aetna Life Ins. Co. v. Lavoie, 475 U.S. 813, 106 S.Ct. 1580, 89 L.Ed.2d 823 (1986).

Jurisdiction
Northbrook National Ins. Co. v. Brewer, 493 U.S. 6, 110 S.Ct. 297, 107 L.Ed.2d 223 (1989).
Underwriters Nat'l Assur. Co. v. North Carolina Life & Accident & Health Ins. Guar. Ass'n, 455 U.S. 691, 102 S.Ct. 1357, 71 L.Ed.2d 558 (1982).
Rush v. Savchuk, 444 U.S. 320, 100 S.Ct. 571, 62 L.Ed.2d 516 (1980).
Clay v. Sun Ins. Office, 377 U.S. 179, 84 S.Ct. 1197, 12 L.Ed.2d 229 (1964).

Labor Disputes/Picketing
N.L.R.B. v. Retail Store Employees Union, 447 U.S. 607, 100 S.Ct. 2372, 65 L.Ed.2d 377 (1980).

Life Insurance
Dick v. New York Life Ins. Co., 359 U.S. 437, 79 S.Ct. 921, 3 L.Ed.2d 935 (1958).
U.S. v. Bess, 357 U.S. 51, 78 S.Ct. 1054, 2 L.Ed.2d 1135 (1958).
Daniel v. Family Sec. Life Ins. Co., 336 U.S. 220, 69 S.Ct. 550, 93 L.Ed. 632 (1949).
Williams v. Union Cent. Life Ins. Co., 291 U.S. 170, 54 S.Ct. 348, 78 L.Ed. 711 (1934).

Marine Insurance
Czaplicki v. The Hoegh Silvercloud, 351 U.S. 525, 76 S.Ct. 946, 100 L.Ed. 1387 (1956).
Wilburn Boat Co. v. Fireman's Fund Ins. Co., 348 U.S. 310, 75 S.Ct. 368, 99 L.Ed. 337 (1955).
Maryland Cas. Co. v. Cushing, 347 U.S. 409, 74 S.Ct. 608, 98 L.Ed. 806 (1954).
Calmar S.S. Corp. v. Scott, 345 U.S. 427, 73 S.Ct. 739, 97 L.Ed. 1125 (1953).
Lanasa Fruit Steamship & Importing Co. v. Universal Ins. Co., 302 U.S. 556, 58 S.Ct. 371, 82 L.Ed. 422 (1938).
Great Lakes Transit Corp. v. Interstate S.S. Co., 301 U.S. 646, 57 S.Ct. 915, 81 L.Ed. 1318 (1937).
Standard Marine Ins. Co. v. Scottish Met. Assur. Co., 283 U.S. 284, 51 S.Ct. 371, 75 L.Ed. 1037 (1931).
Gulf Refining Co. v. Atlantic Mut. Ins. Co., 279 U.S. 708, 49 S.Ct. 439, 73 L.Ed. 914 (1929).

McCarran-Ferguson Act
S.E.C. v. Nat'l Securities, 393 U.S. 453, 89 S.Ct. 564, 21 L.Ed.2d 668 (1969).
Robertson v. California, 328 U.S. 440, 66 S.Ct. 1160, 90 L.Ed. 1366 (1946).
Prudential Ins. Co. v. Benjamin, 328 U.S. 408, 66 S.Ct. 1142, 90 L.Ed. 1342 (1946).

Medicare
U.S. v. Erika, Inc., 456 U.S. 201, 102 S.Ct. 1650, 72 L.Ed.2d 12 (1982).

Premiums
Lyon v. Mut. Benefit Health & Accident Ass'n, 305 U.S. 484, 59 S.Ct. 297, 83 L.Ed. 303 (1939).

Punitive Damages
Pacific Mutual Life Ins. Co. v. Haslip, 111 S.Ct. 1032, 113 L.Ed.2d 1 (1991).
Aetna Life Ins. Co. v. Lavoie, 475 U.S. 813, 106 S.Ct. 1580, 89 L.Ed.2d 823 (1986).

Retaliatory Taxes
Western & Southern Life Ins. Co. v. State Board of Equalization of California, 451 U.S. 648, 101 S.Ct. 2070, 68 L.Ed.2d 514 (1981).

Right to Benefits
Order of United Commercial Travelers of America v. Wolfe, 331 U.S. 586, 67 S.Ct. 1355, 91 L.Ed. 1687 (1947).

Servicemen's Group Life Insurance
Ridgway v. Ridgway, 454 U.S. 46, 102 S.Ct. 49, 70 L.Ed.2d 39 (1981).

Sex Discrimination
Newport News Shipbuilding & Dry Dock Co. v. E.E.O.C., 462 U.S. 669, 103 S.Ct. 2622, 77 L.Ed.2d 89 (1983).

Taxation
Colonial Amer. Life Ins. Co. v. Comm'r of Internal Revenue, 491 U.S. 244, 109 S.Ct. 2408, 105 L.Ed.2d 199 (1989).
C.I.R. v. Stern, 357 U.S. 39, 78 S.Ct. 1047, 2 L.Ed.2d 1126 (1958)

APPENDIX D

GLOSSARY

Agent - The agent is the person authorized to act on behalf of the insurer in dealing with third parties and insureds. Agents are essentially employees of insurers.

Americans with Disabilities Act (ADA) - The ADA, 42 U.S.C. § 12101 *et seq.*, went into effect on July 26, 1992. Among other things, it prohibits discrimination against a qualified individual with a disability because of that person's disability with respect to job application procedures; the hiring, advancement or discharge of employees; employee compensation; job training; and other terms, conditions and privileges of employment. It also prohibits such discrimination with respect to public transportation services, and facilities that are open to the public.

Annual Aggregate Liability Insurance - The total amount of coverage available for a given year under a policy of liability insurance. This limits the total loss an insurer will suffer in exchange for a lower premium to the insured.

Arbitration - Refers to bringing a dispute to an impartial third person chosen by the parties to adjudicate the dispute. The parties agree in advance to be bound by the arbitrator's decision or award (after having an opportunity to be heard).

Bad Faith - The opposite of good faith. Generally implies fraud or an intent to deceive — the conscious doing of a wrong because of dishonest purpose or moral impropriety.

Binder - A written memorandum which gives temporary protection to an insured. It contains the important terms of the insurance contract.

Bona fide - Latin term meaning "good faith." Generally used to note a party's lack of bad intent or fraudulent purpose.

Broker - The broker is a middleman who solicits insurance business from the general public, but without being employed by a specific insurer. Generally, a broker will be construed as working for the insured's benefit, and his or her acts will be imputed to the insured.

Cancellation - Typically, state laws provide for the effective cancellation of insurance policies only upon the insurer's meeting certain stringent requirements. For example, a notice of cancellation usually has to be mailed to the insured at least 30 days prior to the effective date of the cancellation.

Compensatory Damages - These are damages which are awarded to make the plaintiff "whole." They compensate for the loss suffered, but do not go beyond that.

Double Indemnity - Usually seen in life insurance contracts — where the indemnitor agrees to pay twice the contracted-for amount — in the case of, e.g., accidental death.

Due Process - The idea of "fair play" in the government's application of law to its citizens, guaranteed by the Fifth (federal government) and Fourteenth (state & local governments) Amendments. Substantive due process is just plain *fairness*, and procedural due process is accorded when the government utilizes adequate procedural safeguards for the protection of an individual's liberty or property interests.

Duty of Care - That degree of caution or care which is owed by a person or entity to another. Breach of the duty of care will result in liability. Usually, the duty of care owed by a person is the amount of care that a reasonable person would exercise in the same or similar circumstances.

Duty to Defend and Indemnify - The duty to defend is broader than the duty to indemnify. An insurer must defend its insured where the lawsuit against the insured alleges facts which potentially bring the incident within the purview of coverage. The duty to indemnify arises after the facts clearly establish that there has been a loss covered by the policy.

Equal Protection - The Fifth (federal) and Fourteenth (state & local) Amendments to the U.S. Constitution guarantee the equal protection of the law to all persons.

ERISA (the Employee Retirement Income Security Act of 1974) - Codified at 29 U.S.C. § 1001 *et seq.*, ERISA regulates employee welfare benefit plans and retirement plans. It governs the funding, vesting and administration of pension plans. If a plan is under the scope of ERISA coverage, state law will be preempted by this federal law.

Errors and Omissions Policy - Insurance which indemnifies the insured for loss sustained because of an error or oversight on the part of the insured. Commonly carried by agents, brokers and agencies to protect them for the mishandling of applications and other insurance documents.

Excess Insurance - That amount of insurance which covers a loss over a certain dollar amount or over a particular primary policy. Generally, such insurance is cheaper than primary insurance coverage because the insurer will only have to pay out if the loss exceeds the amount provided for by the primary policy.

Exclusionary Clause - A clause in an insurance policy by which coverage that would ordinarily have to be provided may be eliminated. For example, where an insured under a general liability policy intentionally injures another, no coverage will have to be provided by virtue of the "intentional acts" exclusionary clause. However, the same injury caused as a result of the insured's negligence will yield coverage.

Fidelity Bond - Also known as fidelity insurance and guaranty insurance — it is an insurance policy in which the insurer agrees to pay the insured for loss suffered as a result of the fraudulent or dishonest acts of employees of the insured.

Fiduciary - A person or entity acting basically like a trustee. A fiduciary is held to a higher standard of care, that of acting primarily for another's benefit, rather than for one's own. A fiduciary should not have a self-interest in the transactions for which he or she is acting as a fiduciary.

General Agent - A person or entity who is authorized to act for the principal (insurer) in all matters concerning the business.

Good Faith - A rather abstract concept, good faith requires honesty, absence of malice, no intent to defraud or take advantage of, and faithfulness to duty.

Indemnify - To pay for loss suffered by an indemnitee (usually an insured) — to reimburse for a loss already incurred.

Indemnity - Term used to denote compensation given for a loss suffered so as to make the indemnitee "whole." Also refers to a contract by which a person or entity agrees to secure another against an anticipated loss (shifting loss from one person to another). Most insurance policies are indemnity insurance policies.

Injunction - An equitable remedy wherein a court orders a party to do or refrain from doing some particular action.

Insured - A person or other entity who obtains insurance coverage to protect against loss to life, health or property. The insured can be either the entity named in the policy, or another person or entity covered by the policy, but not specifically named therein.

Insurer - The underwriter or insurance company with whom a contract of insurance is made. This is the entity which assumes the risk of loss, for a price.

Liability Insurance - This is insurance which covers lawsuits against insureds for damages to *others*, rather than indemnity insurance which covers loss to the insured.

Litigation - A lawsuit. Includes not only legal action, but all the proceedings within the suit.

Malpractice - This term is usually applied to people in "professional" occupations such as doctors, lawyers, psychologists and psychiatrists, engineers, accountants and architects. Malpractice is the failure to exercise that degree of skill and learning commonly applied under all the circumstances by a prudent member of the same profession who is in good standing in the community.

McCarran-Ferguson Insurance Regulation Act - Federal law which reserves to the states the right to regulate the business of insurance. Federal law will not supersede state insurance laws unless the federal law specifically relates to the business of insurance. Codified at 15 U.S.C. §§ 1011-1012.

No-Fault Insurance - Type of automobile insurance in which claims are made against the insured's own insurance company no matter who was at fault. This insurance is made available by various state statutes. Restricts the right of the injured insured to sue the other party or the other party's insurer (usually, only when personal injuries or medical costs exceed a threshold amount).

Nonrenewal - This is an action taken by the insurer to drop an insured's coverage at the end of a policy period. Generally, the requirements for nonrenewal are less stringent than they are for cancellation of policies.

Personal Injury - This is an injury or harm done to the *person*. It generally includes more than mere bodily injury, but excludes purely economic loss in most cases. Injuries to reputation and mental distress injuries are often considered to be personal injuries.

Premiums - An amount which insureds agree to pay insurers as the consideration (price) for insurance coverage. The premium for a policy period is the cost of the insurance for that period.

Product Liability - This is the legal liability of manufacturers and sellers of products to buyers, users and even bystanders for damages or injuries suffered as a result of defects in the products sold. In many cases, manufacturers have to foresee reasonable uses of their products beyond the uses intended by them, and take precautions to insure that the products are safe for such uses.

Punitive Damages (Exemplary Damages) - Damages awarded to a plaintiff over and above what is necessary to compensate him or her for the loss suffered. Punitive damages are awarded to punish a defendant and to set an example to others. They are usually awarded in cases of intentional wrongdoing or where a defendant has acted wilfully, maliciously or fraudulently.

Reinsurance - A contract by which an insurer obtains insurance to cover it for loss or liability (usually with another insurer). This helps to spread the risk and keep rates lower. In reinsurance contracts, insurers contract for insurance to indemnify them for losses they may sustain by reason of the primary policies they have with insureds. Thus, when the insured suffers a loss, he or she seeks coverage from the insurer, who seeks indemnification from the reinsurer for part or all of the loss.

Securities - Term used to denote evidences of debt or property. Includes stocks and bonds.

Self Insurance - This is not insurance in the traditional sense at all. Rather, the "insured" sets aside a fund to meet losses. Large companies sometimes do this to avoid paying the cost of high insurance premiums. Usually, the "insured" will only cover itself up to a certain dollar amount, then purchase excess insurance to make up any loss in excess of that amount.

Setoff - This is a remedy employed by a party to reduce the amount of money it has to pay. For example, where an insured has received workers' compensation benefits after an automobile accident, the automobile insurer may be able to reduce the amount of its liability by the amount received by the insured. Often, setoffs are allowed to avoid granting the insured a double recovery.

Stacking - This is a means of increasing the amount an insured can recover by adding together (stacking) two or more policies. Usually, insureds will have to bargain for this right with their insurers, and pay a greater premium.

State Regulatory Authority - By virtue of the McCarran-Ferguson Act, insurers are subject to increasing state regulation in all areas of insurance. Each state has its own comprehensive statutory requirements which insurers must follow in order to do business in that state.

Statute of Limitations - The time period within which a lawsuit must be brought or within which a claim must be filed. If a claim is made after the limitations period has expired, the insurer will have no liability to pay the claim.

Structured Settlement - A settlement in which, rather than being paid out in a lump sum, a payment plan is agreed upon whereby the recipient receives a smaller amount each year — the benefit of such a plan is deferred taxation on the income.

Subrogation - "Standing in the shoes of another." This substitutes one person for another so that, for example, where an insured has a cause of action against another, the insurer can pay the insured for the loss, then be substituted (subrogated) to the insured's position, with the same rights as the insured against the third party.

Surety - One who agrees to pay money in the event that the principal fails to do so. Surety insurance is more like a bond than true insurance. For example, where party X owes money to party Y, the surety guarantees the payment, and if party X defaults on the payment, then the surety will be liable for any amount remaining to be paid to Y.

Umbrella Insurance - This is coverage which is intended to be supplemental, to cover losses not covered by other insurance, and it extends coverage to higher limits for a relatively small additional premium.

Underinsured Motorist (UIM) Coverage - UIM coverage is designed to protect an insured where the other party to the accident does not have sufficient insurance to cover the loss. If an insured has personal injury protection coverage of $50,000 and the other driver's coverage limit is $30,000, there could be a gap of $20,000 if the insured's injuries amount to at least $50,000. UIM coverage makes up this difference.

Uninsured Motorist (UM) Coverage - UM coverage is designed to protect insureds where they have been involved in an accident with an uninsured person. UM coverage is provided by an insured's own insurer.

Workers' Compensation Insurance - Governed by statutes in all states, workers' compensation protects employers by offering an exclusive remedy to employees who are injured in the course and scope of their employment; it also protects employees by offering a recovery that is *certain* regardless of the financial straits of the employer.

INDEX

ACCIDENTAL DEATH BENEFITS
    Generally, 219-223

ADJUSTERS
    Generally, 80-82

AGENCY/BROKERAGE AGREEMENTS
    Bonus renewals, 73
    Breach of contract, 68-71
    No competition agreements, 71-72
    Redlining, 73-74

AGENTS
    Agency agreements, 68
    Binders, 63-65
    Deceptive trade practices, 56-59
    Duty of care, 43-51
    Fraud, 56-59
    Libel and slander, 59-60
    Licensing generally, 65-68
    Misrepresentation, 56-59
    Premiums, 61-63
    Redlining, 73-74
    Releases, 60

AIRCRAFT INSURANCE
    Airworthiness, 372
    Conversions to criminal use, 373-374
    Exclusions, 374-376
    Generally, 369-376
    Pilot qualifications, 369-372

ALCOHOL
    Dram shop acts, 382-386

AUTOMOBILE INSURANCE
    Accidents and occurrences, 95-97
    Arising out of use/maintenance, 86
    Borrowed vehicles, 99, 101, 102-105
    Dealers, 108-109
    Family members, 98-102
    Intentional harm, 97-98
    Misrepresentation, 114-115
    Motor vehicle defined, 86-88
    Motorcycles, 110
    No-Fault legislation, 112-113, 125-126
    Other vehicles, 111-112
    Parked vehicles, 93-95
    Permissive users, 102-105
    Persons covered, 98-105
    PIP benefits, 112-114
    Rental and replacement vehicles, 105-107
    Scope of coverage, 86-115
    Stacking, 126-131
    State/Federal regulation, 121-126, 495

BINDERS
    Generally, 63-65

BROKERS
    See also Agents
    Duty of care, 51-56

BURGLARY
    Exclusions, 328-329
    Preconditions for coverage, 325-327
    Visible force and violence requirement, 327-328

BUSINESS AND INDUSTRIAL INSURANCE
    All risk policies, 352-354
    Business risks, 346-352
    Exclusions
        Generally, 355-360
        Polluter's exclusions, 360-367
    Occurrences, 354-355

CANCELLATION
    Auto Policies, 151-158

CASUALTY INSURANCE
    See Liability and Casualty Insurance

528 INDEX

CONSTRUCTION INSURANCE
Generally, 403-407

CONSUMER INSURANCE FRAUD
Generally, 173-178

DAMAGES
Punitive, generally, 19-36

DECEPTIVE TRADE PRACTICES
Agents, 56-59

DEFENSE
Duty to defend, 1-7

DISCRIMINATION
Employment discrimination, 74-79
Redlining, 73-74

DOUBLE INDEMNITY
See Accidental Death Benefits

DUTIES OF INSURERS AND INSUREDS
Auto Policies, 115-121
Care of agents and brokers, 43-56

EMPLOYEE RETIREMENT INCOME SECURITY ACT (ERISA)
Generally, 471-478

EXCESS INSURERS
Generally, 36-41, 306-308

EXCLUSIONS
Aircraft, 374-376
Automobile insurance, 163-169
Burglary, 328-329
Business pursuit, 284-289
Business risks, 355-360
Farmowner's automobile exclusions, 396-399
Health and medical insurance, 242-253
Liability policies, 310-318
Life insurance, 234-242
Polluter's exclusions, 360-367

FARMOWNER'S INSURANCE
Exclusions, 396-399
Theft losses, 399

FIRE INSURANCE
Arson generally, 330-337
Arson investigations, 330-330
Buildings covered, 340-341
Insureds' misconduct, 337-340
Insurers' rights, 341-343
Joint ownership, 334-337
Mortgagees and mortgagors, 343-344

FLOOD INSURANCE
Generally, 376-378

FRAUD
See Misrepresentation

GOVERNMENT LIABILITY
See State and Local Government Liability

GROUP INSURANCE
"Actively at work" requirement, 214-216
Individuals covered, 202-210
Injuries, 211
Limitations periods, 211-214
Policy dates, 211-214
Scope of coverage, 201-214
Types of claims covered, 202-210

HEALTH INSURANCE
see Life and Health Insurance

HOMEOWNER'S INSURANCE
Domicile, 267-271
Business pursuit exclusions, 284-289
Earth movement exclusions, 289-292
Exclusions generally, 272-292
Intentional acts exclusions, 275-284
Misrepresentation, 292-294
Motor vehicle exclusions, 272-275
Residence, 267-271
Scope of coverage generally, 255-267

INDUSTRIAL CLAIMS
See Business and Industrial Insurance

INDEX 529

LIABILITY AND CASUALTY INSURANCE
"Accidents," 302-306
Burglary, 325-329
Cancellation, 308-310
Exclusions, 310-318
Joint and several liability, 318-319
Liability for payment of premiums, 321-322
Notice, 322-325
Policy terms generally, 298-302
Premiums, 319-322
Primary/excess insurance, 306-308
Scope of coverage, 296-319
Visible force and violence, 327-328

LIBEL AND SLANDER
Generally, 59-60

LICENSING
Agent licensing statutes, 65-66
Revocation, 66-68

LIFE AND HEALTH INSURANCE
See also Group Insurance
Change-of-beneficiary disputes, 228-231
Delivery of policies, 216-219
Double indemnity, 219-223
Incontestability clauses, 195-197
Misrepresentation, 186-197
Missing persons, 232-233
Nonpayment of premium, 197-201
Policies not voided, 199-201
Policies voided, 197-199
Preexisting conditions, 250-253
Rival claimants, 223-228
Sex-based mortality tables, 253-254

LONGSHORE AND HARBOR WORKERS' COMPENSATION ACT (LHWCA)
Generally, 467-469

MALPRACTICE
See Professional Malpractice Insurance

MARINE INSURANCE
Coverage allowed, 378-381
Coverage denied, 381-382

McCARRAN-FERGUSON ACT
Generally, 471, 495

MISREPRESENTATION
Consumers, 173-183
Homeowner's policies, 292-294
Life and health insurance, 186-197

NOTICE
Proof of Loss, 322-325

PREMIUMS
Coverage disputes, 319-321
Liability for agent's payment of, 61-63

PROFESSIONAL MALPRACTICE INSURANCE
Bad-faith refusal to settle claims, 428-429
Coverage dates, 415-420
Employer liability, 423-425
Fraud, 420-422
Liability limits and subrogation rights, 425-428
Scope of professional services, 409-415
Suits based on error or mistake, 422-423

PROOF OF LOSS
Generally, 322-325

PUNITIVE DAMAGES
Against insurers, 19-36

REINSURANCE
Generally, 41-42

RELEASES
Generally, 60

SET-OFF
Automobile insurance, 159-161

SLANDER
Generally, 59-60

STACKING OF AUTOMOBILE POLICIES
Generally, 126-131

STATE AND LOCAL GOVERNMENT LIABILITY
Generally, 391-395

STATE REGULATION
Generally, 121-126, 480-494

THEFT
Generally, 325-329
Preconditions for coverage, 325-327

TITLE INSURANCE
Generally, 386-390

TOXIC WASTE
See Liability and Casualty Insurance

UNINSURED/UNDERINSURED MOTORIST BENEFITS
Accidents and events covered, 134-137
Duty to offer coverage, 145-149
Exclusions, 149-151
Generally, 131-151
Hit-and-run accidents, 137-138
Insurers' obligations, 132-134
Interception of benefits, 145
Persons entitled to coverage, 140-142
Physical contact rules, 138-140

WORKERS' COMPENSATION
Accidents in the course of employment, 435-439
Chronic conditions initially arising out of work-related injuries, 442-444
Claims procedures generally, 461-463
Coming and going rule, 432-434
Death benefits generally, 457-459
Disability payments generally, 451-456
Disputed employee-employer relationship, 440-442
Dual purpose of business and pleasure, 438-439
Exclusive remedy rule, 448-451
"In the course of" defined, 439-440
Incarcerated employees, 463-464
Intentional acts of third parties, 436
Longshore and Harbor Workers' Compensation Act (LHWCA), 467-469
Misconduct by employers, 466-467
Multiple employers, 446-447
Permanent partial disability, 453-454
Permanent total disability, 454-456
Primary employers, 446-447
Setoff, 459-461
Statute of limitations, 461-463
Temporary total disability, 452
Violation of safety laws, 464-465